Kaye Gibbons

McFarland Literary Companions
by Mary Ellen Snodgrass

1. *August Wilson* (2004)

2. *Barbara Kingsolver* (2004)

3. *Amy Tan* (2004)

4. *Walter Dean Myers* (2006)

5. *Kaye Gibbons* (2007)

Kaye Gibbons

A Literary Companion

Mary Ellen Snodgrass

McFarland Literary Companions, 5

McFarland & Company, Inc., Publishers
Jefferson, North Carolina, and London

LIBRARY OF CONGRESS CATALOGUING-IN-PUBLICATION DATA

Snodgrass, Mary Ellen.
Kaye Gibbons : a literary companion / Mary Ellen Snodgrass.
p. cm. — (McFarland literary companions ; 5)
Includes bibliographical references and index.

ISBN-13: 978-0-7864-2943-1
(softcover : 50# alkaline paper) ∞

1. Gibbons, Kaye, 1960– —Criticism and interpretation.
2. Women and literature—Southern States—History—20th century.
3. Southern States—In literature.
I. Title. II. Series.
PS3557.I13917Z87 2007 813'.54—dc22 2006102822

British Library cataloguing data are available

On the cover: Kaye Gibbons ©David Goodwin;
background ©2006 Design Pics

Manufactured in the United States of America

McFarland & Company, Inc., Publishers
Box 611, Jefferson, North Carolina 28640
www.mcfarlandpub.com

Acknowledgments

I owe thanks to Kaye Gibbons for generous email answers to my questions about her family and career and for supplying a cover photo. Also, I acknowledge the advice and research assistance of the following people and institutions:

Christy Allen, reference librarian
State Library of North Carolina
Raleigh, North Carolina

David Bond, reference librarian
Southern Illinois University at Carbondale

Karen Gross, public relations associate
Arden Theatre Company
Philadelphia, Pennsylvania

Mary Harden, literary agent
Harden-Curtis Associates
New York City

Burl McCuiston, reference librarian
Lenoir Rhyne College
Hickory, North Carolina

Mary McDonald, reference librarian
St. Andrew's College
Laurinburg, North Carolina

Elyse Pineau, professor of speech
Southern Illinois University at Carbondale

Aaron Posner, playwright
Arden Theatre Company
Philadelphia, Pennsylvania

Susan Reese, associate director
Braswell Memorial Library
Rocky Mount, North Carolina

Wanda Rozzelle, reference librarian
Catawba County Library
Newton, North Carolina

Mary Taylor, reference librarian
Southern Illinois University at Carbondale

Contents

If death and sorrow and the inexplicable joy
that comes from triumph over death and sorrow,
if these themes are predominant in my work, past and future,
it is because they dominate my memory.
"My Mother, Literature, and a Life Split Neatly into Two Halves" (1991)

Preface

For readers seeking a greater knowledge or understanding of Kaye Gibbons's contributions to feminist, American, and Southern literature, *Kaye Gibbons: A Literary Companion* offers an introduction and guided overview. The text equips the reader, feminist, linguist, student, researcher, teacher, reviewer, and librarian with analysis of characters, plots, humor, symbols, and classic themes from the works of a bestselling, reader-pleasing author. The text opens with an annotated chronology of Gibbons's life, Southern heritage, astounding early career, works, and awards, followed by Gibbons's family tree. The 103 A-to-Z entries combine analysis from feminist historians, reviewers, and critics along with generous citations from primary and secondary sources and comparative literature. Each entry concludes with a selected bibliography. Two maps clarify Civil War battles and settings in downtown Raleigh, North Carolina, which permeate Gibbons's fourth and fifth novels, *Charms for the Easy Life* and *On the Occasion of My Last Afternoon.* Annotated charts elucidate the convoluted genealogies of ten fictional clans, particularly that of quixotic quester Ellen Foster. In addition to clearing up dates and events, the family trees account for the relationships between Grandfather Barnes and Josephine Woodward and between Roland Stanley and Stella Morgan. Extensions to genealogy fill in unusual connections between freedwoman Clarice Washington and the haughty Samuel P. Goodman Tate and between the title character and Stuart in the Ellen Foster novels. Generous cross references point to divergent strands of thought and guide the reader into peripheral territory, e.g., from violence to rape, from powerlessness to vulnerability, from old age to wisdom, and from urbanism to Raleigh, North Carolina.

Back matter is designed to aid the student, reviewer, and researcher. Appendix A orients the beginner with a chronology of historical events and their intertextual importance to crises in the lives of fictional characters, for example, the arrival of Welsh Quakers like Charles Davies in North America, the approach of General George Brinton McClellan's troops to the Tate plantation on the James River in June 1862, the final push toward women's right to vote, and Dr. Julian Stanley's search for bright youth to introduce to scholarship at Johns Hopkins University. The entries feature abbreviated references to the works from which each event derives. Appendix B provides 42 topics for group or individual projects, composition, analysis, background material, enactment, and theme development, notably, motifs of matriarchy and marital discord, character attitudes toward materialism and tyranny, the author's choice of dialect, development of sisterhood and sources of mistrust, and the backdrop of Christmas and the New Year as a shaper of tone and atmosphere.

Back matter concludes with an exhaustive bibliographical listing of primary sources followed by a general bibliography organized by the Gibbons title each elucidates. Many entries derive from journal and periodical articles and reviews of Gibbons's essays, novels, and short fiction in major newspapers. A singular entry reveals critical response to Aaron Posner's stage adaption of *Ellen Foster* for Philadelphia audiences. Secondary sources, particularly those by experienced reviewers, are useful for the study of works that have yet to merit thorough analysis in academic journals. A comprehensive index directs users of the literary companion to major and minor characters, events, historical eras and figures, movements, place names, Gibbons's contemporaries and mentors, published works, sources, authors, literary motifs, period terms, genres, and issues, e.g., Betty Randolph Davies and Pete and Shirley, Sudie Bee and Whately Tate, the battle of Gettysburg and the massacre at Fort Pillow, the Great Depression and Franklin Delano Roosevelt, freedmen's schools and the Works Progress Administration, Joyner's Store and the South, Charles Frazier and Dorothy Allison, Kate Chopin and Eudora Welty, *Trifles* and "My Mother, Literature, and a Life Split Neatly into Two Halves," *The Feminine Mystique* and the Miranda stories, Charlotte Brontë and Gabriel Marcía Marquez, Cinderella and Judith and Holofernes, the Ku Klux Klan and "allotment Annies," trickster lore and the fool tale, and venereal disease and euthanasia.

Introduction

A wonder at creating fictional lives, Kaye Gibbons directs language into the obscure corners of human yearnings and behaviors. At her best, she dramatizes women's natural affinity for sizing up social and domestic situations and for applying intuitive solutions to dilemmas of the moment, from a case of pellagra to a government-mandated IQ test, from dismembering ducks to rescuing a shoeshine man from drowning. From her own mother-daughter camaraderie, she writes of childhood's surmise about adult hurts, particularly those pangs emerging from tribulation, neglect, and madness. From her works come realistic scenarios of coping with hard times and squeezing out the last drops of joy in rural settings. Her expertise at dramatic oddments— selecting books from a bookmobile, releasing tension by scrubbing grout, delighting in flaky pie crust, sharing intimate pillow talk with a sympathetic mate, cooking lunch for farm laborers, reading a Kipling story aloud to a pre-schooler, larking with an all-woman gin rummy club — speak the truths of women's lives. Epiphanies of right thinking emerge from word pictures— Maureen Carlton Ross binding rock-hard breasts against the pain of infant death, Emma Garnet Tate Lowell feeling compassion for Quincy Lowell as he sobs over carnage to come from the Civil War, Charlie Kate Birch escorting her granddaughter Margaret out of a romantic movie to read *The Yearling*, and Ellen Foster measuring with her fingertips on a map the distance from Baltimore to home. Through realism, Gibbons validates the on-the-spot evaluations and choices that elevate humankind for its grasp on goodness, mercy, and sacrifice.

The dominance of male-female differences in Gibbons's writings reveals her concern for gender egalitarianism. Avoiding feminist cant, she replicates the rural womenfolk she grew up with in Nash County, North Carolina, to celebrate female work and ways as the urge to "go and do." From her stories come battles of the sexes alongside the volunteer nurses of the Civil War, the guile of farm wives during the Great Depression, a survey of self-employed veterans of World War I, the desperation of parents during the 1918 influenza pandemic, and the courage of manless wives and mothers during World War II. At the core of her heroines arises a willingness to subvert patriarchy to upgrade family life. For Ruby Pitts Woodrow Stokes, self-reclamation begins with the purchase and concealment of a pistol under her pillow. For Pearl Wiggins, superintending a madwoman follows a demand for car privileges and for twice the salary usually accorded a black female domestic. For Mary Oliver, rescue of her sequestered aunt Maureen begins with doses of sense to negate the humbuggery of Troop, a callous wife-diminisher.

To inform the reader of the worst in gendered behaviors, Gibbons defaults to the classic Greek theater for the rule of decorum. She introduces child endangerment in screened visions of Bill man-handling the breasts of his ten-year-old daughter, through male absorption in the execution of two felons on a gallows in Williamsburg, Virginia, and in an epistolary confirmation that Dr. John C. Gunn tortured Alice Tate to her grave with the anti-female treatments of the mid–1800s. Off-stage from the liberation of Sade Duplin lie the "shot to pieces" remains of a womanizing, tight-walleted husband who got his just deserts. Out of sight of Ruby, a 20-year-old widow, is the pool room death of John Woodrow, a sleazy, mouthy adulterer knifed through the lungs. Beyond the sight of wife Lottie and daughter Betty, the head of skinflint Charles Davies lodges between two river rocks in his final moments of wrestling with a troubled farm economy and independent women.

Gibbons admires the pride and fortitude of protagonists without reducing them to ciphers of goodness and propriety. Her valiant war nurse, Emma Garnet Tate Lowell, falls short of candor by concealing from Charlie, Martha, and Mavis a previous manumission that should have set them free from the Lowell household. Laura, the beloved foster mother, recedes to her room to reframe frenzied thoughts and to suppress misgivings about volunteer parenting. Maggie Barnes, a defender of son Freddy from corporal punishment, cheats her children of protection by betraying them to Grandfather Barnes. Sophia Snow Birch, a man-hunting flirt, stalks businessman Richard Baines in a movie house as a potential second husband. The most painful of human frailties take shape in the lethal cigarette addiction of Ruby Stokes and the suicide of Shine in March 1969 out of acknowledgement that she lacks the strength to mother. By conferring humanity on her heroines, Gibbons enhances their credibility and endears them for their shortcomings.

The centrality of storytelling in Gibbons's writing expresses the vital function of language in human affairs. From cribhood, Marjorie Polly Randolph absorbs family stories dating back four generations to her Irish forebears. Even before her birth, she profited from the birthing charms and jingles valued by midwife Polly Deal. In the rescue of Maureen Ross from a misogynist, Mary Oliver relies on the letters of a stranger, Judith Benedict Stafford, who narrates her sexual liberation from an adulterous mate through vigorous travels in Cuba and Europe in more woman-pleasing male company. From family lore, Hattie Barnes learns that cook-housekeeper Pearl Wiggins offered unconditional mother love to Hattie in lieu of Maggie's ability to function as a normal birth mother and female head of household. Embedded in the coming-of-age of Maureen Tate are lapses in the family history since her sister Emma married and moved to Raleigh. In each instance, oral telling fills in gaps that impede the fulfillment of human potential.

Gibbons commandeers the storymaker's powers to allot fictional justice and retribution. A suitable death for Stanton, a Richmond drug dealer, kills him off with an overdose of ammonia; Ellen Foster's stony-hearted grandmother receives her last breath from the lips of the granddaughter she abases. To the whiny, inept widower "Blinking" Jack Ernest Stokes, the text metes out a querulous solitude in the bed that his wife's ghost visits. Gibbons exiles to Texas Aunt Nadine Nelson and daughter Dora, a mother-daughter fraud team. For Lottie O'Cadhain Davies, the death of an unloving husband entitles her to post-marital freedom and an unforeseen lagniappe, a widow's pension from Social Security. Margaret inherits the intangible wealth of her grandmother's war-time pragmatism and her firm grip on career and community service. In the last hours of Emma's life, the author extends a gauzy vision of a reunion in heaven with her beloved. The satisfying disconnect from character lives leaves readers content with Gibbons's views on sin and nemesis.

The devices of the storyteller attest to Gibbons's mastery of subtlety and nuance. For Gothic humor, she sets the revelation of a snake in "The Headache" by lamplight in an outhouse; juxtaposition places Clarice Washington's making of sausage contemporaneous with the near-beheading of the slave Jacob. For edenic symbolism, Gibbons unveils the initial courtship between Ruby and Jack Stokes under a pecan tree. With situational drollery, the author pictures Stuart untaping quarters from his midriff to fund a trip to the county fair. To upbraid Jack Stokes for unmanly behavior, she engrosses him in Roadrunner cartoons, an ironic form of escapism for a 65-year-old man. To celebrate volunteer parenting, she has the orphaned Ellen opt for "Foster" as a surname and select a new mama on Christmas Day. To honor female qualities, the author awards a diary and toy microscope to her intellectual Ellen, widowhood to disillusioned wife Sophia Snow Birch, mother love to June Stanley, a devoted husband to Amanda Bethune, and the Lowell fortune to Emma. By manipulating names, Gibbons selects jewel names for Pearl Wiggins, Emma Garnet, and Ruby Stokes, "little star" for Starletta, a busy insect name for cook-housekeeper Sudie Bee, and a brightness to crown Clarice Washington.

Gibbons's massive fan base exults in the author's clever plots, honest-to-the-bone vernacular, and witness to female coping skills and daring. Lacing texts are memorable shards of wisdom and exempla of quirky, yet believable graces, including Starletta's enjoyment of light-up shoes on Christmas Eve, a marriage proposal and gift of a glass doorknob from Stuart to Ellen, antique scalpels to Charlie Kate Birch, Lucille Womble's embrace of the Hippocratic Oath, and Martha Greene Oliver's renting of a hotel suite, scene of multiple sexual dalliances with a filmmaker and a levitationist. At readings and book discussions, enthusiasts delight in hearing Ellen's plans to murder her father, Emma's distribution of leeches among septic battle wounds, Maggie's ongoing seduction of husband Frederick, Mary Oliver's first encounter with Southern peculiarities, and Bridget O'Donough O'Cadhain's posturing in a deathbed scenario in Galway, Ireland. For Gibbons fans, literary eccentricities are the stuff of fiction, the reason to read on.

Chronology of Gibbons's Life and Works

A feminist storyteller empowered by redemptive language, Kaye Gibbons is known for depicting sturdy girls and women capable of bearing inhuman burdens. A pervasive motif—the solacing of human need with comfort—derives from the author's experiences with poverty, spiritual emptiness, and limited pleasures that date to early childhood. From those encounters, she came to treasure survival as an art. She writes the recovered stories, motifs, and inklings that honor daring, self-claiming females.

May 5, 1960 Born the last of three children on Bend of the River Road in Nash County, North Carolina, Bertha Kaye Batts Gibbons reflects that she was an odd bird—an over-achiever growing up solitary and apart near semi-literate neighbor kids named Chicken Stew, twins Billy and Buck Baker, and Sap Head. She recalls her maternal grandmother, Martha Griffin Gardner of Elm City, as elegantly dressed in Lillie Rubin frocks, displaying a cigarette humidor, and setting a formal table, yet treating her granddaughter for chicken pox with superstition—locking her in the henhouse. After publishing *Charms for the Easy Life* (1993), Gibbons described how Grandmother Martha influenced the actions of the fictional Charlie Kate Birch: "My grandmother never walked anywhere, she ran; she never talked, she shouted.... All of her motions and words were exaggerated; she was Southern hyperbole" (Madrigal, 1993).

Gibbons's first name came from her paternal grandmother, Bertha Davis Batts of Nash County, the mother of seven daughters. The Batts' neighbors were black farm families, including a beloved friend named Coot, the prototype of the fictional Starletta in *Ellen Foster* (1987) and its sequel, *The Life All Around Me by Ellen Foster* (2006). The author described the Batts family's tobacco farm as a red clay square. Some seven miles outside of Rocky Mount on the Tar River, she lived in farm country in a four-room house roofed with corrugated tin. In a return to roots in 2004, she mused, "It's almost like an out-of-body experience that something that happened in this kitchen is being read by a million people" (Stephens, 2004).

Gibbons's upbringing followed the Southern pattern of the era. She wore Buster Brown bangs and striped ticking dresses, attended a Baptist church, and spoke a Southern agrarian dialect. Her folksay described hardscrabble existence as "going and doing," a utilitarian phrase that the author repeats in reference to the new lives of freed slaves in *On the Occasion of My Last Afternoon* (1998) and in reference to women's independent actions in *Divining Women* (2004). Gibbons's mother, tall and willowy, shopped in town on Saturdays and drove to Elm City to visit her own mother on Sundays. Of the social status of best friend Martha, Gibbons later regretted the child's life of "grinding, gray, hopeless poor of Walker Evans photographs" (Gibbons, "First Grade," 80). The phrase alludes to *Let Us Now Praise Famous Men: Three Tenant Families* (1936), a lengthy photo essay that James Agee wrote for *Fortune* magazine during the Great Depression revealing the labors and malnutrition of Southern sharecroppers. Experience with the laboring-class shaped Gibbons's contributions to New South writing, a departure from the past and stress on the here and now that permeates Dorothy Allison's *Bastard Out of Carolina* (1992) and the stories of Bobbie Ann Mason.

Despite direct descent from the first European settler of North Carolina, the Batts family lacked a dependable head of household. Gibbons recalls her father, Charles "Charlie" Batts, one of seven children, as a brilliant "renaissance" farmer and problem solver. He was also a swiller of liquor, a version of William Faulkner's fictional Snopeses, the Southern slackers who lived by self-serving excuses and cussedness. In *Ellen Foster*, a first novel, Gibbons reprises the childish wishes to kill a ne'er-do-well father. Because of Charles Batts's profligacy, there was no heat or electricity in the tin-roofed house. Child rearing responsibilities fell on the author and her older brother David and a maternal aunt, Susie Vick. Gibbons yearned to live in a brick house, which she connected to a normal father not addicted to alcohol. She tempered criticism of his drinking with comments on his sense of humor and on his service as a photographer on the carrier U.S.S. *Hornet* during World War II, a setting she reprises in *A Cure for Dreams* (1991).

In "My Mother, Literature, and a Life Split Neatly into Two Halves," an entry in the compendium *The Writer on Her Work: New Essays in New Territory* (1991), Gibbons credits her mother, Alice "Shine" Batts, for encouraging the writer's strength and persistence. Shine weakened at age 12 from a bout of strep throat that developed into rheumatic fever. In the author's memory, Shine takes the form of a survivor— a "good country woman," a crocheter of antimacassars, sterilizer of Mason jars for pickles, smocker of dresses, and plucker and dresser of chickens (Gibbons, 1991, 52). In summers, Shine shaded her face with a wide-brimmed straw hat. When times were tough, she crossed the road to talk out her troubles with neighbors Ida Mae and Otha. To drive the farm truck to market, Shine had to scoot down in the seat to reach the pedals. Grinding gears made her husband laugh. In later reflections, Gibbons regretted that her mother remained "artistically mute" (Gibbons, 1999). Longing for the real woman, the author became obsessed with restructuring a lost life from medical records and interviews with relatives about her mother's mood swings.

November 22, 1963 At age three and a half, Gibbons observed her mother in the act of lighting the gas oven when a news announcement of President John Fitzgerald

Kennedy's assassination jolted the family. As Shine Batts sat in the kitchen floor and wept, the vision of motherly emotion embedded itself in the daughter, whom Shine held at the knees.

1964 Gibbons began reading newspapers and admired the lyricism of the King James bible, a standard text to children brought up in the Southern fundamentalist milieu. In this same period, she sat with her mother at the beauty salon each Friday and watched *The Secret Storm*, a soap opera that spawned the author's love of *The Young and the Restless*. Sharing an involvement in serial melodrama became a connection between mother and daughter as well as with Reynolds Price, who echoes Gibbons's love of TV melodrama.

1966 Like Hattie Barnes, the narrator in *Sights Unseen* (1995), Kaye Gibbons felt secure during the last year of her mother's stable health. In "The First Grade, Jesus, and the Hollyberry Family" (1998), the author relives her introduction to Coopers School, which smelled like crayons. Carrying a red bookbag, she wore bobbed hair, patent leather shoes from the Roscoe Griffin Company, lace drawers from Belk Tyler, and a smocked plaid dress that her grandmother purchased at the Bib 'N Tucker, a children's emporium on Main Street. Each day, the author rode bus 72 down a winding road to class. Several times a year, a preacher from New Life Ministries conducted soul-scathing religious classes in the school auditorium. On the upside of the era, she applauded Barbie dolls, Hawaiian Punch, Pop-Tarts, and Jackie Gleason's weekly variety show, which featured the June Taylor dancers. She watched the *Ed Sullivan Show* with her mother and the *Grand Ole Opry* with her father. For fun, she manipulated Slinkys.

Of early reading, the author recalls how books rescued her. To interviewer Nicole Brodeur, Gibbons's confided, "I had nowhere else to go" (Brodeur, 1996). Her home shelves offered limited types of reading material — encyclopedias, a text on cattle castration, and *Graveyard of the Atlantic*, a compilation of shipwrecks on the Carolina coast. She rejected Dr. Seuss and criticized the mind-numbing, goody-goody children's literature common to first-grade primers. From *Child Craft Encyclopedia*, she learned the verse of Emily Dickinson and memorized lines from Edna St. Vincent Millay's elegaic "Renascence" (1917). Gibbons reflected to poet Dannye Romine Powell, book editor for the *Charlotte* (N.C.) *Observer*, that poetry seemed good enough to eat. From practicing the alphabet modeled in the Palmer handwriting text, she began to see herself as a writer.

December 24, 1966 In the preface to *Christmas in the South: Holiday Stories from the South's Best Writers* (2004), Gibbons notes the nostalgia that seizes her when she relives the death of her maternal grandfather, Charles Bennett Batts, on Christmas Eve. He was a lover of children and a giver of joy to a close extended family. As he opened gifts under the watch of his seven children and their children, Kaye's mother, Shine, sat on his lap. He grasped his chest and expired of a coronary amid the shrieks of aunts who shepherded the children upstairs and out of view of death at close range.

1967 Gibbons bore daily class consciousness of the difference between frame-house children and brick-house children, the ones with the nice lunchboxes and parents who didn't drink. In second grade, she suffered a blow to her competitive spirit after losing a spelling bee on the word "boulevard," which principal Thorpe B. Smith passed to the champion, a brick-house classmate named Stuart. Balancing loss with joy, Gibbons flourished under the teaching of Olive Stokes of Battleboro, North Carolina, who identified brilliance in Kaye. Later, Stokes commented, "I didn't know what she was going through. If I had, I would have taken her home with me" (Mosher, 1991).

In class, the author read from *Around the Corner*, the second in a Ginn Basic Reader series edited by Odille Ousley and David H. Russell and introduced to public school curricula in 1949. The elementary school primer offered classic and post–World War II stories plus full-color illustrations, word studies, and a cumulative vocabulary of 223 new words. Two decades later, Gibbons realized that the simmering mix of events and observations from these years coalesced into her first novel.

1968 In the year Gibbons was "saved" at a Baptist altar call and subsequently baptized by full immersion, she had problems with the here and now. During her mother's lengthy illness, Shine Batts was often hospitalized "looking older and older with each return" (Gibbons, "First Grade," 82). On the national level, the author was mystified by television news of riots in Birmingham, Montgomery, and Chicago. In her own neighborhood, mixed-race play was common to rural children like Kaye and her black friend Coot.

1969 In the fourth grade, Gibbons weathered a painless school desegregation. She gained her first boyfriend and developed competence in public speaking at a 4-H Bicycle Safety contest by competing in oratory on the topic "What's Right about America." She angered local dignitaries on the judging panel by defending Jane Fonda's right to oppose the Vietnam War. Shine and Charles Batts made a family joke about threatening to send her to the Richard T. Fountain state girl's reformatory, which opened that year in Rocky Mount.

March, 1970 Before Gibbons's tenth birthday, 47-year-old Shine Batts retreated from incurable manic depression by swallowing a lethal dose of sleeping pills. In adulthood, the author recalled the demise of her mother's hope as past-due bills piled higher. Plagued by ill health, Shine underwent open-heart surgery the previous year. Critic-novelist Jacqueline Carey remarked on the insidious nature of Shine's mental illness, which "seeps into the very fiber of the household" (Carey, 1995, 30). In the aftermath, hormonal shifts precipitated a lethal depression in Shine before the invention of lithium-based treatment and Prozac. Gibbons recalled a legacy of discontent: "I know what it's like to live with someone who's unhappy" (Jarvis, 2005).

To reclaim childhood memories, in 1995, Gibbons completed *Sights Unseen*, an autobiographical account of Hattie Barnes's girlhood with an insane mother who eventually recovers. The action avoids autobiographical scenarios. From her own bouts of bipolarity, Gibbons preserves the manic need for shopping. She laughed, "Let's just say Maggie and I both have outstanding shoe collections" (Paddock, 1995). Composition required eight drafts. She divulged to Polly Paddock, book critic for the *Charlotte Observer*, "It was a grueling process—and I think I'm still trying to suppress the memory" (*ibid.*). Writing as a cure for survivor guilt allowed Gibbons to let go of the "what ifs": "If I had been a better girl, if I had sat stiller and had been quieter" (O'Briant, 2004).

As a result of multiple physical and emotional struggles, Shine abandoned any future vision. In her final moments, she assured her daughter that she was not abandoning her. The sudden suicide evoked chaos in the household, where nice children no longer came to play. A ten-year-old pariah, Gibbons lied to outsiders that her mother died of a heart attack. Gibbons developed a longing to reorder Shine's life. She extracted good memories from maternal aunts, who recalled their sister as clever and witty. In an era of "trying to find ways to mother myself," Gibbons took on the role of housekeeper and bill-payer while her father drank himself into oblivion (Hodges, 2004). She later credited her success to will power. Her repression of the events lasted until 1975, when she embraced Shine's death as a signpost and liberation from the sameness of the farm wife's existence. Nonetheless, 35 years later, anger still stunned the author with daily reminders of unfinished business. It wasn't until the publication of *The Life All Around Me by Ellen Foster* that Gibbons could understand and forgive Shine.

At first, the motherless child filled the empty places with network television shows like *Green Acres* and *Get Smart*, Nancy Drew mysteries, and Madeleine stories. When those palled, Gibbons opted for Edgar Allan Poe's exotica from the Braswell Library bookmobile. The works that remained in her memories were the wistful elegy "Annabel Lee" (1849), the terror story "The Tell-Tale Heart" (1843), and a regional treasure hunt in "The Gold Bug" (1843). From *World Book*'s poetry anthology, she moved on to Shakespeare's Sonnet 116, but concluded that only deceased poets from Great Britain and New England ranked high enough for listing as classic authors. Dreaming in another sphere, she yearned to be a lab technician clad in a white coat and wielding litmus paper and test tubes.

Shine's inheritable emotional instability also gripped the author in a cycle of mental soars and plunges she shares with past masters Lord Byron, Robert Lowell, Herman Melville, J. D. Salinger, Anne Sexton, Thomas Wolfe, and Virginia Woolf. In adulthood, manic states caused Gibbons to blurt out loud comments in public, to hear popular music and Christmas carols, to mount buying frenzies, and to compose elegant prose. In 1995, she referred to "manic binges in which thoughts are looped together by a seemingly inconsequential thread" (O'Briant, 1995). According to Emily Martin's essay "Rationality, Feminism, and Mind" in *Feminism in Twentieth Century Science, Technology and Medicine* (2001), Gibbons's writings about mood disorders are part of a late 20th-century redefinition of unstable emotions as a strength rather than a handicap. In the "up" states, the nervous system is capable of "fluency, rapidity, and flexibility of thought on the one hand, and the ability to combine ideas or categories," all adjuncts to literary achievement (Creager, Lunbeck, & Schiebinger, 2001, 218).

December 25, 1970 For Christmas gifts, Gibbons bought her own presents in town. In adulthood, she recalled a King James bible, a suitable book to begin her shelf of personal favorites and an auspicious blessing to the year's end that left her motherless. Of the 66 scriptural books, she preferred lyric psalms, the generosity of Proverbs, and the evocative images of Revelation, the final and most surreal book of the bible. The value of biblical writing as literature remains a constant in her writing career.

1972 Passed about among relatives like Rudyard Kipling and Truman Capote, the author left a maternal aunt, Susie Vick, for foster care outside Wilson, North Carolina, in a period that Gibbons describes as two hellish years in a toxic environment. With a touch of black humor, she characterized her upbringing as the type that "encourages someone to either become a writer or to rob convenience stores" (Blades, 1991). While enrolled at Spaulding Middle School at Spring Hope, North Carolina, she toiled ten-to-twelve-hour days in the fields and worked on her brother's wedding day barning tobacco. Unwashed and uncombed, Gibbons took her place as a bridesmaid. Vick sewed school dresses for her niece from upholstery cloth scraps. To ennoble herself, Vick claimed that the stress of caring for a motherless child caused the aunt to contract cancer. In church testimonials, she praised a miraculous cure.

May, 1973 Before her father's death, Gibbons was the subject of a custody battle waged by her older brother David, a senior at East Carolina University. Until he graduated, she came under the care of Mary Lee, a surrogate mother. Like the fictional Ellen Foster, Gibbons chose her foster mother after seeing her at church in Rocky Mount. The author packed a suitcase and walked up the hill to the woman's home. The author later recalled, "A new mama pulled me out of the cold and nurtured me. That's why I'm happy now" (McCabe, 1997). By seventh grade at R. J. Wilson Junior High, Gibbons was living in Englewood with David, a fertilizer dealer, and a new sister-in-law, Barbara Atkins Batts, the model for the loving, supportive foster mother in *Ellen Foster*. In May, Charles Batts died. Parentless, but well cared for, Gibbons enjoyed a Schwinn bike and after-school work at Bobby Mears' grocery store and at the Sunset Nursery. Nonetheless, she later remarked, "When you're an orphan, bad days tend to run in long stretches.... [A] rescue falls through and you have to gain the power to hope again" (Brodeur, 1996). She described the feeling of being "hardened off," like a seedling (Jessup, "Kaye," 1995).

Gibbons was grateful to her brother "for taking me in, dusting me off, showing me the virtues of an honest day's work, and smiling over my report cards" (Gibbons, 1993, 7). She credited Barbara with a Pygmalion transformation by introducing Kaye to elocution. Barbara later exulted, "We're not proud of her fame, fortune, and glory. We're glad for her ... that we raised someone as nice as she has turned out to be. Fame hasn't changed her" (Reedy, 1998). Still escaping through literature, Gibbons cast a critical eye on a half page of Mario Puzo's crime saga *The Godfather* (1969). After paying a nickel to a boy extorting change from would-be readers, she admired images that later impacted her own creation of sensory experiences.

1976 By age 16, Gibbons abandoned dreams of lab science for any job that would bring instant wealth, the antidote to a life of poverty. For a profession, she saw herself as a famous trial lawyer battling the death penalty before the U.S. Supreme Court. She later reflected on coming-of-age as a time "I learned to be the kind of girl I needed to be to be a good writer. I learned to observe people and my surroundings" (Reedy, 1998).

1977 At age 17, Gibbons worked after school at B. Dalton's, the Cardinal Theater, Englewood Supermarket, and Sunset Nursery while holding up her grades and playing guitar with the Now Generation Singers, all in the search for college tuition. An anonymous benefactor enlisted her in the 1977 Miss North Carolina National Teenager Pageant. Among well-rounded, athletic girls, she saw herself as bookish and awkward and her dress as a homemade horror of pink and blue floral organza. Her wretchedness among other girls derived from a feeling of being the alienated oddball.

1978 Gibbons felt like Cinderella while living in Rocky Mount with an aunt and cousin until graduation from Rocky Mount Senior High School on South Tillery Street. Her advanced English teacher, Elizabeth "Betty" Hardy, joyed in Gibbons's writing and placed her compositions on the bottom of the stack "so I would have something to come to when I was tired" (Mosher, 1991). Alma Murchison, another English teacher, recalls Gibbons as unique, honest, and unaffected by peer pressure. From history teacher Barbara Taylor, the author learned that "history was a living, breathing and beautiful reality," an impetus to her inclusion of realistic backgrounds in fiction (Reedy, 1998).

The Batts family attended church, but seemed unmoved by religious ethics. Gibbons used regular church attendance as an opportunity to memorize 100 biblical passages, which earned her trips to the Children's Bible Mission Camp at Falls of the Neuse River outside Raleigh. Her reading included biographies of nurses Clara Barton and Florence Nightingale. Gibbons disparaged low chemistry grades that ended hopes of attending medical school and a dream of becoming an emergency room doctor. Her interest in wellness, public health, and treatments for illness retreated into the background until she resurrected them in the novels *Charms for the Easy Life*, the story of a country herbalist, and in *Diving Women*, an historical novel set during the 1918 influenza epidemic and featuring a home birth.

Gibbons recalled the pleasure of reading Eudora Welty's short works, especially the stories "Death of a Traveling Salesman" (1841) and "Moon Lake" (1980) and a 1979 character study of Ida M'Toy, a midwife and used clothing dealer in Jackson, Mississippi. By age 18, Gibbons had added John Steinbeck's Great Depression saga *The Grapes of Wrath* (1939) to her reading list. Subsequent good reads mirror a pattern in bedrock feminist writers—a love of Charlotte Brontë's *Jane Eyre* (1847) and Emily Brontë's *Wuthering Heights* (1847). Gibbons later remarked that the only way to learn to write is to read. In adulthood, she recommended as worthy fiction the P. D. James mysteries, the novels of Allan Gurganus and Amy Tan, and a global classic, Gabriel García Marquez's *One Hundred Years of Solitude* (1967). Marquez's style and themes impressed Gibbons, who admires his balance of dense prose with airy lightness and sturdy convictions.

1979 At the end of her teens, Gibbons entered a sane, predictable school, North Carolina State University in Raleigh, first as a political science major before switching to history. She roomed with Sarah Durant, worked part-time at the D. H. Hill

Library technical information center, and drove to the Rathskeller and on shopping sprees at used clothing stores in a dilapidated white Volkswagen beetle that sported a coat hanger for a radio antenna. Already a writer obsessed with bringing characters to life, she felt drawn to the sermons of Cotton Mather and Roger Williams. Author-teacher Lee Smith, the Guy Owen Writer in Residence at the university, marveled, "Everybody was kind of blown away at how smart she was" (Jessup, "Kaye," 1995). Despite her brilliance, Gibbons labored under the myth that country girls don't become famous writers. Unknown to her were the success stories of North Carolina novelists Allan Gurganus and Reynolds Price.

1980 On the proceeds from three waitressing jobs, one at MacGregor Downs Country Club, and from tutoring members of the football team, Gibbons pursued a degree in British and American literature. She pored over the intricacies of poems by T. S. Eliot and Gerard Manley Hopkins and the history of literature, from early Medieval Caedmon to late 20th-century poet Ted Hughes. She planned to teach college English and publish in learned journals, a next-door neighbor to actually writing literature. While enrolled in creative writing, she quailed at an assignment to compose haiku. Between her jobs waiting tables and working in the library, she cribbed a haiku. After only one session, Gibbons quit the creative writing course and began writing a novel as a literary exercise.

August, 1981 Gibbons concluded her sophomore year at N.C. State and enrolled at the University of North Carolina at Chapel Hill. On a governor's scholarship and a stipend from the Veteran's Administration, she discovered a campus she described as "a crazed vortex. It really does need a fence around it" (Reedy, 1998). In the scholarly ferment, she began to think of study as an end in itself. A Southern literary master, Cleanth Brooks, taught her in-depth reading and analysis, but she took no more courses in writing. She later came to perceive intellectualism and art as redemptive. In this formative era, doctors diagnosed her as manic-depressive and prescribed anticonvulsants to control frenzied states. By age 45, she realized that they overreacted to her post-adolescent restlessness and misread her creative extremes of reading all night.

1982 College introduced Gibbons to a breed of women different from tobacco farmers like Shine Batts. The author studied the range of young womanhood from sorority belles and "society idlers" to feminist organizers of the National Organization of Women, which got its start in Washington, D.C., on October 29, 1966, for the purpose of bringing women into the mainstream of American life (Gibbons, 1993, 154). Interrupting her studies, manic depression forced her hospitalization in Raleigh for seven months. She later noted, "I couldn't remember from paragraph to paragraph what I was reading" (Kenney, 1995).

May 12, 1984 Instead of following the extremes of her mother's life, Gibbons married 36-year-old landscape architect Michael Gibbons, a native of Queens and former Manhattan taxi driver, New York, whom she met on campus at N.C. State. Although Gibbons admitted, "My mama would have shot him if he'd drove up in our yard," the match proved uplifting as well as satisfying (Romine, June 1987). On the subject of people who marry outside their class, like Ruby Pitts in *A Virtuous Woman* (1989) and Samuel P. Goodman Tate in *On the Occasion of My Last Afternoon*, the author revealed a life-long sense of inferiority: "If I had married beneath me, I would have had to marry a snail or a rock or something" (Madrigal, 1989). At the Gibbons family duplex apartment on Cole Street in west Raleigh, North Carolina, Kaye found a need to simplify down to the fundamentals of self. She delighted in thrift and impressed Michael with savings on groceries from coupons she clipped from *Red Book*. She later acknowledged that the birth of daughter Mary and the publication of *Ellen Foster* saved the author's life. At that point, Gibbons "became an adult" (Edgers, 1997).

1985 As a new parent, the author surprised family and friends with her ability to organize a home and to tend the first of three daughters. Gibbons recalled her husband's welcome to Mary and his unexpressed delight that his wife was capable of domesticity. For guidance, she read *Dr. Spock's Baby and Child Care* (1946), a best-selling handbook to everyday choices and quandaries. She determined to reclaim her mother's strengths in maternal lore and pass them to her own girls. In looking back, she quipped, "I mainly learned how to raise them by watching *Leave It to Beaver*. If June said so, it must be so" (Spurr, 1995).

Contributing grit to the author's literary horizons were readings in William Blake's *The Book of Thel* (1789), an allegory on the confrontation between innocence and experience. More influential on her writing is James Weldon Johnson's introduction to *Book of American Negro Poetry* (1922), which validates vernacular speech. No longer ashamed of her rural Southern roots, she chose image and symbol as introits to the gutsy colloquialisms of Ellen Foster, a *naif* too early thrust into hardship. Begun as the focus of a poem, Ellen was a persona to be shaped over a series of glimpses as she grew up, adapted, and prevailed.

Summer, 1985 While majoring in American literature with a combination of lower- and upper-level courses, Gibbons studied Southern fiction at a graduate seminar led by Southern literature scholar Lewis D. Rubin, Jr., an editor at Algonquin Press, which he founded in 1983. He taught critical thinking and respect for language and fostered the writing success of Clyde Edgerton and Jill McCorkle. Gibbons reflected to Martha Waggoner in an interview for the Durham, North Carolina, *Herald-Sun*, "He helped teach me to read from a writer's point of view and ask questions.... So when I read, I tear things apart. It takes me forever to read a book" (Waggoner, September 1999). One of her papers he assessed with an H for "highest honors."

Rubin struck a respondent chord in Gibbons by explaining how authentic voicing in Mark Twain's *The Adventures of Huckleberry Finn* (1884) resulted in the first great American literature. In an early assessment of her interests, Rubin predicted that she would focus on female burdens and their spiritual reclamation through language. At the beginning of her career, she bought a door from Lowe's, balanced it on two sawhorses, and began work on a typewriter purchased on credit. Her choice of a profession centered on self-expression, "If I could use my own voice, then I was doing literature for a living" (Willett, 2004). Upon launching into a first novel, she chortled, "It scared my pants off" (Romine, April 1987). She described the feeling of drilling into an underground stream of "all art and good things" (*ibid.*).

November, 1985 Lewis Rubin admired a 30-page manuscript that Gibbons credited to a deep mysterious place in her psyche. He offered $1,500 for publication rights. With his encouragement, she wrote an autobiographical female quest novella, *Ellen Foster*, during a six-week manic episode that resulted in three months of psychiatric treatment. The author structured the novella around the domestic violence that isolated the title character from normal girlhood. Critic Valerie Sayers, reviewing for the *Washington Post*, compares Ellen to Huck Finn for facing moral challenge "with her dukes up" (Sayers, 2006). The story begins with a line picturing 11-year-old Ellen plotting to murder her father, perhaps the most cited of Gibbons's writing. The plot possessed a life of its own: "It was like something running in a path ahead of me, and I ran behind it with a stick and kept whipping it back into the path" (O'Briant, 1989). Drained by the oneness with Ellen's persona, Gibbons completed the manuscript and vomited. She denied to interviewers that she modeled Ellen after herself.

January 1, 1986 Gibbons turned the completed manuscript over to Rubin. Its command of authentic voice amazed and delighted novelist Lee Smith, who introduced Gibbons to Liz Darhansoff, a New York literary agent. Smith admired Gibbons's early post-modernism for compressed, urgent action. In retrospect, the author admitted the subconscious influence of J. D. Salinger's picaresque classic *The Catcher in the Rye* (1951). When *Seventeen* magazine proposed serializing *Ellen Foster*, Gibbons refused to punctuate dialogue, thus ending hopes of publishing in a popular teen venue. The loss came at a time that Gibbons suffered gestational diabetes and anticipated giving birth to daughter Leslie in 1987 without insurance to cover hospital costs. Two days after completing the manuscript, Gibbons began 12 weeks of therapy in a psychiatric ward for fluxuating between numbness and lightning-like flashes that muddled her thinking. She later denigrated psychotherapy for substituting mantras for anxiety.

January 12, 1987 *Ellen Foster*, a Literary Guild alternate, created a stir among readers and critics. It earned a citation from the Ernest Hemingway Foundation, a Louis D. Rubin Writing Award from the University of North Carolina, and the admiration of authors Alfred Kazin, Walker Percy, Elizabeth Spencer, John Barth, and Eudora Welty and of Jacqueline Kennedy Onassis. More important, the first novel established the author in a career that suited her talents and temperament. One admiring listener of Gibbons's reading from *Ellen Foster* described a gradual disconnect as author merged into character.

Gibbons was surprised by the novel's success. She discovered an immediate response from "people who had suffered as Ellen did" (Brennan, 1997). To those in need of mothering, she urged a search for inborn courage: "Find those who will love you, who will help you find a space to bloom" (*ibid.*) The author became the first North Carolina State University D. H. Hill Library author-in-residence, a post she continues to hold. As visiting lecturer, she supported the Friends of the Library program and established a fifth-floor office at the library, the former office of Thomas Wolfe scholar Richard G. Walser.

April, 1987 After numerous breaks in her education, Gibbons completed a few missing credits in geography, geology, and physical education and graduated from the University of North Carolina at Chapel Hill.

June, 1987 At her first American Booksellers Association convention, held in Washington, D.C., Gibbons discovered that Vintage Contemporaries outbid Dell, Viking Penguin, and Washington Square Press for paperback rights to *Ellen Foster.* The price — $33,000 — was the highest Algonquin ever negotiated for one of its books. The negotiation was propitious for both author and publisher, a female-friendly firm that critic Linda Tate credits for "[providing] a culturally significant corrective to the myopic male vision of southern women" (Tate, 1994, 183). Of Gibbons's rise to stardom, the author stated, "If my work is honest and speaks anywhere near to the heart of things, it is because Louis [Rubin] raised my mind and heart right" (Weaver, 2002). Gibbons praised him as a father figure who "sent me out into the larger world" (*ibid.*). In this same period, she published "The Headache," a short story in *St. Andrews Review.* The touch of Southern Gothicism in a snake-in-the-pocketbook prank and in the wee female physician who solaces heroine Lucille Womble suggest the influence of Flannery O'Connor and Eudora Welty, both Southern short fiction masters who valued encounters with the grotesque as reflections on human foibles.

1988 Gibbons received a surprisingly large royalty check as *Ellen Foster* flourished in the United States and France, where it appeared in excerpts in *Elle* magazine. The novel rose to fifth on the bestseller list and created demand in England, Denmark, and Sweden. In thanks to Louis Rubin, the author named her third daughter Louise and declared that motherhood and publication were life-savers. Gibbons, who was tempted to substitute indolence for work, disciplined her days for the writing of a second book. Opting for a literary career, she said of her novels, "I would rather go for the art and have them just happen to be popular" (Gretlund, 2000, 153). In this same period, Paramount Pictures bought film rights to *Ellen Foster*, a project to be directed by Randa Haines, the director of *Children of a Lesser God* (1986). Gibbons was embarrassed by an honorarium for "The Headache," awarded by Fred Chappell, North Carolina's poet laureate. She later claimed that her attempts at writing short fiction turn into chapters of novels.

May 10, 1988 *Ellen Foster* won a $2,500 award — the Sue Kaufman Prize for First Fiction from the American Academy and Institute of Arts and Letters. Gibbons received the honor in New York at the same time that her friend Reynolds Price was inducted into the academy. Of the prize, she remarked, "I feel like an artist now. I really do" (Romine, 1988). The next month, she began a promotional tour for the paperback edition of *Ellen Foster.*

1989 *A Virtuous Woman*, perhaps Gibbons's least favorite of her works, demanded less emotional involvement during composition. The writing of four drafts coincided with the breast-feeding of toddler Leslie and newborn Louise, whom the author nestled while typing. Daily composition felt like "yanking a stubborn mule up a hill" (O'Briant, 1989). By the time the book was edited and published by Louis Rubin, the author was hospitalized during a manic state and could not initiate a book tour. She faced the published author's dread that critics would compare her successful first novel with its successor. She realized that she was no longer "twenty-seven years old, quirky and cute" and that the public demanded more from her (Gretlund, 2000, p. 1138). Meanwhile, in October, her husband quit work to stay home with their three daughters.

Unlike *Ellen Foster*, the second novel required two distinct voices to recapture a marriage. The pro-woman story features widower "Blinking" Jack Ernest Stokes, who summons from death the words, fragrance, and presence of his wife, Ruby Pitts Woodrow Stokes. The novel, a Doubleday Book Club and Literary Guild main selection, remained on the *New York Times* bestseller list for weeks. Reviewer Elliot Krieger summarized part of the reason for the novel's popularity—the author's "affectionate portrayal of tenants and migrants" that counters Erskine Caldwell–style ridicule and discounting of the rural poor (Krieger, 1989). To critic Roz Kaveney, the writing distilled with "quiet dignity" biblical themes and traditional values, two elements that give a country-and-western feel to the narrative duet (Kaveney, 1989, 998).

In an interview with the Rocky Mount *Evening Telegram*, Gibbons regretted the "recent dispersal and watering down of language, the lost language in the South," a gradual diminution of regional traits that she intended to halt in her third novel (Wallace, 1990, 8). With a $20,000 grant from the National Endowment for the Arts, she began a more mature novel, *A Cure for Dreams*, at the same time that her first marriage foundered. The writing of a three-generation matrilineage based on scraps from Susan Glaspell's one-act play *Trifles* (1916) allowed Gibbons to vent frustrations with men and to laud women for taking responsibility for rearing children. The first of two multilayered female sagas, the novel honors women who better their lives and those of their offspring by maintaining and learning from feminist stories. It is significant to Gibbons's motif that she herself extracts from Glaspell a kernel of womanly wisdom to reshape and pass on to subsequent generations.

At the suggestion of Duke University professor Lee Smith, Gibbons began her first research as a basis for fiction. Within the Southern Historical Collection at UNC's Wilson Library, the author located source material that the North Carolina Historical Society began amassing in 1844. Essential to her project was the authentic voicing in transcripts of the Federal Writers' Project of the Great Depression. From the manuscripts featuring ex-slaves, mill hands, cotton farmers, smallholders, working women, housewives, and the jobless, she incorporated such locutions as "pink of the evening" for sunset and "when nature left me" for menopause. Of the poignant self-disclosures of plain people, she remarked, "You'd have to be a hard-hearted person to come away from those interviews not admiring the human voice" (Blades, 1991).

The discovery of unaltered vernacular from the American working class solidified the author's faith in ordinary speech as an art form. The text comprises 19 vignettes in the life of Betty Davies Randolph, a 20-year-old woman still dominated by her mother. The author visited Lee Smith's classroom, presented students notes and anecdotes from the Works Progress Administration (WPA) tapes, then read aloud passages from *A Cure for Dreams* to illustrate how research impacts fiction. In Smith's summation, "You do it all and it soaks in and then a voice has got to emerge to tell the story, because you cannot be writing history" (Smith, 2001, 102).

At an American Booksellers Association convention in Washington, D.C., Gibbons grew more confident during interviews. For the first time, she admitted that she used her own life as the basis for the Ellen character. She regretted cover-ups and thanked Adult Children of Alcoholics meetings with expunging self-blame that her mother committed suicide and her father drank himself to death. It was another two years before Gibbons could address her manic depression without feeling stigmatized. She admitted to the need for candor: "I can't lie to myself and say, 'Oh, it's a thyroid disorder'" (Kenney, 1995).

1991 As her girls entered nursery school and kindergarten, Gibbons helped out at the Montessori school. At home, she encouraged painting at easels. The author beamed, "Sitting on the deck watching the children paint is everything. It is hard to have much more" (Mosher, 1991).

March, 1991 *A Cure for Dreams*, edited by Louis Rubin, featured a cover photo that Charles Batts made of Shine in California in 1943, when she wore a turban while cleaning the family apartment. It won a $5,000 Nelson Algren Heartland Prize from the *Chicago Tribune* and a PEN Revson Foundation Fiction Fellowship of $12,750 for the best fiction by an American under age 35. An independent cinema company optioned the novel for film. Returning to Gibbons's regard for the storyteller, the plot pictures Marjorie Polly Randolph extending her dead mother's presence by relating her story. In the opinion of Ralph C. Wood, a critic for *Christian Century*, Gibbons's fiction up to this point "reveals how ordinary people live, thanks both to gumption and grace, quite extraordinary lives" (Wood, 1992, 842).

April–May, 1991 *A Cure for Dreams*, like Gibbons's two previous novels, was translated into eight languages. It earned a 23-city promotional tour, which she described as a "46-cheeseburger trip" (Romine, 1991). The novel, written in daily stints from 9:00 A.M. to 12:30 P.M., received the North Carolina Sir Walter Raleigh Award, presented by the North Carolina Literary and Historical Association and the Federation of North Carolina Historical Societies. The novel's success buoyed the author after the sale of Algonquin Books to Workman Publishing, when she chose to sign with G. P. Putnam's Sons. Guided by Putnam editor Faith Sale, Gibbons overcame personal obstacles. Reinvigorated, she began an 18-month project, *Charms for the Easy Life*, which Linda Parent Lesher lists in *The Best Novels of the Nineties* (2000). During give and take with the publisher, Gibbons realized that her editor was also advising novelists Alice Hoffman, Lee Smith, Amy Tan, and Kurt Vonnegut. In the company of major authors, Gibbons felt overpaid when she first signed a million-dollar contract. Out of gratitude, she dedicated *Charms* to agent Liz Darhansoff.

Written during a stable, happy time in her life, the new novel taxed Gibbons's resilience and ingenuity. The three-layered matrilineal saga required three drafts to zing her female characters with life and purpose. The author characterized the finished work as "three splinters of my personality"—acerbic bluntness, passion, and intellect (Madrigal, 1993). She chose period details from Colombian author Gabriel García Marquez's *One Hundred Years of Solitude* and *Love in the Time of Cholera* (1986) and from Cuban-American author Oscar Hijuelos's Pulitzer Prize–winning novel *The Mambo Kings Play Songs of Love* (1990). Contributing to the text were WPA interviews, motifs from Studs Terkel's *The Good War* (1984), and consultations with Dr. Robert Farnham, a clinical pathologist in Charlotte, North Carolina, and Dr. David Henderson, an obstetrician-gynecologist in Raleigh, North Carolina.

January, 1992 Traveling in a crowded Volvo station wagon, the Gibbons family resettled at Woodacre in Marin County, California, an area that Michael Gibbons loved from a former residence there. The relocation, which lasted 40 days, did not provide the cure for a troubled marriage. The couple separated on the drive west. The author later summarized the move as an "expensive and stupid venture" (Madrigal, 1993). Upon return to Raleigh, in March, Gibbons fleshed out the text of *Charms for the Easy Life* with historical anecdotes and diction from a supportive boyfriend. After a divorce, she completed the manuscript in her rumpled bedroom on an antique wood table. For her skill, she earned from Ann Alexander, critic for the *Greensboro* (N.C.) *News & Record*, the sobriquet of "North Carolina's shooting star" (Alexander 1992).

February 2–9, 1992 Selections from Gibbons's works accompanied pieces by Doris Betts, Wilma Dykeman, Gail Godwin, Jill McCorkle, Ruth Moose, and Lee Smith in the stage miscellany *Dear Ms. Dare*, a collection of vignettes, verse, and song. Directed by Bo Thorpe, the showcase opened at the Cape Fear Regional Theater in Fayetteville before its reprise at the North Carolina Women Writers' Conference in Winston-Salem on March 14.

1993 Gibbons began to relax and let herself venture into essays and children's fiction. She remarked, "I've finally gotten to the point where my children are old enough that I can branch out and do some creative playing" (Giffin, 1993). For her writing career, she received a University of North Carolina Distinguished Alumnus Award.

March, 1993 G. P. Putnam's Sons issued *Charms for the Easy Life*, a *New York Times* bestseller and notable book of 1993 that Gibbons began writing within 20 minutes of completing *A Cure for Dreams*. Originally titling her fourth novel *Eagle Avenue*, Gibbons settled on the final title 20 minutes before submitting the manuscript to the publisher. During relaxing moments, she enjoyed a friendship with North Carolina novelist Allan Gurganus, author of *The Oldest Living Confederate Widow Tells All* (1989), but the two writers refrained from discussing their careers. In an interview, Gurganus confided his admiration for Gibbons: "There something extremely personable in her work that engages you" (O'Briant, 1995).

May, 1993 While caroming from New York to Boston, Minneapolis, and Detroit on a 30-city book tour, Gibbons suffered a bout of exhaustion. She was elated when *Charms for the Easy Life* made the *New York Times* bestseller list, her first time at the top of the list. She began seeing her work in airports, a sure sign of the novel's popularity.

September 25, 1993 Gibbons wed a 48-year-old intellectual—corporate attorney Frank P. Ward, Jr., a graduate of Yale, Duke, and New York University who specializes in labor, employment, and civil rights cases at the firm of Maupin, Taylor, Ellis, and Adams. According to society page news, the bride wore an ivory damask Laura Ashley gown for the service, which took place at Christ Episcopal in Raleigh. She knew him first as a book reviewer for the *Raleigh News & Observer*. Drawn to her "strong sweetness," he met her in 1989 and introduced her at gatherings of Friends of the Library at North Carolina State University (Jessup, "Kaye," 1995). She became stepmother to his two children, Frank, III, and Victoria, and keeper of four terriers and a poodle from the pound (one pregnant with four pups), five cats (two named Earl and Huey Long), three gerbils, and a crab. From Frank's mother, Mary Alice Ward of Lumberton, North Carolina, Gibbons adopted the habit of keeping a reading journal.

In the exclusive Hayes-Barton district of Raleigh, Gibbons enjoyed a close-knit family. At 8:00 P.M. each night, she sat in bed with her children and read for an hour. Ward treated Gibbons with old-style courtesy, providing her daily fix of toasted pimiento-cheese-on-white sandwiches from the Glenwood Pharmacy on the corner, stocking their home collection of some 4,000 volumes, and introducing her to the verse of early 20th-century Greek poet Constantine P. Cavafy. Ward refers to her scripturally as "the word made flesh" (Miller, 1995). In a personal essay for *Paris Review*, she identified Ward as her first love and added that "his power of transformation saw me through the metamorphosis from little girl to woman," a statement refuting her earlier maturing from marriage to Michael Gibbons (Gibbons, winter 1999, 146).

1994 In a state of misery, Gibbons undertook her fifth novel, *Sights Unseen*. She observed, "I was disappointed that writing about [manic depression] didn't give me this sense of relief" (Jessup, "Disease," 1995). At the novel's completion, she activated grammar-checking software and discovered that her writing suited a ninth-grade reading level. She joked, "I'm expecting a wide readership" (Walcott, 1996, 116). To relieve her toil, Frank gave her "the Mixmaster of my dreams for my birthday" (Olney, 1994.) Simon & Schuster released a two-cassette abridgement of *Charms for the Easy Life*, which Gibbons read in her distinctive piedmont Carolina drawl. Patricia Holt, reviewing for the *San Francisco Chronicle*, admired the oral flow, which "lures us into its rich languid storytelling power" (Holt, 1994).

February 3–20, 1994 Scenarist-director Aaron Posner, co-founder of Philadelphia's Arden Theatre Company, adapted *Ellen Foster* for the stage, starring Stephanie L. Gatschet and Alexis Schulman as young Ellen, Suzanne O'Donnell as the older Ellen, and Marcia Saunders in the dual role of Aunt Nadine Nelson and the new mama. The production, held at the St. Stephen's Alley Performing Arts Center, earned stellar comments. In a preview for the *Philadelphia Daily News*, critic Nels Nelson lauded Ellen's "steadfast good humor and healthy skepticism" (Nelson, 1994, 40). Clifford A. Ridley, theater critic for the *Philadelphia Inquirer*, admired "larger-than-life melodramatic characters" (Ridley, 1994). He questioned an aspect that stymied book critics—Gibbons's intermingling of a picaresque quest tale with "Ellen's gradual shedding of her acquired notions of racial superiority," a secondary plot that winds unevenly through the text (*ibid.*).

1995 G. P. Putnam's Sons published a 90,000-copy first run of *Sights Unseen*, the focus of the author's two-month tour of 32 cities. The dedication page notes the help of Gibbons's three daughters and two stepchildren as well as the influence of agent Liz Darhansoff, editor Faith Sale, and proofreader Anna Jardine. The text reflects anecdotes related by the author's mother-in-law, Mary Alice Ward. Central to place, time, and characters is Gibbons's girlhood in Bend of the River, North Carolina, and the sufferings of her mother from mental turmoil. The memories of cold hands and panic at straitjackets, seizures, and loss of control carry a verisimilitude too shattering to be fictional. To ease her fears of the stigma of mental illness, her psychiatrist urged her to think of cyclical moods like diabetes, a controllable illness. Gibbons later reflected, "I have not been sick in so long that I was able to, as Wordsworth said, 'recollect it in tranquility'" (Waggoner, 1995). Composition gave her courage. She explained, "[It] made me reaffirm my pledge to stay well. I try hard every day, even though it's much easier to give in to this illness" (Paddock, 1995).

The story, which is a frequent feature on high school and college reading lists, touches on Southern racism and the pejorative "nigger," but Gibbons, like her icon Eudora Welty, chooses not to crusade for civil rights (Gibbons, 1995, 197). The original text contained two books, which she split into two stacks on her dining room table. She retained the unpublished part for another book. *Sights Unseen* won a Critics Choice Award from the *San Francisco Chronicle* for its starkly powerful reunion between a girl and her mentally reconditioned mother. Gibbons anticipated that writing about mental illness would yield insights into the effects of her own emotional illness on her daughters. In *When a Parent Is Depressed: How to Protect Your Child from the Effects of Depression in the Family* (2002), Dr. William R. Beardslee lists *Sights Unseen* as a source for families dealing with chronic manic-depression.

Versions of Gibbons's work increased her impact on the fiction market. The Hallmark Hall of Fame bought rights to *Ellen Foster*. At Southern Illinois University at Carbondale, Elyse Lam Pineau adapted *A Cure for Dreams* for narrative presentation at the 110-seat Kleinau Theatre of Quigley Auditorium. A live broadcast in Russia paired Gibbons's reading with that of Yevgeny Yevtushenko and Mordecai Richler. A list in *Village Voice* placed Gibbons's work third after Albert Camus and Colin Powell. One reviewer declared that Gibbons could write a manual on garden hoses and come up with a bestseller. She reflected on the joy of success: "I realized I was in charge and if I wanted to be happy, I could make that happen" (Jessup, "Kaye," 1995). Part of her self-motivation was the ability to retain "healthy patterns of insight" from manic states (Kenney, 1995). Contributing to her self-esteem was receipt of the first Mary Frances Hobson Family Foundation Award, presented at Chowan College.

January, 1995 Her fifth novel complete, Gibbons took a deliberate ten-month hiatus from fiction to research Civil War history, the background of *On the Occasion of My Last Afternoon*. The working title, "Her Ordinary Grace," suggests the focus on female composure during racial, political, and economic upheaval. She included in her survey the notable abolitionist Lowells of Boston, Major Robert Gould Shaw's father, General Robert E. Lee's daughter Mildred, Wade Hampton, Varina Davis, and Dorothea Dix. From books dispatched by fellow author Jeanne Braselton, Gibbons researched battlefield surgery and the treatment of "female hysteria," a misogynistic diagnosis of normal women's yearning for independence (Gibbons, 2004, 62). Rather than compose on her Macintosh computer, Gibbons took 350 pages of notes in longhand and distributed throughout the text the details that heighten realism — the Southern's odium toward generals Benjamin Franklin Butler and William Tecumseh Sherman, the haphazard departure of slaves to freedom, the slave-baiting by ignorant white children, the hiring of saloon drunks as messengers, and the postwar malaise that engulfs widows whose worlds crumble before their eyes. One remarkable reply to a dear-John letter came from a Confederate soldier who stated, "Dear Erstwhile Sweetheart, God will now have time to punish you" (Hodges, 1998). The miffed boyfriend signed himself "No more love for you, Jack."

August–October, 1995 In spite of pain from a slipped disc, Gibbons remained on the move. When Kim Weaver Spurr, a reviewer for the Durham, N.C., *Herald-Sun*, interviewed the author, she found a confident professional — "funny and cheerful, elegant and poised ... a woman of quiet strength" (Spurr, 1995). At the Eudora Welty Writers' Symposium at the Mississippi University for Women in Columbus, Gibbons shared the podium with author Will Campbell and poet Dannye Romine-Powell. The event, begun in 1989, showcased Southern writers reading from their works. Gibbons noted the predominence of female attendees, the traditional supporters of Southern literature. Also in 1995, Gibbons completed three projects based on her state heritage. For a video, *Second Sunday Reading*, she collaborated with Lenard D. Moore. A seven-part series of radio broadcasts for *Soundings*, a production of the National Humanities Center, featured Gibbons in a half-hour discussion of her work.

December, 1995 Gibbons joined Laura Argiri, Jerry Bledsoe, Michael Chitwood, Clyde Edgerton, Fred Chappell, Philip Gerard, Marianne Gingher, Jaki Shelton Green, David Guy, William McCranor Henderson, Margaret Maron, Jill McCorkle, Tim McLaurin, Bland Simpson, Lee Smith, and John Welter in composing a serial novel. The completed murder mystery, edited by David Perkins, appeared as *Pete & Shirley: The Great Tarheel Novel*, issued by Down Home Press in association with the Raleigh *News & Observer*. Replete with Southern Gothic, the parody became an inside joke for residents of the Triangle area, which encompasses North Carolina's most prestigious university communities. At month's end, Gibbons earned a squib in *New Yorker* for rewriting the dedication in *A Virtuous Woman* to replace her first husband's name with that of Frank Ward. With her usual fervor, she sniped, "It was irritating to me every time I opened the book" (Malinowski, 1995, 46).

January 12–February 25, 1996 Aaron Posner's 1994 adaptation of *Ellen Foster* flourished in the South. Lisa Adler directed a reprise in Atlanta at the Horizon Theatre, a southeastern premiere for the work. It starred wispy thin Jarrett Horne in the title child role with Shari Garretson as Ellen's mother, Heather Heath as the adult Ellen, and Kimberley Hammett as Starletta. Reviewer Dan Hulbert lauded Adler's feel for subtle realism. When the play opened at Meredith College later in February, Gibbons attended with her brother David. She noted to Byron Woods, a correspondent for the Raleigh *News & Observer*, "I haven't completely uncovered the psychology of it all" (Woods, 1997). After a break from the audience to distance herself from harsh memories, she returned to sit by her brother. Of the heavy emotion of the autobiography, she observed, "It was tough for both of us" (*ibid.*).

March, 1996 In a summation of Southern strengths, author Willie Morris contributed to Olympic Games spirit in Atlanta, Georgia, by spotlighting the people who have made the New South. In mentioning Kaye Gibbons, he pictured her "taking her place prominently in that remarkable nexus of Southern women writers who have always greatly mattered to our culture and tell us who we are" (Morris, 1996). He situated the author among Southerners "who are well-rounded and well-grounded in their lives and values ... [and] contribute their gifts and strengths to others without recompense" (*ibid.*). Morris admired Gibbons most for her versatility and sense of fun.

April 12–14, 1996 Gibbons was the Wilson Lecturer at the Second Southern Women Writers' Conference, a showcase of emerging authors held annually at Berry College in Mount Berry, Georgia. For the occasion, she delivered a personal essay, "The First Grade, Jesus, and the Hollyberry Family," a humorous retrospective of growing up in the eastern piedmont among religious fundamentalists.

May, 1996 After jettisoning 900 pages on January 3 and rewriting her text by March 15, 1997, Gibbons issued *On the Occasion of My Last Afternoon*, an historical novel based on women's lives before and during the Civil War. She abandoned the title *Seasons of My Discontent* and voiced the text in imitation of Katherine Anne Porter's Miranda stories. Of authorial frustrations, Gibbons explained that, "after three years of digging ditches" and compiling 350 pages of notes on yellow legal pads, she never felt luminosity in the story (Gossett, 1998). To Ben Steelman, a journalist for the Wilmington (N.C.) *Morning Star*, she declared, "I felt I'd been dragged behind a tractor-trailer for a couple of miles," the preface to a long rest with her family at Wrightsville Beach (Steelman, 1998). She joked, "It's something which every Southern writer has to do ... write a book on the Civil War" (Kenney, 1995). During the project, she became a "nocturnal mother," her term for keeping odd hours that limited contact with her children (Gibbons, *Occasion*, n.p.). At the end of the writing, she entered a hospital to recover from sleep deprivation.

Gibbons extracted the pervasive sense of loss in 19th-century female lives from consultations with Southern Civil War historian Shelby Foote, from Bruce Catton's Civil War books and Clarence Poe's *True Tales of the South at War: How Soldiers Fought and Families Lived* (1865), and from letters, 53 journals, Confederate medical reviews, and 175 women's post-war writings for the vanity press. Among letters were women's testimonials to hardships. Gibbons explained, "They wanted their children and grandchildren to remember what they had to endure" (Steelman, 1998). Heartened by the encouragement of Oprah Winfrey and by the guidance of editor Faith Sale, the author completed the novel in 40- to 60-hour sessions over a three-month period of what protagonist Emma Garnet calls "livable chaos," the result of fame and a day that brought 65 phone calls. Gibbons dedicated the work to Sale, whom she called "the Queen of Love and Beauty" (Gibbons, 1998, n.p.). Throughout the text, the character seems to speak the author's delight in a happy marriage with her adoration of a man who arrives home "loving me, loving me, loving me" (*ibid.*, 127). Critic Corinna Lothar, a reviewer for the *Washington Times*, called the novel a powerful, poignant, detailed "evocation of the war years and their effect on the lives of Southern civilians" (Lothar, 1998).

At a high point in Gibbons's critical acclaim, she became the youngest recipient of the Chevalier de L'Ordre des Arts et des Lettres. One of many Southern authors prized by the French, she attained best-selling status with *Ellen Foster*. Nominating the author for knighthood was documentary filmmaker Catherine Berge, director of *Fortune Cookie* (1993). The public presentation occurred in Paris in October. Bestowing the formal title was the French Minister of Culture, Philippe Douste-Blazy, in token of the author's contribution to French literature.

While serving as keynote speaker at the Southern Women Writers' Conference at Berry College in Rome, Georgia, Gibbons befriended author Jeanne Braselton and read a draft of her first novel, *A False Sense of Well-Being* (2001). That same year, Gibbons taped a three-hour abridged version of *Ellen Foster* for Simon & Schuster. Reviewer Trudi Miller Rosenblum admired the flat, chilling voice that not only relates the child's story, but also reveals an emotional trauma so terrible that Ellen wrings herself dry of feeling.

September 5, 1996 Gibbons conveyed to interviewer David G. Spielman and photographer William W. Starr her dismay at the uprooting of a tree, part of the havoc of Hurricane Fran. Stoic in the aftermath of water-damaged books and photos, she stated that destruction made it easier for her to "write about what devastation means" (Spielman & Starr, 1997, 70).

1997 In tandem with Terry Beaver, Kaye Gibbons narrated the part of Ruby Stokes for a three-hours abridged version of *A Virtuous Woman* for Simon & Schuster Audio. The reading won the approval of Rochelle L'Gorman, a reviewer for the *Los Angeles Times*, who admired the authenticity of a duet of Southern voices.

In the writer-helps-writer tradition, Gibbons read the first 100 pages of Charles Frazier's *Cold Mountain*, a novel he began in 1990. The response was instantaneous: "It vibrated my system" (Waggoner, October 1999). In hopes of a bidding war, she alerted editors and passed Frazier's beginnings to her agent, who quickly contracted the manuscript to Atlantic Monthly Press for a six-figure sum. Gibbons compared the historical fiction to Civil War novels by Shelby Foote and Michael Shaara and added, "This novel deserves any and all prizes that might be lying about" (Gossett, 1997).

March 20–23, 1997 Gibbons appeared at the 21st Annual Tennessee Williams/New Orleans Literary Festival, a venue she revisited in 2000 and 2005.

Late May, 1997 Closer to home, Gibbons received honors at the 13th Annual Raleigh Medal of Arts award ceremony. In addition to her fame for authorship, she earned esteem for establishing libraries in state orphanages.

May 31, 1997 In an address to 85 attendees of the annual session of the Mental Health Association in Orange County, North Carolina, Gibbons spoke on "Frost and Flower, My Life with Manic Depression Thus Far," which Wisteria Press published in 1995 as a monograph. In a recap of her experiences with mental illness, she admitted, "It is a rare moment to feel well" ("Author," 1997). She queried, "Who rules my body, me or the disease?" (*ibid.*). She noted that drugs further complicated her search for sanity and caused her to ask if she were behaving inappropriately. She later joked, "Lithium flatlines me and makes me want to join the Junior League" (Steelman, 1998). For her candor, mental health professionals and patients and their families gave her a standing ovation. She realized, however, that taking medication generated wellness: "If I didn't, I'd destroy the children. I'd go down, and I'd drag three innocent children down with me" (Jessup, "Disease," 1995).

December 8, 1997 During an interview on the Oprah Winfrey Show before 15 million viewers, Gibbons gravitated toward the actor's warmth: "I don't know how much of that was her and how much was an act, but she was very helpful" (Reedy, 1998). The author admitted to being the real Ellen Foster and confessed a need to tell stories about childhood trauma. In the swirl of public acclaim, Vintage printed an additional 2.2 million paperback copies of Gibbons's chosen works; Algonquin kicked in 45,000 hardback reprints. The author's elation at being one of Oprah's authors and at the boost to her earnings preceded a housewifely concern: "I'll be able to get my hardwood floors done before finishing my next book" (Edgers, 1997). Gibbons was particularly supportive of Oprah's attempt to elevate readers from a limited diet of bible readings and the novels of Tom Clancy and Danielle Steele. Gibbons beamed, "[Oprah]'s feeding people literature, real quality. I'm proud to be part of it" (Gossett, 1997).

December 14, 1997 *Hallmark Hall of Fame* aired *Ellen Foster*, a two-hour CBS-TV screenplay adapted by William Hanley and Maria Nation and directed by John Erman. It starred Jena Malone, whose role as Ellen echoed her portrayal of Bone Boatwright in the Showtime film *Bastard Out of Carolina* (1996). Supporting Malone as Ellen was Julie Harris as Grandmother Leonora and Ted Levine as the predatory father, Bill Hammond. Rounding out the cast were Glynis O'Connor as Ellen's mother Charlotte, Barbara Garrick as Ellen's aunt Betsy, Debra Monk as Betsy's sister Nadine, Kimberly Brown as Dora, Nadine's daughter, and Lynne Moody and Bill Nunn as Starletta's parents. Filmed in Vancouver, British Columbia, the family drama discloses the result of grudges and vengeance. Harris remarked of her character that the combination "creates poison in your system and that poison eventually kills you" (McCabe, 1997). The film featured the song "Remember Christmas," by composer Harry Nilsson. Critics compared the Southern setting and feminist themes to the films *Wildflower* (1991), *Before Women Had Wings* (1997), and *All the Little Animals* (1998).

1998 The author received the 35th annual North Carolina Award for Literature, which the General Assembly established in 1961 as the state's highest civilian honor for excellence in the arts, literature, public service, and science. She quipped that a country girl from Nash County could expect to pour champagne or collect plates at such a function, but not to be the honoree. At her urging, James H. Watkins edited *Southern Selves: From Mark Twain and Eudora Welty to Maya Angelou and Kaye Gibbons: A Collection of Autobiographical Writing* (1998). Gibbons contributed "The

First Grade, Jesus, and the Hollyberry Family," a tart, witty review of her life at age six.

Mid-January, 1998 Gibbons, accompanied by her husband, Frank Ward, addressed the Junior League of Winston-Salem's 1998 Author Luncheon, a fund-raiser for the "Read to Me" program. The couple relished the job of stocking children's homes and a center for abused women and children in Johnston County with 2,000 books. Of the need for new books, Gibbons explained, "Children in these situations too often get used things, and feel used themselves" (Brodeur, 1996). She described the new books as "spiritual possessions" (*ibid.*).

June 26, 1998 Reviewers applauded the release of Simon & Schuster's audio version of *On the Occasion of My Last Afternoon*, a four and a half-hour abridged version read by Polly Holliday, who earned more kudos than did reader Sally Darling for the six-cassette unabridged version issued by Recorded Books. Cassandra West, a reviewer for the *Chicago Tribune*, praised Holliday's blend of "sweetness and light that makes Gibbons' language sing" (West, 1998). The book won a Notable Book of 1998 designation from the *New York Times Book Review*. Of its timing, Gibbons explains, "I felt pressure, not from the publisher, but from myself to get it out as close to the Oprah hoopla as possible" (O'Briant, 1998).

October, 1998 Along with works by Bill Cosby, Ernest Gaines, Maya Angelou, and Wally Lamb, talk-show host Oprah Winfrey touted two of Gibbons's books—*Ellen Foster* and *A Virtuous Woman*—for the Oprah Book Club. Winfrey described the latter novel as the love story that Americans were waiting for. Within the month, readers bought three million copies. Although Gibbons at first feared that talk-show notoriety would trivialize her work, the honor elevated her to a greater fame and a broader, more egalitarian readership. The shift in public response caused her to dub the before and after as "pre–Op" and "post–Op" ("Author Lavishes," 1998). The recognition came at a time when she carried 75 extra pounds from 19 types of medication that left her listless and muddle-headed. In response to Gibbons's honor by the Oprah Book Club, Recorded Books issued an unabridged four-hour audio version of *Ellen Foster*, a three-tape version read by Ruth Ann Phimister.

November, 1998 In late November, Gibbons addressed a dinner meeting of the Literary and Historical Association in Raleigh concerning the centrality of true language to her writing. She claimed the rural South as her touchstone and real people as the sources of her fictional personae. Endowed with a love of "a human voice talking," she remarked, "Way down town or way out of town, ... we still glory in imaginative talk" (Hodges, 1998). For vernacular refreshers, she valued walking through K-Mart to eavesdrop on normal human conversation.

February 12, 1999 At the John H. Mulroy Civic Center in Syracuse, New York, Gibbons delivered the Rosamond Gifford Lecture, "My Life with Manic Depression So Far." With seriocomic drollery, she revealed bizarre delusions and plunges into depression that warped her sanity, but fueled verbal sprees for twenty years. Critic Jane Nordby Gretlund compared the author's self-revelation to William Styron's *Darkness Visible* (1990), a confessional treasure on depression.

April, 1999 Along with Southern novelists Allan Gurganus, Terry Kay, and Dori Sanders, Gibbons tweaked Margaret Mitchell's *Gone with the Wind* (1936) by proposing a zany conclusion. In the reprise, Rhett Butler sires a son by Prissy, who elopes with Frederick Douglass. The child, a legless deaf-mute, begs on Atlanta streets, drawing donors by pounding a tin drum. After he opens a school for fiction writers, Gibbons continues, "Scarlett, a frenzied shopaholic, is his first published student. She blows her hefty advance on shoes, and to make ends meet, is forced to waitress at a barbecue hut" ("Mammy," 1999).

May, 1999 In an interview for *Book* magazine, Gibbons revealed the gnawing mother hunger that drove the author to plan a biography of Shine Batts as a catharsis to decades of obsessive curiosity. Gibbons remembered Shine as "a Rosie the Riveter from an aristocratic Southern family" (Steelman, 1998). The author explained the purpose of her investigation: "I want to find out who my mother was as a woman.... I have very few memories of her. I want to find out how she operated as a woman, find out what she liked, what jokes she thought were funny" (O'Briant, May 1999). That same month, Gibbons received an honorary doctorate of letters at the North Carolina State University spring graduation ceremony. She exulted that the ceremony gave her an opportunity to "wear my big green medal for my contribution to French literature and a really great robe" (Reedy, 1998).

2000 After five novels, Gibbons discovered that her placement in book stores migrated from the "Southern writer" category into the mainstream. In *Southern Writers at Century's End* (2000), editors Jeffrey J. Folks and James A. Perkins listed her as a member of a "flowering of Southern writers, perhaps a third generation Southern Literary Renascence" (Folks & Perkins, 2000, 113). Included in this elite cadre are Gail Godwin, Allan Gurganus, Randall Garrett Kenan, Jill McCorkle, and Lee Smith. The authors' commentary lauds the intimacy and affection of Gibbons's blue-collar vernacular style. Common talk creates an aura of reality in her woman-centered fiction, as though the author were merely passing on a stock of anecdotes from a circle of female acquaintances.

Gibbons tended to tour and speak outside the South, but limited her speeches to two or three per year to assure time at her desk and with her daughters. When city developers planned to turn a small park in the Hayes Barton section into a pond, she joined neighbors in defending "one of Raleigh's oldest remaining green spaces" (Lindenfeld, 2000). With the aid of her daughters, Gibbons notified 300 households of the project that would deplete the area of a gathering place for trick-or-treaters and wintertime sledders. Her own family used the spot for making movies. Of one effort, the author recalled, "It was just perfectly hilarious to see Louise running through a park dressed like an orangutan" (*ibid.*).

The author punctuated writing time with other projects. The audio version of *Charms for the Easy Life*, read by actor-producer Kate Fleming for Sound Library, retained the range of emotions in narrator Margaret, an adult looking back on life in an all-woman household. The reading earned the regard of Joanna M. Burkhardt, a reviewer for *Library Journal*. Gibbons provided Modern Library with an introduction to a new edition of Kate Chopin's *The Awakening and Other Stories* (1899).

Among Gibbons's comments was her complaint that readers tend to judge Chopin on the basis of *The Awakening* to the exclusion of her short fiction in *Bayou Folk* (1894). Gibbons's accolade could also apply to her own career: "[Chopin] rebounded from her losses first to preserve her spirit and that of her children" (Gibbons, 2000, xii).

December 22, 2000 The author separated from Frank Ward. In middle age, she reassessed her life options and maintained an amicable relationship with her children's father and grandmother. Some months later, in a review of two biographies of Edna St. Vincent Millay, Gibbons congratulated herself for avoiding the dependencies and dangerous living of writers like F. Scott Fitzgerald and Ernest Hemingway. She acknowledged that "a life well-lived" can produce art as readily as "a life lived in a perpetual cycle of panic and recovery" (Gibbons, September 2001). Still at home in a 77-year-old two-story brick manse at 918 Cowper Drive in Raleigh, she vowed to remain on the premises until death: "The owner of Brown-Wynne Funeral home who lives across the street will have to come get me" (Spurr, 1995).

2001 Gibbons thrilled a European audience by addressing a gathering at the Pompidou Center in Paris. That same year, she wrote an introduction to an anthology, *I Cannot Tell a Lie, Exactly and Other Stories*, by Mary Ladd Gavell. The opening paragraph contains Gibbons's credo: "The principal aims of literature are to create joy, to delight, and to instruct, not in the sense of changing our politics but in leading us to a full, vibrant, and authentic sense of purpose" (Gibbons, *I Cannot*, 2001, ix).

April, 2001 While recording *Ellen Foster* for Audioworks, Gibbons admitted a need for the missing punctuation as visual guides to tone and atmosphere. In another venture into audio publication, she co-narrated an abridged cassette version of *The Best American Essays of the Century* (2000), edited for Houghton Mifflin by Joyce Carol Oates and featuring the work of James Agee, Maya Angelou, James Baldwin, F. Scott Fitzgerald, Langston Hughes, Zora Neale Hurston, Martin Luther King, Jr., Mary McCarthy, John Muir, Susan Sontag, and Mark Twain.

September 11, 2001 The terrorist attacks on the World Trade Center and the Pentagon forced Gibbons into a new mindset. She began living in the moment and writing more directly about emotional truth.

December 26, 2001 An acrimonious divorce from Frank Ward left the author broke and grasping at loans from friends to tide her over. As the financial gap ended the dream of Gibbons's daughter to attend college in New York, the household sliced expenses. The author gave up alcohol and, in January 2001, all prescription drugs as well as a chic wardrobe and partying with friends. She intended to "get my children to a good place and get myself there first" (Krentz, 2006). The effort required 18-hour workdays, but she congratulated herself for running an orderly household "big enough to allow for those flare-ups that happen when you're a single parent with three teenage girls" (O'Briant, 2004). She compared her new life to a "dress with plenty of room in the seams' (*ibid.*) The new self encouraged her to travel to Las Vegas to interview comedian-magician Penn Jillette on the subject of authenticity in art. In a short span, he remarked, "I feel like I've known her forever ... a sexy genius with creative energy just flowing out of her" (*ibid.*).

2002 Kaye Gibbons's life received an uptick from a re-diagnosis that declared her untouched by the bipolar syndrome. She gave up pills and lost some 60 pounds. She reflected that "Artistic behaviors are closely akin to the symptoms of bipolar disorder" (*ibid.*).

August 18, 2002 *Charms for the Easy Life* was a vehicle for Showtime-TV, which featured a screenplay written by Angela Shelton, the North Carolina–born author of *Tumbleweeds* (1994), and directed by Joan Micklin Silver. Gena Rowlands and Mimi Rogers starred as the healer Charlie Kate Birch and daughter Sophia. Susan May Pratt played the narrator-daughter Margaret. Gibbons complimented Shelton at the premiere on the quality of the adaptation. Shelton, who became a fan of Charlie Kate, noted, "She's way ahead of her time" (Clodfelter, 2002). An unsigned review for *Cableworld* compared the feminist draw of the screen version to that of Fannie Flagg's *Fried Green Tomatoes at the Whistle Stop Café* (1987) and Rebecca Wells's *Divine Secrets of the Ya-Ya Sisterhood* (1996), both derived from Southern feminist fiction.

January, 2003 Gibbons worked at a number of projects—publication of *Raised by Hand*, copyediting *The Method of Life*, composing magazine articles and a screenplay, and co-production of *Charms for the Easy Life*. To fill a gap for the Penguin Lives series, she composed a biography of Jacqueline Kennedy Onassis, a role model who inspired the author to prioritize the needs of children before the demands of marriage. In spare time, Gibbons traveled, swam, hiked 50 blocks daily, read, studied pottery with Sid Oakley at Cedar Creek, and cooked meals for homeless men in Raleigh. Posing as the Dixie Chicks, in February, Gibbons, Jeanne Braselton, and Lee Smith entertained at the South Carolina Book Festival.

March 30, 2003 The suicide of 41-year-old widow Jeanne Braselton in Rome, Georgia, left Gibbons both sorrowing and angry. The previous year, Braselton won the 2002 Georgia Author of the Year Award. Gibbons did not attend the funeral of the witty, bubbly friend whom Gibbons joined daily in an hour's telephone chat.

Late April, 2003 Gibbons joined the Fellowship of Southern Writers, a literary organization established in Chattanooga, Tennessee, in 1987 by such luminaries as Cleanth Brooks, James Dickey, Shelby Foote, Ernest Gaines, Reynolds Price, William Styron, and Eudora Welty. Gibbons lauded the founders of Southern literature for "[setting] a standard so high that every page and every paragraph and every line had to be the very best it could be" (Zane, 2001). The description is a fair assessment of her own work.

September 20, 2003 Another loss increased Gibbons's bereavement—the death of her editor, 63-year-old Faith Sale of Cold Spring, New York, who died on December 7, 1999, from a rare form of cancer caused by exposure to asbestos. The author joined Patricia Griffith, Heidi Julavits, Lee Smith, and Amy Tan at the Folger Library in Washington, D.C., for the "William Faulkner Birthday Reading: A Tribute to Faith Sale."

October 5, 2003 Gibbons was cognizant of the failed careers of well-intentioned writers. She pictured "bodies and minds crumpled on the side of some notorious highway to hell long before our time" (Gibbons, September 2001). In a review for the *Atlanta Journal-Constitution* of novelist Charles Baxter's *Saul and Patsy*, Gibbons poked fun at authors' worries that "brilliant, swell writers" assess their fiction at parties. She assuaged "prepublication angst" by revealing Baxter's affirmation of her world view and of his intent "to either marry me or adopt me" (Gibbons, 2003). Like herself, Baxter "loves humankind, his characters, and his readers enough to redeem us through the miracle of language and simple will" (*ibid.*)

Late February, 2004 Curious about the later life of fictional heroine Ellen Foster, Gibbons worked at a sequel tentatively titled "Ellen in Love." The author explained, "I wanted to see whether she was happy, how time had treated her" (Gearino, 2004). In this same period, she continued contributing to the *Atlanta-Journal Constitution* by reviewing Thomas Mallon's *Bandbox* and Susan Vreeland's *The Forest Lover*.

April 12, 2004 Gibbons created history-based fiction in *Divining Women*, which she typified as a "sort of *One Hundred Years of Solitude* with Faulknerian characters" (O'Briant, 2004). The story, which honors Alice Batts, Southern author Eudora Welty, and editor Faith Sale, echoes the barbarity of mental wards revealed in Charlotte Perkins Gilman's classic feminist story "The Yellow Wallpaper" (1892). Gibbons captures women's phoenix-like resurgence during the suffragist movement, World War I, and the 1918 influenza epidemic, when the vengeful discrediting of the protagonist's being outranks global oppression in terms of cruelty. In reference to her sympathy for the main characters, Mary Oliver and Maureen Carlton Ross, the author admitted to a passionate interest in womanhood, a good memory for "acts of goodwill," and the layering of the female life into friend, mate, mother, and self (Gibbons, *Divining*, ix). According to reviewers, the novel shares with *Fried Green Tomatoes* and with Allan Gurganus's *The Oldest Living Confederate Widow Tells All* a regard for female friendship.

For background, Gibbons read Edith Wharton's canon, including short stories, *The House of Mirth* (1905) and other novels, travelogues, and early writings on decorating. Gibbons contributed to her predecessor's costume drama a compactness and phrasing that reviewer Nancy Pate characterized as "tensile strength" (Pate, 2004). For themes, Gibbons focused on women's unchanging struggles and spiritual needs that underlie the surface details of a marriage. On the threshold of change initiated by World War I, the era saw the destabilization of from-birth class distinctions. Rounding all into a stirring read are the rhythms of the King James bible and the poems of Emily Dickinson, an insistent iambic tetrameter that paces Gibbons's writing. On a personal note, the author dedicated *Divining Women* to her daughters, Mary, Leslie, and Louise, with an epigraph encouraging them to prevail rather than merely endure, an allusion to William Faulkner's Nobel Prize speech in 1950.

On women's need of men to flesh out their lives, Gibbons remarked in an interview with Art Taylor on her hero-worship of Dr. Phil, a pop-psychology guru who claims that individuals set themselves up for manipulation and mistreatment. The author confided that she empowered herself by writing *Divining Women* and gained from the daily scheduling of writing and revising a sense of personal control. She became so addicted to pounding out fiction on her computer that she teased, "I'm turning into Joyce Carol Oates" (Hodges, 2004).

May 25, 2004 Gibbons received honors from her homeland when 800 attendees applauded her work at "A Night of Notables," which recognized talent from Edgecombe and Nash Counties. The celebration, held at the Dunn Center for the Performing Arts at North Carolina Wesleyan College, gave her an opportunity to reminisce about her childhood. Encouraging her was the thought that "If I did my best ... people around me would support me" (Murphy, 2004).

August, 2004 Gibbons ended her relationship with her first agent and began working with Joy Harris. The author signed a seven-figure contract with Knopf for an eighth novel. The return to Ellen Foster's persona put the author on familiar and reassuring ground. After nine rewrites of her "boomerang book," Gibbons abandoned the original publisher (Hodges, 2004). Retreating to a hotel room, she worked one-on-one with editor Ann Patty at Harcourt Brace. The experience restored the author to joy and personal wholeness. She confided to Jeri Krentz, an interviewer for the *Charlotte* (N.C.) *Observer*, "If I only live twice and one of those times is through Ellen, I may have her avoid all the mistakes I've made" a reference to opportunities to alter her own autobiography through a fictional alter ego (Krentz, 2006). Near deadline for the finished manuscript, Gibbons holed up at the Harcourt office and passed pages directly from printer to copy editor.

October 25, 2004 The *Oxford American* published "Don't Try This at Home," an essay in which Gibbons repudiates notions that writing is not only formulaic, but relatively easy. The text insists that artistic composition takes place alongside housework and everyday struggles. Unlike common myths that writers are more intensely cerebral than non-writers, Gibbons's image of the novelist buying toilet paper at Wal-Mart and losing sleep over re-edits deflates the puffed-up scenario of a tidy writing process. She enumerates the demands that drain the writer — the delving into one's self, withdrawal from distraction, fear of cliché, and haphazard arrival of royalty checks. She also names men as a misdirection of female energies.

After two divorces, Gibbons savored living alone with only one daughter, Louise, still in the nest. The author filled her bedroom with 4,000 books. For relaxation, she crafted jewelry or made collages from flea-market photos. Along First Avenue in Manhattan, she perused the streets and city architecture of Gramercy Park, sipped icy Diet Coke quick-chilled in the freezer, and contemplated the lives of two mice, whom she called Ben and Willard. For movies, she opted for the dialogue of *Pulp Fiction* (1994), the plotting of *The Usual Suspects* (1995), the milieu of *Boogie Nights* (1997) and *Full Metal Jacket* (1987), and the acting of Christopher Walker in *Joe Dirt* (2001), a travesty on redneck culture. For music, she chose Van Morrison, Green Day, and a triad of rappers— Run-DMC, Jay-Z, and Eminem —for their lingual manipulation.

2005 Gibbons earned membership in the Young Women's Christian Association

Academy of Women. She also received the Oklahoma Homecoming Award, an honor that the Oklahoma Center for Poets and Writers presents to a Southern author during the annual Celebration of Books. Contributing to her canon was the six-hour unabridged audio cassette version of *Divining Women*, which the author narrated for Recorded Books. A review in *AudioFile* lauded Gibbons's grace and restraint in carrying the text from its quiet stirrings to a volcanic resolution.

November, 2005 In an interview at the office of her publisher, Gibbons remarked on the fun of repackaging her autobiography as the life of Ellen Foster: "Writing is in many ways an existential form of revenge and correction, a way of reconciling wounds" (Miller, 2005). Through fiction, the author could pursue more creative work by quelling regret and cleansing the hurt of her mother's suicide.

December 25, 2005 In a gesture to desperate females like Shine Batts, Gibbons, in conjunction with a New York City department store, spent the day offering food and clothes to homeless people.

January, 2006 Still writing at her purple divan in the "sonnetarium," a second-floor room in a 3,300-square-foot residence on Lead Mine Road north of Raleigh's beltline, Gibbons began planning a break with the South and a move north after her third daughter graduated from Broughton High School. The author grew weary of the narrow, stratified Southern life in Raleigh, particularly the stultifying Carolina Country Club. After a summer in New Orleans, she planned to keep a townhouse in Raleigh, but shifted her life northward to a small Manhattan apartment overlooking the East River. The venture produced optimism: "I feel like my old self again, with rows and rows of new doors to open, books to write, stories to tell" (Krentz, 2006).

In her New York residence, Gibbons began composing *The Life All Around Me by Ellen Foster*, a sequel to *Ellen Foster*. She developed the sequel amid 20 exuberant 14-year-olds during her daughter's birthday party. Just as the new work was reaching bookstore shelves, *Ellen Foster* won recognition in London as one of the 20th century's Twenty Greatest Novels. Gibbons dedicated the sequel to screenwriter-essayist Connie May Fowler, sister-in-law Barbara Batts, and daughters Leslie, Louise, and Mary. Set in September 1974, the story carries the main character at age 15 beyond girlhood to the end of public school and to courtship by Stuart, her best friend. The author had to tune in to Ellen at a different plateau in her development and reclaim the insistent, saucy voice of an adolescent survivor. Gibbons also read the five-hour audio version for Books on Tape.

According to Gibbons, Ellen's crackerjack retorts and winsome insights allow the author to return to her own girlhood and give backbone and verve to Ellen's developing persona. Changes in the initial story involve definite dates and the name "Shine" for Ellen's 40-year-old mother, a loving gesture toward the author's mother. Mixed reviews suggest that readers are less than enchanted with Ellen's word wizardry and intellectual swagger and with the rehashing of events and characters from the first installment. By way of explanation, the author reported a sense of maturity and security that enabled her to recede into her daily work while supporting three children in a single-parent home. In an analysis based on the author's personal life, critic Rheta Grimsley Johnson, reviewing for the *Atlanta Journal-Constitution*, blamed the cheery ending on Gibbons's personal happiness. Johnson reminded readers, "Nobody content ever created Holden, Huck, or Hamlet" (Johnson, 2006).

In a recap of past interviews, journalist Craig Jarvis, a feature writer for the Raleigh *News & Observer*, traced a shift in Gibbons's perception of the Ellen character. He noted that, in 1986, the author denied that Ellen was autobiographical because she battled a dual terror—fear of being judged by her family's circumstances if she confessed and the "fear of being found out, of being caught" if she lied (Mosher, 1991). While completing a 30-city book tour, the author abandoned *Lunatic's Ball*, a feminist novel set in a Baltimore madhouse in 1900, and began composing the third installment in the Ellen saga. Gibbons envisioned an Ellen cycle extending to some six books carrying the protagonist to an Ivy League college and into old age. Concerning the difficult job of shaping future episodes, the author admitted to interviewer Virginia Daniel, a writer for the Raleigh, Durham, Chapel Hill, North Carolina, *Independent Weekly* that menopause was whittling away at memory, forcing Gibbons to scribble notes in notebooks and on envelopes of napkins: "If I can see or imagine an image that wouldn't occur until page 200, I'll just put it where I can see it. I tape up little scraps of ideas, and as I use something, I'll just mark it out" (Daniel, 2006).

March, 2006 In an interview with Associated Press journalist Martha Waggoner, Gibbons confided that she wanted to be William Faulkner. At a high point in her career, she told interviewer Jeri Krentz of the *Charlotte* (N.C.) *Observer*: "What I try to do is focus on how much I can get accomplished.... There's no one stopping me from doing what I want to do" (Krentz, 2006). Her ambition took her over a 60-day tour, which concluded in Toronto on March 15.

October, 2006 Random House issued *The Other Side of Air*, a novel that Gibbons completed after the death of author Jeanne Braselton left three chapters unfinished. The text opens on a dedication to Gibbons, whom Braselton loved in a complex sister/mother/friend/mentor relationship. Gibbons's rewrite took three months. Of the restructuring, Gibbons commented "I pulled the linoleum up. The subfloor was OK. Then I vacuumed and put some more linoleum down" (O'Briant, 2004).

Gibbons appended an afterword to equip Jeanne's departing spirit with "a sort of last-minute gift of memory for a long, long journey" (Gibbons, "Afterword," 2006, 173). In Jeanne, Gibbons observed "hope that women who choose a literary life could be able to manage, to produce a strong and vibrant legacy of fiction" (*ibid.*, 177). The ghostwriter seemed relieved of sorrow by putting into print the words that Braselton left unsaid concerning the death in 2002 of her husband, poet Albert Braselton, from heart disease. Gibbons confided to interviewer Andrea Hoag, "If I never do another literary thing in my life, ... to have let my friend live on through her beloved imaginative world and in her readers' imagination will, simply put, be good enough" (Hoag, 2006).

• *Further Reading*

Alexander, Ann. "Books to Include in Your Beach Bag," *Greensboro* (N.C.) *News & Record* (17 May 1992).

"Author Lavishes Her Support on the Read to Me Program," *Winston-Salem Journal* (13 January 1998).

"Author Speaks on Her Mental Health Struggle," *Chapel Hill* (N.C.) *Herald* (31 May 1997).

Beardslee, William R. *When a Parent Is Depressed: How to Protect Your Child from the Effects of Depression in the Family*. Boston: Little, Brown, 2002.

Blades, John. "A History and a Novel Win Heartland Prizes," *Chicago Tribune* (23 August 1991).

Branan, Tonita. "Woman and 'The Gift of Gab': Revisionary Strategies in *A Cure for Dreams*," *Southern Literary Journal* 26 (spring 1994): 91–101.

Brennan, Patricia. "Mixing Pathos and Spunk Jena Malone Plays a Child Looking for Love," *Washington Post* (14 December 1997).

Brodeur, Nicole. "So They'll Know They're Not Alone," Raleigh, N.C., *News & Observer* (27 November 1996).

Carey, Jacqueline. "Mommy Direst," *New York Times Book Review* (24 September 1995): 30.

Clodfelter, Tim. "Like a Charm — Screenwriter Found Inspiration in Her Own Family for Adaptation of Novel," *Winston-Salem* (N.C.) *Journal* (17 August 2002).

Creager, Angela N. H., Elizabeth Lunbeck, and Londa Schiebinger, eds. *Feminism in Twentieth Century Science, Technology and Medicine*. Chicago: University of Chicago Press, 2001.

Cumming, W. P. "The Earliest Permanent Settlement in Carolina," *American Historical Review* 45, no. 1 (October 1939).

Daniel, Virginia. "The Life All Around Her," Raleigh, Durham, Chapel Hill, N.C., *Independent Weekly* (26 January 2006).

Eckard, Paula Gallant. "Ellen Foster: Survival in the New South," *Five Owls* (25 April 2005).

Edgers, Geoff. "Oprah Books Raleigh Author," Raleigh, N.C., *News & Observer* (28 October 1997).

"*Ellen Foster* and *A Virtuous Woman*," *Wilson Quarterly* 14, no. 1 (winter 1990): 95.

Folks, Jeffrey J., and James A. Perkins, eds. *Southern Writers at Century's End*. Lexington: University Press of Kentucky, 1997.

_____, and Nancy Summers Folks. *The World Is Our Home*. Lexington: University Press of Kentucky, 2000.

Gearino, G. D. "Ellen Foster to Return," Raleigh, N.C., *News & Observer* (26 February 2004).

Gibbons, Kaye. "Afterword," *The Other Side of Air*. New York: Random House, 2006.

_____. *Charms for the Easy Life*. New York: Putnam, 1993.

_____. *Divining Women*. New York: G. P. Putnam's Sons, 2004.

_____. "The First Grade, Jesus, and the Hollyberry Family," *Southern Selves: From Mark Twain and Eudora Welty to Maya Angelou and Kaye Gibbons: A Collection of Autobiographical Writing*. New York: Vintage, 1998.

_____. "First Loves," *Paris Review* 153 (winter 1999): 145–146.

_____. "For Millay, Word Was All," *Atlanta Journal-Constitution* (23 September 2001).

_____. "In 1912, a Lady Painter Meets Her True Nature," *Atlanta Journal-Constitution* (14 March 2004).

_____. "Introduction," *I Cannot Tell a Lie, Exactly and Other Stories*, by Mary Ladd Gavell. New York: Random House, 2001.

_____. "My Mother, Literature, and a Life Split Neatly into Two Halves." *The Writer on Her Work: New Essays in New Territory*. Vol. 2. Ed. Janet Sternburg. New York: Norton, 1991, pp. 52–60.

_____. *On the Occasion of My Last Afternoon*. New York: G. P. Putnam's Sons, 1998.

_____. "Student's Demise Rocks Young Couple's Quiet Michigan Existence," *Atlanta Journal-Constitution* (5 October 2003).

Gossett, Polly Paddock. "After 7 Years, Instant Success," *Charlotte* (N.C.) *Observer* (23 July 1997).

_____. "Author Says New Attention Is Unnerving, But Welcome," *Charlotte* (N.C.) *Observer* (9 November 1997).

_____. "Book Talk," *Charlotte* (N.C.) *Observer* (23 August 1998).

Gretlund, Jan Nordby. "In My Own Style: An Interview with Kaye Gibbons," *South Atlantic Review* 65, no. 4 (fall 2000): 132–154.

Hoag, Andrea. "Death Carves Out a Lasting Impression," *Atlanta Journal-Constitution* (20 August 2006).

Hodges, Betty. "Southern Writer Mines Linguistic Heritage," Durham, N.C., *Herald-Sun* (29 November 1998).

Hodges, Sam. "Writer Says Her New Books Show Difficult Spell Is Over," *Charlotte* (N.C.) *Observer* (27 April 2004).

Holt, Patricia. "A Bounty of Books for Listening," *San Francisco Chronicle* (12 June 1994).

Jarvis, Craig. "The Life All Around Her: Kaye Gibbons Returns to the Character That Made Her in Order to Remake Herself," Raleigh, N.C., *News & Observer* (25 December 2005).

Jessup, Lynn. "Disease Inspires Author's Latest Novel," *Greensboro* (N.C.) *News & Record* (12 November 1995).

_____. "Kaye Gibbons: Another Happy Ending," *Greensboro* (N.C.) *News & Record* (12 November 1995).

Johnson, Rheta Grimsley. "A Spunky Child Grows," *Atlanta Journal-Constitution* (25 December 2005).

Kaveney, Roz. "Making Themselves Over," *Times Literary Supplement* (15 September 1989): 998.

Kenney, Michael. "An Author Confronts Her Inner Demons," *Boston Globe* (20 September 1995).

Krentz, Jeri. "Hard Journey Back to 'Ellen,'" *Charlotte* (N.C.) *Observer* (29 January 2006).

Krieger, Elliot. "Author's Characters Dominate," *Richmond Times-Dispatch* (28 May 1989).

Lesher, Linda Parent. *The Best Novels of the Nineties: A Reader's Guide*. Jefferson, N.C.: McFarland, 2000.

Lindenfeld, Sarah. "Novelist Mustering Opposition to Hayes Barton Pond," Raleigh, N.C., *News & Observer* (25 September 2000).

Lothar, Corinna. "From the Real to the Surreal," *Washington Times* (16 August 1998).

Madrigal, Alix. "Gibbons Writes to Surprise Herself," *San Francisco Chronicle* (15 October 1989).

_____. "A Tough Southern Belle," *San Francisco Chronicle* (2 May 1993).

Malinowski, Jamie. "Dedicated Lines," *New Yorker* (25 December 1995): 46.

"Mammy Turns Tara into a Thriving B&B," *Atlanta Journal-Constitution* (14 April 1999).

McAlpin, Heller. "The Return of Cinderella," *Newsday* (1 January 2006).

McCabe, Bruce. "A 10-Year-Old Finds Happiness," *Boston Globe* (14 December 1997).

Miller, Mary E. "A Charmed But Uneasy Life," Raleigh, N.C. *News & Observer* (29 October 1995).

Miller, Pamela. "Kaye Gibbons' Novel Draws from Her Life," Minneapolis-St. Paul (Minn.) *Star Tribune* (15 January 2006).

Morris, Willie. "Olympic Atlanta," *Atlanta Journal-Constitution* (24 March 1996).

Mosher, Katie. "Family, Career Blossom for 'Ellen Foster' Creator," Raleigh, N.C. *News & Observer* (21 April 1991).

Murphy, Tom. "Chamber Celebrates Area Success Stories," Rocky Mount (N.C.) *Evening Telegram* (26 May 2004).

Nelson, Nels. "Simply Irresistible: Arden Theater Company's 'Ellen Foster,'" *Philadelphia Daily News* (27 January 1994): 37, 40.

O'Briant, Don. "Between the Pages," *Atlanta Journal-Constitution* (20 May 1999).
_____. "Book Signing," *Atlanta Journal-Constitution* (10 September 1995).
_____. "Kaye Gibbons Does the Rewrite Thing," *Greensboro* (N.C.) *News & Record* (14 June 1998).
_____. "Kaye Gibbons Puts Pen Down Long Enough to Talk about Life," *Houston Chronicle* (18 April 2004).
_____. "Writing a Most 'Virtuous' Art for Gibbons," *Atlanta Journal-Constitution* (18 June 1989).
Olney, Judith. "Writers' Gala Pays Homage to 'First Loves,'" *Washington Times* (5 October 1994).
Paddock, Polly. "Kaye Gibbons Recalls 'Sights Unseen' As a Tough Project," *Charlotte* (N.C.) *Observer* (27 August 1995).
Parker, Roy, Jr. "Elegant Family Story," *Fayetteville* (N.C.) *Observer* (14 April 1991).
Pate, Nancy. "Kaye Gibbons Offers Tale of Two Women," *Orlando Sentinel* (7 April 2004).
Perry, Carolyn, and Mary Louise Weaks, eds. *The History of Southern Women's Literature.* Baton Rouge: Louisiana State University Press, 2002.
Reedy, Martha L. "Author, Author!," Rocky Mount, N.C., *Evening Telegram* (7 June 1998).
Ridley, Clifford A. "A Girl in Dire Dickensian Straits Who Lives to Learn the Outcome," *Philadelphia Enquirer* (3 February 1994).
Romine, Dannye. "Gibbons Wins Kentucky Derby," *Charlotte* (N.C.) *Observer* (10 April 1988).
_____. "Literature Liberates: Raleigh's Kaye Gibbons Finds Freedom, Affirmation in 1st Novel," *Charlotte* (N.C.) *Observer* (26 April 1987).
_____. "Victorian Times Inspire Magazine," *Charlotte* (N.C.) *Observer* (28 June 1987).
_____. "With Three Novels Behind Her and a New One Ahead, N.C. Authors Kaye Gibbons Is Taking Control of Her Life," *Charlotte* (N.C.) *Observer* (14 April 1991).
Rosenblum, Trudi Miller. "Audio Books," *Billboard* 108, no. 33 (17 August 1996): 78.
Ryan, Laura T. "Gibbons Says Manic Depression Fuels Her Art," Syracuse (N.Y.) *Herald American* (12 February 1999).
Sayers, Valerie, "Growing Into the Role," *Washington Post* (6 January 2006).
Skube, Michael. "Art of Translation Calls for Ear Attuned to Human Emotion," *Atlanta Journal-Constitution* (21 February 1999).
Smith, Lee. *Conversations with Lee Smith.* Jackson: University Press of Mississippi, 2001.
Spielman, David G., and William W. Starr. *Southern Writers.* Columbia: University of South Carolina Press, 1997.
Spurr, Kim Weaver. "Storied Life: For Gibbons, Words Reflect Part of Herself," Durham, N.C. *Herald-Sun* (27 August 1995).
Steelman, Ben. "Gibbons Takes Much-Needed Rest," Wilmington, N.C., *Morning Star* (26 July 1998).
Stephens, Spaine. "Nash County Still Inspires Gibbons," Rocky Mount (N.C.) *Evening Telegram* (24 March 2004).
Tate, Linda. *A Southern Weave of Women: Fiction of the Contemporary South.* Athens: University of Georgia Press, 1994.
Waggoner, Martha. "Book Addresses Manic-Depression," Durham, N.C., *Herald-Sun* (17 September 1995).
_____. "Kaye Gibbons Happy with Life Around Her," *Wichita Eagle* (10 March 2006).
_____. "One for All, All for One," Durham, N.C., *Herald-Sun* (21 September 1999).
_____. "The Write Stuff in North Carolina," *Greensboro* (N.C.) *News & Record* (3 October 1999).
Wallace, Marybeth Sutton. "Reaping Weeds: Gibbons Brings Words to Fruition," Rocky Mount, N.C. *Evening Telegram* (25 November 1990): 8.
Weaver, Teresa K. "Southern Fiction's Father figure," *Atlanta Journal-Constitution* (29 December 2002).

West, Cassandra. "Listener's Guide," *Chicago Tribune* (5 July 1998).
Willett, Melissa. "Gibbons Brings Her Voice to Fayetteville," *Fayetteville* (N.C.) *Observer* (5 October 2004).
Wolcott, James. "Crazy for You," *New Yorker* (21 August 1996): 115–116.
Wood, Ralph C. "Gumption and Grace in the Novels of Kaye Gibbons," *Christian Century* 109, no. 27 (September 23–30, 1992): 842–846.
Woods, Byron. "Author Watches Her Life on Stage," Raleigh, N.C., *News & Observer* (1 March 1996).
Zane, J. Peder. "Welty's Passing: A Death in the Family," Raleigh, N.C., *News & Observer* (29 July 2001).

Gibbons's Genealogy

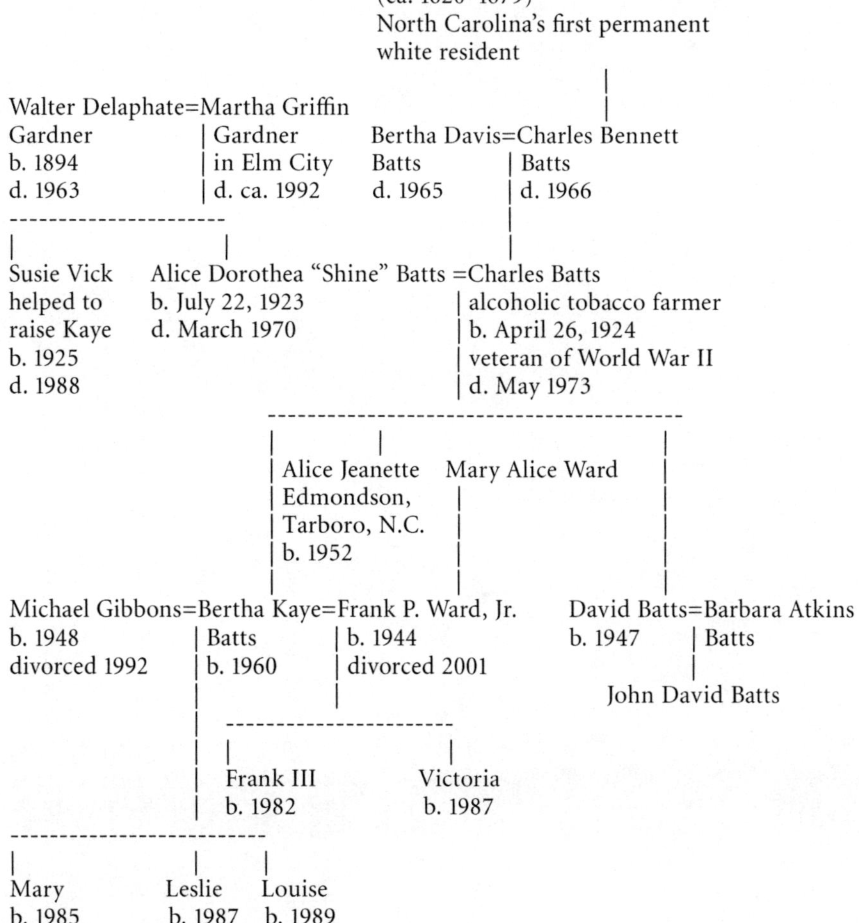

Kaye Gibbons: A Literary Companion

achievement

Gibbons expresses feminism by setting female characters in untenable situations and recording their unique methods of extricating themselves. Beginning with Lucille Womble's survival of farm poverty in a short-short story, "The Headache," published in the June 1987 issue of the *St. Andrews Review*, Gibbons explores community synergy in relieving the protagonist of two weeks of self-inflicted insomnia, weeping, flashbacks, and anxiety attacks brought on by an ethical lapse — the concealment of a purse abandoned in a restaurant ladies' room. Initiating Lucille's recovery from near suicide is her trust in a strong female, Dr. Janet Cowley, who stands by the confidentiality promise in the Hippocratic Oath. Advancing from confession, in obedience to Dr. Cowley's advice, Lucille returns to her one-room dwelling to nestle in marital reassurance from husband Henry and to allow herself to be forgiven. The story implies that Lucille achieves relief from torment by renewing her trust in love and in self.

The author progresses to greater feats in her first novel, *Ellen Foster* (1987), a fictional memoir. Gibbons places the vulnerable, motherless ten-year-old title figure in the clutches of her drunken, morally corrupt father Bill. To escape neglect and manhandling and to stave off rape, Ellen eludes him on New Year's Eve, 1969, by fleeing to the safehouse of Starletta's parents. The text stresses the advance in humanism in Ellen's choice of a black family at a period of Southern history when lower-class whites maintained moral superiority over blacks. During her subsequent residence in a series of four households, she becomes adept at sizing up welcome or the lack of it. Her instinctive discomfort around her cousin Dora, aunts Betsy and Nadine Nelson, and their vengeful mother forces Ellen to a cut ties with her birth family and select a stranger to foster her. A signal leap of faith in humankind, the choice takes Ellen out of danger on Christmas Day, 1970, to a loving foster parent. Out of gratitude for rescue, Ellen celebrates a secure home by sharing it with Starletta. The act of sharing enhances Ellen's triumph over seedy relatives with a self-ennobling defeat of ingrained racism. To the school psychologist who questions Ellen's new surname, she conceals a necessary next step in reclamation. As analyst Linda Adams Barnes explains, the child must "forge her identity on her own, rather than to be influenced by an external force" (Barnes, 1993, 30). Gibbons wrings satire out of Ellen's successful self-analysis and her private ridicule of a bumbling therapist.

Following public and critical acclaim for Ellen's self-extrication from homelessness and orphanhood, Gibbons moved on to adult achievers— Ruby Pitts Woodrow Stokes, the twice-married agrarian survivor in *A Virtuous Woman* (1989), and Lottie O'Cadhain Davies, a devalued wife in *A Cure for Dreams* (1991). Both works portray the female subversion of male-dominated society. Ruby achieves contentment through compromise that allows her to marry "Blinking" Jack Ernest Stokes, an unlikely candidate for a second husband. Although lower in social class and less astute than his wife, Jack offers her a haven of love and respect, two qualities missing from her first marriage to John Woodrow, a wastrel and womanizer. Capping the Stokes' quarter century of marital bliss is the fostering of June Stanley, a neighbor child in need of mothering. Lottie Davies, a similarly disillusioned wife, achieves fulfillment and joy through a different form of compromise — the replacement of marital love with delight in her daughter, Betty Davies Randolph. For both protagonists, Gibbons acknowledges achievement with the everyday pleasures in mothering and the womanly arts—cooking for Ruby and sewing for Lottie.

The trio of first novels leads up to Gibbons's towering grandmother, Charlie Kate Birch, a matriarch and community pillar in *Charms for the Easy Life* (1993). The story of a self-educated herbalist-midwife cuts through professional and social constraints of the 1930s and 1940s to applaud "Dr. Birch," who provides healing, birthing, dentistry, and wellness advice to the poor of coastal Pasquotank County on the Albemarle Sound and of Raleigh in central North Carolina. Like Ruby Stokes and Lottie Davies, Charlie Birch reaps rewards for kindness and volunteerism through the role of mentor. From her example, her granddaughter Margaret develops respect for self-directed reading and for generosity to the needy, including casualties of World War II, for whom she writes letters at the Durham veterans' hospital. Gibbons orchestrates Charlie Birch's death at a height of contentment on Christmas night, 1942, after seeing Margaret welcomed into a family of promising in-laws. The concluding funereal gestures extol Charlie Birch for preparing Margaret for the vicissitudes of life and for accepting death as an inevitable part of the life cycle.

Moving into inner resources, Gibbons creates Maggie Barnes, the recovering manic depressive in the author's fifth novel, *Sights Unseen* (1995). Unlike the housewifely grace of Ruby, the social uplift of female community by Lottie, and the advice and health care administered by Charlie Kate, her daughter Sophia Snow Baines, and granddaughter Margaret, Maggie achieves a massive overhaul of self in 1967. The healing delivers her fractured family from ongoing chaos by restoring her to normality as wife and mother. Following psychotherapy and eight weekly electroconvulsive shock treatments at Duke Hospital, bit by bit, Maggie resumes the demands of female head of household, in her daughter Hattie's words, by "sheer dint of will" (Gibbons, 1995, 208). Crucial to her success is her acceptance of emotional fragility and the need for psychotropic drugs— lithium and Miltown — to help her maintain wellness. For

Maggie and the previous protagonists, Gibbons supplies female survivors with idiosyncracies that guarantee success, from Lucille's acceptance of medical advice and Ellen's refusal to be cowed by dismissive kin to Ruby's arming herself with a pistol against an ego-whittling husband. Working up to Lottie Davies's guidance of Betty toward a worthy husband and Charlie Kate's direction of Margaret into the marriage market, Gibbons pictures the role of family in individual achievement. For Maggie, Hattie Barnes's unfailing trust that her mother will reclaim her sanity and return home cured sets the tone of a renewal of mother-daughter unity.

The author's most praiseworthy achiever, Emma Garnet Tate Lowell, displays the empowerment of the Zeitgeist — the historical concept that the times shape the individual. At a turning point in Southern history in the author's first historical novel, *On the Occasion of My Last Afternoon* (1998), Emma enjoys a comfortable home on Blount Street near the governor's mansion in Raleigh, North Carolina. She keeps house and educates three daughters— Leslie, Louise, and Mary — when the outbreak of the Civil War demands a complete shift of focus. In the words of reviewer Jessica Treadway, Emma partners with her husband, Dr. Quincy Lowell, to bolster "the inadequate medical care of the time" (Treadway, 1998). From him, she acquires a pseudo-military combat decoration — a silver brooch dated 1861, the year of her on-the-job training in tracheotomies, debriding shrapnel wounds, and applying leeches to suppurating tissue, all elements of critical-care nursing. From dealing with unimaginable wartime demands on her home, family, and worldly goods, Emma achieves a more satisfying break with the past in June 1862 by confronting her calculating father, Samuel P. Goodman Tate, for his cruelties and for wasting his wealth on foolish Confederate pipedreams. The stirring novel expresses feminist truths through Emma's willingness to adapt to chaos and to accept loss as a wartime given at all social levels. At life's end in 1900, 70-year-old Emma, content with self, family, and service, crowns her own achievements by embracing mortality in a reunion in the afterlife with her beloved Quincy.

A variant on Emma's love invigorates reclamation in *Divining Women* (2004), Gibbons's seventh novel. During the pregnancy of Maureen Carlton Ross, on September 20, 1918, an in-law dispatches a stranger, 22-year-old Mary Oliver, to guide Maureen through the last 50 days of waiting. Achievement in Maureen's case consists of bearing up to her husband Troop's aggressive rejection and of surviving the home birthing and loss of Ella Eloise Ross, a stillborn infant who arrives on November 8, 1918, only three days before an armistice ends World War I. As though making her own peace with unpromising choices, Maureen follows Mary's lead in preparing the tiny body for burial and in bucking Troop, who shrieks his hatred and demand for control from the front sidewalk. With a victor's calm, Maureen faces him and declares, "I feel a little of the power of God in me" (Gibbons, 2004, 200). Her achievement in motherhood and selfhood prefaces over 20 years of autonomy, a tribute to her determination to be free.

On return to Ellen Foster in 1974 at age 15 in *The Life All Around Me by Ellen Foster* (2004), Gibbons balances intellectual achievement with ordinary coming-of-age landmarks. While awaiting a reply from Dr. Derek Curtis Bok concerning early admission to Harvard University, the title character experiences a series of epiphanies.

At the top of the list, her selection of Laura as a foster parent in 1970 relieves Ellen of homelessness at the same time that it provides a mature sounding board for misgivings and terrifying flashbacks. A succession of accomplishments boosts Ellen to reigning community poet and to first place in the heart of Stuart, a love-sick admirer who fantasizes elopement with Ellen to Pedro's South of the Border, a roadside stop and fireworks emporium in South Carolina. Both humorous and poignant, Ellen's achievement of womanhood ignites its own pyrotechnics from her reunion with a box of personal belongings left by her mother, handholds on reality that still Ellen's quaking hands and satisfy soulful yearnings. The author advances the possession of the dead mother to an awareness that Ellen "could be more than what my mother did, more than the moment she died" (Gibbons, 2006, 218). The mental image of success thrusts Ellen into a hopeful state of mind devoid of the gaps and dismaying echoes of the past.

See also **autonomy, reclamation**

• *Further reading*

Barnes, Linda Adams. "Telling Yourself into Existence: The Fiction of Kaye Gibbons," *Tennessee Philological Bulletin* 30 (1993): 28–35.

Gibbons, Kaye. *Divining Women*. New York: G.P. Putnam's Sons, 2004.

_____. *The Life All Around Me by Ellen Foster*. New York: Harcourt, 2006.

_____. *Sights Unseen*. New York: G.P. Putnam's Sons, 1995.

Treadway, Jessica. "Old Times There Are Not Forgotten," *Boston Globe* (31 May 1998).

adaptation

Kaye Gibbons investigates the personal revamping that enables individuals to survive disappointment and ill fortune. A brief short story, "The Headache," issued in June 1987 in the *St. Andrews Review*, surveys release from guilt in Lucille Womble, a farm wife who nags herself for two weeks into physical illness that approaches suicide. Central to her healing from insomnia, crying jags, head pain, and anxiety attacks is her retreat into marital love. Unquestioning affection and admiration from her husband Henry frees her of self-blame for trashy behavior in concealing a pocketbook abandoned in a restaurant ladies' room. Pared-down expectations provide her with a respite from psychosomatic ills. From standard bearer for family ethics, she reverts to the manageable self-image of female head of household and mother.

At the introduction of Gibbons's long fiction, the title character of *Ellen Foster* (1987) lives the nightmare of her unnamed mother's marriage to Bill, a brutal alcoholic. The multi-stage adaptation begins with Ellen's early girlhood and the gradual demise of her mother from rheumatic fever and the after-effects of open-heart surgery. In the estimation of Valerie Sayers, a reviewer for the *Washington Post*, Ellen "arises from the [mother's] deathbed, fierce and determined to do battle with the world" (Sayers, 2006). Motherless and alone with a monster, the child suppresses panic and manages to feed herself and pay utility bills until her father's drunken lust on New Year's Eve, 1969, sends her fleeing to a nearby black household. Working her way through relatives and a temporary residence with Julia, an art teacher, Ellen triumphs in a Christmas Day, 1970, conquest of the perfect foster home and accompanying new mama, later identified as Laura. Adaptation to a more normal life gives Ellen the leisure and safety in which to reshape her aims and ideals, which a warped upbringing force too soon into adult mode.

Less promising than Ellen's self-transformation is the misery of "Blinking" Jack Ernest Stokes, the anti-hero of *A Virtuous Woman* (1989) who rescues Ruby Pitts Woodrow from early widowhood and despair. The improbable pairing of Jack, a 40-year-old field laborer, with Ruby, the 20-year-old daughter of a prosperous farm owner, nonetheless generates a happy quarter-century of wedlock. Inured to earthly suffering, she exhibits a strong vision of the soul's survival in the afterworld: "My spirit will live and see all and know all it couldn't before" (Gibbons, 1989, 117). At the loss of his beloved mate to lung cancer, Jack, at age 65, exhibits innate emotional limitations. Unlike his tough-minded wife, he retreats to bed, bowls of corn flakes and canned soup, bourbon, Roadrunner cartoons, and the fragrance of Ruby's lilac dusting powder on the sheets. His inability to cope with grief is both a diminution of Jack's manhood and an honor to Ruby, who made him whole.

The author's third and fourth books—*A Cure for Dreams* (1991) and *Charms for the Easy Life* (1993)—deal more directly with the theme of adaptation. The first pictures the success of the O'Donough-O'Cadhain-Davies-Randolph matriarchy in reshaping marriage to suit their needs. After Bridget O'Donough O'Cadhain wearies of a pair of drunks—her loutish husband Sheamus and brother-in-law Bart—she emigrates from Galway, Ireland, in 1918 and resettles their sizeable clan on the Cumberland River in Bell County, Kentucky. The success of her daughter, Lottie O'Cadhain Davies, at mothering Betty Davies Randolph and at surviving the Great Depression precedes the adaptation of the two-family household to the suicide of Lottie's Quaker farmer-miller husband Charles, a soul-less miser and workaholic. Bolstered by housekeeper-midwife Polly Deal and by Betty's newborn, Marjorie Polly Randolph, a four-woman alliance foretokens coping and serenity throughout World War II.

Kaye Gibbons reprises the era and the all-woman motif in *Charms for the Easy Life*, which pictures the coming-of-age of Margaret under the tending and mentorship of her mother, Sophia Snow Birch, and of Sophia's mother, the irrepressible healer-midwife Charlie Kate Birch. Like the Davies family, Charlie Kate's household must outwit poverty and dependence during hard times, gas rationing, and world instability. The author indicates Charlie Kate's balance of business shrewdness with great-heartedness in her practice of herbalism, dentistry, and midwifery in the mill hill district of Raleigh, North Carolina. While aiding the poor and ignorant during house calls, she helps the Birch family to adapt to a manless existence. Her example introduces Margaret to female networking and to an unshakeable confidence that carries the girl through her mother's remarriage on Christmas Eve, 1942, and through Charlie Kate's unforeseen death on Christmas night. At the same time that American forces grapple with a two-phase world war, Margaret's poise presages an ability to manage whatever lies ahead.

A more stirring view of adaptation dominates *On the Occasion of My Last Afternoon* (1998), Gibbons's first historical novel. Make-do becomes a coping mechanism by which people survive shortages of food, medicines, and jobs during the Civil War and Reconstruction. In the absence of hospital surgeries and recovery wards, the city offers the Fair Grounds as a makeshift location for an interim facility. As trainloads of wounded from major conflicts wind into Raleigh, the Lowells convert their home into a receiving center for the overflow from the battles of Manassas, Virginia (July 21, 1861; August 28–30, 1862), Antietam, Maryland (September 17, 1862), Gettysburg, Pennsylvania (July 3–4, 1863), and the Wilderness, Virginia (May 5–7, 1864). Cook-housekeeper Clarice Washington prepares meals night and day to feed family and patients while Emma Garnet Tate Lowell strips the linen closet of anything resembling sheets. The unforgiving element of national turmoil is the expenditure of human energy. Dr. Quincy Lowell develops a knack for napping standing up while leaning against a wall; Emma beds down in a hospital closet. Their ability to endure on scraps of rest and comfort keep them alive and functioning as war tests their inner reserves.

Gibbons creates pathos from a simple truth, that some of the characters cannot survive the punishing pace of civil war. By the time of the surrender at Appomattox Court House on April 9, 1865, Maureen Tate has abandoned her Southern belle posturing, but Clarice, the family mainstay, has died in 1863 from pneumonia. To Emma's dismay, Quincy's vitality is unrecoverable. As he slips into death, Emma begins a new phase of adaptation, living among her Lowell in-laws in Boston while she salves her sorrow by conversing with Quincy at his grave. Shored up with a discovery of the solace in cooking, Emma returns to Raleigh to join Maureen in fighting for social justice for widows, orphans, and the poor and uneducated. Gibbons indicates the value to the grieving of sharing with the have-nots. By 1900, Emma can look back on her emergence as a city benefactor and acknowledge the worth of involvement for reviving her beneficent strengths.

Adjustment takes an unusual twist in *Divining Women* (2004), Gibbons's seventh novel. The restlessness of Mary Oliver, a 22-year-old graduate student at Radcliffe College, precipitates an unusual mission — serving her aunt-by-marriage, Maureen Carlton Ross, as companion and birthing coach. Unprepared for a toxic home environment, on September 30, 1918, Mary arrives by train to Elm City, North Carolina, a bucolic name that belies the ominous atmosphere of her uncle Troop's home. Amid pompous decor and busy William Morris wall coverings, she retreats upstairs to Maureen's domain, a boudoir-sitting room gentled by silvers, blues, violets, and greens, open windows, and womanly comforts. While acclimating to the jerky rhythms of Troop's angry arrivals and departures, Mary rebels against the "broad day-light larceny" of Maureen's will and amplifies in Maureen a more vital type of adaptation, the reclamation of self from a finicky, domineering martinet (Gibbons, 2004, 67). The motif reprises one of feminism's optimistic concepts, that women in need bolster each other.

In her usual manner, the author offsets world events with the daily woman-hindering hurdles erected by patriarchal society. Habituation to difficult times—Southern racism, the suffrage movement, World War I, and the 1918 influenza pandemic — seems less challenging than the women's preparation for Maureen's labor and delivery. On November 7, the reunion of the female householder with her maid

Mamie initiates a three-woman home birthing, an inspiring shift in Maureen's status to mother. The stillbirth of Ella Eloise Ross the next day, troubles Maureen less than the bold burial of her only child at sunset on November 9 against Troop's public hectoring. Once free of daily ego strafing, Maureen, with Mary's help, revives self and courage to begin 21 years of loving friendship. Set in the final months of the suffrage movement, the novel emphasizes the self-direction of women who flourish outside the structure and confinement of marriage.

The adaptation of the title character in Gibbons's *The Life All Around Me by Ellen Foster* (2006) reiterates the strengths of a heroine now entering her mid-teens. No longer furtive and heart-needy as she was at age 11, by 1974, Ellen advances to mind nurturing by requesting from Dr. Derek Curtis Bok early admission to Harvard University. In tune with her foster mother Laura, Ellen commits herself to cohabitating with rambunctious teens who use their rooms for carnal trysts with boyfriends. In her reach toward probity and self-esteem, Ellen makes an unwise phone call to social services, a revelation of home instability that threatens her own placement with Laura. More serious to the inner protagonist is a face-off against Aunt Nadine Nelson and Cousin Dora, two long-standing enemies who seem less formidable than they did in their appearance in *Ellen Foster* in 1970. In possession of a box of her mother's personal items, Ellen finds the courage to relive raw memories and to reach for Laura's steadying hand. In the resolution, Ellen discovers increments of adjustment that anchor and sustain her. Harmonized to Laura's style of mothering, Ellen orients her thoughts and dreams from guilt for her 40-year-old mother's suicide to a future that matures and educates her for a normal life.

• *Further reading*

Chandler, Marilyn. "Limited Partnership," *Women's Review of Books* 6, nos. 10–11 (July 1989): 21.

Gibbons, Kaye. *Divining Women*. New York: G.P. Putnam's Sons, 2004.

_____. *A Virtuous Woman*. Chapel Hill, N.C.: Algonquin Press, 1989.

McKee, Kathryn. "Simply Talking: Women and Language in Kaye Gibbons's *A Cure for Dreams*," *Southern Quarterly* 35, no. 4 (Summer 1997): 97–107.

Sayers, Valerie, "Growing Into the Role," *Washington Post* (6 January 2006).

autonomy

Kaye Gibbons expresses feminist views through the independence and self-motivation of female characters. In the short-short story "The Headache," published in the June 1987 issue of the *St. Andrews Review*, farm wife Lucille Womble directs herself toward wellness after she seizes and conceals an abandoned purse in the restroom of a chicken restaurant. Supporting her reach for money to sustain the Wombles through hard times is husband Henry, a war veteran and farmer who values Lucille for her goodness and family loyalty. Unlike later female heads of household in Gibbons's fiction, Lucille can relax against him in sleep and free her mind of thoughts of suicide and financial fears by dreaming of new hats. The story honors a stable marriage as a source of womanly liberation and self-esteem, but falls short of the fierce handhold on self that empowers Gibbons's more forthright heroines.

The author's first novel spotlights the autonomous female as a self-motivated virago. Essential to the self-rescue of the title character in *Ellen Foster* (1987) is her belief that redemption is solely her responsibility. To Tuesday sessions with the school psychologist, she presents a brazen front that refuses to give him a peek into her sad and wounded spirit. She indicates a willingness to reveal her true self once she settles personal business, which involves selecting a family to accept and harbor her unconditionally. After a judge places her in her maternal grandmother's custody, in mid-summer 1970, Ellen plots a way out of hoeing the old woman's fields by peddling costly knickknacks from the house. Until Ellen can amass enough money to escape, she regards herself as a Gothic stereotype—"an old monster zombie" in the power of an evil witch (Gibbons, 1987, 68). The phrase echoes fairy tale elements of the plot drawn from the quandaries of Rapunzel, Gretel, and Sleeping Beauty, three innocents who tumble into the clutches of malefactors.

Beginning with Ellen Foster's resolve to find a home, Gibbons's canon persistently views the risks of female daring. In *A Virtuous Woman* (1989), 18-year-old Ruby Pitts Woodrow Stokes struggles under the consequences of inadvisible elopement intended to rid her of boredom in a rigidly gendered homelife. Her first husband, 26-year-old farm laborer John Woodrow, forces her to accept the working-class modes of migrant workers, who occupy substandard housing short term as they move from job to job. His sour criticism and inconstancy so unsettle Ruby that she arms herself with a pistol to end his skirt chasing. When an unforeseen pool hall knifing to John's lungs snips her marital tether, at age 20, she again marries a poor man, "Blinking" Jack Ernest Stokes, who ends her youthful widowhood. Emotionally bereft, she accepts a life of penury because of his love and adoration. In quirky fashion, she rewards herself for marrying a celibate male and for being "every bit of his experience" (Gibbons, 1989, 69).

Gibbons admits that love, on its own merit, can raise unique obstacles. Constant cherishing demands a price from Ruby, who must contend with her 40-year-old husband's immaturity, secret drinking, and his expectation that she will willingly and expertly fulfill the role of wife and mother, whom he lost at age fourteen. Although housewifeliness rejuvenates Ruby with the rewards of baking pies and bread, making spaghetti sauce, and fostering June Stanley, an unloved neighbor child, the text reveals frustrations and momentary fears when Jack chooses to fire her pistol, shocking her with memories of a murder plot. A more serious price exacted for autonomy, Ruby's smoking habit ends her life at age 45 from lung cancer. Addiction to tobacco, developed as a shield against John's verbal battery, takes on tragicomic dimensions. Ruby stuns Jack by gesturing from her oxygen tent that she wants a cigarette. He misinterprets two fingers to the lips as blowing a kiss before realizing that Ruby will be Ruby all the way to the grave.

Gibbons's third and fourth novels—*A Cure for Dreams* (1991) and *Charms for the Easy Life* (1993)—picture her most autonomous females. The first of the two titles sketches the female community of Milk Farm Road, North Carolina, where housewives weather the Great Depression by gambling at gin rummy and pinochle in the back room of Porter's store. They have what novelist George Eliot described as "the more independent life—some joy in things for their own sake" (Heilbrun, 1982, 76).

Lottie O'Cadhain Davies, the card club's founder, recognizes in rural women the need for enough mad money to relieve them of poverty and the tedium of threadbare clothes. By purchasing organza, venise lace, chiffon, and beaded English netting, she sews for herself and daughter Betty Davies Randolph the fetching outfits that express their uniqueness and flair for fashion. Within a woman-made milieu, Lottie and Betty thrive despite the suicide in 1937 of farmer-miller Charles Davies, Lottie's work-obsessed Welsh Quaker husband. The women's sisterhood with other oppressed females surfaces after the murder of Roy Duplin, a shotgun slaying unsolved by part-time Deputy Sheriff John Carroll, but obviously the work of Roy's widow, Sade Duplin. Lottie and her community of women friends encircle Sade with compassion and affection until Sade can realign her aims following her violent rupture of corrosive marriage vows. Independent once more, in widowhood, Sade creates a support system through visits from her older children. On cash recovered from Roy's stashes, she finances a fireside nest where she can enjoy womanly comforts without a man's objections.

Charms for the Easy Life pictures another type of autonomy in the career-driven life of Charlie Kate Birch, the herbalist-midwife who forms a phalanx of female caregivers with her daughter, Sophia Snow Birch, and Sophia's daughter Margaret. Essential to their freedom from male control is the merger of a three-woman household, the choosing of financial investments, and the sharing of domestic tasks like clock repair rather than turning to a man for help. As Margaret reaches the end of public school in spring 1940, she charts her own path as her grandmother's assistant. During their volunteer rounds at the veterans' hospital in Durham, Margaret selects a recovering casualty, Tom Hawkings, III, as a future husband. Though out of school at the time of Charlie Kate's death, Margaret apparently intends to enroll in college at war's end and to marry Tom. The text convinces the reader that a bright girl reared by two tough women certainly knows her own mind.

Girlish independence surges in importance in the author's fifth novel, *Sights Unseen* (1995), the story of a rural family reborn through the healing of a crazed wife-mother. For the sake of contrast, Gibbons reveals a Jekyll-and-Hyde version of autonomy. Maggie Barnes, wife of a North Carolina farmer and mother of two, experiences mood swings from depressive retreats to bed to rambunctious talking, arguing, flirtation, and misbehavior. At the height of manic states, she requires the surveillance of her husband Frederick and her father-in-law, Grandfather Barnes, as she acts out an independence from normal restraint. Her forays include sizeable purchases of new outfits, shoes, and bedroom furniture. At her return in 1967 from months of psychotherapy and eight electroconvulsive shock treatments at Duke Hospital, she exhibits the Dr. Jekyll version of autonomy — the firm, but well-mannered lady of the house who silences her father-in-law for chiding her children at the table after they reject servings of oyster dressing. Self-assured by therapy and psychotropic drugs, Maggie once more paces her days from sewing sun suits, driving daughter Hattie to school, shopping for children's clothes, and returning home to canning vegetables, pleasant naps, and low-key visits to Hattie's room at bedtime. Maggie's duality persists, but rehabilitation allows her to express the controlled self, the persona that recognizes her emotional weaknesses while asserting her strengths.

A complex wartime awakening of autonomy during social and economic upheaval reconfigures Emma Garnet Tate Lowell, the narrator of Gibbons's first historical novel, *On the Occasion of My Last Afternoon* (1998). Coddled in childhood by cook-housekeeper Clarice Washington, Emma develops backbone by relaying grit to her acquiescent mother, Alice Tate, a plantation mistress schooled in polite submission. When marriage tears 17-year-old Emma away from home and mother in 1847, an abiding guilt reminds the bride that Alice remains at Seven Oaks under the rule of planter Samuel P. Goodman Tate, a pitiless wife abuser. Losses of both parents and of Clarice and Quincy, Emma's paternal husband, shove the protagonist into a survivor's post-war nightmare. Standing at Quincy's Boston grave, Emma acknowledges that, to be whole, she must return south to the corruption and graft of Reconstruction in Raleigh, North Carolina. Intolerable conditions for the white underclass and for freed slaves point her toward a renewing enterprise, a late-in-life mission to the needy and unemployed. Bankrolled by the Lowell fortune, she develops a spontaneity that ignores snooty aristocrats and the Ku Klux Klan while restoring dignity and sustenance to the poor. Gibbons awards her a peaceful end to 70 years and anticipation of meeting Quincy in heaven, a restoration of love and companionship.

A parallel to Lottie and Sade in *A Cure for Dreams* and to Alice Tate in *On the Occasion of My Last Afternoon*, Gibbons's heroines in a seventh novel, *Divining Women* (2004), revisit the issue of female liberation from male grasp. Martha Greene Oliver, newly widowed and grieving for son Daniel, who hangs himself from a Baltimore hotel room chandelier in 1913, chooses to exit the mansion her parents and in-laws share on Dupont Circle in Washington, D.C. The purpose of a two-female household — Martha and her 17-year-old daughter Mary — is the breaking of old bonds to ensure female identity. Without the too-close supervision of an older generation or of a housekeeper or governess, Martha believes herself capable of cultivating Mary's individuality. The motif echoes the contentment of Emma Garnet Tate Lowell, whose mothering of Leslie, Louise, and Mary Lowell expresses autonomy at the same time that it advances matrilineage.

The text leapfrogs from a mother's self-freeing to the maturing of her daughter. By age 22, Mary, a graduate student at Radcliffe College, seems ripe for her own adventures, which Martha promotes by dispatching her south. On September 30, 1918, Mary becomes female companion to Maureen Carlton Ross, Mary's diffident aunt, who faces a last trimester of pregnancy under the mental torment of her tyrannic husband Troop. Without coaxing, Mary instinctively begins rebuilding Maureen's confidence to reflect the emerging New Woman of the suffragist era. Gibbons rewards Mary for benevolence and courage by molding a life-long friendship between the two women. Tempered by a difficult birthing process and by the stillbirth of Maureen's daughter, Ella Eloise Ross, on November 8, 1918, the emotional growth of both Mary and Maureen parallels two historical monuments to freedom — the triumph of the suffrage movement in 1920 and the emergence of the United States from World War I, a test of national autonomy in a complex era of global renegotiation.

Gibbons returns to autonomy in her first sequel, *The Life All Around Me by Ellen Foster* (2006), a reprise of the author's redoubtable young title heroine. Living with foster mother Laura, Ellen continues to test willfulness by perusing her bedroom shelf of books chosen by educators of gifted students at Johns Hopkins University. Certain that life demands more training than what she gets at the local high school, on September 20, 1974, Ellen dares to write a personal letter to Dr. Derek Curtis Bok at Harvard University requesting early admission. On the home scene, Ellen reports unruly teen foster daughters to social services and edges away from a glass door knob, a love token from Stuart, who removes the hardware from Ellen's old home. Still shaky at determining her path, she answers to the still small voice within that directs her toward a box of personal items, her only handhold on her dead mother, who committed suicide in March 1969 at age 40 from an overdose of prescription digitalis. Alternating between retreats to Laura's assurances and advances toward a scholarly education, Ellen navigates the familiar peripheries of teens at the shores of adulthood.

See also **feminism, powerlessness**

• *Further reading*

Gibbons, Kaye. *Ellen Foster*. New York: Algonquin Press, 1987.

_____. *A Virtuous Woman*. Chapel Hill, N.C.: Algonquin Press, 1989.

Heilbrun, Carolyn G. *Toward a Recognition of Androgyny*. New York: W.W. Norton, 1982.

Wood, Ralph. "Gumption and Grace in the Novels of Kaye Gibbons," *Christian Century* 109, no. 27 (September 23–30, 1992): 842–846.

Barnes, Hattie

One of Gibbons's self-reliant and reliable females, Harriet Pearl "Hattie" Barnes, the narrator of *Sights Unseen* (1995), develops backbone from native intelligence and situational demands. In the summation of novelist-critic Jacqueline Carey, a critic for the *New York Times Book Review*, Hattie examines her childhood "at a delicate intersection of the ordinary and the horrific," a metaphor for the 12-year-old's daily encounters with a bipolar mother (Carey, 1995, 30). Hattie shares a daunting lack of assertive mothering with the title character of *Ellen Foster* (1987) and with Emma Garnet Tate Lowell, the narrator of *On the Occasion of My Last Afternoon* (1998). Born to Maggie Barnes, a volatile manic-depressive farm wife incapable of normal human affection, Hattie experiences rejection from the moment of birth in 1955. As reviewer Michael Harris describes the family's quandary in a critique for the *Los Angeles Times*, Maggie "is the most important person in their lives, but they have no real presence in hers" (Harris, 1995, 5).

Hattie's salvation is one of Gibbons's volunteer mothers, Pearl Wiggins, the maid and housekeeper who parallels the black neighbor and rescuer of Ellen Foster and prefigures the reassuring presence of Clarice Washington, surrogate mother to Emma. In reference to Hattie's hurt, Susan L. Nelson states in *The Other Side of Sin: Woundedness from the Perspectives of the Sinned-Against* (2001), "Ambiguity and conflict happen in the human situation but ... they can be attended to and healed" (Park & Nelson, 2001, 84). In a chaotic home environment that Hattie compares to "total eclipses or meteor showers," Pearl's surrogate parenthood assures Hattie stability as well as education in motherhood and housekeeping (Gibbons, 1995, 6–7). To sustain order, Hattie maintains exemplary behavior and, following the example of her older brother Freddy, retreats to her room to read and study, the beginning of a life of scholarship. Cleansing Hattie's uneasy, yet lucid memories of ostracism and public humiliation for Maggie's crazy stunts is storytelling, a cathartic disburdenment at a crucial point in early girlhood that enables Hattie to forgive her mother and to heal her wounded pride. Relieving Hattie's story of sorrow are the 15 years of wellness that Maggie enjoys before her death.

See also **Barnes genealogy**

• *Further reading*

Carey, Jacqueline. "Mommy Direst," *New York Times Book Review* (24 September 1995): 30.

Gibbons, Kaye. *Sights Unseen*. New York: G.P. Putnam's Sons, 1995.

Harris, Michael. "Scenes—and Skeletons—of a Troubled Southern Family," *Los Angeles Times* (9 October 1995): 5.

Perry, Carolyn, and Mary Louise Weaks, eds. *The History of Southern Women's Literature*. Baton Rouge: Louisiana State University Press, 2002.

Park, Andrew Sung, and Susan L. Nelson. *The Other Side of Sin: Woundedness from the Perspectives of the Sinned-Against*. Albany: State University of New York, 2001.

Barnes, Maggie

Gibbons claims a kinship with Maggie Barnes, whom the author created after a year's struggle with manic depression and suicidal urges. Seen through the memories of her daughter Hattie in a psychological novel, *Sights Unseen* (1995), Maggie is a beloved, but pitied figure whose infrequent lapses into sanity uplift and bless her children and exhausted husband. Hattie recounts the first days of World War II, when her mother agrees to marry an old friend, Frederick Barnes. Goading him to court Maggie is Frederick's dictatorial father, Grandfather Barnes, who sees Maggie as an erotic, slightly dangerous female given to exhibitionism in a polka dot bikini and to nonstop talking and jitterbugging after five highballs. Detached from social and internal control, Maggie develops into the family's constant affliction from her thralldom to mental demons. In a pseudo-romantic relationship, Grandfather Barnes indulges Maggie and serves as her buffer against social and legal consequences of her actions after she runs down a pedestrian in Rocky Mount with her car to stop the woman from stealing her soul. The metaphor of soul stealing personifies bipolarity, a disease that thwarts and belabors the spirit, thus gutting the will.

In her role as narrator, Hattie critiques the treachery of insanity in mothers. Dooming the family structure is an absence of maternal responsibility and role modeling to the Barnes children. At the depths of delusion, Maggie fears that the theft of her soul will leave behind a dry husk, a shell depersonalized by madness, treatment, and debilitating drugs. To her antics before her son Freddy's baseball team, she feels the need to atone for saddling her children with an erratic parent. Freddy's memory of a loony mother lurking behind the batter's cage symbolizes Maggie's pivotal family role at the nexus of action. The incident prefigures her eventual commitment in 1967 to the psychiatric ward of Duke Hospital. After fifteen years of counseling and anti-depressives, she experiences a resurgence of health and mental balance that releases both her true self and her ability to nurture and love her family.

Maggie's illness results in a dual nature. To the reader, she first appears like a domestic invader, a wraith-like banshee who gives her husband, children, and house staff no rest from badgering and terrorizing. In the plot resolution, at age 57, she becomes the pitiable victim of eight electroconvulsive treatments, jolts to the brain that cloak her memory in fog. After the initial zapping, she must reintroduce herself to Hattie and Freddy, who tiptoe around a woman who is a virtual stranger to them. At a more pathetic crossroads, she fails to recognize her husband. The text uplifts Frederick for his gentle telling of events in their lives that tugs Maggie back from post-treatment amnesia toward their marriage, early parenthood, and early home life in Louisiana. The recap of events serves Gibbons as a rehumanizing of Maggie.

The change in the female head of household blesses the Barnes family with unforeseen calm, order, and hope. The new Maggie behaves with such self-restraint that she speaks openly of the nursing staff's watchfulness for her former suicidal urges. By the time that she returns home, Hattie does not know which mother to anticipate. A critique in *Belles Lettres* declares that Gibbons could have elicited more sympathy for Maggie with greater development of the reconciliation of mother with child. Restored to sanity, Maggie speaks knowledgeably of rehabilitation — the need for rest, doses of lithium and Miltown, and a smooth routine. Her decision to cook two nights a week and to drive Hattie to school indicates a thoughtful survey of wifely and motherly duties and a new prioritizing from willfulness to a sane independence.

See also **Barnes genealogy**

• *Further reading*

Gibbons, Kaye. *Sights Unseen*. New York: G.P. Putnam's Sons, 1995.
Glass, Julia. "To Comfort the Comfortless Kaye Gibbons Writes of a Girl's Life with Her Mani-Depressive Mother," *Chicago Tribune* (20 August 1995).
Gretlund, Jan Nordby. "In My Own Style: An Interview with Kaye Gibbons," *South Atlantic Review* 65, no. 4 (Fall 2000): 132–154.
Harris, Michael. "Scenes— and Skeletons— of a Troubled Southern Family," *Los Angeles Times* (9 October 1995): 5.
Johnson, Rheta Grimsley. "A Skewed Life with Mother," *Atlanta Journal-Constitution* (3 September 1995).
"Review: *Sights Unseen*," *Belles Lettres* (January 1996).

Barnes genealogy

An insular North Carolina farm clan, the Barnes family draws inward to shelter Maggie Barnes, whose insane antics leave her open to ridicule. Gibbons leaves open to debate how much of the family's harboring derives from love and how much from protection of the family reputation:

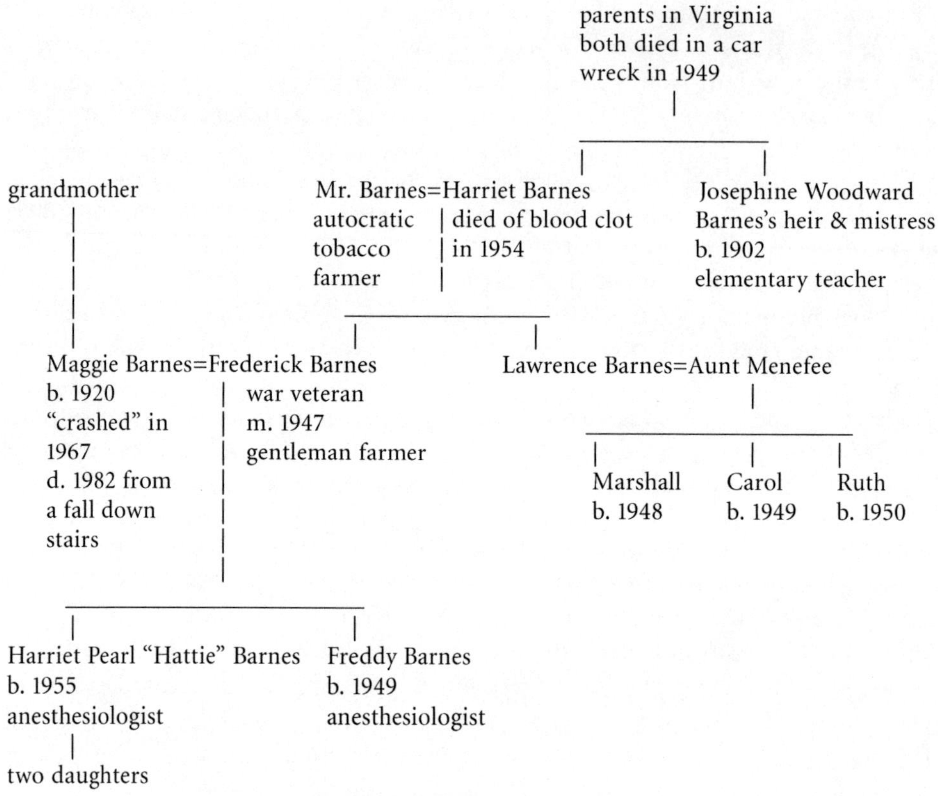

• *Further reading*

Gibbons, Kaye. *Sights Unseen.* New York: G.P. Putnam's Sons, 1995.

belonging

The acceptance of individuals into human community underlies the plots of Kaye Gibbons's fiction. In a short-story story, "The Headache," issued in June 1987 in the *St. Andrews Review,* farm wife Lucille Womble alienates herself through two weeks of self-punishment with head pain, sobbing, insomnia, and flashbacks. At the source of her torment is guilt for having concealed a handbag abandoned by a prankster in a restaurant ladies' room. Lambasting herself for white trash behavior, she retreats to a mental island of blame and visions of suicide until a physician, Dr. Janet Cowley, convinces her to share the incident with Lucille's husband Henry. Belonging for Lucille involves a supine retreat to Henry's side of the bed and a renewal of their marital oneness. In belonging, there is hope for her liberation from psychosomatic anguish.

In Gibbons's first novel, *Ellen Foster* (1987), the title character learns about belonging from observing the families of Starletta and Mavis. In flight from her father Bill, a drunken bootlegger and aggressive molester, on New Year's Eve, 1969, ten-year-old Ellen wills herself out the window into freezing weather and straight to Starletta's home, where Ellen overcomes racist fears long enough to rest from constant vigilance. After a court judge passes her to her maternal grandmother, a prominent landowner, Ellen realizes that the unbalanced old woman harbors a grudge that Ellen looks and behaves like her dissolute father. Although housed in a wealthy environment, Ellen is no closer to acceptance than she was in a nuclear family. From a hiding place, she observes an uproar of camaraderie and love on the front porch of a black laborers' shack, where Mavis, an agricultural superintendent, enjoys family in a way that Ellen has never seen.

Gibbons builds dramatic irony out of a destitute white child's selection of black family values as a model for belonging. Subtextually, experience with unified households inspires Ellen. On Christmas day, 1970, she makes her own place in a family by selecting a foster mother at church and by lugging personal items to the woman's home. The quest concludes with sensory perceptions of homelife — the smell of frying chicken, the feel of the pony Dolphin beneath her on leisurely afternoons, the delight of homemade curtains and pillow shams, and the sound of other girls contributing to meal planning. Monetarily, the securing of Ellen's bag of $166 in cash in the linen closet reassures a child who has no reason to trust the adults who sub for her dead mother. For Ellen, belonging envelopes her like the towel that her foster mother monograms with an S for Starletta. Ensured of welcome, Ellen is able to lie quietly on her bed in her own room and share the comfort with Starletta, who sleeps peacefully at her side. The pose suggests the interlinkage of giving and receiving as bases for emotional stability in a damaged psyche.

A study of a mature sense of belonging and of marital happiness empowers *A Virtuous Woman* (1989), Gibbons's second novel. Through fateful coincidence, 40-year-old farm laborer "Blinking" Jack Ernest Stokes stumbles on 20-year-old Ruby Pitts Woodrow at a crisis— the stabbing death of her worthless, exploitive husband John in a pool-room free-for-all. In his inarticulate style, Jack muses on "how it all lined up for me," his term for the encounter of a womanless farmhand with a love-hungry domestic worker (Gibbons, 1989, 17). Resigned to farming-class hopes and perspectives, Ruby and Jack work out a satisfying marriage in what critic Marilyn Chandler, writing for *Women's Review of Books*, calls "the language of feelings limited by customs of taciturnity and contempt for complaint" (Chandler, 1989). Paradoxically, the couple remains wedded over a quarter century of pragmatic give and take that allows Ruby to overlook Jack's secret drinking and reconciles Jack to Ruby's cigarette habit. The text attests to a constant rebalancing of expectations along an axis of love, the gimbal that supports an unlikely union.

Fellowship undergirds Gibbons's third and fourth novels, *A Cure for Dreams* (1991) and *Charms for the Easy Life* (1993). Set in female milieus, the stories depict protagonists as the mainstays of women and families in trouble. For Lottie O'Cadhain Davies, the queen bee of Milk Farm Road in *A Cure for Dreams*, the organization of a women's social club for penny-ante games of gin rummy and pinochle in the back of Porter's store counters the decade of financial blows from the Great Depression. A cadre warring against female hurts, the card players support Trudy Woodlief's need for food for her five children and Sade Duplin's fear of arrest by part-time Deputy Sheriff John Carroll for gunning down her ill-tempered womanizing husband Roy. The understated plottings of women in defense of women makes life bearable in a patriarchal Southern community.

In similar fashion, herbalist-midwife Charlie Kate Birch, the protagonist of *Charms for the Easy Life*, triumphs through female synergy. She relies on daughter Sophia Snow Birch and granddaughter Margaret for housecalls on patients requiring emergency treatment, birthing, and medical advice. For home-wearied women in her dental chair, Charlie Kate dispenses significant amounts of ether as short-term respites from home toil and marital disillusion. The three-woman healing team is particularly gentle to Maveen, the 70-year-old retired domestic whom a dismissive doctor abandons to starve in pain from stomach cancer. Allied in acts of healing and altruism, Charlie Kate's household parcels out similar benevolent gestures and advice to each other to ensure Charlie Kate's recovery from the reappearance of a fickle husband in 1938, widow Sophia Snow Birch's building of a new love life after her farm agent husband dies of stroke in August 1936, and Margaret's introduction to dating and higher education during the first months of World War II. As Sophia drifts away to a new husband on Christmas Eve, 1942, and Charlie Kate dies on Christmas night, Margaret stands alone supported by the years of upbringing in a sturdy all-female environment. Gibbons implies that marriage into the prominent Hawkings family will renew marital belonging to a matrilineage dogged by failed unions.

Belonging becomes a racial and social issue in Gibbons's first historical novel, *On the Occasion of My Last Afternoon* (1998). Homelife is so threatening to the Tate children at Seven Oaks plantation in Bruton Parish, Virginia, that they shelter in the kitchen with cook-housekeeper Clarice Washington. Life is less stressful apart from the rages of their father, Samuel P. Goodman Tate, and from their mother Alice's ineffectual vapors. For son Whately Tate, disownment results from a last return from Washington College in Lexington, Virginia, to report his sexual misbehavior with a barmaid. On Sullivan's Island, South Carolina, in 1845, at age 20, he dies alone of malnutrition and self-treatment for syphilis. For his sister Emma Garnet, in 1847, a permanent retreat from her blustering, menacing father takes her to Raleigh, North Carolina, in the company of her husband, Dr. Quincy Lowell, and Clarice. By establishing Clarice as housekeeper, Emma retains the familiar sounds and smells of the kitchen and ensures herself frequent advice on deportment and courage that steadied her in childhood.

The Greek concept of *philios* or membership in a group at first eludes the newlywed Lowells. Among pro-slavery Confederates, Emma and Quincy must traverse the social scene by avoiding disruptive topics like slave ownership, manumission, and threats to the plantation economy. Eventually, the couple form their own small enclave of liberal friends who share the patriotism and benevolence of the Boston Lowells. In the early 1860s, constant disruptions and losses of the Civil War strip Emma's sanctuary of mainstays. Following the deaths of Clarice in 1863 and Quincy in 1865, Emma must re-create belonging in Raleigh by joining sister Maureen Tate in welcoming the oppressed to their home and by outlining new aims to sustain Emma during late widowhood and old age. Gibbons describes Emma's renewed sense of nesting as the result of culinary training in Boston, where she lives with in-laws shortly after Quincy's final collapse on the train north. In the feminine domain of kitchen and pantry, Emma survives end-of-life solitude and loss by giving of self through hospitality and meal service.

Gibbons's seventh novel, *Divining Women* (2004), turns an amalgam of support and new-found courage into an emotional belonging. To Mary Oliver, a 22-year-old graduate student at Radcliffe from Washington, D.C., travel south by train to Elm City, North Carolina, on September 30, 1918, displaces her from a tight clan of two sets of grandparents on Dupont Circle. The Gothic oppression of her aunt, Maureen Carlton Ross, by a villainous husband replicates the sequestering of the heroine in Victorian potboilers. In an atmosphere bristling with menace, the two women find each other — Maureen out of need and Mary from empathy and involvement in Maureen's final 50 days of pregnancy. A tender processional to the cemetery allies a bicultural extended family — Mary, Maureen, and the stillborn Ella Eloise Ross accompanied by house servants Zollie and Mamie. Gibbons speaks through Mamie the verbal test of belonging: "We all love you" (Gibbons, 2004, 201). The text implies that the women's birthing of Ella Eloise on November 8, 1918, and her burial the next day at sunset forges a sure and unending sisterhood. Left opaque is the core of the 21-year relationship of Mary and Maureen, whether friendship or lesbian union.

See also **displacement**

- *Further reading*

Chandler, Marilyn. "Limited Partnership," *Women's Review of Books* 6, nos. 10–11 (July 1989): 21.

Gibbons, Kaye. *Divining Women*. New York: G.P. Putnam's Sons, 2004.

_____. *A Virtuous Woman*. Chapel Hill, N.C.: Algonquin Press, 1989.

betrayal

Betrayal undermines the stability of female union in Kaye Gibbons's feminist fiction. In a short-short story, "The Headache," published in the June 1987 issue of the *St. Andrews Review*, protagonist Lucille Womble draws comfort from a statement from the Hippocratic Oath guaranteeing that Dr. Janet Cowley divulges none of the patient confessions she hears in her medical office. Under the promise of secrecy, Lucille feels free to disclose the guilt and thoughts of suicide that condemn her to two weeks of head pain, insomnia, weepiness, and night terrors. For the title character in Gibbons's first novel, *Ellen Foster* (1987), betrayal ranges far beyond Lucille's fears of being labeled white trash. For Ellen Foster, the ultimate treachery is a father who sells bootlegs liquor to a houseful of black boozers and who allows them to sully her tender girlhood with filthy words and implications. Before Bill can attack her virginity, on New Year's Eve, 1969, Ellen flees into the cold to shelter with a nearby black family. In a twist on the theme of betrayal, Ellen must abandon her own race to find rescue and comfort. An epiphany illuminates her gradual awareness that blacks endure an ongoing ousting from the community, where whites degrade and belittle the black laboring class solely for the color of their skin.

A deluge of wrongs swells the initial treachery to a ten-year-old into a life-threatening flood. Compound betrayals await Ellen at the homes of three maternal relatives. Her Aunt Betsy offers temporary shelter, a shopping trip, and cursory parenting to the mother-hungry orphan. From a witchy grandmother demanding slave labor, Ellen receives little better than the housing and feeding of a migrant farm worker. Before Christmas 1970, the child journeys on to the home of Aunt Nadine Nelson, who smothers daughter Dora with love and attention while relegating Ellen to the outskirts of hospitality. Wearied by undependable sources of security and affection, Ellen succeeds at what she does best — she jettisons unreliable people and solicits the love of strangers by selecting her own foster parent. The end of a string of treacheries suggests that Ellen has an innate armor that shields her from spiritual and emotional rebuffs.

Ellen's youthful self-harborage foretokens the late blossoming of Ruby Pitts Woodrow Stokes, the protagonist of *A Virtuous Woman* (1989). Pampered in childhood, Ruby enters womanhood unbraced by the instruction in mate selection necessary to a satisfying marriage. The trickery of 26-year-old John Woodrow, her first husband, blindsides her, leaving her too ashamed of their elopement to return to the Pitts family. Innocent of his connivance, at age 18, she accepts a raw marital arrangement that lowers her economic status to house drudge in a migrant shack. Her response to his mean-mouthing and adultery belies the title of *A Virtuous Woman*. Rather than continue in a hopeless union with a manipulative slacker, she places her pillow over a pistol and awaits his return from a fling with a 16-year-old slut. In later years, after Ruby marries "Blinking" Jack Ernest Stokes, his discharge of the pistol for target practice refreshes memories of the dismay and determination of a 20-year-old wife search for a one-shot exit from a bad bargain. Perpetuating her restlessness are a barren womb from John's spread of sexually transmitted disease and her addiction to smoking, an escape from his badgering that eventually kills her at age 45 from lung cancer. Warned that her life nears its end, she perpetuates her belonging to Jack with the stocking of the freezer with meals of pork with corn and beef with beans to perpetuate their togetherness after her death. Gibbons enhances their tragic separation by depicting Jack as the inconsolable widower. After death robs him of Ruby, he belongs nowhere.

Like Ellen Foster's mother and Ruby Stokes, Irish-American immigrant Lottie O'Cadhain Davies, the protagonist of *A Cure for Dreams* (1991), falls victim to romantic illusion. Lured by the vague promises of a suitor, Welsh Quaker farmer-miller Charles Davies, at age 18, she leaves home on the Cumberland River in Bell County, Kentucky, and, in 1918, finds herself wed to a soulless workaholic at Milk Farm Road in North Carolina. Treachery in Lottie's life extends to the girlhood of her daughter, Betty Davies Randolph, who longs in vain for a father's affection. Gibbons indicates that the oral traditions of the female community prepare the untried girl for the realities of marriage. Through Lottie's manipulations, Betty passes up Luther Miracle and his dirty hair and deserts Stanton, a druggie addicted to Neurol Compound, who demeans Betty as "girlie" (Gibbons, 1991, 131). Too smart for betrayal, Betty grooms Herman Randolph for wedlock and retains her virginity as a hedge against trickery and abandonment. Betty's strategy triumphs. A war bride left with her mother and mother-in-law in February 1942, Betty thrives in a female matrix that welcomes her daughter, Marjorie Polly Randolph, the inheritor of womanly wisdom that dates back four generations. Gibbons implies that storytelling frees Marjorie of the forms of betrayal that beleaguer her foremothers.

Gibbons turns to a problematic view of female victimization in *Charms for the Easy Life* (1993). In 1902, the focus, herbalist-midwife Charlie Kate Birch, chooses an unschooled waterman as her husband, but she gradually outgrows him. As she develops intellect and stamina through calculated regimens of reading and clean living, her unnamed husband slowly slips away in mind and spirit and, finally, in body. Desertion does not dim the love of daughter Sophia Snow Birch for her father, who returns in 1938 long enough to lure Charlie Kate to the Sir Walter Raleigh Hotel for a three-day tryst. Worldly wise from her experiences with neighbors and patients, Charlie Kate engineers her own treachery by seizing $1,365, her husband's entire bankroll, before abandoning him. The incident offers a female subversion of the more common man-leaves-woman motif. Unfazed by manlessness, she attends his funeral without tears and bargains with his mistress for a mantel clock, a symbol of reality to a woman disabused of girlish illusions about men.

The novel's betrayals fan out to the next generation. Overlaying Charlie Kate's loss to a feckless male is Sophia's marriage to a farm agent, a shameless bounder who makes a joke of wearing yellow shoes to their wedding. Sophia misses wedlock, but, like her mother, she is less wide-eyed and vulnerable in her courtship by businessman Richard Baines, a stabler, more devoted mate. Their Christmas Eve 1942 contretemps brought on by the arrival of the former Mrs. Baines to town concludes with triumph and tragedy. During Richard and Sophia's elopemenet to the Carolina shore, they learn of Charlie Kate's unexpected death on Christmas night, a departure from an all-woman home at a propitious moment in its history. Gibbons portrays Sophia's new-found backbone and the emerging independence in her daughter Margaret as shields against future male falseheartedness.

In Gibbons's first historical novel, *On the Occasion of My Last Afternoon* (1998), treachery adopts numerous guises. During girlhood at Seven Oaks plantation in Bruton Parish, Virginia, protagonist Emma Garnet Tate Lowell endures the perfidy of Alice Tate, a genteel Southern-bred mother who is too weak to defend her children against their father, Samuel P. Goodman Tate, an overbearing monster. Secure in marriage and a new home in Raleigh, North Carolina, 17-year-old Emma once more experiences the duplicity of a woman when Lucille McKimmon, a social contact, sends Emma into a swoon by asking indirectly about the suicide of Whately, Emma's 20-year-old brother. Shunned by the city's elite, Emma fights her way out of double dealing by establishing her own social milieu, which includes a bishop, physicians, Raleigh literati, and two state governors. The formation of a coterie of like-minded people exhibits Gibbons's belief that avoidance of the faithless is the best protection against deceit.

Gibbons pictures mortal treachery as the most devastating double-cross. Emma's success at integrating a liberal life apart from racist snobs survives until the end of the Civil War, when death twice pummels her. Her first loss is Clarice Washington, the faithful surrogate mother and cook-housekeeper who dies of pneumonia in 1863. Two years later, overwork snatches Quincy, the beloved husband who works himself to death treating combat victims. Gibbons provides a resurgence of self-confidence in the plot resolution as Emma accepts the support of her Boston in-laws and retrieves from the past her sister Maureen Tate, a late-blooming activist. Their unified action against community hunger, ignorance, and poverty survives until Maureen, like Clarice and Quincy, slips away in an unforeseen demise. Because of Emma's religious faith, she meets her own end-of-life farewells secure in the knowledge that the faithful Quincy awaits her across the great divide. Although the resolution echoes the sentimental motif of Victorian romance, Gibbons clings to a post-modern belief in love as a buttress against disappointment and loss.

In her seventh novel, *Divining Women* (2004), Gibbons reinvestigates insincere matrimony as a model of dissimulation. To outsider Mary Oliver, a 22-year-old graduate student at Radcliffe traveling from Washington, D.C., to Elm City, North Carolina, an evil husband's fakery masks the cause of his wife's retreat to an upstairs hermitage. Candid in the face of an ogre, beginning on September 30, 1918, Mary chips away at the bravado of her uncle, Troop Ross, who cows his wife, Maureen Carlton Ross, with daily denunciation mantled by regular deliveries of hothouse roses. To outflank the dissembler, Mary successfully restructures Maureen's self-esteem at a fearful moment, the stillbirth on November 8, 1918, of Ella Eloise Ross, a child already betrayed by a father who refers to her as "it" (Gibbons, 2004, 203). He signs off from his shattered marriage with heinous denunciation of a woman he slanders as "too goddamn worthless to be somebody's mother" (Ibid., 200). As is true of Gibbons's previous malefactors, Troop damns himself through bitter, undeserved aspersions to his wife. Maureen caps the family schism with thanks to Mary and Mamie, who lie next to Maureen to warm her body and revive her spirit during and after the delivery of Ella Eloise. The alliance of the unknown niece with her aunt and the Ross family domestic embodies Gibbons's familiar situational groupings that come together out of need rather than reliance on the undependable nuclear family.

Gibbons's first sequel, *The Life All Around Me* by Ellen Foster (2006), treachery clings to the title character's psyche. Long separated from the personal items belonging to her dead mother, Ellen faces down her grasping Aunt Nadine Nelson, a forger and thief of Ellen's sizeable inheritance. In the view of Laura, Ellen's foster mother, the mill of retribution has "been grinding, slowly as it always does and exceedingly small" (Gibbons, 2006, 173). Although wealth and personal items repay Ellen for years of family lying, the real antidotes to betrayal come from Cousin Dora, who repudiates Nadine, and from Laura. She hugs Ellen with a verbal testimonial, "I know, I know, and I love you, I know" (Ibid., 205). In the resolution, Christmas 1974 redeems Ellen from the self-blame and family angst of five past Christmases, endowing her with the self-assurance to accept early admittance to Harvard University as an appropriate reward for not giving up.

• *Further reading*

Gibbons, Kaye. *A Cure for Dreams*. New York: Algonquin, 1991.
_____. *Divining Women*. New York: G.P. Putnam's Sons, 2004.
_____. *The Life All Around Me by Ellen Foster*. New York: Harcourt, 2006.
Williams, Lynna. "For Ellen Foster, There's Finally Light at the End of the Tunnel," *Chicago Tribune* (8 January 2006).

Birch, Charlie Kate

A seasoned wisewoman and model of the New Woman in *Charms for the Easy Life* (1993), Clarissa "Charlie" Kate Birch, Gibbons's sturdy activist and folk healer, is the self-educated bulwark of an intergenerational all-female household. Critic Jay Strafford, in a review for the *Richmond Times-Dispatch,* describes the truth-telling protagonist as "the chief matriarch of a matriarchal family," a force for "female solidarity before that phrase became politicized" (Strafford, 1993). In the estimation of reviewer Judith Beth Cohen, Charlie Kate is "mythic [for] her subversive vision of women's possibilities" (Cohen, 1993). Born in 1882 and married in 1902, Charlie Kate possesses what granddaughter Margaret refers to as a "muscular soul," a bossy facade and an exemplary spirit too resolute and too motivated to be easily daunted (Gibbons, 1993, 46). Unlike a weak twin named Camelia, who commits suicide in 1910 after the death of her hydrocephalic son, Charlie Kate flourishes during the Great Depression and World War II by applications of tough-mindedness and will. Her firm voice and clear perception mirror the strength and foresight of Carson McCullers's Berenice Sadie Brown in *The Member of the Wedding* (1946), Toni Morrison's Grandma Baby Suggs in the Pulitzer Prize–winning novel *Beloved* (1987), and Gloria Naylor's title figure in *Mama Day* (1988), all examples of feminist fortitude.

Key to Charlie Kate's success in midwifery, internal medicine, surgery, and dentistry is an astute pragmatism. For training, she reads the *New England Journal of Medicine*, a farmer's almanac, Dr. John C. Gunn's *Domestic Medicine, or Poor Man's Friend* (1830), and secondhand medical books. After saving a millhand from an accident by sewing him up with red thread, she uses the incident as leverage against the mill owner to extort an addition to her Beale Street residence. He complies because she threatens to reveal the appalling factory conditions that expose workers to loose gyrating parts in unoiled machinery. Similarly moved to intervene in the coming-of-age of her daughter, Sophia Snow Birch, Charlie Kate fosters the education of Charles Nutter, a potential beau who completes medical school with financial aid from Charlie Kate. Although Nutter does not pair up with Sophia, Charlie Kate considers her expenditure a wise investment, a form of benevolence that strengthens all of society.

Just as she readies Charles Nutter for medical practice, Charlie Kate attacks problems with logic, moral clarity, and background study. She and Sophia plot investments by reading each company's prospectus and accompany Margaret in close order to her first wake, a receiving for Ida O'Shea, a playmate killed by influenza. In August 1936, the packing of Sophia's dead husband's belongings is matter-of-fact and devoid of grief for a man whose leaving generates no sorrow. On a post-funeral visit to Morehead City, Charlie Kate gazes out to sea and prophesies World War II. In similar direct style, she demands that the management of the Atlantis hotel halt the jitterbugging of debutantes, a restoration of order that her autocratic powers fails to accomplish. Without regret, she establishes domestic order a few months later by merging her household with that of Sophia and Margaret. To rescue a crumbling herbal compendium and to secure Margaret's interest in herbalism, Charlie Kate insists that her granddaughter copy the text of the old handbook into a notebook.

Similarly practical in day-to-day matters, Charlie Kate blames a host of human ills on dissolute living, unhygienic conditions, and lack of sleep.

Margaret admires her grandmother for two extremes— a crusty exterior impervious to sentiment and a sympathy for the ignorant and destitute. Charlie Kate promotes public health by blackmailing bigoted city officials into laying a boardwalk and sewer lines in the poor district and by teaching her patients to use flush toilets. She pities women trapped in unfruitful, loveless marriages to drunkards or selfish cads like her first son-in-law. Upon encountering her own strayed husband in 1938, at age 56, she robs him of $1,365 and awards the wad of cash to the Confederate Ladies' Home, which opened in 1900 on Grove Avenue in Richmond, Virginia. To relieve the tedium of the spinster teachers retired from Miss Nash's School for Young Ladies, Charlie Kate earmarks the donation for entertainment and edification — a radio and Victrola, magazine subscriptions and leather-bound copies of classic literature, and rejuvenating jaunts to Charleston and Savannah. The gesture echoes other networking in Gibbons's pro-woman fiction.

Although awed by her grandmother's generosity and moral rectitude, Margaret is able to identify human flaws— Charlie Kate's admiration for gentrified manners and her temerity in criticizing the battle strategy of a Southern paragon, General Robert E. Lee. As the novel concludes with Sophia's remarriage and Margaret's apparent pairing with Tom Hawkings, III, according to Maureen Harrington, book critic for the *Denver Post*, Gibbons "isn't foolish enough to let a novel end without the dollop of the bittersweet that is life" (Harrington, 1993). Suddenly snatched from the trio of strong women on Christmas night, 1942, Charlie Kate is absent in person, but pervasive in practical and spiritual influence. Gibbons indicates a feminist truth, the value of memory to survivors of strong women who marked the trail ahead.

See also **healing and health**

• *Further reading*

Cohen, Judith Beth. "Review: *Charms for the Easy Life,*" *Women's Review of Books* 11, no. 1 (October 1993).

Gibbons, Kaye. *Charms for the Easy Life*. New York: Putnam, 1993.

Harrington, Maureen. "Child's Vision Right on Target," *Denver Post* (4 April 1993).

Lothar, Corinna. "'Charms' Are Many in Gibbons' New Novel," *Washington Times* (6 June 1993).

Madrigal, Alix. "A Tough Southern Belle," *San Francisco Chronicle* (2 May 1993).

Strafford, Jay. "'Easy Life' Comes Hard to Women," *Richmond Times-Dispatch* (27 June 1993).

Birch genealogy

The original Birch genealogy established with anecdotal humor in *Charms for the Easy Life* (1993) lauds a female family line blessed with sense and backbone as well as a surprising number of suicides:

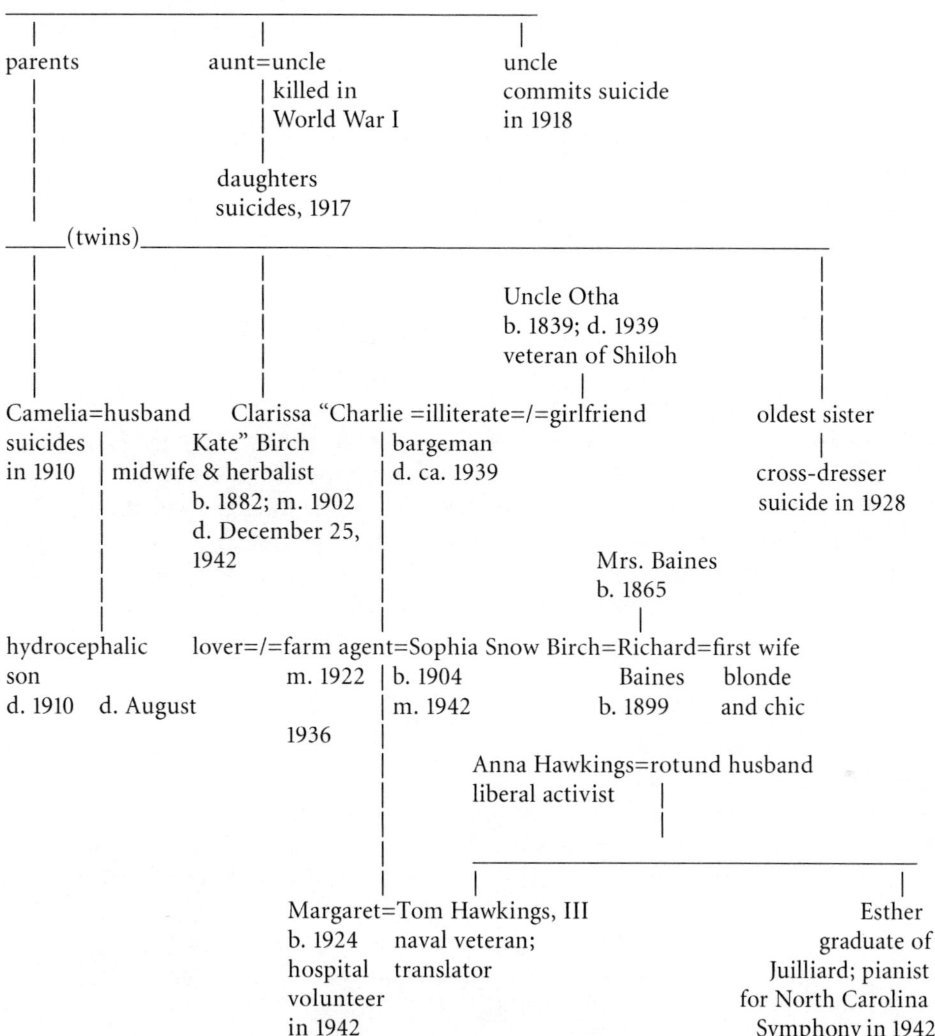

See also **Birch, Charlie Kate; Margaret**

• *Further reading*

Gibbons, Kaye. *Charms for the Easy Life*. New York: Putnam, 1993.

Charms for the Easy Life

In the wake of *A Cure for Dreams* (1991), Kaye Gibbons's second female saga, *Charms for the Easy Life* (1993), covers a North Carolina matrilineage from 1902 to 1942. Jay Strafford, a reviewer for the *Richmond Times-Dispatch*, described the novel as "a realistic picture of women alone," a reference to a manless household of three generations (Strafford, 1993). Because of the synergy of protagonist Charlie Kate

Birch, her daughter Sophia Snow Birch, and granddaughter Margaret, residents of the mill district of Raleigh, North Carolina, receive quality birthing, dentistry, advice on hygiene, sex education, and general health care. As described by Maureen Harrington, book reviewer for the *Denver Post*, the three healers flourish amid human drama: "Death, birth, the humiliations of the flesh are everyday matters of importance to these three" (Harrington, 1993). Because of the ongoing challenges, the trio relies on skill and optimism to carry them through the Great Depression and into home guard volunteerism during World War II.

In an essay for *Library Journal*, critic Nancy Pearl lauded the feminist text for its portrait of vigor and toughness in an elderly female protagonist. Through the memories of her granddaughter Margaret, the persona and career of eccentric healer Charlie Kate Birch take shape. A self-taught herbalist, dentist, and midwife, she is initially well rooted to a spot in coastal Pasquotank County on the Albemarle Sound, where her family has lived for five generations. Unaffected by Southern racism and class distinctions, she develops a working relationship with age-old Indian cures. With the aid of an Indian midwife, Sophia Snow, Charlie Kate gives birth to Sophia Snow Birch, the second generation of the family tree. The naming replicates a thankful gesture in *A Cure for Dreams* (1991), in which Betty Davies Randolph names her daughter Marjorie Polly to honor cook-midwife Polly Deal and prefigures a similar naming of Harriet Pearl "Hattie" Barnes for her black surrogate mother, Pearl Wiggins, in *Sights Unseen* (1998). The choice affirms a traditional relationship between mothers and folk health providers that dates into prehistory.

Gibbons describes female tragedy as the introit to Charlie Kate's resettlement in Wake County, the center of state government. After the death of a hydrocephalic nephew, the razor slashings with which his unconsolable mother Camelia, Charlie Kate's twin, kills herself triggers despair in the boy's father, who stretches out on railroad tracks to await a quick death. Nevertheless, the trio of losses only stimulates Charlie Kate, who centers her life on motherhood, education, and service to the unfortunate. In token of her granddaughter's intellectual promise, Charlie Kate cultivates Margaret's mind and brags about her reading Rudyard Kipling's *The Jungle Book* (1894) in first grade and Robert Louis Stevenson's *Kidnapped* (1886) the next year. The author tempers the grandmother's pushiness with a genuine affection for Margaret and concern for her welfare. The trio's adventures, in the estimation of Colleen Kelly Warren, book reviewer for the *St. Louis Post-Dispatch*, disclose "a family that takes eccentricity for granted" (Warren, 1993).

The novel tests the all-female cast during unproductive encounters with a variety of men. Charlie Kate's marriage in 1902 to an illiterate ferryman proves insubstantial, but it awards her a dutiful daughter. After Sophia's rakish husband dies of cerebral hemorrhage in August 1936, Charlie Kate moves into the household to help rear her granddaughter, whose datelessness concerns Sophia. Family strengths concentrate good sense and sober living in Margaret, who rejects flirting in favor of cures, midwifery, and principles of hygiene learned while she accompanies her grandmother and mother on house calls. Mirroring the worthlessness of two unreliable husbands is an aristocratic Raleigh doctor who disdains Charlie Kate's expertise. By face-to-face blackmail, she defeats him and wins for herself professional access to the Hayes Barton Pharmacy as well as a reputation for impeccable ethics. The qualities that Charlie Kate models instill themselves in Margaret, who cherishes a legacy of female zest and individualism.

See also **Birch, Charlie Kate; Birch genealogy; Margaret**

• *Further reading*

Gibbons, Kaye. *Charms for the Easy Life.* New York: Putnam, 1993.
Harrington, Maureen. "Child's Vision Right on Target," *Denver Post* (4 April 1993).
Pearl, Nancy. "Companion Reads for Your Next Book Club," *Library Journal* 128, no. 1 (1 January 2003): 192.
Strafford, Jay. "'Easy Life' Comes Hard to Women," *Richmond Times-Dispatch* (27 June 1993).
Warren, Colleen Kelly. "Three Generations of Feisty Women," *St. Louis Post-Dispatch* (6 June 1993).

Civil War

For good or ill, the Civil War is an omnipresent subject in Southern literature, which gravitates toward unsettled issues and lingering regrets. In an introduction to the Modern Library volume of Kate Chopin's *The Awakening and Other Stories* (1899), novelist Kaye Gibbons reflects on the hardships of women who survived the fearful and destructive era. In Gibbons's view, "The War was a widow-maker, and for younger women of the common classes with children to support on no pension and no legacy, the options of employment were as rare as they were dismal" (Gibbons, 2000, xxv).

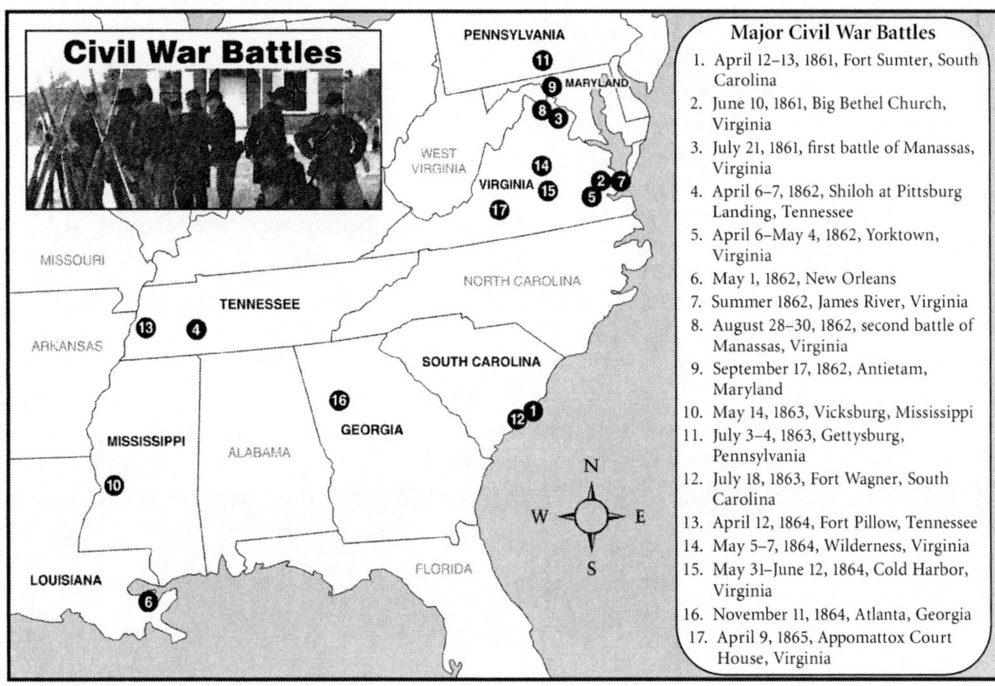

RAYMOND BARRETT, JR.

With sympathy for impoverished genteel females, the author pictures them teaching music or Latin, living with relatives, and trying to be as unobtrusive as possible. The loss of female verve and pragmatism further depletes the South at a time when it requires both.

Gibbons introduces the subject of the war years by describing the family lineage of Charlie Kate Birch, the midwife-herbalist of *Charms for the Easy Life* (1993). On Christmas Day, 1942, Charlie Kate receives a set of authentic Civil War surgeon's scalpels in token of her care of the underclass in the mill district of Raleigh, North Carolina. She cherishes an unexpected gift from her son-in-law — the four-volume biography of Robert E. Lee, a classic written by Douglas Southall Freeman in 1934. She wears an heirloom black dress that became the daily uniform of her mother, who mourned until her death the defeat of the Confederacy from the date of General William Tecumseh Sherman's scorched-earth ravaging of Georgia and the Carolinas from September 1 to December 22, 1864. Another minor character, 100-year-old Uncle Otha, regales mourners at his son's wake with details of the battle of Shiloh, an horrific carnage that began on April 6, 1862, at Pittsburg Landing in southwestern Tennessee and continued into the next day. Although the retelling occurs in 1939, the loss to the Confederacy of 10,500 soldiers still touches the hearts of Southern listeners who, in one way or another, carry the scars.

Through tableau and selected detail, Gibbons's first historical novel, *On the Occasion of My Last Afternoon* (1998) presents Southern loss in a retrospect of 130 years. During an upsurge of period novels, her writing coincided with Madison Jones's completion of *Nashville 1864: The Dying of the Light* (1997), the story of the Union occupation of Nashville, Tennessee, and with Josephine Humphreys's *No Where Else on Earth* (2000), a Civil War novel set among the outcast Lumbee in eastern North Carolina. In Gibbons's fiction, planter Samuel P. Goodman Tate's slashing of the slave Jacob's throat in hog-slaughtering season, 1842, precipitates family disaffection that causes Emma Garnet Tate to marry a liberal Northerner, Dr. Quincy Lowell of the Boston abolitionist Lowells. The murder symbolizes the savagery of bondage that presses Southern slavery toward ruin. In 1847, at age 17, she dissociates herself from Seven Oaks plantation, her childhood home in Bruton Parish, Virginia, and settles on Blount Street in Raleigh, North Carolina. In 1900, reflecting over her 70 years, she recognizes the euphemisms and locutions that allowed Southerners to live with slavery's horrors, the waste of sectionalism and war, and the collapse of the Southern plantation system, the corrupt economic order that sustained the gentry and elevated them above blacks and crackers. Feminist critic Linda Wagner-Martin notes that Emma's poised retrospect glimpses the "dignity that could penetrate, and civilize, the Southern wilds" (Wagner-Martin, 1999, 4).

Gibbons views social upheaval through the compromises and privations of females, both real — Varina Davis, Fannie Farmer, Dorothea Dix, and General Robert E. and Mary Custis Lee's daughter Mildred — and fictional. In chapter 9, Emma details the labors of women to tend fields and to cook scarce staples into meals for starving children. Of the fears of women whose sons are of age to join the fighting, Emma remarks, "Mothers smell blood before the wound is given" (Gibbons, 1998, 173). She repines over energies and time devoted to killing people. In addition to the sapping of women and children, Emma regrets the pathetic sufferings of blurred figures in the photos of Mathew Brady, the era's visual historian. She reports the death of Colonel Robert Gould Shaw, who sacrificed himself and much of the 54th Massachusetts Regiment, America's first black militia, at the siege of Fort Wagner, South Carolina, on July 18, 1863. After the counting of 43,000 casualties following the battle of Gettysburg, Pennsylvania, on July 3–4, 1863, the Lowell family extends their charity by opening a home recovery ward to relieve overcrowding at the Fair Grounds tent hospital and to support the outreach of the African Zionist church. The emphasis on philanthropy retrieves the novel from a long list of privations and sacrifices and renews faith in survivors, particularly women.

Gibbons honors noncombatants for their resourcefulness. In the absence of cots during the setting up of makeshift wards, nurses bed down the wounded on straw. For afternoon tea, recuperating men sip hot drinks made from peppermint, an herbal stimulant that grows wild near the Lowells' house. Pragmatism requires Quincy to perform surgery on the grand piano and to teach Emma to perform tracheotomies, to apply leeches to necrotic tissue, and to extract shrapnel from the backs of battle-weary boys retreating from Yorktown, Virginia, where General George Brinton McClellan faced General Robert E. Lee and the Confederate line from April 6 to May 4, 1862. In contrast to Quincy's humanitarianism is the bull-headedness of his father-in-law, Samuel P. Goodman Tate, who bankrupts himself by outfitting and arming Colonel Wade Hampton's South Carolina infantry, which Tate drills near the Shirley Plantation, a grand estate 35 miles west of Williamsburg. Emma lumps her father among those "foolish enough to court the dream of a Confederate victory" (*Ibid.*, 251). At the nadir of his fortunes, Samuel juxtaposes the image of his dying wife Alice as a contrast to plantation anathema, the quartering of Yankee officers and "their camp-following whores" in the estate's master bedroom (*ibid.*, 215). Samuel's well deserved defeat and the Lowells' survival of wartime exigencies provide Emma a short-lived satisfaction. Because of Quincy's sudden collapse from exhaustion in 1865, she shelters with her Lowell in-laws in Boston, safely out of sight of the Reconstruction era that, like the war, beleaguers Raleigh. Her next civil combat involves her with sister Maureen in uplifting, feeding, and educating North Carolina's war-damaged poor.

• *Further reading*

Gibbons, Kaye. "Introduction," *The Awakening and Other Stories*, by Kate Chopin. New York: Modern Library, 2000.

_____. *On the Occasion of My Last Afternoon*. New York: G.P. Putnam's Sons, 1998.

Hobson, Fred C., ed. *South to the Future: An American Region in the Twenty-First Century*. Athens: University of Georgia Press, 2002.

Wagner-Martin, Linda. "Kaye Gibbons' Achievement in *On the Occasion of My Last Afternoon*," *Notes on Contemporary Literature* 29, no. 3 (May 1999): 3–5.

coming of age

The blossoming of youth into adulthood undergirds the feminist themes of Gibbons's novels. In *Ellen Foster* (1987), the author's first novel, mature burdens of tending a motherless household and caring for a drunken father push the ten-year-old title figure too soon toward adult decisions and compromises. Reprised in the author's first sequel, *The Life All Around Me by Ellen Foster* (2006), in fall 1974, Ellen reaches her mid-teens still befuddled and waylaid by flashbacks to a toxic home environment. Old enough to realize that she needs a scholarly atmosphere, she rejects the mooning of Stuart, who courts her with a glass door knob removed from her old house and a proposal to enjoy a "valentime bed" after they elope to Pedro's South-of-the-Border fireworks emporium and motel (Gibbons, 2006, 139). Closer to her heart is the box of personal belongings of her deceased 40-year-old mother Shine and a psychiatric evaluation from September 10, 1968, that presents the first objective revelation of Shine's illness. By letting the mother grow up, Ellen herself moves into a more mature realm of perceptions and inklings about the depression that forced Shine to commit suicide.

More tenuous and less dramatic are the yearnings for autonomy in Gibbons's second novel, *A Virtuous Woman* (1989). Teen restlessness and rebellion against authority thrust 18-year-old Ruby Pitts, a coddled daughter of landowners, out of the nest toward union with 26-year-old farm laborer John Woodrow. Lacking the nurturance of her mother and of Sudie Bee, the family do-all, Ruby abruptly learns the reality of married life for the underclass woman, from a brutal loss of virginity to cooking for two in a migrant shack. At John's death from a knife wound to the lungs in a bar brawl two years later, Ruby shelters with 40-year-old "Blinking" Jack Ernest Stokes, another farm worker twice her age. In retrospect of her choices, she admits that returning home to the Pitts family to confess unwise girlish choices is more atonement than she can muster. In both Ellen Foster and Ruby, the absence of readiness generates false starts and hurtful regrets.

Coming of age supplies mother-daughter conflict in *A Cure for Dreams* (1991), a matrilineal saga that follows the O'Donough-O'Cadhain-Davies-Randolph women from hunger and squalor in Galway, Ireland, in 1918 to the banks of the Cumberland River in Bell County, Kentucky. After an unsound courtship similar to that of Ruby Pitts, protagonist Lottie O'Cadhain Davies makes her way to Milk Farm Road, North Carolina, as the outcome of a common teen error, the perception of a marriage proposal as escape from unhappiness. During the Great Depression, maturity disabuses her of the notion of male rescue and fosters self-salvation from a withered marriage to miserly farmer-miller Charles Davies, who discounts both his wife and daughter. Too late to spare herself lengthy regret, Lottie uses storytelling as a means of educating her daughter, Betty Davies Randolph, on the real obstacles to female contentment.

Essential to the maturity of Lottie's daughter is a parting of the ways with her beloved widowed mother. During years of shadowing her mother out the door to escape bitter domestic fights, Betty cozies up to games of pinochle and gin rummy with neighboring women in the back of Porter's Store. Gibbons indicates, however, that Betty must cut the umbilical cord to claim her individuality. Significantly, Betty circumvents her bossy mother through rebellion — by studying a secretarial course and working at Kresge's in Richmond, the Virginia metropolis that once headquartered the Confederacy. A suitable site for a failed secession, the city claims Betty for only a short time, during which she falls for Stanton, a flashy deceiver addicted to Neurol Compound. Her choice of a beau suggests that she is still too green to abandon maternal guidance, however domineering.

For untried girls like Betty, coming-of-age struggles are both emotionally necessary and intellectually instructive. The mother-daughter tension helps her to see the flaws in Luther Miracle, her dirty-haired boyfriend, and to accept Herman Randolph, a navy enlistee, as more promising husband material. Without overt duplicity, Lottie manages to seal Betty's union with Herman, who departs in February 1942 for service aboard the U.S.S. *Hornet* during World War II, leaving the Davies women to each other's company. Gibbons enlarges on female strengths on November 25, 1942, when midwife Polly Deal delivers Betty and Herman's daughter, Marjorie Polly Randolph, the fourth in the chain of women. The event implies that Betty has achieved motherhood and, in Lottie's absence from the birthing, has secured independence as a keystone of matrilineage for at least one more generation.

The motif of leaving home and learning by doing informs Gibbons's seventh novel, *Divining Women* (2004). Restless during World War I, Mary Oliver, a 22-year-old graduate student at Radcliffe, sheds the security of home to develop autonomy. On September 30, 1918, she travels from Washington, D.C., to Elm City, North Carolina, to become the companion and defender of Maureen Carlton Ross, a pregnant wife harried by Troop Ross, her emotionally stunted husband. As love for Maureen grows in Mary, she finds the indignation and guts to batter Troop to a standstill and to uplift Maureen from the stillbirth of Ella Eloise Ross on November 8, 1918. Leaving the ruins of a marriage on the sidewalk, Mary whisks Maureen back to Washington, D.C., to thrive among normal folk. Like Betty Davies Randolph in *A Cure for Dreams*, Mary values both self-rule as well as the familiar moorings of home and mother.

The layered household dealings of *Charms for the Easy Life* (1993), Gibbons's fourth novel, describes a similar fine-tuning of mother-daughter symbiosis. As Margaret approaches college age, she lives under the at-home tutelage of mother Sophia Snow Birch and grandmother Charlie Kate Birch, a revered folk doctor. However, the lessons conflict: from mother Sophia, Margaret learns that women seduced by romanticism suffer from the lack of practical expectation; from grandmother Charlie Kate, Margaret acquires respect for logic and a healthy skepticism of human perfectibility. To Sophia's urging that Margaret go to college and size up marriageable men, Margaret chooses to live out 1942 as a volunteer at a Durham veterans' hospital while her grandmother continues to manipulate Margaret's encounters with young men. Unlike Betty Davies Randolph, Margaret does not have to slip away from the two female role models. After Sophia elopes with businessman Richard Baines on Christmas Eve, 1942, and Charlie Kate dies unexpectedly on Christmas night, Margaret has no need to rebel or force her way into adulthood. Aptly armed for womanly roles as healer and wife, Margaret gently smooths her grandmother's corpse and awaits the return of life choices. Gibbons proves that the pre-arranged selection of Tom Hawkings, III, for a husband and Charlie Kate's wooing of the Hawkings family completes Margaret's coming-of-age without the need for child-against-adult confrontations.

In a more personal view of a young woman's struggle to birth individuality and self-confidence, Hattie Barnes, the adult narrator of *Sights Unseen* (1995), reflects on childhood attempts to compensate for a crazed mother. In the description of novelist-reviewer Jacqueline Carey, a critic for *New York Times Book Review*, Hattie sets her sights "at a delicate intersection of the ordinary and the horrific [while] Maggie's illness seeps into the very fiber of the household" (Carey, 1995). By reliving Barnes family crises, Hattie extols the love of a surrogate mother, cook-housekeeper Pearl Wiggins, while forgiving Maggie Barnes for decades of bedroom sulks and insane escapades, which climax in the deliberate wounding of a pedestrian with her car in Rocky Mount to stop the unsuspecting woman from allegedly stealing Maggie's soul. At the crossroads of tragedy, coming of age for Hattie involves overt reconciliation. She bears an inner awareness that reading and scholarship compensate her for cultivating no close friends and for avoiding home visits by outsiders. Symbolically, Hattie's choice of anesthesiology as a career reflects her narrative cure for a troubled life — the quieting of subconscious hurts through mature introspection and measured storytelling.

In addition to educating and liberating the young, coming of age tests Gibbons's most emotionally assailed characters. Like Ellen Foster, Ruby Pitts Woodrow Stokes, and Betty Davies Randolph, plantation heiress Emma Garnet Tate Lowell, protagonist of *On the Occasion of My Last Afternoon* (1998), contemplates choices and decisions that exceed her experience. A timorous figure in a post-wedding carriage in 1847, 17-year-old Emma bids farewell to her refined and loving mother Alice while Samuel P. Goodman Tate fires verbal salvos at his rebel daughter for stealing Clarice Washington, the family cook-housekeeper. As the Lowells depart for a European honeymoon, Samuel curses their unborn offspring in a spiteful spectacle. Through poetic justice, Gibbons pictures him in June 1862 in the extremes of coronary failure when his three granddaughters retreat from his presence, leaving him to rail at the house staff and at Emma and her husband Quincy. As Samuel's heart withers, Emma's grows with love of family, neighbors, and the suffering young men who either flourish or die under her medical care. The motif of selflessness embodies the author's faith in service to others as a form of self-broadening and spiritual reclamation.

Gibbons describes Emma's coalescing womanhood as the result of both inner strength and marital support. She exclaims, "I became a lady of my own" (Gibbons, 1998, 113). In retrospect, Quincy, like a patient father, guides his wife to a scrutiny of the past and an examination of familial ruins that challenge her self-confidence during the 12 years she lives apart from Alice. Through his steadying influence, Emma relives the baths that Clarice once scented with lavender to calm and reassure her in childhood. The interweaving of motherly images casts doubt on Emma's complete maturity and on her readiness to manage a household and children. As a gesture to the historical milieu, Gibbons depicts the Civil War as Emma's true coming of age, a test of stability and unselfishness for the entire nation. Nursing rewards her with competence in the critical ward as her husband's surgical assistant. Emma's continued emotional development scrolls on toward the last afternoon of the title, the death that approaches in 1900 in her 70th year, when she looks forward to an otherworldly reunion with Quincy. At this phase of character ripening, she achieves reader approval for her willingness to grow and change, a human trait that moots the question of when and under what circumstances people come of age.

See also **vulnerability**

• *Further reading*

Carey, Jacqueline. "Mommy Direst," *New York Times Book Review* (24 September 1995): 30.

Gibbons, Kaye. *A Cure for Dreams.* New York: Algonquin, 1991.

_____. *The Life All Around Me by Ellen Foster.* New York: Harcourt, 2006.

_____. *On the Occasion of My Last Afternoon.* New York: G.P. Putnam's Sons, 1998.

McKee, Kathryn. "Simply Talking: Women and Language in Kaye Gibbons's *A Cure for Dreams,*" *Southern Quarterly* 35, no. 4 (Summer 1997): 97–107.

community

For Kaye Gibbons, community is a side of human involvement that enables people of differing temperaments to support and comfort each other while retaining individuality. The concept invigorates "The Headache," a short-short story issued in June 1987 in the *St. Andrew Review.* Protagonist Lucille Womble, a self-crucifying farm wife, recovers from two weeks of psychosomatic illness with the help of a trio of supporters—employer Mae Bell Stokes, Dr. Janet Cowley, and Lucille's husband Henry. For the title character in *Ellen Foster* (1987), Gibbons's first novel, community consists of those people willing to volunteer time, effort, and advice to a ten-year-old orphan in need of deliverance. The varied human facilitators in Ellen's milieu include overnight housing with Starletta's parents on New Year's Eve, 1969, short-term residence with Aunt Betsy, loving words from a field hand named Mavis in July 1970, and sheltering by an art teacher named Julia and her domestically inclined husband Roy. Ellen's nomadic existence concludes on Christmas Day, 1970, when a foster mother named Laura introduces her to the lessons of girlhood that she missed after the death of her birth mother. In a racist society, Gibbons stresses the irony of unconditional love from Starletta's mother and from Mavis, both black parents who model the kind of acceptance that Ellen hungers for and eventually locates among strangers.

Despite critical claims that Gibbons is a sexist author, "The Headache" and her second novel refute notions that females are the only solacers. In a male-centered community, Burr Stanley and "Blinking" Jack Ernest Stokes, rural contemporaries in *A Virtuous Woman* (1989), compensate each other's needs. Jack thinks of Burr as a son and delights in his wangling of 48 acres of farmland from Lonnie Hoover, who needs a husband for his pregnant daughter Tiny Fran. In a lopsided pseudo-family, the Stanleys and the Stokes support and uplift each other—Jack and his wife Ruby by sheltering Burr's daughter June from her shrewish mother Tiny Fran, and Burr and June by comforting Jack, a 65-year-old widower who retreats to a bedroom hermitage to mourn Ruby's death. In a touch of well-deserved grace, Jack accepts from Burr a parcel of land to see him through the rest of his days spent without Ruby among a farming class that values his experience and husbandly example.

In *A Cure for Dreams* (1991), Gibbons describes a similar communal embrace of the bereaved — the tenderness of local women on Milk Farm Road toward Sade Duplin, whose shotgun murder of her husband Roy goes unsolved. Lottie O'Cadhain Davies, a sympathetic female visitor and canny observer, joins other women in protecting Sade from arrest by the inept investigator, part-time Deputy Sheriff John Carroll, who is incapable of thinking like an enraged housewife. In womanly fashion, Lottie overcompliments Sade's piecrust, the culinary skill that Sade takes pride in. Other female neighbors dose Sade with paregoric to erase her terrors of a vengeful ghost. The absence of Roy, a philandering, overbearing head of household, lures Sade's older children home to tend and pamper their remaining parent. The gradual restructuring of Sade's family is an appropriate gift from local women, who console and aid each other during the Great Depression like one extended sisterhood.

Community on Milk Farm Road provides coming-of-age support during Betty Davies Randolph's teen years. Lottie, who has no intention of approving Betty's interest in her scruffy boyfriend, Luther Miracle, musters gin rummy- and pinochle-playing lady friends as a dramatic chorus. After Lottie belittles Luther for filthy hair, a dishonest mother, and lackluster father, fellow card players chime in with their own disparagements of Betty's beau. In contrast to the vigorous female community that bolsters and edifies Betty, her father, Quaker farmer-miller Charles Davies, is a friendless drone bound to a day's work and the profits he amasses. While an economic decline bedevils Charles with money worries, Betty discerns that her father accumulates wealth and land, but he "had no friends accumulated" (Gibbons, 1991, 69). Lacking the female bonding that Lottie and Betty cherish, in 1937, Charles ends his life of miserly deterioration by neatly folding his clothes before drowning himself in the river. Significantly, his choice of death allies him permanently with the antithesis of stability and buoyancy, the current that concludes his striving for comfort from tangible wealth and sweeps away his life as his head lodges between two rocks.

In the final scene of *A Cure for Dreams*, the author particularizes members of the community according to their ability to answer the needs of a vulnerable female. In a summation of the fictional impact, critic Roy Parker, Jr., reviewing for the *Fayetteville* (N.C.) *Observer*, described the novel as intense and disciplined — "a no-holds-barred story" devoid of "preachiness or prissiness" (Parker, 1991). In a one-on-one setting, Betty gives birth to Marjorie Polly Randolph, the fourth generation of O'Donough-O'Cadhain-Davies-Randolph women. Intentionally apart from Lottie during labor and childbirth, Betty accomplishes a womanly feat without the officiousness of her mother, who tends to steamroll Betty and her choices. For a surrogate parent, Betty accepts the mothering of Polly Deal, the family's housekeeper and community midwife, who makes a "deal" with Betty to birth the baby before summoning Lottie. Polly ushers the tiny girl from the womb under the oral spell of childbed chants, a folk tradition that dates to primitive forms of communal birthing, such as those practiced by Greek obstetrician Agnodice and colonial Massachusetts midwife Anne Hutchinson. As though preparing Betty's daughter for a place in the female saga, Polly protects the infant's ears and rounds out her head with gentle hands, much as women knead a delicate pie crust. Marjorie's successful passage into a female community lies in her early ability to focus on women talking, the oral product of sisterhood.

The extended female community gives place to an insular compound in *Charms for the Easy Life* (1993), Gibbons's fourth novel. Unlike the women of Milk Farm Road, in August 1936, herbalist-midwife Charlie Kate Birch retracts her microcosm to an even smaller milieu — a tri-level female household comprised of grandmother, daughter Sophia Snow Birch, and granddaughter Margaret. Before the triad forms, Charlie Kate and Sophia survive the perfidy of worthless husbands. The lesson extends to daughter Margaret a truism that men leave and women stay. Learning to depend on women is Margaret's introduction to maturity and socialization. By the time that she readies for college, she uses World War II as an excuse to extend her residency with mother and grandmother and to enjoy their literate sharing of healing methods, books, and mental stimulus. Gibbons proposes that the trio cannot hold out against a bi-gendered world by matchmaking Sophia with businessman Richard Baines, whom Sophia meets at an auspicious film, *Gone with the Wind* (1939), a fictional view of black and white female bonding in Georgia during and after the Civil War. For Margaret, Sophia's marriage on Christmas Eve 1942, the day before Charlie Kate dies in her sleep, fractures the tight community, but reveals Margaret at a stage of life where she is capable of fending for herself.

In similar feminist style, Gibbons shapes a closed community in *Sights Unseen* (1995), an autobiographical reprise of the assaults of a madwoman on a farm household. Because of the Barnes family's fear of ridicule, for over 20 years, they shield their secret from outsiders by closing up ranks. The complicity of farm hands, housekeeper Pearl Wiggins, and Grandfather Barnes with Maggie Barnes's immediate family conceals from the prying rural neighborhood the extremes of Maggie's misbehaviors. Vacations involve only insiders at the coastal retreat where Maggie's manic aberrations remain sheltered and closeted within the clan. For Hattie and her older brother, Freddy Barnes, growing up amid curious friends causes the siblings to seclude themselves and to depend on each other and a mutual love of books for emotional respite and intellectual cultivation. The author describes brother and sister as anesthesiologists in adulthood, a shared interest in medicine and in the quieting of hurt that began in their childhood home.

For her first historical novel, *On the Occasion of My Last Afternoon* (1998), Gibbons abandons character autonomy in previous works to depict the intrusion of the Civil War on the human landscape. In the preliminaries to slavery's downfall, protagonist Emma Garnet Tate Lowell survives the grandiose regionalism of her father, planter Samuel P. Goodman Tate, who murders a slave during hog-slaughtering season in 1842 for sassing his master. Married in 1847 at age 17 and resituated in Raleigh, North Carolina, Emma enjoys a peaceable urban household far removed from the James River community of her childhood home at Seven Oaks plantation in Bruton Parish, Virginia. Although conservative society rejects the Lowells, they draw friends to their home through communal love of altruism and public service to slaves, wounded soldiers, bereft women, and the underclass. Gibbons asserts that like bonds with like through the agency of goodness and eagerness to help the less fortunate.

When war threatens all layers of Raleigh society, human relationships alter with the times. Out of necessity, Emma narrows community to the Lowells' three daughters, Leslie, Louise, and Mary and to household staff, all ably managed by cook-housekeeper Clarice Washington. By war's end on April 9, 1865, the limited home community is worn thin from making do. Clarice's death from respiratory illness in 1863 and Quincy Lowell's sudden collapse from exhaustion at war's end leaves Emma to venture once more into safe harbors, first among her in-laws in Boston, then in a return to her Blount Street residence in Raleigh. The female-centered household, devoid of Clarice, embraces one of the balms of womanhood, a renewed sisterhood with Emma's unmarried sister, Maureen Tate. By extending their community to enfold widows, orphans, and the destitute, Emma and Maureen create a common bond that uplifts them both, one from widowhood and one from spinsterhood. After Maureen's unexpected death, Emma assuages multiple losses by encircling herself once more with family — daughters and sons-in-law and grandchildren — and, in 1900, by preparing for a departure from life. Rather than dread death, Emma treasures a new opportunity to bond with Quincy's spirit in a heavenly community.

In her seventh novel, *Divining Women* (2004), Gibbons characterizes a similar kinship of women as a restorative matrix. After the loss of son Daniel and husband Grammar Oliver in 1913, Martha Greene Oliver travels to New York to reunite with Judith Benedict Stafford. The two reclaim a friendship that daughter Mary Oliver describes as the recovery of a dropped stitch, a retrievable lapse that allows the pattern to advance unchanged. The visual image reprises the needlework and quilting metaphors that permeate and enrich feminist literature, including the description of Lottie's sewing and Sade Duplin's quilting in *A Cure for Dreams*. By modeling female community-building as patchwork, the author honors the ability of female quilters to recycle domestic scraps into a useful item resplendent with woman-crafted beauty.

A headlong pacing forces the story to a late climax — the dramatic female collaboration in the birthing of Ella Eloise Ross, the stillborn child of Maureen Carlton Ross. Symbolically, the end of Maureen's pregnancy and marriage occurs over November 7–9, 1918, two days before an armistice ends World War I. After Mary Oliver experiences vicarious motherhood by collaborating with Maureen and midwife Mamie during the communal delivery, the three women clasp the cooling infant corpse and share body heat, a symbol of life-giving motherhood that saves Maureen from shock and grief. The strength of female synergy invigorates Maureen, who, on November 9, manages the walk from home to the cemetery at sunset with the tiny coffin, borne by Mamie's husband Zollie. In contrast with the moribund fatherhood of Maureen's husband Troop, the affectionate trio and Zollie prefigure the "holy city" that Maureen describes in her brief eulogy (Gibbons, 2004, 207).

With the aid of a similar fervent alliance, Gibbons's first sequel, *The Life All Around Me by Ellen Foster* (2006), works through the muddle of her title character's past and future. In fall 1974, at a turning point in Ellen's 15th year, her foster mother Laura joins Starletta and Starletta's mother in a woman-to-woman confrontation with Ellen's Aunt Nadine Nelson and Cousin Dora Nelson. Like a military vanguard, Laura rejects Nadine's rude remarks about Ellen's cropped haircut and returns the discussion to Nadine's theft of Ellen's inheritance through forgery of legal documents. Surprising to Ellen is Dora's siding with Laura against a mother guilty of fraud. To Nadine's snarls, Ellen addresses 15 years of rejection: "Nothing's expected from whom nothing was given" (Gibbons, 2006, 178). Safe and loved by Laura and

Starletta's mother, on Christmas Eve, 1974, Ellen describes her feeling of support as not fearing that the floorboards will part or the ground swallow her bed. The graphic description of community as refuge captures the progress that Ellen has made in the past five years.

- *Further reading*

Gibbons, Kaye. *A Cure for Dreams*. New York: Algonquin, 1991.
_____. *Divining Women*. New York: G.P. Putnam's Sons, 2004.
_____. *The Life All Around Me by Ellen Foster*. New York: Harcourt, 2006.
McKee, Kathryn. "Simply Talking: Women and Language in Kaye Gibbons's *A Cure for Dreams*," *Southern Quarterly* 35, no. 4 (Summer 1997): 97–107.
Parker, Roy, Jr. "Elegant Family Story," *Fayetteville* (N.C.) *Observer* (14 April 1991).

A Cure for Dreams

A verbal matrix of female narratives from four generations, Gibbons's third novel creates a cumulative whole from individual stories of survival, friendship, redemption, and renewal. The text demonstrates what philosopher Charlotte Perkins Gilman termed a "mobilization of women" (Gilman, 1899, 347). The characters do battle silently, subconsciously with the gendered customs that belittle or degrade them. For the work's complexity, Padgett Powell, a critic for the *New York Times Book Review*, compared *A Cure for Dreams* (1991) to a stage drama by Lillian Hellman, a Southern feminist playwright. Gibbons took the novel's title from a real cure for dreams found in a folk medicine manual published in 1915. In the view of critic Ann Alexander, in a review for the *Greensboro* (N.C.) *News & Record*, the work is "more measured, more polished, more intentionally literary" than Gibbons's first two novels, which focus on individual character development (Alexander, 1993). Unlike the monologue of the title figure in *Ellen Foster* (1987) and the repining of farm wife, Ruby Pitts Woodrow Stokes, in *A Virtuous Woman* (1989), the female community of Milk Farm Road grows through story swapping that expands into a verbal highway from make-do to joy.

The author maintains her faith in language as the common denominator of human interaction. In the background of *A Cure for Dreams*, the great-grandmother, Bridget O'Donough O'Cadhain, lacks true communication with her lineage because she prefers Gaelic over English, even after her emigration in 1918 with Sheamus, her blustery husband, from Galway to a family enclave on the Cumberland River in Bell County, Kentucky. The Americanization of her daughter, granddaughter, and great-granddaughter produces a vibrant matrilineage that heartens and uplifts through shared oral stories of coping and endurance. As described by Jeffrey J. Folks and Nancy Summers Folks in *The World Is Our Home* (2000), by repeating the verbal wisdom of past decades, the female storykeepers use recollection as a balm for grief, guilt, and uncertainty, a trio of emotions that engulfs the text and threatens character stability. At the same time, retellings confer immortality on fragile strands of the Irish-American family's history, which surface as handholds during the Great Depression.

Gibbons tinges her good-hearted heroines with a streak of jolly wickedness. After the birth of Betty Davies to Lottie O'Cadhain Davies in 1920, the two become co-conspirators against Lottie's miserly Welsh husband, Charles Davies, a slavish Quaker farmer-miller. The two-against-one factor enables the female duo to weather a barren homelife and hard times with flair. Lottie tricks him into believing that she buys the lowest-priced fabrics out of respect for his pursy ways. From lengths of venise lace, chiffon, and beaded English netting, she updates her and Betty's wardrobe with chic styles. In collusion with the Davies women, two sales clerks conceal in their purchases surprise buttons and ribbon, a tangible reward for womanly spunk. The pulse of the O'Cadhain-Davies female line quickens hope in neighboring women, who join Lottie for a radical diversion — penny-ante gambling on gin rummy and pinochle in the back room of Porter's store. The illusion of trouncing penury and of risking loss on low-stakes card games combines with Lottie's snappy sewing styles to relieve a decade of patching, skimping, and going without.

The novel's subtext involves the basics of an endearing womanly wisdom and of surreptitious empowerment in a closed society dominated by lower middle-class men. As explained by analyst Linda Adams Barnes, the characters literally "tell themselves into existence" (Barnes, 1993, 35). From Betty's observations of Lottie at full tilt as the queen bee among rural woman come inklings of women's hidden sorrows and intimate delights, particularly the womanizing of Sade Duplin's husband Roy and the long-lived romance of Amanda and Richard Bethune, the rural community's model couple. Lottie teaches her daughter to value wifely sacrifice through stories of Grandmother Bridget's privations. The themes have a predictive power that shields Betty during her tender years. Before her coming-of-age, she learns to spot marital discord in the discourteous ways men summon their wives and in the unfortunate circumstances of white trash neighbor Trudy Woodlief and her brood of five children, left to hunger by their larcenous father Tommy. When Betty ventures into dating, Lottie vetoes Luther Miracle as unpromising and immediately spies something amiss in Stanton, a Richmond suitor who conceals addiction to Neurol Compound. More significant to female survival on Milk Farm Road is Lottie's eyes-only investigation of a shotgun murder by observing the post-traumatic response of Sade Duplin, the husband-killer. Like scraps for a quilt, these and other folk episodes contribute to the stories that pass down to Marjorie Polly Randolph, the lucky recipient of matrilineal narratives.

See also **Davies-O'Donough-O'Cadhain-Randolph genealogy; storytelling**

• *Further reading*

Alexander, Ann. "Book of Changes for Kaye Gibbons," *Greensboro* (N.C.) *News & Record* (21 March 1993).

Barnes, Linda Adams. "Telling Yourself into Existence: The Fiction of Kaye Gibbons," *Tennessee Philological Bulletin* 30 (1993): 28–35.

Folks, Jeffrey J., and Nancy Summers Folks. *The World Is Our Home.* Lexington: University Press of Kentucky, 2000.

Gibbons, Kaye. *A Cure for Dreams.* New York: Algonquin, 1991.

Gilman, Charlotte Perkins. "The Woman's Congress of 1899,"http://wyllie.libvirginia.edu:8086/perl/toccer-new?id=SteWoma.sgm&images=images/modeng&data=/texts/

english/modeng/parsed&tag=public&part=1&division=div1,1899, accessed on October 10, 2006.
McKee, Kathryn. "Simply Talking: Women and Language in Kaye Gibbons's *A Cure for Dreams*," *Southern Quarterly* 35, no. 4 (Summer 1997): 97–107.
Wood, Ralph C. "Gumption and Grace in the Novels of Kaye Gibbons," *Christian Century* 109, no. 27 (September 23–30, 1992): 842–846.

Davies, Lottie O'Cadhain

In *A Cure for Dreams* (1991), Gibbons creates an intricate North Carolina matrilineage of rural folk from Milk Farm Road, an agrarian microcosm. From Lottie O'Cadhain Davies through her daughter Betty Davies Randolph and granddaughter Marjorie Polly Randolph come life-smart antidotes to female silencing, victimization, and powerlessness. Lottie is what reviewer Sharon Lloyd Stratton, a critic for the *Richmond Times-Dispatch*, terms "an attractive, genteel social leader who moves authoritatively through life" (Stratton, 1991). As described by reviewer Dannye Romine, book editor of the *Charlotte* (N.C.) *Observer*, Lottie "has blind spots big as cannon balls," which include deceit, bossiness, jealousy, and a firmer than necessary grip on her daughter. (Romine, 1991). Overshadowing her faults, a canopy woven of cunning and will shields her from reader and reviewer disdain.

Self-direction is Lottie's strong suit. At a turning point in Betty's life, Lottie refuses to be constrained by standard grammar and syntax, which she reconfigures to suit her thought patterns. In an intimidating letter to her prospective son-in-law, Works Progress Administration worker Herman Randolph, blasting his enlistment in the navy, Lottie levels a stream of sibilance dotted with D's and T's that pock her salvo with militance. The impact is fair warning that any man daring to court Betty can expect an involved and judgmental mother-in-law. After Betty weds her sweetheart in February 1942, Lottie maintains her autonomy by rejecting Herman's mother's request for home-baked goods to accompany him to war. Asserting a nonconformist self, Lottie, in the kitchen style of her stubborn mother Bridget, states, "Cooking for enlisted men was not my pleasure" (Gibbons, 1991, 153). Like subsequent resolute protagonists—Charlie Kate Birch in *Charms for the Easy Life* (1993) and, to a lesser degree, Emma Garnet Tate Lowell and Clarice Washington in *On the Occasion of My Last Afternoon* (1998) and Mary Oliver in *Divining Women* (2004)—Lottie insists on an idiosyncratic method of combating the difficulties of the war years and the challenges of Betty's coming of age.

For Lottie Davies, the transmission of her family's past forms an ongoing tutorial for Betty. Lottie's forceful orality battles the era's standard of acceptable femininity for its attempt to subdue women, regulate their lives, and suppress their unique talents and contributions to community. From her mother's example and from stories of Irish grandmother Bridget O'Donough O'Cadhain, an immigrant to America in 1918, Betty internalizes methods of female combat against the despair and want of the Great Depression. Just as Bridget refuses to cower under her husband Sheamus's drunken bluster in Galway before she resettles in Bell County, Kentucky, Lottie develops into a similar man-tamer. In the broad view, she exemplifies the broadening of life choices by gambling at gin rummy and pinochle and by sewing spiffy outfits for herself and her daughter. In contrast to males who flaunt mantalk to assert authority over women, both Bridget and Lottie cherish womantalk as an embodiment of female empowerment, consolation, and joy. Thus, the legacy that passes to Betty's daughter Marjorie forms a tri-partite celebration of female hardihood.

• *Further reading*

Balingit, JoAnn. "Review: *A Cure for Dreams*," *Magill Book Reviews* (1 September 1991).

Branan, Tonita. "Woman and 'The Gift of Gab': Revisionary Strategies in *A Cure for Dreams*," *Southern Literary Journal* 26 (Spring 1994): 91–101.

Gibbons, Kaye. *A Cure for Dreams*. New York: Algonquin, 1991.

McKee, Kathryn. "Simply Talking: Women and Language in Kaye Gibbons's *A Cure for Dreams*," *Southern Quarterly* 35, no. 4 (Summer 1997): 97–107.

Romine, Dannye. "A Dream Come True — Third Time Out Is a Charmer for Raleigh Novelist Kaye Gibbons," *Charlotte* (N.C.) *Observer* (31 March 1991).

Stratton, Sharon Lloyd. "Family Talk Is Backbone of 'Dreams,'" *Richmond Times-Dispatch* (5 May 1991).

Davies-O'Donough-O'Cadhain-Randolph genealogy

One of Kaye Gibbons's most successful female lineages, the female line from Bridget O'Donough O'Cadhain to Marjorie Polly Randolph grows strong from a blend of cunning and tolerance:

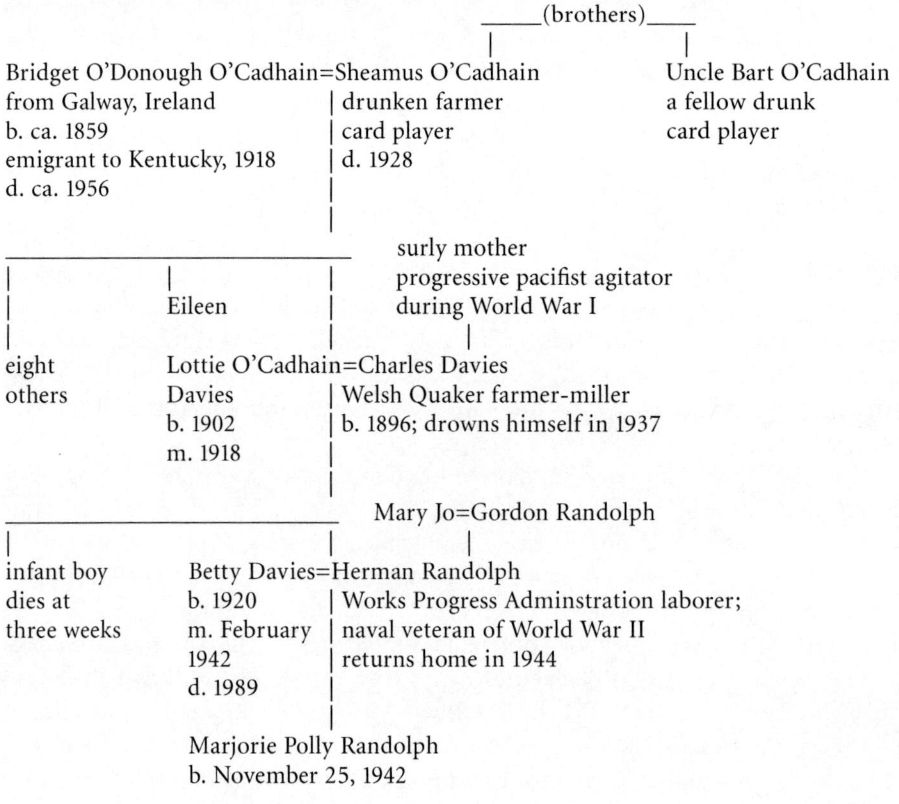

• *Further reading*

Gibbons, Kaye. *A Cure for Dreams.* New York: Algonquin, 1991.

death

Gibbons confronts death as an unavoidable reordering of character lives. She turns mortality into a liberator in her first novel, *Ellen Foster* (1987), in which the 40-year-old mother's deliberate overdose of prescription digitalis for the after-effects of open-heart surgery ends her suffering. The suicide frees the title character from a frail tether to home at the same time that it deprives her of mothering and patrimony. A quiet death in bed eases into the text with Bill's insistence that his wife sleep off the pills. The text discloses that Bill slays his wife by choosing not to intervene and by threatening to kill Elllen if she telephones for help. Snuggling with her dying mother, Ellen wills her heart to beat for herself and for the corpse that shares the other half of the bed. The image rejects Southern Gothic overtones and asserts pathos as a means of building mother-daughter drama. For Ellen, the quiet that follows her mother's struggles introduces a welcome rest that precedes domestic chaos. Gibbons recycles the symbolic child's mothering of the mother in the falling action of *On the Occasion of My Last Afternoon* (1998). In 1863, Emma Garnet Tate Lowell bids farewell to her surrogate mother Clarice Washington, the beloved black cook-housekeeper whose "daily miracles" turn a succession of family residences into homes (Gibbons, 1998, 241). Like Ellen, Emma absorbs the fleeting warmth of Clarice's body as though storing up both human energy and love.

For Gibbons's first novel, death precipitates maturity in a pre-teen girl who has borne more responsibility than childhood accommodates. The loss of a loving mother forces Ellen to apply ingenuity and guile to rescuing herself from Bill, who turns profligacy, unrequited desire, and spite against her. Defiant of Southern social codes, Ellen relieves loneliness outside her home by cultivating friendship with Starletta, a black child who becomes a figurative "little star" on Ellen's horizon. Relieved by Bill's death from alcoholism in 1970, Ellen wills him into oblivion in a coffin nailed tight to prevent stalking by the undead. She reaches back to gentler times and retraces the path that her mother leaves behind. Through maternal stories, catalog fantasy games, and gardening lessons, Ellen begins constructing her own family and selecting values that negate the dissipation, menace, and squalor that is Bill's legacy. In a testimony to Charles Darwin's theory of survival of the fittest, she proves herself capable of securing a nest in which to rest and grow into womanhood at a more appropriate pace.

At a telling moment in Ellen's character development, she shepherds her maternal grandmother toward death. The elderly shrew, suffering from flu, requires the 11-year-old's feeding and bathing as life ebbs away shortly before Christmas 1970. According to analyst Linda Adams Barnes, the third family death is a liberating moment for Ellen, who, out of a need to shed guilt, "[makes] an enormous bound in her psychological growth" by freeing herself of responsibility for her parents' demise (Barnes, 1993, 30). Out of a desire to ready the grandmother's corpse for presentation to Jesus, Ellen supplies a Sunday hat and artificial flowers as adornments to a vengeful, unlovely crone. The effort startles Aunt Nadine Nelson, whose greed predisposes her toward her own concerns rather than the earthly preparation of her mother for the grave. Gibbons interweaves the dramatic passage with humor from Ellen's scorekeeping, her assumption of blame for her mother's death and the conferral of two souls—"my daddy's and your own"—for the deceased woman to manage (Gibbons, 1987, 80). The allotment of soul supervision tires Ellen, who hopes that death has ceased its invasion of her life, a multiple intrusion that overtaxes so young a mourner.

In a second novel, *A Virtuous Woman* (1989), the author surveys regret as a human reaction to loss. In contrast to Ellen Foster's self-motivation are the whining and withdrawal of "Blinking" Jack Ernest Stokes, the 65-year-old husband of Ruby Pitts Woodrow Stokes. Unlike the mother of Ellen Foster, Ruby ponders ridding herself of John Woodrow, a loutish first husband who conveniently dies of a punctured lung in a pool hall brawl before she can shoot him with her pistol. Like the orphaned Ellen, Jack finds himself adrift after Ruby becomes addicted to cigarettes and, at age 45, coughs and spews herself to death from lung cancer. The final struggle for breath gives him the cold shudders. Ruby has her own memories of her grandmother Sophie's gradual demise amid the friendly chatter of Big Daddy. Ruby stresses the falsehood of pretending—"It's a bigger cheat than having to die" (Gibbons, 1989, 13). In a dual metaphoric glimpse of mortality, Gibbons depicts death first as Ruby's betrayer and next as the thief of Jack's solace and helpmeet, whose demise leaves him dazed and emotionally disarmed. Illusion edges out sanity after Jack senses Ruby's spiritual presence on his bed during the night. The fantasy of her return to the fragrance of lilac dusting powder mirrors the depth of Jack's sorrow and the extent to which his imagination will go to lure her back.

Like the marital scenario that begins *A Virtuous Woman*, the disaffection of a neglected, under-valued wife surges in a death scene in *A Cure for Dreams* (1991), Gibbons's third novel. Lottie O'Cadhain Davies, the mate of Welsh Quaker Charles Davies, a work-crazed, money-mad farmer and miller, refuses to honor his sudden passing. Preceding his depression, he discounts the maiming of a 17-year-old laborer in a baler, a dismembering death common to operators of farm machinery and to Southern Gothicism. In a graphic depiction of Charles's suicide in the river in 1937, the author pictures his head wedged between rocks like bookends. The image suggests the unyielding terrors of the Great Depression at the same time that it implies the suitability of gripping his head between rocks, which are as adamantly dense as his view of husbandly duties to wife and daughter Betty. Out of spite at his intractability, Lottie refuses to be solaced during the wake in the parlor, where she sits upright among local women. Her posture implies a widowhood in which she refuses to manifest phony grief or to capitulate to loss.

Lottie becomes the apt choice of companion to accompany her tough mother, Bridget O'Donough O'Cadhain, to Ireland for a premature leave taking. Gibbons extracts drollery from the failure of Bridget's plan to inveigle her dissolute husband Sheamus to escort her home to Galway. In the emotionless one-line note, daughter Eileen O'Cadhain describes how, in 1928, Sheamus has shad for dinner, then drops dead, an image that allies him with the hapless fish. Eileen and her sisters feed Bridget the notion that Lottie bears a debt to her mother since Lottie's marriage in 1918. Just as Lottie rejects fake widow's sorrow, Bridget outlives a community farewell by proving herself equal to the specter of death. Stubborn in early life and in old age, she returns to her home on the Cumberland River in Bell County, Kentucky, to live out nearly a century of matriarchy. The two role models bode well for Lottie's daughter Betty and granddaughter Marjorie, both of whom live out World War II without the comfort and backing of Betty's husband Herman, a sailor on the U.S.S. *Hornet* in the Pacific conflict.

In her fourth novel, Gibbons retreats from life-and-death drama to portray mortality as a given in human affairs. A daily communion with all aspects of human life in *Charms for the Easy Life* (1993) contributes to the well-rounded education of Margaret, the narrator. Under the tutelage of her herbalist-midwife grandmother, Charlie Kate Birch, Margaret accepts late-night death calls as a normal part of the family's unlicensed medical practice. Accompanied by Charlie Kate and Charlie Kate's daughter, Sophia Snow Birch, Margaret expertly sizes up suffering and death and hands her grandmother the essential instruments and wrappings that answer each need. Gibbons develops durability in Margaret, the inheritor of the grandmother's skills. During Sophia's Christmas Eve honeymoon to South Carolina in 1942, Margaret copes with Charlie Kate's sudden death on Christmas night by performing the traditional tasks and by calmly awaiting the community's discovery that they have lost their beloved protector and healer. The image of Margaret posed by Charlie Kate's corpse attests to the natural order of death preceding the emergence of a robust new generation. Predicting success is Charlie Kate's furtherance of romance between Margaret and Tom Hawkings, III, the son of liberal, cultivated Raleigh aristocrats.

In like fashion, Gibbons's first historical novel on the Civil War, *On the Occasion of My Last Afternoon* (1998), turns death struggles into the training ground of another heroine, narrator Emma Garnet Tate Lowell. Just as Margaret learns how to treat wounds and dose the afflicted, Emma's experience of comforting 85 victims of the Civil War who die sequentially on her lap precipitates a deepening humanism. Newspaper accounts of combat loss alert her to the imprecision of genteel Southern euphemisms. She reports that journalists avoid "die" and "dead" by referring to people who "pass" as though they glide noiselessly away from the battles of Manassas, Virginia (July 21, 1861; August 28–30, 1862), Vicksburg, Mississippi (May 14, 1863), and the Wilderness, Virginia (May 5–7, 1864). Her husband, Dr. Quincy Lowell, confers dignity on casualties and honor to their families by demanding that newspapers identify death by its name. His imperative symbolizes a shift in society as the vigorous survivors of civil war reject Victorian euphemisms for vitiating the language.

The daily impact of suffering and death readies Emma for more losses— the demise of cook-housekeeper Clarice Washington in 1863 and, two years later, the unforeseen collapse of Quincy. Unlike the pious leave-taking of Little Eva and the title figure in Harriet Beecher Stowe's *Uncle Tom's Cabin* (1852), Clarice departs in a realistic family gathering marked by sorrow and fear for the loss of her wisdom and energy. In contrast, Quincy slips away as quietly and unobtrusively as he lives, a suitable death for Gibbons's unassuming family man. Re-educated in the ineluctability of death, Emma embraces longevity, an old lady's reward/punishment for outliving loved ones. From daily visits to Quincy's grave in Boston, she draws strength and guidance. She graduates to cooking classes, where conversation and food-sharing with other women restore her zest for life. Returned to the Lowells' Blount Street home in Raleigh, North Carolina, to "pat things down," she reclaims her spirit while rescuing her sister, Maureen Tate, as well as the sorrowing, downtrodden survivors of war (Gibbons, 1998, 276). By the time that Emma reaches her last afternoon in 1900, 70 eventful years have conditioned her to the natural fate of humankind.

The comfort of shared pre-death moments opens *Divining Women* (2004), the author's seventh novel. The dawn death of Maureen Carlton Ross on September 12, 1939, strikes the mourner, Mary Oliver, with the retreat of a vertical body into a fetal position as mental faculties loosen themselves for a flight to eternity. Gibbons balances the comfort of a peaceful letting-go with a quirky series of family battles against ghosts at the Dupont Circle manse shared by the Greenes and Olivers in Washington, D.C. Other family departures include the demise in 1913 of Mary's father, Grammar Oliver, a beloved parent much mourned by his wife Martha. Most unlike Maureen in death, Daniel Oliver, the spoiled 16-year-old *"enfant terrible,"* hangs himself from a Baltimore hotel room chandelier that same year (Gibbons, 2004, 41). To his sister Mary, Daniel's abrupt self-slaying relieves the household of a demanding, selfish sybarite who destroys their pleasures and vacations with tantrums. Mary's wry comment on the return of Daniel's body in the baggage car satirizes the abasing of the ostentatious rich in their last earthly travels.

In her typical life-affirming style, Gibbons stocks scenes of World War I and the 1918 influenza pandemic with death jokes and pathos. In October, at Troop Ross's over-decorated home, the genteel comportment of a family gathering before dinner time makes Mary think of the composure of mourners awaiting the laying out of a corpse. In the resolution of Maureen's marital face-off against Troop, her punitive husband, the couple engage in a morning squabble over the Awake!, a casket intended to rescue people from premature burial. The jokes presage the tiny coffin of Ella Eloise Ross, strangled at birth on the umbilical cord. Reposed with honor and guarded her by mother, at sunset on November 9, 1918, Ella Eloise journeys to the cemetery for a brief family burial. A year later, Maureen expresses her truncated motherhood on a granite marker that takes comfort in the child's dwelling "in the heart of the Lord" (*Ibid.*, 207). The uplifting epitaph echoes Emma Garnet's sentiment that death prefaces a reunion of the blessed.

In *The Life All Around Me by Ellen Foster* (2006), the sequel to *Ellen Foster*, the title character bears a common death stigma, the regret of mother loss. Paralleling her mother's open-heart surgery, Ellen feels in her own body a deep black hole, a "raw, gouged place" made surreal by the absence of any foreseeable filling (Gibbons, 2006, 66). The dread of seeming different from normal people causes Ellen to envision the outcast, an "old odd vampire girl" aged and stooped before her time by ill-fitting shoes (*Ibid.*, 67). The classic Gothic image suggests a living form burdened by premature decrepitude. Gibbons neutralizes the orphan's morbidity with love from Laura, the foster mother. In Laura's arms, Ellen absorbs like breast milk an unending flow of acceptance and support. One of the author's uplifting scenes of womanly love, the novel's resolution reassures both Ellen and the reader that the power of *agape*, the Greek concept of selfless love, is the sole antidote to human sorrows.

• *Further reading*

Barnes, Linda Adams. "Telling Yourself into Existence: The Fiction of Kaye Gibbons," *Tennessee Philological Bulletin* 30 (1993): 28–35.
Chandler, Marilyn. "Limited Partnership," *Women's Review of Books* 6, nos. 10–11 (July 1989): 21.
Gibbons, Kaye. *Divining Women*. New York: G.P. Putnam's Sons, 2004.
_____. *Ellen Foster*. New York: Algonquin Press, 1987.
_____. *The Life All Around Me by Ellen Foster*. New York: Harcourt, 2006.
_____. *On the Occasion of My Last Afternoon*. New York: G.P. Putnam's Sons, 1998.
_____. *A Virtuous Woman*. Chapel Hill, N.C.: Algonquin Press, 1989.
Town, Caren J. *New Southern Girl: Female Adolescence in the Works of 12 Women Authors*. Jefferson, N.C.: McFarland, 2004.

dialect

For Southern fiction, dialect is an overt means of communicating and legitimizing regional flavor. Kaye Gibbons chooses the vernacular out of a belief that "there is nothing grander than the voice of the common man" (MacLellan, 1998). In an early short story, "The Headache," issued in the June 1987 *St. Andrews Review*, protagonist Lucille Womble establishes her rural background in the admission of having "birthed ten children, one weighed thirteen pounds" and of a confrontation with a snake, from which she "ain't been right since" (Gibbons, June 1987, 6, 7). In the estimation of Roy Parker, Jr., a literary critic for the *Fayetteville* (N.C.) *Observer*, Gibbons is best suited for replicating "the down-to-earth vernacular of the Southern countryside ... the voice of plain people," his term for people like Lucille, the agrarian folk of eastern piedmont North Carolina (Parker, 1991). Of her own Southern drawl, the author describes the result as sounding like Daisy Mae in Al Capp cartoons or like Elly May Clampett on *The Beverly Hillbillies*, but her literary application of regional dialect rings true to real Southern society.

In regard to replicating Carolina low-country sounds, novelist Ann Tyler credits Kaye Gibbons with "perfect pitch" (Tyler, 1991). As though bearing a nodding acquaintance with her characters, Gibbons sinks into local patois almost like a familiar posture or gait, but she manages to capture quaintness without denigrating her fictional casts. In a second novel, *A Virtuous Wife* (1989), she mines humor from Sudie Bee's set-to with her employer about feeding farm workers indoors on good china. Sudie Bee mutters, "Be like telling the pig family make theyselves at home," a comic use of a folk pronoun (Gibbons, 1989, 34). For a third novel, *A Cure for Dreams* (1991), the author works into female conversations "taking foot in hand," "the pink of the evening," the onset of menopause "when nature left me," and tea "strong enough to trot mice on," Southern metaphors that seem natural to Milk Farm Road vernacular (Morris, 1991). The authenticity of "splinter barefoot" and "wizzled up" rings true to Gibbons fans, who embrace her illiterate and semi-literate characters with a fierce possessiveness. Reviewer Ann Morris, in a critique for the *Greensboro* (N.C.) *News & Record*, elevates the author's compilation of folk speech as "a hope chest of sorts, a putting up of lost language for future generations" like icicle pickles in a Mason jar (Morris, 1991).

For Gibbons, succinct dialect contributes to fictional compactness. A reviewer for *Wilson Quarterly* lauds her for avoiding hard-handed folk talk in favor of a Southern idiom that is "dry and practical as a farmer's skin" ("Review," 1990, 95). In *A Cure for Dreams*, the folk locutions of Irish-Americans range from Irish Catholic swearing to the rural North Carolina "can-see to can't-see," a variation of "dawn to dusk" (Gibbons, 1991, 11). Narrator Betty Davies Randolph describes the emergence of twins, whom midwife Polly Deal "caught," the back-country verb for birthing (*Ibid.*, 167). A more caustic metaphor pictures Betty's grandmother, Bridget O'Donough O'Cadhain, "[backing] her ears," a mulish gesture that captures her stubbornness in demanding a family escort to Galway a half century after her emigration to a family enclave on the Cumberland River in Bell County, Kentucky (*Ibid.*, 103). Like the writings of William Faulkner, Flannery O'Connor, and Eudora Welty, the language distinguishes the poorly educated without scorn, as with cook-housekeeper Pearl Wiggins's reference to Freddy and Hattie Barnes in *Sights Unseen* (1995) as the "best chirrun," the description of anger in *Ellen Foster* (1987) as chewing nails and spitting tacks, and the pronunciation of "jubus" (dubious) in *The Life All Around Me By Ellen Foster* (2006) (Gibbons, 1995, 190; 2006, 15). All three models of semi-literate laboring-class sound and metaphor acclaim Southern dialect for its uniqueness and its harmonizing of common speech with vivid onomatopoeia.

Gibbons outfits characters with utterances as idiosyncratic as fingerprints. Tenant farmer "Blinking" Jack Ernest Stokes, a 65-year-old widower in *A Virtuous Woman* (1989), speaks a Carolina strain common to eastern piedmont tobacco country. He epitomizes the home-bred local who has never ventured beyond the land of his forebears. His syntactic patterns include the indigenous subjunctive in "it won't so much like I felt like" and the mischosen pronoun in "trying to shove Jesus down I and mama's throats" (Gibbons, 1989, 60, 16). Native to the coastal Carolinas are "might could," "bout as well," "telefoam," "bitch bites," and "off away from out here," a characteristic adverb string that imparts four degrees of separation. In disgust at the immorality of Tiny Fran Hoover, Jack chooses a barnyard image, "showing her tail" (*Ibid.*, 96). In reference to the withering effects of lung cancer in his wife, Ruby Pitts Woodrow Stoke, he sums up malignancy with a general distaste for "such as that," an inexplicit term that bears his desperation to distance himself from unimaginable physical deterioration (*Ibid.*, 5). To differentiate the social status of Jack from his more genteel wife, Gibbons discloses intellectual thoughts to reflect an upbringing among the Pitts clan, a more educated landed gentry. Contemplative and self-revelatory, Ruby is capable of a depth of expression unencumbered by her husband's rural diction and folk syntax.

A skillful depiction of dialect differentiates race as well as socio-economic strata in *On the Occasion of My Last Afternoon* (1998), Gibbons's first historical novel. Along the James River in 1842, the mix of African and Southern language creates what the author calls a "*mirepoix* (blend)," a culinary term that refers to the aromatic vegetables that serve as a base for savory cooking (Gibbons, 1998, 13). Amid the hubbub arising from a slave murder during winter hog-slaughtering at Seven Oaks Plantation, standard English merges with Afro-American dialect and Gullah. The latter is a West African argot of the newly enslaved Guinea negroes just arrived from Charleston, exemplified by "jubus" for "dubious," "bluegum" to describe oral racial traits, "Missa Tate" to name the master, "bidness" for business, and freedwoman Clarice Washington's "might oughten" for "should" and her description of her foster son, Samuel P. Goodman Tate, as "so come apart" from family trauma (*Ibid.*, 7, 13, 12, 14, 239). With a survivor's finality, she declares an end to plantation rumblings about Samuel's murder of the slave Jacob: "And what I say 'bout this one, *he* dead? I say, Let it go" (*Ibid.*, 14). The monosyllabic utterance captures Clarice's rhythm and fire as well as her authority over serious plantation matters.

From so horrific a beginning, Gibbons maintains a path between good and evil on her way toward the novel's serene conclusion. During the fostering of Lavinia Ella Mae Dawes, an underclass child from the flats, the Quincy Lowell family invites her to a staging of *Macbeth*. She asks to read along with the dialogue so nothing will "alarm up at" her (*Ibid.*, 118). Long after Clarice's death from pneumonia in 1863, her idiosyncratic commentary survives in a female compendium, the annotations recorded in a family copy of *The Williamsburg Art of Cookery*, a reliquary of foods and cooking styles dating to the earliest European settlement of tidewater Virginia. While Emma Garnet Tate Lowell acquires a late-in-life competence in the kitchen, she hears an echo of Clarice rebutting plantation mistress Alice Tate's critique of egg pudding. Clarice's note retorts in idiom, "Your mouth must be off," a written example of her monosyllabic utterances (*Ibid.*, 266). Implicit in the comment is Clarice's repudiation of over-refined tastes and false words. Her renunciation of black subservience injects backbone into Emma at a needy moment in Emma's adulthood.

The toney background of Gibbons's seventh novel, *Divining Women* (2004), seems devoid of dialect until the arrival of narrator Mary Oliver in Elm City, North Carolina. On September 30, 1918, her first train trip from Washington, D.C., to the South introduces her to Mamie and Zollie, the black family retainers who exhibit the residue of slave times—economic peonage and personal and social obsequiousness to their white employer, Troop Ross. Mamie, like Clarice Washington, makes short work of her kitchen duties, which she describes as "up to my elbows in lard" (Gibbons, 2004, 55). Unfortunately for the novel, a letter from Zollie after the death of his two boys and his sister strains the reader's acceptance of so garbled a model of semi-literacy. In less mawkish black dialect, on November 8, 1918, Mamie summons Mary to share a two-sided warming of Maureen's body after she gives birth to Ella Eloise, a stillborn daughter. In Mamie's terms, "All over. We have to bring up her thermometer" (*Ibid.*, 187). The pressing of black flesh on white so heartens Maureen that she orders Mary to telegraph Maureen's mother about the extraordinary love of a black domestic.

Dialect in Gibbons's sequel *The Life All Around Me by Ellen Foster* (2006) perpetuates a low-key survey of speech in North Carolina working-class communities. Tweaking the professional class, the text pictures the school librarian referring to the attacker of a retarded girl as a "hulking, sonabitch, grain-fed fool," a testimonial to the tangy, field-bred insults that pepper Southern speech (Gibbons, 2006, 163). While sitting on the stone wall outside school with friends Luther, Marvin, and Stuart, the title figure joins the others in remarking "Huh" to Martha to acknowledge her late arrival after opening the family store (*Ibid.*, 59). Stuart repeats the interjection to emphasize annoyance with Ellen for sharing her attention with the others. To stifle Luther's exhibitionism, Martha's retort begins with "boy howdy," a standard introduction to a snappy comeback (*Ibid.*). Marvin, who is failing English, refers to a hot fall when he and "deddy like to of [almost] had to sleep in the chimley," a fair estimation of eastern piedmont agrarian argot (*Ibid.*, 59–60). Less believable are Ellen's colloquialisms, such as her quotation of William Faulkner's descriptive "narrow-assted" for "thin-hipped" (*Ibid.*, 212). So regressive a trait in a brilliant student disquiets journalist Lauren Collins, a critic for the *New York Times Book Review*, who describes the unnatural language as "forcing a thoroughbred to behave like a trick pony" (Collins, 2006, 15).

See also **language; writing**

• *Further reading*

Collins, Lauren. "Older, Wiser," *New York Times Book Review* (5 March 2006): 15.
Gibbons, Kaye. *A Cure for Dreams*. New York: Algonquin, 1991.
_____. *Divining Women*. New York: G.P. Putnam's Sons, 2004.
_____. *Ellen Foster*. New York: Algonquin Press, 1987.
_____. "The Headache," *St. Andrews Review* (June 1987): 3–8.
_____. *The Life All Around Me by Ellen Foster*. New York: Harcourt, 2006.
_____. *On the Occasion of My Last Afternoon*. New York: G.P. Putnam's Sons, 1998.
_____. *Sights Unseen*. New York: G.P. Putnam's Sons, 1995.
_____. *A Virtuous Woman*. Chapel Hill, N.C.: Algonquin Press, 1989.
Lanham, Fritz. "Truths Unplotted," *Houston Chronicle* (15 October 1995).
MacLellan, Erin. "More on Gibbons," *Greensboro* (N.C.) *News & Record* (12 July 1998).
Morris, Ann. "Gibbons' 'A Cure for Dreams' Is a Hope Chest of Language," *Greensboro* (N.C.) *News & Record* (31 March 1991).
Parker, Roy, Jr. "Elegant Family Story," *Fayetteville* (N.C.) *Observer* (14 April 1991).
"Review: *Ellen Foster* and *A Virtuous Woman*," *Wilson Quarterly* 14, no. 1 (Winter 1990): 95.
Souris, Stephen. "Kaye Gibbons's *A Virtuous Woman*: A Bakhtinian Iserian Analysis of Conspicuous Agreement," *Southern Studies* 3 (Summer 1992): 99–115.
Tyler, Ann. "Fiercely Precise: Kay Gibbons' World of Southern Womanhood," *Chicago Tribune* (24 March 1991).
Wood, Ralph C. "Gumption and Grace in the Novels of Kaye Gibbons," *Christian Century* 109, no. 27 (September 23–30, 1992): 842–846.

displacement

Kaye Gibbons portrays character comfort and discomfort in terms of positioning in time, place, and socio-economic milieu. The short-short story "The Headache," issued in June 1987 in the *St. Andrews Review*, pictures farm wife Lucille Womble enjoying a rare dinner out at a chicken restaurant, a treat financed by her oldest son Franklin. Upon seizing and hiding a purse abandoned in the ladies' room, she distances herself from family with self-accusations of trashy behavior. At the extreme of her mental torment lie visions of suicide. Reclamation of Lucille requires dual female intervention — the advice of employer Mae Bell Stokes to make an appointment with a new physician, Dr. Janet Cowley. Acting on the doctor's advice, Lucille replaces herself in social status and personal regard by snuggling close to husband Henry and offering to confess the source of psychosomatic crying, insomnia, head pain, and flashbacks. Gibbons indicates that marital intimacy returns to Lucille her former status as goodwoman.

The author chooses displacement as the focus of her first novel *Ellen Foster* (1987), which launched the author's career. In 1969 at age ten, the title character suffers a multi-faceted dislocation of self from family and from mothering. Precipitating homelessness for Ellen is her mother's marriage out of socio-economic class to Bill, a truculent ne'er-do-well who earns a living selling bootleg liquor to blacks. The familial rift alienates the gentrified mother from Ellen's maternal grandmother, who damns Bill by association as a nigger. On Saturdays, when he passes out on the bathroom floor, it is Ellen's job to roust him out of the way and to shepherd her mother back to bed as though Ellen parents both adults. Because the child lacks physical powers of intervention, she chooses to be a silent and disapproving presence in a toxic atmosphere. When the couple meets alone in the kitchen, Ellen feels responsible for defending her mother against Bill, a virulent model of the brooding slacker who bad-mouths his subservient wife. To supervise the bedroom, Ellen further displaces herself further by demanding to sleep in her crib, a retreat to infancy that allows her temporary supervision of her mismated parents.

In the rising conflict, the author imagines a storm approaching, an image of an amorphous, ungovernable cosmic uprising that foreshadows the implosion of Ellen's household. Upon the 40-year-old mother's suicide in March 1969 from an overdose of prescription digitalis, the loss both overwhelms and frees Ellen from ongoing misery at the same time that it isolates her from caring society. She seizes some stability through a standard American outlet — by joining a Girl Scout troop and by making up requirements for merit badges. Alone at Christmas, she purchases and wraps her own holiday surprises as a fantasized celebration. Because the father morphs into a potential rapist, on New Year's Eve, 1969, an inborn sense of danger propels Ellen into the cold to seek shelter with Starletta, daughter of a black family. Ellen's flight manifests an extreme choice of haven for a white girl born in the racist South. Gibbons reveals that eating and drinking at Starletta's table and sharing a bed with a black sleeper worsen the sense of dislocation. Ironically, a subsequent spying on the family of Mavis, a field hand, leaves Ellen yearning for the kind of love she has found only among blacks. Four nomadic moves to the homes of art teacher Julia, Aunt Betsy, Ellen's grandmother, and Aunt Nadine Nelson and Cousin Dora serve as intermediate steps in the choice of a foster parent, an outsider who accepts and loves Ellen for herself at Christmas, 1970, a blessed day on the Christian calendar. Comfortable at last in a safe milieu, the child relinquishes the adult burdens that rob her of belonging.

Loss of place in an older girl undergirds the restlessness of Ruby Pitts Woodrow Stokes in *A Virtuous Woman* (1989), Gibbons's second novel. Reared among the landed gentry, at age 18, she unwisely fights boredom by eloping with 26-year-old

John Woodrow, an overbearing migrant laborer. His constant goading of "little Miss Vanderbilt" reminds her that she seems too privileged to belong to the itinerant farm class (Gibbons, 1989, 40). His death in a pool hall knifing through the lungs ends her two-year marriage to a drunken womanizer, but she feels unworthy to return to the Pitts farm to seek her family's reclamation. Ruby's inability to reroot on home soil arises from gender boundaries. Male dominance situates her brothers, Jimmy and Paul, on the Pitts acreage, but relegates Ruby to the kitchen window to watch the men at a distance. Through a dual husband-and-wife narration, the author stresses Ruby's need for "Blinking" Jack Ernest Stokes, her second husband, a tenant farmer twice her age whose acceptance and love outweigh the class and background differences that separate them. Securing her place in their home is Jack's need for tending and feeding, a void that she leaves unfilled after her death at age 45 from lung cancer. The text implies that Jack becomes displaced in his own home when he retreats into canned soup, bowls of corn flakes, bourbon, Roadrunner cartoons, the fragrance of Ruby's lilac dusting powder, and fantasies of her ghostly visitation to his bed. Burr Stanley's gift of land to Jack solaces another part of his petulance — to own the fields he has worked all his life.

In her fifth novel, *Sights Unseen* (1995), Gibbons reverses displacement to describe the self-exile of narrator Hattie Barnes. While living in a household ravaged by her mother Maggie's surges of moping and insanity, Hattie occupies a closed compound to which she invites no playmates. Rather than develop friendships with peers, she chooses the motherliness of Pearl Wiggins, the family cook-housekeeper. Hattie accounts for her standoffishness from other families as a protection of the self from visiting a normal home, an orderly household that contrasts the chaos in the Barnes residence. She admits to feeling a strong affection for dolls, but she avoids open-armed embraces of friends or membership in the Girl Scouts as methods of shielding the family secret of a madwoman on the loose. Ultimately, alienation comes to an end in 1967 after Maggie Barnes returns from Duke Hospital a changed woman from psychotherapy and eight weekly electroconvulsive shock treatments. After she rights herself as self-controlled wife and mother, Hattie breathes easier and abandons the walling off of the family secret from potential pity, curiosity, or ridicule from outsiders. Symbolically, Gibbons places her narrator in a life-affirming job: Hattie aims her considerable intellectual talent at a career in anesthesiology, a job that allows her to relocate the suffering in temporary serenity.

In Gibbons's first historical novel, *On the Occasion of My Last Afternoon* (1998), interwoven forms of uprooting undergird a story of wretched childhood and wartime hardship. Emotionally displaced at Seven Oaks plantation in Bruton Parish, Virginia, narrator Emma Garnet Tate Lowell, like Hattie Barnes in Pearl's kitchen, seeks communion with women in the domestic domain. In 1842, after her father, planter Samuel P. Goodman Tate, murders the slave Jacob during hog-killing season, 12-year-old Emma retreats to the work space of freedwoman Clarice Washington, a cook-housekeeper who sets the child to a slave chore seasoning pork and patting out sausage. The respite serves two purposes— shielding Emma Garnet from plantation mayhem and training her in household duties, a haven that she returns to in widowhood.

The protagonist's disjuncture with family parallels the growing national unease during the death pangs of Southern sectionalism and the flesh trade. As Emma reaches her teens, the rantings of her father worsen at threats to the slave economy from abolitionism and secession. The plot portrays the disparate effects of outrages on Emma and her brother Whately, a student at Washington College in Lexington, Virginia. After Samuel ousts Whately from home at Christmas for impregnating a barmaid, at age 17, Emma looks to marriage to Dr. Quincy Lowell to rid her of Samuel's daily blow-ups and to bind her to the type of family she has never known. Contributing to her mixed feelings about home are the loss of Whately, who dies in 1845 at age 20 of syphilis on Sullivan's Island near Charleston, South Carolina, and Emma's separation from Alice, who has parted from her two oldest children at a time when the mother has little control over her own domain. Of the whole Tate family, Alice seems the most seriously expatriated from the decorum and values of the Old South. In 1847, worries about Alice follow Emma across the state line to her new home in Raleigh, North Carolina, where mother hunger nags at Emma's contentment. Gibbons depicts her restiveness as an inner landscape devoid of the birth parent who truly treasured her.

While establishing herself as wife, female head of household, and mother, Emma juggles variances in belonging. In a house on Blount Street run by Clarice, the Lowells relish an edenic calm and joy in parenthood. Simultaneously, the betrayal of social maven Lucille McKimmon forces Emma to resituate herself in polite society. In the urban milieu a few blocks from the governor's mansion, both Lowells readily befriend liberals who establish their own ground rules by disdaining slavery and Southern arrogance. When the Civil War threatens Lowell family stability, Emma embraces home for a different purpose — a reprieve from duties as a volunteer nurse in the critical care ward at the Fair Grounds hospital and a brief daily reunion of her family circle of three daughters— Leslie, Louise, and Mary — and a badly overtaxed husband. Although the Confederate surrender at Appomattox Court House on April 9, 1865, secures the nation, disruption resurfaces over the course of subsequent losses—first Clarice from respiratory illness in 1863, then Quincy from exhaustion in 1865. Gibbons heightens the end of a marriage with a graceful observation that Quincy "slipped away as gently as he had lived" (Gibbons, 1998, 260). The ebb and flow of Emma's life toughens her, but the loss of her supportive husband once more dislodges her from a secure orbit.

Gibbons describes discomposure as an element of perspective. Moved by train from the South to her in-laws in Boston, Emma silently gnaws the back of her hand as Quincy's casket descends into the earth much as her husband quietly recedes from her life. She clings to a shred of wedlock by visiting the grave and by listening for his voice in her memories. In her view of acclimating to widowhood, she is helping Quincy to "settle," an incongruous term that contrasts her post-funeral emotional agitation. As self-centering returns, like a lamp on a gimbal, she rights herself in a new persona emerging from the "short rows of grief" (*Ibid.*, 267). The term resonates with irony from a woman enriched in girlhood by the stoop labor of field hands, one of whom her father nearly beheads for failing to observe slave-master decorum. Like newly freed blacks, Emma sheds the onus of sorrow and moves up the row toward an unknown destiny.

Gibbons extols Emma for her ability to absorb hurt with determination and fortitude. To a Union veteran, the protagonist differentiates between social uprooting and a loathing of the North, a post-war attitude she characterizes as unreasonable. Stabilized by classes in cookery, she gradually distances herself from Quincy's remains and returns to the South. In Raleigh once more with sister Maureen, Emma follows Clarice's example by energizing the Blount Street kitchen. In charitable mode, Emma ensconces herself in a womanly sphere of cooking and supporting the unfortunates hardest hit during the Reconstruction era. She becomes a living example of the Christian concept of receiving through giving. In 1900, on the last day of her 70 years, she feels prepared for the final disunion with earth, a liberation she expects to remate her with Quincy. The grace of her demise expresses Gibbons's notion of displacement as a state of mind rather than a shift in locale.

The action of Gibbons's seventh novel, *Divining Women* (2004), perpetuates the author's interest in character habituation to an unsettling time, place, and social milieu. On September 30, 1918, Mary Oliver, a 22-year-old graduate student at Radcliffe from Washington, D.C., has no inkling of what to expect from her first journey into the South. Her intent is to ease the final days of a difficult pregnancy of her aunt, Maureen Carlton Ross, a spiritually bashed wife. On the scene in Elm City, North Carolina, Mary expresses the attitude of the New Woman toward the denigration of women. Demanding ingenuity and guile, the home situation horrifies Mary for the unnerving torments that Troop Ross heaps on his dispirited wife. For Maureen, wedlock to a despot becomes a life-threatening displacement from self.

Maureen's emotional shackling replicates the straits of Danaë and Andromeda in Greek mythology, fairy tales of Rapunzel and Snow White, the nursery rhyme "Peter, Peter, Pumpkin Eater," and the jailing of Hester Prynne, heroine of Nathaniel Hawthorne's Puritan fable *The Scarlet Letter* (1850). Troop, a turnkey emotionally stunted by an upbringing based on spite and self-aggrandizement, harasses Mary for intruding and siding with Maureen and for demanding baskets of fruit and tender care of swollen feet. The two women withdraw into a private refuge, the feminine boudoir that Maureen creates for herself in an eyesore house decorated to suit a social climber. Gradually, Mary, like Laura in *Ellen Foster* and Emma Garnet in *On the Occasion of My Last Afternoon*, breaks through the double standard. She discovers an unforeseen reward of volunteerism, an emotional haven shared with a damaged loved one. Gibbons stresses that the financial worth of belonging and residence matters little after Maureen delivers Ella Eloise Ross, a stillborn daughter strangled on the umbilical cord on November 8, 1918. After committing Ella to her grave the next day at sunset, Mary maintains spiritual union with Maureen by shepherding her north by train to Washington. The departure accounts for the tone and atmosphere of the opening scenario, in which Mary shares with Maureen over two decades of serenity and contentment in a more salubrious setting.

Gibbons resumes her interest in Ellen Foster's uprooting in a sequel, *The Life All Around Me by Ellen Foster* (2006). Living with foster mother Laura in fall 1974 allows Ellen to feel "looser in the neck than usual" with the rightness of her placement (Gibbons, 2006, 151). Although physically secure and emotionally welcome among high school students, Ellen suffers flashbacks to homelessness and orphanhood that struck at age eleven. Rattling around in her head are loose images of mother-daughter love in childhood and of rejection from relatives' homes. As her intellectual accomplishments press her toward womanhood, she must resolve the emotional issues that demand answers. Like a sheriff-to-outlaw walk-down on Main Street in *High Noon*, she confronts her aunt, Nadine Nelson, and demands restitution of property and tangible evidence of a mother's love. In the novel's resolution, a quiet perusal of personal belongings and a hospital summation of mental disorder in Ellen's mother Shine on September 10, 1968, acquaint Ellen with the woman she knew only from a child's perspective. A dramatic example of rerooting, Ellen's retreat from outsized fears and personal misgivings strips her of dissociation with place and time. Like the lost lamb in Jesus's parable in Luke 15:3–7, Ellen embraces her foster home as a final stop on her quest for security.

See also **belonging; social class**

• *Further reading*

Gibbons, Kaye. *The Life All Around Me by Ellen Foster*. New York: Harcourt, 2006.
_____. *On the Occasion of My Last Afternoon*. New York: G.P. Putnam's Sons, 1998.
_____. *Sights Unseen*. New York: G.P. Putnam's Sons, 1995.
_____. *A Virtuous Woman*. Chapel Hill, N.C.: Algonquin Press, 1989.
Harris, Michael. "Scenes— and Skeletons— of a Troubled Southern Family," *Los Angeles Times* (9 October 1995): 5.
Munafo, Giavanna. "Colored Biscuits: Reconstructing Whiteness and the Boundaries of 'Home' in Kaye Gibbons's Ellen Foster," *Women, America, and Movement*. ed. Susan L. Roberson. Columbia: University of Missouri Press, 1998, pp. 38–61.

Divining Women

Divining Women (2004) characterizes the strengths of women to overcome domestic misery. Opening with a rhapsodic ode to sisterhood, Gibbons supersedes suspense by looking two decades beyond the story to the serene lives shared by female co-protagonists, Mary Oliver and Maureen Carlton Ross. The conflict depicts the male coercion of Maureen by her husband Troop, a psychologically rough-hewn industrialist. The setting, a graphic model of the double standard, undulates with malice. As feminist author Louisa May Alcott describes in "A Whisper in the Dark" (1863), "The air is poison, the solitude is fatal" (Alcott, 2000, 57). Troop uses as an excuse for acrimony Maureen's episodes of self-expression, which he interprets as "female hysteria," a sexist descriptor of the female demand for autonomy (Gibbons, 2004, 62). The conflict allows Gibbons to dramatize a central feminist issue, female autonomy in what novelist George Sand called a "condition of inequality, inferiority, and of the dependence of one sex upon the other" (Schneir, 1972, 30)

Set during World War I in Elm City, North Carolina, the plot, according to critic Donna Seaman, a reviewer for *Booklist*, is a "gorgeously moody and piquant fairy tale, an updating of the madwoman in the attic in Charlotte Brontë's *Jane Eyre*" (Seaman, 2004). Like Brontë's attempt to acclimate governess Jane Eyre to Thornfield, the manse of Edward Rochester, Gibbons pictures in little the daily anguish of a pregnant woman enmeshed in domestic hostility that hovers in the atmosphere like a pernicious aura. The safe birth of Maureen's first child and her release from torment become the missions of Troop's niece, Mary Oliver, a 22-year-old graduate student at Radcliffe. Arriving by train from Washington, D.C., on September 30, 1918, Mary recognizes Troop's verbal lashings as the equivalent of brutalizing a prisoner of war. At a fragile point in Maureen's selfhood, Mary tempers a woman hovering on the raw edge of insanity, a concern of female protagonists in Gibbons's short story "The Headache" (1987) and her novels *Ellen Foster* (1987) and *Sights Unseen* (1995).

Writer-reviewer Judi Goldenberg, a critic for the *Richmond Times-Dispatch*, praises Gibbons for creating a palpable sense of time and place. On the first confrontation between Troop and Maureen, Mary speaks her candid observations of an unorthodox marital environment. The unpredictable home scene, a domestic parallel to the bomb blasts and machine gun strafings of the Western Front, centers Maureen's private combat — a home birthing on November 8, 1918, that ends in her daughter Ella Eloise's strangulation by the umbilical cord. To the chagrin of the pompous Troop Ross, Gibbons orchestrates the end of his marriage the next day in a public place — the sidewalk outside the house. At sunset, Mary, Maureen, and the family servants, Zollie and Mamie, transport the small white coffin to the cemetery in full view of neighbors who censure Troop's tirades. The date coincides with the winding down of world war only two days before the armistice. A brief coda words Maureen's farewell to her newborn with honor to mothers who deliver their babes "into the arms of grace" (Gibbons, 2004, 207).

• *Further reading*

Alcott, Louisa May. *The Portable Louisa May Alcott.* New York: Penguin, 2000.

Gibbons, Kaye. *Divining Women.* New York: G.P. Putnam's Sons, 2004.

Goldenberg, Judi. "To Endure, Women Form Bond," *Richmond Times-Dispatch* (9 May 2004).

Schneir, Miriam, ed. Feminism: *The Essential Historical Writings.* New York: Vintage, 1972.

Seaman, Donna. "Review: *Divining Women,*" *Booklist* 100, no. 13 (1 March 2004): 1133.

Smith, Starr E. "Review: *Divining Women,*" *Library Journal* 129, no. 5 (15 March 2004).

dreams

Dreams infest Kaye Gibbons's fiction with night-time battles against day-time terrors. In a short-short story, "The Headache," published in the June 1987 issue of the *St. Andrews Review*, protagonist Lucille Womble inflicts herself with two weeks of psychosomatic ailments that range from weeping, insomnia, and anxiety attacks to dreams of a fanged monster. The result of concealing a purse abandoned in a restaurant ladies' room, the mental barrage assails the farm wife, who already battles home chores for a family of twelve. At the looming edge of her self-punishment lie visions of suicide. After confessing her ethical lapse to a physician, Dr. Janet Cowley, Lucille successfully rids herself of nightly phantasms. Clasped in the arms of her husband Henry, she accepts his compliments of her goodness and looks forward to the gift of two hats, a symbolic head protector that doubles the potency of her cure.

Similarly, for the title figure in *Ellen Foster* (1987), reveries become battlefields for the fantasies and dreamscapes that dramatize insecurity and pent-up fury. In 1969, a maelstrom of hostility and vengeance churns in ten-year-old Ellen, causing her to dream of vomiting the tensions that wrack her waking moments. At the center of the nightmare whirls a circus image — her maternal grandmother wearing a "big clown smile," a blaring symbol of duplicity and spite (Gibbons, 1987, 73). The specter suits a family matriarch who decorates her home in expensive baubles while forcing Ellen into mid–July field labor. Redeemed from the downward swirl of hatred and vengeance, Ellen reports in chapter 12 that she awakens in a foster home refreshed and optimistic, an indication of psychic wholeness among strangers that is unattainable among blood kin.

Gibbons projects an adult fantasy in the dreams of "Blinking" Jack Ernest Stokes, a 65-year-old widower in her second novel, *A Virtuous Woman* (1989). Deflated by the loss to lung cancer of his 45-year-old soulmate, Ruby Pitts Woodrow Stokes, he retreats to bed, a symbol of their physical and spiritual union throughout a quarter century of marriage. In his sorrow, he perceives his wife's spirit lying on top of the covers and struggles to separate reality from wishful thinking that Ruby "can do anything she wants to" (Gibbons, 1989, 146). Like a love-smitten suitor, he ponders wooing her back the next night by sprinkling lilac dusting powder on clean sheets. Frustrated with grief and loneliness, he can only grasp her pillow and sob for his beloved "haint." Gibbons's most troubling conclusion, the decline of Jack into dreams and fantasies honors his devotion to Ruby while questioning a grown man's inability to accept human mortality.

As examples of the threat of gauzy unreality to female characters, the author chooses ephemeral illusions for her third novel, *A Cure for Dreams* (1991). The title seems rooted in Ruby's declaration in *A Virtuous Woman*, "Daydreaming, loving the wrong man, smoking, all habits hard to break" (*Ibid.*, 78). The source of conflict in heroine Lottie O'Cadhain Davies arises by the confluence of Brownies Creek and the Cumberland River, a symbol of her infortuitous dive into a more treacherous vortex than she anticipates. Mooning over an imaginary rescuer approaching on horseback, she pictures a violently erotic scenario — a one-shot cowboy capable to putting a hole through her ball of worsted, a graphic symbol of female deflowering. Central to her self-restraint, the dream rider's exit always leaves her alone and unclaimed, like damaged goods. Unfortunately, Charles Davies, the man who does propose wedlock in 1918, lacks even the dash and promise of the phantom lover. Perhaps through self-denial, Lottie condemns herself to disaffection by uniting with a farmer-miller whose dream centers on money as a palpable reward for constant toil. Faithful to the title, Gibbons concludes the novel two generations later with a glimpse of baby Marjorie Polly Randolph, Lottie's granddaughter, who shakes off sleep to absorb the sounds of women talking, the conversational cure for dreams that redeems women by pressing them into action.

The resolution of Gibbons's fifth novel, *Sights Unseen* (1995), inflates residual fear of mother loss in 1967 after Maggie Barnes returns from successful psychotherapy and eight electroconvulsive shock treatments at Duke Hospital for manic depression. Frederick, her faithful husband, has a recurrent nightmare of field hands recovering Maggie's drowned remains from an irrigation pond and dumping her on the doorstep like a cat revelling in a successful hunt. Clothed in white eyelet robe weighted with rocks, she mirrors the self-liberating suicide of feminist writer Virginia Woolf, who, in 1941, used a similar method of escaping mental torment. The dream immobilizes Frederick until the imaginary Maggie revives and lambastes him for firing the Mexican laborers before the seasonal cucumber harvest. A touch of black humor, the revived corpse reprises sci-fi trickery, like the Vincent Price film ploys that invest Freddy Barnes's imagination. Both funny and ghastly, the talking dead suggests Maggie's retreat from white-clad femininity to the raving banshee who once haunted the Barnes household.

In a more hopeful conjugal scenario, a dual dreamscape dramatizes marital harmony in *On the Occasion of My Last Afternoon* (1998). Because of Lucille McKimmon's cruel reminder of 20-year-old Whately Tate's death from syphilis in 1845 on Sulivan's Island outside Charleston, South Carolina, narrator Emma Garnet Tate Lowell sinks into a three-day stupor self-induced by laudanum purloined from Quincy Lowell's medical bag. In and out of a surreal state, she is able to "bob up once in a while and touch his shirt," a palpable reality that ensures her survival (Gibbons, 1998, 63). As the husband hovers over his pregnant wife and shares her troubled visions, Quincy sleep-talks and demands that Emma revive. Pressed down with sorrow for Whately and with fear that an unwise dose of sedative threatens her unborn baby, she responds to his request for popcorn by sleep-walking to the kitchen and returning with his snack, the only food she knows how to prepare. The real-unreal aura of her dreams persists after his death, when conversations at his grave prefigure her final afternoon. In 1900, at age 70, Emma reverts to a benevolent dream-state — half on earth and half in the beyond with Quincy. The reverie rounds out a life of harsh realities that slides effortlessly toward eternal rest.

See also **vulnerability**

• *Further reading*

Gibbons, Kaye. *Ellen Foster.* New York: Algonquin Press, 1987.
_____. *On the Occasion of My Last Afternoon.* New York: G.P. Putnam's Sons, 1998.
_____. *A Virtuous Woman.* Chapel Hill, N.C.: Algonquin Press, 1989.
McKay, Mary A. "Gray Ghosts: Civil War and Remembrance through the Eyes of Another Compelling Kaye Gibbons Character," *Times-Picayune* (16 August 1998): D6.

education

In real and fictional environments, Gibbons surrounds her family and characters with opportunities for learning and intellectual advancement. Undergirding her regard for education is a respect for personal tastes and dislikes, such as guilt for never having read Leo Tolstoy's epic *War and Peace* (1869), which she proposed consuming in Cliffs Notes form. In a book review of Susan Vreeland's *The Forest Lover* in the March 14, 2004, edition of the *Atlanta Journal-Constitution*, Gibbons reveals elements of her mothering style, particularly her attempts to educate three daughters. To rescue them from overly descriptive literature she chooses to "load them up and haul them off to buy Cliffs Notes," a source of summary and explanation that relieves tedious passages (Gibbons, "In 1912"). Fueling her rebellion against outdoorsy prose is a psychological failing she calls "exteriors neurosis," a personal distaste that she readily acknowledges to her children (*Ibid.*).

The author equates learning with an innate hunger, like a longing for water and nourishment. The title character in *Ellen Foster* (1987), Gibbons's first novel, absorbs experience with the same fervor that impels her toward the county bookmobile. From her gentle mother, Ellen learns to select beans at the height of their goodness, an image that comforts and sustains her like home-cooked meals and borrowed books. Following discriminating reading, Ellen acquires a respect for literature, especially verse, which tranquilizes her during the disintegration of her home and family. The memorization of poems, an intellectual activity that Gibbons enjoyed in childhood, girds Ellen for hardship, providing a rhythm for hoeing and a mental oasis that "breaks up the day" from insecurity and worries about overbearing relatives (Gibbons, 1987, 64). The flight of a troubled mind into abstractions reflects the intellectual escapism of Robert Frost's poem "Choose Something Like a Star" (1947), which exalts the selection of ideals "to stay our minds on and be staid."

Like the home learning of Ellen and her mother, in *A Cure for Dreams* (1991), Gibbons allies Betty Davies Randolph with her mother, Lottie O'Cadhain Davies, a wiley Irish-American survivor of the Great Depression. During local women's gin rummy and pinochle games in the back of Porter's store, Betty observes Lottie's deliberate uplift of downtrodden housewives. The same chutzpah enables Lottie to circumvent her miserly, unloving husband, farmer-miller Charles Davies, and to overrule Betty's first choice of a boy friend, the unkempt Luther Miracle. Well trained in gendered behaviors, Betty leaves home to try her girlhood education on the single life in Richmond, Virginia, where she studies secretarial courses with funds allocated by President Franklin D. Roosevelt. Upon her retreat to Milk Farm Road from a failed romance with Stanton, an addict to Neurol Compound, Betty allows Lottie to intervene once more and guide her toward marriage and motherhood. Upon the departure of son-in-law Herman Randolph to the navy during the Pacific war in February 1942, Lottie keeps at home both Betty and Marjorie Polly Randolph, the next female generation in need of life skills. Contributing to the triad of women is Polly Deal, the in-house wisewoman and midwife who births Marjorie and sets Betty on the way to independence. The simultaneous birthing of mother and child epitomizes the human need to continue growing and learning during momentous life shifts.

Gibbons presents a paradigm of the self-educated woman in *Charms for the Easy Life* (1993). In an intergenerational female household, reading, discussion, and humanitarianism dominate family life. In the view of critic Corinna Lothar, a reviewer for the *Washington Times*, Charlie Kate Birch, a self-educated midwife and herbalist, snatches training where she finds it, "in the secrets of the North Carolina backwoods folk medicine, in the wisdom acquired by years of keen observation of the human body, and in the knowledge contained in books" (Lothar, 1993). The satisfaction of the autodidact passes down to daughter Sophia Snow Birch and to granddaughter Margaret, who prefers home and on-the-job training to enrollment in college. For the same reason that education strengthens female independence, Margaret develops autonomy from self-directed learning in a liberal gynocentric environment. With a solid front, the three-woman household remains actively reading and discussing ideas throughout, with an interest in the biography of Robert E. Lee engaging Charlie Kate on the day she dies.

Gibbons peruses a less sanguine reason for education in Hattie Barnes, narrator of *Sights Unseen* (1995), for whom study is a respite from an unpredictable household. Like her older brother Freddy, to avoid the manic excesses of her insane mother Maggie, 12-year-old Hattie frequently withdraws to her room to read or do homework. In less fearful moments, Hattie shelters in the kitchen with Pearl Wiggins, the cook-housekeeper and pseudo-parent who stands in the breach created by Maggie's frequent emotional surges, sulks, and tantrums. Gibbons describes Hattie's reliance on literature and scholarship as a refuge and a compensation for the playtime and relaxation that the Barnes family misses. From physics, Hattie learns about gravitational pull and the tensions of attraction-repulsion "that keeps planets from banging into each other," an intellectual concept that mirrors the surging forces of Maggie's warring mental states (Gibbons, 1995, 155). Ultimately, education salvages the past for Hattie during her training in anesthesiology. From clinical experience with bipolar patients, she is able to view Maggie's rehabilitation in 1967 objectively and to forgive the constant threat of madness that overshadows Hattie's girlhood.

The author treasures learning as an appropriate gift from educated people to the underclass. In *On the Occasion of My Last Afternoon* (1998), in contrast to Samuel P. Goodman Tate, who retreats to his study for self-education in the classics, his son Whately, a student at Washington College in Lexington, Virginia, teaches the cook-housekeeper Clarice Washington to read. For a text, Whately chooses copies of *Godey's Lady's Book*, a fashion magazine that appeals to Whately's refined mother Alice. In the spirit of sharing, knowledge passes from hand to hand. An altruistic couple — Whately's sister, Emma Garnet Tate Lowell, and her husband, Dr. Quincy Lowell — and Clarice bestow lasting introductions to literacy on those in need of drilling in standard English. The bedraggled Dawes family becomes an ongoing welfare project that involves baskets of fresh vegetables, presentable clothes and shoes, and academy training for Lavinia Ella Mae Dawes and her brothers. Lavinia is already familiar with cattleyas, dendrobiums, oncidiums, and vandas, the orchid families her grandmother tended. The episodes increasing Lavinia's potential reveal a familiar down side of learning — the resentment of ignorant Primitive Baptist parents, whom the children quickly surpass in understanding and vision. Frank Dawes words his father's concerns that the children "get above [their] raisings," a familiar backwoods Southern chastisement of progressive offspring (Gibbons, 1998, 245).

Gibbons salts her historical novel with educational landmarks. Among the household's retainers, Charlie, Martha, and Mavis acquire reading and writing skills far above those of most black servants. Over a period of nine years at the kitchen table, they study *Murray's Grammar* (1795), the standard text on parsing, spelling, punctuation, syntax, and writing compiled by Pennsylvania-born Quaker attorney Lindley Murray. As proof of his influence, his practical handbook also crops up in Charles Dickens's *Nicholas Nickleby* (1839), Herman Melville's *Moby Dick* (1851), Harriet Beecher Stowe's *Uncle Tom's Cabin* (1852), George Eliot's *Middlemarch* (1872), and

Mark Twain's *Christian Science* (1907). Following the charitable example of their parents, Leslie, Louise, and Mary Lowell supplement the servants' education with stories from Washington Irving's *History of the Life and Voyages of Columbus* (1828) and from *Peter Parley's Winter Evening Tales*, a compendium of verse and fable that Samuel G. Goodrich published in 1829. The three girls' penchant for reading the classics derives from homeschooling. Emma superintends curriculum with the help of her brother Whately's library, Quincy's medical texts, and mail-order books that include Herodotus's *Histories* (440 B.C.), the Western world's first history anthology. Quincy develops his own pedagogical style for his children's Latin lessons and for late evening studies of the skies and myths about heavenly constellations. Emma states a brief apologia that learning is the springboard to excellence, a cornerstone of virtue, an ideal of the Victorian era.

A more poignant form of education occurs in *Divining Women* (2004), Gibbons's seventh novel. Mamie, the cook and maid of the Ross household in Elm City, North Carolina, worries that her boys have to compete in the world with only the three-month schedule of a negro subscription school. She teaches her husband Zollie to read from an American classic—*The Eclectic First Reader*, a developmental primary textbook for young children published in Cincinnati in 1838 by William Holmes McGuffey, a founder of American classroom method. Because of the elementary nature of lessons on animals and children at play, Zollie suffers an assault to his dignity. Mamie thanks Mary Oliver, a 22-year-old visitor to the Ross home, for replacing childish reading material with a daily newspaper. For Zollie, absorbing news about the Hindenburg Line, Woodrow Wilson's war plan, and violations of world peace encourages intelligent comprehension and analysis suited to an adult literacy student. Simultaneously, Gibbons implants the events as historical background and as reflections of a domestic milieu bristling with hostility.

At the novel's climax, Gibbons depicts a different reason for learning. To Maureen Carlton Ross, a severely discounted wife, one avenue out of a debilitating domestic imbroglio is enrollment at a women's college near her home in Elm City, North Carolina. The reference suggests the University of North Carolina at Greensboro, a women's college that gained its fervor for female education from crusading founder Charles Duncan McIver. For Maureen, classes with other women would provide "something for myself," her term for individualized intellectual development (Gibbons, 2004, 142). Mary, Maureen's niece and caretaker, who arrives on September 30, 1918, for the last 50 days of Maureen's pregnancy, alerts Maureen to the warped thinking of her husband, Troop Ross, for whom an educated wife equates with intellectual competition and marital abandonment. The tug of war exhibits the author's feminist beliefs that women attain wholeness through exploration of brain power and talents.

When Ellen Foster returns in *The Life All Around Me by Ellen Foster* (2006), she moves more vigorously toward a college degree. In the view of Marjorie Gellhorn Sa'adah, a critic for the *Los Angeles Times*, Ellen is "off-the-charts smart" (Sa'adah, 2006, R7). In an introductory application letter to Harvard University president Dr. Derek Curtis Bok, she indicates an innate curiosity that impels her toward scholarly rigor, the preface to a career in research in contagious disease. In contrast to her out-the-top scores in government-mandated IQ tests, she wastes her imagination and natural affability in independent study with Mrs. Delacroix, a wheelchair-bound librarian whose reading experience is limited to a popular classic, *The Power of Positive Thinking* (1952), a non-denominational bromide published by the Reverend Norman Vincent Peale. Other choices for advancement include the high school across the street, night classes at a community college, or the Academy of the New Dawn Apocalypse, a white-flight private school operated by fundamentalist bigots to avoid racial integration. To suit Ellen's needs, instructors at Johns Hopkins University in Baltimore create an individualized plan, the result of Dr. Julian Stanley's effort in 1972 to search out talented youth to challenge and reward for excellence. Ellen follows the syllabus in a home library from her Mamie Eisenhower floral chair until some intuitive thrust forces her to look beyond the rural community to a campus milieu.

Gibbons creates humor out of Ellen's equating learning with tuition. Underpinning Ellen's zest for reading and mental stimulus is a negative impulse, a fear that she may not earn continued employment at the "countinghouse," her term for a perpetual assessment of her strengths and weaknesses (Gibbons, 2006, 67). To reimburse Laura for tuition to the Johns Hopkins camp and to college, Ellen embroils herself in underworld financing by writing poems for other students on a sliding scale from one to five dollars, a level she reserves for composing sonnets. A *deus ex machina* conclusion rewards Ellen with a family inheritance and a scholarship to Harvard, an example of overcompensation to an orphan on a par with similar excesses in the social novels of Horatio Alger and Charles Dickens.

See also **reading**

• *Further reading*

Gibbons, Kaye. *Divining Women*. New York: G.P. Putnam's Sons, 2004.

_____. *Ellen Foster*. New York: Algonquin Press, 1987.

_____. "In 1912, a Lady Painter Meets Her True Nature," *Atlanta Journal-Constitution* (14 March 2004).

_____. *On the Occasion of My Last Afternoon*. New York: G.P. Putnam's Sons, 1998.

Lothar, Corinna. "'Charms' Are Many in Gibbons' New Novel," *Washington Times* (6 June 1993).

Sa'adah, Marjorie Gellhorn. "You Can't Go Home Again," *Los Angeles Times* (8 January 2006): R7.

Ellen Foster

An American literary classic, *Ellen Foster* (1987) is a book club and classroom staple that Londoners honored as one of the 20 top novels of the 1900s. Critic Carrie Brown of the *Chicago Tribune* called the writing a "bravura performance" (Brown, 2004). Reviewer Sharon Lloyd Stratton, on staff at the *Richmond Times-Dispatch*, compared narration through flashbacks to the style of Robert Cormier's young adult thriller-spy novel *I Am the Cheese* (1977), a fictional ordeal similar to Ellen's for its claustrophobic interior monologue. Told by the title character, Gibbons's story, set in a small Southern town, takes shape with clarity and vision as the ten-year-old survivor, like a maple seedling, struggles to set roots. In the estimation of critic Veronica Makowsky, an essayist for *Southern Quarterly*, the author intends to "rewrite the saga of the American hero by changing 'him' to 'her' and to rewrite the Southern female *Bildungsroman* by changing its privileged, sheltered, upper-class heroine to a poor, abused outcast" (Makowsky, 103). Makowsky's regard for the novel echoes similar critical reverence for a new wrinkle in feminist fiction.

Set from 1969 to 1971, according to the dates in the sequel, *The Life All Around Me by Ellen Foster* (2006), the initial plot follows the conventions of the female quest myth. Analyst Giavanna Munfo describes the goal as a reconstruction of "the figurative and literal dimensions of 'home'" (Munafo, 1998, 39). Picturing an emotionally needy only child, the plot reveals an innately strong title figure confronting both a volatile homelife and Southern patriarchy. To her credit, Ellen is willful, verbally aggressive, and smart, a self-rescuing orphan whom analysts compare to Mark Twain's protagonist in *The Adventures of Huckleberry Finn* (1884), to the heroine Mattie Ross in Charles Portis's western adventure novel *True Grit* (1968), and to Mick Kelly and Frankie Addams, the respective female seekers in Carson McCullers's *The Heart Is a Lonely Hunter* (1940) and *The Member of the Wedding* (1946). In each instance, children from compromised home situations look inward for the strength to save themselves.

Like the household descriptions in *Sights Unseen* (1995), *On the Occasion of My Last Afternoon* (1998), and in *The Life All Around Me by Ellen Foster*, the text of *Ellen Foster* deliberately oscillates between memories of past uncertainties and the joys of a wholesome present. Ellen's experience with mothering affirms the belief in Louisa May Alcott's *Little Women* (1868–1869) that "Mothers are the *best* lovers in the world" (Alcott, 1983, 409). Like a cactus on a waterless landscape, in an odious, demoralizing environment, Ellen survives her 40-year-old mother's suicide in March 1969 from an overdose of prescription digitalis. Through the conventions of the *Bildungsroman*, Gibbons follows her heroine over a complex landscape of false starts and dead ends. Refusing to be marginalized or cheated of her heritage, Ellen harrows her family for suitable kinship and, one by one, culls a heartless grandmother, two aunts, and a cousin who don't deserve family loyalty. To Dannye Romine, book editor of the *Charlotte* (N.C.) *Observer*, the odyssey passes "through the scruffy outposts of the heart" (Romine, 1987). Through horticultural symbolism, the author follows Ellen down a garden path and uses vegetable cultivation as an emblem of motherly nurturing. The text remarks that "weeds do not bear fruit" (Gibbons, 1987, 49). In the summation of novelist-reviewer Jacqueline Carey, Ellen is "hounded from household to household by dead bodies and drunks," a reference to the lowest points in the child's fortunes (Carey, 1995, 30). Rather than flee toward her extended family, on Christmas Day, 1970, at age 11, she runs toward her first real family, strangers whom she selects from fellow church attendees. Appropriately, the choice of an auspicious home setting created by foster mother Laura occurs in the week preceding the new year, a symbolic time of relaxation and renewal.

See also **Foster, Ellen; Foster genealogy; *The Life All Around Me by Ellen Foster***

• *Further reading*

Alcott, Louisa May. *Little Women*. New York: Bantam, 1983.
Brown, Carrie. "Kaye Gibbons' Focus Is on Female Fortitude," *Chicago Tribune* (4 April 2004).

Carey, Jacqueline. "Mommy Direst," *New York Times Book Review* (24 September 1995): 30.

Gibbons, Kaye. *Ellen Foster*. New York: Algonquin Press, 1987.

Gray, Richard, and Owen Robinson, eds. *A Companion to the Literature and Culture of the American South*. Malden, Mass.: Blackwell, 2004.

Groover, Kristina Kaye. "Re-visioning the Wilderness: Adventures of Huckleberry Finn and *Ellen Foster*," *Southern Quarterly* 27, no. 3/4 (Spring/Summer 1999): 187–197.

Makowsky, Veronica. "The Only Hard Part Was the Food: Recipes for Self-Nurture in Kaye Gibbons's Novels," *Southern Quarterly* 30 (Winter–Spring 1992): 103–112.

Munafo, Giavanna. "Colored Biscuits: Reconstructing Whiteness and the Boundaries of 'Home' in Kaye Gibbons's *Ellen Foster*," *Women, America, and Movement*. ed. Susan L. Roberson. Columbia: University of Missouri Press, 1998, pp. 38–61.

Romine, Dannye. "'Ellen Foster' Takes you on Poignant Search," *Charlotte* (N.C.) *Observer* (26 April 1987).

Stratton, Sharon Lloyd. "Magnolia Grows Out of Rough Soil," *Richmond Times-Dispatch* (21 June 1987).

Town, Caren J. *New Southern Girl: Female Adolescence in the Works of 12 Women Authors*. Jefferson, N.C.: McFarland, 2004.

Ellen Foster (adapted for stage by Aaron Posner)

Playwright Aaron Posner's selection of Kaye Gibbons's first novel *Ellen Foster* (1987) for staging attests to the work's engaging dialogue and character confrontations. Adapted to three acts and 23 scenes, the play, performed by the Arden Theatre Company, debuted in Philadelphia's St. Stephen's Alley Performing Arts Center from February 3–20, 1994. In the estimation of Clifford A. Ridley, theater critic for the *Philadelphia Inquirer*, the adaptation replaces Ellen's evocative memoir with a graphic "plot that brims with incident," which he summarizes as a "picaresque childhood journey" (Ridley, 1994). Opening on David Gordon's circular, multi-level domestic set, the action requires mood lighting and incidental music of banjo, double bass, dulcimer, and guitar. Posner makes multiple application of the quilt on a brass bed as the scene of three deaths and a friendly sleepover, scraps of Ellen's life that coalesce into a meaningful whole. He features surrealistic enactments of the title character's murder of her father Bill by shooting him with a pistol, dispatching him with tainted whiskey and a poisonous spider, and smothering him with a pillow. By alternating between Ellen's birth home and her foster home, Posner retains Gibbons's reciprocating tone and atmosphere, which contrast the quiet order of Ellen's foster home with her grandmother's rudeness at the funeral and the minister's babbling about a dead woman he knows nothing about. Posner contributes to Ellen's mother the name Sarah, a suitable choice from Genesis of a matriarch who heads the Hebrew race.

Essential to the first act is Ellen's need to relive the traumas of young girlhood, which she does with the aid of two actors, one the young Ellen and one older. The duo balances narration with action. Posner enhances domestic conflict by having Ellen's loutish father Bill regret not marrying Sarah's healthy sister Nadine and by voicing Bill's threat of murder if Ellen telephones for help for her suicidal mother. Vivid deviations from the novel depict Bill calling his daughter "Sugar Blossom Britches," Starletta inviting Ellen to play with her Lincoln logs, and Starletta's father paying the electricity bill and taking Ellen shopping to buy a winter coat (Posner, 1994, 9). A shift in Starletta's father has him refer to her as "Star" and recite a folksy blessing over Christmas dinner (*Ibid.*, 11). Posner's touches shift the preponderance of womanly aid to Ellen by fleshing out Starletta's father as a responsible parent and generous male neighbor.

In Act I, Posner's briskly paced, if stagy extensions of the novel pelt the audience with sense impressions. To relieve Ellen's tension, the new mother shampoos her hair; to add dimension to short-term fostering by flower children Julia and Roy, the adapter inserts family improvisations of Prince Valiant in the Sunday newspaper cartoons and the trio's enriching the garden with chicken manure, a symbol of the detritus that enriches their garden much as adversity builds Ellen's character. More dramatic are Bill's drunken trouncing of the marigold bed at the elementary school, Julia's reassurance that Ellen is safe from Bill, and intervention by an elderly judge in Ellen's placement. Dialogue by Mavis, the field supervisor, pads her importance to Ellen's life during the child's miserable residence with her maternal grandmother. The contrast of good and bad elements in Ellen's life energize the text by extending shreds of hope for her survival.

The adapter labors over the issue of Ellen's actual words and the dialogue in her head — the retorts she wished she had made or that she was wise enough to suppress. In Act II, she carries on an extensive exchange with Starletta over the black child's crush on Tom, a white boy. Another pairing particularizes the psychiatrist's probing into Ellen's identity problems each Tuesday against her hostile stonewalling. Autoharp chords punctuate a more complex dialogue by which Aunt Nadine Nelson demeans Ellen through complements to Cousin Dora, who edges the intruder out of a private mother-daughter holiday celebration. The older Ellen words suppressed hostility toward the twosome for their insults by identifying Ellen's fantasy boyfriend, a deliberate taunt at Dora, who has no beau. Instead of Gibbons's choice of Nick Adams, a character in short stories by Ernest Hemingway, Posner chooses the more familiar David Copperfield, Charles Dickens's autobiographical character whose inept, whiny wife is named Dora. Upbeat exchanges mark the play's resolution as Ellen trudges to the foster home on Christmas Day, 1970, and explains her need of rescue to the attentive new mother. The success of Posner's dramatization earned the praise of Clark Groome, drama critic for the *Chestnut Hill* (Pa.) *Local*, who claimed the work as "the most successful, most honest, most engaging dramatic adaptation" in the reviewer's experience (Groome, 1994, 39).

• *Further reading*

Cofta, Mark. "Arden Triumphs with 'Ellen Foster,'" Montgomery and Delaware County, Pa., *Main Line Times* (10 February 1994).

Gibbons, Kaye. *Ellen Foster* (adapted for stage by Aaron Posner). Philadelphia: unpublished, February 1994.

Groome, Clark. "Fine 'Ellen Foster' Another Triumph for Arden Theatre," *Chestnut Hill* (Pa.) *Local* (3 February 1994): 39.

Northam, Greg. "Recounting a Woman's Troubled Childhood," *Philadelphia Gay News* (4 February 1994).

Ridley, Clifford A. "A Girl in Dire Dickensian Straits Who Lives to Learn the Outcome," *Philadelphia Enquirer* (3 February 1994).

fears

A forthright and unflinching author, Kaye Gibbons dissects the terrors that stalk her fictional characters. In an early short-short story, "The Headache," issued in June 1987 in the *St. Andrews Review*, protagonist Lucille Womble disables herself through two weeks of psychosomatic illness brought on by seizing an abandoned handbag and concealing it in her underwear. Terrified that the greedy act is symptomatic of trashy behavior, she sinks under insomnia, nonstop head pain, hysteria, and night terrors of a serpent with flashing fangs. Brought on by the snake-in-the-lost-purse trick, the crippling misery drives her to the brink of suicide. Subtextually, Gibbons reveals the real terrors of living on a failing farm, scrubbing dirty overalls by hand, and surviving the bank's repossession of two farm machines. Countering the struggle of living in a one-room house and caring for ten children, Henry Womble encircles his wife with respect and affection. His antidote to fear takes the form of a promise to buy Lucille two new hats, a lavish outlay from a cash-strapped farmer for his ailing wife. Gibbons honors his intuition and generosity as examples of marital support and protection.

At an extreme of menace to a preteen orphan, Gibbons's first novel, *Ellen Foster* (1987), pictures a homelife so volatile that the title character monitors the minute disruptions caused by her blinks and breaths. Her terrors are kinesthetic — instinctive retreats from amorphous whirling and from gaping chasms. In the opening paragraphs, the title character discusses her response to an ink blot test, the common name for Hermann Rorschach's psychological evaluation of personality traits and emotional function. To the school psychologist, each Tuesday, Ellen describes deep black holes, the bottomless pits that yawn before the daughter of a mother sick with heart disease and of a self-indulgent bootlegger named Bill, who has no business rearing a ten-year-old. In a fragmented family, Ellen pictures her only moorings as the ailing mother with tired-looking skin and the argumentative, infantile monster-father who swears at the world. A graphic image describes a carnival ride left unattended to spin itself off its rails, forcing Ellen to restore order to a chaotic world. For good reason, she trembles at school and plunges her tell-tale hands beneath the desktop. The constant tension derives from the pressure of responsibilities far beyond a child's grasp.

Gibbons undergirds her novel with sound psychological foundations. Throughout Ellen's day, the control of subconscious terror makes her fidgety, combative, and suspicious, particularly of questions from teachers and other authority figures. In an effort to restore harmony, she claims to read before going to sleep to stop her mind from rambling. In the mortuary car before her mother's funeral service and burial, Ellen wants to sit by the door to facilitate a quick getaway. On the edge of domestic catastrophe, she pictures red foliage on a tree bursting into flame and burning a home and barn, a vision of the combustible nature of her relationship with Bill. On a conscious level, her fear focuses on pasture snakes, which a pony scares away. At school, Ellen shields herself from grief and prying eyes by wearing her mother's stockings under her dress. At home with Bill, Ellen stays in her room and looks to the window as an escape if she needs one. When he manhandles her on New Year's Eve,

1969, she retreats to the edge of the woods and to Starletta's house before abandoning home permanently. The inborn dependence on flight connects Ellen with small forest animals and birds that share her innate readiness to elude danger.

Gibbons rims Ellen's waking hours with anxiety. Returned home after a weekend with Aunt Betsy, Ellen resorts to wedging a chair at her bedroom door and by arming herself against Bill's predations. Even in the safety of Julia and Roy's home, the demonic parent lives in Ellen's head. A sudden command to make a wish on her 11th birthday scares her by its abrupt violation of her private thoughts. The day Bill makes a scene and exposes his genitals at the elementary school, fright generates spots before her eyes. Gibbons enhances Bill's evil by picturing his car parked on marigolds planted by handicapped students, a double symbol of vileness and vulnerability. At Ellen's maternal grandmother's house, the child connects quaking hands with the old lady's accusations that Ellen is just like Bill, a wastrel and cohort of black derelicts. In the falling action, a peaceful pre-meal meditation at a foster home defines more normal anticipations— in place of constant confrontation and safeguarding, she awaits a home-cooked dinner at a table where she receives welcome as a trusted family member.

Departing for the child's perspective, Gibbons's second novel, *A Virtuous Woman* (1989), contrasts adult male-female responses to death and loss. In a narrative duet, 45-year-old Ruby Pitts Woodrow Stokes expresses the apprehensions of dying with terminal lung cancer while her husband, 65-year-old "Blinking" Jack Ernest Stokes, recoils from a life sentence of surviving without her. For Ruby, the finality of ending a life as farm wife leaves her pondering unfinished earthly business. A diagnosis of malignancy causes her to cry, heave, and sob, yet increases her introspection on gender differences. She acknowledges that she can do little from the grave to help her widower. She correctly predicts Jack's terror at wifelessness. Although he survives bachelorhood to age 40, he relives his mother's demise from eating tainted meat and his own questioning of God's indifference to human suffering. The defiance of an absent god recurs in Ruby's last days, when Jack shouts down Cecil Spangler, a pious Primitive Baptist who offers only smug religious legalism to her plight. Three months after her death, Jack's hallucinations of Ruby's benevolent ghost depict the far edge of fear and a venture toward madness.

In *Sights Unseen* (1995), a more intricate study of insanity, narrator Hattie Barnes reprises the uncertainty of being unloved in girlhood and her father's dread of losing his wife to bipolar instability. During Hattie's coming-of-age, at age 12, she survives the down times of her mother's nadirs and the riotous upswings that jeopardize normal family activities. Hattie's longing for a sane mother reaches a turning point late in 1967, when Maggie undergoes psychotherapy and eight weeks of electroconvulsive shock treatment at Duke Hospital. In the interim, Hattie ponders the shadow of the "maternal role in passing on the marked gene," an erudite statement masking an understandable anxiety of future madness in herself or in her older brother Freddy or their children (Gibbons, 1995, 163). The shift from raving mother to organized, resolute patient leaves Hattie uncertain of what to expect when Maggie returns home. The amorphous fears gradually subside as Maggie establishes herself as wife, parent, head of household, and, most important, controller of self. Although she is never able to compensate for Hattie's years of insecurity, the change in Maggie's mothering establishes for Hattie a solid base of expectations devoid of anxiety. By day, mother and daughter read and nap together; at night, Maggie hovers at Hattie's bedside, a standard pose of the nurturing parent intended to precipitate restful sleep. In adulthood, Hattie narrates her family history as an intellectual mode of exorcising "the worry and the wounds of my childhood" (*Ibid.*, 209).

In Gibbons's first historical novel, *On the Occasion of My Last Afternoon* (1998), the text moves beyond individual childhood fears to the terrors of war and economic chaos that sweep the American South. In youth, narrator Emma Garnet Tate Lowell battles a household scourge, the outrageous demands and dreams of regional glory in her father, planter Samuel P. Goodman Tate. Marriage in 1847 at age 17 to Dr. Quincy Lowell and relocation from the James River area of Virginia to urban Raleigh, North Carolina, moderate Emma's immediate troubles. On the down side, contentment produces guilt and a constant ache for her delicate mother, Alice Tate, who remains behind under Samuel's constant verbal bashing. When war invades both states, fears take on palpable shapes from trainloads of wounded needing Quincy's care and Emma's nursing and from a sizeable household dependent on Clarice Washington, the cook-housekeeper who superintends the kitchen and child care. Unlike Gibbons's poorer protagonists— Lucille Womble, Ellen Foster, Ruby Stokes, and the women of Milk Farm Road in *A Cure for Dreams* (1991)— Emma has the security of gold coins stashed in the cellar in false-bottomed peach baskets, but Quincy's death catapults his widow into an emotional morass similar to that suffered by Jack Stokes. In the novel's falling action, Gibbons replaces Emma's fear with boldness as her heroine survives widowhood and redirects her assets and energies toward philanthropy and the mothering of children and grandchildren. Love and war-time experience soothe her cares when, in 1900 at age 70, she embraces mortality as an opportunity to reunite with Quincy.

During another war, the basis of realism in Gibbons's seventh novel, *Divining Women* (2004), grows out of a wretched domestic situation. On September 30, 1918, Maureen Carlton Ross, a gentle wife in the last trimester of pregnancy, suffers the unremitting oppression of her husband Troop, an icy-hearted taskmaster. He dismisses her as a drama queen given to bouts of "female hysteria," a gendered medical slur implying an inborn lapse of logic and self-control in women (Gibbons, 2004, 62). As Maureen's due date looms, the stagy home scene depletes her of energy and hope, two essentials to a parturient woman. Tremulous in her upstairs haven, she muses that she already feels dead. Combating her malaise, niece Mary Oliver, a 22-year-old graduate student at Radcliffe, lobs enough retorts to Troop's blustering to remind Maureen that she's not only living but that she'll "stay that way" (*Ibid.*, 88). The synergy of Mary and Maureen proves equal to a poignant resolution in which the two women and the family servants, Mamie and Zollie, complete the funeral of Ella Eloise Ross, Maureen's stillborn infant, at a sunset interment on November 9, 1918. Gibbons words an encomium to the child with a reminder that God relieves human suffering much as he stilled the weeping of Lazarus's mother. Filled with Christian comfort, the brief farewell to Ella doubles as the author's comforting gesture to readers.

In *The Life All Around Me by Ellen Foster* (2006), the sequel to *Ellen Foster*, Gibbons enlarges on the terrors that inhibit the title figure's relaxation. In fall 1974, her memories of losing both parents deepen the black holes that yawn during anxiety attacks. At the county fair, she refuses slinging rides that replicate the feeling of centrifugal jostling. Laura, her foster mother, offers maternal handholds on trust—a viewing of *Willie Wonka and the Chocolate Factory* (1971) and a ride home in the car with Ellen's head in Laura's lap. Even a child's movie leaves Ellen fearful of Willy Wonka's "dark undersoul," a suggestion of overly acute sensibilities that suspend Ellen's enjoyment of normal amusement (Gibbons, 2006, 14). Far beyond her peers in intelligence, she is capable of wording the challenge of the moment: "facing another span of time I'd had to get to the other side of, not live wholly inside" (Gibbons, 2006, 15). In the final paragraphs, she summarizes Laura's love as a spotlight on the inner reaches. Instead of dreading the future, Ellen is able to envision the progression of days as "turning over like plowed ground folding" (*Ibid.*, 218). The image suits the agrarian milieu as well as the author's upbringing within predictable seasonal shifts.

See also **superstition**

• *Further reading*

Barnes, Linda Adams. "Telling Yourself into Existence: The Fiction of Kaye Gibbons," *Tennessee Philological Bulletin* 30 (1993): 28–35.
Gibbons, Kaye. *Divining Women*. New York: G.P. Putnam's Sons, 2004.
_____. *Ellen Foster*. New York: Algonquin Press, 1987.
_____. *The Life All Around Me by Ellen Foster*. New York: Harcourt, 2006.
_____. *Sights Unseen*. New York: G.P. Putnam's Sons, 1995.
Munafo, Giavanna. "Colored Biscuits: Reconstructing Whiteness and the Boundaries of 'Home' in Kaye Gibbons's *Ellen Foster*," *Women, America, and Movement*. ed. Susan L. Roberson. Columbia: University of Missouri Press, 1998, pp. 38–61.
Romine, Dannye. "'Ellen Foster' Takes You on Poignant Search," *Charlotte* (N.C.) *Observer* (26 April 1987).

feminism

Kaye Gibbons is more a philosophic feminist than an activist. Early in her career, she set out on a quest "to investigate the phenomenon of being female," especially the lives of poor women in the rural South (Burleigh, 1989). To reviewer Polly Paddock, book editor of the *Charlotte* (N.C.) *Observer*, the author described her notion of women's rights as "freedom of choice [rather than] a rejection of femininity" (Paddock, 1993). Shaping her literary style is the influence of feminist masters—Grace Paley, Katherine Anne Porter, Elizabeth Spencer, Jean Stafford, and Eudora Welty, all of whom examine the female life as a lesson in empowerment and autonomy. The themes resonate in tandem in all of Gibbons's writing, beginning with the early short-short story, "The Headache," issued in June 1987 in the *St. Andrews Review*. The plot depicts the moral quandary of Lucille Womble, who peers down the dark slope of suicide. Her self-punishment is the result of an ethical lapse, the concealment of a handbag she finds abandoned in the ladies' room of a chicken restaurant. Forgiving herself requires trusting three people — her employer, Mae Bell Stokes, a physician, Dr. Janet Cowley, and Lucille's husband Henry. Strengthened by the benevolence of others, Lucille re-commissions herself to do the good works for which she is known and loved. The story bodes well for Gibbons's longer fiction.

The author equates feminism with resilience. In an interview conducted by Don O'Briant of the *Atlanta Journal-Constitution*, she scorned the idea that Southern women are empty-headed clotheshorses who strip off their white gloves to caress the family silver. She explained her image of strong, self-confident women: "[They] wait in the corners for the moment to take over a situation, and then they manipulate it with their hands and get a grasp on it" (O'Briant, 1995). The tactile image summarizes the prehensile quality of her heroines, from Lucille Womble's seizure of an abandoned purse and preteen orphan Ellen Foster's search for a foster home to sober survivor Ruby Pitts Woodrow Stokes's clutch of a pistol and the hands-on healing performed by unlicensed herbalist-midwife Charlie Kate Birch, her daughter Sophia Snow Birch, and granddaughter Margaret. Rounding out 20 years of clearly delineated female strength, Laura, the single-parent fosterer in Gibbons's first sequel, *The Life All Around Me by Ellen Foster* (2006), bolsters herself for mothering with lengthy conferences with Starletta's mom, a sounding board who shares the role of female mainstay of two needy households.

Gibbons's characters contest oppression and disappointment through restorative narrative that disburdens and elates. In *A Cure for Dreams* (1991), she pursues what Roy Parker, Jr., a literary critic for the *Fayetteville* (N.C.) *Observer*, describes as a "[James] Thurber-like 'war between the sexes,'" (Parker, 1991). Protagonist Lottie O'Cadhain Davies reveals immediate disillusion with her Quaker husband, Charles Davies, who turns farm and mill toil into a religion. Largely abandoned during daylight hours, she creates her own diversions, which include sewing clothes for herself and daughter Betty and visiting local housewives. After forming a women's social club in the back room of Porter's store, Lottie introduces pinochle and gin rummy and insists on gambling with pennies, a bit of daring to dispel the tight budgets and travel restrictions necessitated by the Great Depression. Gibbons notes that rural males disapprove of female pleasure that derives "from something other than home and hearth," a free-floating male suspicion bordering on paranoia (Gibbons, 1991, 31). She extends the feminist implications in a mother-daughter alliance against Charles, an unloving mate-father. During menacing times, Betty learns about odds and betting from her mother, who takes pride in a daughter skilled enough to challenge riverboat gamblers. The image sets Betty in a fluctuating milieu that, like a strong current, challenges her ability to stay afloat. Ironically, it is the river that claims Charles, who, in 1937, drowns himself in despair of the economy, leaving Lottie and Betty to soldier on.

In a reworking of Susan Glaspell's classic one-act play *Trifles* (1916), Gibbons turns Lottie into a silent sleuth at the scene of Roy Duplin's death from a shotgun blast. While part-time Deputy Sheriff John Carroll studies the front yard for footprints and shell casings, Lottie comforts Sade, the new widow, listens to her terrified keening, and scans the domestic scene. The evidence reveals a woman's furor in uneven stitches on a Dutch doll quilt pattern and the wailing of a wife fearing arrest for an out-of-patience retaliation against domestic oppression. Gibbons concludes with delight in the inability of Deputy John Carroll to retrace the motivation of a killer mate who took all she could stand from a vile-natured adulterer. The transcendence of solitary widowhood is one of the truisms of feminist literature — the ability of single women to rehabilitate themselves in an orderly household devoid of men. In the aftermath, Sade thrives by turning Roy's room into a fetching parlor adorned with a quilt, a universal symbol of women's knack for recycling scraps into a useful work of art. Concealed by tacit agreement is the line of stitches that Lottie resews in an effort to console Sade and protect her from the law, a male-structured institution that ignores men's ongoing assaults on female esteem.

Gibbons's pro-woman credo in her fourth novel, *Charms for the Easy Life* (1993), reveals the reciprocal nature of charity and grace. For its accomplished survey of womanhood, reviewer Corinna Lothar, in a critique for the *Washington Times*, proclaimed the author the "heir to Edith Wharton's keen understanding of the yearning heart of Everywoman" (Lothar, 1993). Self-educated healer Charlie Kate Birch works steadily at improving the lives of impoverished and defenseless patients. She expands her clientele by offering dental treatment. Her gendered use of chloroform involves anesthetizing only women in token of their home labors and marital afflictions. As a gauge for dosage, she studies the fatigue in the patient's face and increases the amount meted out to the sorely taxed. The gesture illustrates a covert form of female networking that acknowledges unending domestic tribulation. Providing evidence of need are Charlie Kate's two female cousins, who commit suicide with shards of a glass pitcher in mourning for their father, a casualty of World War I. Unlike the weak-willed cousins and her suicidal twin Camelia, Charlie Kate exults in self-motivation and prevails over adversity.

In a lengthy critique of Gibbons's depiction of inept and overbearing men, critic James Thompson, writing for *World & I*, faults the author for plotting an overt anti-male text expressing her personal qualms about the men in her life. Thompson sums up Gibbons's theme in colloquial terms: "Women must stick together because men aren't much good" (Thompson, 1993, 354). The self-sufficiency of Charlie Kate's all-female household is openly hostile to males who have, so far, mostly disappointed or irritated. Thompson implies that the author sets up for her virago Charlie Kate a series of straw men — a nearly lynched negro, the hapless Hermit Willoughby, whiny wounded veterans, Sophia's womanizing husband, an inept medical practitioner, and Dr. Charles Nutter, a homeboy-does-well who owes his education to Charlie Kate's sponsorship. Thompson scores a feminist point in characterizing the beloved, but bossy healer as controlling her daughter Sophia "as ruthlessly as would any man" (Thompson, 1993, 351).

James Thompson's generalization falls short of encompassing the multi-dimensional Kaye Gibbons. In her first historical novel, *On the Occasion of My Last Afternoon* (1998), she takes the war-time opportunity of raising from petticoats and propriety the New Woman, a feminist paragon who emerged in the 19th-century novels of the Brontës, the dramas of Henrik Ibsen, and the philosophy of John Stuart Mill and his wife, Harriet Taylor Mill, the author of a formal feminist manifesto, "The Enfranchisement of Women" (1851). During the Civil War, Emma Garnet Tate

Lowell partners with her husband, Dr. Quincy Lowell, in the surgical treatment of maimed soldiers. Usually well mannered and conventionally dressed, in 1861, Emma strips stockings and shoes and commandeers staff during an influx of wounded to the critical ward. By night, she snatches sleep on a cot in the supply closet. One surgeon balks at taking orders from a woman, but Emma shouts him down with evidence of sloppy stitches in his surgical patients. To Quincy's overflow of emotion at trainloads of war wounded, Emma cradles him, reversing the stereotypical order of husband solacing wife. In 1861, he decorates her with a monogrammed silver pin for advancing from a refined Southern lady to an unswooning hero of combat casualties. In financially secure widowhood during Reconstruction, she directs the Lowell fortune toward new business and philanthropy, two essentials in the South's rebirth.

An unusual retreat from women's liberation occurs in Gibbons's seventh novel, *Divining Women* (2004), a deceptively unfeminist work until a burst of pro-woman action in mid-text. Set among the wealthy Greene and Oliver families in Washington, D.C., the exposition portrays Mary Oliver, the 22-year-old narrator, as a bored Gaucher graduate and M.A. candidate at Radcliffe who resists joining the volunteer nurses of World War I. She also rejects more involvement in the women's suffrage movement than marching in parades, a common form of public protest during the final months of the drive for full citizenship rights for women. Perhaps because of a life of ease and privilege, Mary and her widowed mother, Martha Greene Oliver, feel no kinship with the crusaders at headquarters, which derives volunteer energy from "mannish and combative women" (Gibbons, 2004, 34). Mary's avoidance of any feminist organization belies her true feelings about powerless victims like her aunt, Maureen Carlton Ross. In token of "woman's dense and marathon existence," Mary envisions tracking down the divine power distributor and overturning collusion between God and patriarchs (*Ibid.*, 77).

In the estimation of writer-critic Judi Goldenberg, in a review for the *Richmond Times-Dispatch*, Gibbons's text displays "a deep underlying respect for the sisterhood that binds all women," an empathy that the characters of *Divining Women* express through letters, conversation, communal birthing, and gentle restorative acts (Goldenberg, 2004). As the conflict heightens, in chapter eight, Mary Oliver muses on her mother's perception of love and beauty. Martha believes that affection nourishes wedlock and that a "furnished mind," like nutmeg in a vanilla cake, spices up an ordinary union into a memorable taste experience (Gibbons, 2004, 96). Warring against on-the-spot infatuation, she reminds Mary that the heart — Freud's id — seeks immediate gratification, but the intellect — the ego — approaches the issue from a more realistic perspective. Corroborating Martha's credo, the mini-tragedy of Judith Benedict Stafford on May 3, 1912, portrays a double-crossed wife who abandons a sleazy husband caught *in flagrante delicto* with a street chippy. Judith searches European cities for a valuable life truth — that freedom validates a woman far more than living a marital lie. In a letter to her best friend Martha dated April 24, 1915, Judith declares that a vulnerable female risks more harm from living among the wrong people than from walking unescorted down a dark alley by night in Washington, D.C. No longer a husband-pleasing "princess," she resorts to a Parisian version of sexual liberation, a refutation of the Puritanic principle of wedding for life and contending in private with a faithless mate (*Ibid.*, 101).

Gibbons addresses feminism more directly in her first sequel, *The Life All Around Me by Ellen Foster*, a return to the title character in fall 1974 at age fifteen. An unusual friendship between foster mother Laura and Martha's mother encourages the latter to visit on Sunday afternoons for a nap away from a noisy household. While the guest rests and regroups, Martha's father vegetates in stereotypical American style — in front of a televised football game. Laura, preparing tea for Martha's mother, explains to Ellen that "Women hide women," a profound summation of universal sisterhood in an androcentric world (Gibbons, 2006, 37). The layered giving and receiving in Laura's female circle sets an example for Ellen of self-empowerment through synergy and loyalty. As the ideal volunteer mother, Laura epitomizes Ellen's inborn drive to elude poverty, orphaning, and powerlessness by grasping opportunity.

See also **achievement; autonomy; mothering; powerlessness; self-esteem; *Trifles*; women; "The Yellow Wallpaper"**

• *Further reading*

Burleigh, Nina. "Maternal Inspiration Fuels Southern Writer's Work," *Chicago Tribune* (1 October 1989).
Gibbons, Kaye. *Charms for the Easy Life*. New York: Putnam, 1993.
_____. *A Cure for Dreams*. New York: Algonquin, 1991.
_____. *Divining Women*. New York: G.P. Putnam's Sons, 2004.
_____. "Introduction," *I Cannot Tell a Lie, Exactly and Other Stories*, by Mary Ladd Gavell. New York: Random House, 2001.
_____. *The Life All Around Me by Ellen Foster*. New York: Harcourt, 2006.
_____. *On the Occasion of My Last Afternoon*. New York: G.P. Putnam's Sons, 1998.
Goldenberg, Judi. "To Endure, Women Form Bond," *Richmond Times-Dispatch* (9 May 2004).
Lothar, Corinna. "'Charms' Are Many in Gibbons' New Novel," *Washington Times* (6 June 1993).
O'Briant, Don. "Book Signing," *Atlanta Journal-Constitution* (10 September 1995).
Paddock, Polly. "Kaye Gibbons: A Writer's Journey," *Charlotte* (N.C.) *Observer* (30 May 1993).
Parker, Roy, Jr. "Elegant Family Story," *Fayetteville* (N.C.) *Observer* (14 April 1991).
Thompson, James. "Man-Taming Granny," *World & I* 8, no. 9 (September 1993): 349–354.

food

Kaye Gibbons details food and meals in her fiction as elements of lifestyle, socioeconomic class, retreat from adversity, and spiritual refreshment. In 1989, she revealed to critic Nina Burleigh, a journalist for the *Chicago Tribune*, an initial straying from the hard-fried menu of the Southern table to steaming light meals without adding fat. In contrast to her older sister Alice in Tarboro, North Carolina, who "makes biscuits with lots of salt and lard three times a day every day whether there is someone there to eat them or not," Gibbons chose the lo-cal diet of yuppiedom (Burleigh, 1989). Five years later, she reverted to the tastes and aromas of her mama's kitchen.

Her own wedding luncheon included Southern staples—country ham, stewed okra and tomatoes, collards, potato salad, biscuits, and corn bread, the home-raised foods of piedmont North Carolina.

An early fictional example, the chicken dinner in "The Headache," a short-short story issued in June 1987 in the *St. Andrews Review*, characterizes luxury for a barely coping farm family. The night out prefaces a two-week crisis in Lucille Womble's life after she retrieves from the restaurant ladies' room an abandoned purse, a symbol of treasure to a despairing farm wife. The motif of food as an antidote to need returns in *Ellen Foster* (1987), the author's first novel. Before easing her desperation for a secure dwelling, the title character dines with a black family, but stops short of drinking after Starletta or eating a "colored biscuit," a point of honor to a Southern child brought up in backwoods racism (Gibbons, 1987, 31). Ellen reveals a deep hunger that causes her to "stay starved," a reference to emotional and physical malnutrition that Starletta's family temporarily relieves (*Ibid.*, 58). While living on her own in the absence of her father Bill, Ellen settles for frozen meals, an innovation that provides only a dab of dessert, a bleak commentary on a life short on sweetness.

Reclamation sets Ellen Foster on a trajectory that targets both nourishment and joy. Settling with a new mother translates into enough money to buy groceries and to enjoy soft biscuits, the smell of chicken frying, and egg sandwiches spread on both sides with mayonnaise, Ellen's endearing symbol of bounty and extravagance. Hurrying home from church to Sunday lunch, she slips out of her dress fast enough to break a zipper and two collars. Sunday afternoons involve preparing the week's menu, a tactile assembly-line process that acknowledges her previous cooking experience and her need for long-distance care through home-packed school lunches. Physical hunger causes her to appreciate a stranger who is a more substantive parent than Ellen's limited choices among extended family.

In contrast to Ellen's strivings for sustenance, Gibbons's second novel, *A Virtuous Woman* (1989), depicts the preparation of ample meals at the Pitts home. Each involves a division of labor based on age and social class. While the cook Sudie Bee wrestles a flapping turkey to the ground with her axe and guts it for baking, Ruby Pitts, the family's pampered daughter, takes no part in the farmyard essentials. At age 18, she elopes with John Woodrow without taking stock of a farm laborer's existence minus hired help like Sudie Bee. Two years later, after Ruby departs early widowhood to marry a 40-year-old bachelor farmhand, "Blinking" Jack Ernest Stokes, she views food from a laboring-class perspective. Lacking kitchen skills, she stirs a honeymoon meal out of "two kinds of canned something" and heats them in one pot atop a grimy hot plate (Gibbons, 1989, 77). The haphazard pairing of canned goods parallels the hasting union of Ruby with Jack, two unlike mates who yoke into wedlock under unpromising conditions.

Ruby's story illustrates the worth of will in salvaging a marriage. Out of necessity, she learns cookery and takes pride in watching her loaves rise, an image of domestic promise. To assuage the longing for a child, which John destroyed by infecting her with a sexually transmitted disease, she mothers June Stanley, a poorly parented neighbor and family friend whom Ruby teaches to weave potholders, a homely portent of kitchen work. The growth of culinary skill parallels an expansion of self-regard, Ruby's reward for choosing a stable and loving mate who loves her cooking. Jack's contentment under Ruby's care spools out in frozen meals of pork with corn and beef with beans that see him through three lonely spring months after her death in March of her 45th year. In token of his sorrow for losing a memorable cook, he resorts to corn flakes, watery canned soup, and bourbon while dreaming of Ruby's spaghetti sauce, a hearty comfort food rich in aroma, color, and flavor. In his fantasies of Ruby's return as a spirit, he envisions her eating yogurt in bed, a lascivious image with erotic overtones.

Food in Gibbons's fourth novel, *Charms for the Easy Life* (1993), ventures from pure nourishment into therapeutic herbs, hygiene, and healthful diet for the underclass. After the death of her errant husband, Charlie Kate Birch, the self-educated herbalist and midwife, brews clover tea to salve her grieving granddaughter Margaret. For her own nourishment, Charlie Kate creams two cloves of garlic in a mortar as a spread for morning toast, a humble nutritional supplement dating to medieval dietary manuals. She trusts lemon balm and evening primrose tea for restorative sleep and an occasional brandy to soothe frazzled nerves. On her last evening, she doses herself with papaya tablets and gingerroot tea for the "irritatingly vague nausea" that foretokens her death (Gibbons, 1993, 252). Margaret's first indication that the family matriarch is gone is the absence of sounds in the kitchen from knife on cutting board and pestle scraping mortar. The culinary implements resound in the resolution of Charlie Kate, who weathers life's raw edges and constant impact.

The author's fifth novel, *Sights Unseen* (1995), sets in the kitchen and at the family table the struggles of a family with an insane female head of household. As Maggie Barnes ranges out of control in meteoric streaks of craziness, Frederick Barnes has no choice but to hire Pearl Wiggins, a domestic, cook, and keeper who is equal to Maggie's bipolar mood swings. Together, the two women carry out a familiar harvest-time chore, the setting of an outdoor table for 20–30 field hands. At issue in less peaceable scenes are the meals that Pearl attempts to prepare while coaxing Maggie out of some petulant extreme. From a female perspective, Maggie pictures herself cooking flounder for an imaginary guest, Senator Robert Kennedy, who creates a minor contretemps because of Maggie's inexperience planning meals for Catholics. Upon her recovery in 1967 after psychotherapy and eight electroconvulsive shock treatments at Duke Hospital, she returns to the kitchen, which she long before abandoned to Pearl. At Maggie's first appearance as mother-in-charge, she reins in Grandfather Barnes, her tyrannic father-in-law, for scolding the children for refusing to eat oyster dressing. The tense scene ensures the Barnes family that Maggie is once more a healthy wife, parent, and hostess. As her sanity stabilizes, she surprises daughter Hattie by helping Pearl can vegetables, an image rife with nurturing as well as hope for the future.

For the pre–Civil War era, Gibbons's first historical novel, *On the Occasion of My Last Afternoon* (1998), conveys the female perspective on short rations and on substitutes for scarce or nonexistent dyes, fabrics, and pantry staples. She chooses lard-rendering and sausage-making as a symbolic denunciation of human bondage and a foreshadowing of the military carnage to come. Set at five or six boiling cauldrons in the yard of a Bruton Parish plantation on the James River, the messy job of pig slaughter and food preservation in 1842 mirrors the master's murder of Jacob, a slave who violates the courtesies demanded of an underling. In the home's inner sanctum, cook-housekeeper Clarice Washington and her assistants, Bertha and Suzy, carry out the woman's work of turning pigskin into cracklings, a byproduct valued for flavor and crunch. The women promise a deep-fried pig tail to Emma Garnet Tate, the novel's narrator, who inhales the aromas of sage and thyme, the seasonings that turn oddments of pork into savory sausage. In the slave quarter, blacks enjoy Brunswick stew, a Southern specialty that has its beginnings in the humblest down-east cookpots. After Emma's father, Samuel P. Goodman Tate, precipitates fear of a slave revolt on a par with the Nat Turner rebellion from August 22 to October 30, 1831, Clarice receives Jacob's widow into the kitchen and extends small pantry consolations in gifts of side meat and lard to the plantation staff. Emma's experience with the grisly murder and its aftermath elicits silent sorrow for disempowered blacks. Like the runaway slave-woman weeping into the soup kettle in Toni Morrison's *Beloved* (1987), Emma adds a personal touch to the sausage from salty tears falling into the mix.

Less portentous examples of food lore in the novel express Southern hospitality. In 1847, the newlywed Quincy Lowells live well and enjoy glasses of Madeira on the veranda in the evening to end the day. While social maven Lucille McKimmon courts them on their arrival to Blount Street in Raleigh, North Carolina, she chooses food gifts as temptations—butter, pepper, and fresh basil. Presentation of three live ducks at the kitchen door poses a stand-off between Emma and Clarice, who follows the Lowells to their new home. Averse to ducks as food, Clarice refuses to prepare birds she deems unfit for human consumption, an ironic pre-war rejection of food before rationing and shortfalls reduce citizens to starvation. After Emma matures into the female head of household, she celebrates holidays with "crown roasts and stuffed hams," an image of majesty and satiety on the tables of gentry (Gibbons, 1998, 127). She makes her own pantry gifts to the poorly fed Dawes family, to whom she sends a cartload of foodstuffs. Unlike the social-climbing Lucille, Emma distributes nourishment for altruistic reasons. The gesture prefaces an adulthood in service to the less fortunate. Ironically, Emma's charity fails to protect Lavinia Ella Mae Dawes, whose husband beats her with a sack of oranges, an unusual weapon suggesting a bizarre burst of male rage.

More poignant are Civil War exigencies, which challenge both Clarice and Emma. Before the war, Clarice coddles the Lowell sisters—Leslie, Louise, and Mary—with raisin scones, ash cakes, and broiled pig tails, the treat that their mother enjoyed in childhood. Emma takes her daughters to Yarborough House for turtle soup, sourdough crackers, and trifle until war puts an end to extravagance. From the substitution of sweet potatoes for lard candles and the cooking of corn into bread, dodgers, dumplings, and pudding, makeshift staples and short rations worsen with the offering of rats at $2 per pound in 1864, when a Raleigh grocer no longer has poultry to sell. Gibbons respects resourceful Southerners for charring okra into pseudo-coffee beans, for fermenting scuppernong juice into wine, and for adapting standard baking to Fannie Farmer's recipe for pumpkin bread. The most pathetic sources of sustenance are lone corn kernels that malnourished children gather from horse stalls, a scavenging that places humankind and beasts in contention for sustenance.

Colonial values undergird the South and its empty pantries. No longer shopping for goods, Emma's staff hunts rabbits and squirrels to make stew for hungry women and children and for wounded soldiers quartered at the Lowell home after the battle of Gettysburg, Pennsylvania, on July 3–4, 1863. The men who subsist on army hardtack cherish memories of their mothers' menus of "salted ham and cabbage, collards, suet cake, black-eyed peas," a culinary indication of working-class origins (*Ibid.*, 197). From Virginia come Maureen Tate's reports on stragglers begging at the door, a last-ditch effort that she and her father eventually adopt to rescue themselves from General George Brinton McClellan's ravaging of the James River area in June 1862. At war's end, Emma, bowed low with new widowhood, retreats to Quincy's Boston family and attends a cooking school, a suitable training ground for a woman whose only culinary talent is popping corn. In the traditional respite of women, she shares skills and healing conversation with other females. Like June Stanley in *A Virtuous Woman*, Lottie Davies in *A Cure for Dreams* (1991), and Charlie Kate Birch in *Charms for the Easy Life*, Emma reshapes her life based on female strengths and acts of charity.

Descriptions of food in *Divining Women* (2004) enhance subtleties of wifehood, sisterhood, mothering, and mourning. In a feminist motif, the "madwoman in the attic," Maureen Carlton Ross retreats from her vicious husband Troop by creating a second-floor haven. Because he lords his power over the household, he cows the cook and forbids fruit in Maureen's room on the pretext of keeping out insects. On September 30, 1918, the arrival from Washington, D.C., of 22-year-old companion Mary Oliver, a graduate students at Radcliffe, preempts his role as jailer. As Maureen's caretaker, Mary conveys nourishing snacks upstairs during the final 50 days of a difficult pregnancy. After stuffed peppers upset Maureen's stomach, Mary treks to the kitchen at 4:00 A.M. for a household antidote, gingerroot, the source of a tea that quells nausea. A poignant conclusion to Maureen's escape from *de facto* house arrest derives from the flow of breast milk that dampens her garments after the birth of a stillborn daughter, Ella Eloise, on November 8, 1918. The unneeded nourishment offends Troop with its womanly odor at the same time that it marks Maureen's motherhood, however brief, with a spot of normality previously lacking during her confinement. At Troop's downfall, Mary and Maureen test his limits by eating lunch with the house staff, Mamie and Zollie. In defiance of Troop's inhumanity, Maureen commands him to share a meal with the "human beings who keep the damn house running" (Gibbons, 2004, 199). An irredeemable fiend, Troop snarls, "Better off dead than suckle an ingrate," one of the most unsettling lines in Gibbons's fiction (*Ibid.*, 200).

Gibbons composes her first sequel, *The Life All Around Me by Ellen Foster* (2006), with food images appropriate to another feminist study of womanly strength and benevolence. When Ellen helps her foster mother Laura comfort Martha's mother from housewifely drudgery, a two- or three-hour nap concludes with a pot of English tea and shortbread biscuits, two comfort foods common to women's restorative snacks. Ellen reflects on Halloween 1971, when she and Starletta costume themselves as macaroni and cheese, a child-pleasing menu staple suggesting the inseparability of friends. On the negative side, a private joy for Ellen, a box of Little Debbie cakes, aggravates antipathy with two difficult foster placements after their boyfriends sneak in, eat the contents, and leave an empty box on the shelf. Ellen's need for the sweet snack symbolizes her yearning for reward after four years of orphanhood. Fortunately, her life with Laura supplies physical sustenance — Moravian cookies, Cokes, and Methodist hot dogs at the county fair, home-packed school lunches, fried chicken on Sundays— as well as the emotional nourishment that edges out a gnawing mother hunger. In the afterglow of Christmas 1974, Ellen says, "We rested from the giving and taking and stayed still together," a quiet acknowledgement of satiety (Gibbons, 2006, 218).

• *Further reading*

Burleigh, Nina. "Maternal Inspiration Fuels Southern Writer's Work," *Chicago Tribune* (1 October 1989).

Gibbons, Kaye. *Charms for the Easy Life*. New York: Putnam, 1993.

_____. *Divining Women*. New York: G.P. Putnam's Sons, 2004.

_____. *Ellen Foster*. New York: Algonquin Press, 1987.

_____. *The Life All Around Me by Ellen Foster*. New York: Harcourt, 2006.

_____. *On the Occasion of My Last Afternoon*. New York: G.P. Putnam's Sons, 1998.

_____. *A Virtuous Woman*. Chapel Hill, N.C.: Algonquin Press, 1989.

Munafo, Giavanna. "Colored Biscuits: Reconstructing Whiteness and the Boundaries of 'Home' in Kaye Gibbons's *Ellen Foster*," *Women, America, and Movement*. ed. Susan L. Roberson. Columbia: University of Missouri Press, 1998, pp. 38–61.

Foster, Ellen

Kaye Gibbons's resilient 10-year-old self-rescuer, Ellen Foster, has become the author's fourth daughter, a needy fantasy child who stopped in for a weekend and remained for two decades. In the estimation of author-critic Lynna Williams, a reviewer for the *Chicago Tribune*, Ellen is "bereft of any childhood worth that word" (Williams, 2006). Her plight resonates with the Cinderella motif, a paradigm of ostracism and motherlessness. Characterized by Madonna Kolbenschlag, author of *Kiss Sleeping Beauty Good-bye* (1979), Ellen is the female striver "deliberately and systematically excluded from meaningful achievement," a condition that Ellen eventually corrects (Kolbenschlag, 1979, 63). Rather than wait for rescue by the male on the white horse or the fairy godmother with the magic wand, Ellen takes the feminist stance and saves herself from unfair judgment and exclusion. She becomes the female quester who is willing to undergo hardships and to accept risks as the necessary prelude to triumph.

Gibbons is so attuned to Ellen's inner landscape that she feels "like I should lay an extra place at table for her" (Kenney, 1995). For a moral compass, according to interviewer Ann Alexander of the *Greensboro* (N.C.) *News & Record*, Ellen relies on her "old soul," an intuitive inner sonar blessed with profound discernment of human nature (Alexander, 1993). In an interview with Virginia Daniel, a reporter for the Raleigh, Durham, Chapel Hill, North Carolina, *Independent Weekly*, Gibbons agreed that "Ellen feels ancient, like she's been alive since the dawn of man" (Daniel, 2006). For her old-as-dirt wisdom, the character has sparked comparison with Charles

Dickens's title waif *Oliver Twist* (1838), Mark Twain's title river rafter in *The Adventures of Huckleberry Finn* (1884), J.D. Salinger's tough-talking Holden Caulfield in *The Catcher in the Rye* (1951), and Harper Lee's feisty Scout Finch from *To Kill a Mockingbird* (1960), all four of whom grow up amid social and emotional disorder. Like the wounded children in these classics, Ellen surveys her defeats from a child's perspective, which lacks full understanding of the anguish that alienates her parents from Ellen's maternal relatives. In a feminized version of the *Bildungsroman*, Ellen reprises the griefs of Charlotte Brontë's orphaned governess in *Jane Eyre* (1847) by struggling to exonerate herself for surviving and for outliving her fractious kin.

Blessed with immediacy and dark humor, the plot of *Ellen Foster* describes the child's picaresque search for home ground after her 40-year-old mother commits suicide in March 1969 from an overdose of prescription digitalis. Along the way, according to book critic Lynn Jessup, a reviewer for the *Greensboro* (N.C.) *News & Record*, Ellen draws insight about human behavior and "spits out her observations like watermelon seeds" (Jessup, 1995). To avenge her father Bill for devaluing and dishonoring his wife, Ellen wears her mother's stockings, a form of internalizing the lost parent by mimicking her daily appearance. Intimate contact with the mother's garments provides post-funereal comfort at the same time that it cloaks uninterrupted private grieving. Contributing to the orphan's search for belonging are memories of two subsequent deceased family members, her father and maternal grandmother. World-wise at a tender age, by Christmas Day, 1970, Ellen has already discerned that there is no Santa Claus on her horizon. To control the work's negative elements, Gibbons blesses Ellen with an outlet—a gift for homespun similes and the exuberant hyperbole of the young. The method reprises the style of James Weldon Johnson, who shaped character from everyday folksay.

Left to ambiguity is the question of Ellen's relationship with a sinister father whose unpredictable menace echoes the fanged phantasm in Gibbons's short-short story "The Headache," issued in June 1987 in the *St. Andrews Review*. Before his sudden death from cerebral hemorrhage in 1970, he pawed her breasts and may or may not have raped her. The hazy reflection derives from the author's screened memory, which allows through the defense only the amount of reality that Ellen can tolerate. Among the gauzy secrets of Ellen's short past are the side-by-side sharing of her mother's deathbed, the willing of one heart to beat for two, and obedience to her father, who forbids the child from telephoning for medical intervention. For day-to-day survival, Ellen retreats into her mother's passivity by following the overt and covert instructive trails her mother left behind in the kitchen and vegetable garden. At a breaking point, Ellen becomes a feminist heroine by abandoning a just-getting-by mode for self-salvation.

Too soon, Ellen shoulders the double onus of grief and guilt, which betray her secrets to the world through outsized fears, anxiety attacks, nightmares, nail chewing, rolling stomach, and tremors. Her psychic shield is a compulsion to organize, list, and rearrange to hold at bay an intrusive swirl of memories and terrors. Long after the fact, she ponders her mother's romantic illusions about a future mate who turns into a feckless, low-class batterer. Similarly ingenuous, Ellen pours over a catalog to select images of the ideal family and accoutrements for their make-believe home, where ideal parents treasure their children. In a seventh novel, *Divining Women* (2004), Gibbons characterizes such romantic fantasizing as the "lunatic optimism" that women accrue from girlhood onward (Gibbons, 2004, 149).

Ellen's triumph is an act of faith that somewhere awaits a female community that will accept her for all her shortcomings. Like June Stanley, the quasi-orphan of Gibbons's *A Virtuous Woman* (1989), and Bone, the victimized child in Dorothy Allison's *Bastard Out of Carolina* (1992), Ellen Foster looks back on the detritus of a ruined family; like Homer's Odysseus, she sets sail on unpredictable seas in search of home. After praying to Jesus for a sign of better fortune, she worships a lace-necked dress. Gibbons creates the sashed outfit from green and navy, colors symbolizing hope and duty. At church the next day, Ellen's dress pays off on her first glimpse of a foster mother and her girls. As a second Christmas nears, Ellen asks for white drawing paper, a suggestion of Aristotle's *tabula rasa* (clean slate), which she intends to inscribe with the particulars of a new self. Pondering what to draw, she thinks of cats and a covered bridge, emblems of softness and secure passage. More revealing of the inner child is her consideration of a seascape, a complex world view that is simultaneously "strong and beautiful and sad" (Gibbons, 1987, 106).

In Gibbons's sequel, *The Life All Around Me by Ellen Foster* (2006), the character remains calculating and sassy but "sore-armed" from past troubles (Gibbons, 2006, 118). In the opening lines, she states her credo that no human effort should be "watered down," a belief that returns in the novel's resolution (Gibbons, 2006, 1). The motto belies a subsequent description of her mother Shine's decline, when she "became too sad and died," a memory worded in the style of a ten-year-old witness (*Ibid.*, 4). Ellen has no patience with government dilly-dallying regarding permanent placement with Laura, a loving surrogate mother fierce enough to shield Ellen from social services paper shuffling. Laura is womanly wise enough to delight Ellen with a jaunt to the movies and with tennis socks adorned with "blue dingleballs," an endearing affectation in a pre-teen (*Ibid.*, 17). For all Laura's running interference to spare Ellen pain, the protagonist must follow her own cognitions, a style that Lynna Williams calls "worrying ideas and memories until they come clear for her" (Williams, 2006).

Critics accuse Gibbons of overselling Ellen's brilliance. *Kirkus Reviews* describes Ellen's previous charm as "curdled into self-congratulatory superiority" ("Review," 2005). Author-reviewer Valerie Sayers, writing for the *Washington Post*, accuses Ellen of "strutting her own prodigious talents and sterling qualities," a failing disdained by other readers (Sayers, 2006). Essential to Laura's mothering is a counterbalance — a reminder to Ellen that she must share the foster home with two rambunctious pre-delinquents who also rate attention. Through Laura's patient discussion of human failings and needs, Ellen learns that behaviors vary in neglected children and that Ellen's perspective on human yearning is unique to her. Increasing alienation are subsequent scenarios in which Ellen's tendency toward divergent thinking sets her outside the norm, a displacement she maps with her fingers on an atlas at a high IQ camp in Baltimore at Johns Hopkins University. Exposure to a college environment increases Ellen's fear that she can never belong in the world. Ruminating to the point of hysteria, she learns from Laura a feminist truth: that giving to others— Stuart,

Marvin, Martha's mother, Starletta, Cousin Dora — steadies the resolve and eases the restive spirit.

See also ***Ellen Foster***; **Foster genealogy**; ***The Life All Around Me by Ellen Foster***

• *Further reading*

Alexander, Ann. "Book of Changes for Kaye Gibbons," *Greensboro* (N.C.) *News & Record* (21 March 1993).

Daniel, Virginia. "The Life All Around Her: Kaye Gibbons Talks to the *Indy* about *Ellen Foster's* Return," Raleigh (N.C.) *Indy* (25 January 2006).

Gibbons, Kaye. *Divining Women*. New York: G.P. Putnam's Sons, 2004.

_____. *Ellen Foster*. New York: Algonquin Press, 1987.

_____. *The Life All Around Me by Ellen Foster*. New York: Harcourt, 2006.

Jessup, Lynn. "Kaye Gibbons: Another Happy Ending," *Greensboro* (N.C.) *News & Record* (12 November 1995).

Kenney, Michael. "An Author Confronts Her Inner Demons," *Boston Globe* (20 September 1995).

Kolbenschlag, Madonna. *Kiss Sleeping Beauty Good-bye: Breaking the Spell of Feminine Myths and Models*. Toronto: Bantam, 1981.

Miller, Pamela. "Kaye Gibbons' Novel Draws from Her Life," Minneapolis-St. Paul (Minn.) *Star Tribune* (15 January 2006).

Munafo, Giavanna. "Colored Biscuits: Reconstructing Whiteness and the Boundaries of 'Home' in Kaye Gibbons's *Ellen Foster*," *Women, America, and Movement*. ed. Susan L. Roberson. Columbia: University of Missouri Press, 1998, pp. 38–61.

"Review: *The Life All Around Me by Ellen Foster*," *Kirkus Reviews* 73, no. 19 (1 October 2005).

Sayers, Valerie, "Growing Into the Role," *Washington Post* (6 January 2006).

Town, Caren J. *New Southern Girl: Female Adolescence in the Works of 12 Women Authors*. Jefferson, N.C.: McFarland, 2004.

Williams, Lynna. "For Ellen Foster, There's Finally Light at the End of the Tunnel," *Chicago Tribune* (8 January 2006).

Foster genealogy

The family of Ellen Foster takes shape out of the oddments of a child's memory and nightmares. From experience, she learns that blood kinship ensures no refuge from a cruel fate. Her choice of "Foster" as a surname is an idiosyncratic retreat from unloving relatives:

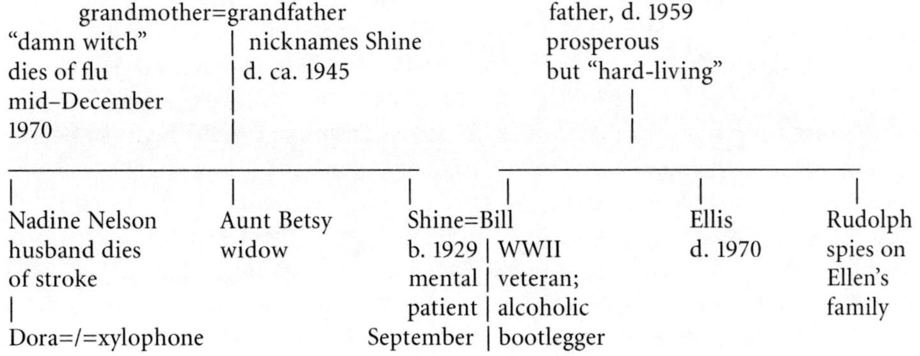

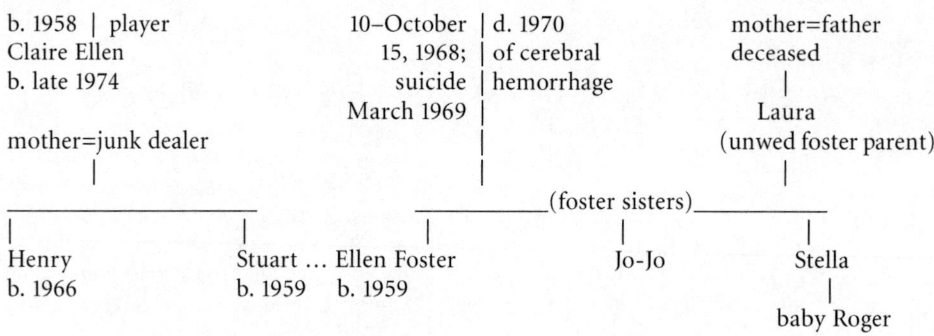

• *Further reading*

Gibbons, Kaye. *Ellen Foster*. New York: Algonquin Press, 1987.
_____. *The Life All Around Me by Ellen Foster*. New York: Harcourt, 2006.

foster parenting

Kaye Gibbons contributes to readers a realistic picture of volunteer child care. In the estimation of Dannye Romine, book editor for the *Charlotte* (N.C.) *Observer*, the source of realism is genuine concern: "Kaye Gibbons knows orphans to the core" (Romine, 1989). In her first novel, *Ellen Foster* (1987), the title character receives more love and attention from her art teacher Julia and Julia's husband Roy than from extended family. At a significant upturn in Ellen's muddled home life, the couple prepares an 11th birthday celebration that startles Ellen with its acknowledgement of her individuality and worth. The unexpected joy of living among normal, unvengeful people sets Ellen on the road to a more lasting relationship with Laura, the foster mother she selects at church and petitions for motherhood on Christmas Day, 1970. Essential to stability are Laura's gifts of sleepovers, fried chicken on Sundays, rides on Dolphin the pony, home-packed school lunches, and relaxation techniques that combat Ellen's tremors, flashbacks, and anxiety attacks. Left unsaid is Laura's perspective on motherly patience and compromise, two essentials of volunteer parenting.

The strand of regard for the unparented child winds through other of Gibbons's works. In *A Virtuous Woman* (1989), the barren marriage of "Blinking" Jack Ernest Stokes and Ruby Pitts Woodrow Stokes draws them to a neighbor, June Stanley, whose mother, Tiny Fran, extends mothering only to her son Roland, a delinquent turned felon. In Ruby's care, June poses for family photos, learns to weave potholders, and acquires instruction in menarche, a mother-daughter passage that Tiny Fran fails to initiate. June flourishes by leaving the agrarian neighborhood to earn a college degree in architecture, a profession suggesting dedication to home building. Supporting her ambition, her foster father comments, "You have to get off somewhere to do something makes some money," a promotion of female independence through financial autonomy (Gibbons, 1989, 62). The reciprocity of woman-to-woman love bolsters Ruby at age 45, when she declines from lung cancer. In addition to loving care, June offers Ruby soft gowns, robes, and slippers, the human touches that spare the dying unnecessary discomfort. Gibbons carries the foster parenting model forward into 65-year-old Jack's first three months alone, when June washes dishes, tidies up, and oversees his welfare. Encircling her like loving arms are the ties of Ruby's apron, a domestic legacy to a beloved foster daughter.

Additional models of fostering grace Gibbons's fifth and sixth novels. Pearl Wiggins, the cook-housekeeper-caregiver in *Sights Unseen* (1995), accepts a difficult challenge in a troubled household. At the birth of narrator Harriet Pearl "Hattie" Barnes, Pearl furnishes the nursery and encourages the lapsed maternity of Maggie Barnes, whose bipolarity supercedes instinctive cuddling and breastfeeding. For 12 years, Pearl cossets and comforts her namesake, who longs for Maggie's attention. Out of respect for the rightful mother-daughter relationship, Pearl reminds the child that Maggie is the real parent and Pearl the surrogate. After psychotherapy and eight electroconvulsive shock treatments at Duke Hospital restore Maggie to normality in 1967, Pearl offers a touching acknowledgement of wellness in the female head of household by slipping back into the hireling's role, leaving Maggie the task of building trust in a wary child.

To a lesser degree, Emma Garnet Tate Lowell, the narrator of Gibbons's first historical novel, *On the Occasion of My Last Afternoon* (1998), fosters an underclass girl to polish her rough edges. Lavinia Ella Mae Dawes, a perceptive daughter of semi-literate parents, requires nourishment as well as a role model of female intellect and excellence. She flourishes in the Lowell residence in Raleigh, North Carolina, where she admires trailing irises on the wallpaper and recognizes orchid varieties on the dinner table from her grandmother's tutelage in horticulture. Dr. Quincy Lowell and his wife further Lavina's opportunities by escorting her to a staging of *Macbeth* and by paying for two years' tuition to Saint Mary's, an introduction to learning suited to Lavinia's considerable talents. In thanks, Lavinia writes, "Did you not, Mrs. Lowell, send me the future?," an acknowledgement of the abstract joys and opportunities contained in education (Gibbons, 1998, 122). The upshot of the Lowell family's love for Lavinia takes shape after her death from neglect and abuse by a cruel mate. Quincy retaliates against her husband, a foul-mouthed wife-basher incapable of loving a woman whose "beauty and grace and care ... warranted somebody's taking a concern for her" (*Ibid.*, 124). In spiritual union with Quincy after his death in 1865, Emma hears his voice urging her to continue tending the needy: "A hundred Lavinias need you.... Go home, hurry" (*Ibid.*, 268). The ghostly commission attests to the reciprocity of volunteer parenting, which comforts both children and their foster parents.

The author returns to her first mother-hungry heroine in a sequel, *The Life All Around Me by Ellen Foster* (2006), a detailed examination of foster mothering. In September 1974, Laura, a single parent, becomes Ellen's mainstay against an uncertain future and against uncontrollable flashbacks to a chaotic home life and the death of both parents. At age 15, Ellen admits that a basic knowledge of the nuclear family wasn't "installed in me young" (Gibbons, 2006, 44). She is mature enough to recognize the honeymoon period that begins a foster placement and to examine Laura's low-key methodology, which includes quiet talks about smart-mouthing and breaking rules. Ellen respects the occasional separation of parent and child for necessary cooling-off periods and for contemplation of the boundaries that discipline demands of both parties. For contrast, Gibbons juxtaposes Ellen's intellectual and emotional demands on Laura with the misdeeds of two "strumpets" who steal Laura's only perfume and consort with boyfriends when Laura drives away on an all-day errand (*Ibid.*, 44). Through Laura, Gibbons states the fundamentals of sanity—the ability to love and work. The author adds a third footing for mental health, a need for rest to balance activity. The triad simplifies for Ellen target areas that she must refine before she can mature.

See also **Laura; Lowell, Emma Garnet Tate; Stokes, Ruby Pitts Woodrow; Washington, Clarice**

• *Further reading*

Gibbons, Kaye. *The Life All Around Me by Ellen Foster.* New York: Harcourt, 2006.
_____. *On the Occasion of My Last Afternoon.* New York: G.P. Putnam's Sons, 1998.
_____. *A Virtuous Woman.* Chapel Hill, N.C.: Algonquin Press, 1989.
Romine, Dannye. "The Struggle for Support," *Charlotte* (N.C.) *Observer* (30 April 1989).

Gibbons, Kaye

A lyric master, Kaye Gibbons regularly wins accolades from respected sources and from fans and book clubs that anticipate each new publication. From her first ventures into fiction —*Ellen Foster* (1987) and the short-short story "The Headache," issued on June 1987 in the *St. Andrews Review*— Gibbons's work has targeted the emotionally troubled. After publishing her second work, *A Virtuous Woman* (1989), a portrait of a rural marriage, she earned a touching salute from Dannye Romine, book editor for the *Charlotte* (N.C.) *Observer*: "Writers who write out of the depths of themselves write with the soul's authority. They trust themselves" (Romine, 1989). Two years later, Jay Strafford, a book critic for the *Richmond Times-Dispatch*, typified the author as "a talented creator of little gems," a reference to Milk Farm Road, the miniature world of *A Cure for Dreams* (1991), Gibbons's third novel, which she peopled with humble, but assertive womenfolk (Strafford, 1991).

Candor accounts for the immediacy of Gibbons's writing. A review in *America* rightly credits her with "unflinching honesty, her foregrounding of hatred and violence and their destructive consequences" (Redding, *et al.*, 1999). Interviews disclose the same sincerity and intense involvement in Gibbons's personal life. In December 1997, she rebelled against the remodeling of the Hayes Barton Grill, source of her favorite lunch. Her reason echoes her respect for Southern traditions: "I can't eat pimiento cheese in Art Deco-type booths!" (Brodeur, 1997). With dramatic hyperbole, she threatened to stand in "pajamas out in front of the pharmacy with a picket sign," a declaration rife with her to-the-bone reduction of issues to the basics (*Ibid.*). From the same directness in fiction come humor and dignity, disparate strands of character strength. Frank examination of mental illness in *Sights Unseen* (1995) generates the quandary of farmer Frederick Barnes, a panicked husband whose bipolar wife Maggie turns him into her sex slave. Beyond coping with her mercurial moods, he institutionalizes her, then reclaims her through a gentle talk cure, a re-introduction to their courtship and early marriage. Gibbons rounds out Maggie's life with 15 years of normality crowned by worthy motherhood. The juxtaposition of pathos with comic touches acknowledges a literary truth as old as Aesop's fables, that human conflicts exhibit a range of intertwining moods, from grave to incongruous.

Gibbons earns critical regard for honing episodes to few words. Concise scenarios reveal the subtleties of blue-collar and gentrified family life, particularly that of North Carolina farm folk and urban newcomers. In 1990, a reviewer for *Wilson Quarterly* ranked Gibbons's villains with those of English social novelist Charles Dickens, creator of Ebenezer Scrooge and Fagin, and placed Gibbons in a league with Southern literary superstars William Faulkner, Katherine Anne Porter, Tennessee Williams, and Thomas Wolfe. By 1993, critic James Thompson, in an essay for *World & I*, considered Gibbons a "serious contender [for] the next queen of Southern Letters" (Thompson, 1993, 349). He admired her for decorum and for a succinctness that is both dynamic and graceful. His assessment rates her the equal of authors Ellen Glasgow, Carson McCullers, Flannery O'Connor, and Eudora Welty, four Southern feminists who influenced Gibbons's style.

To maintain nuance and elegance in her work, Gibbons lives a tightly controlled routine that she calls a "boiled down, purified existence" (Willett, 2004). Early on, she disclosed that she extrudes artistry through bouts of manic depression, a paradoxical syndrome that has limited and enhanced her work since age twenty. She prefers to write during periods of hypomania, a transitional state between self-control and frenzy. Treatment for emotional instability has its liabilities. Under heavy doses of anticonvulsants, she loses the edge that is her gift to Southern feminism. For self-preservation, she values a home sanctuary and the company of three daughters, Leslie, Louise, and Mary, who give her a reason for getting out of bed and going through the motions of normality. Typically, she pictures motherhood as a battle against laundry, an insightful symbol of purification and restoration of order.

Some critics fault Gibbons for maintaining a gynocentric world in fiction that mirrors her own four-woman household. In *Charms for the Easy Life* (1993), heroine Charlie Kate Birch, aided by her daughter, Sophia Snow Birch, and granddaughter Margaret, operates an unlicensed medical practice that draws the sick "like the loaves and the fishes," a food image that blends domestic bounty with Christian charity (Gibbons, 1993, 22). To maintain stasis, Charlie Kate tolerates a parade of lackluster males only for stud service and professional relationships, including men suffering from boils, industrial accidents, near drowning, near lynching, alcoholism, leprosy, and syphilis. After the men make their contributions to the story, they retreat from her fictional stage by a variety of exits—an aristocratic physician out of shame for mistreating female patients, her husband by abandonment, and her skirt-chasing son-in-law by a well-timed cerebral hemorrhage, which kills him dead in bed in August 1936 in answer to his wife Sophia's surreal pleas to Jesus. Three foils to the sorriest males—protégé Dr. Charles Nutter, businessman Richard Baines, and naval veteran Tom Hawkings, III—function like Charlie Kate's well handled puppets, dancing on cue, offering gifts and adoration, and behaving admirably in public. The overview of the herbalist's home life and career corroborates critical inclusion of Gibbons within feminist bounds.

Despite a preference for woman-to-woman support and community, Gibbons maintains a panoply of human characters and conflicts. Her research into the Civil War era for a first historical novel, *On the Occasion of My Last Afternoon* (1998), attests to the author's admiration for male-female synergy. Heroine Emma Garnet Tate Lowell pairs well with her husband, Dr. Quincy Lowell, as a wife and parent, in surgery and the recovery ward, and in home scenes where combat casualties recuperate. In an introspective mode, for *Sights Unseen*, a bruising psychological novel, Gibbons examined her own extended family for insights into insanity. The story features narrator Hattie Barnes, an under-mothered girl, her brother Freddy, imperious Grandfather Barnes, and the family cook-housekeeper, Pearl Wiggins, who pinch-hits as parent until the birth mother, Maggie Barnes, recovers her wits. Gibbons chose sisterhood for the controlling theme of *A Cure for Dreams*, a paean to emotional networking that elevates Lottie O'Cadhain Davies to queen bee of Milk Farm Road during the privations of the Great Depression. Similarly reverential of female strengths within needy communities, Gibbons's first sequel, *The Life All Around Me by Ellen Foster* (2006), creates a model of nurturing and charity in Laura, the title character's foster mother. As in her earlier works, Gibbons's evenly paced survey of Ellen Foster's choices and decisions sustains the author's appeal to a variety of readers.

• *Further reading*

Brodeur, Nicole. "A Grill That's Perfection Just As It Is," Raleigh, N.C., *News & Observer* (10 December 1997).
Brown, Kurt, ed. *Facing the Lion*. Boston: Beacon Press, 1996.
"*Ellen Foster* and *A Virtuous Woman*," *Wilson Quarterly* 14, no. 1 (Winter 1990): 95.
Gibbons, Kaye. *Charms for the Easy Life*. New York: Putnam, 1993.
Redding, Sean, Jane Fisher, and James S. Torrens. "Review: *On the Occasion of My Last Afternoon*," *America* 180, no. 1 (2 January 1999).
Romine, Dannye. "The Struggle for Support," *Charlotte* (N.C.) *Observer* (30 April 1989).
Strafford, Jay. "Ordinary Life Has Meaning," *Richmond Times-Dispatch* (3 April 1991).
Thompson, James. "Man-Taming Granny," *World & I* 8, no. 9 (September 1993): 349–354.
Willett, Melissa. "Gibbons Brings Her Voice to Fayetteville," *Fayetteville* (N.C.) *Observer* (5 October 2004).

Greene-Carlton-Oliver-Ross genealogy

A complex contrast of families and married love, *Divining Women* (2004) depicts the emergence of 22-year-old Mary Oliver from a clannish extended family in Washington, D.C., to attain full humanity in the rescue of her aunt-by-marriage, Maureen Carlton Ross:

grandfather
leaser of convict labor in 1863

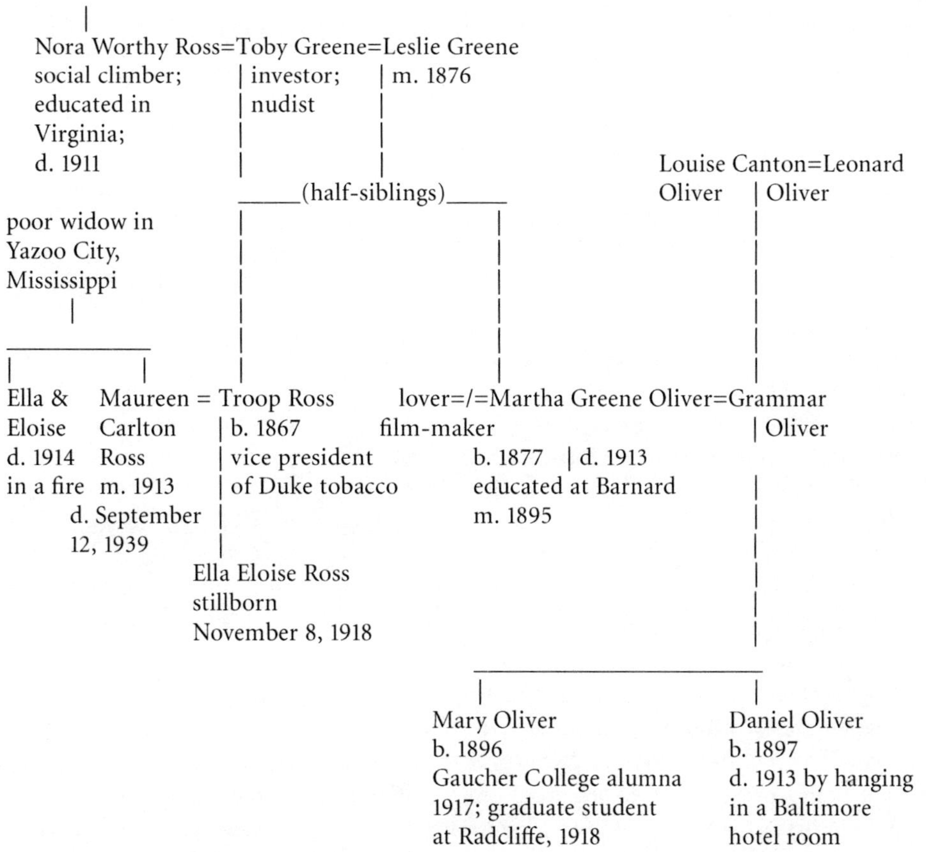

• *Further reading*

Gibbons, Kaye. *Divining Women*. New York: G.P. Putnam's Sons, 2004.

"The Headache"

A model of Gibbons's skill at female vernacular, "The Headache," published in the June 1987 issue of the *St. Andrews Review*, reveals the roots of petty theft in rural poverty. The driving force of the text is a plain-spoken woman in search of comfort. Lucille is one of the unique characters in Gibbons's subsequent fiction who, in the words of analyst Linda Adams Barnes, "must use language of their own to come into being through telling the stories of their own lives" (Barnes, 1993, 29). A commentary on social and economic insecurity in the farming class, the short-short story moves into a realm that Gibbons calls "the hearts of hurting souls" (Avery, 1998). She pictures farm wife Lucille Womble confessing to a physician, Dr. Janet Cowley, the source of two weeks of head pain, horrific visions of serpents, weepiness, and insomnia. The motif of the prank pocketbook derives from Southern trickster lore, which often uses snakes as elements of cruel jest and as symbols of corrosive evil. Like a gnawing censure of lax morals, the image of a beady-eyed snake with protruding fangs haunts Lucille's imagination. Sleeping and waking, she fears to close her eyes and encounter the phantasm. Nocturnal terrors alert her husband Henry to Lucille's two-week anguish, an unusual symptom in their otherwise placid marriage.

The action dots in enough details to endear Lucille to the reader. She mentions a hard summer when the bank repossesses two farm machines, a rare Saturday night supper at a chicken restaurant, and the lure of a "town lady's" purse abandoned in the ladies' room (Gibbons, 1987, 3). Her work as a domestic for Mae Bell Stokes and the scrubbing of overalls on a washboard in a one-room residence attest to unremitting poverty. A symbolic stretch of drop cords to lamp, television, and record player implies the stretch of farm proceeds to support the family of two adults and ten children. Central to Lucille's character are honesty and a rejection of welfare, two qualities common to proud Southern agrarians. Gibbons rewards her protagonist with Henry, a war veteran and loving husband who "spoons" with his wife in bed, cuddling her to his chest to stave off the unmanageable fears that reduce her to tears and thoughts of suicide (*Ibid.*, 5). A common scenario in domestic fiction, the late-night intimacy pictures male-female relations as a dependable solace for women who receive few material rewards.

Gendered behaviors in Gibbons's characters leave tantalizing opportunities for development. The text implies that, while Henry was fighting for his country, Lucille gave birth at home with the aid of her father-in-law. The author introduces Mae Bell as judgmental and intrusive in the positive sense of the words. Contributing to an aura of female community, she promotes the professional office of Janet Cowley, an abnormally small doctor who deserves the patronage of women. Janet's gift to her patient hangs on the wall of Room C—a framed statement from the Hippocratic Oath promising doctor-patient confidentiality, a reassurance to a shamed, troubled person like Lucille. At the end of a difficult day, the patient retreats to Henry's embrace to confess her theft of the abandoned handbag.

Gibbons's skill at novella and novel emerge in the story's unpursued loose ends, which are the beginnings of a much longer work. She speaks her humanism through Henry, who chooses to forestall for two days Lucille's recital of moral wrongs. At a turning point in her recovery, he wisely reminds her that people are prone to faults. A tender outline of private quandary and marital unity, the story teases the reader with its affectionate view of psychosomatic illness generated by a forgivable failing. Too soon, Gibbons rewards Lucille the promise of two new hats and leaves to the reader's speculation how the gifts will eradicate guilt and restore wellness, a pervasive aim in the author's subsequent longer fiction.

See also **Womble genealogy**

• *Further reading*

Avery, Sarah. "The Book of Love," Raleigh, N.C., *News & Observer* (24 November 1998).

Barnes, Linda Adams. "Telling Yourself into Existence: The Fiction of Kaye Gibbons," *Tennessee Philological Bulletin* 30 (1993): 28–35.

Gibbons, Kaye. "The Headache," *St. Andrews Review* (June 1987): 3–8.

healing and health

Throughout her novels, Kaye Gibbons expresses a girlhood interest in ailments, medicine, and recuperation. An early story, "The Headache," issued in the *St. Andrews Review* in June 1987, focuses on the debilitating headache, weepiness, flashbacks, and insomnia arising from mental anguish. The combined onslaught presses the sufferer, farm wife Lucille Womble, to thoughts of suicide. At the heart of the protagonist's two weeks of suffering lies a guilty conscience overladen by a trick, the seizure and concealment of an abandoned pocketbook carrying a snake that a jokester placed in a restaurant ladies' room as a prank. The text indicates that the concern of her employer, Mae Bell Stokes, wise counsel by a physician, Dr. Janet Cowley, and the regard and physical embrace of husband Henry Womble see Lucille through a difficult time in mothering ten children on a failing farm. At the root of successful treatment lies Lucille's forgiveness of herself for lapsing into behavior she associates with white trash.

In Gibbons's first novel, *Ellen Foster* (1987), a more debilitating form of guilt harrows a ten-year-old for failure to rescue her 40-year-old mother from suicide. In restive orphanhood, the title character entertains herself with a toy microscope, which she values as a "good buy" that comes with a warranty, a valuable document to a child who distrusts much of her milieu (Gibbons, 1987, 47). The microscope serves a dual purpose — a proof of Ellen's intellectual pragmatism and a symbol of the introspection that scrutinizes human action and relationships for signs of disaffection and betrayal. The sad irony of Ellen's interest in minutia is her inability to steady quaking hands or to stave off unsettling nightmares, anxiety attacks, and fears of her father Bill, even though he is long dead from alcoholism. At a climactic point in her healing, she states her method of warring against the past: "Every day I try to feel better about all that went on when I was little" (*Ibid.*, 121). Her stoic persona satisfies readers for her ability to nest in unlikely places, to ease inordinate blame for her mother's death, and to reach out for stability in a topsy-turvy world.

In a second novel, *A Virtuous Woman* (1989), the author ponders two incurables, a couple nagged by regret and parted by death. Farm wife Ruby Pitts Woodrow Stokes adopts cigarette smoking as a physical release from her badgering, belittling first husband, migrant worker John Woodrow. After a quarter century of marriage to long-term bachelor "Blinking" Jack Ernest Stokes, she flourishes in a loving environment, but clings to her smokes, perhaps as a solace to harsh memories. In her last hours, lung cancer fails to lessen her need to light up. Her gesture — like blowing a kiss with two fingers — vexes Jack, who bears a wounded heart back to an empty house. After 45-year-old Ruby succumbs to lethal disease, 65-year-old Jack bungles his attempt to live alone once more. Healing eludes him in indoors respites — bourbon, Roadrunner cartoons on television, clean sheets, and the lilac fragrance of Ruby's dusting powder. At sorrow's extremes, he hallucinates a reunion with Ruby's ghost. The double tragedy draws succor from neighbors, June and Burr Stanley, who entice him from inertia back to the world of the living. Like Gibbons's first novel and first short story, the Stanleys' altruism validates the volunteer's intervention in the needs of a fellow human being.

In Gibbons's third novel, *A Cure for Dreams* (1991), real and fabricated symptoms mark the childhood of Betty Davies Randolph, the sole surviving child of Quaker farmer-miller Charles Davies and Irish emigrant Lottie O'Cadhain Davies. Gibbons describes the faux frailties of Betty's infancy as her mother's inventions to keep mother and child out of Charles's cotton fields along Milk Farm Road in rural North Carolina. By age 12, Betty becomes so obstinate that she eats only cornbread and molasses, ironically, the daily crumbs of the underfed. The author embroiders details— malaise, dark swollen tongue, and patchy skin from pellagra and the daily doses of Lydia Estes Pinkham's black cohosh and alcohol elixir, first marketed in 1875, which keeps Betty intoxicated. The episode dramatizes a parental battleground on which Charles militates against Lottie for her ignorance of nutrition. Later, ignorance and inexperience ill prepare Betty for another encounter with self-endangerment from drugs. To her surprise, Stanton, her Richmond beau, turns out to be a cyclical patient in the "dope ward" from casual indulgence in Neurol Compound, a sedative crutch containing bromide (Gibbons, 1991, 129). The author pictures Betty shedding Stanton and forming a healthy, promising relationship with Herman Randolph, a fellow farm child unfettered by urban indulgences.

Gibbons stocks *A Cure for Dreams* with herbalism and woman-to-woman comforting. At the emotional collapse of Sade Duplin after she slays her husband Roy with a shotgun, Lottie and her friends prescribe chamomile tea, a mild sedative and tonic, and paregoric, an analgesic tincture of opium. On the advice of midwife-baby doctor Polly Deal, Betty ensures a healthy pregnancy from drinking strong haw root tea, a sedative that lowers blood pressure and relaxes the uterus. After giving birth to a daughter on November 25, 1942, during Herman's absence in World War II, Betty accepts from Polly a cup of horehound tea, a harmless folk cure intended to settle the nerves of the mother and her breastfeeding infant. Polly's traditional healing methods contrast the scientific training of Odessa Hightower, a public health nurse whose surname suggests the attitude of country folk toward intrusive educated healers. As a reward for Polly's home health care, Betty offers a lasting reward by naming the baby Marjorie Polly Randolph. The name links Polly to a four-generation matrilineage, Gibbons's all-female extended family that looks to inner strengths for health and happiness.

The author wrings drollery from additional folk cures in her fourth novel, *Charms for the Easy Life* (1993), the story of a self-educated herbalist-midwife. The cast of characters features a trio of women that reviewer Carol Anshaw, a book critic for the *Chicago Tribune*, calls a "healing SWAT team" (Anshaw,1993). The story provides a subtextual history of medicine from crude kitchen-table surgery, iron tablets donated by the Hayes Barton Pharmacy for treating anemia, antipyrine to reduce fever and pain, and a salt-and-soda scrub for pyorrhea to the advent of antibiotics. Civil War field techniques include the pressing of a squashed silver dollar into the head of Uncle Otha, who sustains a cranial injury at the battle of Shiloh, fought at Pittsburg Landing, Tennessee, on April 6–7, 1862. His niece, protagonist Charlie Kate Birch, a pioneering North Carolina folk healer, trains herself in midwifery, herbalism, and clinical practice by reading issues of the *New England Journal of Medicine*, discarded medical textbooks, and a Southern home medical handbook, *Dr. John C. Gunn's*

Domestic Medicine: The Poor Man's Friend in the House of Affliction, Pain and Sickness (1830). Published in Knoxville, Tennessee, the classic text contains "Principles of Common Sense" and recommends simples and tinctures for the healing of rural and pioneer families lacking cash for doctor bills or living too far from medical aid to seek outside help. The description still holds true during and after the Great Depression among Charlie Kate's clientele in Raleigh, North Carolina.

Gibbons applauds the common sense that governs Charlie Kate's diagnoses, treatments, and curatives, some of which she grows in her front yard. Daily calls for laxatives, treatment of colicky babies, the setting of broken bones, educating teens about masturbation and sexual experimentation, and the laying out of the dead build her practice. One of her patients, Hermit Willoughby, suffers a huge boil on the neck that he fails to heal with quaint hexes; another sufferer walks all the way from the Atlantic coast to seek treatment for leprosy. A third patient sets up a perpetual payback to Charlie Kate for curing him of syphilis. A hapless Christian Scientist requires stitches after he walks into a fan. Lacking suturing materials, Charlie Kate opts for red sewing thread, a dual symbol of her pragmatism and boldness in initiating a home-based practice. At a family gathering on Christmas Day, 1942, she removes warts, a daily complaint to folk doctors. She also engages a surgeon in discussion of Sister Kenny, the Australian nurse who formalized the treatment of polio with hot, wet wraps and muscle flexing. Although the professional exchange gives Charlie Kate an opportunity to crow over her embrace of unorthodox therapies, she wins her granddaughter's admiration by concealing medical innovations.

Gibbons blesses Charlie Kate with ambition and foresight, two qualities the healer passes to her daughter, Sophia Snow Birch, and, to a greater degree, to granddaughter Margaret. To expand Charlie Kate's range to dentistry, she orders a wrench and needle-nose pliers from Sears, Roebuck and purchases chloroform from a veterinary supply house, two sources of necessities that bypass her lack of a medical license. For suffering casualties of World War II at the veterans' hospital in Durham, she orders the hospital administrator to stock standard supplies:

- aloe (a skin soother and burn treatment)
- chaparrel (liver and spleen detoxicant and treatment for cancer and auto-immune disease)
- comfrey (an expectorant, stool softener, and astringent)
- echinacea (a boost to healing of respiratory and urinary ailments)
- St. John's wort (a treatment for nervousness, sleeplessness, and wounds).

All are readily available in the herbalist's garden of folk cures.

Essential to Charlie Kate's skill is an eye for poor hygiene and the accrual of insults to the body from dissolute living. From treating the derelict and unclean, her outreach extends to a two-year-old endangered by whooping cough, the nearly drowned shoeshine man, cases of piles and inflamed testicles, and a Tar River family of five down with malaria. Gibbons details the standard cures of the day:

- croup kettle and tent for whooping cough
- suma root for energy
- sarsaparilla for blood purification
- gingerroot tea for nausea
- papaya tablets for indigestion
- garlic to boost healing and prevent high blood pressure
- quinine to reduce fever.

For dysmenorrhea (menstrual cramps), Charlie Kate recommends two common palliatives:

- false unicorn (a natural form of estrogen for treatment of pelvic pain and morning sickness, as a uterine tonic, and for prevention of miscarriage)
- evening primrose oil (a panacea for joint inflammation, menstrual dysfunction, eczema, heart disease, and breast pain).

She is particularly kind to the pathetic homeless clustered in uptown Raleigh around the City News and Candy. Pretending to shop for copies of the *New Yorker* and the *Saturday Review of Literature*, she offers diagnosis and humane medical care and sends alcoholics suffering gastric ulcer to the Mary Elizabeth Hospital for free barium tests. Although unorthodox in practice Charlie Kate refuses to violate professional ethics. She stocks no love potions and rejects girls seeking abortions. To her daughter Sophia's request for a hex on her philandering husband, Charlie Kate states with authority that voodoo is unnecessary — the man is ripe for a stroke, which occurs eight weeks later in August 1936. Ironically, the master healer fails to diagnose her own fatal illness, which presents only a vague nausea on Christmas night, 1942, before her sudden death. The gentle passing graces the character with a worthy rest from her labors at the same time that it allies her with all sufferers of mortal ills.

Moving from acutely ailing bodies to chronically ailing minds, Gibbons opens her fifth novel, *Sights Unseen* (1995), with a first-person account of bipolarity. Writing from experience with her mother Shine's illness and with her own bouts of extreme mood swings, she felt rather than created fictional dynamics. She stated to Polly Paddock, literary critic for the *Charlotte* (N.C.) *Observer*, "I had the authority to write about the black holes of depression and the elated highs of the manic cycle. But I never want to experience them again, or give my own children any new memories of what it's like to live with" (Paddock, 1995). With a nod toward medical technology, the text opens on narrator Hattie Barnes's awe in 1967 at electroconvulsive shock therapy, the "medical magic" that cures her manic-depressive mother of ravings and withdrawals to bed (Gibbons, 1995, 4). In Hattie's world view, real healing should flow from the nuclear family and from the love between mother and daughter rather than from medical wizardry. Reviewer Julia Glass refutes

Hattie's disillusion with the fact that Maggie Barnes, the madwoman in residence, has no chance of recovery so long as the "air in the Barnes household is thick with collusion" from family members who defend and cover for her craziness (Glass, 1995).

In the resolution, Gibbons settles for a compromise between familial wellness and medical technology by defaulting to Hattie's faith in home healing and Maggie's trust in psychotropic drugs. The curative power of a normal household routine resurges to importance when Maggie emerges from a period of post-treatment amnesia. Reacquainted with her husband, Frederick Barnes, and with children Hattie and Freddy, Maggie returns from Duke Hospital to declare the need of smooth days with a minimum of unforeseen upsets. Aided by lithium carbonate, a standard antipsychotic, and by Miltown, a standard anti-anxiety drug of the era, she shops for her children, sews sun suits for Hattie, and regains control over dinner-table give and take, even the racial sniping of the autocratic Grandfather Barnes. Like a major battlefield conquest, her return to power as female head of household occurs in a womanly domain co-ruled by cook-housekeeper Pearl Wiggins, the family's surrogate mother. Gibbons concludes the novel with Maggie's longing for spring, a symbol of hope and revival.

The lengthy commentary on disease and human hurts in Gibbons's first historical novel, *On the Occasion of My Last Afternoon* (1998), elucidates a litany of suffering and doctoring before, during, and after the Civil War. Before Christmas 1842, the slave Mintus relieves joint pain in planter Samuel P. Goodman Tate by wrapping swollen ankles in mustard and vinegar, a treatment listed in medieval pharmacopia. Samuel treats himself for gorging by purging; the cook-housekeeper Clarice doses his son Whately with lobelia for over-indulgence in barbecue. At a down-turn in the narrative, Whately self-administers calomel purgative and mercury ointment to rid him of syphilis, which he contracts from a barmaid while he attends Washington College in Lexington, Virginia. At his death in 1845 at age 20 on Sullivan's Island, South Carolina, the near-suicide of his sorrowing sister, Emma Garnet Tate Lowell, from an overdose of laudanum proves palliative by sedating her for a three-day sleep. In a similar motif of rest and recuperation, Dr. Quincy Lowell surmises that his mother-in-law, Alice Tate, needs deep sleep and lithium from the waters of Shocco Springs in Talladega, Alabama, to combat chronic migraine headaches caused by domestic tension. After her death in 1859, a lengthy letter from the attending physician, Dr. John C. Gunn, details strenuous treatments—bleeding, cupping, scarification, and cold toweling of the head followed by purging with calomel and jalap, clystering, and foot wrapping. Gunn's quaint gendered postmortem charges an over-exertion of the female brain, which he describes as suited only to "quiet domesticity" (Gibbons, 1998, 156). In Lowell's estimation, Gunn violates the Hippocratic principle, "*Primum non nocere*" (First, do no harm) (Gibbons, 1998, 157). The feminist author appends a more damning response to the lengthy, male-generated torments that end Alice's sad life.

The novel jumps headlong into the grisly immediacy of wartime healing, beginning with the battle of Big Bethel Church, Virginia, on June 10, 1861. After 40 hours without sleep, Emma, unnaided, faces a rush of 48 patients. The chapters on Quincy

Lowell's service at a Civil War hospital thrown together at Raleigh's Fair Grounds disclose the era's dependence on a limited pharmacy:

•opium (a narcotic analgesic)

•morphine (an analgesic and soporific derived from opium)

•quinine (an analgesic and anti-inflammatory)

•silver chloride (a blood purifier and anti-infective)

•sulfuric ether (an anesthetic and analgesic).

All are in critical shortage. Lacking such necessary equipment as scalpels, scissors, mattresses, and glass to secure sanitation in the operating theater, Emma makes do while treating the worst maimed soldiers by removing shrapnel with tweezers, distributing rosin for plasters and straw for bedding, stretching painted canvas over gaping windows, and quarantining contagious patients in the measles tent. She draws a stunning comparison — the packing of men into recovery wards with the layering of African captives in the holds of slave ships, the historical and economic underpinnings of civil disunion.

With her idiosyncratic demand for order and decorum, Gibbons refrains from turning battlefield horror into Gothic spectacle. With an historian's skill, she apportions enough details to establish the situation — too many casualties from the battles of Manassas, Virginia (July 21, 1861; August 28–30, 1862) and Antietam, Maryland (September 17, 1862) for triage, gore underfoot and stink in the air, agonizing bayonet rips to the belly, and maggots chewing infection from suppurating wounds. With a salute to female pragmatism, she honors makeshift herbal treatments:

•snakeroot (a stimulant and tonic)

•mint tea (an antidote to diarrhea, nausea, and gastro-intestinal pain)

•hickory leaves (a source of hot plasters to relieve colds, influenza, pneumonia, and pleurisy).

Dependence on rural simples dating to the Middle Ages enhances evidence of Southern privation as Union forces cut supply lines and the Confederacy loses ground.

The fictional agonies derive from Southern history, which Gibbons dug out of diaries and women's post-war memoirs. Civil War slaughter —"torn-up fields and torn-up bodies"— grows more worrisome (Gibbons, 1998, 163). Quincy and Emma Garnet labor in spring and early summer, 1864, over a stream of fallen soldiers relayed to Raleigh by train from the April 12th Fort Pillow massacre north of Memphis, Tennessee, the Wilderness clash the first week of May in north-central Virginia, and Cold Harbor, another Virginia struggle near the Confederate capital of Richmond that encompassed the last day of May and the first two weeks of June. Nightmarish hospital chores earn Emma an informal silver award for nursing in 1861, but, four years later, steal away Quincy, who collapses from exhaustion and failing metabolism. In the aftermath, Emma has herself to heal as well as her rail-thin sister, Maureen Tate, a refugee from the battered James River region of Virginia who tries to nurse soldiers, but quails at the sight of bloody sheets. Gibbons inserts her standard feminist cure for women's emotional trauma — the soothing conversation of women at cooking labs in Boston and in Emma's Raleigh kitchen. In a non-competitive atmosphere, Emma shares and dispenses food to the hungry and spiritual comfort to herself and other needy war survivors. The motif of benevolence as a source of self-healing affirms the novel's feminist focus on the informal, everyday graces of women's lives.

Gibbons furthers her inquiry into mental and physical health and wellness in *Divining Women* (2004), her seventh novel. Martha Greene Oliver reveals her first observations of sister-in-law Maureen Carlton Ross, bride of Martha's estranged brother Troop Ross. The furrows and ridges in Maureen's fingernails attest to childhood poverty and resultant malnutrition in a poor family in Yazoo City, Mississippi. Martha's daughter Mary, a more fortunate child, congratulates herself on living with a widowed parent who provides the hygiene and nutrition to ward off hookworm, lice, pellagra, fevers, and rickets, the banes of poor Deep South children like Maureen. Mary has greater reason to embrace wellness on September 30, 1918, upon traveling among unsalvageable veterans of World War I wounded by machine gun fire and mustard gas. Some of the semi-invalids earn their living by transporting travelers' luggage. Newly arrived in Elm City, North Carolina, Mary lists causes of death among newborns as diphtheria, rubella, and whooping cough, scourges that medical science has not yet warded off with innoculation. The revelation of widespread suffering contributes to Mary's delayed coming of age and foreshadows her development into a compassionate healer on a par with Charlie Kate Birch and Emma Garnet Tate Lowell.

In feminist outburst, Gibbons energizes the plot by picturing niece Mary Oliver's crusade to save Maureen from mutilation. Maureen's ego-smashing husband Troop intends to allow his wife one pregnancy and birth before committing her to a misogynist doctor intent on performing a hysterectomy to rid a domineering spouse of an assertive female. Already battered by galvanic shock therapy, ice water deluges, vibrating belts, and vaginal fumigation, which reviewer Valerie Sayers describes as "medical tyrannies," Maureen nears collapse (Sayers, 2004). In the last 50 days of Maureen's first pregnancy, Mary introduces her to family observations about Troop's twisted psyche. Re-armed against a despot, Maureen reclaims hidden letters from her mother, an astute parent who warns her "zombie" daughter that female abusers like Troop may threaten to "RIP YOUR FEMALES out" (Gibbons, 2004, 135). The alarm suits a time in American medical history when male doctors credited a range of female complaints and restiveness to "wandering womb," a ludicrous term dating to practitioners in ancient Greece.

Subsequent references to healing in *Divining Women* derive from panic in Elm City at the advance of the 1918 influenza pandemic among local citizens. Contributing to widespread suffering and loss are unreliable curatives that do more harm than good. Zollie, a desperate father, leaves his job as Troop Ross's driver and valet to dose two sons with cocaine, morphine, and tar-wine lung oil, a tar-and-ethyl alcohol balm distributed in 1888 by Dr. Milton George Harter and by Dr. J.H. McLean of St. Louis, Missouri, for the treatment of asthma, bronchitis, colds, and consumption. None of the over-the-counter nostrums combats the flu virus, which rapidly drowns oxygen-deprived lungs, turning victims huckleberry blue. Coughing, choking, and splotchy skin signal the final stage of the disease, which conspires with patent poisons to kill both children and to precipitate the suicide of their aunt from guilt. Dr. Morgan hopes that the unnecessary deaths encourage sellers of unregulated patent medicines to sweep quack cures from their shelves.

Emotional health returns to focus in *The Life All Around Me by Ellen Foster* (2006), a sequel to *Ellen Foster* that reprises the internal searing of the pre-teen narrator. In fall 1974, four years after her orphaning, the tight-necked tensions, nail chewing, anxiety attacks, and nightmares from age 11 flash through her during over-coffee discussions of her future with a social worker and foster mother Laura. To Ellen, the engulfing nausea and gut acid merge into a window shade pulled down over her eyes. Resultant faintness demands immediate contact with cool bathroom tile. With Laura's calming touch and a mature understanding of panic, Ellen is able to summon self-restraint that steadies and heartens. Completing her healing is the intake report from September 10, 1968, on her mother, Shine, for treatment of depression at Dorothea Dix Hospital in Raleigh, North Carolina. During a five week stay, Shine, reduced to 98 pounds from a rheumatic heart condition, receives a valium tablet and twice-daily doses of Navane, an anti-psychotic drug. On her person, she carries prescription digitalis, the pulse-suppressing drug she uses to kill herself in March 1969. The objective analysis of Shine's fear of neglecting her daughter realigns Ellen's thinking, ridding her of blame and evoking a new respect for her mother.

See also **"The Headache"; superstition**

• *Further reading*

Anshaw, Carol. "The Healer's Voice: Kaye Gibbons Conjures Up a Woman with a Cure for Almost Everything," *Chicago Tribune* (21 March 1993).

Creager, Angela N.H., Elizabeth Lunbeck, and Londa Schiebinger, eds. *Feminism in Twentieth Century Science, Technology and Medicine*. Chicago: University of Chicago Press, 2001.

Gibbons, Kaye. *A Cure for Dreams*. New York: Algonquin, 1991.

_____. *Divining Women*. New York: G.P. Putnam's Sons, 2004.

_____. *The Life All Around Me by Ellen Foster*. New York: Harcourt, 2006.

_____. *On the Occasion of My Last Afternoon*. New York: G.P. Putnam's Sons, 1998.

_____. *Sights Unseen*. New York: G.P. Putnam's Sons, 1995.

Glass, Julia. "To Comfort the Comfortless Kaye Gibbons Writes of a Girl's Life with Her Manic-Depressive Mother," *Chicago Tribune* (20 August 1995).

Gunn, John C. *Gunn's Domestic Medicine*. Knoxville: University of Tennessee, 1986.

Nostrums and Quackery. Chicago: American Medical Association, 1912.

Paddock, Polly. "Kaye Gibbons Recalls 'Sights Unseen' As a Tough Project," *Charlotte (N.C.) Observer* (27 August 1995).

Sayers, Valerie. "A Woman Moves South into a House of Spirits," *Washington Post* (4 April 2004).

historical milieu

Gibbons has a reputation for researching period details. Her touches of history range from electroconvulsive shock therapy on a bipolar mental patient and the romantic illusion of Elizabeth Taylor and Spencer Tracy's father-daughter relationship in the film *Father of the Bride* (1950) to war brides giving birth in the absence of husbands in the military and the in-house exhortations of a Primitive Baptist to a cancer patient. Of the joy of locating intriguing facts, the author told interviewer Don O'Briant, a book critic for the *Atlanta Journal-Constitution*, "It's like stumbling onto the winning lottery numbers" (O'Briant, 2000). In *A Cure for Dreams* (1991), she maps a direct connection between character motivation and the times. Set in piedmont North Carolina, the story traces the shift in behaviors during the Great Depression, when "homes were in the grip of Mr. Hoover," who was 31st U.S. president from 1929 to 1933 (Gibbons, 1991, 30). Under the pall of "Mr. Boll Weevil," a destructive farm pest during the mid–1920s, fictional farm families make do on flour-and-water gravy; unemployed men scour the countryside for work or a handout (*Ibid.*, 33). For amusement, more privileged people turn to Jack Benny or Lum and Abner on the radio or attend Andy Hardy movies at the Center Theatre. In her mid-teens, Betty Davies of Milk Farm Road takes an interest in the Dionne quintuplets, a Canadian family born in Ontario on May 28, 1934. While her mother, Lottie O'Cadhain Davies, slips around her work-obsessed husband Charles by organizing pinochle and gin rummy socials for local women in the back room of Porter's store, husbands compensate for financial plight by chasing low-priced tarts from the Willifordtown mill. The author notes that womanizing doesn't ease the era's monetary shortfall, but the boost to male egos is worth the expense. Meanwhile, Amanda Bethune, a woman strapped for the finer things in life, profits from the loan of a red barrette and chintz skirt from Lottie. The feminist touch differentiates the methods of male and female by ridiculing men for their carnal exploits and by lauding woman's glamorizing as an esteem-building antidote to hard times.

In retrospect, daughter Betty admires Lottie's methods of "[worming] around trouble" (*Ibid.*, 55–56). To the surprise of mother and daughter, after Charles Davies despairs of profits from his farm and mill and drowns himself in the river in 1937, Lottie qualifies for widow's aid. The financial *deus ex machina* inspires Betty to exalt President Franklin Delano Roosevelt, a four-term champion of the poor who passed through Congress in summer 1935 the Social Security Act, which aided the unemployed, elderly, widows, and orphans. Betty improves herself through Roosevelt-era largesse by moving to Richmond, Virginia, to study secretarial courses financed by the Works Progress Administration (WPA), which began by presidential order in May 1935 to boost skills and work opportunities to the unemployed and unemployable. On her return to Milk Farm Road, she sings for her beau "On the W.P. and A.," a jaunty tune that praises federal assistance to the hard-pressed. Another source of the era's music is Marie Campbell's *Folks Do Get Born* (1946), which supplies midwife Polly Deal with birthing jingles that she sings as she performs post-delivery ministrations to Betty's baby, Marjorie Polly Randolph, the fourth female of the novel's matrilineage.

In setting a fifth novel, *Sights Unseen* (1995), the author stresses the dominance of pop culture in the rural American home, from Madame Alexander dolls to edgy Vincent Price and Steve McQueen films. To the narrator, Hattie Barnes, the tenor of the times resonates in an amorous upset in the soap opera *As the World Turns* and in the moral rectitude of Sergeant Joe Friday, a tight-jawed police inspector on the crime series *Dragnet.* In the crazed thinking of Hattie's mother Maggie, a sedative injection reminds her of tranquilizing darts shot into rampaging beasts on the television nature series *Wild Kingdom.* The influence of the media takes on more realism in light of news of racial rioting in Birmingham and Chicago. In the plot resolution, Maggie uses a classic comedy routine from the Lucille Ball-Desi Arnaz domestic comedy *I Love Lucy* to express her gratitude for sanity. Before entering Duke Hospital, Maggie lives a constant replay of Lucy and Ethel trying to cope with a conveyor belt advancing candy faster than they can box it. The image implies a sweetness to Maggie's reordering of life after she attains sanity.

The background of Gibbons's seventh novel, *Divining Women* (2004), is the era of Alice and Alva Vanderbilt, Mata Hari and Henry Ford, and the afterglow of the *belle epoque.* The text connects Leslie and Toby Greene of Dupont Circle in Washington, D.C., with Teddy Roosevelt's wife Edith and with summer voyages among the elite aboard the S.S. *Lusitania* and the S.S. *Carpathia*, a luxury liner that came to the rescue of passengers trapped aboard the sinking *Titanic* on April 10, 1912. By May 1917, war in Europe so depletes colleges of staff and students that Toby's 22-year-old granddaughter, Mary Oliver, is unable to complete postgraduate studies at Radcliffe College prefatory to teaching a seminar. In January 1918, her options drop to an entry level course that requires less preparation. In a war-time atmosphere, Mary complains of cabin fever, a situation that Gibbons's creates as an introit to the novel's conflict.

Gibbons illustrates how quickly a milieu can shift by placing Mary Oliver on September 30, 1918, aboard a south-bound train in Union Station during World War I. Of the casualties surviving European combat, Mary notes that those shot in the head and upper body evidence the dangers of climbing out of trenches under cannon and machine gun fire. At the depot in Elm City, North Carolina, she witnesses the blistering, blinding, choking effects of mustard gas, a colorless, odorless poison that leaves veterans struggling and gasping. Returned home in moribund condition, they try to earn a living as train station redcaps trundling passenger luggage. The daily newspaper bruits ongoing debate over the maiming, burning, and torment of soldiers in battle lines along the Western Front in unpronounceable places, the author's suggestion of combat at Ypres, Vimy Ridge, Reims, Bapaume, and Liège. Mention of unknown war zones illustrates how far removed Mary is from period struggle.

As the 1918 influenza pandemic emerges in Elm City, shards of national panic seep through Mary Oliver's self-absorption. Letters from her mother warn of the blatherings of Billy Sunday, a zealous Iowa-born evangelist for the Chicago Young Men's Christian Association who describes the influenza pandemic as divine retribution against the wicked. Mary views other historical warning signs—surgical masks, funereal bells, and the infection of Alfonso XIII of Spain with flu. At a poignant moment in the novel, Gibbons describes the over-the-counter nostrums that Zollie buys for his two sons, who sicken and die from a combination of flu virus and patent medicines concocted from codeine, morphine, and tar wine oil, a lung balm intended to cure coughs and lung congestion. The advance of the virus across the United States prompts panic, $15 pine coffins, call-ups of retired doctors to treat the sick, and hasty folk burials for the dead, the dramatic situation that ends the novel.

Over a half century later, the historical background of *The Life All Around Me by Ellen Foster* (2006) centers the title character in the early 1970s during the North Carolina governorship of James Holshouser, the Vietnam War, the criminal behaviors of mass murderer Charles Manson and bank robber Patty Hearst, and the Watergate scandal. The title character shares school chats with rural teens whose vacations take them no farther than Tweetsie Railroad or White Lake or the rare trip to Colonial Williamsburg, Virginia. Ellen's foster mother Laura fails to get her to a showing of *Willy Wonka and the Chocolate Factory* (1971), but vetoes adult titillation in *Carnal Knowledge* (1971), an adult film featuring Art Garfunkel in the nude. In anticipation of a train ride to a camp for gifted students held at Johns Hopkins University in Baltimore, Ellen pictures a sleeping car like the one in the comic film *Some Like It Hot* (1959), a fictional train trip from Chicago to Florida that allies the acting skills of Marilyn Monroe, Tony Curtis, and Jack Lemmon. Ellen's taste in entertainment ranges from Ava Gardner movies, *American Bandstand, Bewitched, Candid Camera*, and *Dark Shadows* to a Phyllis Diller TV special, which Ellen shares with Laura. With an eye to a Harvard medical degree, Ellen impresses her friends as too other-worldly to care about the Lottie Moon Society, a Baptist outreach named for a missionary to P'ingtu and Tengchow, China, from 1872 until 1912. In the resolution, Gibbons reunites Ellen with family treasures, which include toy rings that a shoe store offers to children from the Buster Brown chest. The blend of popular interests enables Gibbons to establish normality in an otherwise unique fictional protagonist.

See also **Civil War; World War II**

• *Further reading*

Clark, Miriam Marty. "Sounds of Women Talking," *St. Louis Post-Dispatch* (9 June 1991).

Gibbons, Kaye. *A Cure for Dreams.* New York: Algonquin, 1991.

O'Briant, Don. "After Four Tries and Nearly 40 years, Joseph Humphreys Delivers a Historical Novel about a Lumbee Indian and her Outlaw Husband," *Atlanta Journal-Constitution* (17 September 2000).

Romine, Dannye. "A Dream Come True — Third Time Out Is a Charmer for Raleigh Novelist Kaye Gibbons," *Charlotte* (N.C.) *Observer* (31 March 1991).

Hoover-Stanley genealogy

In *A Virtuous Woman* (1989), Kaye Gibbons uses the merger of a land-owning family with landless crackers to illustrate disparate economic levels and social class of rural neighbors:

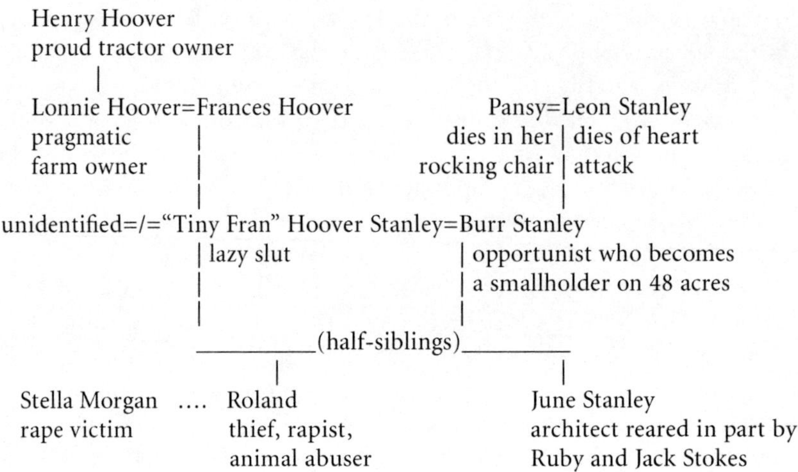

• *Further reading*

Gibbons, Kaye. *A Virtuous Woman*. Chapel Hill, N.C.: Algonquin Press, 1989.

humor

Kaye Gibbons's blend of tragedy and comedy is a high-wire act that attests to creative control and a scholarly grounding in humanism. Her skill at drollery permeates interviews and citations, such as a quote in the *Atlanta Journal-Constitution* of the ease of writing bestsellers: "All you need to create a masterpiece are 26 letters of the alphabet, some assembly required" (O'Briant, 1989). An early example, the snake-in-the-abandoned-pocketbook trick in "The Headache," a short-short story published in the June 1987 issue of the *St. Andrews Review*, illustrates the cruel sufferings of the finder, farm wife Lucille Womble, the mother of ten. Unable to forgive her greed for keeping the lost purse, she suffers two weeks of head pain, insomnia, protracted weeping, and nightly serpent visions that threaten her ability to cope with rambunctious children and failing farm finances. In the distance, she views suicide as a possible solution. After she attains grace from Henry, her loving husband, she falls asleep in his arms engulfed by a touch of authorly wit — a vision of herself wearing two hats, an amazing example of bounty for poor folk.

In Gibbons's first novel, *Ellen Foster* (1987), the title character's humor derives from a more positive source, a natural flair for incongruity. Ellen reduces a perfunctory funeral director to a "smiling man" and childishly mispronounces words like the French *voila* (see there) and "on the up in up," a term that recurs in the sequel, *The Life All Around Me by Ellen Foster* (2006) (Gibbons, 1987, 17, 4, 119; 2006, 2). Ellen refers to her mother's heart disease as the result of "romantic" fever, a misunderstanding of "rheumatic fever" that yields a subtextual criticism of naive women who bank on courtship illusions to better their lives (*Ibid.*, 3). As the action builds conflict, Ellen makes mordant commentary on the substandard relatives who take her in. Of Nadine Nelson's fabrications about her dead husband to her daughter

Dora, Ellen envisions cousin Dora's image of him at the North Pole making toys for Santa Claus to distribute. On Christmas Day, 1970, the author's deft interspersal of puns and gentle humor relieves the tension that sends 11-year-old Ellen into the cold to locate a suitable home. In typical Ellen style, the trek to a foster mother is Ellen's yuletide gift to herself. In retrospect of her new surroundings, she observes, "Nobody has died or blamed me for anything worse than overwatering the terrarium" (*Ibid.*, 121), a symbol of blessing that she showers on a miniature habitat that suggests joy in bounty.

In a second novel, *A Virtuous Woman* (1989), Gibbons lets Southern dialect and back-country situations speak for themselves. At one point, she pictures a make-do grocery and bait shop where the cooler houses chicken and cube steak alongside bloodworms, a juxtaposition still in evidence throughout rural North Carolina. At the heart of fictional conflict, she introduces 40-year-old tenant farmer "Blinking" Jack Ernest Stokes, whose low expectations and self-deprecating style explain a lengthy bachelorhood. The closest he comes to romancing a woman is to petition her to steady a mule while he harnesses the plow. The visual levity continues in his description of meeting 20-year-old Ruby Pitts Woodrow in a burlesque of the Garden of Eden — resting beneath a pecan tree on a smoke break while he transports manure to the vegetable rows by wheelbarrow. To an untraveled homebody like Jack, she has the lure of a car with an out-of-state tag, an image Gibbons repeats in "Joyner's Store," a personal essay printed in the June 1997 issue of *Southern Living*. Embedded in the humor lies Jack's retrieval of self from a medieval form of hand transport to travel in style, a suitable image of a satisfying quarter century of wedlock with Ruby. The author aims satire at Jack's rudderless state at age 65 after Ruby's death. He hires Mavis Washington, the stereotypical overweight domestic, to reorder his life. Because of her portliness and physical decline, she does little more than watch TV soap operas. Ironically, in sorrow for Ruby, Jack recedes into the same electronic escape by staring at Roadrunner cartoons on television and pitying himself.

Returning to satire of female situations, Gibbons summons a mystic woman-to-woman telegraphy in *A Cure for Dreams* (1991). Book critic Roy Parker, Jr., reviewing for the *Fayetteville* (N.C.) *Observer*, described the effect as "sharply etched in ironic humor, but often deadly serious" (Parker, 1991). To ease post-menopausal concerns in Sade Duplin, Lottie O'Cadhain Davies unobtrusively circulates rumors that Roy Duplin's Williffordtown floozy flunked her Wassermann test. Within 48 hours, Roy returns to the nest and thinks up excuses for not sleeping with Sade. During Lottie's visit with newcomer Trudy Woodlief, the shared looks and facial contortions between Lottie and her daughter, Betty Davies Randolph, telegraph disapproval of slatternly white trash. At the revelation that Trudy hales from Baton Rouge, Lottie conveys through body english a prejudgment of people from Louisiana. She suspects Trudy of voodoo, incestuous marriage, and blind support of corrupt Governor Huey Long, a colorful rabble rouser whom a state trooper shot at the state capitol on September 10, 1935. Contributing to the interaction between Lottie and the white trash Woodliefs is Lottie's defense of Porter, the storeowner who refuses Trudy credit. Because of hard times, Porter makes change from a muffin tin after a creditor repossesses his cash register. The episode concludes with rare tears from Lottie, whose meal of ham, tomatoes, and peaches nets two turndowns—one from Trudy and one from Lottie's husband Charles, who receives it secondhand. The rejection spikes a tender spot in female vulnerability, a pride in rural Southern cookery.

A book based on female storytelling, *A Cure for Dreams* skewers women for prolonged conversation, a familiar cliché in jokes about talkative women and telephone party lines. Lonely for daughter Betty, who attends secretarial school in Richmond, Virginia, on a Works Progress Administration grant, Lottie needs to reassert domestic primacy. She summons Betty home to intervene in exchanges with the housekeeper-midwife, Polly Deal. Lottie claims, "I need somebody here to help me listen to her" (Gibbons, 1991, 132). The humor masks a real need to restore the triad of women. In a scene of convoluted maternal control, the three welcome the next generation, Marjorie Polly Randolph, whom Polly delivers in a home birthing in the absence of Lottie. The scheming and one-upmanship predicts an affable power struggle evolving from dynamic women enjoying the camaraderie of their manless domain throughout World War II.

Humor is a welcome given in Gibbons's fourth novel, *Charms for the Easy Life* (1993). Juxtaposed against midwife-herbalist Charlie Kate Birch's no-nonsense philosophy are her loopy twin sister Camelia's self-written letters from President Teddy Roosevelt, which accompany her to the grave. Of the protagonist's chutzpah, Gibbons credits the self-liberation of Southern feminism, which enables Charlie Kate to prevail against a background of self-defeating losers. Of women's quiet subversions, the author elaborated, "Southern women let other people believe that they are vacuous and unintelligent, and meanwhile they're making plans to take over. In the family, they're secretly in charge, and they're OK with the pretense that the man runs things" ("Southern," 1993). The description fits Charlie Kate, who rapidly subsumes her nameless husband in importance to family and community. Like a wet spot on the sidewalk, he gradually evaporates.

Gibbons does not let Charlie Kate slide out of the satirist's spotlight. The protagonist's touchy temper gives way to an acceptance of human foibles, particularly among family members. During a three-day return of her husband to Raleigh, North Carolina, in 1938, Charlie Kate agreeably cohabits with him at the Sir Walter Raleigh Hotel, then rolls him for $1,365 from his wallet as a suitable comeuppance for his fecklessness. Worldly wise, she surveys the pairings of her daughter, Sophia Snow Birch, for signs of womanly weakness toward suitors. When businessman Richard Baines spends the night during a snowstorm, Charlie Kate makes a show of preparing the guest room for him, but she doubts that Baines will remain apart from Sophia, the future Mrs. Baines. The lapse in Charlie Kate's surveillance suggests that she knows she has lost the crusade for an all-female household and that she is willing to accept Richard as a son-in-law.

More serious to Charlie Kate is the maturing of granddaughter Margaret, the herbalist's likely successor. Under the guise of visits to World War II casualties at a Durham veterans' hospital, Charlie Kate chooses diagnosis and treatment for her own tasks and leaves to Margaret the chitchat and letter-writing for recuperating men. After returning from the wards to duty, soldier Tom Hawkings, III, courts Margaret by mail. While censoring letters in a P.O.W. camp in Asheville, he promises to "pass along anything juicy the Germans tell the Fräuleins back home," a humanizing touch that advances German soldiers from demons to war victims much like Tom (Gibbons, 1993, 205). Subtextually, Gibbons reveals a human truth — that combat and distance from home fail to dampen the male-female relationships that undergird the human scenario, even among the enemy.

Perhaps because of painful autobiographical details, Gibbons subdues sportiveness in her fifth novel, *Sights Unseen* (1995), a revealing study of female madness. A comedic situation relieves the family during Freddy's young manhood, when he confounds cook-housekeeper Pearl Wiggins with a gallery of "trailer-park-looking" pinups on his bedroom wall (Gibbons, 1995, 73). Wry period memories of *Dragnet*, a television detective series, and the selling of hard rolls in the Colonial Store to please Yankee interlopers help to gentle Maggie's public humiliation during a manic upsurge of her bipolar illness. The roll-call of electronic influences focuses on a 1967 plot of the soap opera *As the World Turns*, a TV fantasy that Maggie incorporates into the real world. Her aggressive sexuality reaches out to nab Dr. Bob Hughes, a fictional character whom she adds to an enterprising list of seductions achieved only in her delusions. The surreal episode pictures Maggie praising God for flounder, which she intends as a suitable Catholic meal for Senator Robert Kennedy, whom she imagines as a future dinner guest. The female retreat to kitchen chores heralds Maggie's rehabilitation in 1967 through eight sessions of electroconvulsive shock treatment and psychotherapy at Duke Hospital and her restoration to the Barnes family as female head of household. In a painful summation, Hattie is glad that her mother "never decided that the state of mania had felt good enough for a return visit" (*Ibid.*, 208).

Spots of comic relief in Gibbons's first historical novel, *On the Occasion of My Last Afternoon* (1998), offer insight into the stratified folk manners of Tidewater Virginia. Freedwoman Clarice Washington, the cook-housekeeper at Seven Oaks plantation, has known planter Samuel P. Goodman Tate from boyhood, when he begged from door to door in Alexandria. As a counter to his boorishness at table, Alice Tate requests intervention from Clarice when he demands that a dinner guest leave her dress for Alice to copy. Clarice lessens the appeal of the outfit to Samuel by commenting that she has seen a similar outfit on a "high-yellow," a Southern pejorative for a person of mixed race (Gibbons, 1998, 43). Although the remark offends the female guest, it draws a guffaw from 14-year-old Whately Tate. The atmosphere tightens once more from Samuel's double-backhanding his impertinent son, a domestic sacrifice to the father's ego defense.

Additional juxtapositions of heinousness and humor suit the extremes of the Tate household, which Samuel subjugates with incessant blathering and evil outbursts. At the end of Alice Tate's patience is the family outing to Williamsburg to view a double hanging on the square. Contributing to surreality is the guidance of a family friend, a poetaster known as Too-Whit-Too-Woo, a name derived from "Tu-whit! tu-whoo!," a mimetic refrain in William Shakespeare's poem "Winter," found in Act V, Scene 2 in *Love's Labours Lost* (ca. 1593). The friend proposes a trip to the circus as a post-execution treat. Samuel's bloodthirsty taste advances the alienation of his family. When Emma matures to young womanhood and, in 1847 at age

17, marries Dr. Quincy Lowell, Gibbons completes the nuptial episodes with a departing image of the bride and groom in their carriage. Like a singer delivering an operatic coda, Clarice leans out the window to deliver a sermon to Samuel about a host of wrongdoings that will follow him to the grave. Homily delivered, Clarice requests that the groom reel her in through the carriage window, a sight gag reminiscent of Mae West and W.C. Fields slapstick.

In a seventh novel, *Divining Women* (2004), Gibbons extends the humor of a grandfather's predilection for bizarre behaviors. A Washington, D.C., investor, Toby Greene, alienates his social-climbing wife Nora by joining the American Community of Nudists. Stung and outraged that her upscale husband risks social ostracism to pursue an offensive hobby, she changes her name to Nora Worthy Ross and launches 36 years of emotional battery that befuddles and dismays him. After Nora's death in 1911, Louise Canton Oliver muses that Toby continues to risk a ghost's spite for the simple crime of removing his clothes in public. Gibbons returns to the issue of hauntings by describing the spiritual revenants in Toby's house on Dupont Circle as raising "the racket of the spheres" (Gibbons, 2004, 26). The ongoing din creates merriment that contrasts the central action of the novel and its historical milieu, when victims of World War I and of the 1918 influenza pandemic swell the number of the departed.

In an unforeseen burst of wit, Gibbons blends social satire with psychological dysfunction. The story of Nora's emotionally blighted son, Troop Ross, comes to light through a misdirected letter from his mother-in-law, a resident of Yazoo City, Mississippi. An egregious parvenu, he puts on such a show of gentility at his wedding to Maureen Carlton that her mother and other Deep South guests begin to sniff a con artist, a stock character in frontier and Southern trickster lore. In reference to the nobody from North Carolina trying to impress his wife's rural family and friends, the mother-in-law asserts, "You can't fool Mississippi," her assertion of pride in the delta's backwoods sophistication (*Ibid.*, 133). On the novel's periphery, her resilient voice reminds Maureen that the people who really love and respect her await her separation from Troop, a no-good who deserves to live alone and unloved in his overdecorated house.

A disarming wit in the precocious title character underlies *The Life All Around Me by Ellen Foster* (2006), the sequel to Gibbons's first novel. In the estimation of author-critic Lynna Williams, a reviewer for the *Chicago Tribune*, Ellen exudes "deadpan humor and tart cultural notes" that evidence the protagonist's cunning and perception (Williams, 2006). Valerie Sayers, reviewing for the *Washington Post*, chooses the term "wiseguy one-liners," a possible explanation of critical opinion that Gibbons is trying too hard (Sayers, 2006). In addition to ridiculing the North Carolina advertising motto "Variety Vacationland," the officious mismanagement of social programs, and fundamentalist Christian white-flight academies, Ellen alludes to the grammatically garbled selling point of the United Negro College Fund—"A mind is a terrible thing to waste" (Gibbons 2006, 8). Gibbons creates humor out of the 15-year-old's commentary on gaining entrance to Harvard University. To establish credibility with the admittance staff, Ellen attempts to talk with the town's only Harvard graduate, a comatose patient in a nursing home. In her search for intellectual stimulation, she and her foster mother Laura investigate camps for bright teens that Ellen blows off as "weekends with the chess crowd" dissecting fish (*Ibid.*, 25). Ellen's reversion to working-class argot includes references to children "maldeformed" by toxic smoke and the "digestive track" of a freak cow at the fair (*Ibid.*, 64, 113). The retrieval of Ellen from too high a level of erudition restores her humanity in a Southern foster home where Laura loves her for purity of heart.

See also ***Pete & Shirley***

• *Further reading*

Carter, Ron. "Sisters Flee Father's Tyranny," *Richmond Times-Dispatch* (5 July 1998).
Gibbons, Kaye. *Charms for the Easy Life*. New York: Putnam, 1993.
_____. *A Cure for Dreams*. New York: Algonquin, 1991.
_____. *Divining Women*. New York: G.P. Putnam's Sons, 2004.
_____. *Ellen Foster*. New York: Algonquin Press, 1987.
_____. *The Life All Around Me by Ellen Foster*. New York: Harcourt, 2006.
_____. *On the Occasion of My Last Afternoon*. New York: G.P. Putnam's Sons, 1998.
_____. *Sights Unseen*. New York: G.P. Putnam's Sons, 1995.
_____. *A Virtuous Woman*. Chapel Hill, N.C.: Algonquin Press, 1989.
Lanham, Fritz. "Truths Unplotted," *Houston Chronicle* (15 October 1995).
O'Briant, Don. "Author Offers Tips on Carving Out 'Writing Room,'" *Atlanta Journal-Constitution* (9 July 1989).
Parker, Roy, Jr. "Elegant Family Story," *Fayetteville* (N.C.) *Observer* (14 April 1991).
Sayers, Valerie, "Growing Into the Role," *Washington Post* (6 January 2006).
"Southern Charmers," *Chicago Tribune* (18 April 1993).
Steelman, Ben. "Characters Drag Down a Decent 'Divining,'" *Wilmington* (N.C.) *Star-News* (11 April 2004).
Williams, Lynna. "For Ellen Foster, There's Finally Light at the End of the Tunnel," *Chicago Tribune* (8 January 2006).

injustice

Kaye Gibbons embraces an egalitarian approach to justice, which she pictures as tilted in favor of androcentric whites and the moneyed class. An early short-short story, "The Headache," issued in June 1987 in the *St. Andrews Review*, describes the self-castigation of Lucille Womble, a poor farm wife, after she seizes an abandoned purse in a restaurant ladies' room. Based on the snake-in-the-pocketbook trick, a standard ploy in the fool tale, the incident initiates misgivings about self and social class that unjustly torment her for a temporary lapse of judgment. By examining the trickster motif from the victim's perspective, the story depicts a two-week moral crisis in a woman deserving of rescue from the outfall of a cruel jest. Gibbons places justice in the hands of Henry Womble, Lucille's husband, who extends forgiveness and affection based on marital devotion rather than legalism, which the author mistrusts.

In Gibbons's first novel, *Ellen Foster* (1987), injustice to a naif characterizes the ethical failings of society to its youngest members. The title figure undergoes a lengthy series of faulty treatment by authority figures. The disinclination of the bootlegger Bill to rescue his ailing wife from an intentional overdose of prescription digitalis equates with murder. His protracted neglect, rejection, and sexual menacing of daughter Ellen precedes her permanent flight from home after a dismal New Year's Eve, 1969, a symbol of broken promises to a hapless child. Worsening injustice is her series of short-term residencies with the widowed Aunt Betsy and Aunt Nadine Nelson, mother of Ellen's spiteful cousin Dora. More heinous wrongs await Ellen in court, where a judge removes her from a temporary home with art teacher Julia and her endearing husband Roy to the care of blood relatives. The ping-pong nature of Ellen's odyssey lambastes society for failure to ensure nurture and protection for its youngest members.

Gibbons stresses the disservice that follows the well-meaning judge's flawed thinking about restoring Ellen to a secure environment. Under court order, Ellen passes to her maternal grandmother, an unnamed grudge-bearer who hates her working-class son-in-law and "[wants] me so hard to be like him" (Gibbons, 1987, 68). Gibbons pictures a post-funeral scenario in which the grandmother spits on and burns a flag that covers Bill's coffin, a further punishment of her out-of-favor son-in-law in the after-life. The mid-summer field hoeing that Ellen must perform to her grandmother's specifications concludes with the personal feeding, dressing, and washing of the old lady, who dies of flu in Ellen's care shortly before Christmas 1970. Gibbons turns to tender irony after the grandmother's death, when Ellen attempts to blow breath into still lungs and decks the corpse in a Sunday hat and artificial flowers before calling a mortician. Ellen intends the decoration to delude Jesus into accepting the old lady into eternal grace, a higher level of justice that suggests the author's charging the divine with Ellen's grievances. The naive gestures enhance Ellen's characterization as a well-meaning child who inhabits a callous, unfeeling family circle within a criminally remiss society under the watch of an unfeeling god.

In her second and third novels, *A Virtuous Woman* (1989) and *A Cure for Dreams* (1991), Gibbons expounds on other forms of domestic injustice that drive women beyond rationality to desperate measures. In *A Virtuous Woman*, Ruby Pitts Woodrow rationalizes her hiding of a pistol under the pillow and her plan to shoot her wayward husband John for romancing a teenaged slut in their home. Because the Woodrows are itinerant farm laborers, Ruby assumes that an assault by an angry working-class wife will go unpunished by the local law, which tends to ignore underclass violence. Similarly prejudiced is the search for the killer of Roy Duplin, who dies in his front yard of a shotgun blast in *A Cure for Dreams*. Because of his nasty temper, local people of Milk Farm Road lose interest in locating and punishing the unidentified murderer. In secret from the inept part-time Deputy Sheriff John Carroll, neighbor Lottie O'Cadhain Davies informally diagnoses Sade Duplin's wailing as terror of potential arrest. Lottie surveys erratic stitchery and dinner for one and correctly surmises that Sade, pushed to the limit, gunned down her husband after years of abuse. The novel's feminist logic exonerates Sade, who thrives as a widow by recovering Roy's hidden money and using it to transform a prison-like environment into an inviting nest. Just as Gibbons spares Ruby a felon's punishment, the author awards Sade an expanded family consisting of children who feel welcome in a home that once bristled with antipathy.

The premise of *Charms for the Easy Life* (1993), Gibbons's fourth novel, demands that the reader admire the unlicensed medical practice of herbalist-midwife Charlie Kate Birch. A respected, self-educated healer, she offers counsel, medical and surgical care, undertaking, and dental treatment to the have-nots of Pasquotank County and of the mill district of Raleigh, North Carolina. Along with healing, she delivers sermons on hygiene intended to redirect the wayward and to warn unsuspecting youths of the perils of sexual misadventures. In reward for her moral rectitude, she lives well throughout the Great Depression on a stipend paid by a grateful patient cured of syphilis. Through eyeball-to-eyeball blackmail, she forces an aristocratic physician from the snooty Anderson Heights section out of practice. Her weapons are the words of an irate female — a threat to reveal his incompetent birthing of a lower-class child he blinds with silver nitrate drops and his dismissal of 70-year-old Maveen, Charlie Kate's former maid, who lies suffering and starving from a lack of treatment for stomach cancer. From Charlie Kate's maneuverings come more patients as well as prescription privileges and free iron tablets from the Hayes Barton Pharmacy to treat anemia, a symbol of her potent advancement in the health trade. She also earns the admiration of Anna Hawkings, a liberated aristocrat who values the ethics of a dedicated health care worker who — licensed or unlicensed — caters to the needs of the poor. The extensive character web proves a feminist theory that women, like co-conspirators, battle a common front — a male hegemony. In their efforts, they readily cherish and support each other's crusades.

Injustice on a grander scale emerges during and after the Civil War as revealed in *On the Occasion of My Last Afternoon* (1998), Gibbons's first historical fiction. A review in *America* magazine notes a damning premise — the "intricate structure of lies" that undergirds the slave-generated plantation economy of the James River district of tidewater Virginia (Redding, 1999). Terrorism becomes a built-in liability of human bondage. Prefacing the ineluctable secession of the South and its clash with the Union, planter Samuel P. Goodman Tate's silencing of Jacob, a mouthy plantation slave, with near-decapitation in 1842 with a hog-slaughtering knife precipitates anxiety. He and other slave-owning whites fear retribution from angry blacks on a par with the Nat Turner rebellion from August 22 until his capture on October 30, 1831. The only voice uncowed by homage to the all-powerful slavemaster is one of the author's redoubtable females, cook-housekeeper Clarice Washington. A freedwoman, she has the clout to demand that Tate identify his victim: "You know he gots a name. Ever'body gots a name" (Gibbons, 1998, 4). Samuel worsens injustice by admitting that he doesn't know the slave by name, only as a bluegum field hand, a sneering reference to African coloration. Powerless to demand punishment, fellow slaves, "bowed down with trouble," hear from Clarice the safest way to honor the dead: inter Jacob without ceremony, then break crockery to mark the grave, a folk method of identifying a burial site and of warding off ghosts (*Ibid.*, 16). Clarice's power has its limits: she invites Jacob's wife to shelter at the Tate kitchen and offers slaves pantry solace — side meat and lard from the big house kitchen plus advice on how to avoid the auction block at Williamsburg in January. Although Clarice's ministrations seem small compared to the loss of a life, she must work within the lopsided slave-master paradigm.

With authorial panache, Gibbons awaits the appropriate moment to deal retribution to Samuel and his ilk. His wealth squandered on Confederate bonds and the Tate family's James River property usurped by Union General George Brinton McClellan and his troops in summer 1862, Samuel forces daughter Maureen to transport their few paintings by wagon south to Emma Garnet Tate Lowell's home in Raleigh, North Carolina. Emma's outrage at bruises on Maureen's wearied body and at Samuel's high-handed residency in the parlor fuels confrontations that further distance him from Leslie, Louise, and Mary Lowell, the granddaughters he cursed before their birth. Dr. Quincy Lowell, a long-suffering son-in-law, delivers the *coup de grace* during Samuel's alleged late-night bout with heart failure. In front of Emma, Quincy administers a lethal oral dose of digitalis powder, which slows Samuel's unfatherly heart to stillness and silences the evil mouthings that leave Emma begging for laudanum. A taste of blood, a Southern Gothic embellishment of Samuel's euthanasia, satisfies Quincy that a pro-slavery villain knows the real cost of bondage and war.

With a slower, more measured recompense, Gibbons's seventh novel, *Divining Women* (2004), metes justice to another domestic villain in the final moments of the resolution. Like Samuel Tate, Troop Ross is an emotionally stunted strutter incapable of loving his wife, Maureen Carlton Ross. He sequentially limits her involvement in home and family until she languishes in an upstairs boudoir, a post-modern version of the maiden immured in the tower. Physically immobilized during the last trimester of a difficult pregnancy, she merits the affection and protection of Mary Oliver, her 22-year-old niece from Washington, D.C., who arrives by train on September 30, 1918. The reversal of fortune in the final scenes pictures Maureen allying with Mary and Mamie, the family cook-housekeeper, in a poignant birthing scene. The trio, energized by their collaboration, defy Troop and, on November 9, 1918, prepare the stillborn infant, Ella Eloise Ross, for burial at sunset against the father's wishes. The restoration of justice to Maureen's life erupts on the sidewalk, the perfect setting for the unmasking of a *poseur*. At dusk, the small funeral procession—Maureen, Mary, Mamie, and Mamie's husband Zollie—draws respect from neighbors, who view Troop delivering a tirade. The peeling away of phony respectability denudes him of defenses as he yells "vulgar bitches," "imperious nigger maid," and "lackey" (Gibbons, 2004, 204). The intervention of gentlemen in Troop's fury fades into the background in one of Gibbons's signature applications of dramatic decorum. A poetic touch involves the lighting of a gas streetlamp and a wish from the lamplighter that ladies pass safely down the street by night. The brief benediction restores the proprieties to a spurned wife sorely in need of light and protection.

The author's most drawn-out example of nemesis occurs in her first sequel, *The Life All Around Me by Ellen Foster* (2006). To restore equity to the title character, Gibbons revisits the grievances of *Ellen Foster* and awards Ellen money and satisfaction in reparation for years of bias and foul play. The text builts suspense in fall 1974 concerning Ellen's first confrontation with Aunt Nadine Nelson, who withholds a pitiful box of memorabilia once belonging to Ellen's mother Shine. In bestowing the earthly reminders of the mother's few delights, Gibbons reveals a felony—the forging of documents that accompanies the theft of Ellen's sizeable inheritance from her father and grandmother. In the novel's final pages, rightful ownership of lands and rents promises Ellen money for college tuition at the same time that she receives a full scholarship to Harvard University. More precious to her state of mind is an objective diagnosis of Shine's suicidal state on September 10, 1968, and exoneration of guilt for not saving her. After exiling Nadine and daughter Dora to Texas, Gibbons decks her heroine in the knowledge that "my mother's love was what I was made of," a feminist satisfaction of mother hunger and a promising state of maturity and recovery (Gibbons, 2006, 205).

See also **betrayal; feminism; racism; vengeance; *Trifles;* "The Yellow Wallpaper"**

• *Further reading*

Gibbons, Kaye. *Divining Women*. New York: G.P. Putnam's Sons, 2004.
_____. *Ellen Foster*. New York: Algonquin Press, 1987.
_____. *The Life All Around Me by Ellen Foster*. New York: Harcourt, 2006.
_____. *On the Occasion of My Last Afternoon*. New York: G.P. Putnam's Sons, 1998.
Redding, Sean, Jane Fisher, and James S. Torrens. "Review: *On the Occasion of My Last Afternoon*," *America* 180, no. 1 (2 January 1999).

irony

Kaye Gibbons wields irony like a sword. In a short-short story, "The Headache," published in June 1987 in the *St. Andrews Review*, the author imperils a farm wife, Lucille Womble, from overactive idealism. In a summer fraught with financial loss, she locates an abandoned handbag in a restaurant ladies' room. Contributing to irony is the rare evening out for a chicken dinner, paid for by her grown son Frank. In secret from her husband Henry, Lucille nurses two weeks of blame for concealing the lost purse, a trick set up to terrorize her. She founders from hysteria, throbbing head, sleeplessness, and flashbacks to the snake that rears up from the pocketbook. Through confession to a sympathetic physician, Lucille is able to access home therapy, the loving arms of her husband, who credits her with goodness.

The rescue of the innocent from wrongheadedness grounds Gibbons's first novel, *Ellen Foster* (1987). Key to the delineation of a ten-year-old's homelessness and lovelessness is an ongoing comparison between the title character and her black friend Starletta. While Ellen's father Bill invites negro drunks to his house to buy and consume bootleg liquor on New Year's Eve, 1969, she keeps an eye to a bedroom window and an escape route to Starletta's home. With a child's understanding, Ellen admires Starletta's father, a sober, stable parent who welcomes the runaway to a humble haven. The irony emerges from Ellen's Southern prejudice against blacks, whom she suspects of being unclean, unfit housekeepers. At the same time that she recoils from a drinking glass, biscuit, and bed sharing with Starletta's mother, Ellen receives protection from potential mauling and rape from her white father.

The question of home security and trustworthy parenting recurs in a courtroom scene in which a judge removes Ellen from the temporary care of Julia, a hippie art teacher, and her house-husband Roy and places the child with unfeeling blood relatives. Crucial to the theme of child care is the disturbing disparity between an 11th birthday party given by loving strangers and the callous dismissal of Ellen by her aunts, Betsy and Nadine Nelson, and by cousin Dora Nelson. Compounding familial injustice is the exploitation of Ellen by her hard-handed maternal grandmother, who sets the child to hoeing in the fields in July heat. Gibbons wrests grim humor from the fact that Dora and Nadine attend church only on Thanksgiving and communion Sundays, two religious occasions exemplifying Christian charity and soul searching. Spaced throughout Ellen's story are welcoming scenarios in her foster home, in which Laura, a volunteer parent, satisfies the mother hunger that causes Ellen's hands to shake and her thought patterns to lurch toward terror and loss. A final irony coalesces from Ellen's need to salve Starletta's hurts from racism by treating her to a relaxing weekend at Ellen's new home. The new mother validates Starletta by sewing her initials on towels, a domestic touch that attests to the womanly power to console tender children.

Ironies abound in Gibbons's fictional duet, *A Virtuous Woman* (1989), a pairing of voices that illustrates the mutual affection of a mismated couple. With a more subtle approach to human differences that in *Ellen Foster*, the author departs from the straightforward story of child abuse in her first novel to examine the welter of emotions and needs in a rural household. Ruby Pitts Woodrow Stokes, the pampered daughter of an unnamed landowner and county commissioner, suffers the consequences of a common teen error of judgment — retreat from boredom at age 18 through elopement with 26-year-old John Woodrow, a trashy, unfaithful migrant worker. At his death from a knife blade to the lungs in a pool room brawl two years later, Ruby embraces 40-year-old "Blinking" Jack Ernest Stokes for his offer of paternal protection, respect, and love. Their interaction indicates a need for parenting — Jack's pining for motherly tending that he lacked in childhood and Ruby's flight from a youthful widowhood to wed a man who cherishes her like a father. In a child's language, he says, "'Night, 'night, Ruby. See you in the morning," a verbal talisman intended to ward off harm and keep his cancer-riddled wife with him a little longer (Gibbons, 1989, 123).

The novel rounds out its study of the farm couple with multiple tragic ironies offsetting immaturity with sorrow. A complex dramatic irony kills off both Ruby and her first husband with lung failure. Hers results from the cigarettes that make John Woodrow bearable. The end to a quarter century of marriage leaves 65-year-old Jack in a three-month miasma of a dirty house, a bottle of bourbon, meals of corn flakes and canned soup, and escape into Roadrunner cartoons after Ruby's burial in March. Like a child, he retreats from rationality by imagining visitations from Ruby's ghost, whom he summons with sensory enticement — sprinkles of lilac-scented talcum on clean sheets. Gibbons enhances the sense impression by comparing the fragrance to baby powder, a soother to a grieving child-man. Petulant at the intrusion of neighbors Burr and June Stanley, Jack protects his dreamscape, which he justifies as "all I and Ruby's business" (*Ibid.*, 163). As though taking Ruby's place as mother-comforter, June, the childless couple's surrogate daughter, rubs Jack's head and anticipates a short survival for the widower. Gibbons's most ambiguous conclusion, the fade-out on Jack leaves in doubt the author's ability to pity a character so lacking in manhood.

Unlike the slowly unfolding incongruities of *A Virtuous Woman*, ironic humor electrifies *A Cure for Dreams* (1991). Along Milk Farm Road, the Great Depression deprives rural women of cash for gasoline and clothing. To ease the situation, Irish-American protagonist Lottie O'Cadhain Davies assembles a sisterhood based on penny-ante gambling on gin rummy and pinochle. The sessions take place at the back of Porter's store, a symbol of Lottie's subversion of standard neighborhood economics. Lottie succeeds at jollying her friends by guaranteeing that their children will not starve from the loss of pennies. Gibbons notes the shuffling through aprons for "little dabs of egg and pin money, twirled and tied in the corners of cotton handkerchiefs," a common source of security in the Southern underclass (Gibbons, 1991, 31). Players exude joy in betting, a riposte to economic want that asserts their humanity and community. Lottie achieves additional satisfaction from outfoxing her miserly husband Charles, a Quaker farmer-miller, who attempts to discipline her as though she were an unruly child. Gibbons directs irony toward Lottie's lessons to daughter Betty on the elements of marital happiness that make Amanda Bethune the most contented of neighborhood women. Unlike Lottie, Amanda receives the affection of husband Richard in a marriage based on love rather than manipulation.

In like fashion to *A Cure for Dreams*, dramatic irony leaps into the exposition of *Charms for the Easy Life* (1993), Gibbons's fourth novel. The text reveals the story of a three-woman domain headed by self-educated herbalist-midwife Charlie Kate Birch. In 1902, at age 20, she chooses an illiterate waterman as a mate and settles down to treat the poor of coastal Pasquotank County, North Carolina, on the Albemarle Sound. The replacement of a ferry with a steel bridge restructures the marriage, gradually easing the unnamed ferryman out of a job and out of his wife's esteem. Symbolically, she crosses the bridge into an urban environment in need of her services while her husband slides out of the picture, leaving only his unused place setting at the table. Her rise to prominence as an outspoken healer and counselor to the downtrodden in Raleigh's mill district enables her to live comfortably with widowed daughter Sophia Snow Birch and granddaughter Margaret. From Charlie Kate's loss, Margaret learns two interlinking lessons— that men are prone to leave and that women are capable of providing for themselves.

In a fittingly domestic scene, the novel tilts unexpectedly from its feminist orbit. Without warning, 56-year-old Charlie Kate is hanging clothes on the line in 1938 when her wayward husband appears at the edge of a field. The magnetic pull of wife to husband returns her to girlishness, an unlikely reaction from the steely grass widow. Gibbons pictures the reunion of mates as a brief madness. Charlie Kate, suitcase in hand, leaves with a wanderer who reeks of urine and bourbon. After a three-day tryst in the Sir Walter Raleigh Hotel, Charlie Kate snaps to. She summons her granddaughter and brandishes a roll of bills amounting to $1,365. Margaret's puzzlement gives way in aphorism: Gibbons comments that "love and revenge grow from the same kernel of want," an admission of human frailty in the otherwise unshakeable family matriarch (Gibbons, 1993, 76). Because Charlie Kate sees no reason to justify her actions, the brief fling ends without details. She displays her usual aplomb years later at her husband's burial, where she dickers with his mistress for possession of a mantel clock, a palpable symbol of the effects of experience over time wasted on wispy dreams of romance. Enhancing irony is Charlie Kate's attempt to manage the love lives of Sophia and Margaret. Both appear to choose appropriate mates— businessman

Richard Baines for Sophia and Tom Hawkings, III, for Margaret — who offer stable finances in equal proportion to affection and commitment.

On the national level, Gibbons's first historical novel, *On the Occasion of My Last Afternoon* (1998), tackles a reordering of justice through a recompense to Southern slaves. Irony concludes the Cinderella tale of Emma Garnet Tate Lowell, a treasured daughter from tidewater Virginia. She grows up materially privileged, but emotionally traumatized by Samuel P. Goodman Tate, her hectoring father, the slavemaster and squire of Seven Oaks plantation in Burton Parish. Amid wealth and artistic splendor, Emma seeks refuge in the kitchen, the womanly domain of Clarice Washington, the freedwoman cook and housekeeper. Like a pillar supporting the roof, Clarice maintains Emma's childhood home in the place of Alice Tate, a spineless plantation mistress. After 17-year-old Emma marries Dr. Quincy Lowell in 1847, Clarice begins the feeding and mothering of the couple's three daughters, Leslie, Louise, and Mary. A familiar figure in Southern literature — e.g., Mammy in Margaret Mitchell's *Gone with the Wind* (1936), Berenice Sadie Brown in Carson McCullers's *The Member of the Wedding* (1946), and the deceased slave mother of Amantha Starr in Robert Penn Warren's *Band of Angels* (1955) — the fictional Clarice derives from centuries of negro mammies who perform the lowliest, most intimate services for their owner-employers while contributing order, stability, and wisdom to the household.

Gibbons atones through literature for the discounting of the black surrogate mother's love and service to white children. In a resetting of mother-daughter roles, Emma rids herself of guilt at Clarice's death in 1863, when years of unappreciated labors and loyalty come home to haunt Emma and her younger sister, Maureen Tate, a self-centered prom trotter. Emma elevates her household do-all to equal status with the strong women of the South — Confederate first lady Varina Davis, Sanitary Commission administrator Dorothea Dix, and "three generations of Lee women," a reference to Robert Edward Lee's mother Ann Hill Carter Lee; wife, Mary Anna Custis Lee; and his daughters, Anne Carter Lee, Eleanor Agnes Lee, Catherine Mildred Lee, and Mary Lee (Gibbons, 1998, 232). Obeying Clarice's deathbed dicta, Emma and Maureen humble themselves and take lessons from the house staff— Charlie, Martha, and Mavis— by hacking apart a scalded duck, the crude beginning of an education in kitchen essentials for spoiled plantation belles.

Appropriately demoted from a lifetime of special treatment, shortly after the abolition of slavery, the Tate girls accept Martha's scorn that they have spent their childhood and young womanhood depending on black people for everyday necessities. Martha blares out, "Mr. Lincoln means to teach ya'll ladies how to suffer by," a barbed analysis of Abraham Lincoln's Emancipation Proclamation, issued on January 1, 1863 (*Ibid.*, 242). The repayment for lowering a polite veil over servitude is a season in hell, the last year of protracted civil war, when a stream of victims forces Emma and Maureen to perform the most menial kindnesses for moaning, dying soldiers. In one scene, Gibbons sets Emma to plucking shrapnel from a casualty's back with tweezers; in another, she directs the application of leeches to infected wounds. Guiding the family's ministrations, Dr. Quincy Lowell, the maligned Yankee who directs the makeshift Fair Grounds hospital, elevates himself above slavers like Samuel by opening the Lowells' Blount Street residence to an overflow of casualties inflicted by Union forces at the battles of Fort Pillow, Tennessee, (April 12, 1864) and at the Wilderness, Virginia (May 5–7, 1864) and Cold Harbor, Virginia (May 31–June 12, 1864). A tragic irony ends his service at war's end, when he slips away from exhaustion and metabolic collapse in the arms of his enduring wife, who outlives him by 35 years.

A subsequent elevation of a volunteer rescuer forms the nucleus of Gibbons's seventh novel, *Divining Women* (2004). Like Ruby Stokes, Emma Lowell, and Maureen Tate, 22-year-old Mary Oliver grows up treasured and pampered in a prosperous Washington, D.C., household complete with two sets of grandparents, the Greenes and the Olivers. A lull in Mary's graduate studies at Radcliffe in summer 1918 frees her to tend her aunt, Maureen Carlton Ross, an object of pity to Mary's mother, Martha Greene Oliver. To the hateful salvos and insinuating strafings of Maureen's husband Troop, for 40 days, Mary lobs pro-woman retorts capable of deflecting his constant assaults. Heavy irony empowers the resolution, in which Mary, Maureen, and the household servants, Mamie and Zollie, deliver a comeuppance that strips Troop of his pseudo-refinement. Their departure at sunset on November 9, 1918, to bury Maureen's stillborn daughter, Ella Eloise, leaves Troop blustering on the sidewalk in full view of disapproving neighbors. For the pro-woman author, public mortification of the villain suffices.

In her first sequel, *The Life All Around Me by Ellen Foster* (2006), Gibbons addresses the power of irony. The falling action allows the title figure an after-the-fact glimpse of her mother, Shine, at a low point of physical and emotional stability. According to a medical evaluation in the mother's last year, at her admission to Dorothea Dix Hospital on September 10, 1968, she felt powerless to deliver quality child care to her deserving daughter. Ellen, long burdened with guilt that she couldn't save her 40-year-old mother from suicide in March 1969, experiences an epiphany of human muddles: "I've been miserable since she died because she died so I wouldn't be miserable" (Gibbons, 2006, 203). Deepening Ellen's understanding of doing the best she can is the comparison of the deceased mother to Madame C.J. Walker, a black entrepreneur who exemplifies women "who live on in time, inside their time and did with it," a vernacular expression of female coping (*Ibid.*, 204–205).

• *Further reading*

Gibbons, Kaye. *Charms for the Easy Life*. New York: Putnam, 1993.
_____. *A Cure for Dreams*. New York: Algonquin, 1991.
_____. *The Life All Around Me by Ellen Foster*. New York: Harcourt, 2006.
_____. *On the Occasion of My Last Afternoon*. New York: G.P. Putnam's Sons, 1998.
_____. *A Virtuous Woman*. Chapel Hill, N.C.: Algonquin Press, 1989.
Parker, Roy, Jr. "Elegant Family Story," *Fayetteville* (N.C.) *Observer* (14 April 1991).
Szatmary, Peter. "A Slaveowner's Daughter," *Houston Chronicle* (28 June 1998).

"Joyner's Store"

In "Joyner's Store," a nostalgic piece for the June 1997 issue of *Southern Living*, Kaye Gibbons reflects on childhood memories of "plenty of good things you can have for cheap," a goal indigenous to the rural poor of Nash County, North Carolina (Gibbons, 1997, 204). She recalls her older sister Alice taking the bus to school from the local crossroads store, a rural emporium off U.S. 301 that enticed the author for ten years. The site offers coolers of soft drinks, shelves of dusty canned goods, and pinball, a game machine that Charles Batts feeds with quarters while Kaye watches from the height of an upended crate. Staple lunch items range from sardines, potted meat, Vy-eena (Vienna) sausages, and saltines to sweets—Tootsie Rolls, jawbreakers, Goobers, Raisinets, and Dixie cups, a small serving of ice cream eaten with a short wooden spoon. To pay for treats, she gathers bottles for the deposit money. The simplicity of the economy belies the hardships the Batts family faced while growing tobacco in the eastern piedmont.

The personal essay allows Gibbons to relive endearing childhood tidbits. She recalls that, when she was eight, her father ran against Richard Nixon during the 1968 presidential campaign as a write-in candidate from the voting booths set up at Joyner's store. Attesting to the lack of entertainment in Nash County is excitement over the arrival of Suzie the monkey, the pet of the Sinclair Oil deliverer. Suzie spends a dime for a Fudgsicle, which her pale simian hand retrieves from the ice-cream freezer. The author and her peers also rubberneck at "Yankee license plates at the gas pumps," a common occurrence during the migration of New York snowbirds to Florida for the winter. Greeting the leisure class is Bend of the River at its starkest—"clay soil and wire grass abounded, where hailstorms were the closest we could ever get to even a flurry of snow" (*Ibid.*, 205). She regrets the fact that meadows where she once hid Easter eggs now flourish with "yuppification" (*Ibid.*). The supple nostalgia discloses the roots of the author's empathy for humble rural life.

• *Further reading*

Gibbons, Kaye. "Joyner's Store," *Southern Living* 32, no. 6 (June 1997): 204–205.

language

Kaye Gibbons's ability to pound bristly conflict into plowshares intrigues readers and increases her fan base as well as critical acclaim. The key to the humanity of her characters is their resilient talk, the wry humor that speaks harsh, but unavoidable truths, much like the bumptious retorts of Appalachian hillbillies and the Yiddish witticisms and adages of New York Jews. According to Glenn Giffin, book critic of the *Denver Post*, Gibbons particularizes Southern speech with idiosyncrasy: "There's not an 'everyman' quality to the language" (Giffin, 1993). Southern agrarian cadencing and the textures of her homeland resound in her writing like language ingrained from birth, an image she develops in the childhood and coming of age of Marjorie Polly Randolph in *A Cure for Dreams* (1991). Critic Lynn Jessup, writing for the *Greensboro* (N.C.) *News & Record* described the sound "[reverberating] like a Christmas handbell" (Jessup, 1995). As Gibbons explained at a dinner meeting of the Literary and Historical Association in Raleigh, she has no reason to research characters from other language groups: "All my materials are here.... My language is here," a reference to her home in piedmont North Carolina (Hodges, 1998).

Gibbons's use of grassroots materials is legendary. Critic Valerie Sayers, a reviewer for the *Washington Post*, refers to the author's utterance as "one of the quirkiest narrative voices in contemporary literature" (Sayers, 2006). A model of Gibbons's character study emerges in Lucille Womble, the suffering protagonist of "The Headache," a short-short story published in the June 1987 issue of the *St. Andrews Review*. A bare bones scenario, it pictures a humble woman who feels tempted to hide an upscale purse in her "britches," the rural Southern term for women's briefs (Gibbons, 1987, 3). The contrast in womanly handbags differentiates between female haves and have-nots at the same time that it reveals in Lucille a recognition of social boundaries. She relays to her older son the importance of deportment to the working poor. Acting on her philosophy, he charges the youngest boy with behaving "like you ain't got no raising," a pervasive concern among sensitive poor families (*Ibid.*, 4). Additional misgivings about social class color Lucille's worry that her employer, Mae Bell Stokes, perceives Lucille as a welfare recipient, a lowering of family standards to the social bottom.

Essential to Gibbons's first novel, *Ellen Foster* (1987), is the voicing common to a rural, underprivileged pre-teen who lives on a social and economic par with the Wombles. Reviewer Roger Davis Friedman, in a critique for the *Chicago Tribune*, declared that Ellen's "words don't just hang uselessly but add up to cherished brittle sentences" (Friedman, 1987). Of sharing the pony Dolphin, she remarks that foster children have to "wait your go," an element of Ellen's introduction to egalitarianism in a family comprising more than one child (Gibbons, 1987, 13). Some of the endearing lines of Ellen's monologue indicate a partial understanding of common terms. For a court appearance, she wears "patting leather shoes"; during negotiations with her future foster mother, Ellen offers $166, a hoard intended to keep the relationship on the "up in up" (*Ibid.*, 55, 119). At a crucial point — the death of her father Bill from cerebral hemorrhage resulting from alcoholism — she cowers and pleads that authorities "shut the lid down hard on this one," a suggestion of 19th-century European Gothic vampire lore and the terrors of the undead stalking the innocent (*Ibid.*, 70).

Gibbons's skill at character delineation through language enters a more complex level in *A Virtuous Woman* (1989), a narrative duet for husband and wife. The basis, according to reviewer Roy Parker, Jr., a reviewer for the *Fayetteville* (N.C.) *Observer*, is the "argot of the tobacco country somewhere between the Tar and the Roanoke" rivers in lower Piedmont, North Carolina (Parker, 1989). Ruby Pitts Woodrow Stokes speaks in standard English her introspection into everyday occurrences. When her husband, tenant laborer "Blinking" Jack Ernest Stokes, fires Ruby's pistol, she conceals flashbacks to her first husband, John Woodrow, whom she intended to shoot to end their wretched two-year marriage. Jack, whom diction and syntax identifies as an unlettered rustic, recalls that he "had the big mouth" while courting Ruby, a deviation from a quarter century of saying little to women (Gibbons, 1989, 45). In the plot resolution, he pictures himself as a 65-year-old fool for discovering "what you thought was so ain't so," a reference to his yearning for Ruby's return from death as a "haint" (*Ibid.*, 152). By concluding on Jack's longings for Ruby, whether in the flesh or as a spirit, Gibbons exalts the female described in the novel's title for triumphing over death through Jack's dreams and memories.

By her third novel, Gibbons's works began receiving more scholarly critiques, which tend to focus on animated, insightful vernacular that enhances the membership of women within communities. Of *A Cure for Dreams* (1991), novelist-reviewer Josephine Humphreys, in a critique for the *Los Angeles Times*, remarked on a text that offers "evidence that the English language may be, in the service of fiction, ever refreshed and enlivened" (Humphreys, 1991, 13). She refers to keen-edged diction that gilds the narrative with clarity and sparkle, a visual luminosity that a reviewer for the *Chicago Tribune* called "almost palpable" ("Tribune," 1991). Language becomes the trunk line that channels therapeutic models, universal information, and period details. Essential to the historical milieu are the period terms that the author salts in, including the Works Progress Administration (W.P.A.), Butterick dress patterns, Lydia Pinkham, "Mr. Hoover," "Mr. Boll Weevil," Hitler, and gas rationing, a sore spot with Quaker farmer-miller Charles Davies, an overbearing miser (Gibbons, 1991, 63, 33). The ongoing female issues, as described by Miriam Marty Clark, a teacher-reviewer for the *St. Louis Post-Dispatch*, reveal in "subtle ways what a small world [they] mark out, how narrow the limits" (Clark, 1991).

Similarly, in *Charms for the Easy Life* (1993), the soft Southernisms and Afro-American cadencing mark residents of eastern North Carolina. After the family matriarch, Charlie Kate Birch, emigrates southwest from coastal Pasquotank County on the Albemarle Sound, she reopens her unlicensed medical practice in Raleigh, North Carolina. In contrast to a neighborhood petition blaming "the redio" for a tornado and demanding "git rit ov it," she remains a touchstone of standard English (Gibbons, 1993, 20). The text opts for period diction, the lingua franca of World War II — dogfaces, enlistees rejected as 4-F, Eisenhower jackets, censored mail from a German P.O.W. camp, and Edward R. Murrow's broadcasts on the radio, which typify the military aspects of the 1940s. For noncombatants, details like waiting in ration lines, imitation stockings, low-flying blimps, jitterbugging to wartime tunes, Charles Lindbergh's non-interventionism philosophy, and slang terms like "girlie," "zoot suit," "all dolled up," "swell," and "shake-down dance" establish Gibbons's dedication to the era's social concerns and nervous energy (*Ibid.*, 193, 171, 178, 197).

At a later point in history, precise language defines the family quandary with an insane wife and mother in *Sights Unseen* (1995), Gibbons's fifth novel. Upon welcoming Maggie Barnes and her infant, Harriet Pearl "Hattie" Barnes, home from the maternity ward of Duke Hospital, Pearl Wiggins, the cook and housekeeper, upends the doctor's diagnosis of post-partum depression by summarizing Maggie's behavior as "jumbledy," an apt summation of bipolarity (Gibbons, 1995, 60). Character responses to craziness vary in terms of each viewer's relationship with Maggie. To Josephine Woodward, a replacement for the children's paternal grandmother, Maggie suffers from "spells"; to Maggie's imaginative son Freddy, manic extremes compare to scenes in Vincent Price's horror movies (*ibid.*, 127). A fellow patient on the maternity floor chides, "You, missy, are a mess" (*Ibid.*, 31). Pearl works through Maggie's bad spells by "[talking] herself out," a narrative cure that echoes the word healing in *A Cure for Dreams* (*Ibid.*, 39). Frederick silences his dismay except for the rare curse or plaintive cry, "My life is not my own" (*Ibid.*, 53). For Hattie, the most traumatized of the family, her mother's restoration to normality causes Hattie to forgive the past and to cling to Maggie's alter ego, "peaceful and smiling" (*Ibid.*, 209). Ultimately, according to critic Linda Tate, narration nourishes the family with "a vital fuel for the regeneration of a woman and her community" (Folks & Folks, 2000, 224–225). Through verbalization, Hattie reclaims and immortalizes her mother while accomplishing for herself the grieving necessary for self-healing.

For the author's first historical novel, *On the Occasion of My Last Afternoon* (1998), language becomes the vehicle for transporting readers to the plantation South and its subsequent collapse. Her genius prompted feminist historian Linda Wagner-Martin to declare the author "one of the consummate ventriloquists of twentieth century fiction" (Wagner-Martin, 1999, 3). Period terms like the quaintly euphemistic title proved easy for Gibbons to master. In her words, "The Civil War lends itself to locution" (Kenney, 1995). From the era, she extracts "zinc" (sink), "sangaree" (spiced wine), "floradory" (stage actress), "stepping-babies" (toddlers), and "tussy-mussy" (small bouquet of flowers) (Gibbons, 1998, 4, 6, 9, 20). The shift from niceties to social cataclysm and wartime exigencies forces narrator Emma Garnet Tate Lowell to exonerate herself for setting down "rough language that no Southern lady ... would approve" (*Ibid.*, 62). An upended milieu leaves noncombatants "in a swivet," a mild term for social and economic catastrophe (*Ibid.*, 256). At the foundering of the James River plantation hegemony in June 1862, Samuel P. Goodman Tate retreats to the home of his daughter Emma in Raleigh, North Carolina. To the family's humiliation by General George Brinton McClellan's forces, Samuel issues from the Lowell home letters to editors of newspapers in Atlanta, Knoxville, Nashville, New Orleans, and Vicksburg spewing his Confederate diatribes and racist epithets, the verbal equivalent of cannon salvos.

Silencing villains is a specialty of Gibbons, who kills off father Bill with alcoholism in *Ellen Foster*, knifes John Woodrow through the lungs in *A Virtuous Woman*, drowns the money-grubbing Charles Davies in *A Cure for Dreams*, and doles out a cerebral hemorrhage to Sophia's womanizing husband in August 1936 in *Charms for the Easy Life*. Samuel Tate's evil mouth continues to abrade the Lowell family until Quincy stifles his father-in-law by pouring a late-night overdose of digitalis between his lips, ostensibly to ease heart failure. In reference to a patient's murder, Quincy orders Emma to say nothing of the breach of law and medical ethics. More important to Emma's peace of mind is the recovery of cook-housekeeper Clarice Washington's "receipts," annotations to standard Southern cookery that Emma values as a female legacy (*Ibid.*, 266). From preparing regional dishes, the heroine perceives in her "quick marrow" (innate understanding) the womanly strengths that support her submissive mother Alice and that enable Clarice to bolster three generations of the Lowell-Tate genealogy (Gibbons, 1998, 115).

In her first sequel, *The Life All Around Me by Ellen Foster* (2006), the author dismayed some critics and fans by overblending the title figure's spectacular folk locutions with intellectual fire power. In a fidget on her way by train to Baltimore for classes for gifted children at Johns Hopkins University, Ellen admits to chewing on conundrums like "how somebody first put math and moods together in iambic pentameter" (Gibbons, 2006, 70). Gibbons juxtaposes metaphysical abstractions with the naked terror of flashbacks to childhood, when Ellen has less emotional sophistication to buoy her. In fall 1974, when Aunt Nadine Nelson arrives to brazen out her fraudulant diversion of Ellen's inheritance, her niece recognizes that Nadine relies on an *ad hominem* put-down, willing Ellen "to fear I was funny-looking" for having cropped hair (*Ibid.*, 171). In a reversion to the earlier persona, Ellen checks the dresser mirror and observes that she "looked chaotic" and she forgot "how quickly order flies off the rail," two reprises to images of catastrophe from the novel *Ellen Foster* (*Ibid.*, 202). The reharmonization of her outlook is the gift of Laura, the foster mother, who trusts in loving cajolery to tranquilize a turbulent spirit.

See also **dialect; humor; irony; racism**

• *Further reading*

Clark, Miriam Marty. "Sounds of Women Talking," *St. Louis Post-Dispatch* (9 June 1991).

Folks, Jeffrey J., and Nancy Summers Folks. *The World Is Our Home*. Lexington: University Press of Kentucky, 2000.

Friedman, Roger Davis. "A Girl Escapes a Family to Find a Family," *Chicago Tribune* (22 May 1987).

Gibbons, Kaye. *Charms for the Easy Life*. New York: Putnam, 1993.

_____. *A Cure for Dreams*. New York: Algonquin, 1991.

_____. *Ellen Foster*. New York: Algonquin Press, 1987.

_____. "The Headache," *St. Andrews Review* (June 1987): 3–8.

_____. *The Life All Around Me by Ellen Foster*. New York: Harcourt, 2006.

_____. *On the Occasion of My Last Afternoon*. New York: G.P. Putnam's Sons, 1998.

_____. *Sights Unseen*. New York: G.P. Putnam's Sons, 1995.

_____. *A Virtuous Woman*. Chapel Hill, N.C.: Algonquin Press, 1989.

Giffin, Glenn. "Gibbons Enamored of Southern Style," *Denver Post* (13 April 1993).

Hodges, Betty. "Southern Writer Mines Linguistic Heritage," Durham, N.C., *Herald-Sun* (29 November 1998).

Humphreys, Josephine. "Within the Marriage, a Secret Life," *Los Angeles Times* (19 May 1991): BR13.

Jessup, Lynn. "Kaye Gibbons: Another Happy Ending," *Greensboro* (N.C.) *News & Record* (12 November 1995).

Johnson, Rheta Grimsley. "A Skewed Life with Mother," *Atlanta Journal-Constitution* (3 September 1995).

Kenney, Michael. "An Author Confronts Her Inner Demons," *Boston Globe* (20 September 1995).

Parker, Roy, Jr. "Kay Gibbons Reprise," *Fayetteville* (N.C.) *Observer* (30 April 1989).

Sayers, Valerie, "Growing Into the Role," *Washington Post* (6 January 2006).

"Tribune Books," *Chicago Tribune* (15 September 1991).

Wagner-Martin, Linda. "Kaye Gibbons' Achievement in *On the Occasion of My Last Afternoon*," *Notes on Contemporary Literature* 29, no. 3 (May 1999): 3–5.

Laura

Kaye Gibbons's first novel, *Ellen Foster* (1987), provides a panoply of female ideals and foils as models and warnings to the title figure. At age ten, Ellen rashly retreats from family and seeks harborage among strangers, former hippies Julia and Roy, an art teacher and her husband whose off-beat home life seems like answered prayer. Aunt Betsy, who grudgingly gives Ellen a home after the child's grandmother's death, belies the Christmas spirit by humiliating and rejecting a needy child during the holidays. On December 25, 1970, Ellen makes her own wish come true by leaving a "no-room-at-the-inn situation" and knocking at the door of Laura's foster home (Gibbons, 2006, 10). Ellen finds herself not only welcome, but lavished with proper meals, bag lunches, pony rides, and a room of her own decorated in pink checks, a veneer of innocence and naiveté to turn grim thoughts toward normal girlhood. As satisfaction to the soul, Laura enfolds Ellen in safety, acceptance, and affection. The child responds with awe that a stranger offers more unconditional love than does blood kin. Implicit in Laura's mothering is respect for the long road that Ellen traverses to save herself from despair.

A stellar champion of troubled teen girls, Laura offers a refuge to the afflicted. In church, her forthright step and dignified posture suggest a queen, whom Ellen superimposes over Laura. Through dark romanticism, Ellen pictures Laura as a doomed Anne Boleyn, the former mistress and second wife of Henry VIII, plodding with measured tread toward execution for treason on May 19, 1536. For Ellen, Laura extends her usual heroism to the shielding of a fragile ego during Ellen's search for a permanent dwelling and for the right to a family legacy. On the emotional level, Laura offers Ellen the Aristotelian *tabula rasa* (clean slate)—a place where no old scores threaten the child with shame for her father Bill's loss of furniture to the repo man or with guilt for her mother Shine's suicide in March 1969 at age 40 from an overdose of prescription digitalis. Laura's home is a model of order, a godsend to a child whose universe perpetually careens toward disaster. In Laura's care, Ellen becomes a respectable somebody, a resurrected self wiped free of remorse. At temporary regressions, Laura suggests breath control and relaxing massage that halt Ellen's anxiety attacks, dispel flashbacks, and still quavering hands.

In the sequel, *The Life All Around Me by Ellen Foster* (2006), the title character, at age 15, makes astute observations of Laura, a kind women who takes casseroles to a poor family and donates canned goods at the county fair in lieu of buying tickets. As described by Lynna Williams, a critic for the *Chicago Tribune*, the foster mother is a "compelling, complicated character in her own right," typical of many-sided females like Dr. Jane Cowley in "The Headache" (June 1987), June Stanley in *A Virtuous Woman* (1989), Amanda Bethune in *A Cure for Dreams* (1991), and Mamie in *Divining Women* (2004), all of whom Gibbons chooses to leave only partially fleshed out (Williams, 2006). In understated verbal combat with a social worker, Laura comes off like actor Ava Gardner in the movie *The Night of the Iguana* (1964), a tense film featuring North Carolina's famed screen goddess from Smithfield, southwest of Gibbons's birthplace. Laura's childhood-restoring method of taking Ellen to a kiddie movie once a month illustrates the foster mother's appreciation of such innocent pleasures as *Willy Wonka and the Chocolate Factory* (1971), *American Bandstand* on Saturday-morning television, and window shopping downtown with the other foster children. Because Laura sets viewing standards, she rules out the film *Carnal Knowledge* (1971), which features nude shots of Art Garfunkel. More comforting to Ellen is a ten-mile ride home from intrusive government IQ testing with her head in Laura's lap while gentle fingers stroke Ellen's hair.

Laura's idealism becomes the two-edged sword that both defends and threatens foster placements. Quick to shield girls from the fallout of shattered families, she knows the negative urges that dispose two undisciplined teen girls toward misbehavior, especially sexual experimentation as a substitute for affection. After spending a day introducing Starletta's mother to a new physician at the teaching hospital, Laura returns to domestic uproar and blames herself for letting altruism overshadow the demands for home supervision and discipline. To Ellen's need for more security and for the attention that Laura wastes on the two outlaws, Laura states a psychological truth, the impossibility of willing people to behave responsibly. Her wisdom covers both randy teens and Ellen, whose tipoff of the home situation to social services threatens the entire foster home. In her forgiving fashion, Laura uses the misplaced loyalty as a lesson in thinking before acting in haste.

Gibbons endows Laura with on-the-spot foresight. When Stuart shows up unannounced on his bicycle at an inopportune moment, she urges Ellen to attend to his need for company. To reduce Ellen's tensions, Laura conceals family gossip about cousin Dora's pregnancy and tries to stave off a family visit in fall 1974 that renews Ellen's anguish over boorish, grasping relatives. Picturing Aunt Nadine's arrival, Laura visualizes a circle around the foster home, an invisible rampart that fends off corruption and harm. To Ellen, the home atmosphere has a solidity like ballast, which she needs to stay afloat during the fast-paced resolution. In the falling action, Laura endears herself for loyalty to a foster daughter she cherishes like an unexpected Christmas gift. From Laura's great-hearted perspective, Ellen's presence honors the foster home, which Laura superintends like a domestic bastion. Ellen's extraordinary character corroborates Laura's prediction of an amazing future for them both.

See also **foster parenting**

• *Further reading*

Gibbons, Kaye. *The Life All Around Me by Ellen Foster.* New York: Harcourt, 2006.
Town, Caren J. *New Southern Girl: Female Adolescence in the Works of 12 Women Authors.* Jefferson, N.C.: McFarland, 2004.
Williams, Lynna. "For Ellen Foster, There's Finally Light at the End of the Tunnel," *Chicago Tribune* (8 January 2006).

The Life All Around Me by Ellen Foster

The sequel of *Ellen Foster* (1987) fills in gaps and queries left dangling by the first text. Gibbons picks up the protagonist's story as she writes Dr. Derek Curtis Bok, president of Harvard University from 1971 to 1991, for special permission to begin college. Opening on September 20, 1974, the novel introduces 15-year-old Ellen as witty, loquacious, and ambitious, three qualities that propel the narrative. After acknowledging that she refuses to be "disdone" by a spate of demoralizing life experiences, she reflects on her unusual background (Gibbons, 2006, 2). Her list of qualifications include writing the newspaper column "Ellen's Tellin," working concessions for spending money, school library chores, and aiding a teacher of retarded students. Simultaneously, Ellen maintains top grades and wins essay competitions and an oratory contest held in Washington, D.C. (*Ibid.*, 7). The mid-teen milieu featuring boys in camouflage gear at the beginning of hunting season and a county health nurse teaching about hygiene and sexual abstinence reflects much of the author's own coming-of-age in Nash County, North Carolina.

Gibbons maintains a wry tone tinged with bitterness that recalls her protagonist at age 11 as hostile and defensive. Of long-term emotional damage, the author contrasts the alternatives of living with foster mother Laura or following Social Services placement in a nightmarish orphanage suited to "damaged goods," Ellen's harsh metaphor for homeless children as emotionally frazzled as she (*Ibid.*, 10). The possibility returns Ellen to nail chewing and overachievement, two symptoms resurrected from her years of bad dreams, anxiety attacks, quaking hands, and a distrust of authority figures like school psychologists, social workers, court judges, and psychometrists. Envisioning herself as a crawling babe jolted by a frayed light cord, she ponders the efforts of normal people to cope with terror and spiritual emptiness, threats she shares with Summer, the scared orphan in Cynthia Rylant's award-winning fostering story *Missing May* (1993).

Gibbons pictures her heroine in constant motion. Ellen's urgency vibrates with enough tension and energy to upset the other two foster girls in Laura's household, leaving them huffy and embittered until Ellen intervenes. Her train trip to a high IQ camp at Johns Hopkins University in Baltimore reveals much about her emotional and intellectual makeup. On the way north, she fidgets and paces the aisles, annoying adult passengers with her questions, comments, and edginess. To pass the time, she strolls other compartments and chats with a clerk in the dining car, who treats her to a bagel and coffee at a stop-over at Union Station in Washington, D.C. The journey depicts an intellectual curiosity made manic by misgivings that Ellen must overcome before achieving confidence and stability.

Critics vary in their acceptance of Gibbons's filling in blanks from the original novel. Among pans of the novel are complaints about an unwieldy title, contrived plotting, dense syntax, and rambling, confusing leaps of thought. In a critique of the audio version for *Library Journal*, reviewer Rochelle Ratner charged the cast of characters with unrealistic friends and a "suddenly righteous" cousin Dora Nelson, whom Ellen receives with joy in Dora's incipient motherhood (Ratner, 2006). In the *New York Times Book Review*, Lauren Collins dismisses the plot as "unfortunately unbelievable" (Collins, 2006). Karen Campbell, a critic for the *Boston Globe*, typified the story as "precious" in its cute epistolary beginning and sweet, but sentimental for its conclusion to "one hellacious childhood" (Campbell, 2006). Susan Kelly, in commentary for *USA Today*, posed an ambiguous overview — she disliked the Cinderella quality of the novel's ending, but admired Ellen's "phoenix-like rise from the ashes," two folkloric images of the same outcome (Kelly, 2006).

See also **Foster, Ellen; Laura**

• *Further reading*

Campbell, Karen. "Ellen Foster Returns, Wise Beyond Her Years," *Boston Globe* (January 17, 2006).

Collins, Lauren. "Older, Wiser," *New York Times Book Review* (5 March 2006): 15.

Gibbons, Kaye. *The Life All Around Me.* New York: Harcourt, 2006.

Kelly, Susan. "Ellen Foster Grows Less Endearing with Age," *USA Today* (2 February 2006).

Ratner, Rochelle, "Review: *The Life All Around Me by Ellen Foster,*" *Library Journal* 131, no. 12 (1 July 2006): 118.

Lowell, Emma Garnet Tate

Opinionated and wise beyond her years, Emma Garnet Tate Lowell, the narrator of *On the Occasion of My Last Afternoon* (1998), turns proto-feminist eyes on the American Civil War. She establishes in the novel's opening a gift for storing up observations for later reassembly into timely insights. In the estimation of feminist historian-critic Linda Wagner-Martin, Emma speaks from the poised perspective of the upper middle class an "understanding of privilege," a predictable outcome of living the gentrified life of mid–19th century tidewater Virginia (Wagner-Martin, 1999, 4). In 1842, at age 12, Emma admits being curious and dreamy, a standard pair of descriptives for pre-teens that Gibbons introduces in Lottie O'Cadhain Davies in *A Cure for Dreams* (1991) and, to a lesser degree, in Ruby Pitts in *A Virtuous Woman* (1989). Reared on the James River in Bruton Parish, Emma sets a precedent for clear-eyed human study that validates her memories of plantation life, slavery, submissive womanhood, and the Civil War, an interlinked historical milieu that explodes into social and economic chaos.

Gibbons supplies Emma with spiritual pillars. Strengthening her coming of age are contrasting mothers— Alice Tate, the polite doormat wife of vain planter Samuel P. Goodman Tate, and freedwoman Clarice Washington, the cook-housekeeper who builds confidence through pragmatic surrogate mothering. In adulthood, Emma, still tended by Clarice, thrives on unconditional love that neutralizes a withering girlhood. On evenings on the veranda shared with her husband, Dr. Quincy Lowell, she sips Madeira while allowing memory to cleanse her of the "accretion of past wrongs," a storehouse of the indignities she suffered under her martinet father (Gibbons, 1998, 34). Ironically, the dampening of girlish enthusiasm prepares Emma for a more terrible adulthood, when crisis upon crisis follows the secession of Southern states and the onset of armed conflict. Gibbons sets up Emma's life as a paradigm for survival learned from years of buffeting.

The author poses a multi-sided characterization that abuts strengths with innate weaknesses. Emma exemplies what feminist critic Carol Gilligan depicts in *In a Different Voice: Psychological Theory and Women's Development* (1982)—"the feminine voice [that] struggles to resolve in its effort to reclaim the self and to solve the moral problem in such a way that no one is hurt" (Gilligan, 1982, 71). Gibbons allows Emma a forgiveable failing, her regret for not rescuing Alice from Samuel's evil-tongued barrages. While honeymooning in Paris in 1847, Emma berates herself for enjoying *petits fours* on the Champs-Élysées while her mother cowers under a monster's control. In 1859, when Mintus and Ezekiel, Tate family slaves, deliver a death notice to the Blount Street residence in Raleigh, Emma regresses to childhood to lie in the floor, weep, and demand the return of her husband to console her over Alice's passing. Unable to atone for 12 years of absence from Alice, Emma berates herself to "reprehensible neglect, for profound dereliction of duty" (*Ibid.*, 142). She carries into old-ladyhood a monumental self-blame that humanizes Gibbons's gem-like heroine.

The novel stresses Freudian concepts of the spurned daughter seeking the approval of males. Under Quincy's direction, Emma compensates for her shortcomings by treating the most deplorable combat injuries, by opening the Lowell home to a surfeit of casualties, and by acknowledging the manumission of staff members Charlie, Martha, and Mavis. The novel praises the character's ability to endure loss while displaying the vulnerabilities of a daughter bereft of two mothers—Alice and Clarice—and, at war's end, the widow of a beloved husband. Critic Peter Szatmary, in a review for the *Houston Chronicle*, questions the hurried conclusion to Emma's last 35 years, when she "becomes a veritable pioneer in business, philanthropy, and equal rights" (Szatmary, 1998). In the final accounting in 1900 on Emma's last day, she cradles herself in certainties—that she dignified sister Maureen Tate's sudden passing, that Raleigh's poor profit from cash gifts from the Lowell fortune, and that the Lowell-Tate heritage ensures children and grandchildren a firm grounding in morality. Gibbons clings to the paradigm of the Victorian novel with a coda wreathed in duty to family and steadfast Christian principles. Emma rewards her life's efforts by anticipating a celestial reunion with Quincy, the father figure who made her whole.

See also **Lowell-Tate genealogy**

• *Further reading*

Gibbons, Kaye. *On the Occasion of My Last Afternoon.* New York: G.P. Putnam's Sons, 1998.

Gilligan, Carol. *In a Different Voice: Psychological Theory and Women's Development.* Cambridge, Mass.: Harvard University Press, 1982.

Redding, Sean, Jane Fisher, and James S. Torrens. "Review: *On the Occasion of My Last Afternoon*," *America* 180, no. 1 (2 January 1999).

Szatmary, Peter. "A Slaveowner's Daughter," *Houston Chronicle* (28 June 1998).

Wagner-Martin, Linda. "Kaye Gibbons' Achievement in *On the Occasion of My Last Afternoon*," *Notes on Contemporary Literature* 29, no. 3 (May 1999): 3–5.

Lowell-Tate genealogy

The unsettling maturation of Emma Garnet Tate Lowell into a wife, mother, Civil War nurse, and philanthropist discloses her ability to profit from strong and loving relationships. Exonerated from previous faults, she lives the kind of exemplary adulthood that counters a hate-spattered nuclear family:

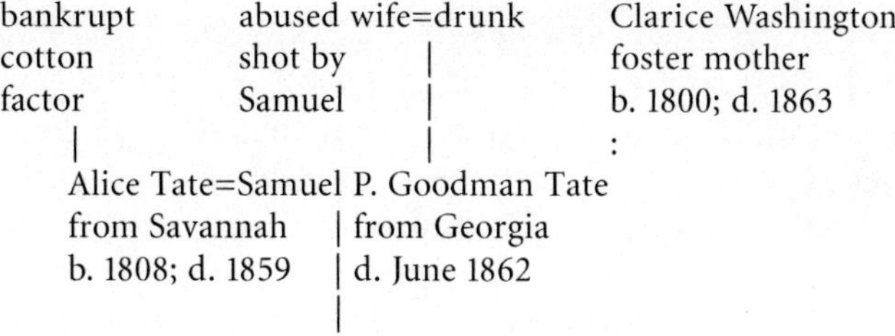

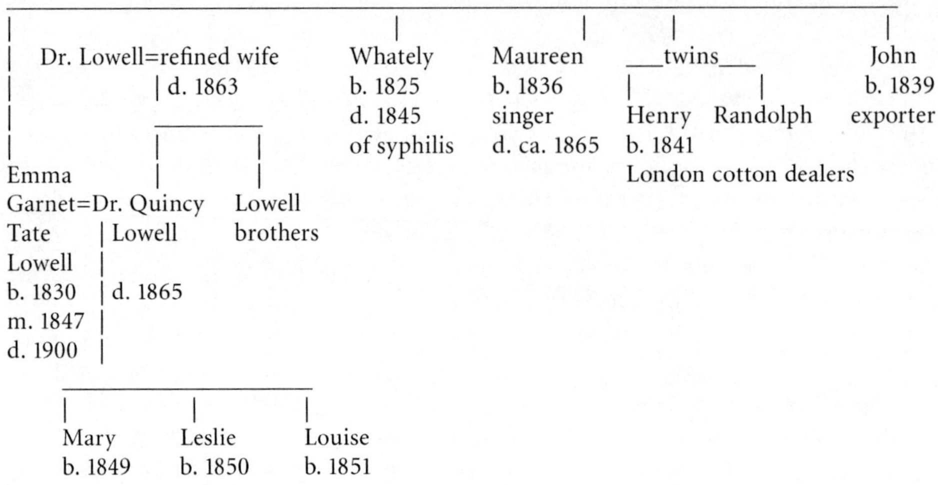

• *Further reading*

Gibbons, Kaye. *On the Occasion of My Last Afternoon.* New York: G.P. Putnam's Sons, 1998.

Margaret

The teller of Gibbons's fourth novel, *Charms for the Easy Life* (1993), Margaret looks back on three generations of female solidarity. Born in 1924 and reared in the pre–World War II era, she navigates the turbulent wake left by an overly romantic mother and overly sensible grandmother. In the view of Maureen Harrington, book critic for the *Denver Post*, Margaret hoists an ambiguous facade—"brilliant, solitary, a bit lost" (Harrington, 1993). A forthright narrator, like Hattie Barnes in *Sights Unseen* (1995) and Mary Oliver in *Divining Women* (2004), Margaret accepts the disappearance of her grandfather and father as tokens of male perfidy. Rather than pursue the flibbertigibbet narcissism of her mother, Sophia Snow Birch, Margaret maintains Ovid's Roman ideal of *medio tutissimum* (going safest in the middle). While awarding affection and good wishes to her man-trap mother, Margaret follows gracefully in the path of Grandmother Charlie Kate Birch, who offers day-by-day instruction in midwifery, benevolent herbalism, and folk dentistry.

In her teens, Margaret ponders the possibilities of a college education. Well read through perusals of quality literature—Samuel Butler, Samuel Taylor Coleridge, Charles Dickens, George Eliot, Thomas Hardy, Ernest Hemingway, Rudyard Kipling, Thomas Mann, Marjorie Kinnan Rawlings, John Steinbeck, Mark Twain, Eudora Welty, Thomas Wolfe, Virginia Woolf—and invigorated by intelligent discussions of literary themes and social issues, she advances from high school at a national turning point, the onset of World War II. Her introduction to battlefield carnage begins with packing Red Cross boxes with cigarettes and Hershey bars. By 1942, she progresses to a Durham veterans' hospital, where Charlie Kate tends to doctoring and leaves Margaret to write letters for recuperating soldiers. The contrast between orderly arrangements of candy and smokes and the anguish of recuperation characterize her unceremonious coming of age. A girlish guile directs her to insert her own versions of dictated letters to sorrowing mothers and unfaithful girlfriends. The experience of challenging Tom Hawkings, III, to abandon his dilly-dallying begins Margaret's lasting relationship with a veteran who proves to be likely husband material. The subtext suggests that their sharing of wartime exigencies strengthens a relationship founded on realism rather than on gauzy dreams like Sophia's immersion in radio and romantic stories, the "romantic fever" of Ellen's mother in *Ellen Foster* (1987), or the chivalric yearnings of Lottie O'Cadhain in *A Cure for Dreams* (1991) (Gibbons, 1987, 7).

Gibbons concludes the novel with Margaret's superintendence of home affairs. As the trio of women dwindles to one, she bids farewell to her mother on Christmas Eve, 1942, when Sophia elopes with businessman Richard Baines to the South Carolina coast. Charlie Kate warns of a shift in the female balance of power: "She'll not be into your affairs. You go on about your business" (Gibbons, 1993, 239). Margaret admits to being awestruck by the newness of the arrangement and confesses to herself that her own "appeal to young men appeared stunted, dwarflike" in comparison with Sophia's skill at flirtation and seduction (*Ibid.*, 240). Accompanied by her grandmother, Margaret moves confidently among future in-laws, a gentrified clan that welcomes Tom's poised, affectionate girlfriend. Upon the grandmother's sudden death on Christmas night, Margaret is equal to a family tragedy she has viewed many times in the lives of Charlie Kate's patients. Obeying the female traditions of stopping the clock and shrouding mirrors, Margaret smooths her grandmother's limbs and readies herself to be discovered, like a treasure as yet unclaimed. The scene predicts an era of mature self-reliance much like that of Charlie Kate. Gibbons stresses Margaret's acceptance of self and her embrace of Tom and the Hawkings family as the rewards due Margaret for her charm, intelligence, and sensitivity.

See also **Birch genealogy**

• *Further reading*

Gibbons, Kaye. *Charms for the Easy Life*. New York: Putnam, 1993.
_____. *Ellen Foster*. New York: Algonquin Press, 1987.
Harrington, Maureen. "Child's Vision Right on Target," *Denver Post* (4 April 1993).

marriage

Kaye Gibbons stages character marriages as the crucibles that test adults for patience, forbearance, and fortitude. In "The Headache," a brief domestic story in the June 1987 issue of the *St. Andrews Review*, the action focuses on the hardscrabble agrarianism of Henry and Lucille Womble, who rear ten children and absorb the loss of two farm machines to the bank within one summer. One of the author's first ventures into the life of the fictional goodwoman, the study of Lucille portrays her as dependent on nightly marital intimacy during her two-week battle with psychosomatic head throbs, hysterical sobbing, insomnia, and recurring serpentine phantasms. Cuddled against Henry's chest, she presses his hands to her belly, a reassuring conjugal posture for two adults saddled with a daytime nightmare — the declining farm income on which the family depends. Appropriately, he forestalls her confession of ethical wrong and awards her right thinking by promising to buy her two hats, a double tribute to the goodwife. The conclusion dramatizes a marriage built on trust and mutual regard.

In contrast to the Wombles' togetherness, Bill's genteel wife, the unnamed invalid in *Ellen Foster* (1987), lacks the physical strength to counter the guile and cruelty of her abusive mate, a bootlegger and layabout. With a child's logic, Ellen attempts to supervise her parents' tenuous togetherness in kitchen and bedroom. Out of spite, in 1969, Bill eases his 40-year-old mate into suicide by doing nothing to rescue her from a deliberate overdose of prescription digitalis. In Ellen's estimation, Bill's truculence advances from the level of everyday drunken snarls to murder. Upon his death in 1970, Ellen longs to see him nailed in his coffin like Dracula, a blood-sucking monster who drains the family of love and serenity. She shelters temporarily with her art teacher Julia and Julia's husband Roy, a standout figure in Gibbons's novels for his willingness to share household cleaning and to alter domestic routine with a festive birthday for 11-year-old Ellen. The only other wedded pair for Ellen's study are Starletta's parents, a black couple who recognize need in the runaway child, who flees neglect, breast groping, and potential incest on New Year's Eve, 1969. At Ellen's settlement in a foster home, Gibbons overrides the value of married love to a family by stressing the single parenting of Laura, the new mother, as a sufficient defender and mentor for needy children.

More detailed than the union of the Wombles in "The Headache" and the disunion of Ellen's parents in *Ellen Foster* are the two marriages of Ruby Pitts in *A Virtuous Woman* (1989), Gibbons's second novel. The author reprises Ruby's type of ennui at home in the resolution of *The Life All Around Me by Ellen Foster* (2006), which depicts Ellen's mother as a bored farm girl who marries as a source of the excitement that her parents disallow. In stark contrast to 18-year-old Ruby, itinerant farm laborer John Woodrow, a sneering pool hall hang-out, mocks his wife's gentrified upbringing, a motif that Gibbons reprises in the background of Shine, the doomed mother of Ellen Foster and in Alice Tate, the well-bred Georgian ill-suited to Samuel P. Goodman Tate in *On the Occasion of My Last Afternoon* (1998). John angers Ruby to the point of murdering him after he takes up with a 16-year-old tart. Pistol in hand, Ruby sleeps in her clothes in minute-man readiness for John's return from a carouse. Ironically, unknown to her, he has already met a violent end. The knifing through the lungs that rids her of a no-good lout generates a *Peyton Place* solution and introduces her to "Blinking" Jack Ernest Stokes, a tenant farmer two decades her elder. At an upturn in Ruby's destiny, Jack reports her unexpected widowhood and offers comfort and friendship. As characterized by Dolores Flaherty, a book critic for the *Chicago Sun-Times*, their union "[grows] into the primary reason each found for living" (Flaherty, 1990). Their meeting under a pecan tree mimics an Adam-and-Eve encounter in Eden, a fortuitous convergence marred by a modern serpent — Ruby's smoking, a self-destructive habit that eventually kills her.

The novel depicts the second marriage as a serendipitous yoking. At a turning point in 20-year-old Ruby's maturation into womanhood, Jack longs to wed the idealized goodwoman. In the flip critique of Roy Parker, Jr., book critic for the *Fayetteville* (N.C.) *Observer*, their wedlock is "Abelard and Heloise in the cornrows, Romeo and Juliet with faces seamed by time and leathered by the summer sun of Dixie," a literary nod toward sweet, but doomed matings (Parker, 1989). The second marriage ties Ruby to a new burden—an adoring, if hard-luck husband who yearns to be mothered and cared for. In the essay "Limited Partnership" for the *Women's Review of Books*, author-critic Marilyn Chandler diagnoses the flaw in the Stokes union: "Their communications are rudimentary and their sensibilities different and largely unexamined" (Chandler, 1989). What seals their oneness is a mutual need for rescue, Jack from solitude and Ruby from disillusion.

Through tense, but poignant intimacy, the novel strives to illuminate shifts in expectation for the post-romantic era. Heavy with irony is the couple's separation after Ruby Stokes's demise at age 45 from lung cancer. In her final days, she busies herself with sewing, cooking, and freezing pork with corn and beef with beans for Jack, an innocent whom she continues to coddle *in absentia* from March through June after her death. Unconsoled by Ruby's pillow, bourbon, and Roadrunner cartoons, Jack fantasizes her resurrection as a wispy, lilac-scented night-time revenant. The off-kilter relationship bemuses critics, who range to extremes in lauding and lambasting the misaligned pair. Reflecting the conjugal stoicism of Ántonia "Tony" Shimerda, an immigrant Bohemian farm wife in Willa Cather's *My Antonia* (1918), Gibbons takes the pragmatic view that flawed people like Jack and Ruby come together out of need and remain soulmates out of compromise and devotion, the core ideals of "for better or worse."

In her third novel, *A Cure for Dreams* (1991), Gibbons advances from realistic romance to a female saga. After Bridget O'Donough's marriage to the card-playing drunkard Sheamus O'Cadhain, their union hardens her in much the same way that wedlock inures O-Lan, the bartered slave-bride of Wang Lung in Pearl Buck's *The Good Earth* (1931). Like the hard-edged Mama Elena and her daughter Rosaura, the unloved wife of Pedro Muzquiz in Laura Esquivel's *Like Water for Chocolate* (1989), Bridget O'Cadhain develops a mean-spiritedness that saps the whole clan, who emigrate from Galway in 1918 to farm on the Cumberland River in Bell County, Kentucky. From this hopeless union comes a willful daughter, Lottie O'Cadhain, who seeks a storybook romance to neutralize an ugly home scene of neglect and patriarchal demands. However, like her mother, 18-year-old Lottie makes a poor choice of husband in Quaker suitor Charles Davies. Dreaming of a gallant mounted rescuer, she marries him less out of dreams of happiness than out of need to escape a wretched extended family that lives compound-style under Bridget's tyranny. On the Davies' North Carolina farm, Charles weds himself to farming, milling, and penny-pinching, his sole delights. In the estimation of Dolores Flaherty, book critic for the *Chicago Sun-Times*, their marriage degenerates into "grudging accommodation" that includes compensation for the death of an infant son (Flaherty, 1992). The truce is poor nourishment for wedlock.

Gibbons describes a joyous Freudian-style compensation as the wife's salvation. During Charles's long daylight absences, Lottie and daughter Betty gad about the neighborhood, form a covert sisterhood of farm wives, and muse on other women's marriages, particularly that of Sade Duplin, whose husband Roy "yaps" at her by brandishing words that express nothing (Gibbons, 1991, 45). Lottie admires the ten-year love match of Amanda Bethune, whose husband Richard is a prize. Out of patience with most males, Lottie considers her own experiences with a loutish father and uncle and a workaholic husband and wonders "what to do with a man who did more than show up for meals" (Gibbons, 1991, 33). Her musing reflects a feminist regard for a mother-daughter duo who have more to share than earning and saving money. Lottie's guidance helps Betty establish a more promising relationship as war bride to Herman Randolph, a sailor on the U.S.S. *Hornet* during World War II and father of narrator Marjorie Polly Randolph, the fourth branch of the O'Donough-O'Cadhain-Davies-Randolph matrilineage.

The author's fourth novel, *Charms for the Easy Life* (1993), describes a variety of mismates along the same pattern as John Woodrow and Ruby Pitts and as Charles and Lottie Davies. The narrative glimpses a husband who searches for voodoo to force his wife into a lifelong state of disappointment, a widow who insists on lurid details from the coroner of her husband's cerebral hemorrhage in August 1936, and a betrayed wife who divvies up responsibility for a funeral bill with her deceased husband's mistress. In 1902, the heroine, Charlie Kate Birch, marries for love, but gradually outgrows her illiterate husband, a former ferryman from coastal Pasquotank County, North Carolina, on the Albemarle Sound who works at a Raleigh livery stable as aide to a blacksmith. Watching her flourish at midwifery and herbalism, he recognizes female self-sufficiency achieved by "hurling [herself] at a desire" (Gibbons, 1993, 25). He studies his spunky wife in silence, sleeps upright in his chair rather than share her bed, and eventually drifts out of her life to settle in Ohio. To questions about post-marriage plans, Charlie Kate, like Christophine in Jean Rhys's *Wide Sargasso Sea* (1966), prefers a dose of poison to another man in her life. With characteristic fervor, Charlie Kate wishes her absent mate in hell, a dramatic condemnation of male distancing and betrayal that flourishes in Gibbons's female survivors.

Rather than belabor the herbalist's grass widowhood, the author transforms the desertion into a topic for pedagogy. The abandonment teaches Charlie Kate's daughter, Sophia Snow Birch, about the unpredictability of an uncommitted male. Symbolizing cyclical faithlessness is a dinner plate that remains at the table from the day he skips town to "that next morning, and the next night, and on and on and on" (*Ibid.*, 26). Despite first-hand knowledge of her parents' marital discord, Sophia must experience her own conjugal fiasco by wedding a sharp-dressing bounder who turns their marriage into a joke by wearing yellow shoes to the ceremony. Rather than charge Sophia with witlessness, Gibbons chalks up the bad choice to father hunger. Charlie Kate takes some of the blame for failing to link Sophia with Charles Nutter, the non-beau whom Charlie Kate grooms for a son-in-law. After Sophia's husband's sudden death from apoplexy in August 1936, she makes short work of a death announcement to her daughter Margaret: "He's gone. Go start the coffee," one of Gibbons's funniest understatements (Ibid., 49). Obviously, Charlie Kate's lessons have struck home.

Gibbons distinguishes among the three women in their styles of compassion and understanding. Charlie Kate seeks a pragmatic union for Sophia, who prefers the type of romance she milks from novels, radio, and movies like *White Cargo* (1942). Charlie Kate is incapable of fathoming loneliness so profound that Sophia weeps mascara-blackened tears into her pillow. Finding businessman Richard Baines during intermission at the matinee of *Gone with the Wind* (1939), Sophia experiences an upsurge in hope that delights her daughter. The chance meeting dismays Charlie Kate, who considers another male under their roof both superfluous and intrusive. Wise beyond her years, Margaret remains neutral during the mother-daughter tiff and concludes that Grandmother Charlie Kate would repopulate the earth with women only, a suggestion of the utopian scenario in Charlotte Perkins Gilman's pastoral idyll *Herland* (1915). Critics have illogically assumed that the shift of humankind to all females represents the author's feelings rather than the musing of a witty fictional character.

Kaye Gibbons retreats from marital combat in a fifth novel, *Sights Unseen* (1995), a study of insanity within an enduring rural clan. Against outrages of a raving mother and the cowering of insecure children stands the stoic Frederick Barnes, a loving, forgiving gentleman farmer who remembers his wife Maggie in the early years of their courtship, marriage, and parenthood. Although weak-willed and acquiescent in the presence of the demanding Grandfather Barnes, Frederick retains his patience and hope during the worst of Maggie's extreme behaviors, which include intemperate demands for sex during Frederick's working day. Driven to tears at her institutionalization in 1967 at Duke Hospital, he spends a long weekend each week in restoring her memory after electroconvulsive shock amnesia and in loving her as tenderly as he did before they wed in 1947. One of Gibbons's exemplary husbands, Frederick deserves the 15 years of happiness with Maggie after her rehabilitation and before her death in 1982 from a fall down stairs. Framed in the recall of his daughter Hattie, he commits himself to the marriage vow "in sickness and in health."

In her first historical novel, *On the Occasion of My Last Afternoon* (1998), Gibbons proposes another model of mated bliss in the union of plantation daughter Emma Garnet Tate with Dr. Quincy Lowell, a Boston brahmin and the antithesis of everything Emma has known about monogamy. A sparsely delineated character whom author-critic Jessica Treadway, in a review for the *Boston Globe*, summarizes as "saint, martyr, and ideal soulmate," Quincy is less lover than adult counselor and consolation for the poor fathering that his wife receives in childhood from the heartless blusterer Samuel P. Goodman Tate (Treadway, 1998). In contrast to Samuel's verbal blistering of recessive wife Alice, Quincy's few faults include dedication to work over family and his all-thumbs gift-wrapping of Emma's Civil War award, an initialed silver brooch that serves as a quasi-diploma for on-the-job medical training in the months following the firing on Fort Sumter, South Carolina, on April 12–13, 1861. In defense of Quincy's lack of dimensions, Gibbons consigns him to 20-hour workdays when he attempts to treat the wounded from the battles of Manassas, Virginia (July 21, 1861; August 28–30, 1862), Antietam, Maryland (September 17, 1862), Gettysburg, Pennsylvania (July 3–4, 1863), and the Wilderness, Virginia (May 5–7, 1864). At his wife's collapse among surgical cases, he can only fan her and urge her to return home. In widowhood, Emma turns to Quincy's spirit, which continues to compensate her for the loss of dear ones. Like a watchful angel, in 1900, Quincy hovers near as his widow completes her earthly work and longs for a heavenly reunion with her husband. Begging the question of husband material, his ethereal qualities set him apart from Gibbons's more mortal mates as a paternal, committed family man.

In a visceral examination of marital extortion, Gibbons creates for her seventh novel, *Divining Women* (2004), a form of house arrest sustained by liveried servants and heightened by salvos of hybrid roses. Troop Ross, a domestic terrorist molded in childhood by his vengeful mother, Nora Worthy Ross, maintains a proprietary attitude toward his wife/captive, Maureen Carlton Ross. A monolithic Bluebeard, he is the predator that Clarissa Pinkola Estes's *Women Who Run with the Wolves* (1992) charges with "[severing] the woman from her intuitive nature..., [leaving her] deadened in feeling, feeling too frail to advance her life" (Estés, 1992, 39). Like a Gothic inquisitor, he turns his manse in Elm City, North Carolina, into a minefield of verbal and situational traps. Set on September 30, 1918, the opening scenes of 22-year-old narrator Mary Oliver's visit to her uncle and aunt echo the climate of World War I, which haunts the railway station in the form of crippled, mustard-gassed veterans earning their living as baggage handlers, a symbol of ongoing emotional and physical burdening. A victim of barbed criticisms and hostile glares, Maureen sinks in her last 50 days of pregnancy and summons Mary to attend her during bouts of "female hysteria," a sexist diagnosis of women's retaliation against a patriarchal society (Gibbons, 2004, 62). By subtle extension, Gibbons affirms a feminist theory, that the same source of male hostility produces both war casualties and quashed wives.

The conflict heightens in chapter seven. In a frontal assault on Mary's liberalism, Troop invites her to a cocktail party. Amid staff at the Duke brothers' tobacco firm, she listens to Troop's well rehearsed diatribe against a woman who drags her husband down to suicide. In Troop's bankerish summation on marriage, he expects "quid pro quo" from an arrangement he equates with long-term usury. Gibbons interposes Mary's analysis of conjugal piracy. She condemns a union that awards Troop his wife's empathy and intelligence, but which discredits Maureen through his methodical pillage of her best qualities. Shoring up Mary's views are letters her mother, Martha Greene Oliver, passes on concerning the abiding need for love and intelligence in marriage. The texts form a choric response from an older, more experienced generation of wives.

For Maureen's edification, Gibbons poses a hypothetical case drawn from letters. The intercalary mini-tragedy in the life of Mrs. Judith Benedict Stafford models the rumblings of feminist revolt — the wretchedness of a wife wearied by the staging and rope pulling producing an outward show of perfect marriage. Judith uses world conflict as a comparative. For her, travel amid politically unsound European cities fails to terrorize as much as the treachery she experiences from returning from a dental appointment on May 3, 1912, to discover her husband's bedroom frolics with a street tramp. For Judith, betrayal reaches intolerable levels after she witnesses a "match girl" wearing Judith's lingerie while fellating Judith's husband on "new Frette linens," luxury bed coverings prized for fine fabric and elegant design (*Ibid.*, 100). Outraged, Judith brandishes a lighted match and threatens to burn alive her husband's "mean little urchin" (*Ibid.*, 101). Emboldened by Judith's rebellion and by stories of Mary's loving family, Maureen stalks out of Troop's life, leaving behind belongings and regrets. Gibbons salves Maureen's racked heart with two forms of parental love — Maureen's farewell to her stillborn daughter, Ella Eloise Ross, at a sunset burial on November 9, 1918, and a long-distance reunion between Maureen and her mother, who demands that Maureen share no more intimacy with "that man" (*Ibid.*, 199). By novel's end, Gibbons reduces Troop from towering intimidator to nonperson, a suitable demotion for a wife persecutor.

• *Further reading*

Chandler, Marilyn. "Limited Partnership," *Women's Review of Books* 6, nos. 10–11 (July 1989): 21.

Estés, Clarissa Pinkola. *Women Who Run with the Wolves: Myths and Stories about the Wild Woman Archetype*. New York: Ballantine, 1997.

Flaherty, Dolores. "...For Her Price Is Far above Rubies," *Chicago Sun-Times* (26 August 1990).

_____. "That Constant Chatter," *Chicago Sun-Times* (23 August 1992).

Gibbons, Kaye. *Charms for the Easy Life*. New York: Putnam, 1993.

_____. *A Cure for Dreams*. New York: Algonquin, 1991.

_____. *Divining Women*. New York: G.P. Putnam's Sons, 2004.

_____. *Sights Unseen*. New York: G.P. Putnam's Sons, 1995.

Parker, Roy, Jr. "Kay Gibbons Reprise," *Fayetteville* (N.C.) *Observer* (30 April 1989).

Treadway, Jessica. "Old Times There Are Not Forgotten," *Boston Globe* (31 May 1998).

materialism

For thematic purposes, Gibbons sets up affluence and material success in counterpoint to emotional stability and contentment. An early short-short story, "The Headache," published in the June 1987 issue of the *St. Andrews Review*, condenses the variables of socio-economic class to a single slip of right thinking. Protagonist Lucille Womble, a cash-strapped farm wife, locates a "town lady's" purse in a restaurant ladies' room and stuffs it down her underwear (Gibbons, June 1987, 3). In further testimony to her threadbare lifestyle, the text spotlights a ragged facial tissue, hard scrubbing at a washboard, and the television and record player tethered to a drop cord in the family's one-room dwelling. More important to the Womble family's level of material gain is a Statue of Liberty lamp, a kitschy gift from the eldest son Frank suggesting the family's patriotism and Henry Womble's wartime service in the military. In ironic contrast, the author pictures Lucille reading an issue of *House Beautiful* in a doctor's waiting room and puzzling over a painting of an English fox hunt, a gentrified scenario that has no meaning to a farm wife of the rural South. Taken together, the details comment on a bedrock theme in Gibbons's fiction, the value of character over things.

In Gibbons's first novel, *Ellen Foster* (1987), the motherless title character plays catalog, a fantasy game involving selection of ideal parents and siblings from posed advertisements. Along with people, Ellen chooses camping gear, a waffle iron, and clothing, the accoutrements that evidence happiness and normality. In the analysis of critic Caren J. Town, the child substitutes "details of the material world to give substance to family," a physical enhancement of daydreaming that makes it seem real (Town, 2004, 99). In comparison of her own thwarted homelife to that of black families, Ellen downgrades Starletta's one-room residence for its dirty plank floors and lack of plumbing and privacy. Nonetheless, in flight on New Year's Eve, 1969, from her lustful father Bill and a pack of drunken rowdies, Ellen accepts solace from Starletta's good-hearted mother, who invites her to the family's table and shares a bed for the night. Echoing the value of home is Starletta's Christmas present, an orange and green town that folds into a carrying case, a symbol of the portability of home values to a more promising setting.

Among kin, Ellen eludes isolation by asking her widowed Aunt Betsy for shelter rather than things. For two days, Ellen enjoys the bathtub and the useless sequin-backed gloves that her aunt buys for her before realizing that Betsy lacks the generosity expected of blood relatives. A more permanent arrangement places the child with her maternal grandmother, a sour grudge holder who hates Ellen primarily because she looks like Bill. Accused of displaying her mother's defiance of social rules in marrying into a lower social level, Ellen feels like an underclass visitor to a museum as she walks through her grandmother's over-decorated house and ponders the waste of money on ostentation. Like the ever-present witch in fairy tales, the grandmother snarls, "I'll break your little hand" for touching a vase (Gibbons, 1987, 62). Ironically, shortly before Christmas 1970, that same hand decks the grandmother's corpse with a Sunday hat and artificial flowers before the funeral home crew carries the old woman away. Ellen assumes that surface decoration will make the embittered old soul more appealing to Jesus.

Ellen states her distaste for her next home in material terms. Passed from grandmother to Aunt Nadine Nelson, Ellen hates her mother's sister for stealing the mother's few personal belongings, a pitifully small inheritance. Ellen envisions Nadine at her job as an in-home demonstrator of a food slicer, an appropriate symbol for a manipulative aunt who calls her niece a bitch and ejects her from shelter on Christmas Day, 1970. For the materialistic aunt, Ellen tries to please by giving her hand-drawn pictures of cats for Christmas. The family excuses their rejection of the gift by explaining that art needs frames, a form of materialistic nitpicking that relieves them of the need to say thanks. In the presence of cousin Dora, whom Nadine surrounds with holiday largess, Ellen experiences a more pressing alienation and loneliness than she did at home. With her signature pluck, she treats the brief stay like residence at a hotel before launching "old Ellen" into a "fresh start" (*Ibid.*, 95). In the meantime, she ponders how to disengage Dora from the belief that Santa Claus always brings surprises, a possibility that a dispossessed child like Ellen would not entertain.

In subsequent pockets of poverty in *A Virtuous Woman* (1989) and *A Cure for Dreams* (1991), Gibbons details material goods for their reflection of hopes and beliefs. For Ruby Pitts Woodrow Stokes, a farm wife in the former novel, the rewards for housewifery consist of lotion on dishpan hands, dusting with lilac-scented talcum, and eating yogurt in bed. In the latter novel, defiance of the Great Depression entices Lottie O'Cadhain Davies to the fabric store to buy English beaded netting, chiffon, and venice lace, goods she pays for with coins plucked from her unwitting husband's pockets. As Lottie's daughter Betty moves toward womanhood, she marks the occasion with a bridal gown suited to post–Pearl Harbor privations—a scooped bodice design with leg-o'-mutton sleeves sewn from a Butterick pattern expressing "the dressing habits of those whose lot was cast for Milk Farm Road" (Gibbons, 1991, 151). Betty reveals her material gain by marrying into a family that owns electrical conveniences, notably a servant's call button. At the wedding shower, Gibbons juxtaposes ceramic bowls, scented soaps, a window pane quilt, and embroidered hand towels alongside the gifts of the humble Woodlief family—a dirt dauber's nest and guinea eggs, domestic tokens of homemaking and procreation.

The amassing of goods in *Charms for the Easy Life* (1993) depicts a family contentment with self-education and service to the poor. Herbalist-midwife Charlie Kate Birch grows medicinal herbs in her front yard and equips her unlicensed dental practice with needlenose pliers from Sears, Roebuck and ether from a veterinary supply house, examples of her ability to skirt the legalities of a medical license like that belonging to a society doctor in Anderson Heights. Her reverence for heirlooms requires the wearing of her deceased mother's good black "Sherman" dress and shoes for special occasions, but awards granddaughter Margaret with books, magazines, and money for movies (Gibbons, 1993, 244). Because of Margaret's rearing in thrift, she is wary of gifts of rayon stockings and love tokens from Tom Hawkings, III. His "artifacts" consist of an ivory Buddha, Hawaiian love songs, a Chinese fan, mementoes from the 1940 world series and the Broadway play *Pal Joey* (1940), arrowheads, a detention slip and report card, and baby shoes and baby photo, a collection encompassing his entire life (*Ibid.*, 231). The return gift is Margaret's grandmother's legacy, the charm for the easy life from a nearly lynched negro, a symbol of rescue and gratitude.

Materialism takes on a different patina in *Sights Unseen* (1995), Gibbons's fifth novel, in which frantically storing up goods equates with mental imbalance. The Barnes family's constant battle against Maggie Barnes's bipolar behaviors requires tact and money. Grandfather Barnes, who urges his son Frederick to marry Maggie in 1947, escorts her on manic shopping sprees and pays for armloads of clothing, shoes, and home furnishings, causing clerks to misidentify him as Maggie's sugar daddy. The text implies that the father-in-law promotes the image of man about town, perhaps out of genuine affection for his son's wife. At a mental breaking point in 1967, Maggie, wearing a Rolex, departs for psychotherapy and eight electroconvulsive shock treatments at Duke University hospital. Her daughter locates irony in her mother's incarceration among the insane "wearing a thousand-dollar watch," a blended symbol of meaningless ostentation and the brevity of human life (Gibbons, 1995, 99). Compounding the inefficacy of wealth is Maggie's discolored face, aged before its time into the visage of a crone. In the final chapter, healing restores her to the material concerns of a normal mother, who cans food for winter, sews sunsuits, and dresses her children appropriately for school and church. The domestic items disclose Maggie's real values.

For a subsequent protagonist, Emma Garnet Tate Lowell, wealth undergirds the vanity of her father, Samuel P. Goodman Tate, a villainous planter-slavemaster in Gibbons's first historical novel, *On the Occasion of My Last Afternoon* (1998).

Advanced from backwoods squalor, the self-made tidewater magnate longs to be admitted to the Society of the Cincinnati, the nation's oldest military heritage society, named for Lucius Quinctius Cincinnatus, the military paragon of fifth-century B.C. Rome. To recreate material success among the landed gentry of Bruton Parish, Virginia, Gibbons sketches the trappings of plantation wealth and refinement—a portrait by English-born painter Thomas Sully, a marble-floored ballroom, blooded Arabian horses and a Hermès saddle, Waterford crystal, Meissen porcelain, Hepplewhite Queen Anne chairs, and velvet curtains. In the background, field hands till the rich soil and tend livestock to provide comforts for the grasping slaver's home and delicacies for his table. To qualify the values of the social-climbing parvenu, Emma describes paintings by Thomas Gainsborough and John Singleton Copley, a Wedgwood Portland vase, Sèvres porcelain and Spode china, and a brocade chaise, all displays of affluence that her father acquires upon the financial collapse of a neighbor ruined by the American Revolution. To Emma, the scavenging of goods from a bankrupt estate equates with "legalized pillage," a characteristic crime for her lavish father (Gibbons, 1998, 23). In contrast, the Landon Carters, who live five miles away on the river road, display Revere silver pieces, tokens of regard for courage at the battles of Trenton, New Jersey (December 26, 1776) and Saratoga, New York (September 19, 1777), which helped to secure American democracy. With a typical allotment of poetic justice, Gibbons pictures the economic reordering that follows the Civil War through the flight of Samuel and daughter Maureen in June 1862 by wagon from General George Brinton McClellan and his Union forces and through Landon Carter's purchase of Tate's Seven Oaks plantation. Contributing to restitution is Quincy Lowell's destruction of a Titian painting after Samuel's death, a minor sacrifice during the family's ridding itself of an irksome intruder.

For the Greene-Oliver family in *Divining Women* (2004), the possession of things seems less important than the advancement of pleasure. Heiress Martha Greene Oliver rears daughter Mary to empathize with the poor. During a Sun and Moon Girls outing at Washington's Rock Creek Park, Martha packs an ornate samovar she purchased in Morocco. The container is a treat for poor children who enjoy no luxuries in their homes. Unlike Mary and her mother, Mary's younger brother Daniel requires accommodations equal to the family's ability to pay. When the Olivers travel to Europe on the S.S. *Carpathia* in 1905, eight-year-old Daniel demands a first-class berth. After his suicide by hanging from a hotel chandelier in Baltimore in 1913, the family continues traveling aboard the S.S. *Lusitania*, a luxury liner that shuttled the rich to and from Europe until German U-boats sank it on May 1, 1915. The loss of Daniel, a mini-despot, prefaces the fictional focus, a bellicose home situation created by Mary's uncle, Troop Ross.

A pathological effusion of goods introduces Mary Oliver, a 22-year-old graduate student at Radcliffe, to her aunt and uncle, Maureen Carlton Ross and Troop Ross. Their stone manse in Elm City, North Carolina, epitomizes the unfeeling atmosphere of conspicuous wealth and snobbery. Unlike Mary's grandparents' shared home on Dupont Circle in Washington, D.C., the interior assaults the senses with "overwrought merchandise"—attention-getting gewgaws, William Morris wallpaper, and portraits bought second-hand (Gibbons, 2004, 48). At a central location, a coat of arms proclaims longevity and nobility. To Mary, the desperation of a status-obsessed homeowner reflects a pathetic insecurity with self and lineage. She imagines Troop and his class-conscious mother, Nora Worthy Ross, poking through the remains of estate sales in search of fraudulent items to betoken family dignity. At the foundering of the Ross marriage, Maureen abandons belongings in delight at freedom from a trophy-hungry husband. Heightening dramatic irony is Troop's indifference to the death of his only child, Ella Eloise, who is stillborn the previous day and buried simply at sunset on September 9, 1918, by family retainers. The decline of light parallels the collapse of Troop's hope for prestige in a minor North Carolina fiefdom.

Gibbons's return to Ellen Foster in a sequel, *The Life All Around Me by Ellen Foster* (2006), contrasts sorrow with material loss. The author reconsiders the orphan's rage that her Aunt Nadine Nelson filches Ellen's inheritance from her mother, Shine. Ellen catalogs a humble legacy—comb and brush, compact mirror, pearls, scarves, dresses, and a pair of hose that Nadine leaves behind. Although surrounded by book shelves overlooking a comfy Mamie Eisenhower chair in her bedroom, Ellen longs for tactile union with her mother. On Christmas Eve, 1974, a return to the family home reminds Ellen of the emptiness of the past and the futility of restructuring memories into a viable future. More valuable than possessions are the love and sanctuary of a foster home. In the final pages, Gibbons blesses her two-novel heroine with a restored inheritance from her grandmother and education paid for by Dr. Derek Curtis Bok, president of Harvard University. Both rewards nurture the "outlandish" birth gifts and talents she received from her beloved mother (Gibbons, 2006, 217).

See also **social class**

• *Further reading*

Gibbons, Kaye. *Charms for the Easy Life*. New York: Putnam, 1993.
_____. *A Cure for Dreams*. New York: Algonquin, 1991.
_____. *Divining Women*. New York: G.P. Putnam's Sons, 2004.
_____. *Ellen Foster*. New York: Algonquin Press, 1987.
_____. "The Headache," *St. Andrews Review* (June 1987): 3–8.
_____. *The Life All Around Me by Ellen Foster*. New York: Harcourt, 2006.
_____. *On the Occasion of My Last Afternoon*. New York: G.P. Putnam's Sons, 1998.
_____. *Sights Unseen*. New York: G.P. Putnam's Sons, 1995.
Munafo, Giavanna. "Colored Biscuits: Reconstructing Whiteness and the Boundaries of 'Home' in Kaye Gibbons's *Ellen Foster*," *Women, America, and Movement*. ed. Susan L. Roberson. Columbia: University of Missouri Press, 1998, pp. 38–61.
Szatmary, Peter. "A Slaveowner's Daughter," *Houston Chronicle* (28 June 1998).
Town, Caren J. *New Southern Girl: Female Adolescence in the Works of 12 Women Authors*. Jefferson, N.C.: McFarland, 2004.

men

The depiction of male behaviors is the Rosetta Stone of Kaye Gibbons's fiction. In caustic commentary on her first three novels, critic Ralph C. Wood, a Baylor religion and philosophy professor writing for *Christian Century*, described the brutishness of her worst male characters as deriving "more from irremediable evil than from remediable patriarchy" (Wood, 1992, 842). Wood's hyperbole correctly sums up the menace of Bill, the bootlegging father of the title character in *Ellen Foster* (1987), and prefigures the bloated narcissism of Samuel P. Goodman Tate in *On the Occasion of My Last Afternoon* (1998) and of Troop Ross, the wife-trampler in *Divining Women* (2004). A loutish miscreant, Bill resents his social superiors and outrages his mother-in-law by arriving drunk to Christmas dinner. At his worst, in 1969, he offers no antidote to his wife's suicidal dose of prescription digitalis. In Ellen's opinion, he represents "a mistake for a person" (Gibbons, 1987, 49). The phrase implies fault in the divine for equipping her with so insufferable a parent.

Bill's depravity reflects the sorriness of Southern white trash. At the arrival of mourners to his wife's wake, he rouses from his usual slouching before the television by corralling beer cans from the yard and tossing them under the porch, a signal to readers of stereotypical redneck disdain for order and sanitation. Unfortunately for Gibbons's literary reputation, Wood and other critics tend to overlook Bill's foils—Starletta's charitable father, the only black male who does not buy liquor from Bill; Jim the fish man who teaches Ellen how to cook bass; a persistent school psychologist; and Roy, the art teacher's husband, who willingly washes dishes and clothes and who offers temporary shelter and a birthday party to the 11-year-old orphan. These models of affection and love for a homeless child receive little acknowledgement from critics galvanized by Bill's opening his fly before elementary school children and his incestuous dreams of Ellen. The enormity of Bill's vices mirrors the oversized villainy of Satan in John Milton's *Paradise Lost* (1667), which requires a massive challenge to Adam to establish his epic presence.

A survey of Gibbons's male figures and their sins against victims disputes Wood's hasty generalization:

male(s)	**female(s)**	**sins**
Ellen Foster **(1987)**		
Bill	wife	drinking, abasement, complicity in her suicide
	Ellen	neglect, sexual harassment, indecent exposure
	mother-in-law	drunkenness, disrespect
Roy	Ellen	none
	Julia	none
Ellis & Rudolph	Ellen	spying
psychologist	Ellen	lack of sympathy
"The Headache" (June 1987)		
Henry Womble	Lucille	none
father Womble	Lucille	none
Lucille's father	Lucille	none
Womble sons	Lucille	none
A Virtuous Woman **(1989)**		
Mr. Pitts	Ruby	gendered discounting of daughter
Paul and Jimmy	Ruby	none

Lester	Sudie Bee	none
John Woodrow	Ruby	deception, abasement, adultery, venereal disease
	mother	arson
	16-year-old	womanizing, abandonment
Jack Stokes	Ruby	drinking, demanding attention
	mother	none
	June	none
Jack's father	wife	religious fanaticism
Big Daddy Pitts	Sophie	none
Lonnie Hoover	Frances	none
	Tiny Fran	lack of discipline
Burr Stanley	Tiny Fran	neglect, drinking
	June	none
Roland Stanley	Tiny Fran	none
	Stella Morgan	rape, assault
	June	menacing

A Cure for Dreams (1991)

Sheamus O'Cadhain	Bridget	drinking, tyranny
	Lottie	drinking, tyranny
Bart O'Cadhain	Bridget	drinking, tyranny
Charles Davies	Lottie	deception, neglect, miserliness
	Betty	miserliness, lack of love, sexism
Stanton	Betty	drug abuse, disrespect
Herman Randolph	Betty	none
	mother	none
	Lottie	none
Tommy Woodlief	Trudy	abandonment, neglect
Porter	Celie	none
Richard Bethune	Amanda	none
Roy Duplin	Sade	drinking, tyranny, womanizing

Charms for the Easy Life (1993)

Charlie Kate's husband	Charlie Kate	abandonment, drinking, adultery
	Sophia	abandonment, drinking
	Margaret	abandonment, drinking
farm agent	Sophia	disrespect, womanizing
	Margaret	disrespect, lack of love
Charles Nutter	Louise	none
	Charlie Kate	none
	Margaret	none
society doctor	female infant	malpractice, abandonment
	Maveen	malpractice, abandonment, sexism
Hermit Willoughby	Charlie Kate	none
alcoholics at the City Grill	Charlie Kate	drinking

Tom Hawkings, IIII	Margaret	none
	Esther	none
	Anna	none
Tom's father	family	none

Sights Unseen (1995)

Grandfather Barnes	Maggie	pseudo-seduction, spoiling
	wife Harriet	tyrannny
	Josephine	compromising reputation
	Pearl	racism, disrespect
	Hattie	chiding, swearing
Lawrence Barnes	Menefee	none
Frederick Barnes	Maggie	none
	Hattie	none
	Pearl	none
Freddy	Maggie	distancing
	Hattie	none
	Pearl	none
deputy sheriff	Pearl	racism

On the Occasion of My Last Afternoon (1998)

Samuel P. Goodman Tate	mother	murder
	Alice	abasement, tyranny
	Emma Garnet	abasement, lack of love
	Maureen	exploitation, abasement, cruelty
	Clarice	verbal abuse
	Mrs. Lowell	verbal abuse
	guest	verbal abuse
cotton factor	Alice	none
Samuel Tate's father	wife	murder
Jacob	wife	none
Whately Tate	barmaid	impregnation, abandonment
	Alice	none
	Emma	none
	Clarice	none
Quincy Lowell	Emma	none
	daughters	none
	Clarice	none
	Lavinia	none
	mother	none
John C. Gunn	Alice	medical malpractice, sexism
Mr. Dawes	Lavinia	neglect
Lavinia's brothers	Lavinia	none
Lavinia's husband	Lavinia	battery

Divining Women **(2004)**

Toby Greene	Nora	disappointing, embarrassing
	Leslie	none
	Martha	none
	Mary	none
Leonard Oliver	Louise	none
	Mary	none
Grammar Oliver	Martha	none
	Mary	none
Daniel Oliver	Martha	bratty behavior
	Mary	bratty behavior
Troop Ross	Nora	none
	Maureen	abasement, tyranny
	Ella Eloise	rejection, abasement
	Mamie	racism, disrespect
	Mary	ingratitude, intimidation
physician	Maureen	sexist diagnosis, mistreatment
Zollie	Mamie	none
	sister	none
	Maureen	none
Stafford	Judith	adultery, tyranny
	trollops	womanizing
lovers	Judith	none
film-maker	Martha	none

The Life All Around Me by Ellen Foster **(2006)**

Bill	Shine	drinking, abasement, complicity in her suicide
	Ellen	neglect, sexual harassment
Stuart	Ellen	none
	mother	none
	Laura	none
Stuart's father	wife	none
Melvin	Ellen	exploitation
Starletta's father	wife	none
	Starletta	none
	Ellen	none
Derek Bok	Ellen	none
attorney	Ellen	none
	Laura	none
Martha's father	Martha's mother	neglect
	Martha	none

Demolishing generalizations about Gibbons's males early in her career is Henry Womble, the affectionate farmer in the short-short story "The Headache," published in the June 1987 issue of the *St. Andrews Review*. In two intimate bedroom scenes, the author pictures Henry soothing his wife Lucille from two weeks of psychosomatic weeping, visions, insomnia, and head pain. His method is conjugal "spooning," snuggling her back against his chest and her bottom against his genitals

(Gibbons, June 1987, 7). Complementing the embrace, her hands clutch his against her lower belly, the source of their ten children. The closeness of the farm couple suggests that a solid marriage rewards a beleaguered farm wife for an endless round of toil and no promise of profit. Henry rounds out a difficult day by promising his wife two hats, a token of husbandly generosity from a man who can ill afford luxuries.

A Virtuous Woman (1989) further refutes Wood's generalization. The story mulls over the complex contrast in 18-year-old Ruby Pitts's first husband, 26-year-old itinerant laborer John Woodrow, and her second, 40-year-old tenant farmer "Blinking" Jack Ernest Stokes. Woodrow fits the Southern stereotype of mouthy, wife-bashing white trash, a drifter with a "twisted up head" (Gibbons, 1989, 39). In each town the roving couple enters, Ruby describes him as quick to "sniff out a pool hall," the retreat of dissolute males (*Ibid.*, 41). She eventually pieces together his ignominy—a three-year term in prison for burning his family's tobacco barns. Sneering and demoralizing, John chips away at Ruby's esteem by deriding the difference in their birth status—he, a migrant soil grubber, and she, the "little Miss Vanderbilt" daughter of a successful farmer and county commissioner (*Ibid.*, 40). Jack, on the other hand, adores the 20-year-old Ruby at first sight and promises to devote himself to her care. Although he is incapable of keeping his vow, the purity of his intent ennobles him as savior of a youthful widow.

Gibbons extends forgiveness to mortal males. She manages a modicum of pity for Jack, a childless husband who regrets Ruby's pining for babies and her distress from terminal lung cancer. The author takes the same pardonning tone in the description of farm owner Lonnie Hoover, who retreats to his tractor to avoid dust-ups between his neglected wife Frances and their shrewish, piggish daughter Tiny Fran. With rural pragmatism, Jack ponders the deal that Lonnie strikes with Burr Stanley to marry Tiny Fran and claim 48 acres of Lonnie's good loam. To Jack, the arrangement is promising enough to entice a landless laborer like Burr to wed a sloven like Tiny Fran and to agree to father her illegitimate child. Burr's punishment for venality takes shape in unending escapism—living his life in drunkenness, farm work, and nightly sessions before a television set. His reward arrives with Fran's departure, which leaves him free to parent their daughter June and to bear comfort and a gift of land to their grieving neighbor Jack. Burr's charity epitomizes Gibbons's vision of the unselfish, egalitarian male.

Gibbons surveys a common pattern in female life in *A Cure for Dreams* (1991), in which ill-favored marriage extends unhappiness from the altar to the grave. In 1918, Irish immigrant Lottie O'Cadhain weds to escape misery at the clan compound on the Cumberland River in Bell County, Kentucky. In a house rocked by the infantile imperatives of her drunken father and uncle, brothers Sheamus and Bart O'Cadhain, and by the yardstick that her mother, Bridget O'Donough O'Cadhain, flashes at the child who obeys those demands, Lottie feels hounded and emotionally spent. By marrying Quaker farmer-miller Charles Davies, she anticipates a loving, serene, and financially secure home life, but she discovers that his promises only "[sound] reasonable and true" (Gibbons, 1991, 7). Gibbons creates irony out of Lottie's move to North Carolina, where Davies expects his wife to glory in grueling labor with the same fervor he feels for toiling in cotton fields and in his gristmill, a symbol of unremitting pressures. In Lottie's opinion, Charles embraces work as his religion. The disappointing men in her life create indifference in Lottie, who looks to motherhood and female friendships as her salvation.

Gibbons takes a feminist stance in describing the detriment an unloving male like Sheamus, Bart, or Charles poses to the family. Lottie's anti-male fervor passes to her daughter Betty, who views Charles's return from work as the raw spot in an otherwise pleasant day. To validate themselves, Betty and Lottie converse in counterpoint to Charles's insistent condemnations and demands. In 1937, his tidy suicide by jumping into a river suggests that their all-female alliance stymies him past the point of coping. Left fatherless, Betty dates Stanton, an addict to Neurol Compound who degrades her as "girlie" before his death three months later from an overdose of spirits of ammonia (*Ibid.*, 131). Gibbons shies away from a follow-up on Betty's marriage by dispatching her husband, sailor Herman Randolph, to the U.S.S. *Hornet* for the duration of World War II. In the meantime, on November 25, 1942, the war bride gives birth to Marjorie Polly Randolph, the next generation of the vibrant O'Donough-O'Cadhain-Davies-Randolph matrilineage. By keeping men in the background, Gibbons focuses on women's abilities to amuse and sustain themselves in a male-dominated world. Subtextually, the conduct of world war by men indirectly charges them with murderous aggression.

In a fourth novel, *Charms for the Easy Life* (1993), Gibbons sprinkles rare ambitious, hard-working men among ne'er-do-wells and bounders. Reviewer Judith Beth Cohen, a critic for the *Women's Review of Books*, accounts for the gendered text as a result of Gibbons's "feminist alternative to the patriarchal myth of man as rescuer or savior" (Cohen, 1993). The husband of heroine Charlie Kate Birch is a nameless failure who flees their moribund marriage to more promising territory in Ohio. Her womanizing son-in-law, a farm agent, also unnamed, does even less to nurture his family. At a dramatic point in altruistic care for the poor of the Raleigh, North Carolina, mill district, Charlie Kate identifies a true villain, a snobbish male physician who blinds a girl with silver nitrate eye drops shortly after her birth. As a literary foil, Gibbons poses the magnanimous Dr. Charles Nutter, Charlie Kate's early find in a rural community of coastal Pasquotank County on the Albemarle Sound. In token of his generosity, he invents a prosthetic hand for combat amputees. While Nutter thrives as director of the veterans' hospital in Durham, the scalawag doctor receives written warning that he owes the maimed child a future to be provided by the Governor Morehead School for the Blind. On the outskirts of characters like a wandering leper from the Outer Banks and the unsanitary Hermit Willoughby, Gibbons indicates that Charlie Kate's daughter, Sophia Snow Birch, thrives in company with her second husband, businessman Richard Baines. In 1942, Margaret nets the true prize in Tom Hawkings, III, scion of an aristocratic Raleigh family who awards Margaret a box of treasures encompassing his boyhood and youth. The gift bodes well for a trio of women in need of proof that men can be trusted.

In her fifth novel, *Sights Unseen* (1995), Gibbons builds counterpoint in the attitudes and deeds of the woman-ogling Grandfather Barnes and his saintly son Frederick. The willful elder Barnes is a "fixer," a Godfather figure who enriches himself through the sale of bootleg liquor out the back door of a pool hall and who flexes his power in the community like a whip (Gibbons, 1995, 13). He tyrannizes his wife, belittles his sons as slackers, and boots his grandson Marshall on the ground for seeking to sit on Grandfather's ankle. The elder Barnes uses money as his weapon: he gives his grandchildren collectible coins for Christmas, but threatens to stop buying them gifts if they waste their cash on candy or frivolities. The standoff between father and son bears a tinge of rivalry for the favors of Frederick's wife Maggie, who mesmerizes both men with her risqué conduct. The complex relationship discloses excellence in Frederick's character at the same time that it exposes his spinelessness in catering to an aging despot.

Frederick maintains their ill-balanced relationship by constantly ceding authority to others. In 1955, Grandfather Barnes demands his way in not visiting his daughter-in-law at the hospital after the birth of grandchild Hattie. Simultaneously, Frederick, "ground-down worried" from guardianship of his bipolar wife Maggie, mediates the difficulties she kicks up in the maternity ward by refusing to breastfeed or cuddle her newborn (Gibbons, 1995, 39). When Maggie develops an inordinate craving for sex, daughter Hattie recalls her father's devolution from bright-and-early farmer to a compliant male concubine who resembles a "hall-walker in a veterans' hospital" (*Ibid.*, 35). In one of Gibbons's most compassionate glimpses of fallen manhood, she pictures the patient, tolerant Frederick in 1967 exhausted to the breaking point, as he weeps on the shoulder of his 12-year-old daughter before committing Maggie to Duke Hospital for psychotherapy and eight electroconvulsive shock treatments. During the 15 years of sanity that Maggie enjoys before her death in 1982, Gibbons rewards Frederick with peace, an orderly household, and well reared children.

In a reprise of the ogreish Bill from *Ellen Foster*, Gibbons's first historical novel, *On the Occasion of My Last Afternoon* (1998), examines the pre-teen memories of Emma Garnet Tate Lowell, another child who hates her father for his lying, bullyragging, woman-baiting ways. Unlike Bill, a lower-class wastrel, the *nouveau riche* planter Samuel P. Goodman Tate bears an ill-gotten reputation for Episcopalian piety in Bruton Parish, Virginia, and for honesty during two terms in the state legislature. However, close-ups of Tate belie his outward show much as Margaret Mitchell undercuts planter Gerald O'Hara, the cheeky Irish upstart in Margaret Mitchell's *Gone with the Wind* (1936). Samuel becomes what theorists Sandra M. Gilbert and Susan Gubar typify in *No Man's Land* (1989) as a 19th-century staple — an "aggrieved defender of an indefensible order" (Gilbert & Guber, 1989, 4). At a social debut, he makes a fool of himself by attempting a genteel dance with his daughter. In private, he rebukes his wife Alice, a gentlewoman who suffers a "nightly-broken spirit," Emma's summation of the effects of crippling verbal battery (Gibbons, 1998, 7). Gibbons stresses that genteel women like Alice are no match for pomposity, vanity, and willful misogyny from a self-made land baron.

In an encompassing view of the Tates' off-balance union, the author reprises a familiar theme in her canon, the clear understanding in children of their parents' faults. To explain the discrepancy between the public boor and the private homewrecker, Emma declares, "Children see into the recesses of the soul" (*Ibid.*, 2). The statement bears out the author's trust in the child witness, who imagines her wrathful father roasting on the kitchen spit, a comic scene dating to the late medieval *Carmina Burana*. For contrast, Gibbons salts in respect for Landon Carter, the plantation owner five miles down the river road, whom Emma commends for his kindness and self-restraint and for courtesies Southern history has stereotyped as the manners of a Virginia gentleman. Landon prefigures the hero to come — Dr. Quincy Lowell, the home-centered husband who, in 1849, rests his ear against his wife's abdomen to enjoy the prenatal sounds of Mary, their first child. Like the courtly lover of 12th-century romanticism, Quincy pledges himself to truth, obedience, and loyalty in an era marked by brutish soldiery, coarse manners, human bondage, and greed. A political progressive with an abolitionist upbringing, he liberates three slaves, Charlie, Martha, and Mavis. A religious man, he displays a commitment to rectitude and ethical service that buoys his wife, three daughters, neighbors, and a constant stream of Civil War casualties in need of medical care. Critics remark that Gibbons is more adept at vivifying Samuel Tate's outrages than at turning Quincy Lowell into a believable physician, husband, and father.

For the punitive villain Troop Ross in her seventh novel, *Divining Women* (2004), Gibbons once more flourishes at creating a unique evil-doer. He espouses what Gilbert and Gubar describe as "patriarchal mythology, [which] defines women as created by, from, and for men, the children of male brains, ribs, and ingenuity" (Gilbert & Guber, 2000, 12). Gibbons stocks the exposition with the keen evaluations of a classroom teacher and with the misgivings of the Olivers— grandmother Louise Canton Oliver, daughter-in-law Martha Greene Oliver, and granddaughter Mary Oliver. In childhood, Troop impresses his teacher as having an "intense singularity" of self, an alarum to the perceptive parent (Gibbons, 2004, 80). He grows into a monstrosity that critic Carrie Brown in a review for the *Chicago Tribune* describes as "mordant, predatory, and psychopathic" (Brown, 2004). Through on-the-scene detective work, the Oliver trio of "divining women" amasses the symptoms of delusion and unbridled anger. Mary concludes that Troop lashes out in retaliation for entrapment by his mother, Nora Worthy Ross, neglect by his distant father, Toby Greene, and envy of the humanity of Troop's blameless wife, Maureen Carlton Ross. Because the concept of family demands respect, affection, and attention to others, Troop recoils from normal behaviors and involvement "to hoard for his own survival," an indication of paranoia borne out by a bizarre remoteness and sadistic stalking (Gibbons, 2004, 18). Spiteful and self-aggrandizing, he uses emotional blackmail to squeeze money from his estranged father, to dupe a loving wife, and to demand a strained gentility in his home.

As in her earlier works, Gibbons moderates the evil of one miscreant male by juxtaposing more humane characters. Opposite Troop stands not only Toby, a thoroughly human family man, but also his daughter's husband, Grammar Oliver, and her father-in-law, Leonard Oliver, a grandfatherly type who shares Toby's home on Dupont Circle in Washington, D.C. To gentle an entourage of ghosts through the mansion, Leonard relieves the bewilderment and sorrow of the newly dead, who increase in number during World War I and the 1918 influenza pandemic. In a humorous conciliation of past with the beyond, Leonard offers to acquit their earthly frustrations by supplying what compensation he can. To women, he sings and cajoles; to a drunkard, he offers liquor as well as counseling on the danger of wandering eternity in a state of inebriation. In the novel's resolution, Zollie, Troop Ross's driver and valet, presents another side of the laudatory male in the deathbed treatment of his two sons for influenza with patent medicine and, on November 9, 1918, in the transfer of Troop's stillborn daughter, Ella Eloise Ross, to the cemetery for a sunset burial. In contrast to Zollie, Troop can think of the tiny body only as "it," a dismissal of the infant's humanity (*Ibid.*, 203).

Suspicions of aberrant males recur in *The Life All Around Me by Ellen Foster* (2006), a sequel to *Ellen Foster*. Retrieved information about Ellen's father Bill depicts a time in his early marriage when he cared for his wife before retreating into postwar angst. During Ellen's mid-teens, she fosters a relationship with Stuart, a comic figure who stands no chance of romancing her or making good on a proposed elopement to Pedro's South of the Border. Symbolic of their dead-end pairing is the glass doorknob that Stuart removes from Ellen's old house as worthy memorabilia of her past. At the novel's climax, when Ellen begins to assess the fortitude of her foster mother, Laura reminds her that an all-female oasis experiences little of the fear or disruption generated by males. Corroborating Laura's contention, the crisis in the life of Starletta's aunt reaches such misery that the aunt stops lactating, leaving her wailing infant in need of feeding. In typical fashion, Gibbons denigrates the cause of the family's misery — a shiftless husband and father — by offering the male no name to dignify his wrongdoing.

See also **marriage; misogyny**

• *Further reading*

Brown, Carrie. "Kaye Gibbons' Focus Is on Female Fortitude," *Chicago Tribune* (4 April 2004).

Cohen, Judith Beth. "Review: *Charms for the Easy Life*," *Women's Review of Books* 11, no. 1 (October 1993).

Gibbons, Kaye. *Divining Women*. New York: G.P. Putnam's Sons, 2004.

_____. *Ellen Foster*. New York: Algonquin Press, 1987.

_____. "The Headache," *St. Andrews Review* (June 1987): 3–8.

_____. *On the Occasion of My Last Afternoon*. New York: G.P. Putnam's Sons, 1998.

_____. *Sights Unseen*. New York: G.P. Putnam's Sons, 1995.

_____. *A Virtuous Woman*. Chapel Hill, N.C.: Algonquin Press, 1989.

Gilbert, Sandra M., and Susan Gubar. *The Madwoman in the Attic*. 2nd ed. New Haven, Conn.: Yale University Press, 2000.

_____. *No Man's Land: Sexchanges: The Place of the Woman Writer in the Twentieth Century: The War of the Words*. New Haven, Conn.: Yale University Press, 1989.

Harris, Michael. "Scenes— and Skeletons— of a Troubled Southern Family," *Los Angeles Times* (9 October 1995): 5.

Heeger, Susan. "Couldn't Live with Her, Can't Live Without Her: *A Virtuous Woman*," *Los Angeles Times* (11 June 1989): 15.

Wood, Ralph C. "Gumption and Grace in the Novels of Kaye Gibbons," *Christian Century* 109, no. 27 (September 23–30, 1992): 842–846.

Miranda stories

In 1988, Kaye Gibbons published in the *Kenyan Review* a scholarly essay on Katherine Anne Porter's Miranda cycle, a Southern literary touchstone that continues to impact Gibbons's writing. Porter, like most feminist authors, focused on the energetic, shrewd female survivor, a prototype that Gibbons echoes in the title character of *Ellen Foster* (1987), in Ruby Pitts Woodrow Stokes, protagonist of *A Virtuous Woman* (1989), and in Lottie O'Cadhain Davies, Betty Davies Randolph, and Sade Duplin, the distraught husband-killer in *A Cure for Dreams* (1991). Gibbons perpetuates the concept of the indomitable female in herbalist-midwife Charlie Kate Birch, her twice-married daughter Sophia Snow Birch, and her independent granddaughter Margaret in *Charms for the Easy Life* (1993), in anesthesiologist Hattie Barnes and cook-housekeeper Pearl Wiggins, who weather cyclical madness in Hattie's mother Maggie in *Sights Unseen* (1995), and in Emma Garnet Tate Lowell and Maureen Tate, the grown daughters of misogynist Samuel P. Goodman Tate in *On the Occasion of My Last Afternoon* (1998). These characters echo Porter's dramatizations of disillusioned agrarian women locked into meaningless relationships, violence, and solitude. Like her mentor, Gibbons works out solutions to fear and loneliness by disclosing internal strengths that both surprise and fortify protagonists for a series of life battles. Gibbons's female character actions demand respect, from Ellen Foster's demand for a new mother and Lottie Davies's formation of a gin rummy and pinochle club during the Great Depression to Charlie Kate's discreditation and blackmail of an unprofessional physician and Emma Garnet's self-reclamation from widowhood to bankroll the rebuilding of the Raleigh economy during post–Civil War Reconstruction.

Like Gibbons, a survivor of a miserable childhood and orphanhood in eastern North Carolina, Porter has reason to retrieve her protagonists from deliberate assaults and to shield them from buffets of ill fortune. Beneath a surface calm, she invigorates her Miranda Rhea novellas, "Old Mortality" (1939) and "The Old Order" (1958), with the female's inner drive and her embrace of risky pathfinding. In "Old Mortality," through transforming narrations of lineage and rememory, a grandmother weeps therapeutic tears that rid her of regret. In "Pale Horse, Pale Rider" (1939), Miranda's reliving of Aunt Amy Gay's reckless passion for her lover Gabriel takes on an immediacy that Gibbons replicates in the multi-level family narratives that form *A Cure for Creams*. In reflections on rites of passage, Betty Davies Randolph remembers most clearly her mother as a talker and storyteller and welcomes her own daughter, narrator Marjorie Polly Randolph, at birth with respect for her ears, the conduits through which pass lessons from foremothers. The stories of these four generations of strong women honor the matrilineage at the same time that they dredge up hope, guile, and coping mechanisms to apply to obstacles in the teller's life.

Gibbons recognizes the artistic pitfalls that yawn in the path of the feminist fiction writer. She admires Katherine Anne Porter's Miranda for embracing "sentiment without nostalgia and distance without dispassion," a fair description of tone and atmosphere in Gibbons's second and seventh novels, *A Virtuous Woman* (1989) and *Divining Women* (2004) (Gibbons, 1988, 75). Gibbons has reason to exemplify Porter's Miranda as an achiever of satisfaction from surveys of the family's troubled past and as a New Women endowed with a resolve to chart her own course. The tight construction of the Miranda stories generates in Gibbons a respect for recreated time and for bizarre details, such as the rabbit's foot charm that a nearly asphyxiated lynching victim confers on Charlie Kate. Similarly, Gibbons applies narrative strictures on her own stories to glimpse the Civil War in the life of Emma Garnet Tate Lowell, World War I and the 1918 influenza pandemic through the experience of 22-year-old Mary Oliver, a graduate student at Radcliffe, the Great Depression years through Lottie Davies's eyes, and the end of the Depression and the onset of World War II through the recall of Betty Davies Randolph and of Margaret, Charlie Kate Birch's self-reliant granddaughter. Just as Miranda orders memories of growth from girlhood to young womanhood, Margaret reflects on growing up under the influence of her mother and grandmother and of the synergy of three women who devote themselves to community hygiene, wellness, and healing. Essential to realism is the stripping of illusion from Margaret during her dealings with her overly romantic mother. Like the abandoned wife Charlie Kate, the fatherless Margaret cultivates a pragmatic view of Sophia's romance with businessman Richard Baines, a more appropriate, more financially promising catch than the farm agent who was her adulterous first husband. The rejection of gauzy illusions enables Margaret to rejoice at Sophia's remarriage on Christmas Eve, 1942, and to prepare the mourning scene for Charlie Kate, who passes away quietly on Christmas night. Sufficient home training renders the granddaughter capable of fending for herself and of anticipating a satisfying future.

In the essay on Porter, Gibbons remarks on Miranda's revolt against community codes, a constant in Gibbons's reordering of marital, religious, and social expectations. In place of the widow's grief, Charlie Kate rebuffs a minister's solace and turns her attention to a mantel clock, which she successfully wrests from her dead husband's mistress. With similar chutzpah, Ruby Pitts Woodrow sheds no tears for her gallivanting husband John, against whom she hides a pistol under her pillow. During the Civil War, Emma Lowell has the audacity to pay Clarice Washington, a black freedwoman cook-housekeeper, rather than to buy a slave to run the Lowells' home and tend their three daughters and a rehabilitation center for combat casualties. At the core of Porter's influence on Gibbons lies a shared regard for imagination and wonder, the release of intellectual control that lets Ruby accept love from an underclass laborer twice her age and that fosters Marjorie Davies Randolph's respect for her mother Betty, grandmother Lottie, and great-grandmother, Bridget O'Donough O'Cadhain, as founts of womanly wisdom and sources of inspiration.

• *Further reading*

Gibbons, Kaye. "Planes of Language and Time: The Surfaces of the Miranda Stories," *Kenyon Review* 10 (Winter 1988): 74–79.

misogyny

Gibbons stocks her woman-centered stories with episodes of wife abuse, child neglect, and other iniquities of lecherous, besotted, lordly males. One of most cited examples of male despoliation of women occurs in 1969 in *Ellen Foster* (1987), when a drunk states that 10-year-old Ellen is a luscious sex object. In reference to his 13-year-old wife Delphi, the speaker salivates, "You gots to git em when they is still soff when you mashum" (Gibbons, 1987, 37). The remark generates terror in Ellen, who retreats to the closet lest she become some male's ideal of a "honey pie" or "sugar plum" (*Ibid.*). The seamy New Year's Eve scenario and Bill's subsequent genital exposure before Ellen's elementary school imply that textual misogyny may extend from neglect to child endangerment, molestation, or incest.

In *A Cure for Dreams* (1991), Gibbons addresses misogyny directly with farmer-miller Charles Davies's Depression-era solution to penury. In 1937, the eighth year of hard times, he charges his wife, Lottie O'Cadhain Davies, and daughter Betty with folly and indolence and demands to know why he is still feeding a 17-year-old spinster. He implies that a girl becomes her father's financial burden after she passes the ideal time for marrying and leaving home. In his opinion, such a failure to snag a husband proves that Betty is worthless. In the author's wry style, the fatherly insult boomerangs by inspiring Betty and Lottie to buy mail-order dresses, a womanly balm to a smarting spirit. The episode contrasts the desperation in Betty's grandmother, Bridget O'Donough O'Cadhain, who wrangles with her husband Sheamus during early morning drunkenness over his demand for "a goddamn egg" for himself and his wastrel brother Bart (Gibbons, 1991, 8). More poignant is Roy Duplin's badgering of his long-suffering wife Sade. To end a dismaying wedlock with a skirt-chaser, she chooses a quick shotgun blow to squelch Roy forever. Through the loving, forgiving actions of Sade's neighbors, Gibbons exonerates Sade for tolerating as much as a woman can bear.

The diminution and maltreatment of women recurs in Gibbons's first historical novel, *On the Occasion of My Last Afternoon* (1998). The strutting, overbearing planter, Samuel P. Goodman Tate, condones gendered gentility—a wife who tats, quilts, and copies dresses from *Godey's Lady's Book* and an elder daughter who plays the piano and paints china. He states outright the contrast between his two girls, the shallow, compliant Maureen and Emma Garnet, the novel's ambitious, but unhousewifely narrator. Samuel suspects Emma of plotting her way into old-maidhood for meddling with issues "beyond a gentlelady's ken" (Gibbons, 1998, 21). He urges her to direct herself to a solid marriage that enhances the prestige of her father, a self-made land baron and slaver. Ironically, the matchmaking he promotes discloses his own social-climbing union with Alice, the genteel daughter of a bankrupt cotton factor from Savannah whom Samuel weds by default. His fortune made, Samuel abandons Alice to languish from extremes of head pain and despair until her death in 1859. His concession to her declining health results in misdiagnosis and brutal treatment by another misogynist, Dr. John C. Gunn, who dismisses female complaints as the result of attempting more than women's brains can manage. For their devaluation of female humanity, both Gunn and Tate deserve placement among Gibbons's insidious woman-haters.

A chilling version of early 20th-century misogyny infects the domestic scene of *Divining Women* (2004), Gibbons's seventh novel. Maureen Carlton Ross, a wife intimidated by a sneering dominator, sinks into episodes of depression that doctors diagnose as "female hysteria," a catch-all term in the 1910s for rebellion against patriarchy that misogynists charged to wandering womb (Gibbons, 2004, 62). Like Offred, the imprisoned breeder in Margaret Atwood's dystopic thriller *The Handmaid's Tale*

(1985), Maureen battles psychic assault and torpor that press her toward madness. To please her husband, Troop Ross, she undergoes galvanic shock, ice baths, therapeutic spinning in a chair, tranquilizers, and vaginal fumigation, all examples of real medical treatments for willful females. He concurs with Maureen's physician that a hysterectomy will return her to normal and rid him of "things that made his skin crawl," a Gothic suggestion of psychotic anti-female fantasies (*Ibid.*, 63). On her arrival by train from Washington, D.C., on September 30, 1918, Mary, Maureen's 22-year-old niece and caretaker, notes that Maureen has reason to be glad that Troop hasn't committed her to the "asylum for nervous women," a state institution in Plymouth, North Carolina (*Ibid.*, 72). The details of medical misogyny illustrate Gibbons's accurate research into women's history at a period when male professional bias prohibited objective diagnosis of female ills.

Divining Women describes cyclical wife battery as an outgrowth of the law of the jungle, by which the strong terrorize the weak. As though doling out reprieves to Maureen's womanhood, Troop, the family tsar, allows her to conceive and carry their only child. He fabricates blame against Maureen for the death of his mother, Nora Worthy Ross, in 1911 and regrets not abandoning a mate he demeans as a "melancholic nag" (*Ibid.*, 64). Maureen's late-pregnancy nausea confirms his suspicion that she favors an atmosphere of high drama, an ironic accusation that reflects his own histrionics. In the falling action, he fails to balance his manipulative act. He charges Maureen with desecrating their stillborn daughter Ella Eloise by lying half-clothed with a "lamentable whore," his description of Mary, Maureen's caretaker. Shortly after the child's death on November 8, 1918, Troop refers to the corpse as "it," a dehumanization fitting to his previous anti-woman tirades (*Ibid.*, 203).

See also **feminism; injustice; men; rape; "The Yellow Wallpaper"**

• *Further reading*

Gibbons, Kaye. *A Cure for Dreams*. New York: Algonquin, 1991.
_____. *Divining Women*. New York: G.P. Putnam's Sons, 2004.
_____. *Ellen Foster*. New York: Algonquin Press, 1987.
_____. *On the Occasion of My Last Afternoon*. New York: G.P. Putnam's Sons, 1998.
McKee, Kathryn. "Simply Talking: Women and Language in Kaye Gibbons's *A Cure for Dreams*," *Southern Quarterly* 35, no. 4 (Summer 1997): 97–107.

mothering

Because of her own loss of a mother at age ten, Kaye Gibbons stresses mother hunger and the matrilineal promise of her fictional families. One of her early good-women, farm wife Lucille Womble in "The Headache," a brief story in the June 1987 issue of the *St. Andrews Review*, overextends herself in disciplining and providing for ten children. In the confessional of Room C at the doctor's office, Lucille confides to Dr. Janet Cowley that the Womble children are ashamed of the family's poverty. From a maternal perspective, Lucille imparts, "I see things. I know" (Gibbons, June 1987, 3). Buried in the subtext is her courage in bearing a child in a home delivery during husband Henry's wartime service in the military. Her reward, embedded in marital intimacy, is Henry's acknowledgement of goodness to him, to their boys, and to everyone Lucille encounters. The simple compliment prefigures Gibbons's later heroines who extend family love to the community, a feminist motif acknowledging the universal benefits of female affection.

In *Ellen Foster* (1987), Gibbons examines mothering from the negative angle of an orphan's mother hunger. The title figure describes gardening as "[working] in the trail my mama left," a poignant image crafted from a child's mother worship and yearning after the 40-year-old woman dies of an overdose of prescription digitalis in 1969 when Ellen is ten years old (Gibbons, 1987, 49). Like Re Jana, the protective daughter in Anne Provoost's biblical epic *In the Shadow of the Ark* (2004), Ellen commits herself to extending her mother's life. With only "one season" to enjoy a healthy mother, Ellen resembles an abandoned nestling not yet ready to fly (*Ibid.*). She craves the attention of Aunt Betsy, a childless widow who enjoys taking Ellen shopping, but who retreats from a permanent commitment to her niece. In contrast to unloving extended family, black nurturers fill in gaps in Ellen's emotional development. A negro neighbor, Starletta's mother, welcomes Ellen on Christmas Day, 1969, and again on New Year's Eve to ease a tense impasse between the child and her roughneck father Bill, who threatens sexual violence against her in the presence of rowdies swilling his bootleg liquor. Jan Nordby Gretlund's summation in *The Southern State of Mind* (1999) tosses off the white-child-in-a-black-home as "almost a Faulknerian cliché" for the standard welcome that blacks extend to whites in "The Bear" (1942) and *Intruder in the Dust* (1948) (Gretlund, 1999, 167). Because of inbred Southern racism, Ellen cannot relax and accept a glass of water, biscuit, or comfort from the black mother, who diagnoses in the runaway white child a serious absence of parental safeguarding and affection. Ellen repays the black mother's kindness with a domestic Christmas gift, a spoon rest, a symbol of female sustenance and support.

Gibbons develops the theme of extrafamilial relationships by inserting Mavis, the black supervisor of field hands working for Ellen's aggrieved maternal grandmother. In the heat of July 1970, Mavis fans Ellen with an apron and instructs her on the need for a hat during hoeing. Maternal love from Mavis takes the form of anecdotes she relates about the beauty and intelligence of Ellen's mother. By assuring Ellen that she resembles her mother, Mavis passes a precious legacy of belonging from the one family member who offers unconditional love. Like a peeping tom, Ellen creeps around Mavis's house to observe a clan unity based on simple joys and good humor. In a more permanent arrangement, Laura, Ellen's foster parent, supervises a baby boy and five foster daughters in her home. In a firmly disciplined, but inviting environment, Ellen joins in tending an aquarium and the planting and watering of a terrarium, microcosms that reflect the mother-rich environments in which she shelters.

In a second novel, *A Virtuous Woman* (1989), Gibbons glimpses the emptiness of Ruby Pitts Woodrow Stokes, a barren woman. To ease her heartache, her husband, "Blinking" Jack Ernest Stokes, considers adopting a child from the orphans reared by Ruth Hartley, an appropriate surname for an adoptive parent. As surrogate mother to June, the neglected child of neighbors Burr and "Tiny Fran" Hoover Stanley, Ruby enjoys camaraderie with a happy, mutually adoring girl. A stand-in parent, Ruby creates an oasis of calm freed from Tiny Fran's snarls and Roland's grappling with his baby half-sister. Ruby photographs June at play and teaches her to weave potholders, a symbol of domestic order and protection from harm. In lieu of home instruction from Tiny Fran on menarche, Ruby fills in for the thoughtless mother and readies June for womanhood. Ruby's reward comes during the last months of her life, when June brings expensive gowns, robes, and slippers to ease Ruby's bout with terminal lung cancer. The pseudo-filial relationship reprises motifs from *Ellen Foster*, in which the most satisfying mothering takes place between people bearing no blood kinship.

To interviewer Jan Nordby Gretlund, Gibbons claimed *A Cure for Dreams* (1991) as her favorite book because of the three generations of females residing together. The variance in parenting marks each stave with matriarchal idiosyncrasies—Bridget O'Donough O'Cadhain's Irish Catholic swearing and Lottie O'Cadhain Davies's joy in rich chiffon, chintz, beaded English netting, and venise lace, from which she makes dresses and slips for daughter Betty. Bridget is expert at massaging guilt to wrest cash from her ten children for a return trip to Ireland. As leverage, she faults them for producing small families, for not learning to speak Gaelic, and for neglecting their aged mother, a standard parental ploy. In reward to a pitiless scold, Lottie transports in a hatbox fragrant gardenias as a gesture of filial regard.

A more substantive maternal love in *A Cure for Dreams* develops in the next generation. In adoration of her cheery, resourceful mother, Betty, Bridget's granddaughter, follows Lottie like a twin. To educate Betty in the nuances of conjugal love, Lottie urges her to study the way that men call their wives. The degree of affection ranges from a no-name command to a respectful use of the wife's first name, the choice of Richard Bethune in summoning his beloved Amanda, whose name in Latin means "she who should be loved." In contrast, Sade Duplin must win back her two estranged children after she kills her evil-tempered husband Roy with a shotgun blast and reclaims their home as an inviting waystation during their children's visits to their widowed mother. Rewarding her sweetness are gifts of taffy, stockings, and a bed jacket, personal comforts intended to honor a goodwoman. In like manner, on November 25, 1942, Betty's adoring welcome to her own infant, Marjorie Polly Randolph, forecasts another successful motherhood augmented by Grandmother Lottie and the family housekeeper-midwife, Polly Deal, for whom Marjorie is named. Critics affirm that Gibbons favors the society of women for the positive energy of good food, congeniality, and unquestioning affection.

In a fourth novel, *Charms for the Easy Life* (1993), Gibbons returns to a tri-level matrilineage in the household of healer Charlie Kate Birch, whose maternal style is officious to the point of absolutism. After the departure of her husband and the death of her despicable son-in-law, she forms a triune medical team with daughter Sophia Snow Birch and granddaughter Margaret. For the herbalist, medical acumen translates into a maternal concern for patients who need either treatment or instruction in nutrition, sexual abstinence, and hygiene. The trio enters the home of a blind child and treats her whooping cough with a croup kettle and tent. When Maveen, the family's 70-year-old retired domestic, dwindles from stomach cancer and starvation, Charlie Kate eases with alcohol rubs the agonies that needlessly accompany the woman's last hours. The pushy sickroom maneuvers soften after Sophia faints during the lancing of Hermit Willoughby's boil. Charlie Kate returns to top-sergeant style in confronting businessman Richard Baines concerning his intentions toward Sophia and toward the party registered at the Sir Walter Raleigh Hotel as "Mrs. Richard Baines" (Gibbons, 1993, 213). To the unplanned Christmas Eve, 1942, elopement of Richard and Sophia to South Carolina, Charlie Kate eases Margaret's anxieties about having a stepfather in short, snappy order: "Sophia will be happy. So will you, and so will I. Go to sleep" (*Ibid.*, 224). Gibbons speaks through Charlie Kate the curt, no-nonsense style of mothering without coddling or sentimentality.

Gibbons ventures into a more complex parenting model in the relationship between Hattie Barnes and her mother Maggie and cook-housekeeper, Pearl Wiggins, in *Sights Unseen* (1995), a fictional survey of a family's battle against insanity. Although mothered by Pearl, Hattie clings to the maternal ideal and longs for Maggie to be "laughing-well" (Gibbons, 1995, 152). In scrolled memories of family stories, Hattie ruminates on her mother's inability to breastfeed after giving birth in 1955 and her rejection of Hattie for being an interminably empty stomach. Recalling Hattie's motherlessness, her brother Freddy calls Hattie a "generic child," reared in the kitchen like a puppy on a short leash (*Ibid.*, 67). At a breaking point in Hattie's tolerance of her drunken, sharp-tongued mother, Maggie refers to her daughter as a freak. The invective forces Hattie beyond the front steps to wait for the bus at the edge of the road, the periphery of home territory out of earshot of more insults. Simultaneous with Hattie's discomfort is a yearning for the inner sanctum, the source of authentic parental affection.

Gibbons indicates early on that Maggie is capable of mothering. In the words of playwright Emily Mann in *Annulla Allen* (1977), "Every woman has this love in her. It may be sleeping but it can be awakened" (Mann, 1977, 29). The unforeseen restoration of Maggie's sanity in 1967 from psychotherapy and eight electroconvulsive shock treatments at Duke Hospital further disorders the disorderly household, leaving Hattie ironically unsure of what to expect. Tentatively, like parted playmates re-exploring each other's friendship, Maggie creeps back into Hattie's trust through sessions of sewing sun suits, reading before naptime, and nightly visitations at the bedroom door. Diffident, but steady, the motherly instinct resumes in Maggie, who gains from Hattie a tacit forgiveness for years of bipolar rampages.

Through a process that Toni Morrison calls "rememory," Gibbons confers respect on a dishonored mother in her first historical novel, *On the Occasion of My Last Afternoon* (1998). Narrator Emma Garnet Tate Lowell, who settles in urban Raleigh, North Carolina, far from her plantation home in tidewater Virginia, torments herself with guilt and grief after the death of her mother, Alice Tate, in 1859. During 12 years of absence from her childhood home, Emma recites for her loving husband Quincy the daily insults and belittlings that Alice bears from her acid-tongued husband, planter Samuel P. Goodman Tate. Gently unpinning and plaiting Emma's hair, Quincy listens to an outpouring of regret and suppressed rage while extolling Emma's mothering by the martyred plantation mistress. Emma relives the hair touches of Alice, who, in 1847, lifts a drooping bun from her just-married daughter's neck as a demonstration of maternal affection. Emma's gesture of touching the moist spot her mother's hand leaves on the carriage window manifests a concern for a female life constrained by a pompous, self-ennobling mate who is not likely to change with age. The author awards Emma a miniature of Alice in Leslie Lowell, a daughter as elegant, graceful, intelligent, and compassionate as the maternal grandmother she has never seen. Gibbons honors Emma's generosity in passing on stored mother-child memories to wounded soldiers, whom she urges to relive the security of being rocked to sleep on their mothers' laps. The easing of distress manifests the intrinsic worth of mothering to families and to the social order.

Four years after Alice's passing, Emma experiences a second painful loss of mothering in the death of Clarice Washington, the cook-housekeeper and surrogate parent for three generations of the Tate-Lowell family. A godly woman blessed with energy and good sense, Clarice so skillfully manages her place in the Lowell household that Emma takes for granted an orderly environment and the encouragement to face tomorrow. At a downturn of Southern hopes of winning the Civil War, in 1863, Clarice coughs out her last breaths from pneumonia. Too late, Emma esteems Clarice as her replacement mother, the "woman who made Seven Oaks a home" (Gibbons, 1998, 232). The Southern conundrum of the undervalued family do-all burdens Emma with sorrow and regret. The inscription of Clarice's name and dates on a brass plaque at Christ Church ennobles her sacrifice and that of myriad Southern mammies who receive much less for their dedication.

The motif of death as a permanent parting between mother and child permeates *Divining Women* (2004), Gibbons's seventh novel. In delight at living alone in Washington, D.C., with daughter Mary, widow Martha Greene Oliver suffers long-term sadness at the suicide of her crotchery 16-year-old son Daniel. After he hangs himself in 1913 from a hotel room chandelier in Baltimore, Martha relives their relationship in terms of his petulance. During a summer trip to Northumberland, she experiences so much sleeplessness from his ghostly visitations that she admits that all mothers maintain closeness with their departed children. Of his hauntings, she declares, "Everything wounds," a suggestion of her regrets and self-incrimination, the predictable burden of the mother of a suicide (Gibbons, 2004, 40).

A mid-text episode involving the Oliver women in the marital despair of Judith Benedict Stafford reveals the sympathetic chiming that harmonizes women in tight community. She mauls herself after discovering her husband on May 3, 1912, in a bedroom frolic with a street tramp. Before Judith can reveal a woe-disfigured face, loose teeth, and fallen hair to her mother in Baltimore, Grandmother Louise Oliver insists that Judith prepare her mother with the truth about Stafford's indiscreet couplings with trollops. Louise insists that Mrs. Benedict will know the truth because mothers recognize malicious damage to their children. The mini-tragedy prefaces the novel's focus, the reclamation of Maureen Carlton Ross in fall 1918. A beleaguered wife from a warm, loving Yazoo City, Mississippi, home, she discovers the one sin that ends her toleration of husband Troop Ross—his denial of postal communication between Maureen and her mother. Still grieving the death of a stillborn child, Ella Eloise Ross, on November 9, 1918, two days before an armistice ends World War I, Maureen hurries north by train with her caretaker, 22-year-old Mary Oliver. Staining Maureen's bodice like war wounds is the milk that leaks from unsuckled breasts, a symbol of the womanly bounty that Maureen offers a moribund marriage.

In *The Life All Around Me by Ellen Foster* (2006), the sequel to *Ellen Foster*, Gibbons compounds the image of foster mothering with multiple views of female nurturers. Soothing Ellen's mind are visions of love from her birth mother. Ellen's thoughts replicate Barbara Kingsolver's essay in *I've Always Meant to Tell You: Letters to Our Mothers: An Anthology of Contemporary Women Writers* (1997), in which she acknowledges, "[You] went right ahead and did what you knew was best for your babies" (Kingsolver, 1997, 260). Memory offers a mental haven that counters some of the invasive anxieties that reduce Ellen to dark flashbacks of death and abandonment. The loss leaves a zero in her life much like the suicide of the mother in Marilynne Robinson's *Housekeeping* (1980). Critic Marjorie Gellhorn Sa'adah, in a review for the *Los Angeles Times*, describes Ellen's free-floating mother hunger as beneficent: "The ghost of a mother is beatified instead of haunting" (Sa'adah, 2006). As a surrogate, Laura regards her duty to Ellen as more than foster mothering. Like a yuletide blessing, Ellen arrives on Christmas Day, 1970, laboring under the personal assaults that bring out the lioness in Laura. Through Laura, Ellen witnesses unselfish acts of restoring Martha's mother to sanity through lengthy Sunday naps and the bearing of casseroles to Stuart's family. When Starletta's aunt visits in so bad a state that her milk won't let down, Laura prescribes rest and hot towels to revive lactation to feed a wailing infant. The sum of kindnesses manifests in mothering the Greek concept of *agape*, a giving of self to those in need without expectation of repayment.

See also **foster parenting; women**

• *Further reading*

Gibbons, Kaye. *Charms for the Easy Life*. New York: Putnam, 1993.
_____. *Divining Women*. New York: G.P. Putnam's Sons, 2004.
_____. *Ellen Foster*. New York: Algonquin Press, 1987.
_____. "The Headache," *St. Andrews Review* (June 1987): 3–8.
_____. *The Life All Around Me by Ellen Foster*. New York: Harcourt, 2006.
_____. *Sights Unseen*. New York: G.P. Putnam's Sons, 1995.
Gretlund, Jan Nordby. "In My Own Style: An Interview with Kaye Gibbons," *South Atlantic Review* 65, no. 4 (Fall 2000): 132–154.
_____. *The Southern State of Mind*. Columbia: University of South Carolina Press, 1999.
Kingsolver, Barbara. *I've Always Meant to Tell You: Letters to Our Mothers: An Anthology of Contemporary Women Writers*. New York: Pocket Star, 1997.
Mann, Emily. *Testimonies: Four Plays*. New York: Theatre Communications Group, 1997.
Munafo, Giavanna. "Colored Biscuits: Reconstructing Whiteness and the Boundaries of 'Home' in Kaye Gibbons's *Ellen Foster*," *Women, America, and Movement*. ed. Susan L. Roberson. Columbia: University of Missouri Press, 1998, pp. 38–61.
Sa'adah, Marjorie Gellhorn. "You Can't Go Home Again," *Los Angeles Times* (8 January 2006): R7.

music

Gibbons stints on the application of music to character interaction. In a first novel, *Ellen Foster* (1987), she describes the title character's displacement on music day among more tuneful schoolmates. In token of Ellen's insecurity, she fights ridicule by pretending to sing with gusto seasonal songs about Easter lilies, Christmas trees, ghosts, "Turkey in the Straw," or patriotism (Gibbons, 1987, 84). The just-pretend involvement reflects the duality of a ten-year-old who deceives the world while re-enacting painful scenarios in her head. Reassurance blossoms during her temporary residence with art teacher Julia and her husband Roy, aging hippies who cling to memories of "good golly Miss Molly," a top-ten vehicle for Little Richard in 1957, and "let it all hang out," a line from the Hombres's hit "Let It Out" (1967) (*Ibid.*, 47). The lack of musicality in the family line returns in the sequel, *The Life All Around Me by Ellen Foster* (2006), in which delayed information informs Ellen that her father played the guitar and thought of himself as a singer.

In later novels, Gibbons positions titles and phrases from songs to establish historical milieu. In *A Cure for Dreams* (1991), the singing of "On the W.P. and A." and Polly Deal's birthing jingles from Marie Campbell's *Folks Do Get Born* (1946) alludes to the assistance of President Franklin D. Roosevelt to victims of the Great Depression. The author's next novel, *Charms for the Easy Life* (1993), continues describing wartime with scenarios featuring radio broadcasts of *Homefront* and songs by pop performers Helen O'Connell, Bing Crosby, and Benny Goodman. Narrator Margaret mentions specifically Nelson Eddy singing Victor Herbert's "Ah! Sweet Mystery of Life" (1910), Johnny Mercer performing June Hershey and Don Swander's "Deep in the Heart of Texas" (1941), and Hazel Scott's piano rendition of the "Minute Waltz," composed by Frédéric Chopin in 1846. The text contrasts the era's musical moods with pre–Christmas 1942 jitterbugging at the veterans' hospital in Durham, slow-dancing to the obligatory "White Christmas," and the 4-F members of the North Carolina Symphony performing Al Jolson's familiar "You Made Me Love You" (1913) and Bing Crosby's wistful "I'll Be Seeing You" (1938), couples' ballads that resurged to popularity during the second world war. More significant to Margaret's future is a piano recital at Peace College, where Tom Hawkings's newly married sister Esther plays classical pieces—Frédéric Chopin's "Revolutionary Étude" (1831), Edvard Grieg's *E Minor Piano Sonata* (1887), and Johann Sebastian Bach's "Minuet in G" (1724). Rather than perform the exhibition works she studied at Juilliard, the pianist chooses Edward McDowell's impressionistic *Woodland Sketches* (1896) and Maurice Ravel's *Le Tombeau de Couperin* (1914–1917). Gibbons draws the final piece into the era by identifying it as a eulogy to a casualty of World War I.

The use of the piano as a surgical table in *On the Occasion of My Last Afternoon* (1998) portrays the exigencies of war as both unpleasant and noble. The gradual wearing out of Dr. Quincy Lowell manifests itself in a service at Christ Church, where his daughters, Leslie, Louise, and Mary, sing "Sheep May Safely Graze," an aria by Johann Sebastian Bach. The contrast between Quincy's daily labors and the promise of innocence and security reduces him to weeping with head in hands and knees bent on a velvet bench. The song returns in 1865 at his funeral, a fitting tribute to his war-time toils. After the hand-to-hand fighting at the Wilderness, Virginia, on May 5–7, 1864, Maureen Tate puts her musical training to good use by singing to sleep the casualties who recuperate at the Lowell mansion. Gibbons states, "They could hide their hurts in music," a rare acknowledgement from the author of the value of melody (Gibbons, 1998, 249). A more positive use of music as a war monument occurs in *Divining Women* (2004), in which vigorous piano playing of patriotic tunes supports military efforts during World War I.

• *Further reading*

Gibbons, Kaye. *Ellen Foster*. New York: Algonquin Press, 1987.
_____. *On the Occasion of My Last Afternoon*. New York: G.P. Putnam's Sons, 1998.

names

Kaye Gibbons fortifies her texts with evocative names for characters and places, such as the replacement of "Clarissa" with the masculine "Charlie Kate" for an aggressive healer in *Charms for the Easy Life* (1998). At the heart of the title character's quandary in *Ellen Foster* (1987), the author's first novel, is her rejection of a reviled surname, which the text never reveals. To a patronym associated with wife abuse, child neglect, alcoholism, and attempted child rape, Ellen negates all ties with her paternal line. Likewise unsuitable is her mother's family, comprised of a dismissive Aunt Betsy, cruel Aunt Nadine Nelson and Cousin Dora, and a surly grandmother. In a touching spot of humor, Ellen chooses to become part of the "Foster" family, an embrace of normality among strangers who are more generous, more humane, than relatives (Gibbons, 1987, 87). During regular Tuesday sessions, the school psychologist charges Ellen with being asocial and describes the renaming as an identity crisis resulting from trauma. To Ellen, the name replaces a two-sided family lineage that shrivels under a burden of callousness and grudge bearing. The pun on "Foster" endears Ellen to readers, who pity the child her two Christmases in search of a permanent haven. In a sequel, *The Life All Around Me by Ellen Foster* (2006), the author rewards Ellen in winter 1974 with the naming of her cousin Dora's daughter, Claire Ellen, a graceful name replete with family forgiveness.

Gibbons continues the naming trend in two subsequent novels. For the women in *A Virtuous Woman* (1991), she chooses Sudie Bee for a housekeeping wonder, Tiny Fran for an overweight slug, and, for Ruby, a visual image strong in color and value. Although the narrative pictures Ruby's virtues interlaced with frailties and a self-destructive dependence on cigarettes, her good qualities live on in the imagination of her 65-year-old husband, "Blinking" Jack Ernest Stokes. His nickname indicates a facial tic that punctuates his diffidence. Suitably, the middle name "Ernest" and the surname "Stokes" characterize his sincerity and warmth in respecting and adoring an exemplary goodwife. In hopes of relieving her hunger for motherhood, he ponders adopting one of the children reared by Ruth Hartley, a female character who bears the first name of the biblical paragon Ruth and a patronym suggesting magnanimity. Serendipity brings the Stokes a needy neighbor child, June Stanley, whose summery given name suits a surrogate daughter blessed with a cheerful disposition and loyalty to Jack and Ruby. In extreme sorrow three months after her death from lung cancer, he grasps at a wispy "haint" in hopes that Ruby has returned to him as a dream-like night revenant.

In contrast to the Stokes' happy union, *A Cure for Dreams* (1991), Gibbons's third novel, pictures Lottie O'Cadhain Davies dreaming teenage reveries at the confluence of the Cumberland River and Brownies Creek, a mystic name subtly attaching her to the folklore of Ireland, her mother country. The daughter of a shrew and a loud-mouth blusterer named Sheamus—pronounced "shame us"—she defies her "lot" as wife to a passionless miser. Contributing to the "lot" of other women living out the Great Depression on Milk Farm Road, a place name blessed with feminine implications, Lottie establishes an all-female card club. In penny-ante backroom games at Porter's store, local housewives gamble small sums on gin rummy and pinochle as harmless counteragents to a long period of doing without new clothes and gasoline for travel. The most loved wife in the card-playing clutch is Amanda Bethune, whose first name is Latin for "she who should be loved." Her surname derives from the Hebrew *beth* for "house," a tidy summation of her domestic bliss—affection and security. Her foil, Sade Duplin, bears an insightful given name suggesting the sadism that she endures from her husband Roy, a "kingly" tormentor. The couple's surname echoes the duplicity of Roy's womanizing and Sade's conclusion to their marital misery by felling him with a blast from a shotgun. Lottie, the manipulator of female fortunes, protects Sade from arrest by concealing from part-time Deputy Sheriff John Carroll evidence of murder.

Gibbons positions *Sights Unseen* (1995), her fifth novel, at Bend of the River Road, a dual image of diversion and containment. The diverted stream suggests both the Barnes family' deviation from the norm and the shift in their fortunes after Maggie Barnes achieves healing and a redirection from years of bipolarity. The author selects for Pearl Wiggins, the black surrogate mother of Hattie Barnes, a precious jewel mirroring the biblical "pearl of great price" that Jesus's parable glorifies in Matthew 13:45–46. Essential to Pearl's beneficence is a reminder to Hattie that her own mother, though crippled by delusions and manic ravings, deserves esteem for being a birth mother. Upon Maggie's return to sanity in 1967 after psychotherapy and eight electroconvulsive shock treatments at Duke Hospital, Pearl weeps with joy at her return and shares domestic duties with a woman whom she once viewed as a daily charge to be coaxed and wheedled into compliance. Maggie awards Pearl a memorable gift by refusing to allow the deputy sheriff or Grandfather Barnes to degrade her race. In the novel's resolution, Pearl remains a cherished companion who shares kitchen tasks with Maggie like a sister.

Character naming in *On the Occasion of My Last Afternoon* (1998), Gibbons's first historical novel, illustrates both denotative and connotive intent. Separating the landed class from their slave-produced wealth in Bruton Parish, Virginia, are the euphemistic Auntie and Uncle or the generalized term "servants" for black people held in bondage. The choice of Lazy for a plantation babysitter reflects both character behavior and a slaveowner's expectations of sorry service from a young slacker. The family cook-housekeeper, freedwoman Clarice Washington, possesses a name rich in the clear-sighted wisdom of a woman who knows her worth. Her surname reminds the reader subtextually that George Washington, founder of his country, was a slaveowner. More significant to Gibbons's fiction are the middle names of villain Samuel P. Goodman Tate and of the narrator, Emma Garnet Tate Lowell. Tate, far from being a "good man," lashes his family with vituperations and sickens them with his vain posturing. In contrast, Emma Garnet, like Pearl Wiggins and Ruby Stokes, bears one of Gibbons's jewel names as testimony to female integrity and worth. After marriage, she joins the Lowell family, one of America's distinguished liberal lineages.

Gibbons continues her allocation of emblematic names in *Divining Women* (2004), her seventh novel. To characterize a victimizing divorcée and her warped son, the author chooses Nora Worthy Ross as a pun on the unworthiness of a vengeful parent to rear a child as her toady. The boy bears the name Troop in token of his mindless following of Nora through serial episodes of bilking her ex-husband of money, parental custody, and reputation. In adulthood, Troop tramples the self-regard of his wife, Maureen Carlton Ross, who marries him in Yazoo City on the Mississippi delta in 1913 and lives with him in Elm City, North Carolina, a deceptively bucolic town name.

To conclude a post-modern Gothic plot, Gibbons wields naming like St. George's sword at the head of the dragon. Like a mid–Victorian heroine in the clutches of evil, Maureen hovers near collapse in her last 50 days of pregnancy from Troop's unstinting manipulation and character assassination. A surprising model of strength arises from letters composed by Judith Benedict Stafford. Vicariously, Maureen retrieves her battered ego by empathizing with Judith, who bears the name of a Jewish widow brassy enough to seduce Holofernes, an Assyrian general, and to hack off his head. The letter writer's moxie both emboldens and blesses, an act conveyed by "Benedict," Judith's maiden name. On September 9, 1918, two days before the truce that ends World War I, the final field of battle pits Troop and Maureen in the choice of a name for their stillborn daughter. By demanding the mellifluous "Ella Eloise" for her babe, Maureen trumps Troop's insistence in "Nora Worthy." Thus, like Beowulf vanquishing Grendel's mother, Maureen silences the lurking virago in her grave.

• *Further reading*

Gibbons, Kaye. *Ellen Foster*. New York: Algonquin Press, 1987.
Rose, Ellen Cronan. "Through the Looking Glass: When Women Tell Fairy Tales" in *The Voyage In: Fiction of Female Development*. eds. Elizabeth Abel, Marianne Hirsch, and Elizabeth Langland. Hanover, N.H.: University Press of New England, 1983.
Wood, Ralph C. "Gumption and Grace in the Novels of Kaye Gibbons," *Christian Century* 109, no. 27 (September 23–30, 1992): 842–846.

old age

Gibbons contrasts the blessings of long life with crabbed old age, a punishment for a life misspent or founded on faulty principles. In *Ellen Foster* (1987), the patrician grandmother spews out hatred for her son-in-law Bill, who marries above his class. At his worst, in March 1969, he wills his heart-sick wife to commit suicide with an overdose of prescription digitalis. At his sudden demise from cerebral hemorrhage in 1970, his mother-in-law spits on and burns the American flag from his casket in a backyard conflagration reminiscent of witches' secret rituals. When life ebbs in the elderly matriarch from a bout of flu, the title character offers bedside washing and feeding to the caretaker who dispatches 11-year-old Ellen to cotton rows to labor in the July sun like a field hand. Contrast continues to highlight the grandmother's twisted behaviors. To a woman who violates the obligation of blood kin, Ellen offers *agape*, the Greek concept of grace, a kindness that the receiver does not have to deserve. Lacking more appropriate forms of decorum, shortly before Christmas, 1970, Ellen decks her grandmother's corpse in a Sunday hat and artificial flowers as tokens of respect. The bizarre deathbed scene serves the author's intent to celebrate a child thrust into mature dilemmas for which she has no preparation and no adult role model.

Likewise intent on reverencing the dead, farm laborer "Blinking" Jack Ernest Stokes regrets the passing of his wife in Gibbons's second novel, *A Virtuous Woman* (1989), the story of a 25-year marriage between unlike mates. A widower at age 65, he grieves from March until June after the death of his 45-year-old soul mate, Ruby Pitts Woodrow Stokes, from lung cancer. To his neighbors' consternation, he refuses responsibility for himself and has an adult-style tantrum in his bedroom. Sitting on a bare mattress drunk on bourbon and immersed in Roadrunner cartoons on television, he refuses to surrender the bedsheets that carry the lilac scent favored by his deceased wife. An irretrievable child-man, Jack is ill-prepared for spending his last years alone in a dwelling he anticipated sharing with a competent housewife and cook. His illogical expectations abandon him to lack-logic solutions to everyday needs. As a result, neighbors Burr and June Stanley predict a limited future for Jack.

Gibbons's next two novels picture demanding, manipulative, and resilient matriarchs. In *A Cure for Dreams* (1991), the bitter wedlock of Bridget O'Donough O'Cadhain precedes emigration in 1918 from Galway, Ireland, to a clan homestead on the Cumberland River in Bell County, Kentucky. With the aid of daughter Eileen, in old age, the unsmiling, mean-spirited, Gaelic-speaking head of household is still capable of coercing her daughter Lottie into escorting Bridget back to the old country. The text creates humor out of a self-dramatizing bedside vigil for a woman who is nowhere near dying. With a miserly grasp on life and the living, she survives into her late nineties. In awe of Bridget's handsome headstone, her great-granddaughter, Marjorie Polly Randolph, puzzles over scraps of information that form an ambiguous memory of the Irish-American materfamilias. Marjorie's mother, Betty Davies Randolph, is more likely to understand dissonant mother-daughter traits because of her rebellion against Lottie. Controlling to the point of smothering Betty, Lottie visits away from home at the time of Marjorie's birth on November 25, 1942. Betty, in collusion with midwife Polly Deal, chooses to complete labor and delivery without Lottie's intrusion. Despite the daughters' need to break tether from mothers, the O'Donough-O'Cadhain-Davies-Randolph matrilineage remains robust and independent from the eldest to the youngest.

Similar in determination to Bridget is Charlie Kate Birch, the self-educated herbalist-midwife who energizes *Charms for the Easy Life* (1993), Gibbons's fourth novel. The surname "Birch" mirrors the upward thrust and resilience of a woman who thrives like birches along a stream. As officious and unwavering as Bridget, Charlie Kate musters her daughter, Sophia Snow Birch, and granddaughter Margaret into a cadre of healers. They go on house calls that call for croup kettles, lancing of boils, setting of broken bones, removal of warts, stitching lacerations with sewing thread, reviving the nearly drowned shoeshine man, and birthing and swaddling of infants. Unlike Bridget, who refuses to learn English, Charlie Kate shares with her all-female household a love of language and reading, two of the author's intellectual treasures. Alert and scholarly, Charlie Kate debates the order of publication of James Fenimore Cooper's frontier classics, *The Last of the Mohicans* (1826) and *The Deerslayer* (1841). On her last evening, Christmas night, 1942, she cherishes a present, a two-volume biography of her hero, General Robert E. Lee, a propitious gift from her new son-in-law, businessman Richard Baines. The holiday bodes well for Richard, who risks marriage into a family of women who suspect male motives.

The three-generational household profits from Charlie Kate's age and experience. The family sits together and, page by page, shares the latest literary works, which they analyze and dissect in even-handed discussions. Crucial to her relationship with her granddaughter Margaret is Charlie Kate's clarity of comment and philosophy. Only hours from death at age 60, she states her approval of the Hawkings family as potential in-laws. After marching in place and hand-to-shoulder exercise to relieve a vague nausea, Charlie Kate leaves life as forthrightly as she lives it, much as General Lee surrendered his Confederate forces to General Ulysses S. Grant at Appomattox. In proof of her vibrant example, Margaret readies her grandmother's corpse for the mortician and performs the funereal rituals of stopping the clock and covering mirrors, a womanly tradition that Charlie Kate teaches her family. Unlike the grudge-clutching crone in *Ellen Foster*, Gibbons indicates that the beneficent matriarch garners home-grown rewards by instructing and edifying subsequent generations.

Geriatric reflections sustain an engaging narration in *On the Occasion of My Last Afternoon* (1998), Gibbons's first historical novel. Through the failing voice of 70-year-old Emma Garnet Tate Lowell, readers relive the excesses of the ante-bellum South and the extremes of suffering, loss of the Civil War, and its aftermath. Emma fine-hones her recount of 12 years of separation from her mother, the gentle, self-effacing Alice Tate, a symbol of the South's gentility before sectionalism turned it to greed and insularity. A model of ineptitude, Alice exemplifies the warning of Sarah Josepha Hale, Philadelphia-based editor of *Godey's Lady's Book*, who warned in the July 1855 issue that a "grossly ignorant woman is unfit to be the mother of an American citizen" (Hale, 1857, 82). Hungry for details of her mother's final illness in 1859, Emma learns of Dr. John C. Gunn's cruel medicines and therapy that cap years of Alice's submission to a vicious husband, planter Samuel P. Goodman Tate. In contrast, a measure of comeuppance chokes off the blatherings of Emma's aged father in June 1862, when war forces him to seek shelter with his nemesis, Dr. Quincy Lowell. Like the childishly petulant Jack Stokes, Samuel retreats into infantile demands and tit-for-tat squabbles with Quincy. As heart failure threatens Samuel's last hours, Quincy offers a dual solution — a lethal oral dose of digitalis powder to end the struggle and to rid the house of a corrosive presence. The two miserable deaths suit the tyrant Samuel and his weak-willed enabler Alice, both of whom prove unworthy parents to Emma and her four siblings.

Emma's fictional memoir embodies an axiom concerning longevity — the longer the life, the more farewells and losses that accrue to the survivor. She outlives a surrogate daughter, Lavinia Ella Mae Dawes, the underclass child whom the Lowell family fosters with food, culture, and education. In Lavinia's past, a beloved grandmother imparted a love of orchids as well as a model of determination. Suffering from shingles, the elderly horticulturist crawled from plant to plant. Lavinia acknowledges that "the daily struggle to keep the stubborn things abloom kept her [grandmother] alive" (Gibbons, 1998, 117). The brief commentary on a faithful orchid grower mirrors Emma Garnet's continuation of nurture to a blossoming female.

Life closures for Emma Garnet continue with cook-housekeeper Clarice Washington's queenly demise in 1863 from pneumonia and her final advice to servants and family. A vigorous surrogate mother, she rasps out goodbyes from the comfort of Emma's bed. With the gravity and authority of an Old Testament patriarch on his deathbed, Clarice extends what wisdom and experience she deems appropriate to Emma's needs. In short order, Quincy's last days follow metabolic collapse after too many hours of service to combat casualties. Weathered by too much suffering and sorrow, during a train ride to Boston in 1865, he slips away from Emma as though reaching heavenward for rest. More pathetic is the abrupt passage of Emma's younger sister Maureen, found naked, cold, and rigid on the floor by her bed. Looking over the remains of her family, Emma entertains a thought that is common to advanced age — that she endures as the last of a passing generation. After a rush to accomplish as much as possible, in 1900, she embraces the notion of dying and reuniting with Quincy in the afterlife. A benevolent touch in Emma's last years derives from her sending money "in an almost gleeful disbursement" to finance the good works she once did in person (*Ibid.*, 272–273). With a satisfying farewell devoid of fear or regret, Gibbons presents the finality of old age and death as a glorious ripeness and espousal of mortality.

The author applies the perspectives of the elderly as contrasts to the sufferings of people in their prime in *Divining Women* (2004). To establish the background of narrator Mary Oliver, a 22-year-old graduate student at Radcliffe from Washington, D.C., Gibbons outlines the eccentricities of two pairs of grandparents, the Greenes and the Olivers, who share a residence on Dupont Circle. Toby Greene, a respected investor, enjoys nudity to such a degree that he destroys his marriage to Nora Worthy Ross and alienates his only son, Troop Ross. A moment of comic relief derives from Toby's fall in the backyard and the consternation of a doctor who treats the elderly nudist he labels a "crackpot" (Gibbons, 2004, 153). More poignant are the ministrations of Leonard Oliver to residential ghosts, whom he eases through regrets about misspent lives. His daughter-in-law, Martha Greene Oliver, laments the press of spirits during the 1918 influenza pandemic, which forces a crush of newly dead to wait in line like travelers at Union Station. The gentle humor offsets news of shocking losses of young and old from a lethal virus. Gibbons extends the theme of life's brevity with the stillbirth of Ella Eloise Ross, an innocent who strangles on her birth cord on November 8, 1918. The paradox of adults mourning the young concludes a cemetery scene in which Maureen Ross and Mary depart from the graveside, leaving the Ross family servants, Mamie and Zollie, to sit near the remains of their sons.

See also **wisdom**

• *Further reading*

Gibbons, Kaye. *Divining Women*. New York: G.P. Putnam's Sons, 2004.
_____. *On the Occasion of My Last Afternoon*. New York: G.P. Putnam's Sons, 1998.
Hale, Sarah Josepha. "Editor's Table," *Godey's Lady's Book* 51, no. 1 (July 1857): 82.

Oliver, Mary

Mary Oliver, protagonist of *Divining Women* (2004), possesses more gumption than her introduction indicates. A trusting 22-year-old alumna of Goucher College and graduate student at Radcliffe, she shares with her aunt, Maureen Carlton Ross, a candid expression that suggests naiveté and vulnerability. According to Mary's widowed mother, Martha Greene Oliver, both Mary and her aunt grow up cognizant of an innate female radar — an alertness that cues the mind to clues from other people's posture, facial expression, and voice. In acknowledgement of Maureen's sensitivity, the family chooses comforting gifts— a shawl and combs for her long dark hair. Martha dispatches Mary on September 30, 1918, to Elm City, North Carolina, as a companion during the last 50 days of Maureen's pregnancy. Ironically, Mary accuses Martha of a violation of trust for believing Mary capable of shielding Maureen from a vicious husband. Like Lottie Davies and Betty Davies Randolph in *A Cure for Dreams* (1991), differences between mother and daughter reflect normal dissonance in a two-woman household in which the younger female needs more life experience to achieve maturity and independence.

In the opinion of reviewer Julia Ridley Smith, a critic for the Raleigh, N.C., *News & Observer*, Mary serves Gibbons as both "spectator and savior" (Smith, 2004). Naturally astute, like Sara Smolinsky in Anzia Yezierska's *The Bread Givers* (1925), Mary is the self-starter and quick study. She sizes up her aunt Maureen's domestic situation and sets out to invalidate her aunt's unfounded misconceptions of womanhood. From past details and from observing the Ross family firsthand, Mary confronts what social scientist Charlotte Perkins Gilman termed a smothering negativity, the stultification of female lives common to American patriarchy in the early 1900s. Mary witnesses the daily delivery of hothouse roses and recognizes them for a husband's "substitution for true emotion," which the Ross marriage lacks from the beginning (Gibbons, 2004, 61). In horror at a battery of worthless medical therapies— galvanic shock therapy, ice water deluges, vibrating belts, vaginal fumigation, towel lashings, and a proposed hysterectomy — to prohibit Maureen's expression of opinions, Mary speaks the mind of the New Woman, who demands the right to fling a tantrum to establish a normal in-home rebalancing of power.

Mary's actions contrast Maureen's behaviors in terms of direction and drive. To Maureen's retreat to a purple divan to await her child's delivery, Mary, like Lottie in *A Cure for Dreams* and Charlie Kate Birch in *Charms for the Easy Life* (1993), refuses to give in to adversity. Mary confronts simple problems, such as demanding fruit for Maureen's diet, retrieving fresh ginger root at 4:00 A.M. to combat Maureen's nausea, choosing to make a sandwich rather than wait for maid service, and phoning in a subscription to the daily newspaper to connect the Ross family with the outside world. The amount of antipathy that can arise from fruit, an herbal remedy, a sandwich, and a daily paper reveals the extent of dysfunction in the household.

Other female actions inform Mary's decisions and strategies. From the letters of Judith Benedict Stafford, Mary extracts wisdom, the letter-writer's self-validation and that sets the record straight for the discounted wife who refuses to blame herself for a withered marriage. Mamie, the maid and cook, supports Mary's mundane rebellions against Troop Ross, the clan ogre. In the falling action, Maureen joins Mary and the staff in challenging his outrage that black and white family members eat together at the same table. The rapid decline in civility leaves Mary little choice but to remove Maureen from North Carolina and to introduce her to Mary's supportive mother and grandparents in Washington. Contributing momentum to the getaway are motherly letters from Mississippi filled with warmth and experience. As the rhapsodic introduction reveals, the withdrawal of Maureen and Mary from Elm City bolsters a woman-to-woman friendship that survives for two decades.

See also ***Divining Women***; **Greene-Oliver-Ross genealogy**

• *Further reading*

Gibbons, Kaye. *Divining Women*. New York: G.P. Putnam's Sons, 2004.
Smith, Julia Ridley. "Gibbons' Latest Novel Is Shy of Divine," Raleigh, N.C., *News & Observer* (11 April 2004).

On the Occasion of My Last Afternoon

Gibbons's sixth novel, *On the Occasion of My Last Afternoon* (1998), reveals a stunning development in her writing interests and a maturing of style. For background material, in January 1995, the author launched a ten-month research project into the Civil War and its impact on women as revealed in histories, letters, and diaries. Intense reading, analysis, writing, and rewriting produced what the editors of the *San Francisco Chronicle* term "a dazzlingly authentic period novel and an unflinching literary indictment" of slavery's proponents and apologists ("Editors," 1998). The reflections of 70-year-old Virginia-born matriarch Emma Garnet Tate Lowell begin in 1900, when she muses on her mismated parents and on her nursing duties in a makeshift Fair Grounds hospital, where staff struggles to treat and house streams of combat casualties. The opening scene, set at Seven Oaks plantation in Bruton Parish on the James River, layers the regional and domestic tensions of 1842—fears among slave owners that Nat Turner stirred from August 22 to October 30, 1831, and 12-year-old Emma's kitchen sausage-making interrupted by the protestations of her father, Samuel P. Goodman Tate, that he didn't intend to slice the throat of Jacob, a foolhardy field hand. Through first-person narrative, the author assesses the role of trauma in her protagonist's character formation.

The breakdown of the Tate family represents in little the dissolution of the plantation South. At the core of Emma's being lie memories of a dear and faultless mother, Alice Tate, who submits to her husband's tantrums as a means of restoring peace and order. Alice's gentility symbolizes the ideal of Southern womanhood ironically embodied in the daughter of a failed cotton factor. Lapsed ideals persist in the household as Alice flees Samuel's rages to visit the Carter plantation, a more stable home five miles away, and as Emma develops the autonomy of the New Woman, the antithesis of the parasitic, self-indulgent Virginia heiress. After Emma's three surviving brothers—Henry, John, and Randolph Tate—leave home to create a trans-Atlantic business in cotton fabrics, Samuel develops in younger daughter Maureen the aristocrat's notion of good breeding and conformity to the Southern paragon of ladyhood. Trained in deportment at a female academy and in singing, Maureen disappoints her father by spurning suitors and remaining unmarried, a suggestion of the sterility of the Southern society and economy in its final years.

Gibbons uses setting as an impetus to change. After marriage in 1847, 17-year-old Emma, Maureen's literary foil, evolves a more realistic style of gentility in the creation of an urban North Carolina home on Blount Street in Raleigh and the rearing of three individualistic daughters, Leslie, Louise, and Mary Lowell, the gems of Emma's motherhood. As war shatters the nation, images of the Wilderness campaign of May 5–7, 1864, mirror her emotional entanglements. Humanitarian concerns force her to strip her Raleigh home of linens, foodstuffs, and amenities to comfort and rehabilitate the wounded. Just as the strain of combat depletes the nation, it steals from Emma her support system, the family cook-housekeeper Clarice Washington in 1863 and, in 1865, Dr. Quincy Lowell, Emma's beloved mate. Gibbons uses these and other losses to strip Emma of dependencies and to disclose inner qualities that revamp courage into defiance and to develop charity into philanthropy.

Through Emma, Gibbons recreates the range of hurts and compromises that inflict on women the terrible price of civil war and social upheaval. At war's end, she enters a spiritually withering widowhood that binds her to Quincy's grave in Boston. In recovery, she returns to Raleigh and outlives her generation. Significantly, with financial and personal loss comes the opportunity to reshape her family and seize selfhood. The final stage in her 70 years attests to the tempering of the New Woman in the crucible of social and economic progress. She reflects on the exigencies of the Reconstruction Era that keep her involved and functioning in the community, to the consternation of a back-biting newspaper editor. On Emma's last afternoon, she, like her contemporaries, can slip into eternity without regret or self-blame for their efforts to restore justice and order to a toppling milieu.

See also **Emma Garnet Tate Lowell; Lowell-Tate Genealogy**

• *Further reading*

"The Editors Recommend," *San Francisco Chronicle* (21 June 1998).

Gibbons, Kaye. *On the Occasion of My Last Afternoon.* New York: G.P. Putnam's Sons, 1998.

Gretlund, Jan Nordby. "In My Own Style: An Interview with Kaye Gibbons," *South Atlantic Review* 65, no. 4 (Fall 2000): 132–154.

Kenney, Michael. "An Author Confronts Her Inner Demons," *Boston Globe* (20 September 1995).

opportunity

In her depiction of ordinary people, Kaye Gibbons sets up prospects of relieving tedium, disappointment, frustration, and want. Her respect for auspicious moments in human lives derives from her own urgency to escape from rural squalor, a milieu she describes in "The Headache," a short-short story issued in June 1987 in the *St. Andrews Review*. In childhood in Nash County, North Carolina, she respected trains, which promised the possibility of escape and adventure far from piedmont tobacco land. She told interviewer Don O'Briant, book editor of the *Atlanta Journal-Constitution*, "I didn't see any reason to grow up and cloister myself in some farm shack, freeze in the winter, sweat in the summer, fight flies, and eat cold collards for the sake of art or anything else (O'Briant, 1989). Paradoxically, she left the farm, but transformed into literature her recall of confrontations, choices, and conversations that echo the environment that shaped her life.

From the beginning of Gibbons's career and the publication of a first novel, *Ellen Foster* (1987), the author has maintained respect for characters who recognize and seize good fortune. Ellen, the title character, excels at outdistancing adults in ridding herself of a faulty home life. Her innate yearning for self-betterment translates into sensible actions—maintaining an upbeat attitude, eating balanced meals frozen onto trays, reading classic literature from the county bookmobile, listing goals, and studying minutiae under her toy microscope, a symbol of introspection and vision. At school, she protects her fragile psyche from intrusive questioning by teachers and, on Tuesdays, by the school psychologist. At church in 1970, she spies a candidate for foster mother, a dignified, confident woman capable of ridding Ellen of the ugliness of her first decade. To the child, so decent and admirable a person is "all that I needed to grab" (Gibbons, 1987, 57). The prehensile quality of Ellen's aim implies both desperation and a willingness to redeem herself from lovelessness and insecurity.

In Gibbons's second novel, *A Virtuous Woman* (1989), opportunity relieves an adult insecurity—the despair of the landless in a milieu dominated by the landed gentry. Farm laborer Burr Stanley jeopardizes future marital and parental happiness by accepting the offer of 48 acres of prime loam. In the risky exchange, he agrees to wed Tiny Fran Hoover, the foul-mouthed pregnant daughter of Frances and Lonnie Hoover, a prosperous and respected farm couple on Milk Farm Road. The meaning of ownership prevails during Burr's dealings with a runaway wife and her bastard son Roland, who embarrass and irk Burr and his neighbors. A quarter century after accepting the two-edged bride price, Burr has an occasion to help a desperate friend, "Blinking" Jack Ernest Stokes, a 65-year-old childless widower who has parented the Stanleys' poorly mothered daughter June. Out of gratitude, Burr awards Jack the land that Jack has tenanted but never owned. The passage of opportunity from one neighbor to another suggests that altruism forms a meandering stream through their rural lives, watering withered spirits with unforeseen bounty.

In Gibbons's third and fourth novels—*A Cure for Dreams* (1991) and *Charms for the Easy Life* (1993)—the theme of opportunity yields both humor and humanism. During the Great Depression, Lottie O'Cadhain Davies, the wife of a money-mad farmer and miller, creates opportunity by hoodwinking her husband Charles with claims of frugality. In addition to rifling his pockets for cash, she convinces him that expenditures on organdy, chiffon, venise lace, beaded English netting, and taffeta save him money on costlier ginghams for the making of her and daughter Betty's wardrobes. An astute observer of her mother's deceptions, Betty develops her own style of opportunism by demanding autonomy during the birthing of her daughter, Marjorie Polly Randolph, during World War II. On November 25, 1942, while Lottie is away from home and Betty's husband, Herman Randolph, serves in the Pacific war aboard the U.S.S. *Hornet*, Betty conspires with midwife Polly Deal to manage a home delivery without Lottie's intrusion. The domestic balance of power remains intact despite Betty's grasp of the reins to establish her own domain in the family matrilineage. The reshaping of opportunity day by day stabilizes the all-woman family for two more years until Herman's return. Gibbons garnishes the rosy conclusion with an assurance that baby Marjorie "thrived on all the attention," a testimonial to the continuum of opportunity that favors a loving household (Gibbons, 1991, 171).

Charms for the Easy Life, another all-female saga, describes the pragmatism of Charlie Kate Birch, a self-educated healer who makes a tidy living from pulling teeth, treating broken hearts and failing bodies, laying out the dead, birthing babies, and dispensing herbs, iron pills, and curatives to needy patients in coastal Pasquotank County on the Albemarle Sound and in Raleigh in central North Carolina. Although her daughter, Sophia Snow Birch, has little skill in finances or medical practice, she attends Charlie Kate on house calls and steers the car over rutted roads. After daughter Margaret reaches late girlhood, she joins the duo and follows her grandmother's directives concerning hygiene, diagnosis, and treatment of the sick. Energized by on-the-job training, Sophia and Margaret establish their own methods of advancement.

Like the nation, the Birch family thrives during the short breather between the Great Depression and the onset of World War II. For Sophia, the landing of a potential husband, businessman Richard Baines, during the intermission of the film *Gone with the Wind* (1939) depicts her reliance on romance, whether in books, on the screen, over the radio, or in the flesh. Margaret, who is slow to attract boyfriends, reaches for opportunity at the Durham veterans' hospital in 1942, when she reads and writes letters for wounded soldiers. Margaret's intent to snag Tom Hawkings, III, and to attend college later in the war years suggests an amalgam of matriarchal talents and ambitions. Like Charlie Kate, Margaret educates herself through reading and studies the possibilities of a medical degree. Like Sophia, Margaret also directs an eye toward domestic happiness, which Charlie Kate predicts from Margaret's acceptance by the elite Hawkings clan. The final scene, which depicts the granddaughter's reverence for her grandmother's corpse, accentuates a feminist dynastic strength, the competence that the elder female generation passes to the younger.

Opportunity in *Sights Unseen* (1995), Gibbons's autobiographical reflection on bipolarity, derives from desperation. In the narration of 12-year-old Hattie Barnes, years of neglect and trial distance her from her manic-depressive mother Maggie. Coddled and defended by her father-in-law, Grandfather Barnes, Maggie pampers herself with shopping sprees for shoes, dresses, and furniture. The spiral of deranged behaviors reaches a breaking point in 1967 after she runs down a pedestrian with her car in Rocky Mount, North Carolina, to halt seizure of her soul. Frederick Barnes, wearied past coping, opts to institutionalize his wife at the Duke Hospital psychiatric ward. The admission of madness to the world leaves the family resolute, but terrified of the effects of psychotherapy and eight electroconvulsive shock treatments. For Maggie, awakening to a normal life follows a swim through amnesia and re-courtship by her husband. Tentatively, the family turns Maggie's reclamation into joyful welcome to a normal female head of household. Hattie reflects on the 15 years of wellness that precedes her mother's death in 1982 from a fall down stairs. The propitious period awards Maggie, Frederick, cook-housekeeper Pearl Wiggins, and the children a long-deserved reunion with sanity.

In Gibbons's first historical novel, *On the Occasion of My Last Afternoon* (1998), opportunity takes the form of wartime crises. Forcing the emergence of maturity and self-direction in narrator Emma Garnet Tate Lowell are the exigencies of the Civil War. In retreat from a childhood oppressed by the twisted behaviors of her father, Samuel P. Goodman Tate, in 1847, 17-year-old Emma grasps a hopeful future through marriage to Dr. Quincy Lowell, a Boston-born humanitarian who grooms her for a life of grace and service to others. In adulthood, Emma finds herself pressed to the breaking point by streams of wounded arriving from Civil War battlegrouds at Big Bethel Church, Virginia (June 10, 1861), and the first battle of Manassas, Virginia (July 21, 1861) by the train-load to the Fair Grounds hospital in Raleigh, North Carolina. The times direct her toward nurse care. She develops the backbone to rebuke an incompetent surgeon for sloppy stitches and to challenge Samuel's brutishness after he shelters at her home in June 1862 from wartime upheaval. Gibbons portrays opportunity for sheltered women in terms of willingness to embrace the moment and to turn historical flux into a training ground for life and identity enhancement.

In an historical period when Union nursing director Dorothea Dix rejected social butterflies for volunteer hospital service, the novel extols the New Woman as the foil of the genteel, apathetic lady of fashion. Unlike her compliant younger sister Maureen, Emma Garnet becomes an urban go-getter, a decisive, financially astute investor in the New South. Freed of the strictures that impaired the plantation belle, she outdistances neighbors in maintaining Clarice Washington as a paid black housekeeper, in freeing three slaves, Charlie, Martha, and Mavis, and in accepting the inevitability of the post-emancipation economic order. By spending the Lowell fortune on job opportunities for needy Southerners at a pottery, bakery, and clothing factory, Emma reaps satisfactions that sustain her in old age. Undaunted by threat, she chuckles at doggerel from the Ku Klux Klan that warns, "Dere nigger-lover.... We no were you live" (Gibbons, 1998, 270). Reflecting on her enterprising daughters and grandchildren, she is pleased that they mirror her altruism and liberal opinions.

Gibbons's seventh novel, *Divining Women* (2004), again validates the feminist motif of investment in other people's happiness. For Mary Oliver, a 22-year-old graduate student at Radcliffe sidelined in May 1917 by World War I, opportunity comes in the form of a mission of mercy on September 30, 1918, to her aunt, Maureen Carlton Ross. In the last 50 days of Maureen's difficult first pregnancy, Mary discovers that being needed rewards the cared-for and the caretaker. While maneuvering Maureen out of the clutches of her destructive husband Troop, Mary experiences the vicarious thrill of the new mother's labor and delivery. Adjacent to Maureen at the height of contractions, Mary observes the "surging of all the elements," the muscular force that ends nine months of anticipation (Gibbons, 2004, 182). Awestruck by raw female courage and determination, Mary respects Maureen as the exemplary mother who, on November 8, 1918, survives birthing and the loss of her stillborn infant, Ella Eloise Ross. Indoctrinated into the mysteries of anguish and sacrifice, Mary shapes the childbed event into an enduring source of woman-to-woman love.

Gibbons's return to her first heroine in a sequel, *The Life All Around Me by Ellen Foster* (2006), answers questions left hanging in *Ellen Foster*. Among the loose threads are 15-year-old Ellen's yearning for emotional and intellectual wholeness, her Aunt Nadine Nelson's seizure of valuable family assets, and Laura's intent to protect Ellen from more trauma. The text honors Ellen's assertiveness on September 20, 1974, in an introductory letter to Dr. Derek Curtis Bok, president of Harvard University, whom she petitions for early college admission. Trial and error introduce her to a whiz kid camp at Johns Hopkins University in Baltimore. Opportunities bob past, offering home-schooling from readings in her bedroom library, the chance of being Starletta's pseudo-mother, and the puppy-dog loyalty and marriage proposal of Stuart, Ellen's first beau. Gibbons hones extraneous events to the long delayed confrontation with Aunt Nadine, who admits to defrauding her niece of a sizeable inheritance. Apart from the issues of money and land, Ellen longs for a more affirming opportunity to dig into the past of Shine, her mentally crippled mother. A box of personal belongings introduces Ellen to her parents in early marriage and discloses the frail mental state that precipitates the 40-year-old Shine's suicide in March 1969 from an overdose of prescription digitalis. Relieved of guilt for failing to rescue her mother, Ellen relaxes into the love of Laura, her foster mother, one of the author's most stalwart maternal figures. The sequel pleases fans of the Ellen character by developing her rescue into a win-win success story.

See also **achievement**

• *Further reading*

Ardis, Ann L., and Leslie W. Lewis. *Women's Experience of Modernity 1875–1945*. Baltimore: Johns Hopkins University Press, 2003.
Gibbons, Kaye. *A Cure for Dreams*. New York: Algonquin, 1991.
_____. *Divining Women*. New York: G.P. Putnam's Sons, 2004.
_____. *Ellen Foster*. New York: Algonquin Press, 1987.
_____. *On the Occasion of My Last Afternoon*. New York: G.P. Putnam's Sons, 1998.
O'Briant, Don. "Writing a Most 'Virtuous' Art for Gibbons," *Atlanta Journal-Constitution* (18 June 1989).
Richardson, Angelique, and Chris Willis, eds. *The New Woman in Fiction and in Fact: Fin-de-Siècle Feminisms*. London: Palgrave Macmillan, 2002.
Stephens, Spaine. "Nash County Still Inspires Gibbons," *Rocky Mount* (N.C.) *Telegram* (24 March 2004).

order

Through writing and speaking, Kaye Gibbons restructures a crisis-ridden childhood to shape a better life for herself. Her retreat from unstinting manual labor on a tobacco farm in Nash County, North Carolina, into authorship of classic feminist literature precipitated what she refers to as a drive to "set order to the universe" (MacLellan, 1998). Contributing to her success is a knack for "aristotelian order," a reference to the classic Greek unities of time, place, and action as described in *Aris-*

totle's Poetics (ca. 340 B.C.) (McFadden, 1997). At the beginning of her career, she told poet Dannye Romine, the book editor for the *Charlotte* (N.C.) *Observer*, "Other people exercise to order their days. I use language to order my past. I feel like if I can get all of that in order then I have a network for the future and everything will be OK" (Romine, 1987). In ordering motifs, the author's novels laud characters like midwife Polly Deal, Irish-American materfamilias Bridget O'Donough O'Cadhain, freedwoman foster parent Clarice Washington, neighbors Lottie O'Cadhain Davies and June Stanley, foster mothers Laura and Ruth Hartley, and cook-housekeepers Pearl Wiggins, Sudie Bee, and Mamie, all of whom impose order on disrupted lives.

For the title character of *Ellen Foster* (1987), making sense of child neglect and brutishness is more than a ten-year-old can manage. She prefers action to doctrine. After her father Bill signs over the family farm to his brothers Ellis and Rudolph, they leave cash each month that Ellen seizes from the mailbox and allots to utilities, food, and incidentals before Bill can waste it on bootleg liquor. Her success with monetary order overlays a more daunting emotional struggle with tattered relatives—Aunt Betsy, Aunt Nadine Nelson, Cousin Dora, and a maternal grandmother—who discount and reject Ellen. Rather than explain them to an intrusive school psychologist during every-Tuesday counseling sessions, she prefers to let the past swirl in her mind. She founders under the brain-wearying task of analyzing a father who cows his dying wife and who eyes his little girl like the wolf sizing up Little Red Riding Hood. New Years Eve, 1969, a symbolic moment in her tenth year, ends the constant tension. Instead of setting fire to the house and immolating Bill and his dissolute pals, she reverts to the fight-or-flight instinct that sends her scurrying from home to home in search of the perfect foster mother. By seeking a worthy rescuer, Ellen intends to pass along to an adult a responsibility that exceeds a child's abilities.

In Gibbons's text, the reordering of Ellen's universe demands both emotional and material fundamentals. To end the cycle of domestic catastrophe, she selects as an adult mediator Laura, a foster mom who superintends domestic tidiness in a brick house with a green lawn and neatly squared hedges, precursors of the greening of Ellen's future and the squaring of family accounts. While napping in her new bedroom, Ellen lies at peace among mother-made adornments—pink-checked curtains and pillow shams, elements of female thrift and creativity in a girlish hue suggestive of innocence. Ellen makes note of the matching decor, a portent that normal childhood may soon match her age and needs. The foster mother rectifies the child's displacement by providing a warm winter coat, freshly shampooed hair, a home-made lunch, and transportation aboard a school bus that stops at the door. The sense of welcome and harmony offers respite from waves of alienation and familial chaos that threaten to engulf an immature orphan.

In a second novel, *A Virtuous Woman* (1989), Gibbons reprises the socioeconomic contrasts of Ellen's world by juxtaposing the decorum and prosperity of the Pitts family alongside the slovenliness and sorry behavior of the Hoovers. After Ruby Pitts demeans herself at age 18 by leaving a home among the landed gentry to marry 27-year-old migrant worker John Woodrow, she plunges into squalor reminiscent of Erskine Caldwell's seamy Deep South shocker *Tobacco Road* (1941). Reduced to domestic drudgery, she scrubs and neatens the Hoover house and endures

John's gibes that she once was "little Miss Vanderbilt," a sneering reference to her gentrified upbringing (Gibbons, 1989, 40). Her labors reach crisis proportions before the wedding of Tiny Fran Hoover, an overweight slug already queasy with morning sickness and too trifling to do more than get in the way. Ruby's future husband, 40-year-old "Blinking" Jack Ernest Stokes, labors in the Hoovers' yard and indicts Lonnie Hoover for allowing his home and daughter to slide along toward disaster. Jack wonders why Lonnie doesn't clamp down on Tiny Fran's misdeeds by taking her to an abortionist. The author poses these examples of personal and domestic disarray to contrast the tidy oasis that Ruby and Jack inhabit after they marry.

Gibbons asserts a Southern stereotype, the ever-faithful black maid-of-all-work who forms a symbiotic relationship with a parasitic white family. For Ruby Pitts, the savior of her childhood is Sudie Bee, the cook-domestic from whom Ruby learns "the meaning of clean" (*Ibid.*, 52). In Ruby's recall of a well-run home, Sudie catches, kills, plucks, and scalds a turkey for the oven and beats a carpet clean faster than it can be vacuumed. Gibbons turns the paradigm of the industrious maid into humor after Ruby's death, when Jack hires Mavis Washington, a subversion of his expectations of restored domestic order. The brief comic relief prefaces an undeniable fact for the 65-year-old widower — without Ruby or a capable hireling to take charge, he must fend for himself. His ineptitude and infantile behavior plunge him into withdrawal to a bare mattress in a dirty house to eat corn flakes and canned soup, drink bourbon, and watch Roadrunner cartoons on television. His only relief from sorrow is a sprinkle of lilac dusting powder, which soothes him with a baby-like fragrance and a fantasy that Ruby has returned as a "haint." The plot resolution implies that Jack cannot survive without the volunteerism of June Stanley, a filial female caretaker whom Ruby groomed from childhood through foster mothering. An embodiment of Ruby's foresight, her apron, a symbol of domestic commitment to order and cleanliness, engirths June like loving arms.

In a third novel, *A Cure for Dreams* (1991), Gibbons's gendered definitions of order vary. For Irish immigrant Lottie O'Cadhain, in 1918, escaping the tug of war between her father Sheamus and mother, Bridget O'Donough O'Cadhain, begins with teen fantasies of a chivalric rescuer and ends badly with Lottie's marriage to Quaker farmer Charles Davies. Retrieved from an Irish-American enclave on the Cumberland River in Bell County, Kentucky, the bride lives on Milk Farm Road in a seemingly harmonious house in piedmont North Carolina. To balance domestic affairs with a workaholic skinflint, Lottie develops lying and deception to art forms that subvert rural Southern patriarchy. The four-stage matrilineage extends female wiles to Lottie's daughter, Betty Davies Randolph, who learns from observation how to outfox a male tyrant. Gibbons poses a standard obstruction to female independence by increasing Lottie's ordering of Betty's personal affairs, including vetoing as boyfriends the scruffy Luther Miracle and Stanton, a razzle-dazzle date addicted to Neurol Compound. To balance female powers, on November 25, 1942, Betty must order her own household by giving birth to Marjorie Polly Randolph in Lottie's absence.

To regulate the four-woman home, Gibbons chooses to triangulate powers. Contributing candor and advice to the new mother, midwife-housekeeper Polly Deal offers an alternate adult female perspective on the difficulties of scheduling duties and allotting control in an all-woman household. Polly's mastery of direction falls short of the expectations of a town lady seeking a laundress specializing in fine linens. Polly "did in good order and sent back and all was well" until the employer slaps her for scorching a handkerchief (Gibbons, 1991, 133). Polly regroups by removing laundry from her list of skills and by focusing on cooking, midwifery, and baby care. In a period of global catastrophe, Betty makes similar alterations by managing a husbandless home until the return of Herman Randolph, a sailor aboard the U.S.S. *Hornet* during the Pacific war. The theme of compromise suits the early 1940s, when women survive loss and hardship by redefining and reshaping domestic order.

The black maid, a peripheral character in *A Virtuous Woman, A Cure for Dreams,* and *Charms for the Easy Life* (1993), epitomizes the white notion of organization. As is often true in domestic novels, Maveen, a domestic similar in responsibilities to Sudie Bee and Polly Deal, remains in the background of the third novel until her retirement at age 70 to her sister's home in the next county. Protagonist Charlie Kate Birch, a self-educated herbalist-midwife, finds no suitable replacement and reveals true affection for Maveen after learning of her illness from terminal stomach cancer, a violation of the healer's ideal. A failed attempt to obtain hospital care for Maveen precedes Charlie Kate's deathbed vigil. The partial restoration of order concludes with the healer soothing Maveen in her last hours by rubbing her torso and limbs with alcohol to bring down her temperature. Charlie Kate charges a unique Southern population for the old woman's needless agony—"white people who seemed to earn a living automatically," a generalized description of the aristocratic physician who discounts Maveen's suffering (Gibbons, 1993, 88). The reference to the elite living in Anderson Heights in north central Raleigh, North Carolina, implies most of the South, where homes attain elegance through the labors of low-paid black servants.

In a farm microcosm in *Sights Unseen* (1995), an entire household lives a nightmare of emotional unrest relieved by the supervision of a black cook-domestic similar in value to Sudie Bee and Maveen. Gibbons pictures a close and loving extended family damaged by intense mad scenes as viewed by a 12-year-old Hattie Barnes. A critic for the London *Times* characterizes the narrative as fraught with "painful and disturbing episodes [that] acquire a surreal humor" ("Review," 15 June 1996). In a home constantly in uproar from Maggie Barnes's bipolar states, Pearl Wiggins, the housekeeper and master at reorganizing chaos, assuages fears in Hattie and calms Maggie's husband Frederick with as much oil-on-troubled-waters as she can muster. Hattie, looking back from adulthood, speculates on the swirling vortex in her mother's brain—a mystic "music of the spheres" that leaves her absentminded and unpredictable (Gibbons, 1995, 84). Because of her aptitude for appeasing Maggie, Pearl has time to locate missing objects and to soft-pedal dissension. Unlike Pearl, who functions amid frenzy, Hattie exhibits the intellectual's coping methods by retreating to her room to arrange her belongings and to fantasize that her father can placate Maggie with a reassuring squeeze of the hand. For Frederick Barnes, the restoration of calm to his wife requires humoring her with sexual dalliance or dosing her with three tablets of Sominex. Even after quiet overcomes Maggie, he feels like a soldier snatching sleep on a troop ship. Until Maggie's healing in 1967 from psychotherapy and eight weeks of electroconvulsive shock therapy at Duke Hospital, the image of wartime discomfort is an apt description of the Barnes household, where subduing Maggie requires battle readiness.

In a shift to historical fiction, Gibbons uses order to stratify Virginia plantation women in *On the Occasion of My Last Afternoon* (1998). In the winter hog-butchering season at Seven Oaks in 1842, narrator Emma Garnet Tate Lowell labors with slaves under the direction of kitchen supervisor Clarice Washington to pat out sausage, fry cracklings, and boil chitterlings. Emma's introduction to the recycling of paltry swine parts into food prefigures her adult service to Civil War casualties, during which she enhances volunteerism with practicality. For her mother, Alice Tate, a sweet-natured plantation wife who prefers quiet to bustle, the best retreat from slaughter is a five-mile ride along the James River road to the Carter plantation, where pigs are already killed, their meat preserved, and equipment and utensils neatly stored away. To escape the outrages of blood odors and slave shouts at home, Alice settles in with the Carter sisters to tat, needlepoint, quilt, and spice oranges into pomanders, all symbols of female-generated uniformity and regularity. She glances over fashion layouts in *Godey's Lady's Book*, a period landmark of ladylike grace and dignity that Sarah Josepha Hale edited from 1837 until 1877. The brief respite fails to allay discontent in Alice, whose husband, Samuel P. Goodman Tate, foments perpetual anarchy.

Gibbons projects from the Tates' disarrayed lives the next phase of Southern history. The novel's narrator restructures her life in similar fashion to her mother's escapes—by marrying a peace-loving Bostonian in 1847 and, at age 17, by journeying to urban Raleigh, North Carolina, far from the turbulence of her tidewater home. The edenic sanctum on Blount Street, efficient staff, and three loving daughters—Leslie, Louise, and Mary Lowell—come at a price for Emma, who lashes her spirit with remorse for abandoning Alice to Samuel's atrocities. The subtext parallels his prideful agitations with the rumblings of secession and civil war that erupt on April 12–13, 1861, with the Confederate firing on Fort Sumter, South Carolina. For Emma, combat poses a new challenge — the admission and treatment of trainloads of injured soldiers at a makeshift hospital comprising a clutch of tents raised at the fair grounds. In her finer moments, she confers hope and serenity on critical cases. As the war reaches its destructive depths in 1864 from the massacre at Fort Pillow, Tennessee (April 12, 1864), the battles of the Wilderness, Virginia (May 5–7, 1864) and Cold Harbor, Virginia, (May 31–June 12, 1864), her family extends its oasis to recuperating soldiers, who fill her bedrooms and parlor to capacity. Her refusal to be stymied exemplifies contributions to the war effort by orderly homemakers. Preparing them for ungovernable influxes of the sick and maimed is traditional womanly training in domestic structure.

The reinstatement of political order comes slowly to Emma's homeland. After confronting Samuel for a lifetime of annoyance and evil-doing, she begins facing the loss of loved ones who sustain her. Samuel's untidy demise on the parlor sofa in June 1862 by a lethal dose of digitalis precedes the deaths of Clarice, Quincy, and Emma's younger sister Maureen. The revival of harmony requires self-renewal, which Emma manages through her childhood mentoring in kitchen order, a preliminary to self-balance. Reconditioned to food preparation and philanthropic service, she establishes a new rhythm to her days, which extend from 1865 to 1900 and her 70th year. In the final paragraphs, she defines order as a healing reconciliation of past frustrations and anger. With death approaching, she can achieve her husband's charge that she "face it all dry-eyed," the novelist's term for stoic restraint (Gibbons, 1998, 273).

Through contrasting settings similar to the plantation and urban manse in *On the Occasion of My Last Afternoon*, Gibbons's seventh novel, *Divining Women* (2004), discloses the roots of domestic disorder. Narrator Mary Oliver, a 22-year-old graduate student at Radcliffe, grows up in a loving extended family on Dupont Circle in Washington, D.C. Management of crises— her 16-year-old brother Daniel's suicide and the death of their father, Grammar Oliver, in 1913, widow Martha Greene Oliver's establishment of a home apart from her parents and in-laws, and the onset of World War I in 1917 and the 1918 influenza pandemic — precedes a daunting personal challenge, the tending of Mary's aunt, Maureen Carlton Ross, during a difficult pregnancy. Prepared for the quirks of Maureen's husband, Troop Ross, on September 30, 1918, Mary arrives by train in Elm City, North Carolina. She quickly surveys Maureen's needs and begins chipping away at Troop's clever scheme to force his wife into an unnecessary hysterectomy to stifle her will. The household undercurrent shows outsiders the adoration of a husband who engulfs his wife with daily deliveries of roses. To accelerate her emotional decline, he forces her to list dates and hybrid rose varieties in her blue notebook, a symbol of sham order that cloaks his daily forays on her sanity.

The disparity between male and female concepts of order empowers *Divining Women* with historical accuracy. When turmoil seizes Maureen's mind, Troop calmly echoes his diagnosis of "female hysteria," a period term for what Betty Friedan, godmother of the feminist movement, called "the problem that has no name" — "a strange stirring, a sense of dissatisfaction, a yearning that women suffered in the middle of the twentieth century in the United States" (Gibbons, 2004, 62; Friedan, 2001, 15). The "problem" arising from the diminution of females found its classic voicings in Henrik Ibsen's play *A Doll's House* (1879) and in a wife's postpartum depression in Charlotte Perkins Gilman's Gothic short story "The Yellow Wallpaper" (1892), a depiction of insanity generated by enforced solitude. In the Ross household, Mary Oliver turns the "problem" into a rallying cry that rejuvenates Maureen. In the falling action, on November 9, 1918, Mary and Mamie, the Ross family's maid-housekeeper, support an abandonment of Troop at his pretentious manse, leaving him with no one to maintain his sham refinement. A new basis of cohesion for Maureen derives from Mary's love and the courage to escape disorder without a backward glance.

In her first sequel, *The Life All Around Me by Ellen Foster* (2006), Gibbons returns to her foundling four years later in September 1974 at age 15 to examine the realignment of a fractured life. The story indicates that relieving a foster child's terrors is not so simple as a TV re-run of *The Waltons*. Symbolic stability takes the form of neatly trimmed hedges, clean brick steps, bleached tile, and a tidy sitting room and guest room. The composure of household routine allows for human error, such as a scoot to the kitchen on the leather ottoman, retreats from chores, and gorging on Little Debbie cakes. Significant to Laura's mothering is the floral Mamie Eisenhower chair she purchases for Ellen's room as a respite and place to gather thoughts. In reference to the neatness of Ellen's mid-teens, author Marjorie Gellhorn Sa'adah, a critic for the *Los Angeles Times*, states the misgivings of other reviewers that "something is awry" (Sa'adah, 2006). She surmises that Gibbons, having lived through Ellen's past challenges, protects her fictional persona from "any more of life" by imposing an unlikely adjustment to unhealthy family alliances and to Ellen's future prospects (*Ibid.*).

See also **"The Yellow Wallpaper"**

• *Further reading*

Friedan, Betty. *The Feminine Mystique.* New York: W.W. Norton, 2001.
Gibbons, Kaye. *Charms for the Easy Life.* New York: Putnam, 1993.
_____. *A Cure for Dreams.* New York: Algonquin, 1991.
_____. *Ellen Foster.* New York: Algonquin Press, 1987.
_____. *The Life All Around Me by Ellen Foster.* New York: Harcourt, 2006.
_____. *On the Occasion of My Last Afternoon.* New York: G.P. Putnam's Sons, 1998.
_____. *Sights Unseen.* New York: G.P. Putnam's Sons, 1995.
_____. *A Virtuous Woman.* Chapel Hill, N.C.: Algonquin Press, 1989.
MacLellan, Erin. "More on Gibbons," *Greensboro* (N.C.) *News & Record* (12 July 1998).
McFadden, Kay. "N.C. Writers Showcased in Hallmark TV Films," *Charlotte* (N.C.) *Observer* (23 November 1997).
Monteith, Sharon. *Advancing Sisterhood?: Interracial Friendships in Contemporary Southern Fiction.* Athens: University of Georgia Press, 2000.
Munafo, Giavanna. "Colored Biscuits: Reconstructing Whiteness and the Boundaries of 'Home' in Kaye Gibbons's *Ellen Foster,*" *Women, America, and Movement.* ed. Susan L. Roberson. Columbia: University of Missouri Press, 1998, pp. 38–61.
"Review: *Sights Unseen,*" London *Times* (15 June 1996).
Romine, Dannye. "Literature Liberates: Raleigh's Kaye Gibbons Finds Freedoms, Affirmation in 1st Novel," *Charlotte* (N.C.) *Observer* (26 April 1987).
Sa'adah, Marjorie Gellhorn. "You Can't Go Home Again," *Los Angeles Times* (8 January 2006): R7.

parenthood

Author Kaye Gibbons grew up outside the requisites for normality. In a personal essay, "What I Won by Losing: Lessons from the 1977 Miss North Carolina National Teenager Pageant" (2005), she remarks that coming of age amid indigence, neglect, family violence, and unstable and alcoholic parents gave her a will to achieve. She admits that writing autobiographical novels helps her untangle the strands of regret and bitterness at past strife. In direct response to readers, in 1997, she urged people to open homes and hearts to the young. In her words, "Our children were not born with the skills needed to parent themselves. That's the most unfair task we could ever require of them" (Brennan, 1997). She stressed the centrality of child guidance over "many dark, lonely and confusing passages in the world," an allusion to the sufferings of her most compelling waif, Ellen Foster (*Ibid.*).

Gibbons's depictions of fictional parents cover a range of human situations—Lucille Womble's concern for her son's shame in "The Headache" (June 1987), the bootlegger Bill's tantrum and exposed genitals outside his daughter's elementary school in *Ellen Foster* (1987), and Frances and Lonnie Hoover's tolerance of their slatternly, amoral daughter Tiny Fran in *A Virtuous Woman* (1989). Contrasting negative scenarios are the joy-filled mother-daughter romps of Lottie O'Cadhain Davies and Betty at the cloth store in *A Cure for Dreams* (1991) and a loving, if unconventional upbringing of Margaret by her mother, Sophia Snow Birch, and grandmother Charlie Kate Birch in *Charms for the Easy Life* (1993). Idiosyncratic parenting reflects the faults and triumphs of adults— Lucille's worry over a failing farm, Bill's alcoholism and brooding hostility, Lottie's advance from failed matrimony in 1918 to devoted motherhood, and Charlie Kate's shielding of Margaret from Sophia's moony romanticism. In the author's view, the chain of lineage passes on sins of omission and commission to subsequent generations. Fortunately for Margaret, her grandmother's ill-chosen union with an illiterate bargeman in 1902 generates a clan revolt against dependence on men for financial and emotional wholeness. Like her grandmother, Margaret develops poise and efficiency in dealing with shifts in personal fortune, even her mother's elopement to South Carolina with businessman Richard Baines on Christmas Eve, 1942, and the unforeseen death of Charlie Kate the next night.

Gibbons orchestrates a complex legacy of parenting styles in *Sights Unseen* (1995), and in her first historical novel, *On the Occasion of My Last Afternoon* (1998). The first example relates the invalidism of a family beset by the bipolar anguish of Maggie Barnes, an unsound female head of household. In trying to cope with her excesses of despair and exuberance, her husband Frederick, son Freddy, and daughter Hattie exhibit their own neuroses. While housekeeper Pearl Wiggins cooks, cleans, and tends to Maggie, narrator Hattie Barnes holes up in her room to read and study. Unlike her older brother, who suffices on hermitism and fantasies about pin-ups and Vincent Price movies, Hattie must venture out to seek Pearl's mothering and to test Maggie's temporary self-control for evidence of parental love. In the background, Frederick Barnes exerts more energy on appeasing Maggie than on fathering his children. Hattie's commitment to the mother-daughter paradigm earns a reward — the tentative realignment of familial order in 1967 after Maggie undergoes psychotherapy and eight sessions of electroconvulsive shock treatment at Duke Hospital. The triumph of hope graces the troubling novel, an autobiographical outgrowth of the precarious parenting that Gibbons recalls from childhood.

In historical fiction, *On the Occasion of My Last Afternoon*, Gibbons poses irresponsible parenting as a model of national misalignment. Through first-person memoir, narrator Emma Garnet Tate Lowell reflects on mixed messages from her soft-voiced mother, Alice Tate, contentious father, Samuel P. Goodman Tate, and take-charge surrogate mother, freedwoman Clarice Washington, the cook-housekeeper at Seven Oaks plantation. As kind as Alice, resolute as Samuel, and pragmatic as Clarice, in 1847, Emma readies herself for parenthood at age 17 by marrying Dr. Quincy Lowell, a fatherly mate who cultivates his wife's best qualities. While rearing daughters Leslie, Louise, and Mary, before the Civil War, the Lowells murmur their personal concerns during evenings on the veranda, an oasis of calm in which to sip Madeira and reflect on their domestic philosophy. Despite the turmoil of sectionalism, the couple concurs on eliciting excellence through home-schooling and free reading among the classics. As a result, the daughters prove themselves well anchored to their parents' liberal views at war's height, when the household stretches and realigns itself to accommodate political and social transition. In 1900 in her 70th year, Emma congratulates herself for quality mothering and for begetting a new tier of the family tree that maintains the family's standards of morality. Through the sifted memories of Emma's declining hours, Gibbons elevates parenthood from duty to a crowning glory that decks maternal triumphs.

An amusing example of parenting introduces Mary Oliver, narrator of *Divining Women* (2004), Gibbons's seventh novel. Before plunging the protagonist into conflict, the author pictures a female view of a "wide and deep universe," (Gibbons, 2004, 13). From her widowed mother, Martha Greene Oliver, narrator Mary, a 22-year-old graduate student at Radcliffe, learns to evaluate women's backgrounds and traits by examining their posture, outfits, and facial expression. From grandmothers Leslie Greene and Louise Canton Oliver and from grandfather Leonard Oliver, Mary acquires a taste for divination and a respect for the ghosts that pass through the family manse on Dupont Circle in Washington, D.C. In contrast to a benignly extended family that includes nudist Toby Greene, Gibbons poses Nora Worthy Ross, a neurotic harpy who cultivates hostility in her son Troop against Toby and the entire Greene clan. By demanding entitlements and handouts, she nourishes a narcissism in Troop that stifles love, rendering him incapable of intimacy with his wife Maureen or of sorrow for their first child, Ella Eloise Ross, who is stillborn on November 8, 1918. In retrospect, Maureen is glad that her daughter does not know Troops's glowering hate. Gibbons replaces Troop in Maureen's life with late-arriving letters from Maureen's mother in Yazoo City, Mississippi, and with flight to Washington, where Mary's beloved household extends welcome and acceptance to a foster daughter.

In her first sequel, *The Life All Around Me by Ellen Foster* (2006), Gibbons juxtaposes model foster parenting with realistic views of birth parenting. Laura, the volunteer mother of Ellen and other needy girls, shares the pro-child attitudes of Starletta's widowed mother, who tends to her retarded daughter while seeking a degree in social work. Contrasting the two are their literary foils, Stuart's parents, Martha's father, and Aunt Nadine Nelson, the widowed mother of Dora and grandmother of Claire Ellen. Stuart's life in a squalid home suffers more from the angry outbursts of his mother than from the lack of parenting from his distant father, a junk dealer. Martha's father vegetates before televised football games, leaving Martha to work at the family store and Martha's mother to retreat to Laura's house for naps and refreshment. More insidious is Nadine's implication of Dora in identity theft and fraud, two crimes that outpace Dora's sins of fornication with a circus xylophone player and conceiving an illegitimate daughter. The lapses in personal and parental ethics serve the novel as proofs that Laura and Starletta's mom deserve honor for molding character in their daughters.

See also **foster parenting; men; mothering; women**

• *Further reading*

Brennan, Patricia. "Mixing Pathos and Spunk Jena Malone Plays a Child Looking for Love," *Washington Post* (14 December 1997).

Gibbons, Kaye. *Divining Women*. New York: G.P. Putnam's Sons, 2004.
_____. "What I Won by Losing: Lessons from the 1977 Miss North Carolina National Teenager Pageant," www.harcourtbooks.com/EllenFoster/essay_whatiwon.asp, 2005.

Pete & Shirley

In 1995, David Perkins, former book editor of the Raleigh, North Carolina, *News & Observer*, launched a literary lark, *Pete & Shirley: The Great Tar Heel Novel*, a serial murder mystery written in 18 chapters by 17 North Carolina authors. Perkins passed off the writers' romp as the result of gathering authors in "his literary pick-up, [passing] around some moonshine, and [waiting] to see what happens" (Perkins, 1995). Participants included editor and novelist Laura Argiri, award-winning columnist and nonfiction writer Jerry Bledsoe, poet and fiction writer Michael Chitwood, Durham-based humor novelist Clyde Edgerton, poet-novelist and university professor Fred Chappell, Wilmington journalist and composition teacher Philip Gerard, award-winning fiction writer Marianne Gingher, dramatist and poet Jaki Shelton Green, columnist and novelist David Guy, novelist and teacher William McCranor Henderson, mystery and short story author Margaret Maron, educator and fiction writer Jill McCorkle, Raleigh-based memoirist and novelist Tim McLaurin, playwright and lecturer Bland Simpson, teacher-author Lee Smith, and columnist and novelist John Welter. Declining to participate were Doris Betts, Allan Gurganus, and Reynolds Price.

Clyde Edgerton, the project initiator, composed the opening chapter and, as a punishment from the group, finished the manuscript. The novel appeared from November 12 to December 3, 1995, in installments issued Monday through Friday and in the Sunday Arts & Entertainment section of the *News & Observer*. The group donated proceeds from a paperback edition to the North Carolina Writers' Network. A tangle of inconsistencies, character shifts, and outrageous cliffhangers, the story parodies politics, religion, and sex through the actions of characters living in the Research Triangle Park in Cary, Chapel Hill, Durham, and Raleigh, North Carolina. At a turning point in the mystery send-up, Gibbons supplies chapter 8, in which Pete studies a diary entry written by Griffin, his band director in 1962. The segment develops the ambiguity about who fathered Samantha's twins, Andi and Mandi Griffin, a suitably woman-centered topic for a feminist writer.

• *Further reading*

Gibbons, Kaye, et al. *Pete & Shirley: The Great Tar Heel Novel* (serial novel). Asheboro, N.C.: Down Home Press, 1995.
Merriman, Ann Lloyd. "Between the Bookends," *Richmond Times-Dispatch* (25 February 1996).
Perkins, David, "The Making of 'Pete & Shirley," Raleigh, N.C., *News & Observer* (12 November 1995).
Steelman, Ben. "On the Path of a Traveling Story," Wilmington, N.C., *Star-News* (26 May 2002).

Pitts-Stokes-Woodrow genealogy

In *A Virtuous Woman* (1989), Kaye Gibbons muses on the close association of landowners and tenant farmers. The marriages of Ruby Pitts to men from the laboring class produce disillusion and bickering in the first union and a quarter century of compromised happiness in the second:

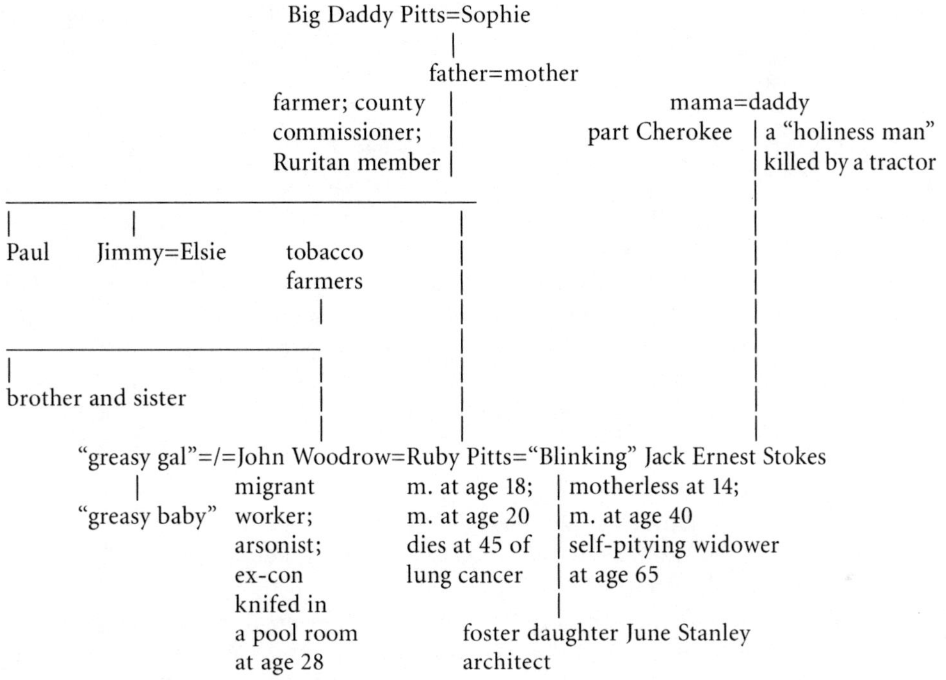

See also **Hoover-Stanley genealogy**

• *Further reading*

Gibbons, Kaye. *A Virtuous Woman.* Chapel Hill, N.C.: Algonquin Press, 1989.

poverty

Kaye Gibbons speaks knowledgeably of the poor from her own red-clay childhood in Nash County, North Carolina. She commented to interviewer Dannye Romine, book editor of the *Charlotte* (N.C.) *Observer*, that she never had a babysitter and, until age 14, knew nothing about dining in restaurants. Gibbons recalled trying to stay out of trouble lest she distract her parents, who "were trying hard just to survive" (Romine, 1987). Like regional writers Dorothy Allison, Rick Bragg, and Barbara Kingsolver, Gibbons shakes up the reader's expectations of behaviors and values among Southern poor whites and laboring-class non-whites. An early retrospect on the effects of poverty, "The Headache," published in the June 1987 issue of the *St. Andrews Review*, portrays want as the motivation of Lucille Womble in retrieving an abandoned purse from a restaurant ladies' room. During a summer of scrubbing overalls on a washboard for her husband Henry and their ten children, she contemplates the bank's repossession of two farm machines. More painful, the shame of her boys at the family's need troubles a mother who despairs at being labeled as trash on welfare. In an ironic gesture, Lucille hands Henry a copy of *House Beautiful*, a waiting room offering ill suited to the needs of a family living in a single room criss-crossed by drop cords. In the resolution, the simple gifts of bedtime snuggling with Henry, acknowledgement of her goodness, and the promise of two new hats alleviates psychosomatic pain in a woman pressed to the ends of coping with farm poverty.

In *Ellen Foster* (1987), Gibbons chooses a background that *New York Times* reviewer Alice Hoffman describes as "a harsh, rural landscape bordered by poverty, brutality, and loss" (Hoffman, 1987). A tender mother-daughter scene in the family bean patch contradicts stereotypes of the shiftless, unclean, and unambitious underclass family. In place of the bumptious Ma Kettle film prototype, Ellen's ailing mother survives as a powerless serf under the thumb of husband Bill, a surly bootlegger and binge drinker. A fragile victim of rheumatic fever, the mother expends what energy she can summon to teach Ellen about plucking ripe beans and about avoiding Bill, whose explosive temper poses a more menacing form of ripeness. Too soon exposed to spousal abuse and threats of molestation, Ellen develops a precocious instinct for self-deliverance. Ironically, after the 40-year-old mother's suicide in March 1969, on Christmas Day, Ellen harbors with a black family that lives in limited circumstances. For the first time, she surveys a level of subsistence lower than her own and acquires respect for hospitable blacks who pity and shelter her.

While examining unwise choices in *A Virtuous Woman* (1989), Gibbons echoes the matrix of *Ellen Foster* by depicting the foolishness of Ruby Pitts, a loved and coddled teenaged daughter of rural gentry. By eloping with 26-year-old tenant farmer John Woodrow, a fractious wife abuser, 18-year-old Ruby, like Ellen's mother, encounters disillusion. Ruby looks at poverty from the other side of the glass by witnessing the everyday squalor of the field hands who cultivate and harvest her father's crops. Deprived of the daily ministrations of Sudie Bee and Lester, the Pitts family domestics, Ruby trains herself to run a home for her second husband, 40-year-old "Blinking" Jack Ernest Stokes, whose need of a woman in his life surpasses Ruby's yearning for marital security. After her death from lung cancer at age 45, Jack's submergence in a domestic mess leaves him sorrowing amid dirty dishes and a bare mattress while he bolts bourbon, munches corn flakes, and watches Roadrunner cartoons on television. Gibbons's subtext indicates that conjugal love is capable of uplifting the poor until loss reduces the couple to a single survivor.

Penury stalks to a lesser degree in Gibbons's third and fourth novels—*A Cure for Dreams* (1991) and *Charms for the Easy Life* (1993), in which female characters have more disposable wealth. In the first work, she pictures the rural families of Milk Farm Road muddling through the Great Depression by ridding their budgets of fashionable clothing and car travel. One stand-out sufferer, Trudy Woodlief, an outsider from Baton Rouge, Louisiana, receives female support to spare the Woodlief children from hunger brought on by the abandonment of their wayward father Tommy.

The plot portrays Quaker entrepreneur Charles Davies, a workaholic farmer-miller, as a victim of poverty because of his miserly attitude rather than from a lack of funds. Although his family suffers little from want, in 1937, he chooses to drown himself, ironically liberating his wife Lottie from an unfulfilling marriage. With the aid of a small widow's pension provided by President Franklin D. Roosevelt's Social Security Act of 1935, Lottie not only supports herself, but garners the riches of motherhood and grandmotherhood after the birth of Betty Davies Randolph's daughter, Marjorie Polly Randolph, on November 25, 1942. Tempering the family's regrets over straitened means are the rationing and belt-tightening that all Americans experience during World War II. Because the Davies-Randolph clan shares privations and blessings, they perceive the period's economic distress as temporary.

In *Charms for the Easy Life*, the author's fourth novel, Gibbons amplifies her regard for resourceful women like Lottie Davies. Contrasting the methods of a farm wife is the success of herbalist-midwife Charlie Kate Birch, who maintains a steady business in birthing and doctoring the poor. During the Great Depression and the first year of World War II, she treats the bottom strata of society — a wandering leper from the Outer Banks, a filthy hermit, mill hill injuries, derelicts at the City Grill, a drowning shoeshine man, and a croupy girl blinded at birth by an uncaring male doctor. The most pitiable of the lot, 70-year-old Maveen, Charlie Kate's retired maid, earns no compassion from the same snobby physician. In the final hours of Maveen's demise from stomach cancer, Charlie Kate can offer only a temperature-reducing massage with alcohol and indignation at Maveen's undeserved suffering and slow starvation. From these slights to the poor, Gibbons stresses the gaps in socio-economic strata and the disaffection of the rich for have-nots, particularly mill hands and the black servant class.

The author generates a more trenchant disclosure of class and no-class behavior in her first historical novel, *On the Occasion of My Last Afternoon* (1998). Miss Lucille McKimmon, an urban social-climber, sends butter, basil, and pear soap to ingratiate herself with the Quincy Lowells, who, in 1847, are prominent newcomers to Raleigh, North Carolina. In contrast to Lucille's social maneuverings, Emma Garnet Tate Lowell prepares her own pantry gifts for the poor. Upon the arrival of 15-year-old Lavinia Ella Mae Dawes with wormy apples as payment for Dr. Lowell's surgery on her father's feet, Emma gathers a cartload of foodstuffs to deliver to the underfed family. Because of Lavinia's delight in the Lowell house, Emma offers a three-day stay in the guest room. The obvious differences in Lucille and Emma support Gibbons's contention that people who move freely among social levels ennoble and enrich themselves for generosity and compassion for the underclass. As a humorous fillip to Lucille, the author pictures the Lowells' house staff robbing the social maven of her ducks to see the family through the meatless meals common to the Reconstruction era.

Gibbons introduces a more subtle investigation of want in *Divining Women* (2004), her seventh novel. In restrained revelations about Maureen Carlton Ross, an abused wife, the text discloses her coming of age in Yazoo City on the Mississippi delta. She endured crowded home conditions and bed sharing and evolved ridged, uneven nails, evidence of childhood malnutrition. Driblets of information depict the

Carlton family as a coterie of seven daughters and two adults surviving on farm proceeds. Maureen's mother, a reader of Emily Brontë's feminist classic *Wuthering Heights* (1847), prefers to indulge in books and love for her children than to clean a house dirtied by nine people. The author enhances the irony of Maureen's misery in fall 1918 in an over-decorated manse in Elm City, North Carolina, and her joy at recovering letters from her mother, a practical parent who extends a trove of good advice.

Gibbons returns to her first heroine in a sequel, *The Life All Around Me by Ellen Foster* (2006). A contrast between levels of subsistence depicts Ellen as a loved and cared-for foster daughter courted by Stuart, son of a junk dealer. She describes Stuart's home in terms of the ever-burning heap of tires in the yard, where he sits on a bucket and stirs the fire with a stick. The blaze suggests a stir in his heart for Ellen. At the height of his infatuation, he proposes his idea of luxury — eloping to Pedro's South of the Border, a fireworks emporium and motel, and staying in a room with a "valentime bed" (Gibbons, 2006, 139). Sealing the proposal, Stuart offers his version of a diamond ring — the glass doorknob that he removes from Ellen's old house and a promise to check his credit at Sears before he shops for a standard love token. The sincerity of his vision of wedlock concludes with more of his picture of the good life — renting the blue house vacated by a worker at the junk yard and serving Ellen chocolate milk and a fried steak. The gentle humor masks Gibbons's sympathy for Stuart, a poor, but great-hearted suitor who matches foster mother Laura in generosity.

See also **materialism; Starletta**

• *Further reading*

Gibbons, Kaye. *The Life All Around Me by Ellen Foster*. New York: Harcourt, 2006.
Hoffman, Alice. "Shopping for a New Family," *New York Times* (31 May 1987): A13.
Romine, Dannye. "Literature Liberates: Raleigh's Kaye Gibbons Finds Freedoms, Affirmation in 1st Novel," *Charlotte* (N.C.) *Observer* (26 April 1987).
Town, Caren J. *New Southern Girl: Female Adolescence in the Works of 12 Women Authors*. Jefferson, N.C.: McFarland, 2004.

powerlessness

Like feminist authors Julia Alvarez, Maryse Condé, Maxine Hong Kingston, and Jean Rhys, novelist Kaye Gibbons navigates an unwavering path through victims of the human condition. A critic for *Wilson Quarterly* accurately sums up her humanistic views as a "vision of hard vicissitudes and necessary graces" ("Review," 1990, 95). The description suits the falling action of "The Headache," a short-short story issued in June 1987 in the *St. Andrews Review*. The protagonist, Lucille Womble, toils for her 12-member family in a one-room house during a summer when the bank repossesses two farm machines. Her venture toward an abandoned pocketbook in a restaurant ladies' room so unnerves her that she languishes under two weeks of head pain, insomnia, crying jags, and visions of the snake that a trickster placed in the purse. Oppressed by want and fears that her children suffer gibes for their poverty, she struggles to avoid the inevitable labeling of trashy people on welfare. Restoring her to wholeness, her husband Henry dispenses a touch of grace, respect for the goodwife and a promise of two new hats, a stroke of bounty to revive her spirit.

In *Ellen Foster* (1987), Gibbons's most wrenching portrait of victimization, unforeseen catastrophes leave ten-year-old Ellen motherless and neglected by Bill, her lustful alcoholic father. Ellen reflects on childish attempts to reduce Bill's spousal abuse by demanding to sleep in her old crib, a retreat to infantile innocence that allows her all-night supervision of her parents. In a moment of self-congratulation, after the 40-year-old mother's suicide from an overdose of digitalis in 1969, Ellen lauds her mother for after-death strength in finally shutting up her evil-mouthed husband. Worsening Ellen's tragedy are the leers of Bill's customers for bootleg liquor. In flight from potential molestation on New Year's Eve, 1969, Ellen launches a complex self-rescue — an odyssey of short-term residences with an art teacher and a string of heartless kin — Aunt Betsy, a maternal grandmother, and Aunt Nadine Nelson and Cousin Dora. Foiling Ellen's plans is the official placement decided by a court judge, a symbol of society's obstruction of a pre-teen's intuitive empowerment. Through thrift, foresight, and swift action, on Christmas Day, 1970, Ellen flees toward an ideal — the proper foster mother, whose institutional designation Ellen adopts as a surname. The protagonist's ingenuity at self-salvage generates a reader following that embraces both the original Ellen and the more mature orphan who narrates a sequel, *The Life All Around Me by Ellen Foster* (2006).

In contrast to Ellen's child-like solutions to neglect and threat, the author's second novel, *A Virtuous Woman* (1989), describes the powerlessness of the adult underclass. The text dramatizes the frustration and exhaustion of landless field hands who share a symbiotic existence with the rural landowners who depend on itinerant spare hands for planting and harvesting. Seen through the eyes of Ruby Pitts Woodrow Stokes, the 18-year-old daughter of a prosperous farmer and a county commissioner, the two-layered farm milieu takes on new meaning after her marriage to 26-year-old John Woodrow, a migrant farm laborer. Two years later, Ruby's life with the shiftless pool hall layabout ends suddenly with his death from a stab to the lungs before she can use the pistol she keeps ready under her pillow for their next marital confrontation. Gibbons portrays Ruby's plot as the result of desperation arising among poor women in a society that discounts the virulence of marital strife.

In the subsequent stave, the author awards Ruby a sturdier, but landless and financially strapped subsistence in a second marriage. Still unaware of her widowhood following John's death from the pool hall fracas, Ruby gravitates toward 40-year-old "Blinking" Jack Ernest Stokes, a dependable tenant farmer. Indicative of his powerlessness is his trundling of manure in a wheelbarrow for his employers when he first courts her. Still a working-class housewife in outback North Carolina, at age 20, Ruby lowers her expectations to nestle into his love. After a quarter century of contentment, at age 45, Ruby faces the greatest threat, a lethal lung cancer brought on by a quarter century of smoking, her self-destructive respite during marriage to John. By advancing the theme of powerlessness to an existential level, the author reminds the reader of the death curse that disempowers all humankind.

In a more uplifting take on gendered powerlessness, Kaye Gibbons delights in female strengths in *A Cure for Dreams* (1991), her third novel. Set during the Great Depression, the work features the women of Milk Farm Road supporting and sustaining each other through conversation. Kathryn McKee, in a critique for *Southern Quarterly*, summarizes the resulting synergy through which the characters "discover in language a power otherwise inaccessible to them as women" (McKee, 1997, 97). In one example, a local physician dismisses Betty Davies Randolph's illness as "more or less popular female complaints" (Gibbons, 1991, 22–23). The generalized diagnosis discounts women's ailments as gendered and therefore flimsy or, at best, suspect. Betty's exuberant storytelling is so beholding to the words and example of her mother, Lottie O'Cadhain Davies, that the deceased woman's spirit literally intrudes on Betty's memories. The ongoing oral exchange undergirds female community, the antidote to unrealized dreams and the suffocating roles of rural daughters and housewives mandated by an androcentric society.

Gibbons portrays other women of Milk Farm Road as more aggressive and less covert in claiming their rights. For Trudy Woodlief, a gutsy white trash newcomer from Baton Rouge, Louisiana, the need for credit at the local grocery store goes beyond negotiation. Because Mr. Porter brushes off her request, Trudy sets in motion her band of children. Rather than beg and cajole the storekeeper, they shoot down aisles "like pool balls" and snatch up supplies (*Ibid.*, 65). In a more desperate setting, a murderer, Sade Duplin, takes a direct approach to ending marital misery. To her husband Roy's bullying, she aims a shotgun. Local women quickly deduce the murderer's identity, which they shield from the bumbling, clueless part-time Deputy Sheriff John Carroll. The feminist reordering of justice characterizes the author's disdain for a one-sided social order that both demoralizes and defeats battered women.

Stronger social commentary emerges in a dramatic episode in *Charms for the Easy Life* (1993), Gibbons's fourth novel. A successful midwife-herbalist, Charlie Kate Birch, builds a case against a class-conscious Raleigh doctor who blinds a poor woman's newborn with misapplication of silver nitrate to the eyes. After the same man refuses to hospitalize Maveen, a retired maid dying of stomach cancer, Charlie Kate rages that he wills the 70-year-old patient to starve to death. In a pique, Charlie Kate mounts a one-woman crusade: she drives to his home in the wealthy Anderson Heights sector and forces him into early retirement on pain of an exposé of his callousness toward the destitute. While her daughter, Sophia Snow Birch, sits outside in the car, she marvels at a home superintended by a butler only blocks from the city's poor. The continguity of rich and poor echoes Gibbons's belief that humanity shares space, but not the world's wealth.

Impotence of a different kind immobilizes Hattie Barnes, the narrator of *Sights Unseen* (1995). The story of a family's struggle against mental illness operates on two fields of combat — the fight to keep Hattie's mother Maggie from harming others or herself and the household's effort to conceal from the public Maggie's bizarre bipolar behaviors. Her delusions reach their height in her running down a pedestrian in Rocky Mount with her car to keep the stranger from stealing Maggie's souls. Gibbons illustrates a psychological strength in the sibling collegiality of 12-year-old Hattie and her older brother Freddy, who channel their energies into reading and scholarship. Although there is little they can do to restore Maggie to sanity or to save their father Frederick from martyrdom as peacekeeper, the children evolve worthy aims for themselves by studying anesthesiology in medical school. Empowered by education and adult autonomy, Hattie relives the chaos of childhood with full knowledge that Maggie recovered in 1967 through psychotherapy and eight electroconvulsive shock treatments at Duke Hospital and enjoyed 15 years of normality before her death in 1982 from a fall. Through Hattie's reflections, the fictional memoir demonstrates the power of storytelling to celebrate triumphs from the past.

In Gibbons's first historical novel, *On the Occasion of My Last Afternoon* (1998), the helplessness of plantation mistress Alice Tate provides dual feminist views of the passive female. Of two minds, Gibbons pities and castigates Alice for submitting to life-draining torment and for surrendering her six children to an antagonistic father. A weak-willed victim of her husband, narcissistic parvenu Samuel P. Goodman Tate, in 1842, Alice allows her 12-year-old daughter, narrator Emma Garnet Tate Lowell, to supply excuses to extricate Alice from Samuel's nightly verbal assaults. By abdicating the role of female head of household, Alice inadvertently prepares Emma for heroism during the Civil War. Emma carries into adulthood a disproportionate amount of guilt for marrying Dr. Quincy Lowell and, in 1847 at age 17, for leaving her mother at Seven Oaks plantation to endure Samuel's pummelling. Exacerbating shame at abandoning Alice, Emma regrets removing herself as a necessary buffer against Samuel's plantation despotism and accepts blame for stealing Clarice Washington, the fearless cook-housekeeper who accompanies the bride to her new home in Raleigh, North Carolina. In 1900, at age 70, Emma reflects on the bizarre events that boost her importance to Raleigh residents both during and after the Civil War.

Fortunately for Gibbons, she retains the fiction writer's control over character and situation. According to literary analyst Veronica Makowsky, the historical novel dooms Alice Tate from the beginning because she is "trained for a southern lady's pedestal and ... [is] consequently unable to ameliorate or curb her husband Samuel's cruelty" or to seek medical treatment for her psychosomatic ailments (Perry & Weaks, 2002, 607). With authorial license, Gibbons not only kills off her passive mother figure from worsening migraine headaches, but also laces the text with an hour-by-hour description of the inept care provided by Dr. John C. Gunn, who practices outdated treatments of bleeding, cupping, purging, and cold-toweling. Doubly crippled and treacherously misdiagnosed, Alice risks destruction by proffering herself as a sacrifice to patriarchal tidewater culture, where polite women remain adornments to their husbands and pawns in the hands of misogynistic physicians.

For a different reason, the impotence of Maureen Carlton Ross in *Divining Women* (2004) reflects the need of pregnant women for husbandly backing. A discredited wife, she suffers the helplessness of Alice Tate in the hands of woman-disparaging physicians. Promised one child before undergoing a hysterectomy, Maureen retreats to her upstairs haven to live out the final 50 days of her confinement. As Simone de Beauvoir describes the motif in *The Second Sex* (1949), Maureen becomes the sequestered maiden: "she is locked in a tower, a palace, a garden, a cave, she is chained to a rock, a captive, sound asleep: she waits" (Beauvoir, 1989, 328). Gibbons turns the increasing physical immurement into an opportunity for a change of heart toward submission to Troop Ross's disparagements. Under the guidance of

22-year-old caretaker Mary Oliver, after September 30, 1918, Maureen shakes off lethargy and strikes back. Doubly wasted by a protracted birthing and by the stillbirth of her first child, Maureen emerges from pregnancy with a valkyrie's spirit. Fresh energies enable her to bury daughter, Ella Eloise Ross, at sunset on November 9, 1918. Only two days before an armistice ends World War I, Maureen takes a train to Washington, D.C., far from domestic conflict, the deflating marriage that threatened her womanhood. As in earlier novels, Gibbons credits a female risk-taker with outwitting a male aggressor.

See also **violence; vulnerability**

• *Further reading*

Beauvoir, Simone de. *The Second Sex.* New York: Vintage, 1989.

Gibbons, Kaye. *Charms for the Easy Life.* New York: Putnam, 1993.

_____. *A Cure for Dreams.* New York: Algonquin, 1991.

Kalfopoulou, Adrianne. *A Discussion of the Ideology of the American Dream in the Culture's Female Discourses.* Lewiston, N.Y.: Edwin Mellen Press, 2000.

McKee, Kathryn. "Simply Talking: Women and Language in Kaye Gibbons's *A Cure for Dreams,*" *Southern Quarterly* 35, no. 4 (Summer 1997): 97–107.

Perry, Carolyn, and Mary Louise Weaks, eds. *The History of Southern Women's Literature.* Baton Rouge: Louisiana State University Press, 2002.

"Review: *Ellen Foster and A Virtuous Woman,*" *Wilson Quarterly* 14, no. 1 (Winter 1990): 95.

racism

In the tradition of authors Harper Lee and Toni Morrison, Gibbons interweaves racial differences and racist opinions throughout her class-conscious Southern fiction. For verisimilitude in her first novel, *Ellen Foster* (1987), the author reprises the overt bigotry of Southerners in the late 1960s, when Ellen's black neighbor sells quilts to whites who profit from the handwork by reselling it at a substantial profit. At the novel's resolution is the epiphany of a friendship between Starletta and the white title character, both victims of poverty and low class status. In courterpoint to the themes of child neglect and homelessness, the author broaches the black-white divide of the rural South, beginning with Starletta's dismay that there is no Girl Scout troop for blacks. In an interview, the author remarked on the proximity of rural whites and blacks who live contiguously in farm communities and who share "the same foodways and folkways" as well as values and religious beliefs (Gretlund, 2000, 139). Despite similarities between laboring-class blacks and whites, Ellen has learned from family assumptions about blacks to be uncomfortable among illiterate field hands who live in filth and have no television or indoor plumbing. An insidious color prejudice creeps into the thinking of children like Ellen in early childhood and remains unquestioned and unchallenged until face-to-face situations force a personal analysis of the racist substructure.

In Ellen Foster's milieu, the pejorative "nigger" resides side by side with other familiar piedmont Carolina dialect, an amalgam of Anglo-Irish terms and West African argot. The epithet voices the hostility of Ellen's father Bill, a white laboring-class monster who makes a living by bootlegging liquor to poor blacks. His vengeful mother-in-law charges him with worthlessness because of his association with a black clientele. To cleanse herself of his spite and sorryness, on Christmas Day, 1970, Ellen launches a quest for a decent family and for a new credo devoid of her father's negativism. Gibbons establishes that Ellen surpasses her father in humanity by accepting a heavy summer tan she acquires during July hoeing when the skin tone of a field hand leaves in doubt her race. Contributing to her contentment with racial ambiguity is the mothering of Mavis, the black superintendent of laborers who models maternal goodness and benevolence.

Critics disagree on Gibbons's juxtaposition of Ellen and her friend Starletta, which shifts the controlling theme from self-salvation to empathy for the black underclass. At the novel's crux evolves Ellen's relationship with a stuttering, mentally deficient black neighbor whose daily miseries seem more onerous, more debilitating than Ellen's white trash upbringing and orphanhood. Ellen expunges the false indoctrination she gained at home by welcoming Starletta to safe harbor, a weekend at the home of Laura, Ellen's foster mom. Validating Starletta as an equal are the monogrammed towels that Laura sews for the occasion and a pre-dinner nap that Ellen shares with her friend. The visit proposes authorial hope that Southern mores have advanced from pre-integration hatred to a more humane, less race-aggrandizing biculturalism.

A more insidious bias erupts in Gibbons's fourth novel, *Charms for the Easy Life* (1993), in which the characters live on Beale Street in the worst section of Raleigh, North Carolina. The location suits the practice of herbalist-midwife Charlie Kate Birch, who invites the curious to listen to the radio while she offers the ailing homemade laxatives and excision of bunions and warts. To shame white factory owners into extending sewer service to the mill district in Wake County, the protagonist baits them with a guarantee that all residents are white. To her granddaughter Margaret, Charlie Kate fumes, "That it mattered one iota was criminal" (Gibbons, 1993, 22). The author expands on the insult to citizens by mentioning a letter of commendation from the director of public works, who pleads ignorance of the plight of local whites. In a later episode involving the slow starvation of 70-year-old Maveen, the family's former maid who is dying of stomach cancer, Charlie Kate threatens an unethical male doctor, who dismisses black female complaints as fibroid tumors and a diet too rich in fat. Gibbons plots Charlie Kate's private war on white bigotry as a two-stage combat — not just upbraiding the physician, but forcing him out of practice. The example of one woman's indignation expands on Ellen Foster's outreach to Starletta by applauding adult solutions to racial exclusion.

Although bigotry is less virulent in *Sights Unseen* (1995), Gibbons reminds the reader that Southern attitudes rarely stray from stereotyping and injustice. At the Barnes farm near Rocky Mount, North Carolina, the theft of a car requires an official investigation. Because the vehicle belongs to Pearl Wiggins, a black cook-housekeeper, and because it disappears in the custody of Hubert, the Barnes's black farmhand, the sheriff's deputy refuses to involve himself in a "nigra mess," a vague term that discounts black-on-black crime as a form of social disorder rather than a felony (Gibbons, 1995, 189). Like Charlie Kate Birch, the female head of household in *Charms for the Easy Life*, Maggie Barnes fights racism in a significant foray against white male hegemony. To the rude table talk of Grandfather Barnes, her judgmental father-in-law, in 1967, she retorts that Pearl is "part of the family" and not a hapless servant expected to tolerate slurs (*Ibid.*, 197). Situated at the rise of Maggie from bipolar mental patient to family hostess, the incident validates two females who reject ethnic and gender oppression.

The height of racial vitriol in Gibbons's fiction boils up during the Civil War, the background of her sixth novel, *On the Occasion of My Last Afternoon* (1998). Amid superficial harmony in which plantation mistress Alice Tate distributes Christmas candy canes to the trash crew and furnishes newlywed slaves with staples from her pantry and root cellar, enslavement founders from its inborn savagery. As troop trains ferry more casualties into North Carolina's capital during the Civil War, the Lowell family beds soldiers, white and black, on every available surface of their home. For their generosity, the Raleigh *Register* publishes a poison-pen note accusing the family of immorality akin to miscegenation for juxtaposing black males so close to the three Lowell daughters, Leslie, Louise, and Mary. The ploy characterizes the speciousness of bigots who capitalize on the long-standing canard of unbridled lust in black men for tender white virgins. Media blasts against liberalism strike Emma Garnet Tate Lowell once more in widowhood because she dares to open a freedmen's school in the United States Bank building. A coy editorial supports the formation on December 24, 1865, of the Ku Klux Klan in Pulaski, Tennessee, by former Confederate soldiers. The terrorist cult issues an unsigned warning that Emma's promotion of black rights will produce "a nigger ... that wil lord hisself over the wite man" (Gibbons, 1998, 270). The pathetic spelling and grammar reveal the fount of racial hate—the competition of dispossessed whites and newly freed blacks in the post-war juggernaut economy. The note produces two reactions in Emma—first, laughter, then the reorganization of the school into private tutorials hidden away in family hovels. Once more, Gibbons portrays female brass as the equal of white male bias.

The racial layering of Elm City, North Carolina, in *Divining Women* (2004), Gibbons's seventh novel, extols a loyalty and subservience of blacks to undeserving white snobs. At the height of selfishness, Troop Ross, the villain, fires his house staff, Mamie and Zollie, for leaving work to attend their two children, victims of the 1918 influenza pandemic. Upon investigation, Troop's 22-year-old niece, Mary Oliver, discovers a note delivered by a black minister that states Zollie's need for money to buy coffins and burial clothes for his sons and for Zollie's 19-year-old sister, who kills herself out of guilt that she fails to save the boys. Troop, an acerbic hypocrite, vilifies his wife's reliance on Mamie, who creeps back to the house on November 7, 1918, to deliver Maureen's stillborn daughter, Ella Eloise Ross. Appalled at the reunion of Maureen and Mary with the servants, Troop sneers, "Two women and two niggers. Hardly God's chosen people" (Gibbons, 2004, 200). Immediately out of his mouth, the slur damns Troop for racist sanctimony against the four people who treasure his hapless infant.

Gibbons enhances the Southern racial climate through dramatic irony. While driving the family preacher to the cemetery, Mary Oliver discovers that the elderly black man is wary of being seen in a car driven by a white female. To ease his fear of being accused of raping a white woman, Mary takes responsibility for transporting him through city streets. The motif recurs that same afternoon when she drives Zollie to the Ross house and ponders the "hateful trivia" that troubles the world on a day of advancing pestilence and death (*Ibid.*, 174). Contradicting the chop-logic of regional prejudice is the loving care with which Zollie, on November 9, 1918, transports Ella Eloise's coffin to the cemetery for a private sunset burial. Allying his humanity with Maureen's grief, Gibbons pictures the house servants making their way from Ella's grave to that of their sons for an evening visit. The three mourners contrast the corrosive hatred of Troop, who abandons the funeral cortege to indulge in a sidewalk conniption against a wife and servants who refuse to obey him. With skillful understatement, Gibbons lets Troop's bile speak for itself.

• *Further reading*

Gibbons, Kaye. *Charms for the Easy Life*. New York: Putnam, 1993.

_____. *Divining Women*. New York: G.P. Putnam's Sons, 2004.

_____. *On the Occasion of My Last Afternoon*. New York: G.P. Putnam's Sons, 1998.

_____. *Sights Unseen*. New York: G.P. Putnam's Sons, 1995.

Gretlund, Jan Nordby. "In My Own Style: An Interview with Kaye Gibbons," *South Atlantic Review* 65, no. 4 (Fall 2000): 132–154.

Monteith, Sharon. *Advancing Sisterhood: Interracial Friendships in Contemporary Southern Fiction*. Athens: University of Georgia Press, 2000.

Munafo, Giavanna. "Colored Biscuits: Reconstructing Whiteness and the Boundaries of 'Home' in Kaye Gibbons's *Ellen Foster*," *Women, America, and Movement*. ed. Susan L. Roberson. Columbia: University of Missouri Press, 1998, pp. 38–61.

Raleigh, North Carolina

The shape and flavor of Raleigh, North Carolina, permeates Kaye Gibbons's fiction, beginning with her fourth novel, *Charms for the Easy Life* (1993) and continuing through *The Life All Around Me by Ellen Foster* (2006), a sequel to *Ellen Foster* (1987), the author's first novel. *Charms for the Easy Life* describes Charlie Kate Birch's career in unlicensed midwifery, dentistry, and herbalism on Beale Street in a mill district neighborhood, where the pregnancies and ills of white and black workers shape her practice. Episodes involve the three-woman household in a deathbed watch over Maveen, a 70-year-old maid dying of stomach cancer in the next county, the charging of a doctor in the wealthy Anderson Heights section in north-central Raleigh with malpractice, and the rescue of a poor child from whooping cough and of five children down with malaria on the Tar River due east of the state capital in Edgecombe County. The author authenticates the female outreach to the poor with details:

- the diagnosis of the ailments of alcoholics clustered around the City News and Candy
- their testing for bleeding ulcers at Mary Elizabeth Hospital northeast of the city center

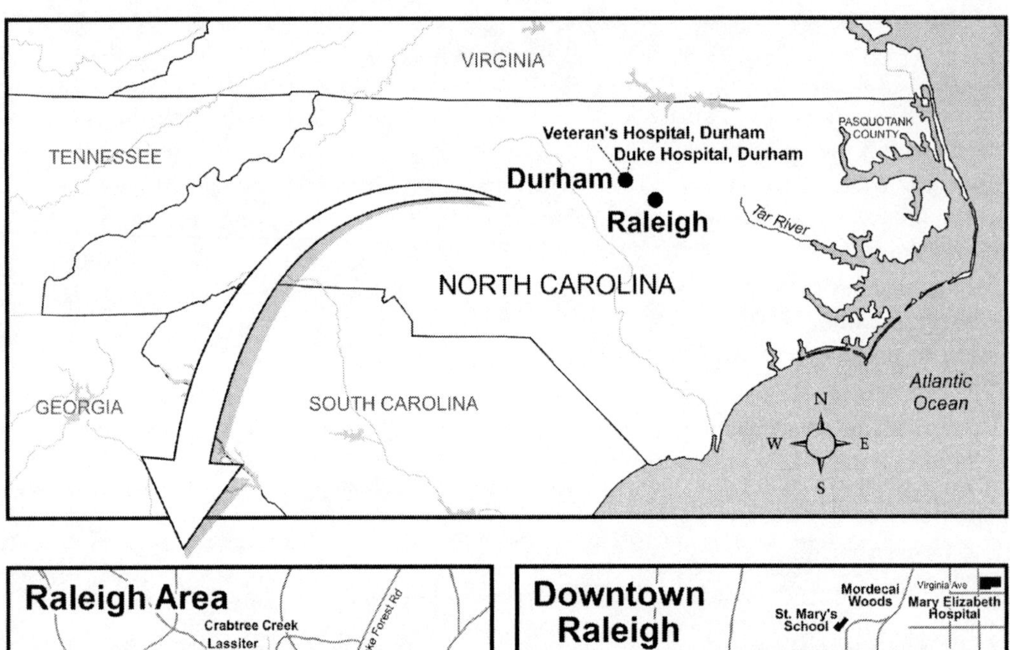

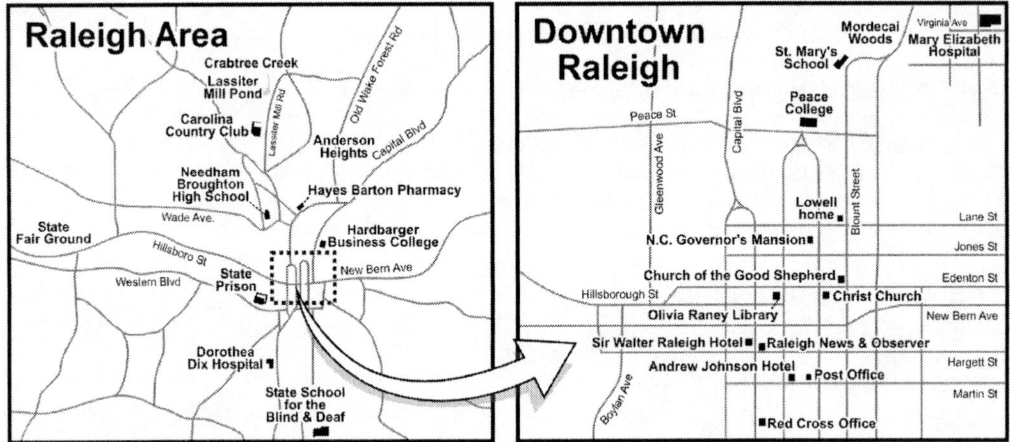

ALL MAPS BY RAYMOND BARRETT, JR.

- the institutionalization of a boy suffering Tourette's syndrome at Dorothea Dix Hospital on South Boylan Avenue west of the city center
- the filling of Charlie Kate's prescriptions and the offering of free iron tablets at the Hayes Barton Pharmacy at the corner of Glenwood Avenue and Fairview Road north of the city center
- the healer's self-education from books checked out of the Olivia Raney Library at the corner of Hillsborough and Salisbury streets in the city's heart.

An admirer of Charlie Kate, Louise Battle Nutter comes from a line of aristocratic Episcopalians who scorn Louise's volunteerism among the poor of coastal

Pasquotank County on the Albemarle Sound and who obliterate her name from the family pew at the Church of the Good Shepherd on Hillsborough Street. The contrast of socio-economic strata attests to Gibbons's intent to survey even-handedly the people of the state capital.

Raleigh landmarks recur throughout the narrative, from the military recruitment center to a piano recital at Peace College, a presbyterian school on East Peace Street, and private parties at Carolina Country Club on Glenwood Avenue. As the life of Charlie Kate's daughter, Sophia Snow Birch, takes an upturn, she encounters businessman Richard Baines at a showing of *Gone with the Wind* (1939) at the Center Theater. During the winter of 1939–1940, she walks with him by lantern light along Crabtree Creek, which winds around the city's northwestern periphery. For winter amusement, he slides her in a chair on the frozen surface of Lassiter Mill Pond. At a crucial point in their courtship, the former Mrs. Richard Baines arrives on Christmas Eve, 1942, for a two-week stay at the Sir Walter Raleigh Hotel, a landmark southwest of the city center since 1924 and the meeting site for the exclusive Sphinx Club. The hotel is also the setting for the awkward three-day reunion of Charlie Kate and her husband in 1938 as well as their final parting three days later.

After the focus shifts to Sophia's daughter Margaret, more Raleigh place names crop up. Margaret spurns enrollment to Hardbarger Business College on Capitol Boulevard and agrees to a blind date for dinner at the Andrew Johnson Hotel at the corner of Martin and Salisbury streets. While she avoids young men, flirts and war brides bid farewell to enlisted and drafted soldiers at the railroad station, which opened across from Nash Square in 1892. Margaret chooses to join her grandmother and mother in packing cigarettes and Hershey bars into boxes for soldiers at the Red Cross office on South McDowell Street. Margaret's first productive encounter with eligible males occurs during her volunteer duties to disabled soldiers at a Durham veterans' hospital near Duke University. After reading their mail and writing their dictated replies, she sends letters from the Raleigh post office, located at the corner of Fayetteville and Martin streets. One of the patients is Tom Hawkings, III, a graduate of Needham B. Broughton, the state's second oldest high school, established in 1929 on St. Mary's Street. His aristocratic Anderson Heights mother, Anna Hawkings, writes political columns for the Raleigh *News & Observer*, a newspaper begun in 1880 at 415 Fayetteville Street.

Additional regional details particularize Gibbons's later fiction. In *Sights Unseen* (1995), in 1955, Maggie Barnes is eight months pregnant with daughter Hattie when she begs for a ride on the Twister at the state Fair Grounds west of town on Blue Ridge Road. In 1967, when Hattie is 12 years old, Maggie's mental meanderings worsen and precipitate a hit-and-run incident in Rocky Mount, which results in the possibility of her confinement to Dorothea Dix State Hospital for the Insane on the town's "bad side" (Gibbons, 1995, 94). Maggie's son Freddy pictures electroconvulsive shock therapy in terms of his visit to the electric chair in the state prison, which opened on Western Boulevard in 1884. The similarities between shock treatments and electrocution of prisoners exemplify punitive attitudes of the era.

The author glimpses Raleigh in ante-bellum days in *On the Occasion of My Last Afternoon* (1998), her first historical fiction. To account for social rejection of Emma

Garnet Tate Lowell and her Northern husband Quincy, the text describes the design of the newlyweds' house by Henry Hobson Richardson, who made his reputation in 1872 as the architect of Boston's Trinity Church. Situated on Blount Street northeast of the city's heart, the Lowells live near the governor's mansion on Wilmington Street, which is occupied from 1848 to 1850 by a family friend, Governor Charles Manly. According to an article in the Raleigh *Weekly Standard*, published on Fayetteville Street, Quincy supervises the Mary Elizabeth Hospital, an authorial anachronism at Glascock Street and Wake Forest Road that wasn't opened until 1914. After services at Christ Church on Edenton Street, he rests from his six-day week with family outings at Lovejoy Park and at Sunday suppers at Yarborough House on Fayetteville Street for turtle soup with sourdough crackers and trifle for dessert. The children make their own forays to Mordecai Woods on Mimosa Street, where they release pet rabbits into the wild.

Secession alters Raleigh and the lives of its citizens. During the Civil War, the Lowells' chickens cease to lay eggs because of constant rifle shots ending military burial services at Oakwood Cemetery, an historic landmark northeast of the city center. Quincy assists Lavinia Ella Mae Dawes by enrolling her at St. Mary's School, a private Episcopalian school for girls founded on Hillsborough Street in 1842. The campus served as a Civil War retreat for Mildred Lee, the youngest daughter of Mary Anne Randolph Custis Lee and General Robert E. Lee. In the plot resolution, Quincy's spirit returns to Emma to urge her to "pat things down" at the state school for the blind and deaf on Tryon Road in south-central Raleigh (Gibbons, 1998, 267).

See also **urbanism; World War II**

• *Further reading*

Anderson, Norman D., and B.T. Fowler. *Raleigh*. Charleston, S.C.: Arcadia, 1996.
Gibbons, Kaye. *Charms for the Easy Life*. New York: Putnam, 1993.
_____. *On the Occasion of My Last Afternoon*. New York: G.P. Putnam's Sons, 1998.
_____. *Sights Unseen*. New York: G.P. Putnam's Sons, 1995.
Kulikowski, Jenny, and Kenneth E. Peters. *Historic Raleigh*. Charleston, S.C.: Arcadia, 2002.

Randolph, Betty Davies

A robust female talker in Kaye Gibbons's pantheon of storytelling women, Betty Davies Randolph, protagonist of *A Cure for Dreams* (1991), models mid–20th century feminism. She flourishes in a fatherless home superintended by a life-hardened Irish-American mother, Lottie O'Cadhain Davies. A dominant voice on a par with the tough Southern protagonists of Reynolds Price, Betty grows up, according to Sharon Lloyd Stratton, reviewer for the *Richmond Times-Dispatch*, "reliving births and deaths, meetings and partings, friendships and feuds" (Stratton, 1991). Betty relays the stories of Irish immigrant Grandmother Bridget O'Donough O'Cadhain and of Lottie as though unearthing the vein of iron that sustains female North Carolinians during the Great Depression. The delving into the matriarchal past illustrates the importance of a chain of female stories that celebrates womanly stamina and guile generation by generation.

Central to the plot is the tradition of women's storytelling, a corrective of misperceptions and a warning to the unwary. Roy Parker, a critic for the *Fayetteville* (N.C.) *Observer*, reduces the story to its feminist framework: "A female grows up, fights for her being in a male-dominated milieu, perseveres, preserves her humor, passes on her strength to a new generation" (Parker, 1991). Brought up coddled and woman-centered, Betty learns from Lottie how to sew dresses and play penny-ante gin rummy and pinochle in the back of Porter's store, two skills that promote female solidarity and endurance during hard times. To test her autonomy, she clerks at Kresge's dime store in Richmond, Virginia, and studies secretarial courses offered with funding from the Works Progress Administration while dating Stanton, a charming drug dealer. Gibbons stresses the dangerous periphery of an urban world far from the mother-controlled agrarian microcosm that Betty leaves behind on Milk Farm Road.

Assuring Betty's survival as a war bride and single parent is her dependence on feminist indoctrination through storytelling. Bonded to Lottie during the gradual burn-out of Charles Davies, a workaholic farmer-miller, Betty compensates her mother for the death of a baby brother and for Lottie's inability to bear more children. In no way diminished by the absent father and brother, Betty realizes that her relationship with Lottie is a candid partnership that demands constant renewal. She accepts Lottie as a pal until maturity, marriage, and impending motherhood on November 25, 1942, force Betty to seek autonomy. In feminist style, Gibbons pictures the final break in mother-daughter intimacy as the birthing of the fourth generation, Betty's daughter Marjorie Polly, delivered by housekeeper-midwife Polly Deal. Lottie's granddaughter arrives two days after Thanksgiving, a symbolic occasion for a matriarchal renewal during the absence of Marjorie's father, Herman Randolph, a sailor aboard the U.S.S. *Hornet* in the Pacific. Reviewer Miriam Marty Clark, in a critique for the *St. Louis Post-Dispatch*, identifies in the story Gibbons's own pleasure in telling the matrilineal saga "with grace and plain eloquence" (Clark, 1991).

See also **Davies-O'Donough-O'Cadhain-Randolph genealogy**

• *Further reading*

Clark, Miriam Marty. "Sounds of Women Talking," *St. Louis Post-Dispatch* (9 June 1991).

Gibbons, Kaye. *A Cure for Dreams*. New York: Algonquin, 1991.

Parker, Roy, Jr. "Elegant Family Story," *Fayetteville* (N.C.) *Observer* (14 April 1991).

Stratton, Sharon Lloyd. "Family Talk Is Backbone of 'Dreams,'" *Richmond Times-Dispatch* (5 May 1991).

rape

Kaye Gibbons characterizes rape both as male-on-female violence and as a predictable yield of women's social and economic subjugation. In her first novel, *Ellen Foster* (1987), the author creates an ambiguous subtext of child endangerment and sexual abuse. Pivotal to Ellen's survival is flight from an unsafe environment controlled by Bill, her bingeing, bootlegging only parent. As feminist analysts Judith

Herman and Lisa Hirschman explain in *The Signs Reader: Women, Gender and Scholarship* (1983), "the greater the degree of male supremacy in any culture, the greater the likelihood of father-daughter incest" (Herman & Hirschman, 1983, 263). On New Year's Eve, 1969, Bill grabs his 10-year-old with rape in mind and admires her "girl ninnies" (Gibbons, 1987, 43). Ellen recoils from groping hands and from the babbling of his dead wife's name, a suggestion that a boozy fog causes him to mistake daughter for wife. Without indulging in prurient specifics, Gibbons reveals the title character's fear and her dash to the woods, a reversal of direction from the stereotypical fairy tale stories of sylvan seduction sites. Rather than speculate on her father's intent, like the Maya character in Maya Angelou's *I Know Why the Caged Bird Sings* (1969) and like Pecola Breedlove in Toni Morrison's *The Bluest Eye* (1970), Ellen describes the scenario as a claustrophobic trap limiting options to a girl who is "just about ripe" for male despoliation (*Ibid.*, 37). The image of ripeness implies an opportunism in men who equate parenthood with the breeding of female offspring for future plucking.

A poignant mental image juxtaposes children's literature with the reality it conceals through euphemism and metaphor. In a fairy tale moment, Ellen pictures herself as the antithesis of Little Miss Muffet by envisioning putting a poisoned spider in Bill's bed. In reality, Ellen is more willing than Miss Muffet to combat evil with evil, a justification of rage and vengeance in victimized children. Scenarios of near-capture and self-preservation precede Ellen's New Year's Eve flight from home, where passed-out black men litter the floor. By seeking safe harborage — the home of Starletta — Ellen puts herself into the care of a stable black family. Without fanfare, Gibbons erases the villainous Bill by attrition from drinking himself to death, a demise that she recalls from her own family's experience. Shuddering at a close call, Ellen bids the mortician to nail Bill into an inviolable coffin guaranteed to curtail his menace.

Gibbons is less successful in accounting for the emergence of perverts from childhood purity. Roland Stanley, a misbegotten son in *A Virtuous Woman* (1989), develops a defensive attitude from the overmothering of Tiny Fran, who conceives her "demon child" out of wedlock (Gibbons, 1989, 97). In boyhood, he shoves his baby sister June, forcing her to flee to Ruby Pitts Woodrow Stokes for sanctuary. Roland demonstrates a sadistic streak by hanging a hapless mule named Sugar Pete, a name suggesting a gentle, blameless dray animal. From cutting the crotches out of women's briefs in a department store at age 18, Roland graduates to mauling a date named Stella Morgan and serving ten years in prison for raping her. In a reflection on mid–20th century mayhem, co-narrator "Blinking" Jack Ernest Stokes juxtaposes Roland alongside Hitler, thus comparing local barbarity with global evil.

In a fifth novel, *Sights Unseen* (1995), the author poses flimsy reasons for the channeling of boyhood callousness into crime against females. Following a foreseeable institutionalization of Maggie Barnes at Duke Hospital for madness in 1967, her 12-year-old daughter Hattie tries to read the reaction of Pearl Wiggins, the family cook and housekeeper. Hattie ponders the glib, lying males who once pursued Pearl when she was younger and 100 pounds lighter. The awkward passage projects Pearl's experience onto Hattie's older brother Freddy, whom Pearl pictures morphing into an adult "rape artist" (Gibbons, 1995, 168). Corroborating Pearl's fear is Freddy's pinup collection, a pubescent fantasy lineup that disgusts Pearl. The groundless suspicion comes to nothing after both Freddy and Hattie study medicine and become anesthesiologists, a symbolic profession that stifles human volition.

See also **sex; violence**

• *Further reading*

Gibbons, Kaye. *Ellen Foster.* New York: Algonquin Press, 1987.

_____. *Sights Unseen.* New York: G.P. Putnam's Sons, 1995.

_____. *A Virtuous Woman.* Chapel Hill, N.C.: Algonquin Press, 1989.

Goodwyn, Ann, Anne G. Jones, and Susan V. Donaldson, eds. *Haunted Bodies: Gender and Southern Texts.* Charlottesville: University of Virginia Press, 1997.

Gretlund, Jim Nordby. *The Southern State of Mind.* Columbia: University of South Carolina Press, 1999.

Gwin, Minrose. *The Woman in the Red Dress: Gender, Space, and Reading.* Champaign: University of Illinois Press, 2002.

Herman, Judith, and Lisa Hirschmann. "Father-Daughter Incest" in *The Signs Reader: Women, Gender and Scholarship.* Chicago: University of Chicago Press, 1983.

reading

Kaye Gibbons is a champion of libraries, books, and literacy and a grateful fan of her readers. In girlhood, she retreated into prose and verse in the Batts family's *Child Craft Encyclopedia.* After absorbing Reynolds Price's Southern teen romance novel *A Long and Happy Life* (1962), she declared to interviewer Dannye Romine, book editor of the *Charlotte* (N.C.) *Observer,* "I met Rosacoke Mustian and was never the same" (Romine, 1989). Gibbons's nominations for favorite North Carolina fiction range from Price's *Kate Vaiden* (1986) to the verse of Archie Richard Ammons. The list covers the span of North Carolina history and culture:

•William Byrd's *History of the Dividing Line Betwixt Virginia and North Carolina* (1733)

•*The Frank C. Brown Collection of North Carolina Folklore* (1952–1964), compiled in collaboration with the North Carolina Folklore Society

•editor Richard Walser's compendium *Tarheel Laughter* (1983)

•Frank Warner and Anne Warner's compilation *Traditional American Folksongs* (1984)

•editors Tom E. Terrill and Jerrold Hirsch's compendium *Such as Us: Southern Voices of the Thirties* (1987)

•William S. Powell's award-winning survey history *North Carolina Through Four Centuries* (1989)

•Margaret Anne Doody's *The True Story of a Novel* (1996).

In the logic of "you are what you eat," Gibbons has become what she reads—witty, humorous, and grounded in Southern history, culture, and literature.

Still devouring books at age 33, Gibbons stated, "I read about three hours a day, so I tend to cover a lot of ground," which included the works of Peter Taylor, Calvin Trillin, and John Updike (Miller, 1993). In 2005, she described her escape into the printed page as a spiritual gift, a serendipitous reward for self-salvation. When she reached adulthood, the Deep South dialect of William Faulkner's fiction and the feminist strengths of Katherine Anne Porter's Miranda stories impacted Gibbons's style. Of self-healing through reading, Gibbons observed to Nicole Brodeur, an interviewer for the Raleigh (N.C.) *News & Observer*, "Books calm people, no matter how bad the day" (Brodeur, 1996). She isolated despair as the target of escapist reading, which revives the power to hope.

From studying the short works of three "living wonders"—Grace Paley, Elizabeth Spencer, and Eudora Welty—Gibbons mastered the use of details and female rememory as markers of historical milieu (Gibbons, 2001, ix-x). In winter 2006, she admitted to a fascination with the magical realism of Gabriel García Marquez's *One Hundred Years of Solitude* (1967). To a question about her favorite works, she selected ten titles and annotated the list with each writer's artistry. Of James Joyce's *Ulysses* (1922), she remarked on inventive language, potent imagery, and the craftsmanship of the first modern novel. She selected Irving Welsh's *Trainspotting* (1993) for its command of dialect and extolled Gustave Flaubert's *Madame Bovary* (1856) for turning a regional story into a testimony to the universality of solitude, envy, yearning, and the consequences of unwise choices. For syntactic mastery, Gibbons named William Faulkner's *The Hamlet* (1940), the first of a trilogy covering Mississippi history. Its tour de force engineering of grammar and phrasing illuminates a scene in *Charms for the Easy Life* (1993) in which an arrogant blind date tries to impress a young high school graduate with his erudition. Another Southern master, Flannery O'Connor, impressed Gibbons with *The Habit of Being* (1979), a posthumous collection of personal correspondence that reveals O'Connor's vision of divine grace.

Gibbons's choices of essential reading material range from the classic to the popular, including the works of Amy Tan and Charles Frazier and the mysteries of Colin Dexter, Sue Grafton, and P.D. James. Gibbons named Berton Rouche's *Eleven Blue Men and Other Mysteries of Medical Detection* (1955) for its compassion and lyricism. For current reading, she listed Michel Faber's *The Crimson Petal and the White* (2003), a dense and insightful pseudo–Victorian novel that contrasts a man's weak-willed wife and his brilliant and resourceful mistress. Of his skill, Gibbons exclaimed, "He writes for keeps. Beside this work, so much other [fiction] is soaked in easy sentiment and cliché" (Zane, 2006). For history, Gibbons selected Perry Miller's *Intellectual History of America* series (1933–1965), an overview of the national mindset from its Puritanic beginnings to the rise of secular thought. Another non-fiction work, Arthur Schlesinger's *The Cycles of American History* (1986), arranges eras by cause-and-effect revelations that range outward from individual acts to their impact on politics, economics, and art. Segueing back into fiction, Gibbons lauded Mario Puzo's crime classic *The Godfather* (1969), which influenced her love of rich sense impression at her first reading in the seventh grade. Rounding out Gibbons's ten best books,

Benjamin *Spock's Baby and Child Care* (1946) and the King James Bible address more personal needs. The former directed her through a new mother's qualms; the latter remains a touchstone of lyrical language embedded with wisdom and majesty.

Gibbons's characters share her enthusiasm for print. An unlikely pairing puts *House Beautiful* in the hands of Lucille Womble, a poor farm wife awaiting a doctor's appointment in "The Headache," a short-short story issued in June 1987 in the *St. Andrews Review.* The disconnect between Lucille and trophy houses exemplies the popular press's targeting of upper-middle-class readers, the substratum of the population most likely to invest in glossy magazines. Disdaining everyday reading of comics books and newspapers, the title character of Ellen Foster (1987) asks a librarian for a list of must-read classics, which includes Chaucer's *Canterbury Tales* (1387) and the novels of Charlotte and Emily Brontë, the twin founts of feminist literature. The bookmobile circuit excites Ellen, who anticipates new books like Christmas gifts. During June mornings of weeding in her grandmother's fields, Ellen meters the chop of her hoe to poetry she has memorized. After her father's death, she yearns for the encyclopedias that had once been hers to peruse at will. At the home of art teacher Julia and her husband Roy, Ellen emerges from introspection to join Sunday improvisations of the Prince Valiant comic strip. The hunger for quality writing prefigures her development into a teen prodigy in the sequel, *The Life All Around Me by Ellen Foster* (2006), in which she recalls with dread weeping while napping at the elementary school library "on a pallet in the Easy Reader section," an ironic implication of innocence to a child recovering from terror (Gibbons, 2006, 16).

In Gibbons's third novel, *A Cure for Dreams* (1991), literature helps to defeat the romanticism implied in the title. Protagonist Betty Davies Randolph, the child of an unsatisfactory marriage, adapts naturally to school and reading, including *Grier's Almanac,* published in 1807 by Robert Grier in Taliaferro County, Georgia, under the title *Georgia and South Carolina Almanack* and continuing for two centuries with an annual circulation of 2.5 million copies. Betty uses the work less as a source of edification or information than as an impetus to selling rosebud salve, a complexion clarifier. After a summer of illness from self-induced pellagra, in 1933, she receives a book of poetry for her 13th birthday. She delights in hearing her mother, Irish-American immigrant Lottie O'Cadhain Davies, read "The Tide Rises, the Tide Falls" (1880), a dramatic elegy by Henry Wadsworth Longfellow. Lottie expresses her own love of literacy in swirly handwriting and conceals from others her regret for ending her education at age fifteen. By interlacing mothering with a love of reading, the author generates positive, hope-filled images in a novel set during the privations of the Great Depression.

In a fourth novel, *Charms for the Easy Life* (1993), Gibbons reprises her own love of books in the self-education of a tripartite matrilineage. She explained to interviewer Polly Paddock, book editor of the *Charlotte* (N.C.) *Observer,* the significance of making her heroines bookish: "There's nothing that will open up life like reading" (Paddock, 1993). Margaret, the narrator, delights in her second grade studies and in hearing her grandmother, Charlie Kate Birch, read aloud. The granddaughter educates herself by perusing Greek classics much as Charlie Kate learns medicine, dentistry, and midwifery by reading outdated medical texts, copies of the *New England*

Journal of Medicine, a farmer's almanac, and Dr. John C. Gunn's *Domestic Medicine, or Poor Man's Friend* (1830), a classic handbook of home remedies. Charlie Kate's daughter, Sophia Snow Birch, shocks the teacher at Miss Nash's School for Young Ladies by carrying to class a copy of Mark Twain's *The Mysterious Stranger* (1910), a dark study of human greed left unfinished after 30 years of composition and rewriting. While Sophia reads Washington Irving's Gothic fool tale "The Legend of Sleepy Hollow" (1819) with Margaret, Charlie Kate recalls her childhood pleasure in books from the Olivia Raney Library, the first public library in Wake County. A landmark in central Raleigh, North Carolina, the library earns respect for its trove of works on local genealogy and history.

Classic books crop up frequently in *Charms for the Easy Life*. Compelled by intellectual curiosity, the Birch women discuss the novels of Thomas Hardy and impatiently take turns reading John Steinbeck's *The Grapes of Wrath* (1939). Margaret is well versed in feminist fiction: George Eliot's *The Mill on the Floss* (1860), Eudora Welty's short fiction anthology *A Curtain of Green* (1964), Virginia Woolf's *The Years* (1937), and the writings of Katherine Anne Porter, Edith Wharton, and Ellen Glasgow. Margaret memorizes Samuel Taylor Coleridge's ghoulish ballad *Christabel* (1797–1800), reads Thomas Wolfe's *Of Time and the River* (1935) and Charles Dickens's *Great Expectations* (1860–1861), cites from Samuel Butler's posthumous classic *The Way of All Flesh* (1903), and receives at Christmas a subscription to the *Saturday Review of Literature*. She begins Marjorie Kinnan Rawlings's Pulitzer Prize–winning novel *The Yearling* (1939) after her grandmother stalks out of the film version of another Pulitzer Prize winner, Margaret Mitchell's *Gone with the Wind* (1936). The granddaughter is puzzled that Charlie Kate refuses to watch the lavish Civil War epic, yet spurns *The Yearling* for lacking action. In a later episode, Sophia earns regard for reading Ernest Hemingway's widely banned novel *To Have and Have Not* (1937) and for confronting a school librarian for banning the works of Nobel Prize–winning author Sinclair Lewis. Typical of Margaret's command of world literature is a discussion of Thomas Mann's *The Magic Mountain* (1924), which eases conversations with Tom Hawkings, III, her first and only beau. For patients at the veterans' hospital in Durham, she is not too high-toned to slip clippings of "Little Orphan Annie" cartoons into letters home.

The confident child reader, a shadow of the author herself, recurs in *Sights Unseen* (1995) in Hattie Barnes. Like Margaret, Hattie has uncensored privileges to her mother's library. The text indicates that Hattie's grandfather and parents curry scholarship in their children with gifts of magazines, books, encyclopedias, and other reference works. In contrast to his own taste in the field hand Hubert's pornographic stash, Freddy caters to his little sister with gifts of *World Book* and *American Heritage* magazines. Gibbons notes the downside of well-read youth — a teacher's accusation of plagiarism against Hattie, whose vocabulary in an essay on the D.H. Lawrence classic story "The Rocking-Horse Winner" (1926) extends to the word "distraught" (Gibbons, 1995, 172). Hattie's choice of reading material echoes themes and motifs from the novel, in which she, like the winner in Lawrence's short story title, struggles to win the love of an obsessed mother. A late view of Maggie Barnes pictures her reading John Steinbeck's *East of Eden* (1952), a complex saga featuring the duality of Cathy/Kate, whose cunning outpaces Maggie's trickery at its worst. During Maggie's relaxing read, Hattie chooses Mary Shelley's *Frankenstein* (1818), an unsubtle reminder of the fractured being her mother has been.

Reading identifies character traits in *On the Occasion of My Last Afternoon* (1998), Gibbons's first historical novel. Prepping for the task, she scanned Burke Davis's *Sherman's March* (1980) and Bruce Catton's Pulitzer Prize–winning *A Stillness at Appomattox* (1953), the third volume of *The Army of the Potomac* series, which lends insight into character motivation. The well-read, but cowardly slavemaster, Samuel P. Goodman Tate, who flies into a rage in 1842 and slices the throat of Jacob, a sassy field hand, fears the hard looks of plantation negroes. During a retreat to an inner sanctum, the slave-killer plunges into volumes by Dante and Goethe, ostensibly to improve his understanding of European languages. Ironically, both authors produced world classics on the subjects of hell and damnation—*The Inferno* (1321) and the tragic play *Faust* (1829). In the confines of the library, Samuel's secret reading allows time for slave tempers to cool and belays a resurgence of retaliation that occurred during Nat Turner's rampage August 22–October 30, 1831. However, the respite is short-term. Samuel faces his own recompense in June 1862 from the social and economic collapse of the James River plantation milieu after General George Brinton McClellan headquarters at Samuel's beloved Seven Oaks estate.

Gibbons credits Samuel Tate with introducing his family to literature. His daughter, narrator Emma Garnet Tate Lowell, relishes her own escapist favorites—Horace Walpole's Gothic classic *The Castle of Otranto* (1764), the frontier novel *The Deerslayer* (1841) from James Fenimore Cooper's Leatherstocking Tales, and the romances of William Gilmore Simms, all gifts of Emma's worldly brother Whately. Unfortunately for Samuel's son, the growth of humanism during his education at Washington College in Lexington, Virginia, alienates him from a father who expects filial devotion to shallow values based on the posturing of a faux scholar. For her own edification, Emma chooses the Niger River exploration featured in Mungo Park's *Travels in the Interior Districts of Africa* (1816) and Mark Twain's whimsical *Innocents Abroad* (1869) rather than the romantic narratives of Sir Walter Scott, a source of unrealistic romantic ideals that, according to Emma's brother Whately, "lull the mind into sweet stupidity" (Gibbons, 1998, 81). In the resolution of *On the Occasion of My Last Afternoon*, Emma makes light of Old Guard disapproval of her liberalism toward freed slaves and poor whites. In conjunction with her younger sister Maureen's aid to poor women and orphans, Emma attends a book discussion of Charles Dickens's *Bleak House* (1852–1853) at which "snippety" ladies stare at their shoes rather than welcome the input of declassé women (Gibbons, 1998, 271). The choice of *Bleak House* symbolizes the bleakness of the Reconstruction Era as well as the frail hopes of Raleigh aristocrats that their slave-based economy can reinvigorate itself.

For widow Martha Greene Oliver and 22-year-old Mary Oliver, the mother-daughter duo in Gibbons's seven novel, *Divining Women* (2004), respect for intellectualism begins at the home of Martha's parents, Leslie and Toby Greene. Although frugal in terms of food budgets, the Greenes, residents of the prestigious Dupont Circle in Washington, D.C., satisfy their intellectual curiosity with conversation sparked by Chautauqua lectures and personal investigations of hydroelectricity as a model of scientific advancement. On their journeys, they purchase boxes of books on such contemporary issues as psychoanalysis and socialism. To grandson Daniel, Toby explains the investment, "We pay to understand" (Gibbons, 2004, 31). Perpetuating their example, granddaughter Mary loses herself in the works of American statesman-historian George Bancroft and plunges into an urbane tragedy, Leo Tolstoy's *Anna Karenina* (1875–1877), for Mary's first travel to the South. The choice of a novel about a women who hurls herself under a train suits the situation, which reminds Mary of her elitist brother Daniel, whose body returns to Washington from Baltimore aboard a baggage car.

Mary continues to assess the world through a literary lens. Upon arrival at her uncle Troop Ross's tacky manse on September 30, 1918, she studies an egregious coat of arms and thinks of the social-climbing peasants in Thomas Hardy's *Tess of the d'Urbervilles* (1895). Mary's pregnant aunt, Maureen Carlton Ross, inhabits a blue-violet-green-silver upstairs hideaway fragrant with hybrid roses and stocked with good books. In addition to an unread collection of feminist writer Edna Ferber's short fiction, Mary locates travel guides to places that might relieve Maureen's in-house misery. In thanks for the Olivers' kindness, Maureen selects a significant return gift — Edith Wharton's *The Decoration of Houses* (1897), a rejuvenating composition that Wharton undertook during a case of nerves brought on by marriage to a lunatic. As the home situation worsens for Maureen and Mary under Troop's absurd, self-serving rules, Mary pictures herself as Lily Bart, the protagonist of Edith Wharton's *The House of Mirth* (1905), an ominous choice of a protagonist who loses traction in a slippery social milieu and chooses suicide with an overdose of chloral hydrate over spinsterhood and poverty.

In *The Life All Around Me by Ellen Foster* (2006), the sequel to *Ellen Foster*, Gibbons extends a respect for reading to praise for self-education. The title character relies on the bookmobile driver as a source of intellectual advice on Harvard graduates in the area. A discriminating reader, Ellen wins a scholarship to the gifted class at Johns Hopkins University by writing an essay, "The Cell Wall and the Surface of Hemingway's Stories: A Compare and Contrast" (Gibbons, 2006, 7–8). From ages 12 to 15, she advances intellectually in a bedroom library tall enough to require a ladder. As part of her in-home weekend training, she tackles economist Thorstein Veblen's *Theory of the Leisure Class* (1899) and Paul Goodman's social treatise *Growing Up Absurd* (1960). Laura's influence on Ellen's intellectual growth becomes palpable in the living room grouping of three books, the biography of Eleanor and Franklin Roosevelt, T.S. Eliot's *Four Quartets* (1945), and *We Are Your Sons: The Legacy of Ethel and Julius Rosenberg* (1975), an apologia for a couple executed for espionage written by Michael and Robert Meeropol, the Rosenbergs' only children. Snippets of readings indicate Ellen's familiarity with David's psalms, *Madame Bovary*, Henry James's *Daisy Miller* (1878), and J.D. Salinger's *The Catcher in the Rye* (1951) and with Edgar Allan Poe's death.

Ellen's taste, like that of Margaret and Charlie Kate Birch, reflects her social and emotional milieu. Ellen's sense of the absurd endears to her Walter Mitty, the fantasy-obsessed character in James Thurber's "The Secret Life of Walter Mitty" (1945). She cites James Joyce and knows the meter and imagery of Robert Frost's "Stopping by Woods on a Snowy Evening" (1923) and John Edward Masefield's "Sea-Fever" (1902), lines from John Crowe Ransom's "Bells for John Whiteside's Daughter" (1924), and details of Charles Dickens's *A Christmas Carol* (1843), in which Ebenezer Scrooge blames bad dreams on an undigested bit of cheese. The four works suggest Ellen's roiling emotions, the first three because of death images in Frost's "the darkest evening of the year," Ransom's goose call of "alas" for a dead child, and Masefield's anticipation of life's "quiet sleep" and the last from Dickens's harrowing of Scrooge with unshakable ghosts and a glimpse of his own tombstone. The merger of literary gleanings with Ellen's personal dilemmas illustrates the value of reading to life-altering choices.

• *Further reading*

Brodeur, Nicole. "So They'll Know They're Not Alone," Raleigh, N.C., *News & Observer* (27 November 1996).

Cohen, Judith Beth. "Review: Charms for the Easy Life," *Women's Review of Books* 11, no. 1 (October 1993).

Gibbons, Kaye. *Divining Women.* New York: G.P. Putnam's Sons, 2004.

_____. *Ellen Foster.* New York: Algonquin Press, 1987.

_____. "Introduction," *I Cannot Tell a Lie, Exactly and Other Stories,* by Mary Ladd Gavell. New York: Random House, 2001.

_____. *The Life All Around Me by Ellen Foster.* New York: Harcourt, 2006.

_____. *On the Occasion of My Last Afternoon.* New York: G.P. Putnam's Sons, 1998.

_____. *Sights Unseen.* New York: G.P. Putnam's Sons, 1995.

Miller, Mary E. "Summertime and the Readin' Is Easy," Raleigh, N.C., *News & Observer* (1 June 1993).

Paddock, Polly. "Kaye Gibbons: A Writer's Journey," *Charlotte* (N.C.) *Observer* (30 May 1993).

Romine, Dannye. "North Carolina: Read All about It," *Charlotte* (N.C.) *Observer* (5 November 1989).

Zane, J. Peder. "Books on the Tar Heel Mind," Raleigh, N.C., *News & Observer* (11 June 2006).

realism

For the sake of truth, Kaye Gibbons demands verisimilitude. In a criticism of Lean Cuisine's frozen meals, she chided, "You don't want to have imitation children, do you? Then why eat imitation food?" (Powell, 1987). The one-to-one comparison resonates with her home-simple view of reality, the source of her fiction. In *The Writer on Her Work: New Essays in New Territory* (1991), she recalls from her college days the loose assortment of images in her mind that defied chronology. She accounts for lapses in accuracy as a natural filtration system by which the brain excises hurt, the kind of suffering that expatriate American poet T.S. Eliot referred to as an overload of reality. Undaunted by a swirl of vivid mind dramas, Gibbons continues to frame one-of-a-kind word pictures— the rescue of a man from strangling in a noose, an ex-slave delivering to a Southern belle a lesson in dismembering a duck, a woman jettisoning a snake from a pocketbook down a privy toilet, a pregnant woman imprisoned by vases of hothouse roses, and the hand-to-lips I-want-a-cigarette gesture of a dying farm wife in an oxygen tent. A reviewer for *Wilson Quarterly* notes that the author toes a fine line between realism and sentimentality by stressing "hard vicissitudes and necessary graces," notably, the hanging victim's gift of a charm promising an easy life and the reclamation of a former Virginia belle from widowhood through female kitchen skills ("Review," 1990, 95). In an essay for *New York*, critic James Wolcott created a more compelling image of Gibbons's canon as "living scrapbooks," like the novels of Anne Tyler, that "[refuse] to primp or pander" (Wolcott, 1996, 115). Both summations commend Gibbons's gift for candor and integrity.

Critics read the novel *Ellen Foster* (1987) and its sequel, *The Life All Around Me by Ellen Foster* (2006), as authentic voicings of an uncherished, unanchored rural North Carolinian. Tricia Stringstubb states in a critique for the *Cleveland Plain Dealer* that such authenticity grounds Gibbons's fiction. The blend of humor and humanity validates children like Ellen, who are born with a visceral grasp on survival. In one instance, Ellen acknowledges the pseudo-finality of a foster home. The food sack and thermos she takes to the pasture on Saturdays are hers only until a foster home shift replaces her with another child. Like the warehoused belongings of a jailed prisoner, a sack containing $166 in coins and bills awaiting her in the closet bears her name and the date that she offered them in payment for hospitality. Stringstubb declares that the true-edged voice of Ellen at age 11 does not retain its realistic thrust after the character reaches her mid-teens. One explanation of critical disappointment in the older Ellen is the author's stage of life — the contentment of middle age too far removed from childhood trauma to revive the raw, grating verities from the introit of the Ellen Foster saga.

Gibbons's second novel, *A Virtuous Woman* (1989), overloads the life of protagonist Ruby Pitts Woodrow Stokes with matter-of-fact hurts and disappointments. She and surrounding characters, according to Jay Strafford, a critic for the *Richmond Times-Dispatch*, are "the people you can count on in trouble, the ones you can truthfully call 'the salt of the earth'" (Strafford, 1989). Foolishly seduced from a comfortable girlhood on a family farm, she marries 26-year-old John Woodrow, whose wedding night maulings divest Ruby of virginity and romantic illusion. The pace of Ruby's downward spiral quickens at age 20 when she slips a pistol under pillow to await John's return from a carouse with a teenage tart. Gibbons deflects a possible shooting with John's unforeseen knifing through the lungs in a pool room affray. In token of the second phase of Ruby's education in reality, the author pictures her smoking a cigarette under a pecan tree when 40-year-old bachelor "Blinking" Jack Ernest Stokes ambles by with a wheelbarrow loaded with manure. Symbolic of the removal of ordure from Ruby's life, the encounter informs her of her widowhood after three days of wondering about John's absence.

Realism amplifies a complex interlinkage of asset and liability in the Stokes' marriage. Ruby flourishes as a wife and housekeeper, but internalizes her distress every time Jack fires her pistol. At the bourbon-sweet breath of his good-night kiss, she forgives him his secret stash in the shed. Their uneven mating survives for a quarter century until cigarettes generate malignancy in Ruby's lung, killing her at age 45 and leaving Jack stunned at the emptiness of a wifeless house. Gibbons turns to realism for his selection of infantile escapes— more bourbon, meals of canned soup and corn flakes, and Roadrunner cartoons on television. Further into infancy, Jack escapes sorrow by sprinkling clean sheets with Ruby's lilac dusting powder, which smells like baby products. The ultimate reality for Jack is mothering, which returns to him through the housework and cheer of June Stanley, the neighbor girl whom the Stokes fostered. Gibbons suggests that, without June's volunteerism and her father Burr's gift of land to Jack, the widower might lack a reason to go on living.

In reference to daily hardships during the Great Depression, Gibbons moves directly to theme with the evocative title of her third novel, *A Cure for Dreams* (1991). In the view of Jay Strafford, the author "writes with such heartfelt empathy for her characters that their lives become real—and important to the reader" (*Ibid.*, 1991). The text portrays rosy illusion as an invasive disease requiring a home remedy. Through retellings of matrilineal stories covering three generations, Marjorie Polly Randolph discerns that real-life challenges demand grit rather than self-trickery. The formula for survival suits Bridget O'Donough O'Cadhain, an emigrant from Galway, Ireland, who sustains herself on Irish Catholicism, a bleak antidote to life with an alcoholic husband, Sheamus O'Cadhain, and his boozy brother Bart. To navigate the straits of hard times and the daily onus of a controlling, work-obsessed head of household, Bridget's daughter, Lottie O'Cadhain, wife of Quaker farmer-miller Charles Davies, employs creative guile. Ignoring strictures on her daily activities, she snatches coins and bills from her husband's pockets when she launders his clothes. Bankrolled for fun, she shepherds her daughter Betty to instructive gin rummy and pinochle games in the back room of Porter's store. Like an open-ended seminar, the conversation of local women schools Betty in the uncertainties of married life and the needs of wives for love and acceptance. Contributing to Betty's education, on November 25, 1942, the family cook, domestic-midwife Polly Deal, tends the birth of Betty's first child, Marjorie Polly Randolph, the fourth generation of O'Donough-O'Cadhain-Davies-Randolph women. The stalwart clan wraps Betty and her babe in security during World War II, when Betty's husband Herman serves in the pacific aboard the U.S.S. *Hornet*. Gibbons's female safety net establishes that women are capable of salving their own hurts and fears.

The combined wisdom of mentors creates a female reality that discounts and defies the patriarchy of Milk Farm Road. At home in their milieu, Lottie, Betty, Polly, and Marjorie embrace strength and pragmatism as antidotes to pipedreams of happily-ever-after wedlock. In the critique of Kathryn McKee for *Southern Quarterly*, Lottie, the skilled seamstress and husband manipulator, "cuts and sews ... a self she wants Charles to see, a self who will pacify his unreasonable nature" (McKee, 1997, 100). Lottie's ability to engineer her own world takes a bizarre turn when she fabricates for her Irish emigrant family in Bell County, Kentucky, a heroic death for Charles in the rescue of a hobo. In place of Charles's cowardly suicide in a river in 1937, she pictures a noble sacrifice from the idealized man she wanted Charles to be. More than a loving gesture to her husband, Lottie's lie saves her from admitting that an improvident marriage freighted her previous life with unhappiness.

With similar character development, *Charms for the Easy Life* (1993) thrives on realism. Gibbons covers such disparate topics as suicide on train tracks, teen masturbation, and the racist nature of medical and civic services in Raleigh, North Carolina. Critic Judith Beth Cohen applauds the potency of Gibbons's female characters, who "don't accept the reality they are given, they alter it" (Cohen, 1993). At a dramatic face-off between Sophia Snow Birch and her husband, they squabble over the wake for flu victim Ida O'Shea, which the father fears will upset their 12-year-old daughter Margaret. Following graphic details of Ida's strangulation on vomit, the narrative describes Sophia's anger at a mate who prefers leaving Margaret to fantasy rather than introducing her to mortality and respect for the dead. The episode moves deftly toward grief and terror after Sophia and her mother guide Margaret to the coffin, where the smell of camphor assaults Margaret's nose. The four-day convalescence that returns her to normalcy succeeds in part from Grandmother Charlie Kate's herbal nostrums— valerian root (a folk sedative and sleep aid) under the pillow and cups of clover tea (a blood purifer).

Gibbons positions the episode about Ida's funeral as a foreshadowing of Margaret's loss of her father to stroke. Unmoved by the passing of a distant, unloving parent, she helps pack his belongings away in the attic and anticipates a fuller life with her mother and especially with her grandmother. An experienced parent and a respected healer of the sick and washer of the dead, Charlie Kate maintains high standards that reject voodoo along with romantic whimsy and requests for abortions. To a young wife overcome by grief for a strayed mate, Charlie Kate chops her advice down to three words, "Get over him" (Gibbons, 1993, 48). Margaret's upbringing in a no-nonsense environment steers her toward service to others— packing Red Cross boxes with Hershey bars and cigarettes and writing letters for wounded veterans of World War II. Well versed in reality, Margaret proffers an unsentimental farewell to Charlie Kate, who dies on Christmas night, 1942, on the threshold of Margaret's womanhood.

Gibbons's narration of treatment for bipolarity places *Sights Unseen* (1995) on a separate plane from her earlier works. Slowly paced and vivid, the childhood of Hattie Barnes stretches out alongside the rampages of her unpredictable mother Maggie. For 12 chapters, the text carries to great length Maggie's unforeseen outbursts, sexual demands, and splurges on fashions and furniture before detailing the remedy of the times— psychotherapy and eight weeks of electroconvulsive shock treatment in Duke Hospital in 1967 amid a "stew of sickness" (Gibbons, 1995, 181). Drained of memory from jolts to the brain, she returns home a changed woman and gradually rebuilds a relationship with husband Frederick, children Hattie and Freddy, and housekeeper Pearl Wiggins. The author turns into dramatic irony the difficulty of family conversation devoid of Maggie's incessant lunacy.

Gibbons's ability to disclose horror with brevity and control reaches a pinnacle in her first historical novel, *On the Occasion of My Last Afternoon* (1998). Reviewer Polly Paddock Gossett, book editor of the *Charlotte* (N.C.) *Observer*, admires the work for its understatement. Without sensationalism, details from the preface, conduct, and aftermath of the Civil War attest to the outfall of the flesh trade. The opening chapters focus on one atrocity— the near-beheading of Jacob, a field hand foolhardy enough to advise the cold-blooded slaveowner Samuel P. Goodman Tate on pig killing. The episode, set in 1842, echoes through subsequent scenes as Emma

Garnet Tate Lowell embraces an adult life devoid of bondage and barbarism, like her father's nightly rebukes to his submissive wife Alice and the double hanging in Williamsburg that Samuel insists on attending for amusement. Settled in Raleigh, North Carolina, with her refined husband, Dr. Quincy Lowell, in 1847, Emma creates an inviting nest for her family with the aid of freedwoman Clarice Washington, the cook-housekeeper who follows Emma from her wedding to her new life apart from crumbling tidewater Virginia's aristocracy. Unfortunately for the nation, war spares no one the horrors that end slavery.

Gibbons views the beginning and end of the Civil War through a domestic lens. Coping for Emma and Quincy involves maintaining a sane, functional home while working at a killing pace to save combat casualties. The narrative reveals no combat or actuarial details of the battles of Manassas, Virginia (July 21, 1861; August 28–30, 1862), Gettysburg, Pennsylvanina (July 3–4, 1863), or the Wilderness, Virginia (May 5–7, 1864). In place of strategic plotting and vainglory, Gibbons substitutes the death rattles of men bayonetted through the gut, suppurating wounds, and the grasping hands that seek Emma's care. During one misstep, she falls prone over a dying soldier and experiences the release of his last breath, a ghoulish symbol of war at close range. Glimpses of letters to parents, surgery performed on casualties atop the Lowells' grand piano, maggots gorging on infected incisions, and carols sung at Christmas 1864 parallel the gradual extinction of the Confederacy. For Emma, realism takes the form of trainloads of wounded who have no hope of the medical treatment they deserve and of a husband who expends his energy to end suffering and save lives. At war's end, victory coalesces into a tripartite portrait of the despairing upper class, starving and unemployed laboring class, and newly freed slaves who lack a vision of their upended social condition.

Realism in Gibbons's seventh novel, *Divining Women* (2004), advances on two fronts— the humor of misaligned family relations and the afflictions of World War I and the 1918 influenza pandemic. At a time when European warfare assaults soldiers with blistering mustard gas, when automatic gunfire strafes doughboys huddled in trenches, Maureen Carlton Ross plots her own combat against her husband Troop, an emotionally frozen fiend. Contributing sensible counsel to the physical care of Maureen during the last 50 days of her pregnancy, niece Mary Oliver, a 22-year-old graduate student, arrives on September 30, 1918, in the last six weeks of the war. She demands an accounting from Troop for abasing and discounting his wife and for imposing "flagrant misinterpretations of reality" on the household (Gibbons, 2004, 89). To Mary, retrieving ginger root from the kitchen at 4:00 A.M. is a necessary mission to combat nausea, which concludes with Maureen's "spewing last night's stuffed peppers into the wastepaper basket" (*Ibid.*, 86). Gibbons augments realism in the final scene when Maureen turns her private regurgitation into a public execration against Troop, who is too self-obsessed to accompany his wife to the burial of their stillborn daughter Ella.

Ribbons eighth novel, *The Life All Around Me by Ellen Foster* (2006), weakens her reputation for straight-up realism. Critics differ on the credibility of a complete retrieval of the title character from a dismal life. On her own initiative, Ellen successfully petitions Dr. Derek Curtis Bok, president of Harvard University, for early college admission. Before securing tuition in his return letter, she follows a roller-coaster track to a high-IQ camp at Johns Hopkins University, a family outing to the state fair, and a private hearing of Stuart's marriage proposal to be followed by elopement to a fireworks emporium at Pedro's South of the Border. Qurky humor gives place to serious confrontations with the past after Ellen takes possession of her mother's personal belongings and reads a psychiatric evaluation of the mother's decline toward suicide in March 1969 from an overdose of prescription digitalis. On Christmas Eve, 1974, Ellen views her family's abandoned property and returns to Starletta's house to celebrate the holiday. Overpowering the resolution is Ellen's control of a family inheritance that leaves her richer than she anticipates. To fans of the Ellen Foster saga, the overturn of bad fortune bears more Cinderella traits than realists can accept.

See also **healing and health; historical milieu**

• *Further reading*

Cohen, Judith Beth. "Review: *Charms for the Easy Life*," *Women's Review of Books* 11, no. 1 (October 1993).

Gibbons, Kaye. *Charms for the Easy Life*. New York: Putnam, 1993.

_____. *Divining Women*. New York: G.P. Putnam's Sons, 2004.

_____. *Sights Unseen*. New York: G.P. Putnam's Sons, 1995.

Gossett, Polly Paddock. "She Sees No Glory in the Gore of War," *Charlotte* (N.C.) *Observer* (7 June 1998).

McKee, Kathryn. "Simply Talking: Women and Language in Kaye Gibbons's *A Cure for Dreams*," *Southern Quarterly* 35, no. 4 (Summer 1997): 97–107.

Perry, Carolyn, and Mary Louise Weaks, eds. *The History of Southern Women's Literature*. Baton Rouge: Louisiana State University Press, 2002.

Powell, Lew. "Lean, Mean, Frozen Cuisine," *Charlotte* (N.C.) *Observer* (28 November 1987).

"Review: *Ellen Foster and A Virtuous Woman*," *Wilson Quarterly* 14, no. 1 (Winter 1990): 95.

Strafford, Jay. "Kaye Gibbbons Creates a Stirring Tale," *Richmond Times-Dispatch* (28 June 1989).

_____. "Ordinary Life Has Meaning," *Richmond Times-Dispatch* (3 April 1991).

Stratton, Sharon Lloyd. "Family Talk Is Backbone of 'Dreams,'" *Richmond Times-Dispatch* (5 May 1991).

Wolcott, James. "Crazy for You," *New Yorker* (21 August 1996): 115–116.

reclamation

Kaye Gibbons endows characters with the inner strength to recoup lost selves. In an early short-short story, "The Headache," issued in June 1987 in *St. Andrews Review*, protagonist Lucille Womble, a poor farm wife, requires prodding from her husband Henry and her employer, Mae Belle Stokes, to unload two weeks' worth of self-torture that generates head pain, insomnia, weepiness, and nightly visions of a rearing snake's head. To ensure secrecy, Lucille questions a physician, Dr. Janet Cowley, about a framed line from the Hippocratic Oath guaranteeing doctor-patient confidentiality, a symbolic canopy shielding Lucille's unethical behavior in concealing an abandoned handbag. Cowley wisely advises Lucille to initiate a talking cure to detoxify an unsettling prank that thrusts a snake-bearing pocketbook into her possession. Through tender husband-wife bed chat, Lucille elicits the reassurance that she is loved and appreciated. Reclamation for Lucille, an early model of Gibbons's vibrant womenfolk, involves a cathartic disburderning and her husband's promise of two new hats, symbols of dual crowns for conscientious womanhood.

For the title character of Gibbons's first novel, *Ellen Foster* (1987), reclamation requires the selection of a new family. The court system fails her by removing her from the voluntary caregiving of Julia and Roy and by entrusting her to relatives as the appropriate source of child-rearing. At age 11, Ellen extricates herself from the hostility of a maternal grandmother and aunt Nadine Nelson and, on Christmas Day, 1970, enters a temporary homeless state until she can locate a worthy surrogate mother. Ellen is proud to live with Laura, a foster parent who sets an ample table and who maintains pleasant mealtime decorum. Living in a normal household surrounds Ellen with the decency and courtesy that assuage and hearten an edgy preteen who is accustomed to snarls, grabs, and verbal badgering from her alcoholic father Bill, a wife killer and child endangerer. Contemplating her day, Ellen comments on the foster family's custom of taking turns riding Dolphin the pony, a lesson in sharing and socialization far removed from life among a biological family that "never was a Roman pillar" (Gibbons, 1987, 56). Ellen's self-rescue endears her to readers and critics, who compare her to Mark Twain's Huckleberry Finn and J.D. Salinger's Holden Caulfield, both emotionally destitute children.

A more common pattern of self-restitution in Gibbons's novels involves women in ridding themselves of disastrous marriages. In *A Virtuous Woman* (1989), the 20-year-old protagonist, Ruby Pitts Woodrow Stokes, tolerates the carping and two-timing of itinerant farm hand John Woodrow, who romances a greasy trollop at their home. Rather than return to brothers Jimmy and Paul or to her father for help, Ruby arms herself with a pistol, which she slides under her pillow for quick access. The plot takes an unexpected side trail after John dies of a knife blade to the lungs during a pool hall fracas. Ruby's salvation occurs later at the Hoover farm, where she meets "Blinking" Jack Ernest Stokes, a bachelor twice her age who offers devotion and genuine affection. Textured with compromise, the Pitts-Stokes marriage nonetheless satisfies both parties. In place of the children she can't conceive because of a sexually transmitted disease from John, Ruby mothers June Stanley, a neighbor in need of womanly love and guidance. Gibbons's theme of reclamation discloses that pragmatism grounds Ruby's contentment and extends to June a serendipitous mothering. The situation reverses in the falling action with June's filial gifts to Ruby in her last days and to Jack, the sad widower who retreats from reality in fantasies of Ruby's return from the dead.

With more humor and moxie, Lottie O'Cadhain Davies, the protagonist of Gibbons's third novel, *A Cure for Dreams* (1991), reshapes a withered marriage into a mother-daughter lark. In collusion with her daughter Betty, Lottie avoids her money-mad husband, Quaker farmer-miller Charles Davies, and gads about Milk Farm Road in search of gossip and low-stakes gambling on gin rummy and pinochle, the amusements of female society during the Great Depression. Beyond sewing new outfits and betting pennies on cards, Lottie acquires an enlightening overview of moribund wedlock. As a lesson in clues to a man's validation of his wife, in the mid-1930s, Lottie urges Betty to listen to the male voice when he summons his mate. Encounters with Amanda Bethune, the rare happily-ever-after wife, introduce Betty to the possibilities of a stable union. To reinstitute marital joy in the O'Donough-O'Cadhain-Davies matrilineage, Betty avoids the errors in judgment that condemn her mother and grandmother to domestic woe. The strategy for happiness exemplifies the value of woman-to-woman storytellling, which edifies at the same time that it entertains.

Gibbons describes Lottie, the daughter of Bridget O'Donough O'Cadhain, a vigorous Irish emigrant from Galway to Bell County, Kentucky, as a passive-aggressive scrapper. Lottie refuses to give in to her domineering husband by avoiding, ignoring, and outfoxing him. While conversing above his droning complaints, she shifts table talk away from his attempts to rule the household with sour frugality. In 1937, his choice of suicide in the river liberates Lottie and even rewards her with a small allotment to widows, an unforeseen benefit of manlessness instituted by President Franklin Delano Roosevelt through the Social Security Act of 1935. Her reclamation is less a makeover than a sweeping aside of a minor annoyance, like a fly buzzing over dinner. With Betty and the family cook, Polly Deal, the all-woman household flourishes into World War II, when Betty claims a worthy mate, Herman Randolph, a sailor aboard the U.S.S. *Hornet*. Before he departs for the Pacific war, he sires the next family female, Marjorie Polly Randolph, the fourth generation of females who set their own agendas.

A similarly enlivening recovery occurs in *Charms for the Easy Life* (1993), which echoes female discontent during the Depression and second world war. Gibbons pictures a band of females—a self-educated grandmother, mother, and daughter—working as unlicensed healers in the mill district of Raleigh, North Carolina, during the 1930s and early 1940s. Like Lottie Davies, both Grandmother Charlie Kate and her daughter, Sophia Snow Birch, rid themselves of paltry mates and the emotional residue of widowhood. Charlie Kate outgrows her husband, who slips away to Ohio; Sophia prays to Jesus to claim her husband, who conveniently dies of cerebral hemorrhage in August 1936, leaving her to box his possessions and stow them out of sight in the attic, a symbol of exile into oblivion. Although both women claim their liberty, Sophia edges back into the marriage market to land businessman Richard Baines, a gallant, generous beau. Charlie Kate, who survives a more problematic alliance with an illiterate ferryman, plunges anew into wedlock during her straying husband's three-day visit at the Sir Walter Raleigh Hotel in 1938. At her departure, she swipes a wad of cash—$1,365—from his wallet. In the aftermath of a well deserved female abandonment of a worthless mate, she brandishes an anti-male wisdom that prepares granddaughter Margaret for womanhood. In a gynocentric environment, Margaret carefully selects as a likely husband Tom Hawkings, III, an adoring, open-hearted boyfriend from respected Raleigh aristocracy. Gibbons implies that the examples set by grandmother and mother spare Margaret the trial and error that force her elders into arduous self-renewal.

In *Sights Unseen* (1995), Gibbons draws on childhood memories for a fictional version of restoring her own spirit. The process of rehabilitating Maggie Barnes from bipolar rampages ends her alienation and terrorizing of family. In the novel's resolution, in 1967, she returns from months of psychotherapy and eight electroconvulsive shock treatments at Duke Hospital. Her retreat from past infractions of decorum prepares her for the long resuscitation of her roles as wife, mother, and female head of household. The tentative response of her children, 12-year-old Hattie and her older brother Freddy, mirrors Maggie's gradual reordering of self and household. Like a swimmer easing into chill waters, Maggie draws Hattie close for an afternoon book talk and nap, cuts and sews sunsuits, and lingers at Hattie's door at night as a silent, but beneficent maternal presence. Gibbons portrays the Barnes family as willingly, forgivingly complicit in making Maggie whole again. Of particular value is the caretaking of Pearl Wiggins, the cook-housekeeper, who substitutes for the insane mother without usurping her place. In the resolution, the author pictures Maggie and Pearl sharing kitchen work like sisters.

A surprising reclamation concludes Gibbons's first historical novel, *On the Occasion of My Last Afternoon* (1998). Protagonist Emma Garnet Tate Lowell grows away from her pampered younger sister Maureen, who remains at home at Seven Oaks, their Virginia homeplace, while cultivating flirtation and a singing career. The collapse of the plantation South finds Maureen unwed in her mid-20s and rapidly losing her looks. A thematic epiphany acknowledges the moral and emotional redemption of Southern women through suffering, a new experience for Maureen. After the death of her mother Alice in 1859 and the displacement of her father, Samuel P. Goodman Tate, by General George Brinton McClellan's occupation forces in June 1862, Maureen flees to Emma and observes authentic strength of character from the Lowell family's daily service to the wounded in Raleigh, North Carolina. Although Maureen lacks the fortitude for treating the maimed in the critical ward or for washing gory sheets, she develops self-respect by singing to men quartered at the Lowell home. From holiday carols and serving tea, she advances to dismembering live chickens, an unforeseen gift in a largely meatless era. Emma witnesses the emergence of a survivor as the "comportment school graduate" scalds, plucks, cuts, and fries poultry that restores the Yule spirit to the household on Christmas Day, 1864 (Gibbons, 1998, 253). In the feminist tradition, Maureen passes on her culinary expertise to the three Lowell daughters, Leslie, Louise, and Mary. Echoing Maureen's salvation are cooking lessons for Emma, who, in widowhood, looks to fellow home economics students for conversations that restore wholeness. The creation of appealing dishes exalts a womanly strength at sustaining others.

Gibbons's most endangered adult, Maureen Carlton Ross, reclaims self in *Divining Women* (2004), the author's seventh novel. In the midst of spiritual warfare, Maureen takes hope from four disparate female sources—the spunk of 22-year-old niece Mary Oliver, support from the maid Mamie, and letters from Maureen's mother and from a stranger, Judith Benedict Stafford, who escapes a failed marriage on May 3, 1912, to embrace personal and sexual freedom in Europe. Upon Mary's arrival by train on September 30, 1918, to Elm City, North Carolina, Maureen, in the last trimester of pregnancy, rethinks the years of bullying by which her punitive husband, Troop Ross, shoves her deeper into cringing compliance. A transcendent moment emerges at Mary's disclosure of messages from Maureen's mother that Troop conceals. Although miserable and off-balance in the last few days of pregnancy, Maureen dispatches Mary to halt the delivery of husbandly floral bribes and to reclaim letters and telegrams from the Carltons in Yazoo City, Mississippi. The restoration of contact with family and home turf begins Maureen's rejuvenation.

A common scenario in feminist fiction is communal birthing, a group effort dating to ancient times that retrieves a parturient female from isolation. When labor on November 7, 1918, grips Maureen, Mary shares the childbed and consoles Maureen while Mamie inserts a crochet hook into the membranes to break the waters that hold the baby in the birth canal. Buoyed by womanly affection, Maureen survives both a harrowing delivery and, the following morning, the death of Ella Eloise after the umbilical cord strangles her. Even in loss, Maureen glories in motherhood. Following directly upon self-regard comes long-distance reunion with a mother endowed with an unshakeable love and devotion to her daughter. Dispatching a postal order to needy kin, Maureen proclaims herself living and thriving, her first self-affirmation since marrying a petty despot. A tender preface assures the reader that Mary and Maureen enjoy over 20 years of shared bliss.

In Gibbons's first sequel, *The Life All Around Me by Ellen Foster* (2006), the title figure reclaims self and future through direct action and serendipity. A frontal assault on the problem of tuition for college results in a letter from Dr. Derek Curtis Bok, president of Harvard University, who offers a scholarship and early admission to replace the inferior education of local schools. More to the core of Ellen's difficulties is the first face-off against Aunt Nadine Nelson, the thief who possesses all that is left of Shine, Ellen's 40-year-old mother. While familiarizing herself with personal items, Ellen reclaims a doctor's description of a difficult period, her mother's fatal decline into mental illness on September 10, 1968, and suicide six months later. The knowledge of Shine's insecurity relieves Ellen of guilt that she couldn't save her mother. Reclaimed as a daughter and heir to family property, Ellen is free to relish the "life all around" her, the loving acceptance of foster mother Laura and of Starletta's mother, who values Ellen like a member of the family. The author's emphasis on calculated self-rescue elevates Ellen to the pantheon of Gibbons's purposeful heroines.

See also **achievement; powerlessness; vulnerability**

• *Further reading*

Gibbons, Kaye. *Ellen Foster*. New York: Algonquin Press, 1987.
_____. *On the Occasion of My Last Afternoon*. New York: G.P. Putnam's Sons, 1998.
Smith, Starr E. "Review: *Divining Women*," Library Journal 129, no. 5 (15 March 2004).

religion

Through fiction, Kaye Gibbons publicly cleanses herself of Southern religious fundamentalism and its attendant ignorance and wrong-headedness. In a personal essay, "The First Grade, Jesus, and the Hollyberry Family" (1998), she recalls several annual chapel programs delivered by an evangelist of the New Life Ministries, who stresses the dangers of Communism and the landscape of hell. Gibbons notes that renegade Baptists are so indoctrinated with terror sermons that they "could've gone to the bathroom in Hell in the dark" (Gibbons, 1998, 75). In retrospect, she blames doomsday diatribes for hardening congregants into mean-spirited individuals who gloat at imperiled non-believers. On the upside, from the extremes of a pulpit pounder, she learns hyperbole, metaphor, and simile, all essentials of her writing style.

The title character of her first novel, *Ellen Foster* (1987), maintains a paradoxical relationship to the almighty. She introduces a jaundiced view of sanctimony at her mother's funeral in 1969. In mental duel with the smug minister at the chapel, who makes unfounded speculations on the goodness of the deceased, Ellen nurtures good memories of her mother. Nonetheless, Ellen fears that suicide is an unforgivable sin. After Ellen's grandmother's death before Christmas, 1970, the child frames a lengthy request to Jesus to allow the second death vigil to negate the first, when Ellen was unable to save her beloved mother. At a necessary flight from a hostile environment, Ellen asks Jesus to purify her and find a surrogate parent to love her. Upon locating a foster home, she adopts the demeanor of her new mother, who finances the shelter with a stipend from the church collection plate. With the rest of the foster family, Ellen attends services regularly, but conceals her opinion that the sermon is "horse manure," an unsurprising response from a sorely tried orphan (Gibbons, 1987, 56).

In reference to piety and godliness, Gibbons scatters bitter bits of criticism throughout her later novels. In *A Virtuous Woman* (1989), "Blinking" Jack Ernest Stokes describes the extremes of working-class women — either whoring or witnessing, an evangelical term for obsessive zeal and confession that "worried the pure living hell" out of a husband (Gibbons, 1989, 62). He tries to make sense of divine will and of Christian piety, but ends up charging God for producing no-goods like Adolf Hitler and Roland Stanley, a neighborhood thief and mule abuser locked in jail for ten years after he assaults and rapes Stella Morgan. Like Ellen Foster, Jack struggles to rationalize the amount of evil and suffering in the world. He lumps together with criminality the lung cancer that deprives him of his 45-year-old wife, Ruby Pitts Woodrow Stokes, after a quarter century of happy marriage. His inchoate musings foster pathos for a sorrowing widower, but deliver no compelling arguments for devotion to God.

Setting her fiction within a rural Southern cosmos, Gibbons exposes the pat certainties of North Carolina evangelicals in a harsh, unpredictable world. Before Jack's evening theological debate with Cecil Spangler, a religious fanatic from the Ephesus Free Will Baptist Church, Ruby expresses an existential notion of cosmic disarray: she views life and fate as random and, in her case, lethal. Gibbons darkens the humor of Cecil's cliché of "[extending] the right hand of Christian fellowship" before Ruby's death in a hospital oxygen tent (*Ibid.*, 118). Jocularity fades as Cecil mouths the standard judgmental greeting that fundamentalists foist on non-believers who lack a "personal savior" (*Ibid.*). Jack's retreat into sarcasm makes no inroads against Cecil's smug negativity, an entrenched world view in the Southern backwoods. Subtextually, the author counteracts Cecil's judgments with Jack's unfailing devotion to his wife, who becomes a spiritual comforter to him after her death.

Gibbons perpetuates a mild interest in characters' religious background in *A*

Cure for Dreams (1991), which pictures the Davies-Randolph women as descendents of Bridget O'Donough O'Cadhain. In her native Galway, Ireland, Bridget consoles her papist paranoia with the belief that God decreed that Irish peasants can never prosper in a milieu controlled by British Anglicans. Bridget's granddaughter, Betty Davies Randolph, is more direct in her disdain for organized religion, particularly the "*Watch Tower* crowd," whom she lumps with drummers and other intruders on domestic order (Gibbons, 1991, 74). More welcome is the door-to-door seller of good luck amulets—beans and roots bearing connections with Jerusalem, the Hebrew capital established by King David, and with St. Jude of Thaddeus, a decapitated martyr and patron of lost causes. Superstitions linked to Jude suit the tenor of the times, when women look beyond realism for magic to dispel the Great Depression. At an uptick in family luck, Lottie qualifies for a widow's fund provided by the Social Security Act of 1935, a sign of grace from the federal government that assures Betty that "Mr. Roosevelt" must truly love God (*Ibid.*, 91). The statement reveals the era's hero-worship of the four-term president and extols the quest for salvation less from zealotry than from human goodness.

In her fourth novel *Charms for the Easy Life* (1991), Gibbons launches small jabs at various faiths. She charges Baptists with distorting sex education for the teens of Wake County, North Carolina, and blames a Christian Scientist for risking the blasphemy of bleeding to death rather than violating the teachings of Mary Baker Eddy by allowing the suturing of a cut. In a Durham veterans' hospital, a patient's horsehair crucifix agleam with grinning teeth receives brief satire. A wry mini-biography of Louise Battle Nutter accounts for her interest in piedmont school children, a violation of class strictures that causes her aristocratic family to efface her name from their pew at the Church of the Good Shepherd, an episcopal congregation founded in Raleigh in 1874. The author rewards Louise's altruism with money, prestige, six children, and happiness while her biased parents lose their fortune in the bank crash of 1929. With a wicked touch of just deserts, Gibbons pictures Louise's husband Charles reinstating the Battle family on their pew, where he has Louise's name reinscribed on the brass nameplate. The only denomination that Gibbons mentions without scorn is the African Methodist Episcopal Zion congregation, to whom the shoeshine man praises Charlie Kate's lifesaving methods that retrieve him from drowning.

Additional snipes at religion derive from the author's growing-up years in a North Carolina setting where Primitive Baptists anticipate the rapture to snatch them up to heaven. *In Sights Unseen* (1995), narrator Hattie Barnes equates ordinary front-door nuisances—tinkers, knife sharpeners, encyclopedia sellers, and drunk panhandlers—with Jehovah's Witnesses, a sect that strives to restore the evangelism of first-century Christianity through one-on-one witnessing. Less frivolous are the author's summations of the South's religious history, which she examines in *On the Occasion of My Last Afternoon* (1998). The evidence of religiosity in Alice Tate and her beastly husband, Samuel P. Goodman Tate, differentiates for their daughter Emma the choice of New Testament over Old Testament philosophy. Alice, a tender-hearted woman who weeps while taking holy communion, displays the piety and loving forbearance found in post-resurrection worshippers. Samuel, the baptizer of plantation negroes, prefers the fulminations of the tyrannic god of Moses and Abraham, which allow Samuel to glorify the Episcopalian work ethic as reflected by slave-powered plantations along the James River. In moments of dramatic irony, he stops reading the evening lesson from the prayer book to sneer at Alice's depression and sick headaches, her excuses for retreating to the bedroom. On Thanksgiving, he mocks the formal blessing of the family retainers with personal and racial jibes. On son Whately's return from Washington College in Lexington, Virginia, Samuel confronts him at dinner with evidence of drinking and dicing and offers "to wager which one of us would rot in Hell first" (Gibbons, 1998, 74). Emma retorts with a charge of "more sinned against than sinning," a line from Act I, Scene II of William Shakespeare's tragedy *King Lear* (ca. 1603) that is often misquoted as scripture. At a lighter moment, Gibbons can't resist snickering at the gullability of the devout: the Tate family observes Harold the Baptist, a shyster preacher at a double hanging in Williamsburg, who sells letters from Jesus to unsuspecting negroes. Harold's fraud stresses the need of the opportunist for superstitious, illiterate prey.

Gibbons returns to issues of sanctimonious schemers in *Divining Women* (2004), her seventh novel. In the panic that sweeps Elm City, North Carolina, in fall during the 1918 influenza pandemic, a black minister struggles to tend the needs of his parishioners, who lack funds for medicine, burial clothing, and coffins. In contrast, a huckster named Arthur waves signs about the town square warning passersby that the almighty intends to carry them off by gales or fever. Maureen Carlton Ross characterizes such charlatans as lazy, alert to possibilities of a quick windfall, and, like Harold the Baptist, quick to exploit the panic of the gullible. Arthur's monomania precedes Maureen's initial labor pain on November 7, 1918, a life-giving struggle that cancels Arthur's fear-mongering about plague with real earthly pathos.

In a sequel, *The Life All Around Me by Ellen Foster* (2006), Gibbons remains true to her secondary crusade against Southern fundamentalism, particularly the rude Moravian lady at the fair who embarrasses Stuart and Starletta for their ignorance. The author lobs mild criticism at Jehovah's Witnesses who discount the religious themes of T.S. Eliot's poetry and at the Academy of the New Dawn Apocalypse, a fundamentalist segregation institute that cloaks under a facade of bible-based family values a lurking racism. More devastating is Ellen's war against the "sliver" of time between waking and sleeping when she wards off memories of her mother Shine's funeral in March 1969, when a preacher delivers a hellfire tirade against suicide (Gibbons, 2006, 34). Ellen speculates on the free passes to special cases—pygmies and coma victims—who bypass standard salvation. The inflexibility of fundamentalism forces her on a "doubt holiday," a semi-permanent leave of absence from obsessive condemnation of individuals who fall outside church legalism (*Ibid.*, 35). To comfort herself, she cites a heartening line from Psalm 102:9 and concludes with an invocation to the mother of God. The choice of deity unearths from Ellen's inner core the mother hunger that haunts her waking moments.

• *Further reading*

Gibbons, Kaye. *A Cure for Dreams.* New York: Algonquin, 1991.

_____. *Ellen Foster*. New York: Algonquin Press, 1987.
_____. "The First Grade, Jesus, and the Hollyberry Family," *Southern Selves: From Mark Twain and Eudora Welty to Maya Angelou and Kaye Gibbons: A Collection of Autobiographical Writing*. New York: Vintage, 1998.
_____. *The Life All Around Me by Ellen Foster*. New York: Harcourt, 2006.
_____. *On the Occasion of My Last Afternoon*. New York: G.P. Putnam's Sons, 1998.
_____. *A Virtuous Woman*. Chapel Hill, N.C.: Algonquin Press, 1989.
Morris, Ann. "Gibbons' 'A Cure for Dreams' Is a Hope Chest of Language," *Greensboro* (N.C.) *News & Record* (31 March 1991).

Ross, Maureen Carlton

The aunt-by-marriage of Mary Oliver in *Divining Women* (2004), Gibbons's seventh novel, Maureen Carlton Ross offers a trusting face and engaging smile as evidence of her openness and vulnerability. Born in Yazoo City, Mississippi, she settles in Elm City, North Carolina, and, in 1913, weds Troop Ross, a deceptive bruiser suffering from free-floating hostility born of narcissism. To ensure marital control, he suppresses his emotions by rejecting spontaneity and by undermining his wife's self-esteem with revulsion at her womansmell and charges that her skin lacks loveliness and appeal. She becomes a model of what philosopher Betty Friedan's *The Feminine Mystique* (2001) calls depersonalization — the "progressive dehumanization" of an imprisoned woman who complies with her keeper by "[forfeiting] self" (Friedan, 2001, 282, 310). The physical symptoms vary from crying jags, fitful digestion, and headache to lassitude, vacuity, and the inability to concentrate.

By abasing Maureen with truculence and intimidation, Ross maintains a false superiority instilled by his vindictive mother, Nora Worthy Ross. To escape his self-ennobling at their ostentatious stone house, Maureen creates a female sanctuary — an ocean-blue sitting room where she opens the windows to refresh the air, a suggestion of nature's cleanliness in a home fouled by bombast. In 1918 in the fifth year of their marriage, the tall, Italianate beauty impresses her sister-in-law, Martha Greene Oliver, as a tastefully dressed, confident, and pragmatic woman capable of willfulness. Grandmother Louise Canton Oliver, on hearing a description of Martha's black silk dress, deduces that Maureen has come from poverty but trusts herself enough to turn four yards of expensive fabric into a stylish shift. The woman-to-woman assessment prefigures a narrative based on the synergy of strong females.

The author creates from Maureen a model of innate female potency over unloving, unwarranted marital supervision. Like Faith McNulty in *The Burning Bed* (1980), Celie in Alice Walker's *The Color Purple* (1982), and Winnie Louie in Amy Tan's *The Kitchen God's Wife* (1991), Maureen at first morphs into the obedient drudge. While her 22-year-old niece Mary volunteers as companion on September 30, 1918, during the final 50 days of Maureen's confinement, the pregnant woman lies on a purple chaise that supports her back and unborn child. She searches for mental engagement to relieve tension. Feverish with anxiety, she admits to Mary that she needs help in restoring good spirits to a depressed and depressing household. Obvious to an outsider, Maureen's color and aroma therapy groups fragrant hybrid roses amid the blues, greens, violets, lavenders, and silvers that shield an in-house oasis from Troop's outbursts. His daily emotional blackmail with gifts of hothouse flowers fails to atone for husbandly contempt for a woman born of an undistinguished rural delta background. The motif illustrates through Maureen's diminution that wives slip into a self-accusatory rut by trying to please domineering mates.

In a confessional to Mary, Maureen discloses a variety of faulty conclusions. Because of her grief at the burning deaths of sisters Ella and Eloise in 1914, she feels guilty of "female hysteria," a misogynist diagnosis of normal emotion (Gibbons, 2004, 62). Mary begins overturning absurd notions, such as Troop's denunciation of Maureen's longing to decorate her own home and to correspond with her family in Mississippi. Mary asks a revealing question about Troop's protection of his mother from Maureen. In reply, Maureen accepts blame for causing her mother-in-law to decline because Troop paid too much attention to his fiancée. On a more immediate level, he denies Maureen fresh fruit because he fears she will let it draw insects. Maureen harbors so much penitence that she misinterprets a lack of mail from her family. Mary's detective work discloses that Troop robs his wife of intimate correspondence with the only people who could strengthen and hearten. With Mary's help, Maureen liberates herself from a destructive five-year marriage and thrives for over 20 years in a mutually loving relationship with her niece.

See also **Greene-Carlton-Oliver-Ross genealogy**

• *Further reading*

Friedan, Betty. *The Feminine Mystique*. New York: W.W. Norton, 2001.
Gibbons, Kaye. *Divining Women*. New York: G.P. Putnam's Sons, 2004.

secrecy

Covert actions inform much of Kaye Gibbons's character development. An early short-short piece, "The Headache," published in the June 1987 issue of the *St. Andrews Review*, turns secrecy into the source of inner torment. Unable to reveal an act of greed to husband Henry, protagonist Lucille Womble, a struggling farm wife, enlarges on an impulse to conceal an abandoned purse. A standard folk prank, the placement of a snake in a pocketbook, eludes her until she slips away to the outhouse by night and hangs an oil lamp on a peg, a dramatic setting for Gothic terror. The thrust of a fanged head in her face unsettles her thinking and, for two weeks, inflicts headache, insomnia, weepiness, and multiple flashbacks of tossing purse and snake into the toilet. Contrasting her covert search for treasure, the action reduces Gothicism by paralleling terror with comfort in a visit to Dr. Janet Cowley, an understanding female physician, and in the husbandly compassion and affection that restores Lucille to health. Subtextually, Gibbons discloses a theme that evolves from the anti–Puritanism of Nathaniel Hawthorne's *The Scarlet Letter* (1850)—the harm of confining human errors within a guilty spirit.

In like fashion, Gibbons narrates her first novel, *Ellen Foster* (1987), from the private thoughts of the title character, an outspoken pre-teen. At Christmas, 1969, Starletta's mother makes ten-year-old Ellen a pillow featuring a Dutch girl, an evocative shadow figure whose oversized hat cloaks her face much as Ellen's personal deliberations conceal her needy heart. At every-Tuesday sessions, a school psychologist fails to elicit the adult-size dilemmas that agitate Ellen. In the falling action, Laura, Ellen's new mother, employs an intuitive touching that loosens the tangle of emotions. Laura clutches Ellen's quaking fingers and rubs her back to massage free repressed rage and sorrow. Laura's goal — a cathartic sob — remains unachieved as Ellen continues to hold back troubling phantoms. In token of the horrific stain of Ellen's first eleven years, the author chooses a less-than-complete emotional disburdening of indelible heartache.

Secrets in Gibbons's second and third novels derive from an adult dilemma — the female penchant for retaining a private self after marriage. For Ruby Pitts Woodrow Stokes, the dying farm wife in *A Virtuous Woman* (1989), a barren womb and malignant lungs are physical infections left over from marriage to John Woodrow. A sneering cad, he brings venereal disease to their bed and vexes her to the point that cigarettes become her escape from marital misery. The sound of gunshots reminds her of the night that she slips a pistol under her pillow to kill off the disgusting adulterer, who flaunts his 16-year-old "greasy gal" and hangs out with the "sorriest of the sorriest" (Gibbons, 1989, 21, 71). In contrast to her murderous plot, Ruby's second husband, "Blinking" Jack Ernest Stokes, stores up his own ruminations to see him through the first three months after her death. He fantasizes that, by washing his graying sheets and sprinkling her lilac-scented dusting powder, he can lure her spirit to their bed. A pathetic concealment, the night-time enticement of Ruby to his side conveys the depth of his sorrow and the wealth of memories of their quarter century together. Gibbons's counterpoint of the will to kill and the conjuring of the dead to life dramatizes male-female happiness as an earthly trade-off, an ephemeral period of joy that briefly staves off mortality.

Summoning less pain and more humor, *A Cure for Dreams* (1991), Gibbons's third novel, depicts the chicanery of a wife who expects no resurgence of her girlhood romanticism. After marrying Quaker farmer-miller Charles Davies in 1918, 18-year-old Lottie O'Cadhain Davies accepts disillusion as a life sentence, her "lot" for making a bad marriage. Rather than entertain Ruby's choice of shooting a disappointing mate, Lottie cherishes Charles's only gift to her, their daughter Betty. The two, like twin sisters, conspire to wrest fun from a dreary home scene by sewing fashions and by forming a women's club at Porter's store. To bankroll their amusements, Lottie loots coins from Charles's pants and tricks him into believing that the venise lace, chiffon, and beaded English netting she sews come at bargain prices. Collusion with Betty elevates Lottie as a model of the independent woman who quietly rejects disempowerment by men. In his own private world, in 1937, Charles eludes the mother-daughter duo by committing suicide, a retreat that suggests deeper hurt and despair than the text reveals. Turning her attention solely to womenfolk, Gibbons illustrates that early lessons in deception equip Betty for her own secrets. To establish autonomy, she conceals a significant event from her manipulative mother — the birth of third-generation female Marjorie Polly Randolph, who arrives on November 25, 1942. For the sake of independence, Betty chooses to award birthing duties to housekeeper-midwife Polly Deal rather than a domineering mother and future grandmother. Because the female protagonists share an admiration for guile, they maintain their in-house league against wartime despair.

Although equally upbeat, *Charms for the Easy Life* (1993) bears darker, more corrosive secrets than the previous work. Unlike Lottie's pilfering of coins from Charles's pocket, protagonist Charlie Kate Birch successfully rolls her wayward husband of $1,365 after he returns in 1938 for a three-day tryst at the Sir Walter Raleigh Hotel. Destructive breaches of ethics mark another male malefactor, a negligent physician who blinds a newborn with silver nitrate drops and who abandons a retired domestic, 70-year-old Maveen, to starve from stomach cancer because he disdains treatment of black females. In a private tête-à-tête, Charlie Kate pursues her own skullduggery by forcing the miscreant doctor out of the profession and by making him pay for the damaged girl's education at a state school for the blind. A frequent motif throughout the novel, the purging of corpses by the involuntary spewing of dark froth from the mouth relieves the departed of undivulged sins and wishes, an image that takes on grotesque extremes from the death scene in Gustave Flaubert's *Madame Bovary* (1856). In token of Charlie Kate's up-front lifestyle, she has no need to unburden herself of secret desires or longings. Gibbons enlarges the folk image into an encomium for her great-heartedness and service to others.

For *Sights Unseen* (1995), Gibbons departs from Charlie Kate's openness to examine the stonewalling of an unfortunate family quandary. The story pictures characters cloaking the Barnes house in secrecy to keep neighbors and playmates from learning about Maggie's episodes of craziness. Her father-in-law, Grandfather Barnes, a powerful community member, telephones the newspaper office to suppress reports of Maggie's erratic behaviors. Like the families of alcoholics and wife beaters, Hattie Barnes and her older brother Freddy screen their mother's bipolar episodes, which could result in ostracism and ridicule. For the same reason, their father, farmer Frederick Barnes, shields the nuclear family from voyeurs and gossips along Bend of the River Road. Hattie protects herself by shying away from spend-the-night parties and membership in the Girl Scouts. Nonetheless, gossip skewers Maggie as a woman with problems, a period euphemism for insanity. Ironically, the black underground passes along the Barnes family's anguish at Renfrow's Roasted Chicken, where Pearl Wiggins learns from two domestics of Maggie's need for a housekeeper and caretaker. In the words of reviewer Ron Carter, that fierce love "somehow found places to root in the cracks of their lives" (Carter, 1995). For all the masking and dissembling, the Barnes children gain love, acceptance, and a semblance of normality from an outsider, who becomes as protective of Maggie's reputation as a member of the extended family.

In Gibbons's first historical novel, *On the Occasion of My Last Afternoon* (1998), another clannish subterfuge, the female artifice of the Tate family, begins in pre-womanhood. To rescue her genteel mother, Alice Tate, from a dinner-table oration on family shortcomings, in 1842, Emma Garnet Tate Lowell, at age 12, cleverly asks her mother's advice on the younger siblings. By summoning Alice to the nursery, Emma launches a conspiracy against Samuel P. Goodman Tate, the overbearing head of household who aims words like darts at his wife, children, and slaves. Alice admires Emma's interventions and expresses thanks for the strategem that ends another evening's harangue of fault-finding. Emma's reward takes place after her wedding in 1847 in a tacit passing of Alice's velvet purse to the bride. Inside, along with $1,000, Alice tucks a note requesting a continuation of mother-daughter silence about their secret circumvention of Samuel's hard-handedness. Gibbons graces the scene with a truism about mothering — before parting with Emma, the mother of the bride retreats into trifles about English tweed to leave unsaid the sorrow of losing her oldest daughter and confidante.

Additional secrecy complicates the novel. Samuel, along with Emma's younger sister Maureen, comes from Seven Oaks plantation to Emma's home in summer 1862 in flight from the occupation forces of General George Brinton McClellan. As a result, Emma endures protracted strain from her father's japes and his embarrassments of the Lowells, an upstanding Raleigh family. In the night, Dr. Quincy Lowell declares that he hears Samuel in the throes of heart failure. To Emma's surprise, Quincy transgresses medical ethics by administering a lethal dose of digitalis powder that stills Samuel's hate-filled heart. Quincy sends his wife back to bed to enjoy a permanent respite. Neither wife nor husband suffers regrets at the stifling of a reproachful egotist. In 1863, secrecy later places Emma's morals in question at the demise of cook-housekeeper Clarice Washington, a freedwoman who shares Emma's guilt for concealing from Charlie, Martha, and Mavis that Quincy long before manumitted them from bondage. With failing breath, Clarice has a more startling secret to reveal — Samuel's shooting of his mother, a crime that he commits in boyhood at his father's command. The late revelations muddle a hurried plot resolution, leaving in question the author's intent in charging the Lowell-Tate family with hidden crimes.

In more timely order, layers of secrecy emerge in *Divining Women* (2004), Gibbons's seventh novel. Narrator Mary Oliver, a 22-year-old graduate student from Radcliffe, comes of age by observing her widowed mother's discreet life and by reading marital revelations in letters from Judith Benedict Stafford. Mary's mother, Martha Greene Oliver, maintains a private self by concealing hotel trysts with a lover, which she bares only to her friend Judith. To her contemporary, Martha contrasts the duties of mothering a fatherless teenage daughter with the widow's obligation to female sexuality, which demands immediate attention. The two women share Martha's suite at the Jefferson Hotel, a luxurious getaway that Martha obscures from Mary. The love nest serves a double duty. After the implosion of Judith's marriage on May 3, 1912, to a New York philanderer caught *in flagrante delicto* with a street strumpet, the wife's retreat to the hotel for a rejuvenating tryst with a Hindu levitation expert produces a humorous sight gag — the lightening of her spirit and the raising of hopes for her future. Ironically, family cover-ups prepare Mary for the serious task on September 30, 1918, of rescuing her aunt-by-marriage, Maureen Carlton Ross, from Troop, her manipulative husband. Like a domestic Mata Hari, Mary unearths Troop's evasive techniques and frees Maureen to enjoy real love. For the falling action on November 9, 1918, two days before an armistice ends World War I, Gibbons chooses the sidewalk in front of the Ross home, where neighbors scold Troop for unseemly railing at his bereaved wife.

In her first sequel, *The Life All Around Me by Ellen Foster* (2006), Gibbons returns to unfinished business in her debut novel. In out-of-kilter parallelism, in fall 1974, the text depicts the 15-year-old title character listening to the moony elopement plans concocted by Stuart, a devoted schoolmate. Overshadowing his intent to whisk her south to Pedro's South of the Border, a state-line fireworks emporium and honeymoon hideaway, is Ellen's fearful reach to the past. She pictures herself concealing a hidden persona, the "old, odd vampire girl" (Gibbons, 2006, 67). Quaking, anxiety attacks, and nail biting indicate pressures on her psyche as she meets for the first time with Aunt Nadine Nelson, a disgruntled relative. The revelation of Nadine's embezzlement of Ellen's inheritance secures enough money for a college education, but leaves unclaimed the pitiful box of personal treasures bequeathed by Shine, Ellen's deceased mother. More to the point of Ellen's reclamation, a doctor's intake report from September 10, 1968, words the mental turmoil that drives Shine to institutionalization and a suicide plan. After banishing Aunt Nadine and Cousin Dora to Texas, Gibbons exonerates Ellen of failing her mother by disclosing Shine's regret at being too weak, too unstable to mother her child. Freed of guilt and reunited with Shine's beneficent spirit, Ellen finds herself enrobed in love.

See also **security**

• *Further reading*

Carter, Ron. "Children Hide Family Secret," *Richmond Times-Dispatch* (10 September 1995).

Flaherty, Dolores, "When Mental Illness Strains Family Bonds," *Chicago Sun-Times* (17 November 1996).

Gibbons, Kaye. *The Life All Around Me by Ellen Foster*. New York: Harcourt, 2006.

_____. *A Virtuous Woman*. Chapel Hill, N.C.: Algonquin Press, 1989.

security

For Kaye Gibbons, the establishment of personal welfare and refuge from adversity relies heavily on female succor. In an early short-short story, "The Headache," issued in the June 1987 *St. Andrews Review*, Lucille Womble, a dispirited farm wife, clutches at an abandoned purse in a restaurant ladies' room. The thought of easy money drives her to a despicable act that turns out to be a snake-in-the-pocketbook trick, a familiar folk ruse. Concealment of the lost handbag fills her with regret that she plunges dangerously close to the level of "white trash," a dire Southern pejorative. Because guilt assaults Lucille with two weeks of weeping, bad dreams, flashbacks, and head throbs, she takes the advice of employer Mae Bell Stokes and confides in an unknown female, Dr. Jane Cowley. An unforeseen reassurance greets Lucille in Room C at the doctor's office in the form of a framed copy of the Hippocratic Oath, which promises, "Whatsoever I shall see or hear ... I will keep inviolably secret" (Gibbons, June 1987, 5–6). Under the promise of confidentiality, Lucille tells all. Secure in Dr. Cowley's diagnosis and restored to her husband Henry's arms, Lucille feels lightened from the gnawings of conscience. Gibbons ennobles the farm wife by stressing the need for cherishing, which outweighs Lucille's financial and moral plight.

With greater psychological depth, the restoration of normality to the title character of *Ellen Foster* (1987), Gibbons's first novel, requires a restructuring of home and family. As Carolyn Perry and Mary Louise Weaks explain in *The History of Southern Women's Literature* (2002), Ellen's self-reclamation is idiosyncratic. She rejects the gung-ho epigraph from Ralph Waldo Emerson's essay "Self-Reliance" (1841) as well as her submissive mother's passivity. Unlike Mark Twain's Huck Finn, who abandons civilization, Ellen pursues the rudiments of civility that society denies her. Striking out on her own in late December, 1970, at age 11, she stakes out a family at church and selects Laura as her foster mother and protector. The new home, set on a green lawn within clipped hedges, offers a "woman-centered community in which independence is balanced with concern for the welfare of others" (Perry & Weaks, 2002, 605). Ellen rapidly adjusts to sharing and treats her friend Starletta to an illicit visit to a whites-only movie theater. The extension of security to Starletta enables Ellen to reward herself for kindness to someone less socially secure than she.

In subsequent feminist fiction, the author resets the female haven from variant perspectives. In her second novel, *A Virtuous Woman* (1989), a 20-year-old widow, Ruby Pitts Woodrow, first secures her own nest by marrying 40-year-old "Blinking" Jack Ernest Stokes, a bestower of affection and respect. Because their quarter-century marriage produces no children, Ruby wrests parenthood for herself by mothering June Stanley, a poorly parented farm child. To prepare June for female roles, Ruby offers instruction in potholder weaving and in menarche, a physical advance into womanhood that June's mother, Tiny Fran Hoover Stanley, neglects to introduce. The mutual love and sharing of June and her surrogate parents rebound to Ruby and Jack in their last years together. June, a practicing architect, supports the beleaguered Stokes household by visiting Ruby during her battle with terminal lung cancer. Like a dutiful daughter, June brings gifts of robes, gowns, and slippers, comfort items that suggest warmth and pampering. Left with a widower to solace, June demands that her father, Burr Stanley, "fix" whatever is wrong at the Stokes residence (Gibbons, 1989, 62). On her own, she restores some of Jack's security by performing much-needed housewifely tasks—dusting, mopping, washing dishes, wiping cabinets—all skills that she learned from Ruby. In a gesture of womanly tradition, June performs the jobs while wearing Ruby's apron, a homey, motherly token that suggests Ruby's arms around her waist.

In Gibbons's next novel, the lack of security results from the times as well as from personal obstacles. *A Cure for Dreams* (1991) characterizes the Great Depression as a vexing era when women sew gingham rather than chintz and when casual driving is too expensive for the locals of Milk Farm Road. To foster security in her daughter Betty, farm wife Lottie O'Cadhain Davies abandons the romantic illusions that jeopardized her late teens. In the mid–1930s, to continue dressing the two of them in cheerful outfits made from net and chiffon, Lottie draws on trickery and defiance of patriarchy. She finances their wardrobes with coins purloined from the pants pockets of Lottie's skinflint husband, Quaker farmer-miller Charles Davies. Against his grumbling at the table, Lottie and Betty chit-chat amiably and relish afternoons of gin rummy and pinochle games in the back room of Porter's store. As Betty ages out of Lottie's grasp, the mother superintends her dating from a distance by bad-mouthing beau Luther Miracle, a poor prospect for matrimony. After Betty distances herself from Stanton, an addict to Neurol Compound whom she encounters while studying secretarial courses in Richmond, Virginia, Lottie cinches her daughter's future by countenancing a permanent relationship with Herman Randolph, a post–Pearl Harbor volunteer to the navy. True to Lottie' vision of Betty's security, before departing to the U.S.S. *Hornet* in February 1942, Herman sires Marjorie Polly Randolph, the next generation of the matrilineage. In his absence during the Pacific war, Lottie, Betty, and Marjorie join cook-midwife Polly Deal in securing the homefront.

For Gibbons's fourth novel, *Charms for the Easy Life* (1993), security takes the form of a female triad. Against the buffeting of males who humiliate, gallivant, leave, and/or die, Charlie Kate Birch, an herbalist-midwife, gathers her daughter, Sophia Snow Birch, and granddaughter Margaret into a single household in Raleigh, North Carolina. In place of coddling, the beloved healer gives her two charges a dose of reality from house calls to treat malaria, boils, broken bones, hernias, and whooping cough and to perform roadside CPR to save a drowning shoeshine man. From tending Charlie Kate's patients, in 1942, Margaret advances to solacing the wounded of World War II at the Durham veterans' hospital. Sensible advice concerning wellness and self-respect prepare Margaret for a real beau, Tom Hawkings, III, whom Charlie Kate fosters as appropriate husband material. The elopement of Sophia with businessman Richard Baines to South Carolina on Christmas Eve, 1942, and the sudden death of the healer on Christmas night, tests the family's in-house mentoring. Margaret maintains her composure while preparing her grandmother's corpse for the undertaker. Secure in poise and professionalism, Margaret seems not only equal to the collapse of the female triad but also amply prepared for a future as a wife and medical student.

A more gripping view of peril emerges from *Sights Unseen* (1995), an autobiographical coming-of-age story depicting a girl's struggle for ideal mothering on a North Carolina farm. In a Bend of the River household disordered by Maggie Barnes's bipolar extremes, 12-year-old narrator Hattie Barnes experiences loneliness and alienation. She creeps around the shambles of homeyness to take what mothering is available from cook-housekeeper Pearl Wiggins, Hattie's "salvation" (Gibbons, 1995, 70). Rejected at birth, Hattie defaults to Pearl for the surrogate mother-daughter relationship that builds confidence. Ironically, in 1967, after Maggie undergoes psychotherapy and eight weekly electroconvulsive shock treatments at Duke Hospital, the family is even less certain of what to expect after she recovers from post-therapy amnesia. Like strangers acquainting themselves, Hattie tentatively accepts Maggie's outreach in the form of home-sewn play suits, a shared reading session and nap, and nightly visits to the bedroom door, auspicious images based on childhood innocence and vulnerability. Because Maggie once more takes root in home soil, sanctuary flourishes in her home and renews family unity. Ensuring wellness in the next generation are Hattie's stories, a cathartic technique essential to feminist celebration of foremothers.

The American upheaval at the foundation of *On the Occasion of My Last Afternoon* (2004) expands on familial jeopardy as a predictable result of civil war and economic instability. During the waning years of Southern slavery, narrator Emma Garnet Tate Lowell survives the posturing and pro–Confederate ravings of her father,

Samuel P. Goodman Tate. Maturing toward womanhood, in 1842, at age 12, Emma rescues her mother Alice from nightly harangue by summoning her to the nursery to consult on a feverish child. Five years later, after marrying a liberal Bostonian, Dr. Quincy Lowell, 17-year-old Emma flees from Seven Oaks plantation, her childhood home on the James River, to establish her own bastion on Blount Street in Raleigh, North Carolina. Promising a tie with the best of the past, cook-housekeeper Clarice Washington accompanies the bride south and undergirds the new housewife and mother with kitchen competence and advice, a reprise of Gibbons's theme of salutary homemaking.

The novel discloses the ephemeral nature of domestic serenity during economic, social, and political restructuring. As trainloads of soldiers demand Quincy's medical care, Emma juggles home duties with work at the Fair Grounds tent hospital as her husband's surgical nurse. More infringement of residential peace arrives in the form of soldiers recuperating in the manse. Worsening the situation is the flight of Samuel and Emma's younger sister Maureen to the Lowells' home from socioeconomic collapse of the James River plantation community, which General George Brinton McClellan overwhelmed on June 25, 1862, with 90,000 members of the Army of the Potomac. To harbor his wife from her father's malignant mouthings, Quincy does the unthinkable — he over-medicates Samuel with an oral dose of digitalis powder, a heart stabilizer that permanently silences the old man's evil gabble. As the war progresses, Emma's shelter with Clarice and Quincy founders with their deaths. In 1865, Emma, fully mature and capable of wresting her own security from chaos, restores her Blount Street retreat, collaborates with Maureen on charitable works, and creates security for others by spending the Lowell fortune on food, shelter, education, and employment opportunities for the underclass. The altruistic gestures express Gibbons's regard for Christian beliefs put into action.

Just as Ellen Foster shelters Starletta and Emma Lowell extends benevolence to the homeless and jobless, Mary Oliver, the 22-year-old graduate student at Radcliffe and narrator of *Divining Women* (2004), shares her own security with a deserving female. By leaving a circle of loving grandparents at their shared residence on Dupont Circle in Washington, D.C., on September 30, 1918, Mary journeys by train to Elm City, North Carolina, to the unknown. She faces a paradox — a seemingly stable manse that conceals from the world the machinations of her uncle, Troop Ross, a psychologically damaged husband. Flanked by vases of hybrid roses, Maureen Carlton Ross anticipates the birth of her first child while parrying Troop's daily sniping and demands that she have a hysterectomy to correct "female hysteria," a period mislabeling of women's demands for enfranchisement and autonomy (Gibbons, 2004, 62). Cut off from her family at Yazoo City in the Mississippi delta, Maureen seeks Mary's solace and caretaking during a difficult pregnancy that concludes on November 8, 1918, in the stillbirth of a daughter, Ella Eloise. In the resolution, Gibbons instills in Maureen the self-direction of Ellen Foster and the gutsiness of Lottie Davies and Charlie Kate Birch. By outflanking Troop, Maureen claims her baby's remains and, in a sunset burial, secures them in the cemetery before abandoning a sham marriage. The last two decades of her life spool out in Mary's loving care, the security that redeems Maureen from life-endangering despotism.

In Gibbons's first sequel, *The Life All Around Me by Ellen Foster* (2006), harborage remains the goal of the title figure and her volunteer mother Laura. In 1974, a return to Ellen's life four years after she chooses her own foster residence finds her ill-matched with community schooling, which falls short of her intellectual capacity. To secure the future, she wheedles Dr. Derek Curtis Bok, president of Harvard University, into offering her a scholarship and early admission to college. Educational needs pale in comparison with the tides of regret, guilt, and mother hunger that reduce her to anxiety attacks, trembling hands, visions of black holes, and nail chewing. Gibbons orchestrates an operatic falling action by reuniting the protagonist with her arch enemy, Aunt Nadine Nelson. Through the intervention of a clever attorney, Ellen takes control of a sizeable inheritance as well as a treasure trove of her mother Shine's memorabilia, which include a school picture and a hotel reservation for Ellen and Shine at Warm Springs, Georgia. The satisfying conclusion depicts Ellen's firm grasp on stability through Laura's love and Shine's flawed mothering. Together, Laura and Shine weld past and present into a canopy to shelter Ellen from what lies ahead.

See also **autonomy; powerlessness; vulnerability**

• *Further reading*

Gibbons, Kaye. *Divining Women*. New York: G.P. Putnam's Sons, 2004.

_____. "The Headache," *St. Andrews Review* (June 1987): 3–8.

_____. *Sights Unseen*. New York: G.P. Putnam's Sons, 1995.

_____. *A Virtuous Woman*. Chapel Hill, N.C.: Algonquin Press, 1989.

Perry, Carolyn, and Mary Louise Weaks, eds. *The History of Southern Women's Literature*. Baton Rouge: Louisiana State University Press, 2002.

self-esteem

The question of personal worth bedevils Kaye Gibbons's characters, forcing them to specify values and clarify their individual codes of demerits and rewards. She introduces the motif of self-assessment in "The Headache," a short-short story issued in June 1987 in the *St. Andrews Review*. Pummelling protagonist Lucille Womble for two weeks, doubts about the social acceptance of farm families exacerbate head pangs, nightly weeping, flashbacks to a confrontation with a snake, and insomnia brought on by her seizure of an abandoned pocketbook from a restaurant ladies' restroom. Before she can reclaim self-regard, she must unburden herself to a female physician, Dr. Janet Cowley, and to Henry, Lucille's husband. A salute to the reciprocity of marriage, the resolution pictures the farm couple cuddled in bed "spoon" style while Henry massages Lucille and compliments her goodness to family and neighbors (Gibbons, June 1987, 7). The crowning of her restored sense of worth takes the symbolic form of double bounty—two hats that he promises to buy her. The final image of Lucille drifting off to sleep picturing herself the new owner of two hats establishes an ongoing motif in Gibbons's fiction of the human gestures of acceptance and affection.

For the title character of *Ellen Foster* (1987), self-validation for a pre-teen orphan equates with survival. Although doubt riddles her private thoughts, restatements of belief in self echo through her first-person narration of tribulations inflicted by her family. For a model, she chooses her deceased mother, who expresses life lessons during bean-plucking sessions in the family garden. Blessed with the best of her parents' traits, Ellen possesses the sensitivity of her mother and the assertiveness of her father Bill, a dissolute ex-farmer and bootlegger. Like Bill, Ellen demands a decent residence that she chooses and negotiates in person. Like her mother, Ellen cherishes friendship with Starletta, an impoverished black child who stutters and sucks dirt clods for mineral nourishment. The amalgamation of worthy traits with charity readies Ellen for a new phase of her life in foster care, beginning Christmas Day, 1970. Under the intuitive attention of a volunteer mother, Ellen reaps the acceptance and home training that undergird healthy self-regard. Like Jo March, the budding New Woman in Louisa May Alcott's *Little Women* (1871) and frontier heroine Mattie Ross in Charles Portis's *True Grit* (1968), Ellen's do-or-die spirit earns her a place among the admirable females of American literature.

Similar in want and need to Lucille Womble and to 11-year-old Ellen, Ruby Pitts Woodrow Stokes, the female protagonist in *A Virtuous Woman* (1989), has only herself to blame for low self-esteem. The darling only daughter of landed farmers, at age 18, out of boredom and a sense of daring, she chooses to marry 27-year-old John Woodrow, an out-of-bounds farm drifter who severs Ruby's ties with her parents. Whittling away at her ego, he rebukes and aggrieves his young wife, forcing her to contemplate murder to rid herself of a sorry low-life. After his unforeseen death from a knife to the lungs in a pool hall fracas, at age 20, she opts for an equally unlikely marriage with 40-year-old "Blinking" Jack Ernest Stokes, a celibate farmer laborer endowed with devotion and tenderness. Luck favors Ruby with the serendipitous adoration and respect of her second marriage, which rebuilds pride. Content as a farm wife, she becomes one of Gibbons's must complex survivors. Her husband, on the other hand, longs for tangible rewards and fantasizes that Ruby returns from death to grace their marriage bed. He mourns serial disappointments because, in the words of critic Roz Kaveney, he has no children or land "to affirm his continuance" (Kaveney, 1989, 998). A *deus ex machina* drops into his hands the title to his acreage, a late developing upgrade to economic status that promises recompense for losing Ruby.

Prestige in Gibbons's third and fourth novels, *A Cure for Dreams* (1991) and *Charms for the Easy Life* (1993), derives from assertive, motivated women who face uncertainty without qualms. Unlike Lucille Womble and Ruby Stokes, Lottie O'Cadhain Davies, a farm wife and mother during the Great Depression, recognizes the value of self-love. In place of a soulless marriage in 1918 to farmer-miller Charles Davies, a miserly workaholic, she rewards herself and daughter Betty with simple treats—homemade outfits sewn from chintz, venise lace, beaded English netting, and chiffon. Funding Lottie's purchases are coins she rifles from husband Charles's pants pockets. With driblets of money, mother and daughter launch a gin rummy and pinochle club at the back of Porter's store that dispels period anguish through gambling and gossip. Lottie advances to rural primacy as queen bee of Milk Farm Road. A humorous title, the designation portrays the crumbs of renown that relieve the stress of farm women trapped under male authority.

Similarly self-directed, Charlie Kate Birch, the midwife-herbalist in *Charms for the Easy Life*, demands excellence in self and family. For her practice, she secures knowledge of scientific advances through in-depth reading of medical journals, almanacs, and discarded textbooks. By developing extensive patronage from the mill district of Raleigh, North Carolina, she acquires an unofficial title — Dr. Birch — a testimony to the awe in which patients hold her. More important to Charlie Kate is the intellectual growth of her granddaughter Margaret, the un-proclaimed heir to the family medical mission to the poor. Charlie Kate builds credibility in Margaret by introducing her to the best in literature and by discussing complex topics as though conversing with an equal. Reared in ethics and common sense, Margaret ignores ungentlemanly disrepect from her first dates. At the peak of maturity in 1942, she selects a worthy future mate, Tom Hawkings, III, scion of a respectable family. By guiding Margaret through character-building encounters, Charlie Kate prepares her granddaughter to slip effortlessly into control of the three-woman household, which the herbalist's death on Christmas night, 1942, leaves unpiloted. The author parts with her character by picturing her as an unfound treasure awaiting discovery.

Depiction of self-worth in Gibbons's autobiographical fifth novel, *Sights Unseen* (1995), contrasts male and female at the task of reclaiming sagging spirits. Narrator Hattie Barnes, at age 12, regrets the lack of an ideal mother-daughter relationship with her mother Maggie, a victim of bipolar insanity. In retreat from manic ups and depressive downs in a darkened room, Hattie develops a sense of self in the kitchen under the guidance of Pearl Wiggins, the cook-housekeeper and surrogate mother during the worst of Maggie's indispositions. Unlike the womenfolk, Grandfather Barnes, an arrogant despot, displays his self-regard in blustering, swearing, and flaunting a mistress. At his vacation house on the Carolina shore, he dresses in slacks and white shirt, a gentrified uniform. Starched and upright, he demands respect and refinement, even if he must cuff his grandson Freddy into line. Barnes's son Frederick, the martyr to Maggie's whims and oddities, lacks his father's hubris, thus ceding to the older man a unique control over family security. Gibbons applies a feminist twist to the resolution after Maggie's rehabilitation in 1967 from psychotherapy and eight sessions of electroconvulsive shock therapy at Duke Hospital. Newly sane, she rebukes Grandfather Barnes at the dinner table for his racist slur against Pearl. The retort situates Maggie high in the family pecking order in terms of female assertiveness and rejection of white Southern patriarchy.

Gibbons's first historical novel, *On the Occasion of My Last Afternoon* (1998), ventures beyond normal issues of dignity and pride to the problematic self-image of antebellum slaves. During hog-slaughtering season in 1842, at a low moment in affairs at Seven Oaks plantation, Clarice Washington, the big house cook-housekeeper, cajoles workers into swallowing anger at their owner, Samuel P. Goodman Tate, for slaughtering Jacob, a bluegum field hand. Her advice on how to avoid the auction block bears warning as well as honor. To demoralized field hands, she orders, "Be proud to what you is worth" (Gibbons, 1998, 15). Unlike the servility of Alice Tate, the female head of household, Clarice's authority and grace undergird a family threatened by internal disorder and the external predations of a revolt similar to that of Nat Turner, who slew white slave owners from August 22 to October 30, 1831.

Clarice's mothering of Alice's older daughter, Emma Garnet Tate Lowell, implants self-direction, a feminist quality that enables 17-year-old Emma to marry, leave home in 1847, and found a family of her own devoid of fear and cowering. At the passing of her surrogate parent in 1863, Emma awards Clarice burial in Oakwood Cemetery, a suitable interment for an oak-like mainstay, and the crowning title of mother, a filial reward for pinch-hitting for Alice.

In her seventh novel, *Divining Women* (2004), Gibbons recounts the spiritual attrition of Maureen Carlton Ross, a beleaguered wife. Her husband Troop's gambit involves steely self-control in the face of her gradual decline under house arrest and constant carping. Like the madwoman in the attic in Charlotte Brontë's *Jane Eyre* (1847) and Jean Rhys's 20th-century prequel, *Wide Sargasso Sea* (1966), Gibbons's post-modern romance follows classic feminist parameters of male coercion and female diminution. In the last 50 days of pregnancy, Maureen turns to a caretaker, niece Mary Oliver, a spunky 22-year — old graduate student from Radcliffe. After her arrival by train from Washington, D.C., to Elm City, North Carolina, on September 30, 1918, Mary remarks, "I could not fathom why he had dismissed her from his heart and mind," an acknowledgement of sterling qualities in Maureen that Troop foolishly squanders (Gibbons, 2004, 193). The statement, like a seesaw, glorifies Maureen while lowering Troop to dirt level.

The novel concludes with a visually dramatic uplift for reviver and revived. Like restorative blood transfusions, Mary supplies her aunt Maureen with daily infusions of courage, good sense, and spiritual tonic. Prefiguring the re-emergence of pride in Maureen is a death joke—a table conversation between Mary and Troop concerning the Awake!, a burial gadget that alerts the living to the plight of a victim of premature burial. The idle remark captures the nature of Maureen's moribund state as rejected, immured maiden in the tower, a staple of 19th-century anti-female Gothic romance. Female synergy, empowered by midwife Mamie and advocate Mary, quickly reverses the situation in Maureen's favor. Her childbed experience on September 7–8, 1918, and the recovery of letters from her mother in Yazoo City, Mississippi, complete Mary's makeover. In Maureen's first face-off with Troop, she exults in postpartum pain, a resumption of feeling to a numbed self. With plain-spoken courage, she warns him, "Enough has been taken" (Gibbons, 2004, 195). Sweeping out of his life with his firstborn in a tiny coffin for a sunset burial, on November 9, she joys in the unbidden stream of breast milk that testifies to her motherhood. Gibbons's strongest feminist scenario, the resolution depicts the grieving mother, like artistic renderings of Mary Magdalene, as grieved, yet victorious.

In *The Life All Around Me by Ellen Foster* (2006), Gibbons turns autobiographical fiction into acclamation by revisiting the aftermath of Ellen's 40-year-old mother's suicide. At age 15, the title figure delivers a walking-talking paradox of intellectual strutting and insecurity. To compensate for mother hunger and the guilt accompanying Shine's suicide five years earlier, in fall 1974, Ellen exudes a stream of clever sparks, the *mots justes* of a teenager in need of emotional grounding. Ironically buoyed by Stuart's adoration and plans for elopement to Pedro's South of the Border fireworks emporium and motel, Ellen clings to her dream of a college education. With tuition secured by Dr. Derek Curtis Bock's offer of a scholarship and early admission to Harvard University, she turns to the past to caress and meditate on the few objects attesting to Shine's last days. A doctor's intake document from Dorothea Dix Hospital on September 10, 1968, routs Ellen's inordinate guilt-bearing by picturing Shine as a weak victim of mental disorder who faults herself for failed mothering. At an epiphany, Ellen exults, "I've been miserable since she died because she died so I wouldn't be miserable" (Gibbons, 2006, 203). By swapping false accusations for forgiveness, Ellen exonerates herself from a common psychological hazard, the survivor's guilt that engulfs families of suicides.

See also **powerlessness; vulnerability**

• *Further reading*

Gibbons, Kaye. *Divining Women*. New York: G.P. Putnam's Sons, 2004.
_____. "The Headache," *St. Andrews Review* (June 1987): 3–8.
_____. *The Life All Around Me by Ellen Foster*. New York: Harcourt, 2006.
_____. *On the Occasion of My Last Afternoon*. New York: G.P. Putnam's Sons, 1998.
Kaveney, Roz. "Making Themselves Over," *Times Literary Supplement* (15 September 1989): 998.

sex

Libido and carnal images in Kaye Gibbons's fiction serve definite purposes in clarifying an array of human desires and behaviors. In an early short-short story, "The Headache," issued in June 1987 in *St. Andrews Review*, the bedroom intimacies of a rural couple, Henry and Lucille Womble, sustain them during hard times. In a summer of bank repossessions of farm machinery and of two weeks of crippling head pangs, terrifying visions, hysteria, and insomnia in Lucille, the female head of household retreats to her bed as the only available sanctum in a one-room residence. Urged by Dr. Janet Cowley to discuss outsized fears with Henry, Lucille cozies back against his chest and pulls his hands to her belly, a primal posture in marital sleeping arrangements. The parents of ten children, husband and wife value physical and emotional nearness as antidotes to the struggle to feed their family on the proceeds of a failing farm.

For *Ellen Foster* (1987), perversion lurks as a subtext to orphanhood and child endangerment. Bill, the drunken father, scandalizes staff and students at Ellen's elementary school by "yelling and undoing his britches," the child's version of a public display of his genitals (Gibbons, 1987, 54). By exposing himself before young students, he justifies the title character's panic and bolt to a safe harbor on New Year's Eve, 1969. More confusing to Ellen is Bill's drunken fondling on New Year's Eve, 1969, while he murmurs his dead wife's name, as though his incantation can turn Ellen into her mother. With a child's imprecision, Ellen indicates that he "pulls the evil back into his self," a suggestion of sexual threat (*Ibid.*, 38). Gibbons's evidence of child molestation sets a pattern of sexual decorum in her fiction. Ellen staves off the need for details about near-incest at home by remarking to a teacher, "I was used to it so do not get in an uproar over it," a brave dismissal and face-saving ploy that belies serious trauma (*Ibid.*, 44). The comment normalizes sexual improprieties as though they are Ellen's everyday realities. In a sequel, *The Life All Around Me by Ellen Foster* (2006), she reflects on endangerment at her childhood home where "I didn't as much live with my father as hide from him" (Gibbons, 2006, 154).

In Gibbons's second novel, *A Virtuous Woman* (1989), lust takes a diametric turn from perversity toward pleasure. Wed improvidently at age 18 to 26-year-old farm laborer John Woodrow, protagonist Ruby Pitts reassesses her flight from boredom at home in view of subsequent domestic violence. At a vulnerable moment, she experiences the terror of marriage to a mean-mouthed drunk, womanizer, and pool hall hang-out. In token of his disrespect, he rips her wedding night garments, the standard anti-female action of a roué in 19th-century Gothic novels that shreds both modesty and romantic illusions. Gibbons intervenes by awarding John an undignified demise from a knife to the lungs during a public brawl. Like a literary Zorro, the author literally slices the legal tether to a despoiler of women.

Remarriage comes too late to salvage Ruby's virginal sweetness, but overturns the tender wedding-night cliché by awarding vulnerability and anticipation to a celibate male. The sexual inexperience of "Blinking" Jack Ernest Stokes ingratiates the 20-year-old widow, who satisfies him with her naked looks, touch, and fragrance. Delighted in his first experience with male-female intimacy, he requests that she leave the bedside light on so he can enjoy seeing her disrobe. Unfortunately for the loving couple, Ruby's first marriage leaves her barren, ostensibly from a sexually transmitted disease from John's frolics with county tarts. Like a shadowy stalker, the lingering punishment for an unwise teen marriage contributes to the Stokes' multiple disappointments.

More complex is the coital duty in *Sights Unseen* (1995). The author lightens a grim recitation of manic-depressive behaviors by picturing Frederick Barnes as the victim of his own wife, Maggie Barnes, whom a precarious bipolar state turns into an unquenchable siren. He has good intentions in 1955 in siring a second child, Hattie Barnes, whom he hopes will restore Maggie's sanity. Unfortunately, childbirth further muddles the home scene. In the words of reviewer-novelist Jacqueline Carey, a critic for the *New York Times Book Review*, in childhood, Hattie reacts to her parents' unusual conjugal schedule with "distaste, pity, amazement, and even amusement" (Carey, 1995, 30). The ongoing bedroom contretemps sets the tone of narration, embarrassing the Barnes children and titillating the maid Olive to spy on her employers. Like other of Maggie's unbalanced behaviors, her flagrant sensuality threatens the development of normal perceptions of womanhood in 12-year-old Hattie and her older brother Freddy, a purveyor of pornography.

An oddly de-sexed romance, Gibbons's first historical novel, *On the Occasion of My Last Afternoon* (1995), follows Victorian convention by avoiding graphic display of physical pleasures. The recoil of tidewater gentry from promiscuous coupling occurs at a crisis, when a Southern oligarch, Samuel P. Goodman Tate, disinherits his son Whately, a student at Washington College in Lexington, Virginia. On return in shame to Seven Oaks plantation on the James River, on December 20, 1842, Whately must confess to his "fire-eater" parent an encounter with a barmaid and expulsion from school for impregnating her (Gibbons, 1995, 30). The conjoining of guilt and shame exiles Whately to Charleston, South Carolina. On Sullivan's Island, at age 20, he dies alone, wasted, and covered in running lesions following crude self-treatments for syphilis. The text indicates that Whately is doubly guilty for contracting a venereal disease and, even more so, for consorting with a working-class girl, a crime against social class that enrages his social-climbing father.

With less vitriol, Gibbons introduces a family schism in *Divining Women* (2004) as the result of Toby Greene's interest in nudism, which offends his prudish first wife, Nora Worthy Ross. In 1875, she steals his son Troop away from Washington, D.C., to her home in North Carolina and replaces his surname with "Ross." In scorn at unorthodox behavior, she hopes that Toby and his new wife Leslie die of a "fanny disease" contracted from romping unclothed in the woods as part of their membership in the American Community of Nudists (Gibbons, 2004, 4). In a letter dated 36 years later, Nora implies that Toby deserves arrest on a morals charge, a humorous take on a Medusa-like ex-wife whose Puritanic mores authorize a barrage of harassment and vengeance at Toby and promote the perversion of Troop.

The author augments Nora's influence into a contagious psychosis that infects Troop Ross's heart and mind. A reflection of deviance occurs in 1913 after his marriage at age 47 to Maureen Carlton Ross, whom he weds only after Nora's death leaves him free of oedipal strangulation. A graceful beauty from Yazoo City, Mississippi, Maureen is the dupe of a mentally unbalanced adult male incapable of sharing his life with a normal woman. On the January night he begs for forgiveness and sires their only child, Troop accuses her of concealing the Vicks, his protection against the smell of female sex. To Maureen, genital odor reminds her of the delta on a rainy day, a healthy response to innate sensuality unshared by Troop. At their ultimate confrontation after the stillbirth of their daughter, Ella Eloise, on November 8, 1918, Maureen stands close, demanding that he inhale her womanly scent. The challenge, like an ordeal by combat, exerts her gender power over a malfunctioning mama's boy. In her usual style, Gibbons dismisses Troop without pity for his rejection of a lovely, potentially empathetic wife.

The novel portrays carnal stories as a necessary source of enlightenment for Maureen and for her caretaker, 22-year-old graduate student Mary Oliver. The two pore over letters between Mary's widowed mother, Martha Greene Oliver, and her friend Judith Benedict Stafford of New York City. Secure in sharing each other's human weaknesses, Martha and Judith confess to opportunities for sexual release. After Judith catches her randy husband on May 3, 1912, in their bed with a street jade, the spurned wife turns to Martha for advice and solace. Martha offers her own suite at the luxurious Jefferson Hotel, a love nest she keeps private from daughter Mary. On a liberating journey from wasted wifedom to free love in Europe, in April 1915, Judith establishes an instructive model of female entitlement to sexual fulfillment. The paradigm educates Mary at the same time that it heartens Maureen to shake off caustic demands from Troop. His withdrawal and reduction to a public rant at his daughter's sunset burial on November 9, 1918, suggests that little-boy theatrics are his only weapons against an assertive wife.

In a first sequel, *The Life All Around Me by Ellen Foster* (2006), Gibbons addresses teen promiscuity as a common breaking point in foster homes. Among homeless, unloved girls, bold sexual escapades substitute for family affection at the same time that they elevate self-regard. Laura's difficulties with two wayward girls put Ellen in the untenable position of eyewitness to broken house rules. Without specifying infractions hidden behind locked doors, Ellen sums up the threat to health from consorting with youths who are likely to be "diseased down there" and from foster girls who drink alcohol and aspire to jobs at a "take-your-clothes-off place" (Gibbons, 2006, 45, 48). Her outrage implies a variance in maturity levels within the family that robs her of empathy for more worldly wise foster children.

See also **rape**

• *Further reading*

Carey, Jacqueline. "Mommy Direst," *New York Times Book Review* (24 September 1995): 30.
Gibbons, Kaye. *Divining Women*. New York: G.P. Putnam's Sons, 2004.
_____. *Ellen Foster*. New York: Algonquin Press, 1987.
_____. *The Life All Around Me by Ellen Foster*. New York: Harcourt, 2006.
_____. *On the Occasion of My Last Afternoon*. New York: G.P. Putnam's Sons, 1998.
Gretlund, Jan Nordby. *The Southern State of Mind*. Columbia: University of South Carolina Press, 1999.
Wolcott, James. "Crazy for You," *New Yorker* (21 August 1996): 115–116.

siblings

To already complex familial relationships, Gibbons applies the camaraderie, dissonances, and in-house rivalries of siblings. Among her pairings are the older and younger Womble brothers trading insults and bedeviling their parents in "The Headache," a short-short story published in the June 1987 issue of the *St. Andrews Review*. An adult version, the widow Betsy and sister Nadine Nelson, are unsuitable surrogate mothers for their niece, the title figure in the author's first novel, *Ellen Foster* (1987). The aunts, self-centered and shallow, care little about Ellen's kindness to their mother, Ellen's maternal grandmother. To Nadine's surprise, Ellen tends the elderly woman shortly before Christmas 1970 during a lethal bout with flu and dresses her before a mortuary crew arrives. Gibbons describes Betsy and Nadine as haggling and competitive, both jostling for the right to claim concern for a mother whom they failed to aid during her final illness. The ugly squabble contrasts the compassion of Ellen, the unwanted granddaughter who decks the corpse in a Sunday hat and artificial flowers to turn a heartless crone into an appealing gift for Jesus.

In contrast to Betsy and Nadine, the dissimilar natures of the half-siblings born to Tiny Fran Hoover Stanley create a yin-yang disparity in *A Virtuous Woman* (1989), Gibbons's second novel. Tiny Fran's offspring consist of an illegitimate son Roland, an animal abuser and date rapist, and his sunny-natured sister June, an architect who is the birth daughter of Burr Stanley and the surrogate child of Ruby Pitts Woodrow Stokes and "Blinking" Jack Ernest Stokes. Starkly opposite, Roland's propensity for evil and June's for good provide an unforeseen reward in the falling action. A widower at age 65, Jack reaps interest on his investment in June, who shares his mourning and restores order to a house left destitute after Ruby's death at age 45 from lung cancer. The author uses literary license to sort out good and bad characters. While

June tidies up and cheers Jack with home-cooked food, Roland, a family malignancy whom Jack compares to Adolf Hitler, serves a ten-year sentence in prison.

Gibbons peruses more fractious families in her third novel, *A Cure for Dreams* (1991), which features surly drunken brothers, Sheamus and Bart O'Cadhain of Galway, Ireland. Like a family curse, the duo invades the kitchen of Bridget O'Donough O'Cadhain, Sheamus's wife, to demand eggs for breakfast following their nightly binges. The brothers' squawks divide the family, causing Bridget to snipe at her daughter, Lottie O'Cadhain Davies, for obeying a pair of souses. Less united are Lottie, her sister Eileen, and their eight siblings, who tolerate Bridget's stagey bidding. After securing a bank loan to pay for a return to Galway, Lottie ameliorates her lapsed sisterhood by traveling from North Carolina to Bell County, Kentucky, bearing a hatbox lined with wet cotton to nestle "cape jasmines," a Southern term for gardenias (Gibbons, 1991, 104). The fragrant blossoms suggest a sweet, ingratiating attitude in Lottie toward sibling unity. The sweetness wanes at dinner when the sisters play whist while Lottie and her daughter Betty wash dishes dirtied by the entire clan. The quick dust-off of the newcomer establishes a reality in sibling relationships that can rapidly deteriorate from cordiality to business as usual.

Similarly unlike are sisters Camelia and Clarissa "Charlie Kate" Birch, a midwife-healer in *Charms for the Easy Life* (1993), Gibbons's fourth novel. Charlie Kate cherishes life as much as her suicidal twin devalues it by killing herself in 1910 at age 28 over the death of her hydrocephalic son. With grim humor, Gibbons adds that Camelia's husband contributes a third death by stretching out on the railroad tracks, a suicide suggesting the family's shared acquiescence to tragedy. Through contrast, Gibbons illustrates innate differences in children born to the same family. Those like June Stanley, Lottie Davies, and Charlie Kate thrive on powers of renascence. Charlie Kate's optimism and work ethic support her through the Great Depression, two world wars, and the disappearance of her ferryman husband. Instead of giving up, she chooses dedication to midwifery, dentistry, and herbalism and to her daughter and granddaughter. The trio, like siblings, endures on family love and sisterhood.

A gendered contrast in siblings empowers the reflections of Hattie Barnes, the narrator of *Sights Unseen* (1995). In the flux of her mother Maggie's manic-depressive episodes, 12-year-old Hattie takes comfort in the surrogate parenting of cook-housekeeper Pearl Wiggins. Although Hattie adores her older brother Freddy, the two react differently to Maggie's violence, neurasthenia, and sexual demands on her husband Frederick. While Freddy retreats to his room to brood, collect pin-ups, and read, Hattie remains in the eye of the storm, absorbing details that flesh out the novel with evidence of a family's struggle with ongoing mayhem. In adulthood, Hattie and Freddy share career interests in anesthesiology, a symbolic quieting of suffering, but their routes to medicine differ. While Hattie lurks about the kitchen in search of mothering and cherishes her mother for being "present at the events of my life, small and large," Freddy ministers to himself by immersion in pornography, horror movies, and scientific study (Gibbons, 1995, 208). In her succinct, woman-centered style, Gibbons omits a thorough study of Freddy's shedding of childhood trauma. The only glimpse of Freddy's coping mechanism resides in a punishing one-person basketball game. He dresses in sweatshirt and putty-hued slacks, an outfit reflecting the stereotypical loners and misfits that the boy's hero, Steve McQueen, played during his movie career.

Like the Barnes children, Emma Garnet Tate Lowell and her older brother Whately enjoy a brother-sister camaraderie in *On the Occasion of My Last Afternoon* (1998), Gibbons's first historical novel. Remanded to female accomplishments—tatting, quilting, piano, and china painting—Emma jettisons incipient ladyhood to develop her mind by reading her brother's old textbooks and gift novels. The latter—Horace Walpole's Gothic classic *The Castle of Otranto* (1764) and the novels of William Gilmore Simms—replace girlish froth with more muscular Gothic and frontier prose. The alliance of the elder daughter with the eldest son confuses sister Maureen, who puzzles over Emma's opinions and her ongoing sparring with their acrimonious father, Samuel P. Goodman Tate. Whately's rapid decline in Samuel's estimation elicits pity from Emma, who remembers her brother's loneliness and his willingness to teach cook-housekeeper Clarice Washington how to read from issues of *Godey's Lady's Book*. Upon Whately's final disgrace on December 20, 1842, for impregnating a barmaid in Lexington, Virginia, he arrives home in tears, but displays generosity toward his mother and sisters with wrapped Christmas gifts. In Emma's package—an inscribed copy of James Fenimore Cooper's frontier classic *The Deerslayer* (1841)—is a note to her bequeathing Whately's library. Reflecting over a warm sibling relationship, like the Maya character's adoration of brother Bailey Junior in Maya Angelou's autobiography *I Know Why the Caged Bird Sings* (1969), Emma recalls her life with Whately like a "magic lantern show" (Gibbons, 1998, 81). The image projects both enlightenment and warmth in a household lacking in both.

In contrast to Whately, who fades out of Emma's life after he contracts syphilis and dies at age 20 on Sullivan's Island outside Charleston, South Carolina, Maureen fades back in. Dislodging her from home is Union General George Brinton McClellan's commandeering of Seven Oaks from the Tate family in June 1862. The loss of contact between sisters conceals from Emma the fact that she is not the only family member to undergo dramatic change. To her shock, Maureen has aged and declined in health as well as marriageability. In a late paean to sisterhood, Gibbons depicts Emma's influence on Maureen, the beau catcher who waited too long to marry. A feminist summation of Maureen's rise to social awareness occurs late in the novel, when Emma, in widowhood in 1865, returns home to Raleigh, North Carolina, to live out the Reconstruction era and to develop friendship with her sister through lengthy talks. As a team, they channel their energies and much of the Lowell fortune into good works aiding widows, orphans, and the illiterate and unemployed. Because of the rushed resolution, the novel supplies little motivation for Maureen's sudden metamorphosis. In place of characterization, Gibbons pictures Maureen's cold, lifeless form contorted in death, another loved one left to Emma's ministrations. As though caressing living flesh, Emma reminds herself to be gentle. The image of sisterly love bolsters the characterization of Emma as kind and forgiving in an era when forgiveness is in short supply.

Gibbons reprises the diametric sibling behaviors of Roland and June Stanley, Camelia and Charlie Kate Birch, and Maureen and Emma Garnet Tate Lowell in a sixth novel, *Divining Women* (2004). Martha Greene Oliver, the alienated younger half-sister of Troop Ross, maintains peripheral courtesies by attending his wedding to Maureen Carlton, a poor girl from Yazoo City in the Mississippi delta. Blessed with intuition about mismatched mates, Martha suspects hardship in Maureen's life. Gibbons creates irony out of the sisterly love for a stranger who needs a shield against Troop's life-long self-indulgence and spite. The concern of one woman for another precipitates sisterly union after Martha dispatches her 22-year-old daughter, Mary Oliver, a graduate student at Radcliffe, on September 30, 1918, from home in Washington, D.C., south to Elm City, North Carolina. Martha's intent is for Mary to tend Maureen during the final 50 days of a difficult pregnancy. The Greene-Ross sibling web shrivels as Mary hustles Maureen north by train to renew her spirit in the warmth and support of the Greene-Oliver clan, far from Troop and his meanness. The resolution reveals Gibbons's faith in feminist sisterhood over birth kinship.

A humorous upsurge of sibling love invigorates Gibbons's first sequel, *The Life All Around Me by Ellen Foster* (2006). In his mid-teens, Stuart, the title character's school chum, shadows her like a brother at the county fair, telephones play-by-play episodes of his emotional squabbles with his mother, and promotes Ellen's interests and beliefs. His vision of their fellowship splits into unlikely relationships. He remembers her from their sharing of a wading pool in childhood and wishes that Ellen had chosen his family to foster her in December 1970, when she abandoned her family in search of a new mama. Like Heathcliff, the foundling in Emily Brontë's *Wuthering Heights* (1847), Stuart fantasizes a sexual relationship with Ellen begun by elopement to Pedro's South of the Border fireworks emporium and motel. By juxtaposing images of a sister-bride, Stuart implies a quasi-incestuous relationship with a girl who flees her lustful father Bill. Rather than wade through Stuart's entangled feelings, Ellen remains sibling-less by dismissing his tender proposal of marriage.

• *Further reading*

Fichtner, Margaria. "Review: *On the Occasion of My Last Afternoon*," *Miami Herald* (8 July 1998).

Gibbons, Kaye. *A Cure for Dreams*. New York: Algonquin, 1991.

_____. *On the Occasion of My Last Afternoon*. New York: G.P. Putnam's Sons, 1998.

_____. *Sights Unseen*. New York: G.P. Putnam's Sons, 1995.

Harris, Michael. "Scenes—and Skeletons—of a Troubled Southern Family," *Los Angeles Times* (9 October 1995): 5.

Sights Unseen

For her fifth novel, *Sights Unseen* (1995), Kaye Gibbons returns to the *Bildungsroman*, the genre of *Ellen Foster* (1987). The immediacy of the fictional study of a troubled girlhood provoked a battery of scholarly comments. In the description of Corinna Lothar, a critic for the *Washington Times*, the book is less coming-of-age story than the "history of an illness" composed with "deceptively gentle" rhythm (Lothar, 1995). The author abandons the tight construction of her first novel for a thorough study of family fallout from one member's manic depression. In the description of writer-reviewer Jacqueline Carey, a critic for the *New York Times Book Review*,

"Everything is steeped together in a rich stew of years," a reflection on the continuum that carries Hattie from unwanted infant to rejected pre-teen and adult survivor (Carey, 1995, 30). Gibbons develops depth during narrator Hattie Barnes's progression from pre-teen to adult career in medicine, which she shares with older brother Freddy. Polly Paddock, literary critic for the *Charlotte* (N.C.) *Observer*, summarized the effect as "moving, disarming, compact," a trio of comparatives that describes Gibbons's entire canon (Paddock, 1995).

Pain motivates the underwritten story. At the crux of family conflict lies the household's compulsion to protect the female head of household, Maggie Barnes, from neighborhood scrutiny and ridicule for bipolar mood swings. Secrecy forces individual needs and disappointments inward, walling off neighbors from family, brother from sister, and father from children. Gibbons develops a pseudo-rescuer, Grandfather Barnes, a flirtatious opportunist who coddles Maggie with gallantry and shopping sprees and with bribes to the Rocky Mount newspaper to suppress reports of her bizarre antics. More vital to the family's salvation is Pearl Wiggins, the family cook-housekeeper, who tends to Maggie while pinch-hitting as mother to Hattie and as female head of household. Like Mavis in *Ellen Foster*, Sudie Bee in *A Virtuous Woman* (1989), Polly Deal in *A Cure for Dreams* (1991), Clarice Washington in *On the Occasion of My Last Afternoon* (1998), and Mamie in *Divining Women* (2004), Pearl illuminates the role of black domestic whose membership in a troubled family exceeds the relationship of mere employee.

Gibbons summarized the success of her fifth novel to Kim Weaver Spurr, an interviewer for the Durham (N.C.) *Herald-Sun*. Unlike William Styron's self-analysis in *Darkness Visible: A Memoir of Madness* (1990) or Pat Conroy's adult-centered perspective in *Beach Music* (1995), Gibbons depicts Hattie as a 12-year-old who develops into an adult storyteller, an anesthesiologist and trauma victim recovering from years of her mother's looniness. The dual glimpses produce psychological fiction that probes the use of electroconvulsive shock treatment (ECT), the standard therapy for bipolarity in the 1940s and 1950s. Because of abuse and misapplication, ECT began to lose validity in private hospitals in the mid–1960s. However, unlike the terrifyingly punitive brain destruction in Ken Kesey's *One Flew Over the Cuckoo's Nest* (1962), the weekly sessions at Duke Hospital in 1967 restore Maggie to a more docile, self-controlled state, allowing her to return home to the duties of farm wife and mother.

The falling action honors a female triumph over self. Gibbons stresses the patient's effort to grasp home duties gradually, to avoid emotional imbroglios, and to overcome family dysfunction in small stages. Maggie begins with tentative realliance between mother and daughter through a shared book talk and nap, home-sewing of play suits, shopping for Sunday clothes, and nightly visits before sleep. Crowning Maggie's success before her death in 1982 are 15 years of wellness, which Hattie treasures as a matriarchal legacy.

See also **Barnes, Hattie; Barnes, Maggie; Barnes genealogy**

• *Further reading*

Carey, Jacqueline. "Mommy Direst," *New York Times Book Review* (24 September 1995): 30.

Gibbons, Kaye. *Sights Unseen*. New York: G.P. Putnam's Sons, 1995.
Harris, Michael. "Scenes— and Skeletons— of a Troubled Southern Family," *Los Angeles Times* (9 October 1995): 5.
Lothar, Corinna. "A Gritty, Witty 'Face'; a Spirited 'Oblivion,'" *Washington Times* (17 December 1995).
Paddock, Polly. "Kaye Gibbons Recalls 'Sights Unseen' As a Tough Project," *Charlotte* (N.C.) *Observer* (27 August 1995).
Spurr, Kim Weaver. "Storied Life: For Gibbons, Words Reflect Part of Herself," Durham, N.C., *Herald-Sun* (27 August 1995).

social class

The social stratification of characters in Kaye Gibbons's fiction reveals a constant skirmish between socio-economic strictures and individual ambition. In her first novel, *Ellen Foster* (1987), the author reflects at a distance on the failed union of the title character's genteel mother with ex-farmer Bill, a sluggard who pieces together a living on their neglected farm by selling bootleg whisky to blacks. In summer 1970, the decline of the family position goads Ellen's maternal grandmother to erupt in hateful, scatter-gun accusations that Ellen is just like her bastard, nigger-loving father (Gibbons, 1987, 20, 21). Homeless and rudderless shortly before Christmas, the 11-year-old passes to her uppity Aunt Nadine Nelson, who prods her daughter Dora to snub Ellen. A pathetic moment in family condescension portrays Nadine belittling Ellen's Christmas gift of hand-drawn cats as unsuitable for home display. Heavy with dramatic and situational irony, the novel champions Ellen as transcending social class by dismissing residence with the Nelsons as a temporary hotel stay and by selecting a loving foster mother to replace a clutch of no-class relatives.

A short-short story, "The Headache," published in the June 1987 issue of the *St. Andrews Review*, describes class consciousness in a frazzled farm wife. Protagonist Lucille Womble, the mother of ten children, punishes herself to excess for keeping a lost pocketbook, a prank lure containing a snake. In the privacy of Room C in Dr. Janet Cowley's office, Lucille confesses shame for wanting to keep the lost purse, an act that appears "common," the mark of "trash" (Gibbons, June 1987, 3). Lucille's first viewing of the snake occurs in the outhouse by the light of an oil lamp, a dual token of poverty and limited vision of self. Unable to maintain fealty to abstractions, Lucille struggles for a grasp on any source of income in a faltering agrarian economy. The subsequent throbbing temples, visions of fangs, weeping, and insomnia for two weeks imply internal combat with ethical standards. Gibbons crowns Lucille for her sensitive conscience with the concern of employer Mae Bell Stokes, the compassion of Dr. Cowley, and the promise of two hats from Henry, Lucille's understanding husband. Gently affectionate, the story corroborates critical opinion that Gibbons exalts laboring-class women as models of everyday goodness and right thinking.

Gibbons's second novel, *A Virtuous Woman* (1989), upholds, then negates the issue of social abasement through marriage to a lower class mate. Out of boredom and misplaced daring, co-narrator Ruby Pitts Woodrow Stokes allies unwisely at age 18 with 27-year-old John Woodrow, a jeering hired hand. Reared in a seemly home among landed gentry who always use cloth napkins at mealtime, Ruby admires her mother's good looks, which rescue her from denigration as "country-come-to-town" (Gibbons, 1989, 31). Ruby quickly slides downward from beloved daughter in a proper home to mistreated wife of a drifter. Constant moves to migrant dwellings and housework for the Hoover family introduce Ruby to the social milieu of Lester and Sudie Bee, the Pitts family domestics. In the estimation of reviewer Roz Kaveney, the Hoovers engage Ruby as a maid "for the sheer pleasure of having a genteel white servant" (Kaveney, 1989, 98). After the author kills off John in a pool room knifing, 20-year-old Ruby retreats into reverie and cigarettes, her refuge from class displacement. Vulnerability draws her into a second out-of-class liaison, this time with 40-year-old bachelor "Blinking" Jack Ernest Stokes. Their mutual hunger for love and respect underlies the theme of need as an antidote to class dissonance.

In a third novel, *A Cure for Dreams* (1991), the author ventures into subtler immigrant vs. native-born citizen differences. Born in 1900, Lottie O'Cadhain Davies grows up in Galway, Ireland, in an oppositional household headed by a demanding drunk, Sheamus O'Cadhain, and a defiant Catholic mother, Bridget O'Donough O'Cadhain. Upon the family's emigration in 1918 to a clan compound on the Cumberland River in Bell County, Kentucky, Lottie commits the teenage error in judgment of dreaming of a male rescuer on horseback who offers an ideal marriage and home. In place of a gallant horseman, she chooses Quaker miller-farmer Charles Davies, whose faults remain hidden until after their union and move to North Carolina. Like other of Gibbons's unwise maidens, Lottie gains no social or psychological boost through hasty wedlock.

Blessed with an immigrant perspective on American class distinctions, Lottie claws her way toward respectability in the back of Porter's store. Through social mobility, she elevates herself to queen bee of Milk Farm Road by enrolling local women in a gin rummy and pinochle club. A whiff of gentrified snobbery emerges during her visits to Trudy Woodlief, a newcomer from Baton Rouge, Louisiana, whose white trash behaviors include shaving her legs before company and humbling herself to beg Porter, the storeowner, for credit. Gibbons depicts Lottie as a female guided by sisterhood to help other women, including Trudy and Sade Duplin, a distraught wife who fells her dissolute husband Roy with a shotgun blast. In widowhood, Lottie allows Bridget to orchestrate a command performance of the dying matriarch during a return visit to Galway. Gibbons sets the folk scene among Irish peasants whose traditions honor deathbed melodrama. On return to North Carolina, Lottie displays a normal side of motherhood by micro-managing daughter Betty's dating habits and culling Luther Miracle, a slovenly prospect. Lottie promotes marriage in February 1942 to Herman Randolph, a farming-class beau who bears the added distinction of service aboard the U.S.S. *Hornet* during the Pacific war. The subsequent generations of the matrilineage bear little connection to Irish peasantry, yet remain agrarian and family-oriented much like their grandsires.

Gibbons's egalitarian fourth novel, *Charms for the Easy Life* (1993), sweeps class aside in an embrace of service to the emotionally and medically destitute. The protagonist, Charlie Kate Birch, flourishes at tending the hurts, birthings, buryings, and dental needs of patients in Pasquotank County and in the mill district of Raleigh, North Carolina. She crusades for the poor by shaming city officials into extending sewer lines to the underclass, who are unfamiliar with flush toilets. Her night calls to treat malaria, boils, whooping cough, and broken bones extend during World War II to the herbal treatment and rehabilitation in 1942 of casualties at a veterans' hospital in Durham. In close contact with a Raleigh aristocrat, Tom Hawkings, III, she furthers her granddaughter Margaret's chance of marrying into an intellectually and socially prominent family. The shift from dowdy patients awaiting treatment on Beale Street to a Christmas 1942 dinner with the upscale Hawkings clan suggests that Charlie Kate, the idealist once married to an illiterate ferryman, realizes that Margaret deserves a husband more suited to her good breeding and home schooling in medicine, humanism, and quality literature.

The social order of *Sights Unseen* (1995), Gibbons's fifth novel, replicates the subtle class gradations of *A Cure for Dreams* by distinguishing farm laborers from farm owners. In a proud extended family, Maggie Barnes thwarts gentility by caroming from depression to bipolar madness. Her protector, Grandfather Barnes, exudes sympathy along with a vaguely erotic attachment to his daughter-in-law, whom he cossets with shopping sprees and gallantries that class him as a sugar daddy. In an agrarian milieu, the wealthy Barnes clan shelters Maggie from gossip by veiling her extremes from neighborhood scrutiny, particularly her public rages and private demands for intense lovemaking from husband Frederick. After psychotherapy and eight electroconvulsive shock treatments at Duke Hospital in 1967 restores her to normal behavior, she abandons her manic personae by assuming the appropriate class role of female head of household and mother of two. Essential to her breeding is the upbraiding of Grandfather Barnes at dinner for using the word "nigger" to describe Pearl Wiggins, the cook-housekeeper who tends Maggie like a sister (Gibbons, 1995, 197). The gesture carries double weight — assertion of a proper upbringing and a retort to a usurping male who challenges Maggie's primacy as hostess.

In her first historical novel, *On the Occasion of My Last Afternoon* (1998), Gibbons describes a self-made man, Samuel P. Goodman Tate, whose extremes of domination reek of Southern Gothicism. Like Gerald O'Hara, the upstart Irish planter who weds the socially compromised aristocrat Ellen Robillard of Charleston, South Carolina, in Margaret Mitchell's *Gone with the Wind* (1936), Samuel marries damaged goods — Alice, the daughter of a refined, but impoverished Savannah cotton dealer. Samuel chooses her as a leg up to social prominence. He glories in a showy home and hires for his daughter's tutor a cynic who summarizes high-end art as "Aristocrats [painting] aristocrats" (Gibbons, 1998, 130). Because the oldest son Whately jeopardizes Samuel's veneer of refinement by admitting to fathering the child of a barmaid, on December 20, 1842, the father disinherits a loving family member who displays the graciousness and sensitivity of Samuel's wife Alice. Five years later, their 17-year-old daughter Emma Garnet weds Dr. Quincy Lowell, a Boston brahmin who suffers Samuel's vulgarities before cutting ties with the tidewater fraud. Ironically, out of ignorance and sectional grudge bearing, Samuel drives away an upscale son-in-law from one of America's most respected lineages.

The text opens in 1842 on a rampage by the bullying oligarch, who demands obedience from family and servants. The only holdout is cook-housekeeper Clarice Washington, who is not impressed by a parvenu who rises from a piddling two acres to the gentrification of 2,000 acres in Bruton Parish, Virginia. In the estimation of analyst Veronica Makowsky, Samuel pursues acceptance by "a society that values birth and breeding over achievement" (Perry & Weaks, 2002, 607). Unspoken between Samuel and Clarice is the knowledge that he finagled his way upward from beggary. Surrounded by expensive trappings purchased at auction, he educates himself at night with Greek grammar and elementary readings in Latin authors. The faux patina of the classics and a bogus family crest reveal Samuel's urgency to rid himself of classlessness and to lavish his vanity with proofs of artistic taste and pure blood lines. In a satisfying touch of poetic justice, Gibbons makes him the laughingstock of the James River community, where real esthetes are quick to identify a fake.

Gibbons dramatizes the outing of the *poseur* by juxtaposing the accuser with the accused. Samuel Tate faces an undeniable comeuppance in 1847 from his daughter's marriage to Lowell, a well-bred New England abolitionist. To reclaim philosophical superiority, Tate blusters his way through a pre-wedding dinner with the Lowell parents, pausing to ridicule the Harvard-educated intelligentsia, whose learning is anathema to a self-taught planter who reads Dante, Goethe, and Voltaire. Tate takes refuge in abasing contemplative men and in reviling Boston women with a coarse racial slur. By reaching below caution to mortify his guests, Samuel breaches forever the social divide with Emma's new family. Gibbons intimates that the evening's confrontation is two-edged in humiliating Emma and her future in-laws while liberating her from a monstrous father.

The novel follows Emma through her own acculturation from a James River enclave to snobbish urban society. Safely removed from Seven Oaks plantation to Blount Street in Raleigh, North Carolina, she lives the glass fishbowl existence of the nonconformist. In addition to being publicly demeaned and shunned by social maven Lucille McKimmon, Emma and Quincy draw Old South disapproval of the Lowells' freedwoman servant, Clarice Washington. The Lowells originate their own social milieu from the professional class, including a bishop, a judge, the daughter of General Robert E. Lee, and two governors. After the family makes a project of elevating Lavinia Ella Mae Dawes from white trash squalor and ignorance, she graduates second in her class from Saint Mary's School. A post-graduation party at Milburnie Lodge miffs mothers of elite girls, who disdain rubbing elbows with the "chin-up" daughter of a coal carter (Gibbons, 1998, 122). Gibbons darkens the Lowell project further by indicating secondhand that Lavinia marries a bounder who beats her with a sack of oranges. The girl's unpropitious marriage and early death remind readers of the class defiance of Henry Higgins, antagonist of George Bernard Shaw's *Pygmalion* (1912–1913), which dumps protégé Eliza Doolittle into a classless no-man's-land. Nonetheless, Quincy's spiritual urging sends Emma home to Raleigh, where "a hundred Lavinias need you," his vision of liberal idealism (*Ibid.*, 268).

Unlike Gibbons's earlier protagonists, Emma Lowell possesses the cash, poise, and social clout to live as she pleases. Despite taunts from a Raleigh newspaper editor, she sweeps her path clear of suffering with appropriate disbursals of money, which she once stored in the basement in false-bottomed peach baskets, a token of humble coverings of wealth. Amid Reconstruction Era rancor, she invests in a freedman's school at the United States Bank building and offers employment opportunities for the poor at a pottery, clothing factory, and bakery. A touch of macabre humor emerges from a poison-pen note from the Ku Klux Klan, which states the fear of the white underclass that an educated black "wil lord hisself over the wite man" (Gibbons, 1998, 270). Undeterred by the derisive editor or by semi-literate night riders, Emma develops feminist character strength by retrieving from want and ignorance likely candidates for intellectual and spiritual uplift.

The privilege and autonomy of the former declassé undergird the humor that accompanies the initial conflict in *Divining Women* (2004), Gibbons's seventh novel. Troop Ross's mother, Nora Worthy Ross, a vengeful ex-wife, lambastes his father, accountant Toby Greene, with assaults on his dignity for joining the American Community of Nudists. Persistently irate at his waste of a Washington, D.C., address, Episcopal leanings, club lunches, and social advancement, Nora has the Washington papers delivered to her North Carolina address to supply her with social page commentary on Greene and his new wife Leslie. In contrast to Nora's disgruntlement, Toby and Leslie's daughter, Martha Greene Oliver, evolves serenity by devaluing class perks. Martha amasses enough wealth in widowhood in 1913 to disobey her deceased husband Grammar's order to hire a house-cleaner. Rather than potter about at housewifery, she chooses to travel in Europe with her family. Martha's emotional health distances her from Nora's neurotic need to grab money and social position as indicators of worth.

Gibbons complicates issues of status and public appearance by developing the conflict between the Olivers and Nora's son, Troop Ross, a cocky nabob in Elm City, North Carolina. After Mary Oliver, a 22-year-old graduate student at Radcliffe, travels south on September 30, 1918, to attend her aunt, Maureen Carlton Ross, during the final 50 days of pregnancy, Troop manifests his own version of Nora's fixation on social class. He refers to the parlor as the drawing room and to the car porch by the French *porte cochère* (covered driveway); he insists on niggling rules of decorum concerning behavior, particularly dining at a proper table setting and eating separate from black house staff. In contrast to Mary's grandparents' wartime display of flags and the playing of patriotic songs on the piano, Troop disdains the posting of an American banner as vulgar. In his toney words, "people of quality" avoid the exhibitionism common to barbershops and courthouses (Gibbons, 2004, 83). His exposure reveals Gibbons's skill at rewarding just deserts—at sunset on November 9, 1918, he screams "perverted bitch" at Maureen as she follows the casket of their stillborn daughter, Ella Eloise, to a graveside service (*Ibid.*, 204). Genuine gentlemen of the neighborhood make astute observations that Troop is not in possession of sanity.

In like fashion, overt behaviors mark the boundaries of class in *The Life All Around Me by Ellen Foster* (2006), the sequel to *Ellen Foster*. Commentary on Aunt Nadine Nelson and cousin Dora identifies traits that demean the landed gentry for their greed and duplicity. At a lower social level, Stuart, the son of a junk dealer, lives in a lean-to near a perpetually burning heap of rubber tires, but he clarifies for Ellen a worse form of white trash shiftlessness in the family of four renters who destroy her old house. Their classmate Martha substantiates Stuart's estimation by running down the renters for failure to pay their grocery store charge account for a year. In the falling action, the rapid transfer of a family inheritance to Ellen illustrates the elusive nature of estates and the sudden elevation of an orphaned foster child into an heiress. More precious than wealth is the advancement of Shine, whom Ellen retrieves from records of Shine's mental decline after marriage to Bill, a low-class boozer. For good reason, critics label the novel a Cinderella fable.

• *Further reading*

Blackford, Linda B. "Review: *On the Occasion of My Last Afternoon*," *Lexington* (Ky.) *Herald-Leader* (19 August 1998).

Fichtner, Margaria. "Review: *On the Occasion of My Last Afternoon*," *Miami Herald* (8 July 1998).

Gibbons, Kaye. *Divining Women*. New York: G.P. Putnam's Sons, 2004.

_____. "The Headache," *St. Andrews Review* (June 1987): 3–8.

_____. *On the Occasion of My Last Afternoon*. New York: G.P. Putnam's Sons, 1998.

_____. *Sights Unseen*. New York: G.P. Putnam's Sons, 1995.

Kaveney, Roz. "Making Themselves Over," *Times Literary Supplement* (15 September 1989): 998.

Perry, Carolyn, and Mary Louise Weaks, eds. *The History of Southern Women's Literature*. Baton Rouge: Louisiana State University Press, 2002.

the South

At a Southern Literary Symposium held in Charlotte, North Carolina, in October 1993, Gibbons named a distinctive quality of the region: "The South has always thought of itself as being a separate country. So it's only natural that a literature would grow out of that feeling of separateness" (Paddock, 1993). In the afterword to Jeanne Braselton's *The Other Side of Air* (2006), Gibbons de-mythologizes notions that Southern writers pluck fiction from front-porch sessions of tale swapping. In place of the generalization that Southern writing emerges full-blown from old stories, Gibbons forebears like William Faulkner and Eudora Welty—"people who are so incredibly daring that they are willing to cast a critical eye on [Southern] values and customs while standing in the very center of it" (Gibbons, "Afterword," 2006, 181). The description captures Gibbons's pluck in spinning miseries of her own childhood on a Nash County farm into literary gold.

At first, the author chose not to write about her farm community at Bend of the River, North Carolina, which she dismissed to interviewer Dannye Romine Powell, book editor of the *Charlotte* (N.C.) *Observer*, as a "little postage stamp of space" (Powell, 1994, 129). Although Gibbons reprises childhood memories in the updated fool tale "The Headache," published in the June 1987 issue of the *St. Andrews Review*, and in her first novels, *Ellen Foster* (1987) and *A Virtuous Woman* (1989), the works identify no specific Southern setting other than small agrarian communities populated by smallholders, land-owning gentry, hirelings, and black domestics and field hands. Instead of "[tackling] the broad, meandering landscapes that figure in many Southern novels," according to critic Lynn Jessup, a reviewer for the *Greensboro* (N.C.) *News & Record*, Gibbons situates her characters geographically through voice (Jessup, 1995).

Gibbons acknowledges a precision of language and an absence of clichés among

Southern speakers. Contributing to regional authenticity is situational humor, which maintains the upbeat atmosphere of her third novel, *A Cure for Dreams* (1991). Light fun emerges in the intent of Trudy Woodlief to name her twins Bernard and Barnard and to nickname them Pee Wee and Buddy, choices more suited to beagle pups. Comedy derives complexity and nuance from the underlying rage of the women of Milk Farm Road, who must rely on female wiles to thwart and subvert patriarchal barriers during the Great Depression. Empowering sessions of a gin rummy- and pinochle-playing klatch in the rear of Porter's store are surges of validation and resolve, in particular, the support of Trudy's shoplifting children and the aiding of Sade Duplin after she kills her controlling husband Roy with a shotgun blast. Group solidarity emerges as Lottie and her followers form an all-woman phalanx around Sade to protect her from part-time Deputy Sheriff John Carroll's inept search of the crime scene for spent cartridges and footprints. The Southern Gothic scenario resonates with regional delight in uppity women who wrest their own justice from male-dominant society.

In her first historical novel, *On the Occasion of My Last Afternoon* (1998), Gibbons categorizes the racial and economic strata of tidewater society in ante-bellum Bruton Parish, Virginia. The opening scene contrasts the surface serenity of a James River estate in 1842 with the horrors of the slave quarters. At the crux of master-on-slave murder precipitated by the pretentious Samuel P. Goodman Tate are his feelings of inferiority. Concealing a working-class origin, he struts in the presence of a liberal-minded suitor, Dr. Quincy Lowell, an intellectual progressive from Boston, Massachusetts. Crude beyond the pale of table badinage, Tate engineers the silent departure of Lowell's parents and the near collapse of Quincy's mother through overtly vulgar affronts. Narrator Emma Garnet Tate Lowell, Quincy's 17-year-old fiancée, takes the opportunity to distinguish between the noble English settlers at Jamestown and the likes of Samuel, a beggarly scion of English rejects dropped off at a Georgia debtors' colony, a method of easing England's overcrowded prisons. Gibbons accords some esteem to Tate for being a self-educated up-and-comer, but condemns his vanity as the goad to self-ennobling boorishness. Emma's late-in-life evaluation of Samuel occurs in 1900, when the 70-year-old widow reflects on the two great conflicts that shape her life, the intertwined domestic combat at Seven Oaks plantation and the downfall of the plantation South from the Civil War and Reconstruction.

At novel's end, Gibbons moves her heroine to Boston in 1865 to live with the Lowells following Quincy's death from exhaustion and metabolic collapse. While Emma works at Massachusetts General Hospital, her Southern accent renews questions of North-South antipathies. Feeling like a foreigner, she acknowledges a lifelong commitment to her homeland, but claims no need to live there during a lengthy period of Union debasement and destruction of the Confederacy. Her most damning utterance relegates to hell General Benjamin Franklin Butler for the crushing of New Orleans on May 1, 1862, and to General William Tecumseh Sherman for the burning of Atlanta on November 11, 1864. In token of her love for Quincy, she draws more comfort from his grave than from their home in Raleigh. In the evenings, culinary classes begin the process of "attenuating anguish," her term for lightening personal and regional woes (Gibbons, 1998, 265). Gibbons characterizes the enjoyment of food preparation as an opportunity for Southern and Northern women to rule their domestic domain and to talk away mutual troubles.

The novel applauds Emma Garnet for her ability to select the best of self and to reconcile the rancor around her with benevolence and grace. By reconnecting with cook-housekeeper Clarice Washington's handwritten amendments to the "receipts" in *The Williamsburg Art of Cookery*, Emma rewards Northern friends and family with egg pudding, chicken with stuffing, collards, and grits, elements of traditional Southern cookery (Gibbons, 1998, 266). Unlike plantation estates and slave quarters, a fine table becomes one aspect of a war-ravaged culture that endures and redeems. In the end, Emma obeys Quincy's insistant voice and returns to their Blount Street home, which she shares with her young sister Maureen. In the view of analyst Veronica Makowsky, the racist, patriarchal South leaves to women like the Tate sisters "the building of subcultures of community," a generalized locale devoid of old grudges (Perry & Weaks, 2002, 608). The critique credits feminism with the strength to overcome petty regionalism.

In the initial action of her seventh novel, *Divining Women* (2004), Gibbons takes a comic tack by poking fun at the South from the perspective of an outsider. She voices dismay at regional quirks through the observations of Mary Oliver, a 22-year-old graduate student at Radcliffe, who, on September 30, 1918, heads south by train from Washington, D.C., to Elm City, North Carolina. At Washington's Union Station, she surveys people who appear to be candidates for an asylum. Her mother, widow Martha Greene Oliver, reminds Mary that Washington bears no likeness to the South. On the journey in close quarters, a confluence of idiocies—coughing, limping, boozing, raging, teasing, swindling, terrorizing, and hysterical wailing—overplays Mary's adventure with Southern Gothicism. The episode suggests Gibbons's inept attempt to emulate the freaks and sharpers created by William Faulkner, Flannery O'Connor, and Eudora Welty.

In fairness to the South, more realistic surveillance prevails. Mary Oliver's examination of basket and flower sellers in Union Station captures an era of post–Civil War recovery. Black women merchandising wares near the fountain raise hopeful faces to Mary as though the 50-some years since emancipation obliterates slavery. At the novel's reclamation of Maureen Carlton Ross in September 1918, Gibbons affirms her joy in Southern cussedness with a letter from Maureen's mother in Yazoo City, Mississippi, that bursts with pride in family and birthplace. In a recap of Maureen's marriage in 1913 to the pretentious Troop Ross, the letter summarizes local suspicions that a delta girl weds herself to a grandiose parvenu too good to drink or wash in well water. Maureen's mother asserts to readers that Mississippians may be poor and inelegant, but they have the good sense to recognize a phony.

Gibbons's wry take on growing up in the eastern Carolina piedmont resurges in *The Life All Around Me by Ellen Foster* (2006), where farm children in 1974 still receive days off from school to bale hay and slaughter pigs. In the title character's self-introduction to Dr. Derek Curtis Bok, president of Harvard University, she describes North Carolina's flat tobacco-land as the "variety" in the advertising phrase "Variety Vacationland" (Gibbons, 2006, 1). Ellen's humor indicates ennui with the agrarian lowlands, which contrast the grandeur of the Great Smokies to the west and the refreshing Atlantic shore along the Outer Banks. Another dig at the South skewers the intractability of white-flight bigots who operate the Academy of the New Dawn Apocalypse, a droll name for a fundamentalist segregation institute that offers Ellen an alternative to night classes at the community college "over by the lumber mill" (Gibbons, 2006, 29). By stressing the rural offerings of her homeland, the author imparts to readers the obstacles she overcame to become a writer.

Gibbons wields even-handed humor to smash stereotypes. For Ellen, the South offers a melange of possibilities, from head lice in the school cloakroom to the birth of Virginia Dare mentioned in *The Lost Colony* (1937), an outdoor drama by Pulitzer Prize–winning author Paul Green that describes an English settlement that disappeared in summer 1586 from the North Carolina shores at Manteo. Ellen juxtaposes wrestling shows with Billy Graham crusades, two sources of income from working concessions. The text satirizes rental property "beaten down in a hot hurry," high school boys intent on camouflage gear and hunting, a teen taxidermist who works at the meat counter, and radio news of pork belly and soybean futures, a daily broadcast in the agrarian South (*Ibid.*, 211). While scrutinizing New Englanders at Johns Hopkins University in Baltimore, Ellen discovers herself a "curiosity" among people who label Southerners as illiterates and bigots (*Ibid.*, 76). The generalization overlooks altruists like Laura and ambitious people like Starletta's mother, a single parent who seeks a degree in social work. More specifically, the jab at Southerners slights Ellen, a budding genius with a hunger for excellence.

See also **Civil War; "Joyner's Store"; *Pete & Shirley*; Raleigh, North Carolina**

• *Further reading*

Bennett, Barbara. Comic Visions, *Female Voices: Contemporary Women Novelists and Southern Humor*. Baton Rouge: Louisiana State University Press, 1998.

Blackford, Linda B. "Review: *On the Occasion of My Last Afternoon*," *Lexington* (Ky.) *Herald-Leader* (19 August 1998).

Gibbons, Kaye. "Afterword," *The Other Side of Air*. New York: Random House, 2006.

_____. *The Life All Around Me by Ellen Foster*. New York: Harcourt, 2006.

_____. *On the Occasion of My Last Afternoon*. New York: G.P. Putnam's Sons, 1998.

Jessup, Lynn. "Kaye Gibbons: Another Happy Ending," *Greensboro* (N.C.) *News & Record* (12 November 1995).

Paddock, Polly. "Writers to Discuss Southern Literature's New Story Line," *Charlotte* (N.C.) *Observer* (17 October 1993).

Perry, Carolyn, and Mary Louise Weaks, eds. *The History of Southern Women's Literature*. Baton Rouge: Louisiana State University Press, 2002.

Powell, Dannye Romine. *Parting the Curtains: Interviews with Southern Writers*. Winston-Salem, N.C.: J.F. Blair, 1994.

Starletta

A cherished friend and companion, Starletta is a complex factor in Kaye Gibbons's first novel, *Ellen Foster* (1987). Living in a one-room house near Ellen's home, Starletta bears out the meaning of her name, "little star," for extending welcome at Christmas 1969, after the death of Ellen's mother. The author pictures the black child as undersized, slow-witted, stuttering, pocked with insect bites, and given to spinning and to sitting in garden rows and grabbing chunks of red clay from her mother's hoeing to suck for nourishment. Like a rambunctious pet, Starletta dismantles her toy sets and flaunts holiday lapel pins with the enthusiasm of a "friendly older toddler" (Gibbons, 2006, 57). More a presence than a persona, she interacts peripherally with Ellen, who is obviously her intellectual superior. Social, educational, and racial differences direct the title character toward a valuable epiphany that Starletta, for all her advantages at home, suffers from an indigenous Southern racism that Ellen learns from her father and maternal grandmother.

As a force for good, Starletta contrasts the novel's antagonists, especially the snotty, dismissive Dora Nelson, the title character's cousin. In an urge common to foster children, Ellen needs to invite Starletta to her new home. The gesture offers a homeless foster child an opportunity for giving in an atmosphere of constant receiving. In the analysis of Sharon Monteith, author of *Advancing Sisterhood: Interracial Friendships in Contemporary Southern Fiction* (2000), Ellen needs a friend after she concludes that "home is of limited value if unsupported by wider social affiliations that can help to make it a shared space rather than a lonely sanctuary" (Monteith, 2000, 69). In anticipation of a sleep-over, Ellen alerts the bus driver to Starletta's arrival and has Laura, the new mother, monogram towels, a form of acknowledgement that parallels the gift of a little Dutch girl pattern stitched by Starletta's mother on a pillow as a gift for Ellen. In exchange for shopping and going to the movies together and resting on Ellen's bed before supper, Starletta plaits Ellen's hair and confers quasi-motherhood as though Starletta were a child to be adored and showered with gifts and privileges. In commentary on the lopsided relationship, Jeff Abernathy's *To Hell and Back: Race and Betrayal in the Southern Novel* (2003) describes Ellen's proprietary attitude as a racist slur—a patrician noblesse oblige that denies Starletta's autonomy or value as a friend. He adds that Ellen, just like Mark Twain's Huck Finn in assessment of his relationship with Jim, realizes from her relationship with Starletta that "there is no inherent value in a white identity" (Abernathy, 2003, 124).

Starletta remains a fixed symbol on Ellen's horizon in the author's first sequel, *The Life All Around Me by Ellen Foster* (2006). The action in 1974 depicts Starletta's parents as reduced to a working widow and college student on welfare after Starletta's dad dies. In an amalgam of past and future, Ellen stands hand-in-hand with Starletta while reliving grasping the hand of Shine, Ellen's mother who commits suicide in March 1969. As though infusing Starletta with intellectual curiosity, Ellen projects global travel after college with Starletta as a companion. In the guest room of Laura's home lie an assortment of tin windup toys, mechanical wonders suited to Starletta's level of intellectual development. For in-house activity, Ellen pushes Starletta on the leather ottoman, a cushy ride just for fun. Ellen speaks of Starletta as being "occupied," an indication of the difference in their maturity that makes Ellen seem more adult babysitter than friend (Gibbons, 2006, 39). Reducing the distance between IQs and backgrounds are photos of Ellen and Starletta at Halloween 1971, when they dressed as macaroni and cheese. The pairing lessens their intellectual distancing with an alliance of humble American comfort foods.

Critics view Starletta as remote, yet curious and cherubic—a Christmas wonder wearing a Rudolph pin and racing through the house in blinking shoes. To Valerie

Sayers, a reviewer for the *Washington Post*, the mentally disabled child is a "holy innocent" existing out of the realm of reality (Sayers, 2006). Starletta's torpor in early scenes erupts into flailing rage after a new boy at school tries to steal the money she collects for cartons of milk she distributes from the lunchroom. Secure with Ellen, Starletta allows herself to be pulled off his head and bedded down on satin pillows in the Easy Reader section of the school library, an image of the safeguarding that Ellen wishes for her friend. Defended by an irate mother, Starletta is as worthy of sheltering as Ellen. The mother-daughter pairs— Starletta and her mother, Ellen and Laura — affirm Gibbons's reverence for the natural order of parenting.

See also **Starletta's genealogy**

• *Further reading*

Abernathy, Jeff. *To Hell and Back: Race and Betrayal in the Southern Novel.* Athens: University of Georgia Press, 2003.
Gibbons, Kaye. *The Life All Around Me by Ellen Foster.* New York: Harcourt, 2006.
Hoffman, Alice. "Shopping for a New Family," *New York Times* (31 May 1987): A13.
Monteith, Sharon. *Advancing Sisterhood: Interracial Friendships in Contemporary Southern Fiction.* Athens: University of Georgia Press, 2000.
_____. "Between Girls: Kaye Gibbons' *Ellen Foster* and Friendship as Monologic Formulation," *Journal of American Studies* 33, no. 1 (1999): 45–64.
Sayers, Valerie, "Growing Into the Role," *Washington Post* (6 January 2006).
Wells, Chandra. "Advancing Sisterhood?," *MELUS 27*, no. 3 (Fall 2002): 229–231.

Starletta's genealogy

Although vaguely structured, Starletta's family line impacts the salvation and reclamation of Ellen, the title character of *Ellen Foster* (1987) and its sequel, *The Life All Around Me by Ellen Foster* (2006):

```
                 _______________
                 |             |
         mother=father  Starletta's aunt ... man who upsets her
on welfare;  | dies                        |
seeker of a  | after 1970       crying infant
degree in    |
sociology    |
             |
         Starletta
```

• *Further reading*

Gibbons, Kaye. *Ellen Foster.* New York: Algonquin Press, 1987.
_____. *The Life All Around Me by Ellen Foster.* New York: Harcourt, 2006.

Stokes, Ruby Pitts Woodrow

One of Kaye Gibbons's most compelling female characters, Ruby Pitts Woodrow Stokes suffers the sure punishments meted out to the unwise. Born to landed gentry, she grows up cherished like a "big baby doll" in a farm clan that accords more autonomy to her father and older brothers, Jimmy and Paul, than to the family's baby girl (Gibbons, 1989, 25). Bored and adventuresome, at age 18, Ruby wearies of accommodating males who cut her meat for her. She is a victim of what polemicist Olive Schreiner characterizes in *Woman and Labour* (1911) as male latchkeepers—"strong and generous men eager to turn it for her, almost before she knocks" (Schreiner, 1911). In place of pampering, Ruby longs for wedlock with a storybook mate who will take her places. Visually seduced by a flashy male, she seals her fate by choosing to elope with a farm worker, 26-year-old John Woodrow, who later calls her "bitch" (*Ibid.*, 37). The author pictures the immediate defeat of teen romanticism in the wedding-night rip of Ruby's robe and nightgown, a symbolic rending of her virginal modesty and romantic illusions.

In a retrospect preceding death, at age 45, Ruby struggles to heal the gashes that John leaves in her self-esteem by remaking the choices that are her undoing. Mocked and betrayed, she tolerates two years of wedded misery before fighting back against his vulgarity, lying, and adultery with trashy, disease-carrying women. Gibbons absolves her female protagonist of plotting murder against a layabout who hangs out in pool rooms and flaunts a 16-year-old trollop in front of Ruby. Worsening the scenario is Ruby's anger that the interloper sports Ruby's lingerie, a woman-shattering motif that Gibbons's reprises in the adultery of Judith Benedict Stafford's husband in *Divining Women* (2004). The violation wounds Ruby's womanhood, her most vulnerable spot.

Contributing to Ruby's ruin is her hunger for cigarettes, a self-destructive escape that enables her to tolerate John and, a quarter century later, ends her life with coughing and gasping from lung cancer. The intervening period reveals one of Gibbons's happier unions, the marriage of Ruby within five months of widowhood to farm worker "Blinking" Jack Ernest Stokes, who is 20 years her senior. Unlike her first romance, she succumbs to verbal and spiritual seduction. Like the farm couple Lucille and Henry Womble in the short-short story "The Headache" (1987) and Emma Garnet Tate and Quincy Lowell in *On the Occasion of My Last Afternoon* (2006), Ruby and Jack marry out of mutual need. They cling to each other while making the best of poverty and childlessness, the result of a sexually transmitted disease from John that leaves Ruby barren. The two-person narrative enhances the contrast between husband and wife by depicting Jack as a surface thinker and Ruby as the more contemplative of the couple. Stoic and loving, she spends the last days of her 45th year preparing meals for Jack, who must rely on freezer packs of pork with corn and beef with beans to supplement his inept culinary skills. More important to Ruby's peace of mind is the growth of persona. Analyst Linda Adams Barnes, in an article for the *Tennessee Philological Bulletin*, remarked, "At the end of [Ruby's] life, she knows what it is to become a woman because she has created that identity for herself" (Barnes, 1993, 23).

Gibbons extends Ruby's influence in Jack's half of the narrative through memories that contrast his acid-mouthed Cherokee mother with the sweet-natured Ruby. Over the three months following Ruby's death in March, he recalls a lovely, generous woman who bakes satisfying pies and bread and who fosters June Stanley as a substitute daughter in their childless household. As though breaching the division between life and death, he grieves at what is "gone, gone buried with her in the grave" and, with sprinkles of her lilac-scented talcum, summons Ruby's spirit to their bed, the core of their union (Gibbons, 1989, 19). In the view of Susan Heeger, a book critic for the *Los Angeles Times*, extensive reflection "[dramatizes] the alienating force of grief and its power to summon longstanding resentments between two people who love each other" (Heeger, 1989, 15). Overlaying his sorrow is anger at Ruby's post-diagnosis funk and disgust at her "two ashy-smelling fingers," the source of her fatal illness (Gibbons, 1989, 4). In the same stave, he is able to forgive Ruby's habitual smoking and to bless her for being "a fine partner," a term redolent with marital compromise (*Ibid.*, 5).

See also **Pitts-Stokes-Woodrow genealogy**

• *Further reading*

Barnes, Linda Adams. "Telling Yourself into Existence: The Fiction of Kaye Gibbons," *Tennessee Philological Bulletin* 30 (1993): 28–35.

Heeger, Susan. "Couldn't Live with Her, Can't Live without Her": *A Virtuous Woman,*" *Los Angeles Times* (11 June 1989): 15.

Gibbons, Kaye. *A Virtuous Woman.* Chapel Hill, N.C.: Algonquin Press, 1989.

Schreiner, Olive. *Woman and Labour.* http://etext.library.adelaide.edu.au/s/schreiner_o/woman/woman.html, 1911, accessed on October 10, 2006.

storytelling

Narrative is Kaye Gibbons's birth gift. In the estimation of author-critic Marjorie Gellhorn Sa'adah, a reviewer for the *Los Angeles Times*, Gibbons produces "complex, cruel, and gorgeous family stories set in the American South," her home and inspiration (Sa'adah, 2006). Key to her success is a down-deep honesty that comes from the marrow. In the afterword to *The Other Side of Air* (2006), Gibbons concurs with author Jeanne Braselton's de-mythologizing—"that writing doesn't flourish in the South because we swap stories on the porch" (Gibbons, "Afterword," 2006, 181). In the intuitive style of Fred Chappell, James Dickey, Allan Gurganous, Barbara Kingsolver, and Eudora Welty, Gibbons delves further into heart hurts. She pictures the unspoken distress of Henry and Lucille Womble, a farm couple making do in "The Headache," a short-short story issued in June 1987 in the *St. Andrews Review.* From the powerlessness of a financially strapped farm wife emerges emotional release. With the aid of Dr. Janet Cowley, Lucille abandons invalidism in favor of a cathartic cleansing of conscience. She displays womanly courage on a par with the reclamation of a guilt-ridden mother in Katharine Anne Porter's "He" (1930), a story of dignity and of on-the-spot decision making in a difficult domestic situation. In place of a lengthy resolution of Lucille's guilt over appearing trashy, Gibbons drapes the closing scene in connubial comfort, a touch of grace that honors married love.

Endowed with an ear for subtle human exposition, Gibbons began engaging readers in her late 20s with *Ellen Foster* (1987), already a classic of American literature for its straight-shooting title narrator. Voicing the miseries of the neglected ten-year-old, the award-winning text provokes and unsettles readers with its candor, a truth-to-heart revelation of regional strengths and faults that the author knows from childhood in the tobaccoland of Nash County, North Carolina. Gibbons plunges directly into an emotional maelstrom by depicting the murderous rage of Ellen, who plots patricide. A motherless child, she must ward off her lecherous father Bill on New Year's Eve, 1969, while restructuring a shattered life. Interspersed with the hurt, scenes of Ellen's foster home predict a hopeful future. The flow of memories substantiates Ellen's delight on Christmas Day, 1970, in locating a suitable foster mother and a home devoid of threat. Gibbons introduces her unique blend of Southern Gothic with decorum. Overlaying narrative are strands of horrific challenge — a suicidal mother who dies of an overdose of prescription digitalis in bed in 1969 alongside her grieving daughter, a father who exposes his genitals to elementary school children, a grandmother who assigns Ellen to hoe the fields in July heat, and the lust of a derelict who salivates over Ellen's pre-womanhood. Offsetting terror are the speaker's brief recall of picking green beans with her mother, a foster home with clipped hedges, a ride on Dolphin the pony, and the fragrance of fried chicken on Sunday, sense impressions that express normality in a beleaguered heroine.

In her second novel, *A Virtuous Woman* (1989), Gibbons again chooses to inform and to alert. An adult version of Ellen Foster, co-narrator Ruby Pitts Woodrow Stokes carries the perils of Ellen's parents' mismating to more detailed reality in a similarly ill-fated youthful marriage. Ruby's revelations of living with farm laborer John Woodrow and of working as a domestic for the fractious Hoover family create empathy for the daughter of a farm owner reduced to working-class circumstance. The bulk of her storytelling describes the concessions and rewards of a second marriage. Echoing her contentment are intercalary chapters by husband "Blinking" Jack Ernest Stokes, a tenant farmer and less literate speaker whose joy in marital intimacy turns to crippling woe after Ruby's death from lung cancer ends their 25-year union. To round out the duet of Ruby and Jack, Gibbons assumes control of the resolution to conclude Jack's share of the story with some comfort at age 65 from a gift of the acreage he has worked throughout a lifetime of tenancy. Critics vary in their response to the complex story, which heightens the author's fan base for its unsentimental disclosure of domestic tragedy.

The author's salute to storytellers, *A Cure for Dreams* (1991), expands on the theme of female pragmatism and the pigeonholing of advice for future reference. The feminist saga portrays woman-centered oral tradition as an escape from totalitarian males and as an inexpensive getaway from rural cashlessness during the Great Depression. Roy Parker, Jr., a book critic for the *Fayetteville* (N.C.) *Observer*, summarizes the blended genres as "tragedy, comedy, tragicomedy, comedic tragedy," a phrase expressing the complexity of humanistic literature (Parker, 1991). In a clutch of country women, Irish immigrant Lottie O'Cadhain Davies and her North Carolina-born daughter Betty Davies Randolph relish gossip and family tales as accumulated experience, cautionary information, and versions of universal behavioral and sexual truths based on legendary matriarchs who are the female giants of the past. The tellings spread cheer and exonerate women for exorcising patriarchal demons. From the constant give and take with farm wives emerges endurance and regard for female uniqueness and durability, as demonstrated by admiration for the solid marriage of Amanda Bethune and by support for Trudy Woodlief, an abandoned wife.

As a form of socialization and an alert to trickery and hasty judgment, the novel, like Jane Campion's screenplay *The Piano* (1993), pictures female tellers as an oral regulatory agency of marital extremes. Lottie guides Betty, the credulous naif, in listening for the "dear" and "honey" of male summons to wives for clues to patriarchy or debasement. The understated example of womanly justice in Lottie's shielding of Sade Duplin from arrest for gunning down her two-timing husband Roy exonerates female methods of self-liberation, particularly flashpoints at the end of a wife's patience. After the birth of Betty's daughter, Marjorie Polly Randolph, on November 25, 1942, oral tradition immediately validates her naming for a black midwife, Polly Deal. Storytelling makes immediate inroads into infant thought, shaping patterns of merriment and survival for the fourth generation of O'Donough-O'Cadhain-Davies-Randolph women. The oral quality of the story earns critical regard for what Dolores Flaherty, a reviewer for the *Chicago Sun-Times*, calls Gibbons's "lyric gifts and narrative command" (Flaherty, 1992).

Charms for the Easy Life (1993), Gibbons's fourth novel, expands the range of narration to the reflections of a well-rounded scion of two stalwart women. Critic Maureen Harrington, in a review for the *Denver Post*, characterized the atmosphere as "strange, private, and utterly believable" (Harrington, 1993). In the estimation of Carol Anshaw, a book critic for the *Chicago Tribune*, Gibbons dramatizes her stories with "wonderfully peculiar, slightly off-center, typically Southern and rural voices she uses to relate them" (Anshaw, 1993). From home-schooling under herbalist-midwife Charlie Kate Birch and her daughter, Sophia Snow Birch, granddaughter Margaret advances to a confident maidenhood. According to a regional generalization by author-critic Diana O'Hehir of the *Washington Post*, the novel revels in "the vigorous Southern tale-telling tradition where all family events become exaggerated and legendary" (O'Hehir, C4). Contributing to Margaret's sufficiency are the examples of Charlie Kate's and Sophia's faulty marriages. Groomed from girlhood to profit from the errors of elders, Margaret relates her introduction to World War II in 1942 at the Durham veterans' hospital, where Tom Hawkings, III, catches her eye. The falling action plots a sure arc in Sophia's elopement to South Carolina with businessman Richard Baines on December 24, 1942, and in Margaret's touching farewell to Charlie Kate, who dies in her sleep on Christmas night. Buoyant in its telling, the novel reveals Gibbons at her most heartening through the family escapades and crusades of the three female healers and through the accrual of wisdom in Margaret, the heir to Charlie Kate's good-heartedness.

A difficult narrative, *Sights Unseen* (1995), reveals Gibbons's ability to turn her childhood nightmares into rigorous, benevolent psychological fiction. The story requires teller Hattie Barnes to rearrange chronological detail according to symptom logic. Amplifying the labors of a family to care for an invalid mother, the text offers such realism that bipolar patients, psychiatrists, and group therapists laud the novel for its value to interdisciplinary studies of family adaptation to mental illness. The curative aspect of storytelling champions Hattie's memoir as a method of reliving past impotence and of savoring eventual triumph. At the pivotal age of 12, in 1967, she witnesses the nadir of family fortunes after her mother Maggie deliberately aims her car in Rocky Mount at a pedestrian whom the driver charges with trying to steal her soul. Hattie's vacillation between Hattie's longing for mothering and her uncertainty at Maggie's rehabilitation at Duke Hospital from eight weeks of psychotherapy and electroconvulsive shock treatment enhance a tension that envelops the family like an infection. In the falling action, Hattie draws on adult strengths to exult in the family's welcome to their long-awaited female head of household and to Maggie's 15 years of wellness.

The empowerment of storytelling takes a negative twist in *On the Occasion of My Last Afternoon* (1998) with the silence of Clarice Washington, cook-housekeeper for the Tate family. A free black, she hoards tell-tale episodes in the past of narrator Emma Garnet Tate Lowell's paternal grandfather and father, Samuel P. Goodman Tate, a raging, blustering bully whom Clarice has observed since his rise to wealth. In grim teasers, Clarice mutters, "I know a fat budget of stories, oh yes, oh yes" (Gibbons, 1998, 6). Awed by her wisdom and experience, Emma admits to the habit of "finding out things I was not ready to absorb," her term for the slave rituals that honor the dead and fend off ghosts and, ironically, for the truth about her father's murderous boyhood (*Ibid.*, 16). She stores up episodes for later assembly into a logical pattern, her shield against looming sorrows and her recompense to a father who wraps himself in artiness by buying up the treasures offered at a bankruptcy sale. In comment on her late-in-life narration in 1900, the 70-year-old widow admits, "a receipt [recipe] is only as good as its alterations," a subtextual observation on the open-ended development of women's oral entrees (*Ibid.*, 266).

In an atmospheric seventh novel, *Divining Women* (2004), Gibbons turns to a new source of family stories, a trove of over 300 letters by which Toby Greene instructs his granddaughter Mary Oliver on the peculiar nature of his marriage and divorce in 1875 from Nora Worthy Ross, a straitlaced social climber. The pages of Nora's grievances contribute to a three-layer fund of instructive narrative that Mary describes as a "continuously looping reel of memories" that elate and reward her (Gibbons, 2004, 13). A second stack of letters from Mary's mother, Martha Greene Oliver, to friend Judith Benedict Stafford of New York City poses another view of off-kilter wedlock. In addition to revealing Judith's flight from a lascivious husband who dishonors her bed on May 3, 1912, by frolicking with a strumpet, the pages enlighten Mary to Martha's sexual needs. The jolt of female realities prepares Mary for her mission to Elm City, North Carolina, on September 30, 1918, as companion to Maureen Carlton Ross, a spiritually battered wife whom Mary rescues. Guiding Maureen toward a hopeful future are Mary's stories of her own family, a loving widowed mother and two sets of quixotic grandparents, one given to nudism and the other to reclaiming ghosts from after-death frustrations.

In Gibbons's first sequel, *The Life All Around Me by Ellen Foster* (2006), storytelling serves as a metaphor for the title character's projection of future happiness. While living with Laura, a beloved foster mother, Ellen imagines an autobiography that extends positive home life and friendship with Starletta into adulthood. Ellen sees herself as crossing the international dateline, a symbolic passage into a new identity after she completes university training in infectious disease. The dissonant image of bad weather scattering fall leaves implies unforeseen cosmic distress virulent enough to confuse and disrupt her plans. In the resolution, Ellen's forgiveness of cousin Dora Nelson for rejecting her in childhood extends to joy in the birth of Dora's daughter, Claire Ellen, a "bright" namesake who betokens a sliver of family reconciliation with exiles in Texas. In contrast to past accomplishments, which Ellen dismisses as a miser's "mean little pile of coins," the future of growth and change offer sparkling possibilities of more stories to come (Gibbons, 2006, 218).

See also **education; language**

• *Further reading*

Anshaw, Carol. "The Healer's Voice: Kaye Gibbons Conjures Up a Woman with a Cure for Almost Everything," *Chicago Tribune* (21 March 1993).
Carey, Jacqueline. "Mommy Direst," *New York Times Book Review* (24 September 1995): 30.
Flaherty, Dolores. "That Constant Chatter," *Chicago Sun-Times* (23 August 1992).
Gibbons, Kaye. "Afterword," *The Other Side of Air*. New York: Random House, 2006.
_____. *Divining Women*. New York: G.P. Putnam's Sons, 2004.
_____. *The Life All Around Me by Ellen Foster*. New York: Harcourt, 2006.
_____. *On the Occasion of My Last Afternoon*. New York: G.P. Putnam's Sons, 1998.
Harrington, Maureen. "Child's Vision Right on Target," *Denver Post* (4 April 1993).
Hemley, Robin. "Regional Underbrush," *ANQ* 5, no. 4 (October 1992): 195–196.
O'Hehir, Diana. "Belles That Don't Ring True," *Washington Post* (3 June 1993: C4.
Parker, Roy, Jr. "Elegant Family Story," *Fayetteville* (N.C.) *Observer* (14 April 1991).
Sa'adah, Marjorie Gellhorn. "You Can't Go Home Again," *Los Angeles Times* (8 January 2006): R7.

Stuart

A whimsical, endearing addition to Kaye Gibbons's male characters, Stuart provides short-term contrast to the female concerns of the title character and her foster mother Laura in *The Life All Around Me by Ellen Foster* (2006). Unlike the fantasy boyfriend — Nick Adams from Ernest Hemingway's stories published posthumously in 1972 — that Ellen conjures on the spot in *Ellen Foster* (1987), Stuart is the son of a junk dealer and an unstable mother and the nephew of a farmer who plows the field across from Laura's house. A grungy-fingered, big-footed teen, Stuart wears Wolverine work shoes from Sears and plods through conversation with grunts of "Huh" (Gibbons, 2006, 57). His crush on Ellen dates to babyhood, when they shared a wading pool that Ellen's mother Shine blew up until she ran out of breath, a foreshadowing of her decline from heart disease. The image captures both the ephemeral nature of childhood and the brief period that Ellen's mother enjoyed her daughter's playtime before committing suicide in March 1969 with an overdose of prescription digitalis.

Stuart develops into both champion and obstacle to Ellen's ambition. Obliquely, at age 15, she views him as a "mistake waiting to happen with a heart of gold," a summary of his characterization as a beloved fool, a stock bumbler in Aesopic fable, medieval stage lore, and Renaissance literature (Gibbons, 2006, 88). Her best memory of him pictures a brown paper sack of candy and money and a letter apologizing for whistling on the day of Ellen's mother's funeral. The mix of gifts reflects a tenderness and purity suited to Ellen's pre-teen sufferings. Later, he declines into a nuisance who tenders a bedroom marriage proposal alongside regret that he hasn't had time to request credit from Sears to buy her an engagement ring. The quirky courtship contributes to Gibbons's satire of Southern eccentrics as strange, but lovable.

Gibbons's attempts at turning Stuart into a model of Southern grotesque fail. Least credible are his makeshift spelling—"More Avien [Moravian] cooky," "carrion [carrying] you"—and butchered English, e.g., "mighten ought to," "tooken," "potter [potted] plant," "credick [credit]," and "instadecision" (*Ibid.*, pp, 93, 134, 138). More discordance emerges in Stuart's discussion of dried eye matter, ducking into the men's room to strip off duct tape and quarters to pay for rides at the fair, getting wedged under the bed in the nude, and shaving his entire body and stuffing frozen peas in his ears to stop the bleeding. His vision of a weekend elopement and honeymoon night at Pedro's South of the Border fireworks store and motel with the "Valentime bed" falls short of believable incongruity (*Ibid.*, 139). The characterization violates the literary truism that less is more.

Gibbons perpetuates Stuart's involvement in the plot as a source of comic relief and teen male discomfiture. His development into a multi-dimensional character in Ellen's life takes shape in a one-on-one confessional in which he sheds tears after his hormone-challenged mother backhands him. A damaged child from living in an insubstantial lean-to facing a pile of burning tires heaped up by his junk dealer father, Stuart parallels Ellen in terms of need. He reveals an emotional leaning toward the foster child, whose sufferings he affirms with loving gestures, notably, serving as her security guard at school and squiring her to a viewing of a lard replica of Iwo Jima at the county fair. At a sentimental height, he regrets that his mother did not foster Ellen, who might have loved him as a brother rather than as a schoolmate. His delivery of a glass doorknob from Ellen's house awards her a symbolic entry into the place that lives in her memories.

See also **siblings**

• *Further reading*

Gibbons, Kaye. *The Life All Around Me by Ellen Foster.* New York: Harcourt, 2006.
Sayers, Valerie, "Growing Into the Role," *Washington Post* (6 January 2006).

superstition

Superstition discloses the insecurities and ignorance of Southern characters in Kaye Gibbons's fiction. A curious blend of clinical medicine with herbalism and folk cures concerning infants occurs in *A Cure for Dreams* (1991). Trudy Woodlief maintains that letting horses blow in babies' mouths cures thrush, a common fungal infection of the gums and tongue. On November 25, 1942, a black cook-domestic, Polly Deal, the local midwife-baby doctor, coaches Betty Davies Randolph through labor and delivery of a first child, Marjorie Polly Randolph. To spare the infant possible blindness, Polly applies drops to the eyes, presumably silver nitrate, an antiseptic that wards off gonorrheal infection of the mucous membranes. Following immediately on birthing, she shapes the infant's head with her hands while the cranial bones are soft and malleable. To soothe mother and breastfed infant, Polly serves horehound tea, a restorative and calming drink. The conclusion of birthing requires Betty to blow into a blue bottle to ensure complete expulsion of the afterbirth. Glass has a long history of efficacy against evil in the agrarian South, where rural families slip empty bottles over the limbs of trees and bushes as a living amulet and yard decoration. Demons, attracted to the bottle tree's blue sparkle, fly in and become trapped. Polly's use of blue glass to capture Betty's breath implies that the demons of childbed fever will remain inactive in the blue prison.

The treatment of Betty Randolph contrasts the folk logic of the birth of Sophia Snow Birch in *Charms for the Easy Life* (1993), during which an Indian midwife named Sophia Snow puffs red pepper through a fresh peacock quill to hasten the birth, presumably by making the mother exert abdominal muscles in a sneezing fit. The birthing coach's name, which suggests both the Greek embodiment of wisdom and purity, survives in the infant, who becomes the assistant and driver for her mother, herbalist-midwife Charlie Kate Birch. The birthing precedes the family's migration west to Wake County and their witnessing a lynching. Quick to the rescue, Charlie Kate and her husband earn the gratitude of the victim, who wears the title fetish, a rear paw of a white rabbit. The symbol derives from the author's perusal of a compilation of old North Carolina folk sorcery. Contributing to the charm's power is the stipulation that it was "caught at midnight, under the full moon, by a cross-eyed Negro woman who had been married seven times," a standard folkloric juxtaposition of light and dark alongside the magic number seven, the sum of the magic numbers three and four (Gibbons, 1993, 6). A touch of dark humor, the description of the animistic talisman projects both ignorance and the comic paradox of an object valued for a power that apparently fails its owner.

Superstitions are indigenous to Charlie Kate's clientele, who recoil from urban flush toilets and newfangled radio broadcasts. She treats the Hermit Willoughby, who gives up on a boil he has tried to cure with onion slices, a handkerchief used by an albino, urine, and the tail of a black cat. She dismisses his countrified treatments and the crushing of eggshells to keep witches from sailing seaward in them. Out of professionalism, she denounces any form of black magic, love potion, or abortifacient. An independent thinker tinged with back-country beliefs, she maintains her own stock of home preventatives, including a cure for colic — knotting a string seven times, tying it around a baby's waist, and leaving the encircling protector to rot off. From folk tradition, she follows the post-death rituals of stopping clocks and covering mirrors, an acknowledgement of the cessation of life and being in the deceased. She passes on to her daughter and granddaughter a belief that troubled or sinful people disgorge evils by foaming at the mouth at the moment of death. The disburdening, called "purging," marks the passing of two caddish husbands, both culpable for carnal sins and logjammed with pinings and unspoken sentiments (*Ibid.*, 80, 87, 193, 254). Only a small amount emerges from 70-year-old Maveen, the family's former maid, and none from 60-year-old Charlie Kate, both serene matriarchs who die at peace.

The empowerment of slaves at Seven Oaks plantation in *On the Occasion of My*

Last Afternoon (1998) derives from implication of harm to their owners. Freedwoman Clarice Washington, the Tate family's cook-housekeeper, warns the slavemaster, Samuel P. Goodman Tate, that he should fear Jacob's woman, a "trick negress" or "goomer," a term for a zombie deriving from the Middle Englisher "gaum," the vacant stare of a corpse (Gibbons, 1998, 9). The widow is mean enough to launch destructive incantations and to set fire to the plantation house in retaliation for Samuel's near decapitation of her man. Narrator Emma Garnet Tate Lowell recalls other incidents of voodoo threats from hairballs and bone piles as well as from vindictive slaves who asphyxiate infants by squirting chloroform through a nursery keyhole. In one scene, slaves hang pennyroyal around doors to ward off witchcraft. During the laying-out of Jacob, Emma witnesses a more benevolent superstition, the touching of his toes to save mourners confrontations with his ghost. Clarice instructs Emma to do the same to the toes of her reprobate father Samuel, whom Dr. Quincy Lowell eases out of life in June 1862 with a lethal dose of digitalis. The tactile reassurance of no ghostly visits is worth the compliance of Emma and her younger sister Maureen, both daughters scarred in childhood by a palpable evil. As though exorcising a resident ghoul, Quincy cleanses the sitting room by having his staff burn everything that Samuel touched, including a 16th-century Titian oil painting. The incineration allies standard sickroom sanitation measures with atavistic belief in the beneficence of flame against lurking malevolence.

The title of Gibbons's seventh novel, *Divining Women* (2004), spotlights the otherworldliness of the Oliver matriarchy—grandmother Louise Canton Oliver, daughter-in-law Martha Greene Oliver, and granddaughter Mary Oliver. To assess the present and see into the future, they consult cards, spirits, tea leaves, and fate (Ouija) boards, parlor fads that Elijah Bond and Charles Kennard began marketing in 1890. During her college days at Barnard, Martha encounters her future husband, Grammar Oliver, who performs volunteer settlement work in the building shared by Beautiful Dreamer, a dual business where she seeks a manicure and fortune telling. Their wedding at St. Bart's draws a variety of wellwishers, including astrologers and palm readers. More educated than most women her age, Martha discards the family's stockpiling of signs to promote a psychological approach—the survey of facial expressions and voices as sources of truth, an advance over phrenology or skull reading, which Franz Joseph Gall proposed in Germany around 1800. Nonetheless, Louise predicts a ghostly persecution by Nora Worthy Ross, the obsessive mother whose death in 1911 elicits a sympathy call from Martha to her half-brother Troop, Nora's only child. The call fails to disclose Troop's inherent rancor, the source of conflict in the rest of the story.

A more poignant example of superstition involves expectation of a birth. As demonstrated by Zollie, Troop's chauffeur, people avoid discussing future activities until the baby arrives and survives infancy. Protective measures involve stymying conversation about the baby and postponing the purchase of newborn clothing and gifts. Narrator Mary Oliver, a 22-year-old graduate student at Radcliffe, accounts for the forfending of grief as a barrier against real medical threats from diphtheria, fever, whooping cough, and rubella, the common causes of death in infants and toddlers. In terror of folklore, Maureen, a native of Yazoo City in the Mississippi delta, refuses to allow a Jack Horner spot in the room or to begin welcoming the newborn to the family. Maureen reminds Mary not to "tease God about a baby" (Gibbons, 2004, 76). The omens prepare the reader for the tragedy of the infant's death. Strangled at birth by the umbilical cord on November 8, 1918, Ella Eloise Ross blesses the extended family, consisting of handyman Zollie, his wife Mamie, Mary, and Maureen. The grieving mother dispels anguish by treasuring full breasts and by returning a year later to post a verbal benediction on the gravesite.

See also **symbolism**

• *Further reading*

Gibbons, Kaye. *Charms for the Easy Life*. New York: Putnam, 1993.
_____. *Divining Women*. New York: G.P. Putnam's Sons, 2004.
_____. *On the Occasion of My Last Afternoon*. New York: G.P. Putnam's Sons, 1998.
"Southern Charmers," *Chicago Tribune* (18 April 1993).

symbolism

Gibbons's deft symbolism produces gem-like glimmers and spectacular epiphanies. The dichotomy of greed and recompense fuels conflict in "The Headache," a short-short story in the June 1987 issue of the *St. Andrews Review*. Compounding a folk anecdote with edenic emblems, the action pictures farm wife Lucille Womble entangled in day and night psychosomatic torment after she falls for the snake-in-the-abandoned-purse prank. By lifted oil lamp in the privacy of the outhouse, a subtextual comment on low-level tricksterism, she opens the pocketbook on terror, a fanged reminder of greed and lapsed ethics that, for two weeks, haunts her dreams and wracks her mind with head throbs, weeping, sleeplessness, and flashbacks. Turning to an Adam-and-Eve image, Gibbons pictures Henry and Lucille snuggled in their bed, where he dispels his wife's fears with an embrace and a promise of two hats, a double crowning of her womanhood. One of the author's affirmations of marriage, the conjugal contentment assuages Lucille's overburdened conscience, which bears more guilt than she deserves.

In her first novel, *Ellen Foster* (1987), Gibbons creates symbols from science and nature. She emphasizes the title character's selections of green beans to pick, a reflection of her ripening into womanhood, and her darkening into an ambiguous skin tone in July 1970, when Ellen begins valuing people for other traits than race or ethnicity. In contrast to her search for wholeness, she boards briefly with Aunt Nadine Nelson, a shrew who works as a demonstrator of food slicers. By spitting on and burning the flag from a coffin, a vengeful maternal grandmother continues punishing her low-class bootlegger son-in-law Bill after his death in fall 1970, which left Ellen orphaned and homeless. A glimpse into the title character reveals her joy in a plastic microscope through which she views a paramecium and euglena, simple life forms that contrast the complexity of Ellen's young life and abandonment. Unlike her hate-filled grandmother, Ellen is open-minded in her study of animal life that parallels her search into home situations that offer the basic elements of identity, family, and mothering. To protect her investment in toy lab equipment, Ellen shields the glass slides during frequent moves during her quest for a real home. In contrast to belongings, her emotions and self-esteem lack protective armor against chance buffeting and deliberate endangerment from her father Bill, who threatened sexual molestation on New Year's Eve, 1969. As critic Nancy Lewis explains in *Southern Writers at Century's End* (1997), Ellen herself is fragile, but her curiosity and intelligence foretoken Gibbons's cast of perceptive, intuitive female heroines.

Gibbons's second novel, *A Virtuous Woman* (1989), builds meaning from womanly meal preparation. In her final weeks of a battle with lung cancer, 45-year-old Ruby Pitts Woodrow Stokes struggles to fill her freezer with appealing entrees— pork with corn and beef with beans— to nourish her soon-to-be-widowed husband, 65-year-old "Blinking" Jack Ernest Stokes. Her target date is Thanksgiving, an appropriate time for Jack to take stock and rejoice in a quarter century of marriage to his beloved Ruby, one of a series of jewel-named characters in the author's fiction. In a wry contrast, Gibbons pictures Jack boozing on bourbon and attempting to feed himself on watery canned soup and corn flakes while remembering Ruby as the maker of pies, bread, and fragrant spaghetti sauce, a colorful comfort food. The memory parallels his appetite for her body, which he cherishes for its graceful femininity, willing sexuality, and lilac scent. As with Ellen's grandmother's post-death vindictiveness and Ellen's survey of a foster family in *Ellen Foster*, metaphors enhance reader perception of character emotions about life and death, particularly Ruby's from-the-grave sustenance of Jack and his hunger for her spirit.

Symbolism strengthens the impact of *Sights Unseen* (1993), an autobiographical novel that Gibbons bases on her own childhood with a bipolar mother. The menace of Maggie Barnes to her family takes lethal shape in her hacking up vegetables on the kitchen counter, a representation of her mangling the job of female head of household. To her 12-year-old daughter Hattie, manic-depressive episodes take on a cosmic contrast, from eclipses to meteor showers, which foretoken later epiphanies about Hattie's childhood. A more caustic memory from 1961 involves Maggie's insane notion that she can develop photos of Hattie's sixth birthday party by pouring film into the sink and soaking it in rubbing alcohol, a harsh liquid that destroys the images. The loss of photographic evidence of a normal celebration presents dual evidence of disorder — Maggie's deranged view of reality and Hattie's recall of girlhood scenes spoiled by her mother's unpredictable outrages. Restoring order to the family, in 1967, Maggie's psychotherapy and eight treatments with electroconvulsive shock at Duke Hospital produce a paradox — amnesia followed by piece-by-piece restructuring of self. Hattie contemplates her mother's 15 years of sanity followed by a new disordering, a fall down stairs in 1982 that kills Maggie. Storytelling prioritizes details as Hattie pieces together her recall of Maggie at her worst and best.

For her first historical novel, *On the Occasion of My Last Afternoon* (1998), Gibbons sketches more graphic symbols. The voice of Emma Garnet Tate Lowell opens in 1842 on horror, the slit throat of field hand Jacob in tidewater Virginia for humiliating planter Samuel P. Goodman Tate at hog-slaughtering time. The slippery killing field, slave outrage, and white family cowering in the big house prefigure the Civil War, the novel's focus. While Samuel morphs into what reviewer Peter Szatmary terms a "towering secessionist," he hires an artist to brush his likeness onto a painting of fox hunting, a stereotype of gentility suggesting an effete form of savagery similar to the stalking of Br'er Rabbit in Uncle Remus's animal fables (Szatmary, 1998). To her credit, Emma successfully eludes Southern barbarism by creating sanctuary for her husband and daughters Leslie, Louise, and Mary on Blount Street in Raleigh, North Carolina. Safely separated from constant in-house rampages, in June 1862, Emma reluctantly hosts Samuel in his last hours as he dies from the edema accompanying heart failure. Laying siege from the parlor sofa, he represents the bloated plantation South, drowning in its own excesses and gazing in terror at retribution. To end Samuel's pestilent outbursts, Emma's husband, Dr. Quincy Lowell, administers a lethal oral dose of digitalis powder, which stills a heart that offers no sanctuary to others. In contrast to Samuel's despicable leave-taking is the easy demise of Quincy, who slips into martyrdom in 1865 following years of overwork, metabolic collapse, and exhaustion caused by humanitarian attempts to repair the damage done by bigots like Samuel. Unlike Samuel, who tastes the blood of nemesis, Quincy passes without struggle into the afterlife.

In a frighteningly manipulative, pernicious environment in *Divining Women* (2004), the author uses roses as a symbol of fragrant subterfuge hurled daily at Maureen Carlton Ross as a token of emotional blackmail. Her supercilious husband, Troop Ross, maintains a reputation in Elm City, North Carolina, for spoiling his wife with daily flower deliveries of hothouse varieties with elegant European names— Homère, named for the Greek epicist Homer; Étoile de Lyon, a creamy blossom named the "star of the city of Lyon"; Beauty of Rosemawr, a gesture to the purity of the Virgin Mary; Duchesse de Brabant, named for a Belgian heiress who secured peaceful entry to Luxemburg in January 1355; and Marie d'Orléans, a French memoirist in 1709 involved in bitter familial in-fighting. In truth, Troop's presents carry a paranoid obligation from a depressed pregnant woman who wearies of her husband's meaningless gestures. In a letter to Martha Greene Oliver, Maureen's caretaker, Mary Oliver, a 22-year-old graduate student at Radcliffe, castigates Troop's elegant bombardment of blossoms as a "vicious fraud" (Gibbons, 2004, 68). The statement prefaces Mary's rescue of Maureen on November 9, 1918, from psychological house arrest.

Images abound in the sequel *The Life All Around Me by Ellen Foster* (2006). The home situation in 1974 pictures a swirl of uncertainty as the title character, at age 15, reaches a precocious jumping-off place in her education. Worries about financing genius camps and college degrees shove her back toward the negativism of her nadir in *Ellen Foster*. In contrast to Ellen's shaky moments and inability to trust others, Gibbons offers readers evidence of a stable life. The hedge remains squarely clipped, the clean brick steps that Ellen shares with foster mother Laura suggest a solid home to be proud of. While Laura smooths wrinkles with her iron, Ellen pictures her reduced to penury in a drainpipe in Calcutta from accumulated debt. A wise and patient Laura remarks on Ellen's tendency to watch television reruns of *Dark Shadows*, a metaphor for the hovering mood that holds Ellen inert on the sofa fantasizing a *deus ex machina* from Greek drama swooping down to rescue mortals from disaster. The accumulation of symbols characterizes a common split in adult-teen thinking — Ellen gloomy over extremes of worry about finances and Laura completing home drudgery item by item. She reminds Ellen that planning for college is not as onerous as "bleaching grout," a more unpleasant household task that involves serious transformation of insidious corruption to purity (Gibbons, 2006, 30).

See also **names**

• *Further reading*

Folks, Jeffrey J., and James A. Perkins, eds. *Southern Writers at Century's End*. Lexington: University Press of Kentucky, 1997.

Gibbons, Kaye. *Divining Women*. New York: G.P. Putnam's Sons, 2004.

_____. *The Life All Around Me by Ellen Foster*. New York: Harcourt, 2006.

Romine, Dannye. "The Struggle for Support," *Charlotte* (N.C.) *Observer* (30 April 1989).

Szatmary, Peter. "A Slaveowner's Daughter," *Houston Chronicle* (28 June 1998).

Trifles

A feminist play by Pulitzer Prize-winning dramatist Susan Keating Glaspell, *Trifles* (1916) informs the subtextual action and themes of Kaye Gibbons's *A Cure for Dreams* (1991). The play, a one-act masterwork of pun and symbol, derives from Glaspell's summer playwriting at Cape Cod, Massachusetts, and from staging by the Provincetown Players, who debuted the work at the Wharf Theatre on August 8, 1916. The text, reset in "Jury of Her Peers" (1917), a short story issued in *Every Week*, exonerates women for combating marital misery with murder. Glaspell creates melodrama during an investigation of the strangulation of John Wright in his sleep, an ominous death suggesting premeditation and stalking. Against a background of spousal abuse, Martha Hale discerns in Minnie Foster Wright a streak of revolt "fostered" undetected by the sheriff and county attorney. Unmoved by the murder of Minnie's canary and by her befuddlement over how to sew a quilt scrap, the authorities overlook clues to a housewife's wretchedness. Composed four years before the full enfranchisement of American women in 1920, character naming reveals authorial tone in the diminution of the protagonist as "Minnie" and a surname suggesting the "righting" of pervasive suppression of females.

In a screened examination of Roy Duplin's death in Gibbons's third novel, Irish-American protagonist Lottie O'Cadhain Davies interprets similar marks of marital dysfunction in the life of Sade Duplin, a post-menopausal farm wife "who never hurt anybody" (Gibbons, 1991, 38). Sade shoulders home responsibilities while Roy gallivants with a Willifordtown tart, a waste of scarce farm cash during the Great Depression. He denies Sade tokens of love and appreciation and publicly debases her with "yapping," a term implying the meaningless outbursts of yard dogs (*Ibid.*, 45). Worsening Sade's situation is the threat of losing the Duplins' acreage, which she inherits from her father. While part-time Deputy Sheriff John Carroll surveys the crime scene in the front yard for shell casings and footprints, Lottie straightens irregular quilting on Sade's needlework project, examines a meal for one and a single slice of pie, and serves Sade chamomile tea, a female restorative dating to ancient times for settling internal turmoil. Seemingly insignificant kindnesses, Lottie's ministrations symbolize the gendered validation of a woman in distress.

Gibbons's view of female justice absolves women who abet a murderer. Committed to restoring peace and order to Sade's joyless life, Lottie further advances feminist concerns on Milk Farm Road by keeping to herself evidence that Roy's grisly demise—"shot to pieces"—results from years of Sade's suppressed rage (*Ibid.*, 41). Sade shifts suspicion to a hobo, a gendered trade-off that diverts Carroll's investigation to a roving homeless male rather than a homebody female. Gibbons carries Glaspell's original story forward to view the self-made widow reshaping her home and family from peaceful elements. Sade accepts sedative doses of paregoric from neighbors who help her expunge Roy from her thoughts. From her oldest children, whom Roy had alienated, she receives gifts of stockings, taffy, and an embroidered bed jacket, all suited to a woman's tastes. Compounding her renewal is the recovery of Roy's money hoard, which finances a daybed and a pleasant sitting room, visual symbols of peace and rest. The feminist episode serves as proof of Lottie's empathy for rejected and harassed wives and mothers and as a model of comeuppance to a domestic villain.

See also **injustice**

• *Further reading*

Gibbons, Kaye. *A Cure for Dreams.* New York: Algonquin, 1991.

Glaspell, Susan. *Plays by Susan Glaspell.* New Haven, Conn.: Cambridge University Press, 1987.

Rajkowska, Barbara Ozieblo. *Susan Glaspell: A Critical Biography.* Chapel Hill: University of North Carolina Press, 2000.

urbanism

Despite her shift to a Manhattan apartment, Kaye Gibbons seems loath to abandon rural North Carolina roots, the source of her literary agrarianism, an essential of Southern fiction. Reared in Nash County at Bend of the River outside Rocky Mount, she considers a Southern birth and upbringing on a piedmont tobacco farm as her "tools" and the genesis of earth-based themes, particularly family, mothering, and sisterhood. The trio anchors an early story, "The Headache," published in the June 1987 issue of the *St. Andrews Review*, which celebrates benevolence to a struggling farm wife (Gretlund, 2000, 138). To interviewer Jan Nordby Gretlund, the author described an innate connection to farm communities much like rural Raveloe in George Eliot's *Silas Marner* (1861) and the village of Mellstock in Thomas Hardy's *Under the Greenwood Tree* (1872). Gibbons chooses bucolic microcosms as settings because "there is so much quiet drama there," her term for the undercurrent of basic life decisions and outcomes (Gretlund, 2000, 133). Reflecting the dismay of Eliot and Hardy at cultural changes wrought by the Industrial Revolution, Gibbons added her regret that the Old South seems in a state of metamorphosis that subdues the region's innate spirituality.

The author's casts of characters know insiders from carpetbaggers. Because of a regional love of the land and the ability to "know their way through fields in the dark," she believes that "hardscrabble Southerners ... do not suffer interlopers from the city gladly" (Gibbons, 1998, 129). She tends to center fictional characters away from urbanites, such as Ruby Pitts Woodrow Stokes and her first and second husbands, John Woodrow and "Blinking" Jack Ernest Stokes, the landlocked tenant and migrant laborers of piedmont North Carolina in *A Virtuous Woman* (1989). In the style of testy Southerners, Trudy Woodlief, a white trash mother from Baton Rouge, Louisiana, in *A Cure for Dreams* (1991), speaks the mind of rural Southerners in rejecting the dirt and noise of Northeastern cities along with the obnoxious Yankees who occupy them. Bridging the flight from outback to uptown are the Pasquotank County and low-rent patients that Charlie Kate Birch tends in her fourth novel, *Charms for the Easy Life* (1993), a story that takes the protagonist from the backwoods to the mill-hill district of Raleigh, North Carolina. Because Charlie Kate imports rural values to the city and introduces the underclass to radio broadcasts, sex education, hygiene, and flush toilets, Gibbons cherishes *Charms* for recreating a "time of the great people of the urban area of the South" (Madrigal, 1993).

In her fifth novel, *Sights Unseen* (1995), Gibbons endows a beleaguered farm family with privacy during forays by a bipolar female head of household. In 1967, the narrator, 12-year-old Hattie Barnes, describes escaping her mother Maggie's mercurial japes by taking the bus to school. On return in the afternoon, Hattie joins her brother Freddy, and cook-housekeeper Pearl Wiggins in veiling from public scrutiny a daily onslaught of Maggie's depressions, tirades, fantasies, and sexual ambush of her husband Frederick. The family takes their only vacation to Grandfather Barnes's seaside getaway, where an extended clan tolerates Maggie's vagueries. The turning point arrives after her escape into Rocky Mount and an attempt to run down a female pedestrian to stop her from stealing Maggie's soul. Because her madness infringes on the urban population, the family commits her to Duke Hospital for psychotherapy and eight electroconvulsive shock treatments, a technological solution to manic depression supplemented with psychotropic drugs, lithium carbonate and Miltown. Returned to the country after Frederick draws her out of post-therapy amnesia, until her death in a fall down stairs in 1982, Maggie restores the family to wholeness and to their place in the rural community. Gibbons indicates that Maggie's 15 years of sanity are a life-altering gift.

The author's most forthright contrast of country and city occurs in her first historical novel, *On the Occasion of My Last Afternoon* (1998). The fictional memoirist, Emma Garnet Tate Lowell, grows up among isolated, parochial planters of the James River region of southeastern Virginia. Amid complacent slaveowners of Burton Parish, in 1842 at age 12, she observes her father's phony Episcopalian piety alongside an intemperate outburst that causes him to nearly decapitate Jacob, a field hand daring enough to advise Samuel Tate on pig slaughter. Against a materialistic backdrop of marble-floored ballroom and expensive oil paintings by Titian, Thomas Sully, Thomas Gainsborough, and John Singleton Copley, she seeks security from an ironic source, the kitchen of freedwoman Clarice Washington, the cook-housekeeper who mothers three generations of aristocrats. To make the transition from unmarried belle to the wife of Boston brahmin Quincy Lowell, in 1847 at age 17, Emma clings to Clarice as a bridge to an urban life in Raleigh, North Carolina.

Gibbons portrays housewifery and motherhood near the state capital as a cornucopia of opportunity for women. No longer limited to tatting, stitchery, china painting, and piano lessons in the tidewater community, Emma develops autonomy for herself and educates her three daughters, Leslie, Louise, and Mary, to think beyond gendered restrictions. From their home on Blount Street close to the governor's mansion, Emma takes her girls to Lovejoy Park, romps in Mordecai Woods, services at Christ Church, and meals at Yarborough House. She introduces them to citified culture and prominent citizens and rears them to think independent of the prissy constraints of plantation ladyhood. Unlike Emma's flirtatious younger sister Maureen, a finishing school graduate who "conformed like a satin glove" to social propriety, the Lowell girls attend urban colleges and develop realistic expectations of self, marriage, and family (Gibbons, 1998, 134).

Life in Raleigh places the Lowells on the front row of the Civil War. Combat and economic upheaval force the household to weather short rations and wartime jitters. The Lowell women take pride in service to the "clots of wounded," who arrive in huge trainloads from the battles of Manassas, Virginia (July 21, 1861; August 28–30, 1862), Gettysburg, Pennsylvania (July 3–4, 1863), and the Wilderness, Virginia (May 5–7, 1864) (*Ibid.*, 196). During Emma's sojourn in Boston in 1865 after burying Quincy near the home of his father and brothers, Maureen becomes Emma's eyes and ears on the devastation of Raleigh citizens. On return to Blount Street, Emma walks about the railroad depot to observe comings and goings of people reshaping their lives. To ease local unemployment, she opens a freedman's school at the United States Bank building and begins sizing up Raleigh business opportunities at a bakery, finance company, pottery, clothing factory, and stable, all suitable post-war investments. By 1900, 70-year-old Emma reflects on the rearing of three daughters and their children in an atmosphere of urban liberalism that predisposes them to appreciate literature and culture and to socialize with all races and classes of citizens.

In her next novel, *Divining Women* (2004), Gibbons reverses Emma Lowell's urbanization in the volunteerism of 22-year-old narrator Mary Oliver, a graduate student at Radcliffe, as caretaker of her aunt, Maureen Carlton Ross. The author depicts Mary's departure from Union Station in Washington, D.C., on September 30, 1918, as the introit to Southern Gothicism. Amid peculiar and unwholesome train passengers, she travels southwest toward Elm City, North Carolina, with understandable hesitance. On the journey, she reads an urban classic, Leo Tolstoy's *Anna Karenina* (1875–1877). The new setting fosters the cruelties of her uncle, Troop Ross, against his wife Maureen, a poor girl from the Mississippi delta who lacks advocates in a community that admires and respects her industrialist husband. Like a sequestered heroine in a Victorian romance, she retreats to her upstairs sitting room to wait out the last 50 days of a difficult pregnancy. After restoring Maureen's self-esteem with pep talks and letters from Maureen's Mississippi family, on September 9, 1918, Mary liberates her from the Southern small town and directs her north toward Washington. Gibbons implies that the open-mindedness of the urban Greene-Oliver clan will salve Maureen's hurts.

Gibbons dips gingerly into urban opportunities in her first sequel, *The Life All Around Me by Ellen Foster* (2006). Dismayed at a mediocre education in a rural North Carolina high school, in 1974, the title character home-schools herself through a guided reading program from Johns Hopkins University and researches on genius camps and university offerings. In 1974, at a seminar for bright teens on the Johns Hopkins campus in Baltimore, Ellen feels belittled by people who recoil from her accent. Retreating into silence, she explores a quad, colonade, art gallery, and impressive stone structures and demeans her own school as a "floored pen" (Gibbons, 2006, 79). More content in the library than among classmates and teachers, she studies an atlas and measures with her fingers the distance from Baltimore to home. In the falling action, Dr. Derek Curtis Bok, president of Harvard University, foresees two terms in summer school and membership in the class of 1981 as well as summer study abroad. No longer dismayed by urban challenge, Ellen remarks, "I bet I can do this" (*Ibid.*, 216).

See also **Raleigh, North Carolina**

• *Further reading*

Alexander, Ann. "Book of Changes for Kaye Gibbons," *Greensboro* (N.C.) *News & Record* (21 March 1993).
Gibbons, Kaye. *The Life All Around Me by Ellen Foster*. New York: Harcourt, 2006.
_____. "On *The Borderland*," *Mr. Universe and Other plays*, by Jim Grimsley. Chapel Hill, N.C.: Algonquin Books, 1998.
_____. *On the Occasion of My Last Afternoon*. New York: G.P. Putnam's Sons, 1998.
Gretlund, Jan Nordby. "In My Own Style: An Interview with Kaye Gibbons," *South Atlantic Review* 65, no. 4 (Fall 2000): 132–154.
Madrigal, Alix. "A Tough Southern Belle," *San Francisco Chronicle* (2 May 1993).

vengeance

The simmering spite of mistreated girls and women takes colorful form in Kaye Gibbons's novels. A Freudian tale, "The Headache," issued in the June 1987 issue of the *St. Andrews Review*, depicts the psychosomatic ills that farm wife Lucille Womble inflicts on herself. Worried over failing finances and the bank's repossession of two farm machines, she violates personal ethics by concealing a purse abandoned in the ladies' restroom of a restaurant. Ironically, the pocketbook is a ruse that a trickster loads with a snake. Self-blame charges Lucille with trashy behavior, a betrayal of a blameless father and father-in-law and of community standards. Bashing herself for two weeks with head pain, flashbacks, crying jags, and visions of a fanged monster, she requires the intervention of employer Mae Bell Stokes and Dr. Janet Cowley to begin healing. Gibbons applies a touch of grace as the antidote to a bad conscience — the loving embrace of husband Henry Womble, who nestles Lucille "spoon" fashion in bed (Gibbons, June 1987, 7). Before she confesses her ethical lapse, he confers forgiveness and promises two hats, a double blessing on a head that aches from too much goodness rather than too little.

In *Ellen Foster* (1987), the title character introduces herself in terms of a murderous hatred of her drunken, lustful father Bill, whom she considers killing with a poisonous spider. On New Year's Eve, 1969, she flees his seedy behavior by running away from home with all the money she can steal from him. At his funeral in 1970, she envisions stout nails securing him in a coffin lest he spring forth vampire-fashion to grope and menace her once more. Her maternal grandmother, a study in grudge-holding, stalks into the night to spit on and toss onto a wood fire the military flag from Bill's coffin. Like coals of hatred, the embers devour the striped cloth while the demonic grandmother, a symbolic Satan's helper like attendees in Nathaniel Hawthorne's Gothic fable "Young Goodman Brown" (1835), gloats. She stokes the backyard pyre into the night like a Druid priestess at a sacrificial immolation. Actor Julie Harris, who played the role of Grandmother Harris in the 1997 Hallmark Hall of Fame adaptation of the novel, summarized the grandmother's spite as the result of "[hating] Ellen because she personifies the horrid man who fathered her late daughter's child" (McCabe, 1997). After the old lady's death from flu shortly before Christmas 1970, Ellen performs a childs' version of redemption by decking her corpse in Sunday hat and artificial flowers to render her a suitable gift for Jesus. The juxtaposition of naive goodness with a crone's evil enhances Gibbons's theme of vengeance as a product of long-term loathing.

More lethal than the grandmother's inferno, the end-of-patience solution of Ruby Pitts Woodrow in *A Virtuous Woman* (1989), Gibbons's second novel, threatens outright murder. After catching her trifling first husband, migrant laborer John Woodrow, at their home with a 16-year-old harlot, Ruby arms herself with a pistol, which she slips under her pillow. The shooting she plots proves unnecessary after John runs afoul of knife-wielders in the pool room, a suitable place for his ruination. Ruby, a 20-year-old widow trapped in menial labor for the Hoover family, comforts herself by picturing his corpse running blood. Unfortunately, although rid of him and married to "Blinking" Jack Ernest Stokes, she conceives no children because of a venereal disease that John imported from his philanderings. In addition to being barren, she carries a lethal contamination in the cigarette habit that enables her to endure marriage to a wife-bashing womanizer. The author characterizes Ruby's escapism through smoking as the human price of two years of coping with a bad bargain.

More imaginative, the machinations of Lottie O'Cadhain Davies in *A Cure for Dreams* (1991) depict wifely vengeance without self-incrimination. Saddled with Charles Davies, a money-worshipping Quaker farmer-miller, she retreats from the dinner table to summon the neighbors' hounds, Bill and Woody. After feeding them her dinner, she sics them on Charles, then marvels that she has forgotten how much he fears big dogs. Within weeks, after Charles drowns himself in the river in 1937 in despair over Depression era finances, Lottie gains control of the domestic situation. Rather than lay out her tight-fisted husband in the living room, she decrees that he go directly to the grave. Because her daughter Betty intercedes in the name of propriety, Lottie sits tight-jawed at the wake and rejects the kind words of mourners. The scenario reverses the womanly concern of Lottie's intervention in the blood guilt of Sade Duplin, a brutalized farm wife who dispatches her husband Roy with a shotgun blast. In both instances, Lottie represents female actions as old as the biblical story of Judith and Holofernes and the Greek Clytemnestra's vengeance on Agamemnon, two feminist exonerations of women for liberating themselves from untenable servitude to overlords.

A similar rejection of obligatory wifely grief spotlights feminism in *Charms for the Easy Life* (1993). The heroine, herbalist-midwife Charlie Kate Birch, returns to

Pasquotank County to the laying out of her wandering, boozing husband, whom she rolls in 1938 at the Sir Walter Raleigh Hotel for a "gangster wad" of $1,365 from his wallet (Gibbons, 1993, 75). Rather than pretend to mourn, she dickers with his mistress over the undertaker's bill and over possession of a mantel clock. Rather than play the hypocrite, Charlie Kate turns her back on a minister's mealy-mouthed comforts. Had her husband not purged his backlog of sins and remorse, she intended selling his carcass to the University of North Carolina medical school to "do as they please with him," an appropriate scrapping of a bum (Gibbons, 1993, 80). In emulation of her stony reserve, her daughter, Sophia Snow Birch, prays to Jesus to end her own marriage to a womanizer. At his sudden demise from a cerebral hemorrhage in August 1936, the widow insists that George the undertaker narrate anatomical details of her husband's sufferings. Her daughter Margaret notes that the three manless women look forward to a bachelor-like contentment under one roof, a just reward to females who share only bad memories of shabby heads of household.

Gibbons apparently enjoys delivering recompense to pedophiles, skirt-chasers, binge-drinkers, and persecutors of girls and women. In a first historical novel, *On the Occasion of My Last Afternoon* (1998), she sets up malefactors to fail. A backstage villain, the lawyer husband of Lavinia Ella Mae Dawes, appears to flourish at spousal violence until an eyewitness reports him to Emma Garnet Tate Lowell in Raleigh, North Carolina. Septimus Wrenn, one of Lavinia's former students, develops a crush on her and follows her home, where he observes her attorney husband flailing her with a sack of oranges. Through channels, Emma's husband Quincy has the abuser disbarred. Gibbons concludes poetic justice with a glimpse of the lawyer journeying toward south Texas under an "unforgiving sky," a suggestion of divine judgment symbolized by the hellish heat along the Tex-Mex border (Gibbons, 1998, 126). The phrase implies a feminist's implacable stance on domestic terrorism.

Gibbons orchestrates more end-of-novel satisfaction by killing off Emma Garnet's wicked father, the venomous Samuel P. Goodman Tate. Before the author expunges the plantation nabob, she sets him on wobbly, gouty legs and a cane and plagues him with arthritic hips. Upon Emma's marriage in 1847 to a Yankee intellectual, Dr. Quincy Lowell, Samuel charts a vituperative course by cursing their unborn children. Arriving at Emma's house with daughter Maureen in retreat from General George Brinton McClellan's advance on tidewater Virginia on June 25, 1862, Tate cloaks his beggary in evil retorts, regal pretensions, and demands for service in the very household he blasted. Although the South's collapsing economy dispossesses him of wealth and 2,000 acres of prime Virginia soil, Emma sets limits on her father's residency on Blount Street and on his blatherings at her family and staff. She leaves to Quincy the long-awaited reprisal for the Tate family's sufferings under an evil-mouthed tsar. A petulant *quid pro quo* begins with Samuel's marring an expensive carpet with ink, followed by Quincy's hurling a newly opened bottle of ink at Samuel's Titian painting. As Samuel fails from heart disease, Quincy ends his misery with a deliberate oral overdose of digitalis powder, a mercy killing that offers more mercy to Emma than to Samuel. Gibbons's stresses that the demise of the terrorist patriarch produces no mourners.

A humorous take on female vengeance opens *Divining Women* (2004), Gibbons's seventh novel, a tale of marital persecution. She portrays Nora Worthy Ross, a malignant divorcée in 1875, wishing on her former husband, Toby Greene, and his second wife Leslie a venereal disease contracted from their membership in the American Community of Nudists. Nora believes the couple deserve death for "inborn selfishness," her term for their scandalous behavior, which jeopardizes Nora's intended rise in Washington, D.C., society (Gibbons, 2004, 4). Contributing to her spite is a contention that her son, Troop Ross, could have been successful if Toby had financed a Harvard education for him. The text pictures the scatter-gun effect of vituperation after Nora's evil plotting warps Troop with an overstock of delusion and wrath. Paranoid beyond cure, he lives his adult years devoid of marital or fatherly love for his family.

Another vituperative scenario crops up during the rising conflict. Mary Oliver, the 22-year-old niece and caretaker of Troop's wife Maureen, shares letters from Judith Benedict Stafford, an elegant New York beauty. At the nadir of her marriage on May 3, 1912, she surprises her husband in their bed with a street wench, who drapes herself in Judith's lingerie. At first pondering setting fire to them or dragging the bed to the sidewalk as evidence to the neighbors of connubial desecration, Judith opts for a room at the Waldorf Astoria Hotel. Replacing murderous thoughts with self-pleasure, she orders candy, roast chicken, and a chocolate milk shake. The urge to kill turns inward, causing her to pluck lashes, claw her face into welts, and chew through her lip. Grandmother Louise Oliver describes Judith's tormented face as ghoulish. The purpose of Judith's self-mutilation suggests the backlash of a beauty against the traits that please men, a dramatization of the feminist assault on the beauty myth, a concept that philosopher Naomi Wolf analyzed in *The Beauty Myth: How Images of Beauty Are Used Against Women* (1991). The marring of self precedes Judith's travels in Europe in 1915 and her adoption of an autonomous sex life free of middle-class prudery.

With less drama, Gibbons restores justice and accuses the guilty in her first sequel, *The Life All Around Me by Ellen Foster* (2006). In 1974, the family trouble-maker, Aunt Nadine Nelson, lambastes the 15-year-old title character with rude comments about her cropped hair and ridicules Ellen's academic prizes before admitting to the theft of Ellen's inheritance. Guilty of fraud, Nadine plots an escape to Texas under the guise of settling her unmarried pregnant daughter Dora out of range of community gossip, a shabby ruse that further demeans the future grandmother. Nabbed after funneling Ellen's wealth to her own use, Nadine not only faces the law, but also the betrayal of her daughter, whose scruples reject forging legal documents with Ellen's name. Gibbons allows the guilty aunt to slither south to Texas, a state that Starletta's mother describes as "large enough to make her feel small as she needs to" (Gibbons, 2006, 182). Pre-empting forgiveness are Nadine's claims that she kept a box of Shine's personal belongings as a way of holding on to her dead sister. Ellen takes a noble route in asserting that all families have members who reflect low moral standards.

See also **injustice**

• *Further reading*

Brown, Carrie. "Kaye Gibbons' Focus Is on Female Fortitude," *Chicago Tribune* (4 April 2004).

Gibbons, Kaye. *Charms for the Easy Life.* New York: Putnam, 1993.

_____. *A Cure for Dreams*. New York: Algonquin, 1991.
_____. "The Headache," *St. Andrews Review* (June 1987): 3–8.
_____. *The Life All Around Me by Ellen Foster*. New York: Harcourt, 2006.
_____. *On the Occasion of My Last Afternoon*. New York: G.P. Putnam's Sons, 1998.
McCabe, Bruce. "A 10-Year-Old Finds Happiness," *Boston Globe* (14 December 1997).
Wolf, Naomi. *The Beauty Myth: How Images of Beauty Are Used Against Women*. New York: William Morrow, 1991.

violence

Gibbons employs violence in the style of classic Greek theater—decorous and as far offstage as possible. Examples energize her fiction, for example, the maiming of a farmhand and the hanging of a mule named Sugar Pete in *A Virtuous Woman* (1989) and Maggie Barnes's treatment with eight sessions of electroconvulsive shock treatment and her son Freddy's memories of a visit to the state electric chair in *Sights Unseen* (1995). An early short-short story, "The Headache," published in the June 1987 issue of the *St. Andrews Review*, dramatizes a familiar folk prank—the concealment of a snake in a pocketbook for an unsuspecting person to release. The author refines a horrific encounter into the mental mauling that farm wife Lucille Womble inflicts on herself. Her motive is noble—punishment for greed that threatens to debase her family as white trash. Violence takes psychosomatic shape for two weeks in insomnia, sobbing, head pain, and flashbacks to her first glimpse of the snake by lantern light in the family outhouse. Gibbons counters protracted mental anguish with conjugal love. Before giving his wife an opportunity to confess her ethical lapse, husband Henry Womble nestles her into his embrace and rewards her with forgiveness and the promise of two hats, a multiple palliative to her throbbing head.

The core of Gibbons's first novel, *Ellen Foster* (1987), dramatizes a child's efforts to forestall evil and to overcome despair generated by Bill, her hateful bootlegging father. A miscreant of Gothic proportions, he berates his sickly, subservient wife and, in 1969, abets her suicide by an overdose of prescription digitalis. Compounding his monstrosity, he paws the breasts of his vulnerable ten-year-old. Her only refuge is flight from Bill and his loutish clientele, who fill the house on New Year's Eve, 1969. The aura of endangerment generates aggression toward a challenger more her size. As a result, she threatens a boy at school for ridiculing her relationship with Julia, the art teacher who offers Ellen a home shortly before her 11th birthday. After Bill's death in 1970, Ellen fantasizes demanding that his coffin be nailed tight to secure a stalker in the grave. The vampirish image symbolizes the residue of menace that pollutes the child's thoughts and dreams.

Similarly shielded is the stabbing of John Woodrow, the offensive seducer in *A Virtuous Woman*. Like Ellen's father Bill, John dies out of view of readers. John's murder from collapsed lungs after a knifing in a pool room brawl ends a two-year marriage fraught with his sneers and badgering. His unexplained absence with a whorish 16-year-old prompts his 20-year-old wife, Ruby Pitts Woodrow, to buy a pistol, which she values like a good luck talisman and fortunately has no call to fire. Until Ruby receives confirmation of John's death, the weapon lies hidden under her pillow, a dual image of fractured conjugal commitment and rest from daily wrangles and disillusion. At a fortuitous moment in her life, Ruby turns to a new husband, 40-year-old "Blinking" Jack Ernest Stokes, rather than fire power for reprieve and much-needed affection and respect. Gibbons jolts Ruby at random when Jack discharges the pistol, an action that he fails to connect with his wife's restlessness.

The author is adept at turning potentially grisly scenes into comedy. In *A Cure for Dreams* (1991), the unforeseen suicide in 1937 of Charles Davies, a Quaker farmer-miller, saves his able wife, Lottie O'Cadhain Davies, from unfulfilling wedlock. Gibbons pictures him drowned in a North Carolina river with his head secured between two rocks, a vise-like representation of his hard-headed miserliness and domination of his family. On a visit to the O'Cadhain clan in Bell County, Kentucky, Lottie rids herself of blame by narrating a fantasy to her relatives of Charles risking his life while trying to save a vagrant. Gibbons later spares Lottie and Charles's daughter, Betty Davies Randolph, from potential injury and disgrace. When Betty moves to Richmond and naively dates Stanton, an addict to Neurol Compound, she instinctively departs his hospital room in a dry-out ward while he calls to her in low-class street slang. Thus, name-calling substitutes for actual menace to Betty. Like Lottie, Betty relies on inborn vigor to ward off intimidation and threat to her reputation. With authorial grace, Gibbons kills off Stanton three months later from heart failure, a suitable death for an abuser of ammonia and a shifty exploiter of women.

Gibbons can't avoid unpleasant scenes in *Charms for the Easy Life* (1993), a novel about a folk healer. Herbalist-midwife Charlie Kate Birch sets broken bones and attends a textile worker mangled in a machine accident. Gibbons lightens the horror by picturing Charlie Kate sewing up the wounds with her only suturing material, red cotton thread. Other images of swabbing pyorrhea, removing warts, draining a boil, relieving whooping cough with a croup kettle, saving a drowning shoeshine man, and treating a syphilitic and a leper leave much to the reader's imagination. More detailed is the onset of World War II, when Charlie Kate and her granddaughter Margaret volunteer at a veterans' hospital in Durham, North Carolina. Again, Gibbons sets Charlie Kate's medical treatments of burns and combat wounds offside while focusing on Margaret, the reader of letters and typist of return messages from patients to girlfriends and family. At the Christmas dance in 1942, when Margaret firms up a relationship with patient Tom Hawkings, III, he appears handsome in street clothes and sedated enough with codeine for a semi-lively jitterbug. Moving away from scenes of half-dressed, bandaged soldiers and their harrowing stories, Gibbons stresses Tom's man-smell, a new experience for Margaret that focuses on a positive gender element.

Gibbons deviates from concealed violence by highlighting harm to a child in her fifth novel, *Sights Unseen*, in which a grandfather rebukes a boy for scraping his spoon on the bottom of his ice cream bowl. The flare-up foreshadows a slow-motion study of an extended family beach scene that critic Michael Harris of the *Los Angeles Times* describes as "violent chiaroscuro" (Harris, 1995, 5). In the company of Uncle Lawrence and Aunt Menefee and their children, the Frederick Barnes family blends in at a three-generation visit at the Carolina coast. Hattie's sudden vomiting and her brother Freddy's taunts result in a sharp slap to the boy from their intractable Grandfather Barnes, who deplores male bullying on a young female. Susan L. Nelson, co-author of *The Other Side of Sin: Woundedness from the Perspectives of the Sinned-Against* (2001), observes that the elder Barnes actually produces the opposite behavior in Freddy. The confrontation illustrates through shaming of the young Barnes that the strong have a right to control the vulnerable through random brutality. Nelson predicts that Freddy is likely to emulate the slap as a means of humiliating others.

The adult-on-child assault precedes female intervention in Maggie Barnes's rise from her sickbed to chide Frederick for allowing corporal punishment of their son. Gibbons heightens suspense by following Maggie down the beach to confront her self-important father-in-law. She surprises the family with betrayal after she exonerates the elder Barnes with a cheery welcome home from his jaunt to Bald Head Island with Josephine Woodward, his mistress. Hattie, a budding scholar, rationalizes Maggie's "contradictory behavior" in terms of physics and the laws of repulsion and attraction (Gibbons, 1995, 154). The upshot of the extended family confrontation is greater distancing between Hattie and her unpredictable mother. After another face-off between Grandfather Barnes and Freddy over Maggie's institutionalization in 1967 at Duke Hospital for psychotherapy and eight sessions of electroconvulsive shock treatment, Freddy channels violence into a self-punishing game of basketball as though he wills himself to suffer a broken collarbone or sliced elbow. Gibbons implies that the acting out of aggression merely drains negative energy without harming Freddy.

In an introit to the Civil War, overt barbarism dominates the opening scene of *On the Occasion of My Last Afternoon* (1998), Gibbons's first historical novel. In the words of reviewer Susan Dodd, the focal family "lives in a habitual state of siege," a foreshadowing of widespread combat across the South (Dodd, 1998). Emma Garnet Tate Lowell, the 12-year-old witness, reflects on her father's near decapitation of Jacob, a sassy field hand bold enough to give advice to the overbearing slavemaster, Samuel P. Goodman Tate. Symbolized by hog-killing season, the 1842 slaying suits the "hardness and venomous spite" of a malefactor whose evil the cook-housekeeper Clarice Washington has observed from his boyhood (Gibbons, 1998, 11). Unlike more occluded death scenes in her earlier novels, Gibbons reveals Jacob as a blood-drenched corpse outlined beneath burlap. The blending of slave and animal gore compounds the savagery of a promoter of Southern patricianism and foretokens the price in blood for emancipation of people whom slavers treat like beasts.

Although much of Samuel's aggression takes the form of hateful slurs and insults at the dinner table or behind his bedroom door, he establishes a propensity for violence against the weak. In 1837, he holds his 12-year-old son Whately at gunpoint until the boy abases himself at his father's direction. The victimization of Whately concludes with Samuel's slaps to Emma and Alice for weeping after 20-year-old Whately dies alone and untreated in 1845 for syphilis on Sullivan's Island, South Carolina. In 1859, Alice Tate succumbs under the gruesome treatments of Dr. John C. Gunn, whom her husband abets in attempts to rid her of sick headaches. Samuel's vicious assaults on his wife and children reveal the inner demons that dispose him toward atrocity.

Through Emma as the adult narrator, Gibbons takes a moral stance on the human bondage that prefaces the Civil War. At a breaking point, Emma speaks the feminist view of war by charging rich men with forcing poor youths to inflict devastation on hungry women and children. In the estimation of reviewer Polly Paddock Gossett, book editor of the *Charlotte* (N.C.) *Observer*, the butchery of combat is "the terrible moral consequence of slavery," the recompense to men like Samuel Tate, who bankrupts himself spiritually and financially to promote the Confederate cause (Gossett, 1998). At an unforeseen moment in the dark of night in June 1862, Emma's benevolent husband, Dr. Quincy Lowell, attends Samuel, enthroned on the parlor sofa because of a rapid decline from edema and heart failure. Quincy's *coup de grace*— a lethal dose of powdered digitalis forced into Samuel's mouth — rewards the tormentor with the taste of blood. The murder performs three services to the novel. At the same time that Quincy silences Samuel's secessionist tirades, the good Yankee doctor comforts his wife and retrieves himself from being too good to be true.

The black humor of *Divining Women* (2004), Gibbons's seventh novel, glimpses the horrors of World War I. On narrator Mary Oliver's ride south by train on September 30, 1918, from Washington, D.C., to North Carolina, she encounters a freakish man pacing a second-class car. Hailed as one of the casualties of trench warfare, he tells veterans that he has borne a shriveled visage and receding jaw for over 30 years from a burst of carbolic acid hurled at his face in 1888. The one-on-one violence introduces a more lethal barbarism — handicapped veterans at the train station earning tips for carrying bags. Among them are two victims of mustard gas or Yperite, an odorless sulfur-based weapon that German soldiers began lobbing on Canadian forces in September 1917 to inflict blistering, blinding, and excoriation of the air passages. War debate worsens in Elm City, where citizens recoil from stories of peeled eyelids and severed heads mismatched with bodies. By presenting stories secondhand, the author controls the degree of horror she inflicts on readers.

See also **Civil War; rape; *Trifles*; World War II; "The Yellow Wallpaper"**

• *Further reading*

Dodd, Susan. "A Sentimental Education," *Washington Post* (12 July 1998).
Gibbons, Kaye. *Ellen Foster*. New York: Algonquin Press, 1987.
_____. *On the Occasion of My Last Afternoon*. New York: G.P. Putnam's Sons, 1998.
_____. *Sights Unseen*. New York: G.P. Putnam's Sons, 1995.
Gossett, Polly Paddock. "She Sees No Glory in the Gore of War," *Charlotte* (N.C.) *Observer* (7 June 1998).
Harris, Michael. "Scenes— and Skeletons— of a Troubled Southern Family," *Los Angeles Times* (9 October 1995): 5.
Park, Andrew Sung, and Susan L. Nelson. *The Other Side of Sin: Woundedness from the Perspectives of the Sinned-Against*. Albany: State University of New York, 2001.
Szatmary, Peter. "A Slaveowner's Daughter," *Houston Chronicle* (28 June 1998).

A Virtuous Woman

Kaye Gibbons's second novel reshapes the compromised, self-destructive goodmother of Ellen Foster into goodwoman Ruby Pitts Woodrow Stokes. In the analysis of reviewer Marilyn Chandler, a critic for *Women's Review of Books*, Ruby exhibits "the old virtues of loyalty, tolerance, compassion, and forgiveness that are the real stuff of workable, if limited, partnerships" (Chandler, 1989). Ruby's qualities and first name shine in the title image, an idealized glimpse of the married woman drawn from Proverbs 31:10–25. Within the Old Testament collection of 900 admonitions and aphorisms lie directions for the civilized life. In the words of novelist Charles Johnson, from Proverbs comes a map for a fragile strand of knowledge: "We are not born with culture. Or wisdom. And both are but one generation deep," a summation of the brief family life of Ruby and "Blinking" Jack Ernest Stokes, an unlikely pair who enjoy a quarter century of wedlock without producing offspring (Johnson 1999, vii–viii). Johnson's commentary on Proverbs chimes with Gibbons's depiction of the chancy mating of a gentrified 20-year-old widow with a bachelor twice her age. The pastiche of culture and wisdom that Ruby acquires in 25 years survives in Jack's dreams, which summon his dead wife to their bed to relieve his loneliness.

Reflecting the influence of William Faulkner's *As I Lay Dying* (1930), Gibbons's novel adapts what critic Stephen Souris describes as a "decentered narrative mode," a carefully synchronized form of circular narrative based on a duet of first-person monologues (Souris, 1992, 99, 100). The braided story line alternates chapters between husband and wife, who reflect on the lung cancer that saps Ruby's energies in the last year of their marriage. Rather than address a fictional audience, the two speakers imply a personal communication with the reader over an expanse of time and space. Ultimately, character experience allows each narrator to reflect on Ruby's death as though Ruby and Jack were omniscient viewers of their own lives. According to a *New York Times* critique by Padgett Powell, it is the reader who must shape the disparate monologues into a "constructive union," much as Ruby and Jack forge a satisfying life together (Powell, 1989, 712). Only in the final chapter does the authorial voice take charge and round out the themes of commitment, loss, and regret.

Gibbons applies character differences to create counterpoint, proving, as Dolores Flaherty, a critic for the *Chicago Sun-Times*, states, the worth of "complexity beneath the surface of goodness" (Flaherty, 1990). Throughout the unsentimental love story, Ruby's faults parallel Jack's in a style critic Roz Kaveney describes as straightforward like "a good Country-and-Western song" (Kaveney, 1989, 998). Coddled by a father and two older brothers, Jimmy and Paul, Ruby enters adulthood unprepared for decision making or emotional trauma. Foolishly, at age 18, she escapes boredom by marrying an itinerant low-life, 26-year-old John Woodrow, a cruel mocker who dies two years later of lung damage from a pool hall knifing. In widowhood, she weds Jack, a clingy, indolent loner. In a model of marital reciprocity, he demands mothering from Ruby at the same time that he satisfies her need for a father figure. Significantly, they meet under a pecan tree, an Edenic image that suggests the loving, but ill-fated union of Adam and Eve. Gibbons wrests humor from the scene by depicting Ruby smoking and meditating while Jack hauls a wheelbarrow load of manure. The image presages a lopsided mating that solaces Jack while Ruby outdistances her earthy husband in depth of thought and feeling.

For all their differences, Jack and Ruby unite like magnets out of a mutual hunger for affection and respect. In the opinion of Marilyn Chandler, the union is a "sturdy but unfulfilling compromise reached through a tacit negotiation over the terms of each other's needs" (Chandler, 1989, 21). Jack's manhood blooms late under the tender giving of his bride. He thinks of her as soft and feminine — the kind of woman to apply lotion to dish-pan hands and eat yogurt in bed. Of his childish and inappropriate response to her final illness, she states that men shy away from the sight of a dying wife who was once capable of "kneeling, stooping, pulling, bending, and rising up when they need to go and do what needs to get done" (Gibbons, 1989, 13). In Ruby's view, Jack interprets his wife's terminal illness as a disordering of the universe, a cosmic lurch that severs his moorings beyond repair.

Gibbons balances the poignant end-of-life scenario with comic relief. After Ruby's obsessive smoking kills her, Jack seeks a new female caretaker in Mavis Washington, an ineffectual housekeeper who disappoints at cleanliness at the same time that she entertains readers with her excuses for accomplishing nothing during two days' employment. The folksy humor is shortlived. Over a post-funeral period from March to June, Jack's environment becomes "smeared up ... raggedy, messy" (*Ibid.*, 125). He lamely excuses his household sty with a left-handed compliment — he has relied on Ruby so long for order that he can't be expected to flourish as a house-husband. Susan Heeger, a reviewer for the *Los Angeles Times*, upbraids the author for allowing the novel to grind down to Jacks' ineptitude and his yearning for someone to give his labors meaning and direction. Other critics applaud the opportunity for neighbors to crown the Stokes marriage with honor and a long-delayed reward of land ownership for Jack's deserving steward.

See also **Hoover-Stanley genealogy; Pitts-Stokes-Woodrow genealogy**

• *Further reading*

Chandler, Marilyn. "Limited Partnership," *Women's Review of Books* 6, nos. 10–11 (July 1989): 21.
Flaherty, Dolores. " ... For Her Price Is Far above Rubies," *Chicago Sun-Times* (26 August 1990).
Gibbons, Kaye. *A Virtuous Woman*. Chapel Hill, N.C.: Algonquin Press, 1989.
Heeger, Susan. "Couldn't Live with Her, Can't Live without Her": *A Virtuous Woman*," *Los Angeles Times* (11 June 1989): 15.
Johnson, Charles, intro. *Proverbs*. New York: Grove Press, 1999.
Kaveney, Roz. "Making Themselves Over," *Times Literary Supplement* (15 September 1989): 998.
Monteith, Sharon. *Advancing Sisterhood?: Interracial Friendships in Contemporary Southern Fiction*. Athens: University of Georgia Press, 2000.
Powell, Padgett. "As Ruby Lay Dying," *New York Times* (30 April 1989): 712.
Souris, Stephen. "Kaye Gibbons's *A Virtuous Woman*: A Bakhtinian Iserian Analysis of Conspicuous Agreement," *Southern Studies* 3 (Summer 1992); 99–115.

vulnerability

Novelist Kaye Gibbons is adept at describing innocence and naiveté without turning frailty into a damning or unforgivable fault. One of her early pitiable females is farm wife Lucille Womble in the short-short story "The Headache," issued in June 1987 in the *St. Andrews Review*. Setting aside principle, she snatches an abandoned purse from a restaurant ladies' room and stuffs it down her underwear. Financially strapped and hoping for a chance gift, she saves her perusal of the contents until she can examine it by lamplight in the outhouse, a humorously Gothic setting. The startling release of a snake from the handbag disposes her to two weeks of psychosomatic torment with sobbing, head pangs, insomnia, and flashbacks of fanged jaws leaping up at her. Contributing to her vulnerability is the need to unburden a guilty conscience to Dr. Janet Cowley, a kind physician who guarantees patient confidentiality. The next stage of a two-part redemption occurs in bed in the embrace of Lucille's husband Henry, who declares her a good woman deserving of reward. The motif of worthiness paired with idealism justifies sparing Lucille more suffering.

Gibbons overlays a child's defenselessness on the title character in her first novel, *Ellen Foster* (1987), the first-person story of a casualty of society. At a height of dramatic tension, on New Year's Eve, 1969, the ten-year-old motherless waif retreats from black men who join her father Bill in drinking bootleg whiskey. One boozer compares Ellen to his wife Delphi, a 13-year-old whom he married for her sexual ripeness. The potential endangerment of Ellen by a lustful father justifies her flight from home. Through dreamscape, Ellen fantasizes her father's death and the work of the black ambulance crew in carting him away. The reverie discloses an anxiety at domestic instability at the same time that it overturns the threat of black male trespassers violating the sanctity of home. In subsequent episodes, Ellen's character strength lies in finding ways to achieve her dream of a secure nesting place. To distance herself from painful memories, she abandons present tense and glimpses intimidation in the distant past. The syntactic shift becomes a subconscious shield against harm.

Ellen is constantly on guard against thoughts of Bill intruding on her consciousness. She depicts lapses in control as an unattended "spare room" in which he "[settles] in thinking he might made his self right at home" (Gibbons, 1987, 102). She talks tough, but cowers during naptime at the elementary school. Menace reaches a height when her father drives his car over a marigold bed, exposes his genitals, and yells a foul-mouthed summons to his daughter. The nightmarish aftermath zigs and zags between safety and threat — the police handcuffing Bill, the art teacher Julia soothing the terrified child, and Julia's husband Roy explaining that the court has ended temporary custody and remanded Ellen to her birth family. In the courtroom, Ellen feels "dazey in my head" and helpless before Bill, even though he is flanked by two police officers (*Ibid.*, 55). After she eludes inhospitable relatives and resituates herself in a foster home on Christmas Day, 1970, a new mom urges Ellen to shed the dammed-up tears that cause nightmares, outsized fears, flashbacks, and quaking hands.

Gibbons turns from an intimidated child to adult weaknesses in her next two novels. Vulnerability in *A Virtuous Woman* (1989) derives from the self-jeopardy that teenager Ruby Pitts initiates by marrying beneath her social class. In the clutches of 26-year-old John Woodrow, an unsavory no-count, at age 18, she faces the indignities of poverty foisted on hirelings. Ironically, Ruby turns to cigarettes, an addiction more debilitating than a wretched marriage. Two years later, on the morning preceding John's death from a stab wound to the lungs in a pool room brawl, Ruby encounters serendipity by attracting "Blinking" Jack Ernest Stokes, a steady farmhand who promises to be her caretaker. In a weakened state, 20-year-old Ruby accepts the 40-year-old bachelor, who adores her. Their flawed union, however, juxtaposes the housewifely Ruby alongside a husband who is incapable of looking after himself after Ruby's death from lung cancer. In retrospect, he remembers her two-fingered gesture for a cigarette from her oxygen tent. The paired vulnerabilities characterize a 25-year marriage based on need and concluding with Jack's infantilism — a retreat into Roadrunner cartoons, a fantasy scenario of flight from disaster.

Vulnerability dominates themes and motifs in Gibbons's third and fourth novels. *A Cure for Dreams* (1991) pictures the limited enjoyments of rural women on Milk Farm Road during the Great Depression. The author pictures Lottie O'Cadhain Davies as the queen bee of afternoon card games, at which members of her club bet pennies on rejuvenating rounds of gin rummy and pinochle in the back of Porter's store. With more resolve, Lottie, a recent widow following her husband Charles's suicide in 1937, extends a motherly shield over daughter Betty during her youth, when Betty encourages the attentions of Luther Miracle, a scruffy beau with dirty hair. On her own in Richmond, Virginia, Betty risks dignity and reputation while dating Stanton, a drug addict to Neurol Compound. On her return to rural North Carolina, Lottie influences Betty's interest in Herman Randolph, a more suitable choice for mate. The cycle of vulnerability continues after the birth of Betty and Herman's daughter, Marjorie Polly Randolph, on November 25, 1942, while her father serves on the U.S.S. *Hornet* during World War II. Gibbons implies that the female society that surrounds the newborn extends guardianship to both the war bride and her newborn.

In a fourth novel, *Charms for the Easy Life* (1993), fragility jeopardizes the patients of herbalist-midwife Charlie Kate Birch. In her ministrations to poor women, she offers additional anesthesia to those who suffer most as wives and mothers. At the height of her role as rescuer, Charlie Kate blames an alcoholic physician for blinding a newborn girl with silver nitrate drops and for abandoning Maveen, a 70-year-old retired domestic dying of pain and starvation from terminal stomach cancer. The lessening of female vulnerability becomes a crusade for Charlie Kate, who fosters her daughter Sophia's courtship with businessman Richard Baines and who shepherds granddaughter Margaret into the wartime marriage market. Gibbons orchestrates a triumphant conclusion at Christmas 1942, when Charlie Kate dies suddenly. The loss occurs after Sophia and Richard elope to South Carolina the previous night and Margaret meets the parents of Tom Hawkings, III, her future in-laws, for a holiday dinner. The passing of power from the elder generation illustrates the value of a staunch role model in toughening the untried.

The depiction of impotence in *Sights Unseen* (1995) reverses the usual order imposed by chronic illness. Because of Maggie Barnes's mental aberrations and extreme behaviors, it is her family that falters during ongoing uproar. Their lives in chaos, they struggle to maintain normal activities while hiding from the outside world Maggie's bipolar madness. In 1967, at the height of willfulness, when she runs down a pedestrian with her car in Rocky Mount to stop the woman from stealing her soul, the family takes charge by admitting Maggie to the psychiatric unit of Duke Hospital. The relationship of vulnerable and victimized shifts as Maggie, the former destroyer of peace, lies helpless under eight weeks of electroconvulsive shock treatments. As characterized in *South to the Future: An American Region in the Twenty-First Century* (2002), Gibbons's candid, but decorous account of the Barnes' "trials of the spirit" illustrates how "strong people, usually with help, can survive" (Hobson, 2002, 38). Frederick Barnes's gentle words coax Maggie back from post-therapy amnesia into her duties as wife, mother, and homemaker. Gibbons's perception of a besieged household similar to her birth family reveals to the reader the need for pity and support of the mentally ill as well as for their caretakers.

Gibbons's most detailed portrait of vulnerability, *On the Occasion of My Last Afternoon* (1998), glimpses the South at its economic and political nadir. By describing the girlhood and marriage of narrator Emma Garnet Tate Lowell, the text cameos the region's anguish as slavery declines toward civil war and emancipation. In 1847, at age 17, Emma marries Dr. Quincy Lowell, a Boston intellectual abolitionist, and escapes the verbal barrages of her father, planter Samuel P. Goodman Tate. Weakening her resolve is the abandonment of her mother, Alice Tate, an enlarged version of Lucille Womble who batters herself with sick headaches during Samuel's harangues. Resettled in Raleigh, North Carolina, Emma berates herself for the next 12 years of Alice's misery, yet develops into a sturdy surgical nurse in a makeshift military hospital at the city Fair Ground. By 1900, years of growth and assertiveness enable the 70-year-old narrator to make peace with Alice's submission to patriarchy. Without regret, Emma congratulates the Lowell family for its courage and moral vigor.

In the character exposition of *Divining Women* (2004), Gibbons's seventh novel, the girlhood experiences of narrator Mary Oliver parallel those of Margaret in *Charms for the Easy Life.* Just as Margaret learns her way around male-female situations at the Durham veterans' hospital Christmas party in 1942, Mary, a 22-year-old graduate student at Radcliffe, first encounters social improprieties at unchaperoned late-winter dances, where dates strand her, amuse other girls, and leave Mary to find her own ride home. She transfers her dismay to the dresses she wore for the occasions, a pair of "disappointed" outfits that she remands to the closet of a spare room (Gibbons, 2004, 19). While her mother, Martha Greene Oliver, tries to compensate for the shabby treatment by oafish boys, Mary intuits that her introduction to public mortification need not foretell a lifetime of similar discourtesies. Her good sense prefigures the rescue of her aunt, Maureen Carlton Ross, the vilified wife of Troop Ross. Beginning on September 30, 1918, Mary tends her aunt during the final 50 days of pregnancy until the birth of Maureen's first child, Ella Eloise, on November 8, 1918. Gibbons shifts vulnerability from both women to the infant, who is stillborn from strangulation by the umbilical cord. By claiming the tiny corpse and escorting it over the father's objections to the cemetery for a sunset burial the next day, Mary and Maureen declare conjoined strengths. A blended symbol, spurts of breast milk, identify Maureen's truncated motherhood at the same time that they prophesy abundance.

In Gibbons's first sequel, *The Life All Around Me by Ellen Foster* (2006), helplessness recedes in the formation of child-foster mother synergy, a feminist pairing. In fall 1974, the title figure, still beset at age 15 by nail chewing, trembling, and anxiety attacks, fights on two fronts. From the past loom unsettled issues of failure to protect her 40-year-old mother, Shine, from suicide in 1969. In the future after high school lie insurmountable financial obstacles to a university education. Through character initiative and serendipity, Gibbons frees Ellen to develop her considerable intellectual gifts. Subtextually, Gibbons stresses Ellen's quasi-motherhood of Starletta, a retarded child whose need for advocacy echoes Ellen's lengthy trials and gnawing mother hunger.

The Cinderella rescue requires a face-to-face confrontation with Aunt Nadine Nelson, the thief who steals Ellen's inheritance and bashes her self-esteem with an insult to her cropped hairstyle. Gibbons staves off a bitch fight through the cool disdain of Laura, a foster mother who sizes up threat and meets it with a proportional retort. In the resolution, Ellen weathers the episode and claims a rejuvenating treasure, Shine's personal belongings, which exonerate Ellen of failing her mother. Simultaneously, a letter from Dr. Derek Curtis Bok, president of Harvard University, responds to Ellen's request for early college admission with a full scholarship and additional educational opportunities. Stripped of terrors and insecurity, Ellen is free to bask in the love of a foster mother who extends acceptance and sanctuary.

See also **powerlessness**

• *Further reading*

Barnes, Linda Adams. "Telling Yourself into Existence: The Fiction of Kaye Gibbons," *Tennessee Philological Bulletin* 30 (1993): 28–35.

Gibbons, Kaye. *Divining Women*. New York: G.P. Putnam's Sons, 2004.

_____. *Ellen Foster*. New York: Algonquin Press, 1987.

Hobson, Fred C., ed. *South to the Future: An American Region in the Twenty-First Century*. Athens: University of Georgia Press, 2002.

Munafo, Giavanna. "Colored Biscuits: Reconstructing Whiteness and the Boundaries of 'Home' in Kaye Gibbons's *Ellen Foster*," *Women, America, and Movement*. ed. Susan L. Roberson. Columbia: University of Missouri Press, 1998, pp. 38–61.

Sandefur, Amy Faulds. "Narrative Immediacy and First-Person Voice in Contemporary American Novels" (dissertation), Louisiana State University, 2003.

Washington, Clarice

A monument to righteousness and female coping, Clarice Washington defines the art of homemaking in Gibbons's first historical novel, *On the Occasion of My Last Afternoon* (1998). Symbolically, Clarice stands tall and unshakeable among the seven oaks of the plantation's name. Appropriately, she is buried in Raleigh's Oakwood Cemetery among state governors, congressmen, Civil War officers, and 1,500 Confederate soldiers. Like Dilsey, the beatific cook-caretaker in William Faulkner's *The Sound and the Fury* (1929), Clarice remains unbowed by family and national catastrophe. In the 1842 home crisis that opens the novel—planter Samuel P. Goodman Tate's slaughter of the slave Jacob with a hog-butchering knife—she sends for "Jacob's woman" at the Throckmorton place as a way of soothing hurt in a disenfranchised slave (Gibbons, 1998, 11). In the fallout from the master's effrontery, Clarice mediates the situation by placating slaves in the quarter with a dole of meat and blankets and by proposing that they tolerate bondage, which she correctly predicts will soon end.

Clarice comes to life in face-to-face confrontations. Her gumption and wisdom turn to acid rebuke against Samuel, her polar opposite, a ruthless slave-killer who has harbored a malignant spirit from the time that she mothered him in boyhood. She informs Emma Garnet Tate that he once ripped a shell from a live turtle to make a Lancelot shield, a token of the macho monster the boy becomes. Gibbons ornaments Clarice with the forebearance of a foster mother who recalls a family atrocity in which Samuel's father forces the boy to shoot and bury his mother. Samuel remains on the site to protect the mother's grave from wild dogs. Clarice comprehends how the murder of innocence in the past produces so pitiless and malcontented an adult.

An improvement on Mammy, the loyal maid-of-all-work in Margaret Mitchell's classic saga *Gone with the Wind* (1936) and a contrast to Calpurnia, the soft-spoken housekeeper-nursemaid in Harper Lee's *To Kill a Mockingbird* (1960), Clarice becomes the Tate family's conscience. She contends with the cringing servility of Alice Tate, the female head of household, and models for Alice's daughter, Emma Garnet Tate Lowell, culinary expertise and domestic management in the face of overwhelming odds. During the expulsion of Whately Tate, a disgraced student at Washington College in Lexington, Virginia, for impregnating a barmaid, Clarice voices parental forgiveness and sorrow "to see a son taking his leave" (*Ibid.*, 19). The admission validates her devotion to white children, whom she loves unconditionally.

Clarice achieves liberation in 1847 by accompanying Emma to her new home in Raleigh, North Carolina. Upon permanent severance from Samuel's raillery, the former cook awards Mintus her kitchen cot. The legacy doubles as a promotion that "[pulls] you on up" in a milieu that offers few advancements to bondsmen (*Ibid.*, 50–51). After resettlement in snooty urban society, like a benevolent mother, she helps Emma's husband Quincy birth the Lowells' three daughters—Leslie, Louise, and Mary. As a surrogate parent, Clarice maintains a cheerful atmosphere by serving the children broiled pig tails, ash cakes, and raisin scones and by washing the girls with perfumed soaps. She tames with linseed oil the red curls of Lavinia Ella Mae Dawes, an underclass child in need of motherly hygiene. Clarice commandeers the all-day, all-night kitchen detail demanded by Civil War casualties whom Emma and Quincy bed down in the family manse. In the opinion of critic Ron Carter, a book reviewer for the *Richmond Times-Dispatch*, Clarice works miracles by tending the sick and by shielding the girls from wartime horror while their parents treat the wounded. Her sweet potato candles, backwoods substitutes for elegant candelabra, light the dinner table, symbolically shedding light and sweet fragrance and promoting a domestic glow during a dark period of political, social, and economic tribulation.

The text endows Clarice with Christ-like traits. Hot baths and cups of burnt okra coffee elicit from Emma a biblical compliment: "You could turn water to wine" (*Ibid.*, 190). Clarice absolves Emma's guilt that she left her mother Alice to endure Samuel's extremes of temper and intimidation. The wise older woman reminds Emma that leaving home initiated Emma's motherhood and the training of three bright, ambitious daughters who display none of Alice's groveling before plantation patriarchy. Robust to age 63, Clarice surprises the household by foundering in 1863 from lethal pneumonia and gasps away her last breaths in Emma's arms. Clarice comforts Emma and cajoles the house staff—Charlie, Martha, and Mavis—to accept emancipation with grace and to forgive their former enslavers. The leave-taking bears a scriptural majesty from its emulation of deathbed speeches by Old Testament patriarchs.

In addition to humor and clever retorts, Gibbons grants Clarice the ability to read and write, an educational advantage lacking in stereotypical mammies and housekeepers of Southern literature. Ironically, the primer that Whately chooses for her lessons is *Godey's Lady's Book*, the epitome of 19th-century fashion consciouness for elite, spoiled women. The undertone of Clarice's kitchen rumblings survives long after her in 1865, when Emma faces the loss of Quincy. Widowed and vulnerable during Reconstruction, Emma recovers from her childhood home a culinary text, *The Williamsburg Art of Cookery*, which arrives with copious additions and emendations in the cook's handwriting. A female legacy, the annotated pages restore for Emma a feeling of oneness with her two mothers, Alice Tate and Clarice Washington. Gibbons accords Clarice a telling honor: the epitaph "Kind Mother," an echo of the mother hunger that haunts the author's canon (*Ibid.*, 241).

See also **food; wisdom**

• *Further reading*

Barnhill, Anne. "Broken Promise: Gibbons' Memoir-Like Tale Lacks Drama," *Winston-Salem* (N.C.) *Journal* (12 July 1998).

Carter, Ron. "Sisters Flee Father's Tyranny," *Richmond Times-Dispatch* (5 July 1998).

Dodd, Susan. "A Sentimental Education," *Washington Post* (12 July 1998).

Gibbons, Kaye. *On the Occasion of My Last Afternoon*. New York: G.P. Putnam's Sons, 1998.

Gossett, Polly Paddock. "She Sees No Glory in the Gore of War," *Charlotte* (N.C.) *Observer* (7 June 1998).

Perry, Carolyn, and Mary Louise Weaks, eds. *The History of Southern Women's Literature*. Baton Rouge: Louisiana State University Press, 2002.

Wagner-Martin, Linda. "Kaye Gibbons' Achievement in *On the Occasion of My Last Afternoon*," *Notes on Contemporary Literature* 29, no. 3 (May 1999): 3–5.

Wiggins, Pearl

The surrogate mother in *Sights Unseen* (1995), Pearl Wiggins replays the roles of Starletta's mother in *Ellen Foster* (1987), Sudie Bee in *A Virtuous Woman* (1989), and Polly Deal in *A Cures for Dreams* (1991) and prefigures the goodness of Clarice Washington, the cook-housekeeper and surrogate mother in *On the Occasion of My Last Afternoon* (1998), and of Mamie, the cook-midwife in *Divining Women* (2004). As cook and general domestic for the Barnes family, Pearl rides out the demented ravings that emerge from Maggie Barnes like bursts of lava. When Maggie is too unbalanced to shop for the children, Pearl bears a signed check and a note allowing her to make purchases, a rare privilege for a black woman in the racist South. Subtextually, Gibbons implies that Pearl is lucky to land a job that offers a substantial salary for the times—$20 per week as opposed to the standard $10—plus a car and a job for Pearl's niece Olive. Critic Michael Harris, in a review for the *Los Angeles Times*, questions why an able, intelligent woman like Pearl "has to cater to a mental patient" to earn wages and benefits owing to such a paragon (Harris, 1995, 5).

In retrospect, narrator Hattie Barnes credits Pearl's success to stamina and patience, the qualities that the author expected of her husband, Frank Ward, during the writing of *Sights Unseen*. Pearl moves up from a paltry job in Sharpsburg through networking at Renfrow's Broasted Chicken, where she learns from two failed maids about problems at the Barnes home. From her first appearance at the kitchen door, Pearl carries out household duties while coping with Maggie's fixations and exhibitionism. Before Maggie gives birth to her second child in 1955, Pearl morphs into a surrogate mother by taking charge of setting up a changing table and crib and shelving baby clothes and toys. In token of dependence on her housekeeper, Maggie names her baby Harriet Pearl Barnes, an honor to a non-white family member similar to Betty Davies's Randolph's selection of Marjorie Polly Randolph in *a Cure for Dreams* (1993) to acknowledge the devotion of cook-midwife Polly Deal. Maggie's selection of "Hattie" as a nickname scandalizes a hospital records clerk, who dismisses it as "a little nigger name" (Gibbons, 1995, 31). Nonetheless, Maggie is determined to award Pearl for performing the parental labors that stymy the birth mother.

Like Ruby in *A Virtuous Woman* (1989) and Emma Garnet in *On the Occasion of My Last Afternoon* (1998), Gibbons features the housekeeping "pearl" as the Barnes family jewel. The text pictures her surrogate motherhood through the "carrying" of baby Hattie on her hip (Gibbons, 1995, 57). As though burdened with a fetus, Pearl compensates for Maggie's dismissal of the newborn and for Maggie's inability to breastfeed or to bond with Hattie. To Pearl's credit, she transfers praise for Hattie's upbringing to Maggie. The housekeeper's loyalty suggests that, at some point, she can no longer stand in for Maggie and that she has no intention of robbing the female head of household of her rightful parental place. The housekeeper's vision is a boon to Hattie, whom Pearl relieves of feeling like an abandoned babe. After Maggie's recovery through psychotherapy and eight sessions of electroconvulsive shock treatment at Duke Hospital in 1967, she moves easily into the place that Pearl leaves open and shares canning and kitchen duties in sisterly fashion. Maggie's defense of Pearl from a racial slur hurled at the dinner table by Grandfather Barnes further elevates the housekeeper to a secure place in the family.

• *Further reading*

Gibbons, Kaye. *Sights Unseen*. New York: G.P. Putnam's Sons, 1995.

Harris, Michael. "Scenes— and Skeletons— of a Troubled Southern Family," *Los Angeles Times* (9 October 1995): 5.

Waggoner, Martha. "Book Addresses Manic-Depression," Durham, N.C., *Herald-Sun* (17 September 1995).

wisdom

Gibbons's women establish order in their lives through domestic control and through conversation. Their talk combines astute observation with sage counsel and anecdotes of human foibles. In *A Southern Weave of Women* (1994), critic Linda Tate describes as an organic "story quilt" the verbal sharing of female experience (Tate, 1994, 197). The feminist folk matrix allows women to reshape episodes of coping and survival to suit their gendered microcosm. From the authentic female voice derives the insider's view of marriage, maternity, disillusion, and suffering, the four themes of Lucille Womble's disburdening of guilt and terror to Dr. Janet Cowley in "The Headache," a short-short story published in the June 1987 issue of the *St. Andrews Review*. Afflicted by psychosomatic ills— two weeks of head throbs, insomnia, flashbacks, and crying jags— Lucille accepts from Dr. Cowley a promise of confidentiality and a suggestion to discuss terrors with Henry, Lucille's husband. Cowley's faith in confession proves palliative after Lucille informs Henry that she has something to confide.

In Gibbons's first novel, *Ellen Foster* (1987), the title character, wise beyond her years, chooses a woman-centered foster home to replace a violent father and passive mother. The drive that sustains Ellen in 1969 and 1970 informs her subconscious that mother-daughter love is the natural order of things, the solution to months of spiritual and physical homelessness. Dotted along Ellen's odyssey are encounters with knowing females. From art teacher Julia comes permission to enjoy life by celebrating an 11th birthday and by acting out Prince Valiant comic strips, a substitution of a budding girlchild for a medieval male gallant. From field supervisor Mavis, Ellen gains an eyewitness validation of her dead mother as pretty and smart, two traits that counter the child's memories of a sickly, submissive housewife who chooses death rather than domestic misery. The author summarizes women's intuitive wisdom in the foster mother who welcomes Ellen on Christmas Day, 1970, a propitious occasion that promises a long association with Ellen's volunteer mother.

Gibbons moves from Ellen's monologue to polyphony in the husband-wife duet of her second work, *A Virtuous Woman* (1989). Reviewer Dannye Romine, book editor of the *Charlotte* (N.C.) *Observer*, admired the depth of the saga for its richness. Of the marriage of 20-year-old Ruby Pitts Woodrow Stokes and 40-year-old "Blinking" Jack Ernest Stokes, Romine summarized, "Their stories are lodged deep and have no truck with artifice. Their stories demand to be told and, once told, yield wisdom" (Romine, 1989). Like Ellen Foster's bone-deep hunch about family harmony, Ruby and Jack's trust in mutual affection shores up their May–December union and keeps it sound. Jack successfully blots out his hard-handed part–Cherokee mother, religious fanatic father, and lonely bachelorhood by accepting Ruby as the real beginning of his adult life. Ruby states her own defense of reaching out for happiness: "It's no crime to want and need somebody to love and to be loved by" (Gibbons, 1989, 143). Although neighbors gossip about her choice of another landless farm laborer, she reflects on the disastrous first marriage and contents herself with Jack as a sure thing.

Similarly supported by past female experience, women combating the Great Depression in *A Cure for Dreams* (1991), Gibbons's third novel, cling to the example of their foremothers for models of stoicism. Female storytelling descends the ladder of family members from Bridget O'Donough O'Cadhain and her daughter, Lottie O'Cadhain Davies, to Lottie's daughter, Betty Davies Randolph. During group tellings, the anecdotes and local gossip from Milk Farm Road fan out horizontally to members of Lottie's gin rummy and pinochle club, all rural women in need of diversion, courage, and bolstering during financial shortfalls. In 1937, players discuss

Trudy Woodlief's ability to feed five hungry, fatherless children and Sade Duplin's recovery from a dispiriting marriage and widowhood following Roy Duplin's sudden death from a shotgun blast. In contrast to female durability, Lottie's husband Charles chooses to drown himself. Ultimately, the female role models and trove of wise stories passes to Charles's granddaughter, Marjorie Polly Randolph, born November 25, 1942, who begins absorbing womanly wisdom by listening from the cradle to the talk of Lottie, Betty, and midwife Polly Deal. Looking back from 1989 to her infancy, Marjorie declares that "The first true memory is sound" (Gibbons, 1991, 171). Like crib gifts, female laughter and exempla welcome and strengthen the most vulnerable of their sisterhood.

Gibbons's fourth novel, *Charms for the Easy Life* (1993), brims with the pragmatism of healer-midwife Charlie Kate Birch, another in the author's succession of sage matriarchs. Charlie Kate promotes the blessings of good reading and the promise of health and stamina from a self-protective daily regimen of exercise, hygiene, and nourishing food. At her singular slide into faulty logic, her granddaughter Margaret, steeped in visual and aural lessons from Charlie Kate's example, is equipped to accept and forgive her grandmother's yearning for a reunion with a wayward husband. The failure of Charlie Kate's three-day tryst at the Sir Walter Raleigh Hotel in 1938 prods Margaret to observe that "love and revenge grow from the same kernel of want," a charitable assessment of rare foolishness in her 56-year-old grandmother (Gibbons, 1993, 76). Capping a feminist coup—the female abandonment of a philandering mate—Charlie Kate returns to grass widowhood after pocketing $1,365, a sensible self-reward to a woman who prefers tangible assets to iffy wedlock.

More compelling than Gibbons's previous wisewomen, Clarice Washington, the cook-housekeeper for three generations of the Tate-Lowell lineage in *On the Occasion of My Last Afternoon* (1998), lives her adult life in service to whites. Gibbons creates in Clarice the understated intelligence and forethought lacking in Alice Tate, the ineffectual plantation mistress, and in Maureen Tate, one of the next generation of spoiled Virginia belles. In the estimation of novelist-critic Susan Dodd, a book reviewer for the *Washington Post*, Clarice, "warm and fierce, cheeky and wise," serves as the sole rampart against looming disaster (Dodd, 1998). Skilled at bribing, cajoling, and manipulating irate slaves in the aftermath of the murder of the uppity field hand Jacob during the 1842 hog-slaughtering season, Clarice calms a plantation contretemps that echoes the upsurge of the Nat Turner revolt of August 22–October 30, 1831. At the core of a folksy world view, she recognizes the built-in failings of human bondage, the life blood of the plantation South. In the unavoidable Confederate revolt and resulting Civil War, she applies considerable experience at coping to maintaining a sanctuary at Emma Garnet Tate Lowell's new home in Raleigh, North Carolina. In the resolution of the family saga, Clarice survives as a voice in Emma's mind and the annotater of the family recipe book, a kitchen version of wisdom lore.

Before opening *Divining Women* (2004), Gibbons cites as an epigraph the vision of mythographer Joseph Campbell concerning predestined happiness. The text alerts the reader to an invisible support system that predisposes individuals to success. He describes the internal flow as an invisible current, like life-giving water that constantly refreshes. The commentary prepares the reader for the resilience of Mary Oliver, a

22-year-old graduate student at Radcliffe. On September 30, 1918, she travels from Washington, D.C., to Elm City, North Carolina, to experience the reality of male-on-female brutality while tending her suffering aunt, Maureen Carlton Ross, during a difficult pregnancy. Wisdom sustains Mary and Maureen in their standoff against Maureen's husband Troop, an unloving, unlovable manipulator who threatens Maureen's womanhood. From an outside source — letters passed between Mary's mother, Martha Greene Oliver, and Martha's friend, Judith Benedict Stafford —comes the feminist logic of two women who restore sexual release to their lives through illicit affairs. Additional womanly support comes from Mamie, the cook-housekeeper who delivers Maureen's stillborn daughter Ella Eloise on November 8, 1918. Bolstered by female intuition, Maureen abandons both husband and belongings to seek normality with Mary's mother and grandmothers, Leslie Greene and Louise Canton Oliver, the trio who generate in Mary an empathy for troubled women.

In Gibbons's first sequel novel *The Life All Around Me by Ellen Foster* (2006), the osmosis of wisdom from foster mother Laura to Ellen requires a rough passage before harborage. In fall 1974, because of past sufferings, 15-year-old Ellen lacks compassion for two fellow foster girls, who toss off a welcoming home and gracious surrogate parent by repeatedly breaking house rules. Still plagued by quaking hands, nail chewing, and anxiety attacks roused by memories of homelessness and orphanhood in 1970, Ellen requires frequent touch-ups of Laura's philosophy about emotional wholeness. Chapter four presents Ellen's version of Laura's wisdom in a metaphoric summation of maturity and trust as the expected arrival of October. As the air cools, birds fly south, and leaves drop, Ellen shelters in an unchanging universe that keeps its promises.

See also **reading; storytelling**

• *Further reading*

Curran, Colleen. "A Forgettable Successor to an Unforgettable Debut," *Richmond Times-Dispatch* (26 February 2006).
Dodd, Susan. "A Sentimental Education," *Washington Post* (12 July 1998).
Gibbons, Kaye. *Charms for the Easy Life*. New York: Putnam, 1993.
_____. *The Life All Around Me by Ellen Foster*. New York: Harcourt, 2006.
_____. *A Virtuous Woman*. Chapel Hill, N.C.: Algonquin Press, 1989.
Mabe, Chauncey. "Review: *On the Occasion of My Last Afternoon*," Fort Lauderdale, Fla., *Sun-Sentinel* (24 June 1998).
Perry, Carolyn, and Mary Louise Weaks, eds. *The History of Southern Women's Literature*. Baton Rouge: Louisiana State University Press, 2002.
Romine, Dannye. "The Struggle for Support," *Charlotte* (N.C.) *Observer* (30 April 1989).
Tate, Linda. *A Southern Weave of Women: Fiction of the Contemporary South*. Athens: University of Georgia Press, 1994.

Womble genealogy

A surprisingly full glimpse of a rural clan, Kaye Gibbons's fictional Womble family in short-short story "The Headache" (1987) derives from the author's skill at compression:

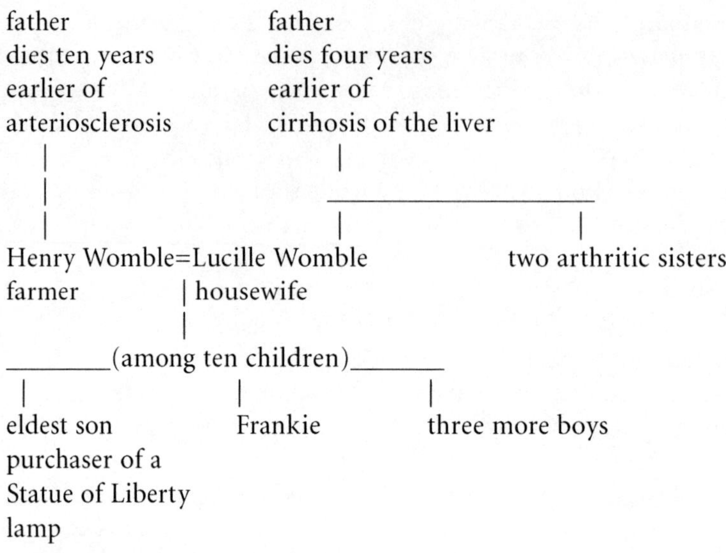

• *Further reading*

Gibbons, Kaye. "The Headache," *St. Andrews Review* (June 1987): 3–8.

women

Kaye Gibbons honors women as complex, multifaceted beings. In her late teens, while scrambling for tuition for college, she doubted that laboring class women could achieve feminist author Helen Gurley Brown's grandiose aims stated in the second wave feminist treatise *Having It All* (1982). When Gibbons began creating her own fictional galleries, the texts starred a more realistic brand of females who relied on spunk, guile, and optimism to see them through disappointments and troubles. From the Southern females she has admired from childhood, she sketches tough, astute, imaginative personae. Yet, as essayist Mary Hunter Austin observed about Comanche, Mojave, Navaho, Paiute, Papago, Shoshone, and Ute women in *The Land of Little Rain* (1903), the proficient female "sees, feels, creates, but does not philosophize about her processes" (Austin 1903, 86). Gibbons declared, "I intentionally made my female characters avid readers and highly intelligent, though unschooled" ("Southern," 1993). The description lauds a raw native discernment of human trials and perils. In the estimation of critic Bret Lott, an author-reviewer for the Raleigh *News & Observer*, Gibbons created protagonists who "worked against their oppressors in close proximity, lending their plights claustrophobic and therefore all the more acute" (Lott, 1998). Like hand-to-hand grappling, her female conflicts earn regard for fierceness.

As a reward for true-to-life dialogue and characterization, Gibbons has developed a faithful following, many of whom are girls and women. One reviewer, Cassandra West, writing for the *Chicago Tribune* declared, "No woman writing in America today captures the spirit — and humanity — of Southern women quite like

Kaye Gibbons" (West, 1998). The author earns plaudits for personal and professional compassion toward mothers and working women. In a gesture of thanks, after a reading, she invites pregnant women and mothers paying babysitters to the head of the line of autograph seekers. Her reasoning derives from personal experience: "I'm too guilt-ridden already to feel responsible for a line of ladies with swollen ankles" (Weaver, 2004). For its respect for women, the quip reveals an ingrained sympathy with the mothering gender.

An early short-short story, "The Headache," published in the June 1987 issue of the *St. Andrews Review*, presages Gibbons's dedication to revealing women's perspectives. The disclosure of psychosomatic head pangs, terror, hysteria, and sleeplessness in a farm wife precedes more detailed images of laboring-class women in Gibbons's longer works. Protagonist Lucille Womble, worried over farm debt and the daily struggles of cooking and washing for a family of 12, agonizes over her concealment of a lost pocketbook that a jokester leaves in a restaurant ladies' room. Dismayed at an ethical lapse — seizing the purse and stowing it in her underwear — for two weeks, she pushes herself toward crippling illness. Gibbons pairs Lucille with Henry, an understanding husband who recognizes that "A woman will wear out," a wise observation of the endless domestic toil that ages and debilitates rural women (Gibbons, June 1987, 5). His gifts to Lucille suggest the basics of marital love — "spooning" in bed during her bouts of crying and a promise of two new hats (*Ibid.*, 7). His wise summation of womanly needs acknowledges the value of physical intimacy, forgiveness, and a touch of frivolity.

Astounding critics for its authentic voicing, Gibbons's first novel, *Ellen Foster* (1987), confronts an orphaned waif with a stony-hearted maternal grandmother and two aunts. Decidedly unmaternal, the grandmother, her daughter Nadine Nelson, and, to a lesser degree, Ellen's Aunt Betsy, protect their own nests while shoving Ellen away from warmth and acceptance. In contrast to rebuffs from family stand the ministrations of Starletta's mother; Julia, a great-hearted art teacher; and Laura, the foster mother whom Ellen hand-picks from worshippers at church. At Christmas, 1969, Starletta's mother offers a safe haven as well as a sweater, a symbol of warmth that heartens and uplifts Ellen at a festive point on the Christian calendar. Julia, a flower child, sets Ellen free from social constraints and celebrates her advance to age 11 with a birthday party. More than her predecessors, Laura liberates Ellen by coaching her through flashbacks to a toxic family. Womanly touches — pink-checked curtains and pillows, back rubs, relaxation techniques, home-packed lunches, and fragrant fried chicken — welcome Ellen to a gynocentric environment. The new home exudes love at the same time that it extends discipline and lessons in sharing and life-affirmation — filling a terrarium with plants, tending fish in an aquarium, and riding Dolphin, the family pony. With a burst of joy, Ellen escapes oversized terrors to reflect on a day she fills with delights. Secure in her room, she rests before dinner and contemplates the blessing of life with her competent new mom. The text earns classic status for revealing Ellen's capacity for renewal.

For *A Virtuous Woman* (1989), Gibbons paces the text to the same domestic rhythms that rehabilitate Ellen Foster — from Pansy Stanley's death at needlework in her rocking chair to her granddaughter June's introduction to female crafts in the weaving of potholders, a humble representation of kitchen duties and the womanly matrix of home and family. The story embraces a cruel element of love and loss with the terminal illness of 45-year-old Ruby Pitts Woodrow Stokes from lung cancer brought on by addictive smoking. Terrified by mortality, she experiences a range of end-of-life emotions and graces. As described by Marilyn Chandler, critic for the *Women's Review of Books*, Ruby "cries, gets angry, and then comforts Jack in his bewilderment over her tears and anger" (Chandler, 1989). In the same time frame, Ruby cooks and freezes enough packets of pork with corn and beef with beans to last Jack for the first three months following her demise in March. The unusual husband-wife relationship in a farm setting, according to Chandler, finds them "unused to the radical kinds of intimacy their situation enforces" (*Ibid.*). Through simple language and childlike admissions, they exalt the marital compromises that require scaling back on expectations and accepting the time they have left together. An unforeseen source of conflict, Ruby's exemplary housekeeping and cooking, leaves Jack unprepared for tending to everyday needs. His pathetic compensation honors his departed wife — longing for a ghostly visitation, he spreads clean sheets on his bed and sprinkles them with lilac dusting powder, the fragrance of Ruby. In her stead comes a surrogate, June Stanley, the child she and Jack nurture in place of the children they can't have. Like a womanly boomerang, a second layer of female order returns to the Stokes home just in time.

Moving toward unsatisfied female needs, Gibbons sets female community in defiance of the Great Depression in *A Cure for Dreams* (1990). The novel depicts generational strengths among rural housewives who rely on woman-to-woman networking. In an article for *Southern Literary Journal*, Tonita Branan describes the conversant women "who talk to each other, talk about each other, gloss old phrases, name their children, weave fictitious accounts of 'what really happened,' write poems, critique men's letters, and read one another's bodies" (Branan, 1994, 91). Born in 1820, Betty Davies Randolph is the scion of forthright females, including a paternal grandmother who risked ridicule by advocating pacifism during World War I. Betty grows up hearing more tales of her Irish Catholic maternal grandmother, Bridget O'Donough O'Cadhain, who brandishes Gaelic curses and a yardstick as weapons against her dissolute husband Sheamus and brother-in-law Bart. In a strictly gendered household, the two brothers sit at the breakfast table drinking and demanding food while leaving labor to the womenfolk. In retrospect, Betty's mother Lottie concludes that Bridget shriveled into a bitter, mean crone in part by hardening herself to her husband's sottish ways and family neglect. Critics — particularly male reviewers — upbraid Gibbons for using male characters like Sheamus and Bart as whipping boys for sundry familial ills. On the other hand, feminists tend to side with Gibbons for blaming Old World patriarchy for belittling and discounting women as whole human beings.

As a balm to women, Gibbons's microcosm on Milk Farm Road in piedmont North Carolina forges union in sisterhood. Female characters inhabit what novelist-reviewer Ann Tyler calls "a shadow world that lies beneath the men's world, skillfully evading men even as they study them from afar," like wild animals surveying predators (Tyler, 1991). By validating mutual sufferings from loneliness, misfortune, treachery, and abandonment, the O'Donough-O'Cadhain-Davies-Randolph women recognize communal strengths and foster backbone. In the summation of reviewer Dannye Romine, book critic for the *Charlotte* (N.C.) *Observer*, the women whom men abandon "may steal, lie, and kill. But they tend to their children, their finances, and each other" (Romine, 1991). During the Depression, Lottie Davies, the community's queen bee, visits housewives and organizes a regular klatch for gin rummy and pinochle playing and conversation at the rear of Porter's store. At the thought of a newcomer, Trudy Woodlief, struggling to rear five children and newborn twins Bernard and Barnard in the absence of her runaway husband Tommy, Lottie rallies aid for the family, even though Lottie's women friends scorn Louisiana-born white trash like Trudy. More terrifying for Lottie, Betty's romance with Stanton exposes her to a dazzling, drug-addicted womanizer from Richmond, Virginia. Like her mother, Betty quickly sizes up his craving for Neurol Compound and stalks from his hospital room, leaving him calling like a trifler to a retreating pair of legs, "Hey, girlie! Come back, girlie!" (Gibbons, 1991, 181). Gibbons applauds Betty for learning from family stories when and how to jettison frivolous, exploitive males. In the absence of husband Herman Randolph aboard the U.S.S. *Hornet*, during World War II, the draw of female sanctuary finds Betty re-ensconced at home. On November 25, 1942, the manless war bride gives birth to Marjorie Polly Randolph, the next generation of the family matrilineage. The text depicts Marjorie's childhood education as crib lessons derived from women's stories.

Gibbons's popular fourth novel, *Charms for the Easy Life* (1993), retreats from romanticism to picture more doughty female noncombatants living manless during World War II. In Durham, North Carolina, in 1942, Margaret, a teenage volunteer at the veterans' hospital, surveys Louise Battle Nutter, an aristocrat reborn as a pro-woman, pro-child advocate. On return from a sojourn in New York City, Louise defies her upscale family by joining the suffrage league and the Transcendental Educational Society and by challenging illiteracy, gendered school curricula, and child labor. Gibbons sets up a similar leader in journalist Anna Hawkings, the mother of Margaret's beau, Tom Hawkings, III, and the admirer of Margaret's grandmother, Charlie Kate Birch, for her unlicensed medical practice among the poor of city's mill hill district. Each example represents a strand of feminism emerging from shifts in American philosophy concerning the interests and capabilities of the first generation of enfranchised women.

Female unity enlivens *Charms for the Easy Life* and supports themes of self-sufficiency and humanitarianism. After one scoundrel husband abandons the family and a second one dies of cerebral hemorrhage in August 1936, Charlie Kate and her daughter, Sophia Snow Birch, emerge as symbols of potency and authority to Margaret, whom they surround with love, encouragement, and possibilities for self-education. The trio lean inward until Sophia's yearning for a husband and Charlie Kate's diminished strength force Margaret to choose for herself a future commitment. Rather than attend college during the first year of World War II, she opts for a stable romance with Tom, a suitable life mate. Critic Judith Beth Cohen, writing for *Women's Review of Books*, notes that the threesome — grandmother, mother, and daughter — "know their collective power is bound to be diluted when they leave the female circle" (Cohen, 1993). Through Margaret's competent preparation for her grandmother's funeral on December 26, 1942, Gibbons dramatizes how Charlie Kate lives on in Margaret's memory, a storehouse of womanly wisdom and a model of advancement.

In *Sights Unseen* (1995), Gibbons's fifth novel, the relationship of daughter, mother, and domestic rests on a darker, more complex appreciation of womanhood than that of *Charms for the Easy Life.* Pearl Wiggins, the Barnes family cook and housekeeper, evens out the cyclic obsessions and rantings of Maggie Barnes, a manic depressive who requires constant monitoring. At the ebb of a kitchen confrontation, Pearl mends mother-daughter rifts by peeling an orange for Maggie and urging her daughter Hattie to share it. The scene concludes with a womanly gesture — Pearl shampooing and setting Maggie's hair and situating her under a hair dryer with a movie magazine, a familiar comfort to women who primp and de-stress at the beauty parlor. When Maggie returns to sanity in 1967 after psychotherapy and eight electroconvulsive shock treatments at Duke Hospital, female roles restore her sense of control and service to family. Once more the lady of the house, Maggie achieves satisfaction by canning vegetables with Pearl and by buying and sewing new clothes for the children. As hostess at the dinner table, Maggie sets boundaries for her opinionated father-in-law, Grandfather Barnes, by rescuing Pearl from his racist debasement. The gesture implies a sisterhood that ensures Maggie's continued rehabilitation in a supportive female environment.

Gibbons's first historical novel, *On the Occasion of My Last Afternoon* (1998), reprises the daughter-mother-surrogate mother triad of *Sights Unseen* with a plantation setting on the James River in Bruton Parish, Virginia. Emma Garnet Tate Lowell, the narrator, reflects on the female hierarchy of her pre-teen years. The female head of household, Alice Tate, quails under the surliness of planter Samuel P. Goodman Tate, her vain upstart husband. As a buffer for Emma's fears and misgivings, Clarice Washington, the wise, stalwart cook-housekeeper, offers situational mothering and shielding from Samuel's outrages, particularly the near-decapitation of Jacob, an intrusive field hand murdered during hog-killing season in 1842. With less drama, Alice models the non-confrontational female by dispatching Emma to her room when the father's dinner-table harangues venture too far into their son Whately's student gambling escapades at Washington College in Lexington, Virginia. As though glimpsing her maternal destiny, Emma takes comfort in rocking one of her younger siblings, a retreat that she continues to enjoy in adulthood. She extends the refuge to Alice by summoning her to the nursery on the pretext of checking baby John for fever. Emma's guile indicates the development of female deception in early childhood and the author's validation of the kitchen and nursery as female domains.

Gibbons recounts through Emma's 70 years the struggles and sufferings of slave times, the Civil War, and Reconstruction. Following ten months of research on the mid–1800s, Gibbons confided to interviewer Don O'Briant, a writer for the *Atlanta Journal-Constitution*, "I was devastated by the constant loss these women felt" (O'Briant, 1998). As the multi-dimensional mate of Quincy, an altruistic physician, Emma hardens herself to chaos by remaining near him at the Fair Grounds tent hospital and by learning nursing from on-the-job training with bandages, splints, tweezers, scalpels, and maggots, an effective exciser of necrotic tissue. Retreating at night to their house on Blount Street, she surrounds herself with female love from Clarice and from daughters Leslie, Louise, and Mary. After widowhood in 1865, womanly strengths continue to brace Emma as she studies cookery in Boston with female companions. At the novel's masterful conclusion, Gibbons inserts a hint of the old Emma in her jest about a good use for grits— a scalding weapon hurled at a philandering husband as his rightful punishment. On Emma's return to Raleigh, she heals her sad heart with days of talk with her younger sister Maureen, a former simpering belle who restores her own spirit by establishing a refuge for women and orphans. The chain of sharing attests to feminist beliefs in female synergy as an antidote to human ills.

In the mold of Emma and Maureen's outreach, the sanctuary one woman provides another dramatizes domestic rescue in *Divining Women* (2004), Gibbons's seventh novel. As the action opens, on September 30, 1918, the narrator, 22-year-old Mary Oliver, departs Union Station in Washington, D.C. through a tunnel, a symbolic birthing of a rescuer. In retrospect, she recalls how her widowed mother, Martha Greene Oliver, separates the men from the women in her house on the excuse that Mary needs the company of women to nullify the trauma of living under the roof of the gruff, punitive Troop Ross. Under the scrutiny of grandmother Louise Canton Oliver, the younger Oliver women sift details about Maureen Carlton Ross, Mary's aunt. In womanly fashion, Louise analyzes character by assessing Maureen's clothing. Mary describes the evaluation as a feminine "method of divination," a gendered sixth sense indigenous to the feminist works of Jane Austen, Margaret Atwood, Grace Aguilar, and Edwidge Danticat. (Gibbons, 2004, 16). Martha exhibits the same clear vision in assessing gifts of a chafing dish, orchid pot, silk wrapper, and scrimshaw hair clasps as evidence of a woman's tastes. Like Lottie's suspicions about a husband-murdering neighbor in *A Cure for Dreams* and Charlie Kate's dosage of chloroform to female dental patients in *Charms for the Easy Life*, the intuitive skills of the Greene-Oliver matrilineage rest on sound evidence.

The Oliver women exhibit more might than the fingertip-maneuvering of a planchette around a Ouija board. After Mary's humiliation at two late-winter dances by her first dates, Grandmother Louise Canton Oliver joins Grandmother Leslie Greene at a showdown with one boy's mother. Set at the lobby of Ford's Theatre, the site of Abraham Lincoln's assassination on April 14, 1865, the humorous confrontation, related with the author's typical decorum, suggests a Mafia-like family support system that protects the most vulnerable of the matrilineage. More daring is Martha's appearance in 1911 at the home of Maureen Carlton Ross and Troop Ross to express sympathy at the death of Troop's harpyish mother, incongruously named Nora Worthy Ross. Because Martha risks a confrontation in the lion's den, she returns to Washington, D.C., in possession of a peace accord that ostensibly ends Nora's 35-year tong war against her ex-husband, Toby Greene, Troop's father. Through understatement, Gibbons indicates that the success of Martha's mission is never in doubt.

Gibbons revisits her motif of interracial female friendships in *The Life All Around Me by Ellen Foster* (2006), a sequel to *Ellen Foster*. Laura, a friend and advocate of Starletta's mother, shares a pack of Kools and discusses the friend's ambition to complete a college degree and become a social worker, a worthy endeavor for the black single parent of a handicapped child. The two women take pride in a decision that has its roots in their mutual involvement in Ellen's chaotic life. At a climactic moment, the author accords Starletta's mother a clarion voice to remind Ellen of her luck in locating Laura, a woman mad enough at Ellen's trials to blow up the road to ward off any more hurt. Restoring stasis to the foster home, in fall 1974, a net of woman-to-woman rumor discloses that Aunt Nadine Nelson owes back rent to Ellen, who inherited her family's house. The female underground successfully unmasks a thief and enables Ellen to take possession of a long-delayed legacy. The celebration in the resolution rounds out another Christmas in Ellen's life with mutual female affection and vision.

• *Further reading*

Austin, Mary Hunter. *The Land of Little Rain.* http://etext.lib.virginia.edu/toc/modeng/public/AusRain.html, 1903.

Branan, Tonita. "Woman and 'The Gift of Gab': Revisionary Strategies in *A Cure for Dreams,*" *Southern Literary Journal* 26 (Spring 1994): 91–101.

Chandler, Marilyn. "Limited Partnership," *Women's Review of Books* 6, nos. 10–11 (July 1989): 21.

Cohen, Judith Beth. "Review: *Charms for the Easy Life,*" *Women's Review of Books* 11, no. 1 (October 1993).

Folks, Jeffrey J., and James A. Perkins. *Southern Writers at Century's End.* Lexington: University Press of Kentucky, 1997.

Gibbons, Kaye. *A Cure for Dreams.* New York: Algonquin, 1991.

_____. *Divining Women.* New York: G.P. Putnam's Sons, 2004.

_____. "The Headache," *St. Andrews Review* (June 1987): 3–8.

_____. *The Life All Around Me by Ellen Foster.* New York: Harcourt, 2006.

Lott, Brett. "Kaye Gibbons Looks Back in Anger," Raleigh, N.C., *News & Observer* (7 June 1998).

McKee, Kathryn. "Simply Talking: Women and Language in Kaye Gibbons's *A Cure for Dreams,*" *Southern Quarterly* 35, no. 4 (Summer 1997): 97–107.

O'Briant, Don. "In Search of a Novel," *Atlanta Journal-Constitution* (2 June 1998).

Romine, Dannye. "A Dream Come True—Third Time Out Is a Charmer for Raleigh Novelist Kaye Gibbons," *Charlotte* (N.C.) *Observer* (31 March 1991).

"Southern Charmers," *Chicago Tribune* (18 April 1993).

Tyler, Ann. "Fiercely Precise: Kay Gibbons' World of Southern Womanhood," *Chicago Tribune* (24 March 1991).

Weaver, Teresa K. "Outside the Writing Room, Reading's Ties Grow Stronger," *Atlanta Journal-Constitution* (8 August 2004).

West, Cassandra. "Listener's Guide," *Chicago Tribune* (5 July 1998).

World War II

The effects of World War II on noncombatants provide details for Kaye Gibbons's down-home fiction. Near the end of *A Cure for Dreams* (1991), Betty Davies marries Herman Randolph, a Works Progress Administration employee who volunteers for the navy after the bombing of Pearl Harbor on December 7, 1941. Following a brief wedding and honeymoon in February 1942, his abrupt departure for the U.S.S. *Hornet* leaves Betty in a situation faced by other manless war brides—coping with pregnancy, birth, and a newborn. Meanwhile, Herman experiences the bloodiest Pacific battles in New Guinea, the Caroline and Marianas Islands, Saipan, Guam, and Iwo Jima. The author stresses the value of sisterhood — a female network that Betty's mother, Lottie O'Cadhain Davies, organizes during the Great Depression. Members in her gin rummy and pinochle club in the back of Porter's store achieve an emotional release usually denied women. Their camaraderie extends to November 25, 1942, through midwife Polly Deal's home birthing of Betty's daughter and the consensus on naming the child Marjorie Polly Randolph. In the pattern of lone women during difficult times, the local females support Betty until Herman's return from the war.

In *Charms for the Easy Life* (1993), World War II creates a more formidable subtext, including the touching separation of lovers and soldiers at the Raleigh, North Carolina, train station and in the port cities of Norfolk, Virginia, and Pensacola, Florida. Gibbons bases some of the details on the prisoner of war camp at Warrenton, North Carolina, and some on her parents' war-time residence on Eagle Avenue in Alameda, California. In the estimation of critic Judith Beth Cohen, a writer for *Women's Review of Books*, "an enduring female household as the world explodes into war" mounts a bulwark against uncertain times (Cohen, 1993). The text notes that, even for previously unmarriageable girls, it was "all but impossible to stay single," a subtextual comment on the need of males for women to come home to rather than the stereotype of man-hungry girls enticing soldiers to the altar (Gibbons, 1993, 139). More insightful of women's years adrift in a manless microcosm is the budding of Margaret, the narrator, who graduates from high school during the early war months. Predicted from 1936 by Margaret's grandmother, Charlie Kate Birch, the European phase of global combat looms in 1940, when Margaret's valedictory warns male graduates from Coopers High School of the draft. Later, the family cringes before radio war news that lists as casualties the boys with whom Margaret grew up. Gibbons applauds in her speaker the patriotism of the female home guard.

At a turning point in her life, the war shapes Margaret's choices and decisions. For two years, she postpones enrolling in college and plots on a map the troop movements announced on radio broadcasts. Sophia Snow Birch, Margaret's frivolous mother, absorbs period trivia — President Franklin Roosevelt's weight and the birthday of his scottie dog Fala. The fears of December 1942 take shape with mention of General Jonathan Mayhew Wainwright, appointed commander of the Philippine war effort in September 1940, as well as Commander Eddie Rickenbacker's marooning at sea from October 22 to November 13, 1942; General Irwin Rommel's retreat from Tobruk, Libya, on December 7, 1941; English Prime Minister Winston Churchill's spat with Benito Mussolini; and the Russian advance across the Volga River against Axis powers in summer 1944, a newsreel feature that interrupts a movie in a Raleigh theater. Commentary on the 4-F's who remain undrafted pictures some of them playing in the North Carolina Symphony, which performs Al Jolson's "You Made Me Love You" (1913) and Bing Crosby's wistful "I'll Be Seeing You" (1938), one of the poignant separation ballads of the war years.

Frivolities wane to accommodate wartime demands and volunteerism. Charlie Kate serves on the War Orphan Board, donates her husband's wedding band to the war effort, and shepherds Sophia and Margaret to the Red Cross office on South

McDowell Street to pack boxes with cigarettes and Hershey bars for American prisoners of war. For volunteering at the veterans' hospital in Durham in 1942, Charlie Kate turns down a free uniform and cafeteria meals, but accepts a C gasoline ration card, which the government began issuing in December 1942 to ministers, doctors, mail carriers, and railroad workers, all of whom the government ranked as essential to home security. During free time, the women's relaxation centers on books, Hedy Lamarr's strapless dress in the film *White Cargo* (1942), caricatures of Churchill in Punch, First Lady Eleanor Roosevelt's *My Day Column*, and radio transmissions of President Roosevelt's fireside chats and of pop tunes by Helen O'Connell, Nelson Eddy, Johnny Mercer, and Benny Goodman. In contrast to the scholarly, patriotic Birch household, female self-decorators are more interested in dyeing shoes, re-feathering and re-veiling old hats, and revamping Easter dresses with trendy shoulder trains and scalloped hems.

More than the list of war dead in the newspaper, the sight of burns, shrapnel wounds, and plaster casts is sobering. Margaret, who is unused to cursing, despairing young men clad only in pajama bottoms and green hospital robes, agrees to read to patients and to type their dictated letters home. Shell-shocked and permanently damaged in mind and body, the most pathetic patients perplex her, particularly Tab, who is blind-sided by a "dear John" letter and subsequently re-assigned to the neurological ward. She pictures his ex-girlfriend Arlene as a tramp given to "mindless ranging around, sampling whatever was handy" (Gibbons, 1993, 194). Equally low on the female horizon are the "allotment Annies" wearing brush-on imitation stockings while attending a hospital Christmas party (*Ibid.*, 195). Like dime-a-dance sirens, each cherishes hopes of landing a husband and a military support check. In opposition to Charlie Kate's denunciation of man-traps, Dr. Charles Nutter insists that opening the dance to local girls lifts wartime morale, a chestnut of male sexual license dating to ancient times.

Gibbons expresses a maternal concern for young veterans by imagining how their mothers must respond to amputated arms, scarred torsos, obsessive thoughts, and dimmed vision in their precious sons. Easing the starkness of recovery wards are Margaret's letters that she makes up and ends with the typed names of unsuspecting sons and boyfriends to ease fears on the home front. Tom Hawkings, III, Margaret's beau, offers repayment for ward care — a gentle jitterbug performed at a Christmas dance in 1942 under the spell of codeine, a dependable alkaloid of opium developed in 1832 that eases the pain of stitches binding shrapnel wounds in his back. At close range, Margaret absorbs the fragrance of men's toiletries, the unmistakable man-smell that is sorely lacking to women during World War II. Acknowledging their romance, at Christmas 1942, she accepts an intimate gift, two pairs of rayon stockings "scheduled for rationing and already in short supply" (Ibid., 231).

Like a familiar tune, elements of the early 1940s recur in other fiction by Gibbons. In *Sights Unseen* (1995), she flashes back to December 24, 1941, only 17 days after the bombing of Pearl Harbor. Frederick Barnes, a recent enlistee in the army, proposes to Maggie, a proud woman who refuses a hurried marriage to save her from being a war bride, a term that implies urgency and desperation. Her rejection reflects a short time-span marked by rapid shifts in personal plans and on-the-spot decisions that affect a generation's marriages, careers, and children. Glimpses of wartime family life place Maggie in a Quonset hut in Louisiana during early motherhood to son Freddy, born in 1949. The temporary nature of late-'40s housing foreshadows the brief contentment of mother with child. As Maggie retreats into manic depression, Frederick pictures his frustrations in war terms— sleeping and pacing on the deck of a troop ship.

An additional comment on the difficult 1940s occurs in *The Life All Around Me by Ellen Foster* (2006). Gibbons imparts Ellen's villainous father Bill's service with actor Robert Stack aboard an aircraft carrier, either the U.S.S. *Hancock* or the U.S.S. *Sitkoh Bay.* The text names the title character's essay for the Woodmen of the World oratory contest as "Franklin Delano Roosevelt: King Arthur or Robin Hood?" (Gibbons, 2006, 7). The theme describes a post-war weakening of loyalty to the leader who directed the nation through world upheaval during an unprecedented four-term presidency. Late in Ellen's discovery of family history, she finds a telegram from 1942 alerting her mother to Bill's return from an aircraft carrier in the Pacific via Hawaii to his wife at Bay View Apartments in San Francisco. Destroying Ellen's homelife is Bill's subsequent aimilessness and alcoholism, a two-edged post-war malaise common to troubled veterans.

• *Further reading*

Cohen, Judith Beth. "Review: Charms for the Easy Life," *Women's Review of Books* 11, no. 1 (October 1993).

Gibbons, Kaye. *Charms for the Easy Life.* New York: Putnam, 1993.

_____. *The Life All Around Me by Ellen Foster.* New York: Harcourt, 2006.

writing

Gibbons is a driven fiction writer who examines the cause and effect of transitions in people's lives. In interviews, she asserts the mystic quality of written language, which emerges from innate wordsmithy rather than through college degrees. In the estimation of Bret Lott, a reviewer for the Raleigh (N.C.) *News & Observer*, Gibbons is a miniaturist, a producer of cameos "perfect in their attention to detail and small enough to be worn like a locket around one's heart" (Lott, 1998). A gift for diction and dialogue undergirds her exploration of inner mysteries, the foundation of a good story much like the dilemmas of folk lives in the fiction of Jane Austen and Thomas Hardy. In an introduction to the works of Southern feminist author Kate Chopin, Gibbons states a credo she shares with Chopin: "Writing into the heart of matters is an inevitable calling" (Gibbons, 2000, xii).

The author credits her knack for characterization and speech to a constant survey of human strengths and failings. Her fiction dramatizes moments that magnify lives, such as the guilty conscience of Lucille Womble in the short story "The Headache" (June 1987), Dr. Quincy Lowell's on-the-spot murder of Samuel P. Goodman Tate in *On the Occasion of My Last Afternoon* (1998), and Laura's retreat to the bedroom to regroup her mothering techniques in *The Life All Around Me by Ellen Foster* (2006). In the estimation of reviewer Kate Mosher, a critic for the Raleigh

(N.C.) *News & Observer*, Gibbons's intent is "to be critical and affectionate at the same time" (Mosher, 1991). Among her fans is North Carolina novelist Reynolds Price, who admires her "no-nonsense, tremendously careful witness of the world" (*Ibid.*). Ralph C. Wood, in a critique for *Christian Century*, accounts for the unusual cadencing of Ellen Foster's run-on sentences as "collisional, not chiefly because she has failed to learn grammar but because her life has been a series of crashes" (Wood, 1992, 843). His observation acknowledges Gibbons's talent for turning hurtful shards of the past into life-affirming storytelling.

The author is addicted to 18-hour workdays, which include the reading of current fiction and reviews. From friend Jeanne Braselton, Gibbons accepted the notion that "combining life and art was a blessing for women writers rather than our plight" (Gibbons, "Afterword," 2006, 177). Making light of grueling work, Gibbons told interviewer Dannye Romine, book editor for the *Charlotte* (N.C.) *Observer*, "At the end of every day I ask two questions: 'Did you have a good time?' and 'Did you do anything that's tax-deductible?'" (Romine, 1987). Gibbons feels emotionally, spiritually, and physically unwell when 30-city book tours and speaking commitments take her away from the task. When ideas pop up out of sync with composition, she scribbles them in notebooks or on napkins or envelopes and keeps them taped in view on her Macintosh computer until the need arises for them. Composing with feet up to ease a bad back, she sits in sight of her children's photos and a sign warning "Sit Down and Don't Get Up Until It's Done," a motto she revisits in *The Life All Around Me by Ellen Foster* ("Interview," 2006).

For over 20 years, Gibbons has honored the writing profession for its respect for language and for the complementary demands of editor, reader, and critic. Of the palpable warmth and humanity of her characters, she declared at a dinner meeting of the Literary and Historical Association in Raleigh, "I was raised 'way back in the country.... And I've never known a stereotypical individual, so why should I people my fiction with them?" (Hodges, 1998). In a description of her labors at creating verisimilitude, she stresses a reclusiveness and abstinence from vacations, telephone and email communication, simple pleasures, and human company. Mercilessly self-critical, she credits patience and a sense of order for her success. She composes in a complex first-person style and forces herself to concentrate through long sessions of rescripting to capture motivation and emotion in a main character's monologue. The result, according to reviewer Roy Parker, Jr., a book critic for the *Fayetteville* (N.C.) *Observer*, is "a steel-hard discipline of exposition and an economy of line," a lingual distillation that sets Gibbons apart from more prolix novelists (Parker, 1989).

For the author, reframing her initial manuscript is the equivalent of warming up members of a symphony or of a pianist playing arpeggios before a concert. She depicts the nitty-gritty of rewriting as merciless paring: "My philosophy is, if it doesn't paddle, throw it out of the boat" (Blades, 1991). The final test of the text is the authentic voicing of characters, for whom words sustain, heal, and regenerate the part of self that withers under stress or when someone close dies. Friend Allan Gurganus remarked, "You wind up wanting to defend the main characters and you become a kind of conspirator in protecting them" (O'Briant, 1995). Through rememory, Gibbons's characters immortalize lost family members while tending their own pangs of severance.

A palpable example of Gibbons's faith in the written word is the gift in *Ellen Foster* (1987) that the title character buys for herself—a diary in which to muddle through bereavement for her dead mother. Of the brilliance of the ten-year-old's diction, writer Mary Karr remarked, "The voice of that kid is so amazing.... There's such emotional conviction" (Weaver, 2005). Gibbons admits to the influence of serendipity on her writing. While she composed Ellen Foster, sessions of watching the TV series *Flipper* inspired the name for the foster home pony Dolphin, a familiar good luck symbol in ancient Roman fable. More significant was the influence of poet James Weldon Johnson, who legitimized the use of everyday speech as a source of art. In applying the precept to the story of Ellen Foster, Gibbons resolved to "see if I could have a child use her voice to talk about life, death, art, eternity—big things from a little person" (Perry & Weaks, 2002, 605). The method also worked in a second novel, *A Virtuous Woman* (1989), which develops the author's skill at vernacular. Critic Roz Kaveney praises the second work for its power to "transfigure the commonplace into a plain language that speaks with as much complexity as the rococo might, but with more appropriateness" (Kaveney, 1989, 998).

Gibbons's mastery of literary nuance pleases at the same time that it informs and instructs. In *A Cure for Dreams* (1991), she rounds out a description of Roy Duplin with understatement. Apart from womanizing and spousal degradation, his reputation sinks lower from the abuse of farm animals, the cheating of tenants, and violations of "race manners," a reference to the rural Southern conventions of black-white relations (Gibbons, 1991, 40). In conclusion, Gibbons sums up his negative traits as the makings of "an unsavory person" (*Ibid.*). The downplay of domestic drama continues after Roy's murder, which Gibbons renders as being "imposed upon" him by a shotgun blast from his belabored wife (*Ibid.*, 41). Taking a feminist stance on gendered injustice, the author brazens that Roy gets what he deserves.

More subtle is Gibbons's ability to survey the wreckage incurred by a dysfunctional home in *Sights Unseen* (1995), a study of bipolarity in a female head of household. The author draws a complicated family portrait derived from her own coming of age with a mentally unbalanced mother in Nash County, North Carolina. Gibbons relied completely on personal experience by working back into pre-teen memories of the suicide of her mother, Alice Dorothea "Shine" Batts, in March 1970. To Polly Paddock, literary critic of the *Charlotte* (N.C.) *Observer*, Gibbons described the process: "All I had was this family and its many problems—I didn't have history to fall back on" (Paddock, 1995). To Kim Weaver Spurr, an interviewer for the Durham, N.C., *Herald-Sun*, Gibbons confided, "I was so afraid of the reviews because it was such a difficult book to write.... Every word was a chore" (Spurr, 1995).

Critics found evidence of enduring art. In the estimation of Michael Harris, a reviewer for the *Los Angeles Times*, the unsettling narrative of madness within a proud landed farm family is "*trompe l'oeil*—an imitation of life so faithful that it conceals much of its own art" (Harris, 1995, 5). With the aid of her training in medicine, narrator Hattie Barnes relives her family's roller coaster chaos and forgives Mattie Barnes, a bipolar mother inhibited from true parenthood. The transformation of home and family, told in flashback, masterfully orders details. In the view of critic Jacqueline Carey, a writer for the *New York Times Book Review*, the text succeeds "without ever being confusing or arty or contrived" (Carey, 1995, 30). A cross-disciplinary classic, the psychological novel reaps rewards from health professionals, loved ones of the mentally ill, and bipolar individuals who gain insight into the invalidism of entire families.

In a critique of Gibbons's first fully realized historical novel, *On the Occasion of My Last Afternoon* (1998), Polly Paddock Gossett places the author "among our finest living writers (Gossett, 1998). Such high praise derives from the vigorous summation of slavery's end as revealed by the gentle, yet unflinching remarks of narrator Emma Garnet Tate Lowell. Gibbons credits successful pre-reading of Southern history, which she treasures as an inborn delight: "I've always been interested in crucibles of history and I love research" (O'Briant, 1998). Among the gems the author turns up are a Fabergé egg that Quincy gives Emma upon their marriage, soldiers conducting lice races, candles made from lard and sweet potatoes, and the sale of rats at the meat market. More bizarre is the extraction of silver fillings from molars of the war dead to mold a silver brooch, an award to heroine Emma Garnet Tate Lowell in 1861 for on-the-job training that turns her into a competent nurse in the critical ward. In the analysis of literary historian Linda Wagner-Martin, such a rise to female autonomy begins as "a candid accounting — though never a sensationalized one — of the trials of the spirit" (Hobson, 2002, 38).

Through a blend of humanism and feminism, Gibbons crowns the achievements of survivors who resort to eating burned okra, wild mint, corn kernels from barn floors, house pets, and stolen ducks to sustain them during widespread hunger. Speaking of moral depravity and social upheaval from the safety of 1900, her 70-year-old heroine looks back on the decline of tidewater Virginia as the South reluctantly cedes its economic prominence. A masterwork of selective reportage, Emma's memories depict the theft of harmonious family times by unstinting trainloads of wounded demanding the surgery and bandaging of Emma and her husband, Dr. Quincy Lowell. Almost as an afterthought, the author rewards a better breed of Southern landed gentry by describing Landon Carter as the new owner of Seven Oaks plantation, the lost patrimony of Emma and Maureen Tate. The bestowal of the Tates' property on their neighbors offers the author an opportunity to dispense literary justice — punishing the entire Tate family for their complicity in human bondage.

During the writing of *Divining Women* (2004), a claustrophobic tale of male-on-female emotional battery, Gibbons jokingly compared her job to a prison guard and a bottler of soda pop for the terror and drudgery of her task. She regretted the loss of her editor Faith Sale, fellow authors, and close friend Jeanne Braselton during the writing, but acknowledged a chance to honor the dead. Like Senegalese novelist Mariama Ba's *So Long a Letter* (1979), the text leaps beyond other feminist fiction for its inclusion of letters from Judith Benedict Stafford, an irate wife who, on May 3, 1912, catches her husband in bed with a street hustler. A review in *Publishers Weekly* considers the shift in perspective erratic, but lauds the work as "atmospheric and unsettling, narrated in hushed Victorian tones and ornamented with period flourishes" ("Review," 2004). As though cueing the orchestra for the finale, Gibbons presses the novel to a glorious conclusion that writer-reviewer Judi Goldenberg, in a critique for the *Richmond Times-Dispatch*, describes as smooth and "eminently readable" for its "silky prose and social portraiture" (Goldenberg, 2004).

For *The Life All Around Me by Ellen Foster* (2006), a sequel to *Ellen Foster*, Gibbons again texturizes a teen memoir. The author sets the action within the protagonist's psyche, which critic Lynna Williams, a reviewer for the *Chicago Tribune*, describes as the "story's landscape" (Williams, 2006). Unlike the guilelessness of the original story, the sequel punctuates the title figure's over-brilliant musings with a personal letter, dialect exchanges among other teens, and an objective psychiatric survey written after the admission of Ellen's mother Shine to Dorothea Dix Hospital on September 10, 1968. Ellen is particularly adept at verse, including phrases from Geoffrey Chaucer's Prologue to the *Canterbury Tales* (1385) and a take-off on Robert Frost's "Stopping by Woods on a Snowy Evening" (1923), which Ellen resets as "The First Day of Hunting Season" (Gibbons, 2006, 61). To save schoolmate Marvin from failing English, Ellen supplies the three-quatrain poem with an aabb rhyme scheme. The parody repeats Frost's choice of "dark and deep," a bifurcated image of stark terror and escapism into the woods, a subtextual commentary on Ellen's inner terrain. Dampering the psychological intensity are the novel's plot twists— Stuart's gift of a glass doorknob and a hilarious bedroom proposal of elopement to Pedro's South of the Border. More problematic is the foundling who turns out to be an heiress cheated of her legacy, a time-worn ploy that Valerie Sayers, reviewing for the *Washington Post*, compares to Victorian sensationalism. The fire-bursts of coy epistolary beginning, disjunctive wordplay, incomprehensible phrasing, and irony earn mixed reviews from critics, including Karen Campbell, a critic for the *Boston Globe*, who accuses Gibbons of "trying too hard" (Campbell, 2006).

See also **dialect; Gibbons, Kaye; humor; irony; language; storytelling; symbolism**

• *Further reading*

Blades, John. "A History and a Novel Win Heartland Prizes," *Chicago Tribune* (23 August 1991).

Campbell, Karen. "Ellen Foster Returns, Wise Beyond Her Years," *Boston Globe* (January 17, 2006).

Carey, Jacqueline. "Mommy Direst," *New York Times Book Review* (24 September 1995): 30.s

Gibbons, Kaye. "Afterword," *The Other Side of Air*. New York: Random House, 2006.

_____. *A Cure for Dreams*. New York: Algonquin, 1991.

_____. "Introduction," *The Awakening and Other Stories*, by Kate Chopin. New York: Modern Library, 2000.

_____. *The Life All Around Me by Ellen Foster*. New York: Harcourt, 2006.

Giffin, Glenn. "Gibbons Enamored of Southern Style," *Denver Post* (13 April 1993).

Goldenberg, Judi. "To Endure, Women Form Bond," *Richmond Times-Dispatch* (9 May 2004).

Gossett, Polly Paddock. "She Sees No Glory in the Gore of War," *Charlotte* (N.C.) *Observer* (7 June 1998).

Harris, Michael. "Scenes— and Skeletons— of a Troubled Southern Family," *Los Angeles Times* (9 October 1995): 5.

Hobson, Fred C., ed. *South to the Future: An American Region in the Twenty-First Century*. Athens: University of Georgia Press, 2002.

Hodges, Betty. "Southern Writer Mines Linguistic Heritage," Durham, N.C., *Herald-Sun* (29 November 1998).

"Interview with Kaye Gibbons," http://btob.barnesandnoble.com/writers/writerdetails.asp?z=y&btob=&cid=883309, Winter 2006.
Kaveney, Roz. "Making Themselves Over," *Times Literary Supplement* (15 September 1989): 998.
Lott, Brett. "Kaye Gibbons Looks Back in Anger," Raleigh, N.C., *News & Observer* (7 June 1998).
Merritt, Robert. "Gibbons Miles Away from 'Ellen Foster,'" *Richmond Times-Dispatch* (7 May 1991).
Mosher, Katie. "Family, Career Blossom for 'Ellen Foster' Creator," Raleigh, N.C., *News & Observer* (21 April 1991).
O'Briant, Don. "Book Signing," *Atlanta Journal-Constitution* (10 September 1995).
_____. "In Search of a Novel," *Atlanta Journal-Constitution* (2 June 1998).
Paddock, Polly. "Kaye Gibbons Recalls 'Sights Unseen' As a Tough Project," *Charlotte* (N.C.) *Observer* (27 August 1995).
Parker, Roy, Jr. "Kay Gibbons Reprise," *Fayetteville* (N.C.) *Observer* (30 April 1989).
Perry, Carolyn, and Mary Louise Weaks, eds. *The History of Southern Women's Literature*. Baton Rouge: Louisiana State University Press, 2002.
"Review: *Divining Women*," *Publishers Weekly* 251, no. 7 (16 February 2004).
Romine, Dannye. "Literature Liberates: Raleigh's Kaye Gibbons Finds Freedoms, Affirmation in 1st Novel," *Charlotte* (N.C.) *Observer* (26 April 1987).
Sayers, Valerie, "Growing Into the Role," *Washington Post* (6 January 2006).
Spurr, Kim Weaver. "Storied Life: For Gibbons, Words Reflect Part of Herself," Durham, N.C., *Herald-Sun* (27 August 1995).
Weaver, Teresa K. "'Liars' Club' Author Still Seeks Truth," *Atlanta Journal-Constitution* (10 April 2005).
Williams, Lynna. "For Ellen Foster, There's Finally Light at the End of the Tunnel," *Chicago Tribune* (8 January 2006).
Wood, Ralph C. "Gumption and Grace in the Novels of Kaye Gibbons," *Christian Century* 109, no. 27 (September 23–30, 1992): 842–846.

"The Yellow Wallpaper"

In one of Kaye Gibbons's salutes to feminist literature, she contrasts a crazy-making situation in *Divining Women* (2004) to a classic impressionist short story. Charlotte Perkins Gilman, herself the victim of a miserable marriage to an unbalanced mate, published the piece in the January 1892 edition of *New England Magazine*. A model of domestic Gothicism, the horror plot of "The Yellow Wallpaper" features delusive madness caused by gendered medical treatment of a hypersensitive new mother. Confined, muzzled, and subdued in a horrific rest cure by John, her physician/husband, the unnamed wife/patient suffers immurement in a locked room away from her baby and friends. Precipitating her psychic disintegration, the emotional violence of being confined in a room decorated with nightmarishly arabesque wallpaper inhibits her ability to refresh creative founts with normal conversation, walks in the garden, visits to relatives, mothering, and constructive outlets. The decline of the patient's faculties presages Betty Friedan's revelation of the "problem that has no name," a term identified in the feminist treatise *The Feminine Mystique* (1963) as classic female malaise.

As helpless as a prisoner of war, Maureen Carlton Ross, the parallel of Gilman's nameless victim, anticipates 50 days of imprisonment in her own home until the birth of her first child on November 8, 1918. Like Gilman's oppressive husband/physician John, Maureen's mate, Troop Ross seems solicitous. He orders daily deliveries of hybrid roses in a show of praiseworthy, but insidious intimidation of his neurasthenic wife. He subjects her to medical treatment for "female hysteria," a misogynistic diagnosis of normal womanly revolt against male coercion (Gibbons, 2004, 62). After arrival by train from Washington, D.C., to Elm City, North Carolina, on September 30, 1918, Mary Oliver, Maureen's 22-year-old niece and caretaker, writes a lengthy comparison to her mother, Martha Greene Oliver, between Gilman's story of a late 19th-century asylum and Maureen's quasi-incarceration. In Mary's estimation, the cause of marital torture derives from Troop's need to establish primacy over his wife by suppressing her gendered yearnings.

Maureen advances her own view of Gilman's crawling, demented madhouse inmate. During treatment with galvanic shock therapy, ice water deluges, vibrating belts, vaginal fumigation, and threats of a hysterectomy, Maureen observes women pushed to the wall by domineering mates. Worse than physical torture are husbandly threats to seize custody of their children. The strategy was one of the rallying points of suffragists in the years preceding full enfranchisement of women in 1920. Maureen recalls head banging, hand chewing, and wailing as overlays of the sputtering life spark, the bit of quick that flickers in maltreated bodies. One doctor opts to jolt a patient out of depression by donning a ghoulish false face and by having her husband report that their children are dead. The images reflect a sadistic trussing of women in a male-dominated medical system that promotes anti-woman diagnoses of female self-liberation.

See also ***Divining Women***

• *Further reading*

Bak, John S., "Escaping the Jaundiced Eye: Foucauldian Panopticism in Charlotte Perkins Gilman's 'The Yellow Wallpaper,'" *Studies in Short Fiction* 31, no. 1 (Winter 1994): 39–46.

Hume, Beverly A. "Managing Madness in Gilman's 'The Yellow Wall-Paper,'" *Studies in American Fiction* 30, no. 1 (Spring 2002): 3–30.

Roth, Marty. "Gilman's Arabesque Wallpaper," *Mosaic* 34, no. 4 (December 2001): 145–162.

Weales, Gerald. "Perera: The Yellow Wallpaper," *Commonweal* 120, no. 3 (12 February 1993): 16–17.

Appendix A: Time Line of Historical and Fictional Events in Gibbons's Works

Each entry contains an abbreviated title for identification of the source of each event. Key: CD = *A Cure for Dreams*, 1991; CEL = *Charms for the Easy Life*, 1993; DW = *Divining Women*, 2004; EF = *Ellen Foster*, 1987; H = "Headache," 1987; JS = "Joyner's Store," 1997; LAAM = *The Life All Around Me by Ellen Foster*, 2006; PS = *Pete and Shirley*, 1995; OOLA = *On the Occasion of My Last Afternoon*, 1998; SU = *Sights Unseen*, 1995; VW = *A Virtuous Woman*, 1989; WIW = "What I Won by Losing: Lessons from the 1977 Miss North Carolina National Teenager Pageant," 2005

1537 October 24: Jane Seymour, the third and favorite wife of Henry VIII, is beheaded (EF).

1776 Through 1777: Landon Carter's family receives Revere silver pieces as rewards for courage at the battles of Trenton (December 26, 1776) and Saratoga (September 19, 1777) (OOLA).

1800 Clarice Washington is born (OOLA). • Early 1800s: Welsh Quakers arrive in America (CD).

1808 Alice Tate is born (OOLA).

1825 Whately Tate is born to Alice and Samuel P. Goodman Tate (OOLA).

1830 Dr. John C. Gunn publishes *Domestic Medicine, or Poor Man's Friend* (CEL, OOLA). • Emma Garnet Tate is born to Alice and Samuel P. Goodman Tate (OOLA).

1831 August 22–October 30: The Nat Turner rebellion terrifies Virginia plantation residents (OOLA).

1833 Samuel Tate sends son Whately to Warren Academy (OOLA).

1836 Maureen Tate is born to Alice and Samuel Tate (OOLA).

1839 John Tate is born to Alice and Samuel Tate (OOLA). • The Tates visit Venice (OOLA).

1841 Twins Henry and Randolph Tate are born to Alice and Samuel Tate (OOLA). • April 4: William Henry Harrison dies a month after becoming the ninth U.S. president (OOLA).

1842 Samuel Tate slashes the throat of the slave Jacob (OOLA). • Before Christmas: Mintus relieves joint pain in Samuel Tate by wrapping swollen ankles in mustard and vinegar (OOLA). • December 20: Whately Tate returns from college to confess to impregnating a barmaid in Lexington, Virginia (OOLA).

1843 January: Slaves anticipate sale on the auction block in Williamsburg, Virginia (OOLA).

1845 Whately Tate dies of syphilis on Sullivan's Island, South Carolina (OOLA).

1847 Marriage tears 17-year-old Emma away from home and mother at Seven Oaks plantation (OOLA). • Emma suffers a three-day stupor from an overdose of laudanum (OOLA).

1849 Emma gives birth to Mary (OOLA).

1850 Emma gives birth to Leslie (OOLA).

1851 Emma gives birth to Louise (OOLA).

1852 Maureen Tate studies voice with Miss Carpentier in Philadelphia (OOLA).

1859 Alice Tate dies under the care of Dr. John C. Gunn (OOLA).

1860 Late December: Emma's twin brothers go to London to persuade the English to back the Southern cotton market (OOLA).

1861 April 12–13: The Confederate firing on Fort Sumter, South Carolina, initiates the Civil War (OOLA). • Mathew Brady hires a staff of 23 men to help photograph Civil War battlefields (OOLA). • June: Dorothea Dix assumes the superintendency of Union nurses (SU). • June 10: After the battle of Big Bethel Church, Virginia, Emma Tate faces a rush of 48 patients (OOLA). • July 21: The first battle of Manassas, Virginia, results in trainloads of wounded to Raleigh, North Carolina (OOLA). • Dr. Quincy Lowell presents Emma a brooch inscribed with the year of her on-the-job training in critical-care nursing (OOLA).

1862 April 6–7: Uncle Otha suffers a head wound at the battle of Shiloh at Pittsburg Landing, Tennessee (CEL). • April 6–May 4: After the retreat from the battle of Yorktown, Virginia, Emma Tate performs tracheotomies and extracts shrapnel from the wounded (OOLA). • May 1: General Benjamin Franklin Butler crushes New Orleans (OOLA). • Summer: Samuel Tate and his daughter Maureen abandon their home after General George Brinton McClellan seizes the James River area (OOLA). • June: Quincy Lowell murders Samuel Tate with an oral overdose of digitalis (OOLA). • August 28–30: More wounded soldiers inundate Raleigh, North Carolina, after the second battle of Manassas, Virginia (OOLA). • September 17: The battle of Antietam, Maryland, overloads Raleigh medical facilities (OOLA).

1863 January 1: Abraham Lincoln issues the Emancipation Proclamation (OOLA). • The grandfather of Nora Worthy Ross leases convict labor (DW). • Quincy Lowell's mother dies (OOLA). • After Clarice Washington dies, Charlie, Martha, and Mavis train Emma and Maureen in kitchen duties (OOLA). • May 14: The battle of Vicksburg, Mississippi, floods the Raleigh hospital with casualties (OOLA). • July 3–4: After the battle of Gettysburg, Pennsylvania, the Lowell family opens a home recovery ward (OOLA). • July 18: Colonel Robert Gould Shaw sacrifices himself and much of the 54th Massachusetts Regiment, America's first black militia, at the siege of Fort Wagner, South Carolina (OOLA).

1864 A meat market in Raleigh, North Carolina, offers rats at $2 per pound (OOLA). • April 12: A stream of casualties arrives in Raleigh after the Fort Pillow, Tennessee, massacre (OOLA). • May 5–7: The battle of the Wilderness, Virginia, overtaxes hospital facilities in Raleigh (OOLA). • May 31–June 12: The Lowells treat victims of the battle of Cold Harbor, Virginia (OOLA). • September 1–December 22: General William Tecumseh Sherman's forces ravage Georgia and the Carolinas (CEL). • November 11: Sherman orders Atlanta, Georgia, burned to the ground (CEL).

1865 Richard Baines's mother is born (CEL). • April 9: General Robert E. Lee surrenders to General Ulysses S. Grant at Appomattox Court House, Virginia (OOLA). • April 14: John Wilkes Booth fatally injures President Abraham Lincoln at Ford's Theatre in Washington,

D.C. (DW). • Later: The corruption and graft of Reconstruction grip Raleigh, North Carolina (OOLA).

1867 Nora Greene gives birth to Troop (DW).

1872 Lottie Moon launches a Baptist mission in P'ingtu and Tengchow, China (LAAM).

1875 Nora Worthy Ross leaves her husband, Toby Greene (DW).

1876 Toby marries Leslie, his second wife (CD).

1877 Martha Greene is born to Leslie and Toby Greene (DW).

1882 Clarissa "Charlie Kate" Birch and her twin Camelia are born in Pasquotank County, North Carolina (CEL).

1886 Emma Lowell visits the women's ward of the Dorothea Dix Hospital (OOLA).

1888 An unidentified man suffers facial mutilation from an attack with carbolic acid (DW).

1892 January: Charlotte Perkins Gilman publishes "The Yellow Wallpaper" in *New England Magazine* (DW).

1895 Grammar Oliver weds Martha Greene (DW).

1896 Martha Greene Oliver gives birth to daughter Mary (DW). • Charles Davies is born to Quaker parents (CD).

1897 Martha gives birth to Daniel Oliver (DW).

1900 Emma anticipates dying and reuniting with her beloved husband Quincy (OOLA). • Lottie is born to Sheamus and Bridget O'Donough O'Cadhain in Galway, Ireland (CD).

1902 Charlie Kate Birch marries a ferryman in Pasquotank County, North Carolina (CEL).

1904 Sophia Snow Birch is named for the Indian midwife who delivers her (CEL).

1905 The Grammar Olivers travel to Europe on the S.S. *Carpathia* (DW).

1910 Charlie Kate Birch's twin commits suicide after the death of her hydrocephalic son (CEL).

1911 Martha Greene Oliver consoles her half-brother, Troop Ross, after the death of his mother, Martha Worthy Ross (DW).

1912 May 3: Judith Benedict Stafford surprises her husband during his bedroom romp with a street whore (DW).

1913 After Daniel Oliver hangs himself from a Baltimore hotel room chandelier, his family travels to Europe aboard the S.S. *Lusitania* (DW). • After Grammar Oliver dies, his widow and daughter establish a private residence apart from their in-laws on Dupont Circle (DW). • Maureen Carlton marries Troop Ross in Yazoo City, Mississippi (DW).

1914 Ella and Eloise Carlton die in a fire (DW).

1915 April 24: Judith Benedict Stafford lives a sexually uninhibited life in Paris (DW).

1916 Mary Oliver graduates from Gaucher College (DW). • Through 1917: German forces erect a system of defenses in northwestern France some 100 miles from Lens to the Aisne River (DW). • August 8: The Provincetown Players introduce Susan Glaspell's play *Trifles* at the Wharf Theatre (CD).

1917 Madame C. J. Walker of Delta, Louisiana, develops the largest U.S. business owned by a black entrepreneur (LAAM). • Charlie Kate Birch's cousins commit suicide after their father dies in World War I (CEL). • A teacher condemns Margaret's reading of Mark Twain's *The Mysterious Stranger* (CEL). • April 6: The U.S. enters World War I after Congress declares war on Germany (DW). • Charles Davies's mother becomes a pacifist agitator against U.S. involvement in World War I (CD). • May: Mary Oliver is unable to complete postgraduate studies at Radcliffe College in Cambridge, Massachusetts (DW).

1918 The family of Sheamus and Bridget O'Donough O'Cadhain emigrates from Galway, Ireland, to Bell County, Kentucky, and settles on the Cumberland River at the confluence of Brownies Creek (CD). • Lottie O'Cadhain dreams of a male rescuer and marries Charles Davies, a Welsh Quaker farmer-miller (CD). • January: Mary Oliver's options drop to an entry level course at Radcliffe (DW). • Promising only one child, Troop Ross impregnates his wife Maureen, who anticipates having a post-birth hysterectomy (DW). • March 11: Influenza emerges in the United States at Fort Riley, Kansas (DW). • April: Alfonso XIII of Spain falls gravely ill with influenza (DW). • Fall: The influenza pandemic besets Elm City, North Carolina (DW). • September 30: Mary Oliver begins taking care of Maureen Carlton Ross in the last 50 days of Maureen's pregnancy (DW). • Maureen's mother writes a letter warning of Troop's spite (DW). • November 7: No physician is available to help Maureen Carlton Ross after she goes into labor (DW). • November 8: Mamie delivers the stillborn child of Maureen Carlton Ross (DW). • That night: Maureen sits by the coffin of Ella Eloise Ross (DW). • November 9: Zollie carries the coffin to the cemetery for a sunset burial (DW). • That night: Mary escorts Maureen to Washington, D.C., by train (DW).

1919 July: Adolf Hitler enters Munich politics as a police spy (VW). • Mid–1919: The boll weevil destroys Southern crops (CD).

1920 Lottie O'Cadhain gives birth to Betty Davies (CD).

1924 Margaret is born to Sophia Snow Birch and her farm agent husband (CEL).

1928 Charlie Kate Birch's cross-dressing nephew commits suicide (CEL). • Lottie O'Cadhain Davies believes that Amanda Bethune "has it all" (CD).

1929 During the Great Depression, the female community of Milk Farm Road, North Carolina, gambles at gin rummy and pinochle in the back room of Porter's store (CD). • Shine is born (LAAM). • March 4: Herbert Hoover is elected the 31st U.S. President (CD). • October 21: The stock market crash begins the Great Depression (CD).

1932 Because Betty Davies's refusal of a healthful diet, she sickens from pellagra (CD).

1933 Betty receives a book of poetry for her 13th birthday (CD).

1934 May 28: The Dionne quintuplets are born in Ontario, Canada (CD).

1935 Through 1962: Eleanor Roosevelt publishes her "My Day" column six days a week (CEL). • May: President Franklin D. Roosevelt orders the founding of the Works Progress Administration (CD). • Summer: Congress passes the Social Security Act, which aids the unemployed, elderly, widows, and orphans (CD). • September 10: A state trooper shoots Governor Huey Long in the state capitol (CD).

1936 June: Sophia Snow Birch asks her mother to place a hex on her skirt-chasing husband (CEL). • August: After Sophia Snow Birch's husband dies of cerebral hemorrhage, her mother moves in with the family (CEL). • On a visit to Morehead City, Charlie Kate Birch predicts World War II (CEL).

1937 Charles Davies drowns himself in a river (CD).

1938 At the Sir Walter Raleigh Hotel, Charlie Kate Birch robs her husband of $1,365 in cash and abandons him (CEL). • September 30: Neville Chamberlain predicts "peace in our time" (CEL).

1939 Southerners reflect on the battle of Shiloh, Tennessee (CEL). • September 12: After 20 years of happiness with Mary Oliver, companion Maureen Carlton Ross dies (DW).

1940 Spring: Margaret's valedictory at the Cooper High School graduation ceremony alerts male classmates to the imminence of World War II (CEL). • September: General Jonathan Mayhew Wainwright assumes command of the Philippine war effort (CEL). • October: The Cincinnati Reds beat the Detroit Tigers in the seventh game of the World Series (CEL). • December 25: Lorenz Hart and Richard Rodgers' musical *Pal Joey* opens on Broadway at the Ethel Barrymore Theatre (CEL).

1941 December 7: The Japanese attack Pearl Harbor, Hawaii (CD, CEL). • General Irwin Rommel's forces retreat from Tobruk, Libya (CEL). • December 8: President Franklin D.

Roosevelt urges Congress to declare war on Japan (CEL). • December 24: Frederick Barnes, a recent enlistee in the army, proposes to Maggie (SU).

1942 Charlie Kate and Margaret volunteer at the veterans' hospital in Durham (CEL). • Tom Hawkings, III, censors mail for prisoners of war in Asheville, North Carolina (CEL). • Bill serves with actor Robert Stack aboard an aircraft carrier, either the U.S.S. *Hancock* or the U.S.S. *Sitkoh Bay* (LAAM). • A telegram alerts Shine to Bill's return from an aircraft carrier in the Pacific via Hawaii to his wife at Bay View Apartments in San Francisco (LAAM). • Late February: Herman Randolph departs for service aboard the U.S.S. *Hornet* (CD). • October 22–November 13: Commander Eddie Rickenbacker is marooned at sea (CEL). • November 25: Polly Deal delivers Marjorie Polly Randolph at the home of Lottie and Betty (CD). • December: The government begins issuing C gasoline ration cards to ministers, doctors, mail carriers, and railroad workers and to volunteers like Charlie Kate Birch (CEL). • December 7: The city of Charlotte changes the name of Lindbergh Avenue in denunciation of Charles Lindbergh's America First policy (CEL). • Christmas Eve: The first "Mrs. Richard Baines" registers at the Sir Walter Raleigh Hotel (CEL). Later: Businessman Richard Baines elopes to the North Carolina coast with Sophia Snow Birch (CEL). • That night: Charlie Kate and Margaret bake Christmas cookies for Mrs. Baines (CEL). • Noon on Christmas Day: Charlie Kate drives to the P.O.W. camp near Warrenton (CEL). • Late afternoon: Tom Hawkings, III, sends a box of memorabilia to Margaret (CEL). • That evening: Tom's sister Margaret performs a piano recital at Peace College (CEL). • Christmas night: After removing warts at a Hawkings family gathering, Charlie Kate Birch dies in her sleep (CEL). • December 26: Margaret observes family traditions by covering mirrors to honor Charlie Kate's passing (CEL).

1944 Summer: Russian forces advance across the Volga River against Axis powers (CEL).

1945 Shine's father dies (LAAM).

1946 Marie Campbell writes a birthing jingle, *Folks Do Get Born* (CD).

1947 Soldier Frederick Barnes marries Maggie (SU).

1949 The parents of Grandmother Harriet Barnes and Josephine Wooward die in a car wreck (SU). • Maggie Barnes gives birth to her first child, Freddy (SU).

1955 Maggie gives birth to Harriet "Hattie" Pearl and names her after the cook-housekeeper, Pearl Wiggins (SU).

1959 Ellen is born to Shine and Bill (LAAM). • Bill's father dies (LAAM).

1962 July 16: Marsha charges Griffin with giving her a sick headache (PS).

1964 Ava Gardner, a native North Carolinian, stars in the movie *The Night of the Iguana* (LAAM).

1967 Maggie Barnes enters psychotherapy and eight weeks of electroconvulsive shock treatments at Duke Hospital (SU).

1968 The author's father, Charles Batts, runs against Richard Nixon during a presidential campaign as a write-in candidate at Joyner's store (JS). January 16: Dennis Baucom is declared missing in action (PS). • September 10: Shine enters Dorothea Dix Hospital in Raleigh, North Carolina. • October 15: Shine completes five weeks of treatment for depression (LAAM).

1969 March: Shine swallows an overdose of digitalis and dies (LAAM). • Christmas: Ellen presents a spoon rest to Starletta's family and receives a sweater (EF). • December 31: Ellen flees drunken males and lodges with Starletta's family (EF).

1970 Bill's brother Ellis dies (LAAM). • After Bill displays his genitals at an elementary school, police arrest him (EF). • Later: A judge remands Ellen to the custody of her maternal grandmother (EF, LAAM). • July: Mavis encourages Ellen to wear a hat while she hoes her grandmother's fields (EF). • Fall: After Bill dies from cerebral hemorrhage, his mother-in-law spits on and burns the flag from his coffin (EF). • Before Christmas: Ellen attempts CPR on her grandmother, who dies of flu (EF). • Later: Ellen decks the corpse in a Sunday hat and artificial flowers before calling the mortuary (EF). • That day: Ellen passes to the care of her widowed aunt, Nadine Nelson (EF). • Later: At church, Ellen sizes up a foster mother who receives funding from the offering plate (EF, LAAM). • Christmas Day: Ellen flees Aunt Nadine and cousin Dora and chooses Laura for her foster mother (LAAM).

1971 Laura allows Ellen to attend *Willy Wonka and the Chocolate Factory* but not *Carnal Knowledge,* which contains nudity (LAAM). • October 31: Ellen and Starletta costume themselves as macaroni and cheese (LAAM).

1972 Dr. Julian Stanley begins a search for talented youth for courses at Johns Hopkins University in Baltimore, Maryland (LAAM).

1974 September: Through massage and relaxation techniques, Laura helps Ellen control flashbacks (LAAM). • September 20: Ellen requests permission from Dr. Derek Curtis Bok to enter Harvard University (LAAM). • Late: Dora gives birth to Claire Ellen, the daughter of a circus xylophone player (LAAM). • Christmas Eve: Ellen visits her family home, which renters vacate (LAAM).

1977 Gibbons remarks on growing up amid indigence, neglect, family violence, and crazed and alcoholic parents (WIW).

1982 After 15 years of sanity, Mattie Barnes dies in a fall (SU).

1989 Betty Davies Randolph dies (CD).

Appendix B: Writing and Research Topics

1. Compare the vision of a nurturing, supportive Southern community in *Charms for the Easy Life* or *A Cure for Dreams* with one of these fictional settings: the muck in Zora Neale Hurston's *Their Eyes Were Watching God*, a Charleston ghetto in DuBose Heyward's *Porgy and Bess* (1935), a small Georgia town in Harper Lee's *To Kill a Mockingbird*, islanders along the Carolina coast in Pat Conroy's *The Water Is Wide* and Gloria Naylor's *Mama Day*, the Florida outback in Marjorie Kinnan Rawlings's *Cross Creek*, and a former plantation in Walter Dean Myers's *The Glory Field*. Include music and dance, food, superstition, faith, learning, shared labor, ritual, fear, betrayal, love, and trust.

2. Discuss variances in Kaye Gibbons's presentation of the feminist motifs of courtship, marriage, birthing, child rearing, abandonment, marital abuse, and widowhood. How does the author's emphasis on one gender applaud female skills at healing? mothering? cooking? coping? survival? crafts? sisterhood? thrift? volunteerism?

3. Characterize elements of dialect in Gibbons's fiction. Note the difference between vernacular in daily conversation, such as preparations for Tiny Fran Hoover's wedding to Burr Stanley in *A Virtuous Woman*, and in the folk expressions that serve as wise adages to elders and authority figures like Starletta's mother, Clarice Washington, Pearl Wiggins, Mavis, Mamie, and Polly Deal.

4. Explain why Gibbons crusades on women's issues, such as poverty in "The Headache," homelessness and incest in *Ellen Foster*, domestic violence and adultery in *A Virtuous Woman*, marital disillusion and injustice in *A Cure for Dreams*, ignorance and abandonment in *Charms for the Easy Life*, mental illness in *Sights Unseen*, male tyranny and violence in *On the Occasion of My Last Afternoon*, medical misogyny and silencing in *Divining Women*, and education and self-esteem in *The Life All Around Me by Ellen Foster*.

5. Summarize the appeal of comic and satiric elements in Gibbons's works. Include childish mispronunciations and small portions of food in frozen meals in *Ellen Foster*, the luring of a ghost with talcum powder in *A Virtuous Woman*, motherly manipulation and a daughter's trickery in *A Cure for Dreams*, a wife's abandonment of a husband and theft of his money in *Charms for the Easy Life*, female sexual demands and an adolescent boy's pinup collection in *Sights Unseen*, the theft of ducks from a haughty neighbor and the departure of a freedwoman from a surly tyrant in *On the Occasion of My Last*

Afternoon, group nudity and communion with the recently dead in *Divining Women*, and a teenaged boy's gift of a glass door knob and his proposal of elopement to a fireworks emporium in *The Life All Around Me by Ellen Foster*.

6. Compose a letter to book clubs, women's studies teachers, and community discussion groups proposing the use the books of Kaye Gibbons during a celebration of Women's History Month. Suggest readings, comparative literature seminars, and the use of fiction to clarify women's concerns and actions during periods of history, particularly the Civil War, Reconstruction, World War I, the 1918 influenza pandemic, the Great Depression, and World War II.

7. Analyze lines that attest to Kaye Gibbons's regard for reading and book ownership, book discussions, community improvement projects, sisterhood, foster parenting, child advocacy, home schooling, literacy campaigns, intervention in domestic violence and child endangerment, sex and hygiene education, midwifery, women's social clubs, cookery and needlework, and activism. Outline your own opinion.

8. Identify and explain references to Christmas in *Ellen Foster, Charms for the Easy Life, On the Occasion of My Last Afternoon*, and *The Life All Around Me by Ellen Foster*. How do Alice Tate, Ellen Foster, Starletta's family, Charlie Kate Birch, Margaret, Sophia Snow Birch, Richard Baines and his mother, Emma Garnet Tate Lowell, Tom Hawkings, III, Maureen Tate, Civil War casualties, Whately, and Laura adapt their needs and emotions to celebration? Why do holidays magnify problems, such as child abuse, poverty, hunger, manlessness, widowhood, banishment, toxic home environments, and wartime wounds? How does each character channel feelings, for example, through visiting friends, attending a piano concert, jitterbugging, making cookies, singing, courtship, feasting, proposing marriage, and exchanging gifts?

9. Account for variant images of death in Kaye Gibbons's fiction. Contrast the passing of these characters: Lottie O'Cadhain Davies's infant son/Maureen Tate, Charlie Kate Birch/Ruby Pitts Woodrow Stokes, Maggie Barnes/Charles Davies, Alice Tate/Maveen, Ella Eloise Ross/Dr. Quincy Lowell, war casualties/Stanton, Ellen's maternal grandmother/Samuel P. Goodman Tate, John Woodrow/Clarice Washington, Camelia Birch/Ellis, Bill/Lucille Womble's father-in-law, Whately/Charlie Kate Birch's husband, and Shine/Roy Duplin.

10. Contrast the parenting in several of Gibbons's works. Include the following models:

- Martha Green Oliver's decision to move Mary from her grandparents' home to a separate residence in *Divining Women*
- Laura and Starletta's mother as single parents in *The Life All Around Me by Ellen Foster*
- Charlie Kate Birch as a preserver of women's traditions and home schooling in *Charms for the Easy Life*
- Bill's assessment of Ellen's "little ninnies" in *Ellen Foster*
- Nora Worthy Ross's perversion of filial love in her son Troop in *Divining Women*
- Julia and Roy's foster parenting of the title character in *Ellen Foster*
- the spiteful punishments of Stuart's mother in *The Life All Around Me by Ellen Foster*
- liberal, intellectual grandparenting of Mary Oliver in *Divining Women*
- the suicidal mother who teaches her daughter how to pick green beans in *Ellen Foster*
- Lucille Womble's concern for her children's social status in "The Headache"
- the housekeeper as surrogate mother in *Sights Unseen* and *On the Occasion of My Last Afternoon*
- Lonnie Hoover's coddling of Tiny Fran Hoover in *A Virtuous Woman*
- Quincy Lowell's storytelling to Leslie, Louise, and Mary in *On the Occasion of My Last Afternoon*
- Maggie Barnes's treachery against her son Freddy at the beach in *Sights Unseen*

- Starletta's Christmas gifts and parental love in *Ellen Foster*
- Sophia Snow Birch's immature mothering of Margaret in *Charms for the Easy Life*
- Maureen Carlton Ross as the grieving parent of Ella Eloise in *Divining Women*
- Samuel P. Goodman Tate's placement of Whately in Warren Academy at age eight in *On the Occasion of My Last Afternoon*
- the Stokes' surrogate parenting of June Stanley in *A Virtuous Woman*
- the grandmother's training of Lavinia Ella Mae Dawes in horticulture in *On the Occasion of My Last Afternoon*
- Lottie O'Cadhain Davies as storyteller and instructor of daughter Betty in *A Cure for Dreams*
- long distance mothering of Maureen Carlton Ross through letters from Yazoo City, Mississippi, in *Divining Women*
- Maggie Barnes's rejection of the infant Hattie in *Sights Unseen*
- Alice Tate as the submissive wife and mother in *On the Occasion of My Last Afternoon*.

11. With a flow chart, contrast the thematic contributions of Kaye Gibbons to feminist literature with the works of Isabel Allende, Julia Alvarez, Margaret Atwood, Charlotte Brontë, Emily Brontë, Charlotte Perkins Gilman, Ellen Glasgow, Susan Glaspell, Barbara Kingsolver, Margaret Mitchell, Flannery O'Connor, Grace Paley, Katherine Anne Porter, Marjorie Kinnan Rawlings, Elizabeth Spencer, Amy Tan, Eudora Welty, and Edith Wharton. Include achievement, adaptation, autonomy, belonging, betrayal, the Civil War, coming of age, community, death, dialect, displacement, dreams, education, fears, feminism, food, foster parenting, healing and health, historical milieu, humor, injustice, irony, language, marriage, materialism, men, misogyny, mothering, music, names, old age, opportunity, order, parenthood, poverty, powerlessness, racism, rape, reading, realism, reclamation, religion, secrecy, security, self-esteem, sex, siblings, social class, the South, storytelling, superstition, symbolism, urbanism, vengeance, violence, wisdom, women, World War II, and writing.

12. Outline the institution of slavery as Emma Garnet Tate Lowell reveals it in *On the Occasion of My Last Afternoon*. Cover the social position of field hand or kitchen worker, the murder of the slave Jacob by owner Samuel P. Goodman Tate, political threats to the slave economy, the Confederate firing on Fort Sumter, the advance of General George Brinton McClellan into coastal Virginia in summer 1862, the collapse of the plantation system along the James River, the flight of Samuel P. Goodman Tate and Maureen Tate to Raleigh, President Abraham Lincoln's Emancipation Proclamation, the end of the Civil War, turmoil among liberated slaves, and the joblessness and homelessness of blacks during Reconstruction.

13. Compare the strengths of sisterhood in two of Gibbons's works, for example:

- Mamie and Mary Oliver's companionship to Maureen Carlton Ross during the birth of Ella Eloise in *Divining Women*
- Starletta and Ellen dressing for Halloween as macaroni and cheese in *The Life All Around Me by Ellen Foster*
- Maureen Tate and Emma Garnet Tate Lowell's outreach to the poor women of Raleigh in *On the Occasion of My Last Afternoon*
- June Stanley's visits and gifts to Ruth Pitts Woodrow Stokes in *A Virtuous Woman*
- the tending of Sade Duplin by Lottie O'Cadhain Davies and other neighbor women in *A Cure for Dreams*
- Charlie Kate Birch and Margaret's volunteer duties at the Durham veterans' hospital in *Charms for the Easy Life*
- Polly Deal's advice about independence to Betty Davies Randolph during the birthing of Marjorie Polly Randolph in *A Cure for Dreams*
- Mae Bell Stokes's concern for Lucille Womble's ailments in "The Headache"

- Pearl Wiggins's sharing of kitchen duties with Maggie Barnes in *Sights Unseen*
- Starletta's overnight visit to Ellen Foster's new home in *Ellen Foster*
- Emma Garnet Tate Lowell's treasury of wisdom from Clarice in a recipe book in *On the Occasion of My Last Afternoon*
- Eileen's summons to Lottie O'Cadhain Davies to assist their mother in *A Cure for Dreams*
- Sophia Snow Birch and Margaret's house calls with Charlie Kate Birch in *Charms for the Easy Life*
- Lottie's gin rummy and pinochle club on Milk Farm Road in *A Cure for Dreams.*

14. Compare the sources of anger and mistrust in Kaye Gibbons's *Ellen Foster* with episodes in Willa Cather's *O Pioneers!*, Toni Cade Bambara's story "Blues Ain't No Mockin' Bird," Terry McMillan's *Mama*, Kate Chopin's *The Awakening*, Sue Monk Kidd's *The Secret Life of Bees*, Toni Morrison's *The Bluest Eye*, Margaret Walker's *Jubilee*, Jamaica Kincaid's *My Mother*, Mariama Ba's *So Long a Letter*, or Barbara Kingsolver's *Animal Dreams.* Determine the impact of racial, social, age, educational, economic, and gender differences on negative emotions.

15. Compare the ambitions and yearnings in unwanted or neglected children in *Ellen Foster, A Virtuous Woman, A Cure for Dreams, Charms for the Easy Life, Sights Unseen, On the Occasion of My Last Afternoon*, and *The Life All Around Me by Ellen Foster.* Determine which text best presents the precarious states of coming of age, autonomy, achievement, and self-esteem.

16. Compare losses and obstacles in *On the Occasion of My Last Afternoon* with similar female sufferings in Margaret Mitchell's *Gone with the Wind*, Zora Neale Hurston's "Sweat," Harriet Beecher Stowe's *Uncle Tom's Cabin*, Jane Smiley's *One Thousand Acres*, Marylynne Robinson's *Housekeeping*, Beth Henley's *Crimes of the Heart*, Margaret Edson's *Wit*, Julia Alvarez's *In the Time of the Butterflies*, Margaret Atwood's *The Handmaid's Tale*, Amy Tan's *The Bonesetter's Daughter*, or Isabel Allende's *Daughter of Fortune.*

17. Compile a brochure or audio tape to accompany a walking tour of Raleigh, noting locales that Kaye Gibbons mentions in her works, particularly Dorothea Dix Hospital for the Insane, Hayes Barton Pharmacy, Olivia Raney Library, Church of the Good Shepherd, Peace College, Crabtree Creek, Sir Walter Raleigh Hotel, railroad station, Red Cross office, Raleigh *News & Observer*, Fair Grounds, governor's mansion, Raleigh *Weekly Standard*, Mary Elizabeth Hospital, Oakwood Cemetery, post office, Mordecai Woods, and St. Mary's School.

18. Summarize the types of advice and counsel shared by these pairs of female characters: Clarice Washington/Emma Garnet Tate Lowell, Starletta's mother/Ellen Foster, Mae Bell Stokes/Lucille Womble, Mary Oliver/Maureen Carlton Ross, Nadine Nelson/Dora, Pearl Wiggins/Hattie Barnes, Lottie O'Cadhain Davies/Betty Davies Randolph, Laura/Ellen Foster, Charlie Kate Birch/Margaret, Mavis/Ellen Foster, Alice Tate/Emma Garnet Tate Lowell, Dr. Janet Cowley/Lucille Womble, and Polly Deal/Betty Davies Randolph. Contrast wisdom from males, particularly Quincy Lowell, Charles Nutter, Grandfather Barnes, Toby Greene, Burr Stanley, Stuart, Grammar Oliver, Henry Womble, Stuart, and "Blinking" Jack Ernest Stokes.

19. Discuss Kaye Gibbons's tendency toward decorum in titillating or grisly scenes, for example, the dosing of two children with deadly over-the-counter drugs, shooting of Roy Duplin, Ida's strangulation on vomit, Tom Hawkings's shrapnel wounds, the stillbirth of Ella Eloise Ross, Martha Green Oliver's secret suite at the Jefferson Hotel, the sexual escapades of foster daughters, Toby Greene's nudity, the suicide of a cross-dresser, Charlie Kate's death in her sleep, the near decapitation of Jacob, the farm agent's cerebral hemorrhage, Ruby Pitts Woodrow Stokes's decline from lung cancer, the rape of Stella Morgan, Freddy Barnes's pinup collection, Ellen's maternal grandmother's death from flu, the diagnosis of alcoholics at the City Grill, Charles Davies's drowning, Maggie's seduction of Frederick Barnes, the

hanging of Daniel Oliver, Judith Benedict Stafford's affairs in Paris, Charlie Kate Birch's three-day reunion with her husband at the Sir Walter Raleigh Hotel, touching the toes of Samuel P. Goodman Tate, and Shine's suicide from an overdose of prescription digitalis.

20. Select contrasting scenes and describe their pictorial qualities, for example:

- Charlie Kate Birch's rescue of a lynching victim and her theft of $1,365 from her husband at the Sir Walter Raleigh Hotel
- Emma Garnet Tate Lowell's performance of tracheotomies at a tent hospital and her farewell words at Quincy's Boston gravesite
- Ruby Pitts Woodrow Stokes's cigarette break under the pecan tree and her filling of the freezer with meals
- Pearl Wiggins's set-up of Hattie's crib and changing table and Pearl's shock at finding Freddy's pinup collection
- Maureen Carlton Ross's record of hothouse flowers in a notebook and her wrapping of Ella Eloise in clean birdseye
- Margaret's jitterbugging with Tom Hawkings, III, and her introduction to the Hawkings family at the train station
- Ellen Foster's decking of her grandmother's corpse with a Sunday hat and fake flowers and Ellen's rescue of Starletta from a fight over milk money
- Maggie Barnes's shopping sprees with Grandfather Barnes and her return from Duke Hospital
- Laura's welcome to Ellen Foster on Christmas Day, 1970, and a face-off against Nadine Nelson over a box of Shine's belongings
- Lucille Womble's scrubbing of overalls and her inspection of the Hippocratic Oath at the office of Dr. Janet Cowley
- June Stanley's housework for "Blinking" Jack Ernest Stokes and June's career as an architect
- Maggie Barnes's appearance at a school baseball field and her attempt to run down a woman in Rocky Mount for trying to steal Maggie's soul
- Lottie O'Cadhain Davies's purchase of English beaded netting, chiffon, and venise lace and her gift of a meal to Trudy Woodlief.

21. Discuss the cultural and familial value of cooking in *On the Occasion of My Last Afternoon* and in other feminist writing, e.g., Laura Esquivel's *Like Water for Chocolate*, Maxine Kumin's "Making the Jam without You," Jean Auel's *The Clan of the Cave Bear*, Erica Jong's *Witches*, Cathy Song's *The Picture Bride*, Laurel Thatcher Ulrich's *Good Wives*, Jessamyn West's *Except for Me and Thee*, Rita Dove's *Thomas and Beulah*, Anna Quindlen's *One True Thing*, Barbara Kingsolver's *The Poisonwood Bible*, or Isak Dinesen's *Babette's Feast*.

22. Account for Gibbons's contrasting opinions about self-endangering behaviors in Dora Nelson, Ruby Pitts Woodrow Stokes, Bill, Maggie Barnes, Quincy Lowell, Whately Tate, Daniel Oliver, Shine, Martha's mother, Judith Benedict Stafford, Stanton, Emma Garnet Tate Lowell, Stuart, "Blinking" Jack Ernest Stokes, Lucille Womble, Alice Tate, John Woodrow, Maureen Carlton Ross, and Troop Ross. Which characters recognize weaknesses? faults? inescapable situations? temporary obstacles?

23. Write an extended definition of *resolution* using as examples the final scenes of Maureen Carlton Ross's departure from Troop Ross, Emma Garnet Tate Lowell's welcome of an after-death reunion with Quincy, Polly Deal's birthing of Marjorie Polly Randolph, Starletta's arrival to spend a night at Ellen's foster home, Henry Womble's cuddling of Lucille, Ellen Foster's examination of Shine's belongings, Maggie Barnes's death from a fall, Margaret's discovery of Charlie Kate Birch's body, and Burr Stanley's gift of land to "Blinking" Jack Ernest Stokes.

24. Compare the skill of females at rhythmic, attitudinal, physical, and vocal methods of countering hurt, anger, shame, and insecurity. Use as models Laura's massage of Ellen during an anxiety attack, Lottie O'Cadhain Davies's gift of chamomile tea

and paregoric to Sade Duplin, Clarice Washington's cheeky farewell to Samuel P. Goodman Tate after Emma's wedding, Laura's payment to the seller of Moravian cookies at the fair, Ellen Foster's nestling with Shine after the overdose of prescription digitalis, Lottie O'Cadhain Davies's description of Charles's rescue of a hobo, Laura's service of a tea tray and shortbread biscuits to Martha's mother, Mamie's directions during Maureen Carlton Ross's delivery of Ella Eloise, Dr. Janet Cowley's advice to Lucille Womble about confession, Judith Benedict Stafford's reclamation of sexual freedom in Paris, and Charlie Kate Birch's advice to Margaret about accepting Sophia's remarriage.

25. Typify family dynamics in Kaye Gibbons's *Sights Unseen* and in Virginia Ellis's *The Wedding Dress*, August Wilson's *The Piano Lesson*, Velma Wallis's *Two Old Women*, Toni Morrison's *The Bluest Eye*, Michel Faber's *The Crimson Petal and the White*, Ernest Gaines's *The Autobiography of Miss Jane Pittman*, Isabel Allende's *The House of the Spirits*, Khaled Hosseini's *The Kite Runner*, Amy Tan's *The Hundred Secret Senses*, Pat Conroy's *The Great Santini*, or Clyde Edgerton's *Walking Across Egypt*. Emphasize the compromises that allow individuals to love unlovable people and to forgive past misunderstandings.

26. Improvise a conference of Samuel P. Goodman Tate, Charles Davies, Bill, Quincy Lowell, Burr Stanley, Landon Carter, Ruby Pitts's father, and Troop Ross on the subject of human happiness in regards to money. As a model, explain through dialogue why home, children, land, prominence, and personal belongings have a different meaning to women than to men.

27. Contrast the use of the supernatural in *Divining Women*, *A Virtuous Woman*, and *Charms for the Easy Life* to that of Marion Zimmer Bradley's *The Mists of Avalon*, Erica Jong's *Witches*, Ann Petry's *Tituba of Salem Village*, Gabriel Garcia Marquez's *One Hundred Years of Solitude*, Jean Rhys's *Wide Sargasso Sea*, Paula Gunn Allen's *Spider Woman's Granddaughters*, or Mary Stewart's *The Crystal Cave*.

28. List and describe a variety of narrative forms and styles in Kaye Gibbons's writings, including saga, dialogue, anecdote, history, satire, serial murder mystery, genealogy, scripture, eulogy, quip, witticism, adage, song, boast, lament, fool tale, hyperbole, verse, short story, personal essay, wisdom lore, book review, autobiography, medical diagnosis, jingle, confession, memoir, literary analysis, parody, and letter.

29. Discuss the repeated motif of the dependable black housekeeper as revealed in the actions and words of Sudie Bee, Clarice Washington, Pearl Wiggins, Maveen, Mamie, and Polly Deal. Explain the humor in the inefficiency of Mavis Washington.

30. With a partner, select literary foils to contrast, for instance, John Woodrow/June Stanley, Grandfather Barnes/Hattie Barnes, Sheamus O'Cadhain/Richard Bethune, Maureen Tate/Lavinia Ella Mae Dawes, Herman Randolph/Stanton, Samuel P. Goodman Tate/Dr. Quincy Lowell, Stuart/Bill, Laura/Nadine Nelson, Nora Worthy Ross/Judith Benedict Stafford, Sophia's husband/Dr. Charles Nutter, Ellen Foster/Dora Nelson, Roland Stanley/Burr Stanley, Charlie Kate Birch/Sophia Snow Birch, Lonnie Hoover/"Blinking" Jack Ernest Stokes, Toby Greene/Troop Ross, Alice Tate/Clarice Washington, and Bridget O'Donough O'Cadhain/Polly Deal.

31. Recap the causes and outcomes of these predicaments: the beating of Lavinia Ella Mae Dawes with a bag of oranges, a proposal of elopement to Pedro's South of the Border motel, Dora Nelson's ridicule of a picture of cats, grumbling of slaves over Jacob's murder, the breaking of waters with a crochet hook, a pool hall knifing, shoplifting at Porter's store, the blinding of a baby girl with silver nitrate drops, a nudist's fall that breaks his arm, too many casualties from the Wilderness campaign at the Fair Grounds tent hospital, the release of a snake into an outhouse toilet, eight weekly electroconvulsive shock treatments at Duke Hospital, Lucille McKimmon's question about Whately Tate's death, Grandfather Barnes's

slapping of his grandson Freddy, lack of graduate courses at Radcliffe, an old woman's return to Ireland to die, the hanging of Sugar Pete, the discovery of a husband committing adultery with a street tramp, negotiation over a mantel clock, the concealment of a pistol under a pillow, and the forging of legal documents.

32. Characterize the importance of secondary character placement in Gibbons's works. For example, note the significance and number of appearances of Whately Tate, Dora Nelson, Zollie, Josephine Woodward, General George Brinton McClellan, allotment Annies, Sheamus and Bart O'Cadhain, Marvin, Richard Baines, illiterate ferryman, Lucille McKimmon, Louise Canton Oliver, school psychometrist, Maureen Carlton's mother, Roy, veterans of World War I, court judge, Lavinia Ella Mae Dawes, Stella Morgan, Dr. Janet Cowley, John Woodrow, Stuart's mother, Cecil Spangler, Mintus, Deputy Sheriff John Carroll, Mavis Washington, Amanda Bethune, and Tiny Fran Hoover Stanley. Which characters offer the most information about major characters? about historical milieu? about feminist themes?

33. Summarize satire of these characters and terms: Methodist hotdogs, fanny disease, Steve McQueen, Cecil Spangler, "valentime" bed, Academy of the New Dawn Apocalypse, IQ camps, Ku Klux Klan, Pete and Shirley, coats of arms, art auctions, exile to Texas, rescuers on white horses, Roadrunner cartoons, pinups, Moravian cookies, Ouija board, newspaper editor, Luther Miracle, lard sculpture, empty hatbox, duct taped quarters, and Mavis Washington.

34. Explain the visual drama in these graphic images: touching the toes of Jacob's body to ward off ghosts, looking at a paramecium and euglena through a toy microscope, carrying a tiny coffin to the cemetery for a sunset burial, taping quarters around the waist, transporting cape jasmine blossoms in a hatbox, waiting for the school bus, examining a pocketbook by lantern light in an outhouse, cooking over a grimy hotplate, hiding a bottle of Vicks, self-treatment for syphilis, warning of God's vengeance in Elm City, burning a flag from a coffin, double lynching and cleaning ducks for a meal.

35. Locate examples of journeys and quests as symbols of ambition, vengeance, and persistence, particularly emigration from Galway to Bell County, Ellen Foster's search for a foster mother, Betty Davies's secretarial course in Richmond, Samuel P. Goodman Tate's flight from Seven Oaks to Raleigh, Ellen Foster's train trip to Johns Hopkins University in Baltimore, Bridget O'Donough O'Cadhain's return for a deathbed vigil in Galway, Charlie Kate's three days at the Sir Walter Raleigh Hotel, Troop's meeting with the Carltons in Yazoo City, Judith Benedict Stafford's escape to Cuba and Europe, the Barnes family's vacation on the Carolina coast, Emma Garnet Tate Lowell's return from Boston, Lottie O'Cadhain Davies's move to North Carolina, Shine's admission to Dorothea Dix asylum, Mary Oliver's train trip from Washington, D.C., to Elm City, Lucille Womble's appointment with Dr. Janet Cowley, the return of Daniel Oliver's body in a baggage car, and General William Tecumseh Sherman's march across Georgia and the Carolinas.

36. Debate the wisdom and efficacy of adages from Kaye Gibbons's works, such as these:

- Clarice Washington's belief in "Happy mother, happy children"
- Ellen Foster's contention that "The way the Lord moves is his business"
- Hattie Barnes's statement "We let the past stay in the past"
- Henry Womble's contention that "People do worse every second the clock ticks"
- Burr Stanley's gloomy comment that "People feed on each other's bad habits"
- the widow Lottie O'Cadhain Davies's declaration, "I've been married enough"
- Bill's philosophy "Wish in one hand and spit in the other and see which gets full first"
- Quincy Lowell's observation, "What a little learning will do to ward off the boogbears of this world"

- Pearl Wiggins's explanation of sex as "People practice having babies"
- Laura's urging Ellen to "Think it, know it"
- Ruby Pitts Woodrow Stokes contention that "The hardest things in the world to see are the ones that are right up on you."

37. Select elements of historical milieus that express women's views of social and economic change in *A Cure for Dreams* and *On the Occasion of My Last Afternoon*, for example, retreat to the movies on Milk Farm Road during the Great Depression, gifts of buttons and ribbon in purchases of yard goods, Emma Garnet Tate Lowell's opening of a freedmen's school at the United States Bank building, and Clarice Washington's circumvention of food scarcity by replacing lard candles with lighted sweet potatoes.

38. Discuss the effectiveness of Gothic elements in Gibbons's fiction, including welcoming dead spirits to a home on Dupont Circle, the rescue of a lynching victim, Roy Duplin "shot to pieces," the hanging of Sugar Pete, sewing up an accident victim with red thread, treatment of a leper, throwing a snake down the toilet, the immurement of Maureen Carlton Ross in an upstairs room, Ellen's grandmother spitting on and burning the flag from Bill's funeral, the near decapitation of Jacob, the lust of drunks for soft young girls, lesions on a victim of syphilis, the electric chair in Raleigh's state prison, the purging of wishes and unspoken words from the mouths of the dead, facial scars from an attack with carbolic acid, the head of a drowning victim trapped between two rocks, a deathbed vigil for Bridget O'Donough O'Cadhain, excision of a boil on the neck of Hermit Willoughby, a ghostly visit to "Blinking" Jack Ernest Stokes's bed, and the vision of Bill as a vampire nailed in his coffin.

39. Survey the rewards of old age in two of Gibbons's characters. Consider Charlie Kate Birch, Toby Greene, Lottie O'Cadhain Davies, "Blinking" Jack Ernest Stokes, Emma Garnet Tate Lowell, Louise Canton Oliver, Clarice Washington, Maveen, Richard Baines's mother, and Bridget O'Donough O'Cadhain.

40. Account for the exclusion or understatement of feminist controversies in Gibbons's female-dominated works, particularly women's right to vote and seek office, equal opportunities for women in the military and in politics, planned parenthood and birth control, workplace stress on women, on-the-job sexual harassment, denigration of women as thinkers and leaders, enrollment of women at universities, and abortion rights.

41. What does Charlie Kate Birch disclose in *Charms for the Easy Life* about underclass poverty? racism? unemployment? inadequate medical care? segregated neighborhoods? What are her personal methods of aiding the oppressed? How would her professional approach work in today's healthcare environment?

42. Summarize examples of emotional stress, crime, madness, suicide, alcoholism, and drug addiction in Kay Gibbons's fiction. Characterize her allotment of fault to the individual in the sufferings of Stanton, Maureen Carlton Ross, Zollie, Bill, Quincy Lowell, Whately, Maggie Barnes, Camelia, Charles Davies, Alice Tate, drunks at the City Grill, Sade Duplin, Roland Stanley, ferryman, Lucille Womble, Shine, Lottie O'Cadhain Davies, Nora Worthy Ross, Zollie's sister, Stuart's mother, and Daniel Oliver.

Bibliography

Primary Sources

"Afterword," *The Other Side of Air*. New York: Random House, 2006.

Birth of a Baby, So Lovely. Chapel Hill, N.C.: Mud Puppy Press, 1990.

Charms for the Easy Life. New York: Putnam, 1993.

Christmas in the South: Holiday Stories from the South's Best Writers (preface). Chapel Hill, N.C.: Algonquin, 2004.

A Cure for Dreams. New York: Algonquin, 1991.

Divining Women. New York: G. P. Putnam's Sons, 2004.

"Don't Try This at Home," *Oxford American* (25 October 2004).

Ellen Foster. New York: Algonquin Press, 1987.

Ellen Foster (adapted for stage by Aaron Posner). Philadelphia: unpublished, February 1994.

"Ellen Foster's Christmas" in *Twelve Christmas Stories by North Carolina Writers: and Twelve Poems, Too*, ed. Ruth Moose. Asheboro, N.C.: Down Home Press, 1997.

"The First Grade, Jesus, and the Hollyberry Family," *Southern Selves: From Mark Twain and Eudora Welty to Maya Angelou and Kaye Gibbons: A Collection of Autobiographical Writing*. New York: Vintage, 1998.

"First Loves," *Paris Review* 153 (winter 1999): 145–146.

"For Millay, Word Was All," *Atlanta Journal-Constitution* (23 September 2001).

Frost and Flower: My Life with Manic Depression So Far. Decatur, Ga.: Wisteria Press, 1995.

"The Headache," *St. Andrews Review* (June 1987): 3–8.

How I Became a Writer: My Mother, Literature, and a Life Split Neatly into Two Halves. Chapel Hill, N.C.: Algonquin Books, 1988.

"In 1912, a Lady Painter Meets Her True Nature," *Atlanta Journal-Constitution* (14 March 2004).

"Introduction," *I Cannot Tell a Lie, Exactly and Other Stories*, by Mary Ladd Gavell. New York: Random House, 2001.

"Introduction," *The Awakening and Other Stories*, by Kate Chopin. New York: Modern Library, 2000.

"Joyner's Store," *Southern Living* 32, no. 6 (June 1997): 204–205.

The Life All Around Me by Ellen Foster. New York: Harcourt, 2006.

A Literary Portrait of Raleigh (videotaped panel discussion). Raleigh, N.C.: Raleigh City Museum, 1997.

"My Mother, Literature, and a Life Split Neatly into Two Halves." *The Writer on Her Work: New Essays in New Territory*. Vol. 2. Ed. Janet Sternburg. New York: Norton, 1991, pp. 52–60.

"On *The Borderland*," *Mr. Universe and Other plays*, by Jim Grimsley. Chapel Hill, N.C.: Algonquin Books, 1998.

On the Occasion of My Last Afternoon. New York: G. P. Putnam's Sons, 1998.

Pete & Shirley: The Great Tar Heel Novel (serial novel). Asheboro, N.C.: Down Home Press, 1995.

"Planes of Language and Time: The Surfaces of the Miranda Stories," *Kenyon Review* 10 (winter 1988): 74–79.

Sights Unseen. New York: G. P. Putnam's Sons, 1995.

"Student's Demise Rocks Young Couple's Quiet Michigan Existence," *Atlanta Journal-Constitution* (5 October 2003).

"Trudy Woodlief" in *The Rough Road Home*.

Chapel Hill: University of North Carolina Press, 1992.
"The '20s Roar Again with Rollicking Energy," *Atlanta Journal-Constitution* (8 February 2004).
A Virtuous Woman. Chapel Hill, N.C.: Algonquin Press, 1989.
"What I Won by Losing: Lessons from the 1977 Miss North Carolina National Teenager Pageant," www.harcourtbooks.com/EllenFoster/essay_whatiwon.asp, 2005.

Secondary Sources

The following sources cover general literary discussion of Gibbons's canon. The following sections list writings about single titles and related works.

General

Abernathy, Jeff. *To Hell and Back: Race and Betrayal in the Southern Novel*. Athens: University of Georgia Press, 2003.
Alcott, Louisa May. *Little Women*. New York: Bantam, 1983.
_____. *The Portable Louisa May Alcott*. New York: Penguin, 2000.
Alexander, Ann. "Books to Include in Your Beach Bag," *Greensboro* (N.C.) *News & Record* (17 May 1992).
Anderson, Norman D., and B. T. Fowler. *Raleigh*. Charleston, S.C.: Arcadia, 1996.
Ardis, Ann L., and Leslie W. Lewis. *Women's Experience of Modernity 1875–1945*. Baltimore: Johns Hopkins University Press, 2003.
Austin, Mary Hunter. *The Land of Little Rain*. http://etext.lib.virginia.edu/toc/modeng/public/AusRain.html, 1903.
"Author Lavishes Her Support on the Read to Me Program," *Winston-Salem Journal* (13 January 1998).
"Author Speaks on Her Mental Health Struggle," *Chapel Hill* (N.C.) *Herald* (31 May 1997).
Avery, Sarah. "The Book of Love," Raleigh, N.C., *News & Observer* (24 November 1998).
Beauvoir, Simone de. *The Second Sex*. New York: Vintage, 1989.
Bennett, Barbara. *Comic Visions, Female Voices: Contemporary Women Novelists and Southern Humor*. Baton Rouge: Louisiana State University Press, 1998.
Bledsoe, Eric. "A Southern Weave of Women: Fiction of the Contemporary South," *Mississippi Quarterly* 50 (1997).
Brodeur, Nicole. "A Grill That's Perfection Just As It Is," Raleigh, N.C., *News & Observer* (10 December 1997).
_____. "So They'll Know They're Not Alone," Raleigh, N.C., *News & Observer* (27 November 1996).
Brown, Kurt, ed. *Facing the Lion*. Boston: Beacon Press, 1996.
Burleigh, Nina. "Maternal Inspiration Fuels Southern Writer's Work," *Chicago Tribune* (1 October 1989).
Chappell, Priscilla A. *Living in Words: Lillian Hellman and Kaye Gibbons*. Chapel Hill, N.C.: unpublished honors essay, 2000.
Cumming, W. P. "The Earliest Permanent Settlement in Carolina," *American Historical Review* 45, no. 1 (October 1939).
Cusick, Claire. "The New Road Home," Durham, N.C., *Herald-Sun* (15 October 2000).
Daniel, Virginia. "The Life All Around Her: Kaye Gibbons Talks to the *Indy* about *Ellen Foster's* Return," Raleigh (N.C.) *Indy* (25 January 2006).
DeMarr, Mary Jean. *Kaye Gibbons: A Critical Companion*. Westport, Conn.: Greenwood, 2003.
Edgers, Geoff. "Oprah Books Raleigh Author," Raleigh, N.C., *News & Observer* (28 October 1997).
"*Ellen Foster* and *A Virtuous Woman*," *Wilson Quarterly* 14, no. 1 (winter 1990): 95.
Estés, Clarissa Pinkola. *Women Who Run with the Wolves: Myths and Stories About the Wild Woman Archetype*. New York: Ballantine, 1997.
Flora, Joseph M., and Linda H. MacKethan, eds. *The Companion to Southern Literature: Themes, Genres, Places People, Movements, and Motifs*. Baton Rouge: Louisiana State University Press, 2002.
_____, and Robert Bain, eds. *Contemporary Fiction Writers of the South: A Bio-Bibliographical Sourcebook*. Westport, Conn.: Greenwood, 1993.
Folks, Jeffrey J., and James A. Perkins, eds. *Southern Writers at Century's End*. Lexington: University Press of Kentucky, 1997.
_____, and Nancy Summers Folks. *The World Is Our Home*. Lexington: University Press of Kentucky, 2000.
Friedan, Betty. *The Feminine Mystique*. New York: W. W. Norton, 2001.
Giffin, Glenn. "Gibbons Enamored of Southern Style," *Denver Post* (13 April 1993).
Gilbert, Sandra M., and Susan Gubar. *The Madwoman in the Attic*. 2nd ed. New Haven, Conn.: Yale University Press, 2000.
_____. *No Man's Land: Sexchanges: The Place of the Woman Writer in the Twentieth Century: The War of the Words*. New Haven, Conn.: Yale University Press, 1989.

Gilligan, Carol. *In a Different Voice: Psychological Theory and Women's Development*. Cambridge, Mass.: Harvard University Press, 1982.

Gilman, Charlotte Perkins. "The Woman's Congress of 1899," http://wyllie.lib.virginia.edu:8086/perl/toccer-new?id=SteWoma.sgm&images=images/modeng&data=/texts/english/modeng/parsed&tag=public&part=1&division=div1, 1899, accessed on October 10, 2006.

Glaspell, Susan. *Plays by Susan Glaspell*. New Haven, Conn.: Cambridge University Press, 1987.

Goodwyn, Ann, Anne G. Jones, and Susan V. Donaldson, eds. *Haunted Bodies: Gender and Southern Texts*. Charlottesville: University of Virginia Press, 1997.

Gossett, Polly Paddock. "After 7 Years, Instant Success," *Charlotte* (N.C.) *Observer* (23 July 1997).

_____. "Author Says New Attention Is Unnerving, But Welcome," *Charlotte* (N.C.) *Observer* (9 November 1997).

Gray, Richard, and Owen Robinson, eds. *A Companion to the Literature and Culture of the American South*. Malden, Mass.: Blackwell, 2004.

Gretlund, Jan Nordby. "In My Own Style: An Interview with Kaye Gibbons," *South Atlantic Review* 65, no. 4 (fall 2000): 132–154.

_____. *The Southern State of Mind*. Columbia: University of South Carolina Press, 1999.

Groover, Kristina Kaye. *The Wilderness Within: American Writers and Spiritual Quest*. Chapel Hill, N.C.: unpublished thesis, 1996.

Guinn, Matthew. *After Southern Modernism: Fiction of the Contemporary South*. Jackson: University Press of Mississippi, 2000.

Gunn, John C. *Gunn's Domestic Medicine*. Knoxville: University of Tennessee, 1986.

Gwin, Minrose. *The Woman in the Red Dress: Gender, Space, and Reading*. Champaign: University of Illinois Press, 2002.

Heilbrun, Carolyn G. *Toward a Recognition of Androgyny*. New York: W. W. Norton, 1982.

Hemley, Robin. "Regional Underbrush," *ANQ* 5, no. 4 (October 1992): 195–196.

Herion-Sarafidis, Elisabeth. "Interview with Lee Smith," *Southern Quarterly* 32 (winter 1994): 7–18.

Hoag, Andrea. "Death Carves Out a Lasting Impression," *Atlanta Journal-Constitution* (20 August 2006).

Hobson, Fred C., ed. *South to the Future: An American Region in the Twenty-First Century*. Athens: University of Georgia Press, 2002.

Hodges, Betty. "Migraine Hits after Oprah's Phone Call," Durham, N.C., *Herald-Sun* (2 November 1997).

_____. "Southern Writer Mines Linguistic Heritage," Durham, N.C., *Herald-Sun* (29 November 1998).

Hodges, Sam. "Writer Says Her New Books Show Difficult Spell Is Over," *Charlotte* (N.C.) *Observer* (27 April 2004).

Hoffert, Barbara. "Writers' Renaissance in North Carolina," *Library Journal* 114 (1 November 1989): 44–48.

Holt, Pat. "Remembering Faith," *Publishing Research Quarterly* 16, no. 1 (1 March 2000): 77–79.

Humphries, Jefferson, and John Lowe. *The Future of Southern Letters*. New York: Oxford University Press, 1996.

"Interview with Kaye Gibbons," http://btob.barnesandnoble.com/writers/writerdetails.asp?z=y&btob=&cid=883309, winter 2006, accessed October 9, 2006.

Jessup, Lynn. "Kaye Gibbons: Another Happy Ending," *Greensboro* (N.C.) *News & Record* (12 November 1995).

Jordan, Shirley M., ed. *Broken Silences: Interviews with Black and White Women Writers*. New Brunswick, N.J.: Rutgers University Press, 1993.

Kalfopoulou, Adrianne. *A Discussion of the Ideology of the American Dream in the Culture's Female Discourses*. Lewiston, N.Y.: Edwin Mellen Press, 2000.

"Kaye Gibbons to Move to Putnam's," *Greensboro* (N.C.) *News & Record* (9 June 1991).

Ketchin, Susan. *The Christ-Haunted Landscape: Faith and Doubt in Southern Fiction*. Jackson: University Press of Mississippi, 1993.

Kingsolver, Barbara. *I've Always Meant to Tell You: Letters to Our Mothers: An Anthology of Contemporary Women Writers*. New York: Pocket Star, 1997.

Kolbenschlag, Madonna. *Kiss Sleeping Beauty Good-bye: Breaking the Spell of Feminine Myths and Models*. Toronto: Bantam, 1981.

Krementz, Jill. *Women Writers: A Book of Postcards*. San Francisco: Pomegranate Artbooks, 1996.

Krentz, Jeri. "Hard Journey Back to 'Ellen,'" *Charlotte* (N.C.) *Observer* (29 January 2006).

Kulikowski, Jenny, and Kenneth E. Peters. *Historic Raleigh*. Charleston, S.C.: Arcadia, 2002.

Ladd, Barbara. "New Directions in Southern Women's Literary Historiography," *Southern Literary Journal* 36, no. 1 (fall 2003): 140–145.

Lanham, Fritz. "Truths Unplotted," *Houston Chronicle* (15 October 1995).

Lee, Eleanor. "Author Kaye Gibbons's Special Brand of Wit and Humor," *Fayetteville* (N.C.) *Observer* (27 May 1988).

Lesher, Linda Parent. *The Best Novels of the Nineties: A Reader's Guide*. Jefferson, N.C.: McFarland, 2000.

Lindenfeld, Sarah. "Novelist Mustering Opposition to Hayes Barton Pond," Raleigh, N.C., *News & Observer* (25 September 2000).

MacLellan, Erin. "More on Gibbons," *Greensboro* (N.C.) *News & Record* (12 July 1998).

Madrigal, Alix. "Gibbons Writes to Surprise Herself," *San Francisco Chronicle* (15 October 1989).

Magee, Rosemary M., ed. *Friendship and Sympathy: Communities of Southern Women Writers*. Jackson: University Press of Mississippi, 1992.

Makowsky, Veronica. "The Only Hard Part Was the Food: Recipes for Self-Nurture in Kaye Gibbons's Novels," *Southern Quarterly* 30 (winter-spring 1992): 103–112.

Malinowski, Jamie. "Dedicated Lines," *New Yorker* (25 December 1995): 46.

"Mammy Turns Tara into a Thriving B&B," *Atlanta Journal-Constitution* (14 April 1999).

Mann, Emily. *Testimonies: Four Plays*. New York: Theatre Communications Group, 1997.

Manning, Carol S. "The Belle Gone Bad — and Just Gone," *Southern Literary Journal* 37, no. 1 (fall 2004): 173–175.

_____, ed. *The Female Tradition in Southern Literature*. Champaign: University of Illinois Press, 1994.

Manning, Martha. *The Common Thread: Mothers and Daughters: The Bond We Never Outgrow*. New York: HarperCollins, 2003.

Manuel, John. *Clear Vision: An Interview with Kaye Gibbons*. Chapel Hill, N.C.: Algonquin Books, 1990.

McAlpin, Heller. "The Return of Cinderella," *Newsday* (1 January 2006).

McFadden, Kay. "N.C. Writers Showcased in Hallmark TV Films," *Charlotte* (N.C.) *Observer* (23 November 1997).

McMains, Victoria Golden. *The Readers' Choice: 200 Book Club Favorites*. New York: HarperCollins, 2000.

Medlin, Nell Joslin. "Louis Rubin, Architect of the Southern Literary Landscape," Raleigh, N.C., *News & Observer* (22 August 1999).

Merritt, Robert. "Gibbons Miles Away from 'Ellen Foster,'" *Richmond Times-Dispatch* (7 May 1991).

Miller, Marcianne. "A Man Would Ruin This...," Asheville (N.C.) *Mountain Xpress* 10, no. 36 (14 April 2004).

Miller, Mary E. "A Charmed But Uneasy Life," Raleigh, N.C., *News & Observer* (29 October 1995).

_____. "Summertime and the Readin' Is Easy," Raleigh, N.C., *News & Observer* (1 June 1993).

Miller, Pamela. "Kaye Gibbons' Novel Draws from Her Life," Minneapolis-St. Paul, Minn., *Star Tribune* (15 January 2006).

Monteith, Sharon. *Advancing Sisterhood: Interracial Friendships in Contemporary Southern Fiction*. Athens: University of Georgia Press, 2000.

Morris, Willie. "Olympic Atlanta," *Atlanta Journal-Constitution* (24 March 1996).

Mosher, Katie. "Family, Career Blossom for 'Ellen Foster' Creator," Raleigh, N.C., *News & Observer* (21 April 1991).

Murphy, Tom. "Chamber Celebrates Area Success Stories," Rocky Mount (N.C.) *Evening Telegram* (26 May 2004).

O'Briant, Don. "After Four Tries and Nearly 40 years, Joseph Humphreys Delivers a Historical Novel about a Lumbee Indian and her Outlaw Husband," *Atlanta Journal-Constitution* (17 September 2000).

_____. "Author Offers Tips on Carving Out 'Writing Room,'" *Atlanta Journal-Constitution* (9 July 1989).

_____. "Between the Pages," *Atlanta Journal-Constitution* (20 May 1999).

_____. "Kaye Gibbons Puts Pen Down Long Enough to Talk about Life," *Houston Chronicle* (18 April 2004).

_____. "Revitalized Author Rides on Creative Crest," *Atlanta Journal-Constitution* (18 April 2004).

_____. "Two Southern Writers to Receive $20,000 Arts Grants," *Atlanta Journal-Constitution* (22 January 1989).

_____. "Writing a Most 'Virtuous' Art for Gibbons," *Atlanta Journal-Constitution* (18 June 1989).

Olney, Judith. "Writers' Gala Pays Homage to 'First Loves,'" *Washington Times* (5 October 1994).

Paddock, Polly. "Kaye Gibbons: A Writer's Journey," *Charlotte* (N.C.) *Observer* (30 May 1993).

_____. "Writers to Discuss Southern Literature's New Story Line," *Charlotte* (N.C.) *Observer* (17 October 1993).

Page, Philip. "From Richard Wright to Toni Morrison," *African American Review* 36, no. 2 (summer 2002): 332–333.

Park, Andrew Sung, and Susan L. Nelson, eds. *The Other Side of Sin: Woundedness from the*

Perspectives of the Sinned-Against. Albany: State University of New York Press, 2001.

Perry, Carolyn, and Mary Louise Weaks, eds. *The History of Southern Women's Literature*. Baton Rouge: Louisiana State University Press, 2002.

Pitavy, François. "Sostenuto e Ostinato: La Petite Musique de Kaye Gibbons," *Europe* 816 (April 1996): 175–187.

Powell, Dannye Romine. "Literary Lady, Love Wed Today," *Charlotte* (N.C.) *Observer* (25 September 1993).

_____. *Parting the Curtains: Interviews with Southern Writers*. Winston-Salem, N.C.: J. F. Blair, 1994.

Powell, Lew. "Lean, Mean, Frozen Cuisine," *Charlotte* (N.C.) *Observer* (28 November 1987).

Reedy, Martha L. "Author, Author!," Rocky Mount, N.C., *Evening Telegram* (7 June 1998).

"Review: *Ellen Foster* and *A Virtuous Woman*," *Wilson Quarterly* 14, no. 1 (winter 1990): 95.

Richardson, Angelique, and Chris Willis, eds. *The New Woman in Fiction and in Fact: Fin-de-Siècle Feminisms*. London: Palgrave Macmillan, 2002.

Romine, Dannye. "Gibbons Wins Kentucky Derby," *Charlotte* (N.C.) *Observer* (10 April 1988).

_____. "North Carolina: Read All about It," *Charlotte* (N.C.) *Observer* (5 November 1989).

_____. "Victorian Times Inspire Magazine," *Charlotte* (N.C.) *Observer* (28 June 1987).

_____. "We'll Let You Go, Kaye Gibbons, So Long As You return," *Charlotte* (N.C.) *Observer* (24 November 1991).

Romines, Ann. *The Home Plot: Women, Writing and Domestic Ritual*. Amherst: University of Massachusetts Press, 1992.

Rose, Ellen Cronan. "Through the Looking Glass: When Women Tell Fairy Tales" in *The Voyage In: Fiction of Female Development*. eds. Elizabeth Abel, Marianne Hirsch, and Elizabeth Langland. Hanover, N.H.: University Press of New England, 1983.

Rothaug, Susanne. "History and Storytelling: Historical Narratives by Women Authors of the Contemporary American South," http://www.uni-regensburg.de/Fakultaeten/phil_Fak_IV/Anglistik/Amerikanistik/copas/PDFs/ArtSusanneRothaugText.pdf+%22kaye+gibbons%22, accessed on September 20, 2006.

Ryan, Laura T. "Gibbons Says Manic Depression Fuels Her Art," Syracuse (N.Y.) *Herald American* (12 February 1999).

Schneir, Miriam, ed. *Feminism: The Essential Historical Writings*. New York: Vintage, 1972.

Schreiner, Olive. *Woman and Labour*. http://etext.library.adelaide.edu.au/s/schreiner_o/woman/woman.html, 1911, accessed on October 10, 2006.

Schweitzer, Ivy. "Advancing Sisterhood?," *Tulsa Studies in Women's Literature* 21, no. 1 (spring 2002): 142–144.

Skube, Michael. "Art of Translation Calls for Ear Attuned to Human Emotion," *Atlanta Journal-Constitution* (21 February 1999).

Smith, Lee. *Conversations with Lee Smith*. Jackson: University Press of Mississippi, 2001.

Snodgrass, Mary Ellen. *Encyclopedia of Feminist Literature*. New York: Facts on File, 2006.

"Southern Charmers," *Chicago Tribune* (18 April 1993).

Spielman, David G., and William W. Starr. *Southern Writers*. Columbia: University of South Carolina Press, 1997.

Starr, William. *Southern Writers*. Columbia: University of South Carolina Press, 1997.

Stephens, Spaine. "Nash County Still Inspires Gibbons," Rocky Mount (N.C.) *Evening Telegram* (24 March 2004).

Sternburg, Janet, ed. *The Writer on Her Work*. New York: Norton, 1930.

Strafford, Jay. "Southern Fiction: Author's Debut Brings New Talent," *Richmond Times-Dispatch* (9 September 1987).

Tate, Linda. *A Southern Weave of Women: Fiction of the Contemporary South*. Athens: University of Georgia Press, 1994.

Terry, Jill. "Advancing Sisterhood?," *Critical Survey* 13, no. 3 (2001): 123–125.

Titus, Mary. "The Wilderness Within: American Women Writers and Spiritual Quest," *American Literature* 72, no. 2 (June 2000): 438–439.

Town, Caren J. *New Southern Girl: Female Adolescence in the Works of 12 Women Authors*. Jefferson, N.C.: McFarland, 2004.

Waggoner, Martha. "Kaye Gibbons Happy with Life Around Her," *Wichita* (Kans.) *Eagle* (10 March 2006).

_____. "One for All, All for One," Durham, N.C., *Herald-Sun* (21 September 1999).

_____. "The Write Stuff in North Carolina," *Greensboro* (N.C.) *News & Record* (3 October 1999).

Walker, Nancy A. "Southern Women Writers: Tradition and Change," *Contemporary Fiction* 34, no. 1 (spring 1993): 150–157.

Wallace, Marybeth Sutton. "Reaping Weeds: Gibbons Brings Words to Fruition," Rocky

Mount, N.C., *Evening Telegram* (25 November 1990): 8.
Waters, Chuck. "Getting Your Work into Print," *Raleigh* (N.C.) *News & Observer* (2 February 1992).
Watkins, James, ed. *Southern Selves: From Mark Twain and Eudora Welty to Maya Angelou and Kaye Gibbons*. New York: Vintage, 1998.
Weaver, Teresa K. "Outside the Writing Room, Reading's Ties Grow Stronger," *Atlanta Journal-Constitution* (8 August 2004).
_____. "Southern Fiction's Father figure," *Atlanta Journal-Constitution* (29 December 2002).
Wells, Chandra. "Advancing Sisterhood?," *MELUS* 27, no. 3 (fall 2002): 229–231.
_____. *Befriending the Other (ed) Woman: Fictions of Interracial Female Friendship*. Storrs: University of Connecticut, 2005.
West, Cassandra. "Listener's Guide," *Chicago Tribune* (5 July 1998).
Willett, Melissa. "Gibbons Brings Her Voice to Fayetteville," *Fayetteville* (N.C.) *Observer* (5 October 2004).
Wolcott, James. "Crazy for You," *New Yorker* (21 August 1996): 115–116.
Wolf, Naomi. *The Beauty Myth: How Images of Beauty Are Used Against Women*. New York: William Morrow, 1991.
"Women in America" *Journal of American Studies* (special issue) 33, no. 1 (April 1999): 1–89.
Wood, Ralph C. "Gumption and Grace in the Novels of Kaye Gibbons," *Christian Century* 109, no. 27 (September 23–30, 1992): 842–846.
Yaeger, Patricia. *Honey-Mad Women: Emancipatory Strategies in Women's Writing*. New York: Columbia University Press, 1988.
Zane, J. Peder. "Books on the Tar Heel Mind," Raleigh, N.C., *News & Observer* (11 June 2006).
_____. "Welty's Passing: A Death in the Family," Raleigh, N.C., *News & Observer* (29 July 2001).

Charms for the Easy Life

Alexander, Ann. "Book of Changes for Kaye Gibbons," *Greensboro* (N.C.) *News & Record* (21 March 1993).
"Also Worth Reading," *Chicago Tribune* (24 April 1994).
Anshaw, Carol. "The Healer's Voice: Kaye Gibbons Conjures Up a Woman with a Cure for Almost Everything," *Chicago Tribune* (21 March 1993).
Barnes, Linda Adams. "Telling Yourself into Existence: The Fiction of Kaye Gibbons," *Tennessee Philological Bulletin* 30 (1993): 28–35.
Bauer, Margaret. "Comic Visions, Female Voices," *Mississippi Quarterly* 53, no. 3 (summer 2000): 479–482.
Burkhardt, Joanna M., and Ann Burns. "Audio Review: *Charms for the Easy Life*," *Library Journal* 125, no. 13 (1 August 2000): 180.
Chadwell, Faye A. "Review: *Charms for the Easy Life*," *Library Journal* 118, no. 33 (15 February 1993): 191.
Clodfelter, Tim. "Like a Charm — Screenwriter Found Inspiration in Her Own Family for Adaptation of Novel," *Winston-Salem* (N.C.) *Journal* (17 August 2002).
Cohen, Judith Beth. "Review: *Charms for the Easy Life*," *Women's Review of Books* 11, no. 1 (October 1993).
Gates, Anita. "Television Review: *Charms for the Easy Life*," *New York Times* (16 August 2002): E27.
Gecan, Carolyn E. "Review: *Charms for the Easy Life*," *School Library Journal* 39, no. 9 (September 1993): 260.
Hanson, Isie V. "Review: *Charms for the Easy Life*," *Southern Living* 28, no. 4 (April 1993): 112.
Harrington, Maureen. "Child's Vision Right on Target," *Denver Post* (4 April 1993).
Haugsted, Linda. "Not Enough 'Charms' Here," *Multichannel News* 23, no. 32 (12 August 2002): 26.
Hepler, Susan. "Period Pieces, Fractured Folktales, and More," *Reading Today* 12, no. 2 (October/November 1994): 28.
Holt, Patricia. "A Bounty of Books for Listening," *San Francisco Chronicle* (12 June 1994).
Lothar, Corinna. "'Charms' Are Many in Gibbons' New Novel," *Washington Times* (6 June 1993).
Madrigal, Alix. "A Tough Southern Belle," *San Francisco Chronicle* (2 May 1993).
Maryles, Daisy. "Review: *Charms for the Easy Life*," *Publishers Weekly* 240, no. 21 (24 May 1993): 32.
McCauley, Stephen. "He's Gone. Go Start the Coffee," *New York Times Book Review* (11 April 1993): 9–10.
McCray, Nancy. "Audiovisual Review: *Charms for the Easy Life*," *Booklist* 91, no. 10 (15 January 1995): 947.
Monteith, Sharon. "Between Girls: Kaye Gibbons' *Ellen Foster* and Friendship as a Monologic Formulation," *Journal of American Studies* 33, no. 1 (April 1999): 45–64.
Nilsen, Allen Pace, and Kenneth L. Donelson.

"Young Adult Literature," *English Journal* 83, no. 7 (November 1994): 99–103.
O'Hehir, Diana. "Belles That Don't Ring True," *Washington Post* (3 June 1993: C4.
Oxman, Steven. "Television Review: *Charms for the Easy Life*," *Daily Variety* 276, no. 52 (15 August 2002): 5.
Paddock, Polly. "Strong Women Seek a True Talisman," *Charlotte* (N.C.) *Observer* (21 March 1993).
Pearl, Nancy. "Companion Reads for Your Next Book Club," *Library Journal* 128, no. 1 (1 January 2003): 192.
"Review: *Charms for the Easy Life*," *New Yorker* 69, no. 18 (21 June 1993): 101.
Sather, Kathryn. "Southern Story with a Bite," *Montreal Gazette* (15 May 1993): K4.
"Showtime 'Charms' Women Viewers," *Cableworld* (15 July 2002): 80.
Steinberg, Sybil. "Review: *Charms for the Easy Life*," *Publishers Weekly* 240, no. 2 (11 January 1993): 52.
Strafford, Jay. "'Easy Life' Comes Hard to Women," *Richmond Times-Dispatch* (27 June 1993).
Summer, Bob, and Sybil Steinberg. "Kaye Gibbons," *Publishers Weekly* 240, no. 6 (8 February 1993): 60–61.
Thompson, James. "Man-Taming Granny," *World & I* 8, no. 9 (September 1993): 349–354.
Warren, Colleen Kelly. "Three Generations of Feisty Women," *St. Louis Post-Dispatch* (6 June 1993).
Weiss, Amelia. "Medicine Woman," *Time* 141, no. 15 (12 April 1993): 77–78.

A Cure for Dreams

Balingit, JoAnn. "Review: *A Cure for Dreams*," *Magill Book Reviews* (1 September 1991).
Blades, John. "A History and a Novel Win Heartland Prizes," *Chicago Tribune* (23 August 1991).
Branan, Tonita. "Woman and 'The Gift of Gab': Revisionary Strategies in *A Cure for Dreams*," *Southern Literary Journal* 26 (spring 1994): 91–101.
Calos, Katherine. "Author Exposes Drama of Ordinary Life in the South," *Richmond Times-Dispatch* (6 May 1991).
Clark, Miriam Marty. "Sounds of Women Talking," *St. Louis Post-Dispatch* (9 June 1991).
Flaherty, Dolores. "That Constant Chatter," *Chicago Sun-Times* (23 August 1992).
Graeber, Laurel. "Review: *A Cure for Dreams*," *New York Times Book Review* 141, no. 49,074 (30 August 1992): 24.
Humphreys, Josephine. "Within the Marriage, a Secret Life," *Los Angeles Times* (19 May 1991): BR13.
Kaganoff, P., and S. Steinberg. "Review: *A Cure for Dreams*," *Publishers Weekly* 239, no. 24 (25 May 1992): 51.
Koenig, R. "Southern Comfort," *New York* 24, no. 13 (1 April 1991): 63.
Larkin, Michael. "Sounds and Messages of the Rural South," *Boston Globe* (25 March 1991).
Lothar, Corinna. "Fine 'Dreams' Tells of Depression, Love," *Washington Times* (29 April 1991).
Lynch, Doris. "Review: *A Cure for Dreams*," *Library Journal* 116, no. 3 (15 February 1991): 220.
McKee, Kathryn. "Simply Talking: Women and Language in Kaye Gibbons's *A Cure for Dreams*," *Southern Quarterly* 35, no. 4 (summer 1997): 97–107.
Morris, Ann. "Gibbons' 'A Cure for Dreams' Is a Hope Chest of Language," *Greensboro* (N.C.) *News & Record* (31 March 1991).
Parker, Roy, Jr. "Elegant Family Story," *Fayetteville* (N.C.) *Observer* (14 April 1991).
Peat, Isie. "Books about the South," *Southern Living* 26, no. 6 (June 1991): 86.
Rajkowska, Barbara Ozieblo. *Susan Glaspell: A Critical Biography*. Chapel Hill: University of North Carolina Press, 2000.
"Review: *A Cure for Dreams*," *Antioch Review* 49, no. 3 (summer 1991): 474.
Sayers, Valerie. "Review: *A Cure for Dreams*," *Washington Post* (8 April 1991): C3.
Shulins, Nancy. "Open Season: Women Authors Take Aim at Abusive Men," *St. Louis Post-Dispatch* (4 August 1991).
Solomon, Charles. "Review: *A Cure for Dreams*," *Los Angeles Times* (16 August 1992): 9.
Strafford, Jay. "Ordinary Life Has Meaning," *Richmond Times-Dispatch* (3 April 1991).
Stratton, Sharon Lloyd. "Family Talk Is Backbone of 'Dreams,'" *Richmond Times-Dispatch* (5 May 1991).
"Tribune Books," *Chicago Tribune* (15 September 1991).
Tyler, Ann. "Fiercely Precise: Kay Gibbons' World of Southern Womanhood," *Chicago Tribune* (24 March 1991).
Wilcox, J. "Escape from Milk Farm Road," *New York Times Book Review* 140, no. 4,859 (12 May 1991): 13–14.

Divining Women

Bak, John S., "Escaping the Jaundiced Eye: Foucauldian Panopticism in Charlotte Perkins Gilman's 'The Yellow Wallpaper,'" *Studies in Short Fiction* 31, no. 1 (winter 1994): 39–46.

Barnhill, Anne. "Strength Does Battle with Calculating Manipulation," *Winston-Salem* (N.C.) *Journal* (4 April 2004).

Brown, Carrie. "Kaye Gibbons' Focus Is on Female Fortitude," *Chicago Tribune* (4 April 2004).

Cook, Elizabeth G. "'Divining Women' Merely Depressing," *Salisbury* (N.C.) *Post* (11 April 2004).

Goldenberg, Judi. "To Endure, Women Form Bond," *Richmond Times-Dispatch* (9 May 2004).

Harris, Karen. "Audio for Adults," *Booklist* 101 no. 19/20 (1 June 2005): 1830.

Hume, Beverly A. "Managing Madness in Gilman's 'The Yellow Wall-Paper,'" *Studies in American Fiction* 30, no. 1 (spring 2002): 3–30.

Lothar, Corinna. "Artists, Immigrants, Determined Women," *Washington Times* (29 August 2004).

McBride, Sharan. "A Pity Gibbons Didn't Move On," *Houston Chronicle* (16 May 2004).

Nostrums and Quackery. Chicago: American Medical Association, 1912.

Pate, Nancy. "Kaye Gibbons Offers Tale of Two Women," *Orlando Sentinel* (7 April 2004).

"Review: *Divining Women*," *Kirkus Reviews* 72, no. 2 (15 January 2004): 52.

"Review: *Divining Women*," *Publishers Weekly* 251, no. 7 (16 February 2004).

Rogers, Amy. "Aligned Between Heartbreak, Hope, 'Divining Women' Fight the Weight of Society's Limitations," *Charlotte* (N.C.) *Observer* (11 April 2004).

Roth, Marty. "Gilman's Arabesque Wallpaper," *Mosaic* 34, no. 4 (December 2001): 145–162.

Sayers, Valerie. "A Woman Moves South into a House of Spirits," *Washington Post* (4 April 2004): T13.

Seaman, Donna. "Review: *Divining Women*," *Booklist* 100, no. 13 (1 March 2004): 1133.

Smith, Julia Ridley. "Gibbons' Latest Novel Is Shy of Divine," Raleigh, N.C., *News & Observer* (11 April 2004).

Smith, Starr E. "Review: *Divining Women*," *Library Journal* 129, no. 5 (15 March 2004).

Steelman, Ben. "Characters Drag Down a Decent 'Divining,'" Wilmington, N.C., *Star-News* (11 April 2004).

Treadway, Jessica. "At War's End, a Loveless Marriage and a Fortuitous Visit," *Boston Globe* (9 May 2004).

Weales, Gerald. "Perera: The Yellow Wallpaper," *Commonweal* 120, no. 3: (12 February 1993): 16–17.

Ellen Foster

Allen, Kimberly G. "Review: *Ellen Foster*," *Library Journal* 112, no. 7 (15 April 1987): 98.

Bell, Pearl K. "Southern Discomfort," *New Republic* 198, no. 9 (29 February 1988): 38–41.

Brennan, Patricia. "Mixing Pathos and Spunk Jena Malone Plays a Child Looking for Love," *Washington Post* (14 December 1997).

Burckhardt, Joanna M. "Review: *Ellen Foster*," *Library Journal* 121, no. 18 (1 November 1996): 120–122.

Busko, Robert. "Scotland County Reads: Author Kaye Gibbons to Visit," *Laurinburg* (N.C.) *Exchange* (15 September 2006).

Clayton, Jay, and Eric Rothstein. *Influence and Intertextuality in Literary History*. Madison: University of Wisconsin Press, 1991.

Dirlam, Sharon. "Review: *Ellen Foster*," *Los Angeles Times* (16 August 1987): 4.

Eaglen, Audrey. "Good Things Come in Grim Packages," *School Library Journal* 34, no. 1 (September 1987): 137.

Eckard, Paula Gallant. "Ellen Foster: Survival in the New South," *Five Owls* (25 April 2005).

Entzminger, Betina. "To Hell and Back: Race and Betrayal in the Southern Novel," *College Literature* 32, no. 2 (spring 2005): 201–204.

Franklin, Melinda L. "Ellen at the Ball: *Ellen Foster* as a Cinderella Tale," *ALAN Review* 23, no. 1 (fall 1995): 16–17.

Friedman, Roger Davis. "A Girl Escapes a Family to Find a Family," *Chicago Tribune* (22 May 1987).

Grahnke, Lon. "This Girl Won't Quit," *Chicago Sun-Times* (12 December 1997).

Green, Mary. "Foster Child," *People* 48, no. 24 (15 December 1997): 17.

Groover, Kristina Kaye. "Re-visioning the Wilderness: *Adventures of Huckleberry Finn* and *Ellen Foster*," *Southern Quarterly* 27, no. 3/4 (spring/summer 1999): 187–197.

Hayward, Dave. "Regional Roundup: Atlanta," *Back Stage* 37, no. 5 (2 February 1996): 37.

Heckman, Don. "Abuse Fails to Devastate," *Los Angeles Times* (13 December 1997): 16.

Herman, Judith, and Lisa Hirschmann. "Father-Daughter Incest" in *The Signs Reader: Women, Gender and Scholarship*. Chicago: University of Chicago Press, 1983.

Hoffman, Alice. "Shopping for a New Family," *New York Times* (31 May 1987): A13.

Joyner, Will. "A Young Girl's Long Road to a Family," *New York Times* (12 December 1997): E34.

McCabe, Bruce. "A 10-Year-Old Finds Happiness," *Boston Globe* (14 December 1997).

Munafo, Giavanna. "Colored Biscuits: Reconstructing Whiteness and the Boundaries of 'Home' in Kaye Gibbons's *Ellen Foster*," *Women, America, and Movement*, ed. Susan L. Roberson. Columbia: University of Missouri Press, 1998, pp. 38–61.

Pennington, Gail. "'Ellen Foster' Showcases a Child's Triumph over Obstacles," *St. Louis Post-Dispatch* (14 December 1997).

Ragas, Meg Cohen. "Age of Innocence," *Harper's Bazaar* (April 1995): 108.

Romine, Dannye. "A Dream Come True — Third Time Out Is a Charmer for Raleigh Novelist Kaye Gibbons," *Charlotte* (N.C.) *Observer* (31 March 1991).

_____. "'Ellen Foster' Takes you on Poignant Search," *Charlotte* (N.C.) *Observer* (26 April 1987).

_____. "Literature Liberates: Raleigh's Kaye Gibbons Finds Freedoms, Affirmation in 1st Novel," *Charlotte* (N.C.) *Observer* (26 April 1987).

_____. "Under the Influence Adult Children of Alcoholics Emerge from Pain," *Charlotte* (N.C.) *Observer* (5 July 1987).

_____. "Vintage Books Buys Ellen Foster," *Charlotte* (N.C.) *Observer* (7 June 1987).

_____. "With Three Novels Behind Her and a New One Ahead, N.C. Authors Kaye Gibbons Is Taking Control of Her Life," *Charlotte* (N.C.) *Observer* (14 April 1991).

Rosenblum, Trudi Miller. "Audio Books," *Billboard* 108, no. 33 (17 August 1996): 78.

Sandefur, Amy Faulds. "Narrative Immediacy and First-Person Voice in Contemporary American Novels" (dissertation), Louisiana State University, 2003.

Stratton, Sharon Lloyd. "Magnolia Grows Out of Rough Soil," *Richmond Times-Dispatch* (21 June 1987).

Town, Caren J. *New Southern Girl: Female Adolescence in the Works of 12 Women Authors*. Jefferson, N.C.: McFarland, 2004.

Tripp, Janet. "Feminism," *Utne Reader* no. 28 (July/August 1988): 114–115.

Weaver, Teresa K. "'Liars' Club' Author Still Seeks Truth," *Atlanta Journal-Constitution* (10 April 2005).

White, Valerie. "Paperbacks for YA," *Emergency Librarian* 19, no. 3 (January/February 1992): 62–63.

Wilkinson, Joanna. "After Oprah 2," *Booklist* 95, no. 19/20 (1 June 1999): 1796–1797.

Yardley, Jonathan. "Child of Adversity: A Young Heroine Finds Happiness Overcoming Prejudice," *Washington Post* (22 April 1987): C2.

Ellen Foster (stage adaptation)

Cofta, Mark. "Arden Triumphs with 'Ellen Foster,'" Montgomery, Pa., *Main Line Times* (10 February 1994).

Groome, Clark. "Fine 'Ellen Foster' Another Triumph for Arden Theatre," *Chestnut Hill* (Pa.) *Local* (3 February 1994): 39.

Hulbert, Dan. "Theater Review: *Ellen Foster*," *Atlanta Journal-Constitution* (19 January 1996).

Nelson, Nels. "Simply Irresistible: Arden Theater Company's 'Ellen Foster,'" *Philadelphia Daily News* (27 January 1994): 37, 40.

Northam, Greg. "Recounting a Woman's Troubled Childhood," *Philadelphia Gay News* (4 February 1994).

Ridley, Clifford A. "A Girl in Dire Dickensian Straits Who Lives to Learn the Outcome," *Philadelphia Enquirer* (1 February 1994).

Woods, Byron. "Author Watches Her Life on Stage," Raleigh, N.C., *News & Observer* (1 March 1996).

The Life All Around Me by Ellen Foster

Campbell, Karen. "Ellen Foster Returns, Wise Beyond Her Years," *Boston Globe* (January 17, 2006).

Collins, Lauren. "Older, Wiser," *New York Times Book Review* (5 March 2006): 15.

Curran, Colleen. "A Forgettable Successor to an Unforgettable Debut," *Richmond Times-Dispatch* (26 February 2006).

Daniel, Virginia. "The Life All Around Her," Raleigh, Durham, Chapel Hill, N.C., *Independent Weekly* (26 January 2006).

Evans, Judith. "'Ellen Foster' Returns, Older and Wiser," *St. Louis Post-Dispatch* (22 January 2006).

Gearino, G. D. "Ellen Foster to Return," Raleigh, N.C., *News & Observer* (26 February 2004).

Jarvis, Craig. "The Life All Around Her: Kaye Gibbons Returns to the Character That Made Her in Order to Remake Herself," Raleigh, N.C., *News & Observer* (25 December 2005).

Johnson, Rheta Grimsley. "A Spunky Child Grows," *Atlanta Journal-Constitution* (25 December 2005).

Kelly, Susan. "Ellen Foster Grows Less Endearing with Age," *USA Today* (2 February 2006).

Larson, Jeanette. "Review: *The Life All Around Me by Ellen Foster*," *Booklist* 102, no. 19/20 (1 June 2006): 108.

Paddock, Polly. "Ellen Foster Revisited," *Charlotte* (N.C.) *Observer* (26 January 2006): 5E.

Quinn, Mary Ellen. "Review: *The Life All Around Me by Ellen Foster,*" *Booklist* 102, no. 1 (1 September 2005): 7.

Ratner, Rochelle, "Review: *The Life All Around Me by Ellen Foster,*" *Library Journal* 131, no. 12 (1 July 2006): 118.

"Review: *The Life All Around Me by Ellen Foster,*" *Kirkus Reviews* 73, no. 19 (1 October 2005).

Sa'adah, Marjorie Gellhorn. "You Can't Go Home Again," *Los Angeles Times* (8 January 2006): R7.

Sayers, Valerie, "Growing Into the Role," *Washington Post* (6 January 2006).

Williams, Lynna. "For Ellen Foster, There's Finally Light at the End of the Tunnel," *Chicago Tribune* (8 January 2006).

Zane, J. Peder. "Authors Add to the Story," Raleigh, N.C., *News & Observer* (4 December 2005).

On the Occasion of My Last Afternoon

Barnhill, Anne. "Broken Promise: Gibbons' Memoir-Like Tale Lacks Drama," *Winston-Salem* (N.C.) *Journal* (12 July 1998).

Blackford, Linda B. "Review: *On the Occasion of My Last Afternoon,*" *Lexington* (Ky.) *Herald-Leader* (19 August 1998).

Carter, Ron. "Sisters Flee Father's Tyranny," *Richmond Times-Dispatch* (5 July 1998).

Dodd, Susan. "A Sentimental Education," *Washington Post* (12 July 1998).

"The Editors Recommend," *San Francisco Chronicle* (21 June 1998).

Fichtner, Margaria. "Review: *On the Occasion of My Last Afternoon,*" *Miami Herald* (8 July 1998).

Gossett, Polly Paddock. "Book Talk," *Charlotte* (N.C.) *Observer* (23 August 1998).

_____. "She Sees No Glory in the Gore of War," *Charlotte* (N.C.) *Observer* (7 June 1998).

Hale, Sarah Josepha. "Editor's Table," *Godey's Lady's Book* 51, no. 1 (July 1857): 82.

Harrison, Kathryn. "Tara It Ain't," *New York Times Book Review* 147, no. 51, 223 (19 July 1998).

Hodges, Betty. "Migraine Hits After Oprah's Phone Call," Durham, N.C., *Herald-Sun* (2 November 1997).

Lothar, Corinna. "From the Real to the Surreal," *Washington Times* (16 August 1998).

Lott, Brett. "Kaye Gibbons Looks Back in Anger," Raleigh, N.C., *News & Observer* (7 June 1998).

Mabe, Chauncey. "Review: *On the Occasion of My Last Afternoon,*" Fort Lauderdale, Fla., *Sun-Sentinel* (24 June 1998).

McKay, Mary A. "Gray Ghosts: Civil War and Remembrance through the Eyes of Another Compelling Kaye Gibbons Character," *Times-Picayune* (16 August 1998): D6.

O'Briant, Don. "In Search of a Novel," *Atlanta Journal-Constitution* (2 June 1998).

_____. "Kaye Gibbons Does the Rewrite Thing," *Greensboro* (N.C.) *News & Record* (14 June 1998).

Parks, Louis B. "Review" *On the Occasion of My Last Afternoon,*" *Houston Chronicle* (19 July 1998).

Redding, Sean, Jane Fisher, and James S. Torrens. "Review: *On the Occasion of My Last Afternoon,*" *America* 180, no. 1 (2 January 1999).

Steelman, Ben. "Gibbons Takes Much-Needed Rest," Wilmington, N.C., *Morning Star* (26 July 1998).

Szatmary, Peter. "A Slaveowner's Daughter," *Houston Chronicle* (28 June 1998).

Treadway, Jessica. "Old Times There Are Not Forgotten," *Boston Globe* (31 May 1998).

Wagner-Martin, Linda. "Kaye Gibbons' Achievement in *On the Occasion of My Last Afternoon,*" *Notes on Contemporary Literature* 29, no. 3 (May 1999): 3–5.

Williams, Lynna. "Narrative Tells This Tale of Life during the Civil War," *Chicago Tribune* (18 November 1998).

Pete & Shirley

Merriman, Ann Lloyd. "Between the Bookends," *Richmond Times-Dispatch* (25 February 1996).

Perkins, David, "The Making of 'Pete & Shirley," Raleigh, N.C., *News & Observer* (12 November 1995).

Steelman, Ben. "On the Path of a Traveling Story," *Wilmington* (N.C.) *Star-News* (26 May 2002).

Sights Unseen

Beardslee, William R. *When a Parent Is Depressed: How to Protect Your Child from the Effects of Depression in the Family.* Boston: Little, Brown, 2002.

Carey, Jacqueline. "Mommy Direst," *New York Times Book Review* (24 September 1995): 30.

Carter, Ron. "Children Hide Family Secret," *Richmond Times-Dispatch* (10 September 1995).

Creager, Angela N. H., Elizabeth Lunbeck, and Londa Schiebinger, eds. *Feminism in Twentieth Century Science, Technology and*

Medicine. Chicago: University of Chicago Press, 2001.

Crellin, John K. *Public Expectations and Physicians' Responsibilities: Voices of Medical Humanities*. Abingdon, Oxford: Radcliffe Publishing, 2005.

Entzminger, Betina. *The Belle Gone Bad: White Southern Women Writers and the Dark Seductress*. Baton Rouge: Louisiana State University Press, 2002.

Flaherty, Dolores, "When Mental Illness Strains Family Bonds," *Chicago Sun-Times* (17 November 1996).

Glass, Julia. "To Comfort the Comfortless Kaye Gibbons Writes of a Girl's Life with Her Manic-Depressive Mother," *Chicago Tribune* (20 August 1995).

Green, Michelle. "Review: *Sights Unseen*," *People* 44, no. 11 (11 September 1995).

Harris, Michael. "Scenes—and Skeletons—of a Troubled Southern Family," *Los Angeles Times* (9 October 1995): 5.

Hendrick Flannagan, Rebecca. "Review: *Sights Unseen*," *Magill Book Reviews* (1 April 1996).

Jessup, Lynn. "Disease Inspires Author's Latest Novel," *Greensboro* (N.C.) *News & Record* (12 November 1995).

Johnson, Rheta Grimsley. "A Skewed Life with Mother," *Atlanta Journal-Constitution* (3 September 1995).

Kempf, Andrea Caron. "Review: *Sights Unseen*," *Library Journal* 120, no. 11 (15 June 1995): 93–94.

Kenney, Michael. "An Author Confronts Her Inner Demons," *Boston Globe* (20 September 1995).

Lothar, Corinna. "A Gritty, Witty 'Face'; a Spirited 'Oblivion,'" *Washington Times* (17 December 1995).

Maryles, Daisy, and Margaret Sanborn. "Behind the Bestsellers," *Publishers Weekly* (16 October 1995): 16.

O'Briant, Don. "Book Signing," *Atlanta Journal-Constitution* (10 September 1995).

Paddock, Polly. "Kaye Gibbons Recalls 'Sights Unseen' As a Tough Project," *Charlotte* (N.C.) *Observer* (27 August 1995).

Park, Andrew Sung, and Susan L. Nelson. *The Other Side of Sin: Woundedness from the Perspectives of the Sinned-Against*. Albany: State University of New York, 2001.

"Review: *Sights Unseen*," *Belles Lettres* (January 1996).

"Review: *Sights Unseen*," *Chicago Tribune* (20 August 1995).

"Review: *Sights Unseen*," *London Times* (15 June 1996).

Spurr, Kim Weaver. "Storied Life: For Gibbons, Words Reflect Part of Herself," Durham, N.C., *Herald-Sun* (27 August 1995).

Timberlake, Barbette. "Review: *Sights Unseen*," *School Library Journal* 41, no. 11 (November 1995): 138.

Waggoner, Martha. "Book Addresses Manic-Depression," Durham, N.C., *Herald-Sun* (17 September 1995).

Warren, Colleen Kelly. "Effect of Mental Illness on Family," *St. Louis Post-Dispatch* (17 September 1995).

Wolcott, James. "Crazy for You," *New Yorker* 71, no. 25 (21 August 1995): 115–116.

A Virtuous Woman

Chandler, Marilyn. "Limited Partnership," *Women's Review of Books* 6, nos. 10–11 (July 1989): 21.

Clark, Marty. "Salvaging Good Out of Grief," *St. Louis Post-Dispatch* (14 May 1989).

Flaherty, Dolores. "...For Her Price Is Far Above Rubies," *Chicago Sun-Times* (26 August 1990).

Flynn, Rochelle L'Gorman. "Sunday Brunch Book Shelf," *Los Angeles Times* (15 February 1998): 2.

Heeger, Susan. "Couldn't Live with Her, Can't Live without Her": *A Virtuous Woman*," *Los Angeles Times* (11 June 1989): 15.

Johnson, Charles, intro. *Proverbs*. New York: Grove Press, 1999.

Kaveney, Roz. "Making Themselves Over," *Times Literary Supplement* (15 September 1989): 998.

Krieger, Elliot. "Author's Characters Dominate," *Richmond Times-Dispatch* (28 May 1989).

Parker, Roy, Jr. "Kay Gibbons Reprise," *Fayetteville* (N.C.) *Observer* (30 April 1989).

Powell, Padgett. "As Ruby Lay Dying," *New York Times* (30 April 1989): 712.

Romine, Dannye. "The Struggle for Support," *Charlotte* (N.C.) *Observer* (30 April 1989).

Souris, Stephen. "Kaye Gibbons's *A Virtuous Woman*: A Bakhtinian Iserian Analysis of Conspicuous Agreement," *Southern Studies* 3 (summer 1992): 99–115.

Strafford, Jay. "Kaye Gibbons Creates a Stirring Tale," *Richmond Times-Dispatch* (28 June 1989).

Taylor, Maurice. "Review: *A Virtuous Woman*," *Library Journal* 114, no. 6 (1 April 1989): 111.

Index

The coded titles after entries are as follows: CD *A Cure for Dreams* (1991); CEL *Charms for the Easy Life* (1993); DW *Divining Women* (2004); EF *Ellen Foster* (1987); H "The Headache" (June 1987); JS "Joyner's Store" (1997); LAAM *The Life All Around Me by Ellen Foster* (2006); OOLA *On the Occasion of My Last Afternoon* (1998); PS *Pete & Shirley: The Great Tar Heel Novel* (1995); SU *Sights Unseen* (1995); VW *A Virtuous Woman* (1989)